Contemporary Sociological Theory

An Integrated Multi-Level Approach

Doyle Paul Johnson

Contemporary Sociological Theory

An Integrated Multi-Level Approach

Springer

Doyle Paul Johnson
Texas Tech University
Lubbock, TX
USA
d.paul.johnson@ttu.edu

ISBN 978-0-387-76521-1 ISBN 978-0-387-76522-8 (eBook)
DOI 10.1007/978-0-387-76522-8

Library of Congress Control Number: 2008923257

Printed on acid-free paper

9 8 7 6 5 4 3 2 1

springer.com

Preface

This volume is designed as a basic text for upper level and graduate courses in contemporary sociological theory. Most sociology programs require their majors to take at least one course in sociological theory, sometimes two. A typical breakdown is between classical and contemporary theory. Theory is perhaps one of the broadest areas of sociological inquiry and serves as a foundation or framework for more specialized study in specific substantive areas of the field. In addition, the study of sociological theory can readily be related to various aspects of other social science disciplines as well.

From the very beginning sociology has been characterized by alternative theoretical perspectives. Classical theory includes the European founding figures of the discipline whose works were produced during the later half of the nineteenth century and the first couple of decades of the twentieth century plus early American theorists. For most of the second half of the twentieth century, a fairly high consensus has developed among American sociologists regarding these major founders, particularly with regard to the works of Durkheim and Weber in analyzing the overall society and of Simmel in analyzing social interaction processes. Since the late 1960s and early 1970s the influence of Marx has also been recognized. Recent decades have also witnessed an increased emphasis on the important contributions of several pioneering feminist perspectives in the early years of sociology.

With the establishment of sociology as an academic discipline, the era of dominant individuals has been largely replaced by dominant theoretical schools. During the middle part of the century, Talcott Parsons' version of functional theory dominated the field—although other perspectives were also advanced as alternatives during that period. These competing theories included conflict theory, critical theory, symbolic interaction theory, and social exchange theory. In more recent decades, several additional theoretical perspective have been elaborated, including, for example, rational choice theory, which is closely related to exchange theory, the sociology of emotions, neofunctionalism, general systems theory, structuration theory, sociobiology, and various postmodern perspectives. The continued development of various forms of feminist theory has also been influential in the field.

The overall organizing framework employed in this book is based primarily on the distinctions among different levels of social reality. Theorists routinely distinguish between micro and macro levels of analysis, even though the distinction is arbitrary in some ways. The micro level involves a focus on human agency and choice and the dynamics of personal relationships and small-scale social systems of various types, particularly those involving face-to-face encounters. The macro level, in contrast, is concerned with larger-scale social systems, typically at the level of total societies.

The specific details of intentional human agency may appear to be submerged in macro-level theories, along with the dynamics of face-to-face relations—despite the fact that the structures of large-scale systems are actually made up of patterns of human action and interaction. Many of the major theoretical perspectives making up the field differ from one another in terms of whether they begin with a micro or a macro level focus, or emphasize one or the other of these levels as primary. In addition, a great deal of recent work in theory has involved explicit efforts to link micro and macro levels.

In addition to micro and macro levels, various intermediate or "meso" levels of analysis may also be identified. The meso-level focus is manifested primarily in the various substantive areas of sociology, many of which have their own somewhat specialized theoretical perspectives. Micro-, meso-, and macro levels certainly do not exist independently of one another, however. Instead, the distinctions have to do with primary focus of attention and the specific concepts and social processes that are most heavily emphasized. This volume will highlight organizations, communities, markets, and socioeconomic classes as meso-level social formations that can be identified between the micro level of face-to-face relations and the macro-level institutional structures of the overall society.

The micro/macro distinction may be compared and contrasted with the more contemporary distinction between agency and structure. The concept of agency may seem initially to be related to the micro level and structure to the macro level. However, both agency and structure are manifested at all levels. Thus, for example, micro-level social relations, such as those among family members or close friends, exhibit definite structural patterns which may either be maintained or transformed through their members' actions. At the same time, meso and macro level systems are also reproduced or transformed through the actions and social relations of the specific individuals involved in them. The influence of different participants as agents in all types of structures may be expected to vary according to their position and the power and resources they control.

In evaluating all of the various contemporary theories to be discussed in this volume, the interdependence of agency and structure at all levels is important to keep in mind. Within the various levels of the social world described above, alternative or competing theoretical perspectives will be highlighted, but not in a way that suggests it is necessary to choose one or the other. Instead, given the complexity of the social world and the variety of ways it can be analyzed, the different perspectives can be regarded as alternative frameworks, or lenses, through which different aspects or features of the social world may be highlighted. All of the theoretical perspectives to be emphasized in this volume are to be seen as providing important insights into the nature of the social world, but all are limited in the specific features of the social world on which they focus.

The four chapters in Part I set the stage. Chapter 1 moves from the implicit common sense theories of everyday life to explicit theories that are developed through intellectual reflection, research, and study. The next two chapters deal with the historical development of sociological theory. Chapter 2 reviews the early European sources, while Chap. 3 deals with the development of American sociology. Chapter 4 describes the strategy of formal theory construction for formulating theoretical ideas as an essential part of the process of scientific inquiry.

The eleven chapters in Part II present the major core perspectives that have long been considered basic in contemporary sociological theory. The presentation moves from the micro to the macro level, with the meso level in the middle. Chapters 5–8 focus on the micro level. The specific theories in these chapters include symbolic interaction theory and the dramaturgic approach (Chap. 5), phenomenological sociology and ethnomethodology (Chap. 6), and social exchange and rational choice theories (Chap. 7). Chapter 8 then relates rational choice theory to variations in the opportunities individuals have to form social ties with different types of people, and how micro-level relationships and social networks develop. Ideas from the sociology of emotions perspective will be incorporated to emphasize that social relationships and networks ties involve emotional exchanges of various types as well as individual rational choice calculations. This applies in personal relationships as well as in more structured institutional settings.

Chapter 9 makes the transition from the micro to the meso and macro levels. The foundation provided by the social exchange and rational choice perspectives will help us understand how larger scale structures are developed to link individuals' own personal interests with conformity to norms that are intended, ideally, to ensure the general welfare. Chapter 10 will then focus on communities and organizations as meso-level social formations. Communities will be viewed as based on subjective emotional bonds and feelings of belonging, though such bonds may involve abstract ideals of solidarity as well as actual social relations. Formal organizations will be analyzed through the social exchange and rational choice perspective as involving the coordination of people's activities to achieve various collective or overlapping goals. However, the process of bringing people together in an organizational context may lead to the emergence of socioemotional ties and feelings of solidarity.

Chapter 11 will be devoted to markets and socioeconomic classes as meso-level social formations. The highly individualistic utilitarian assumptions of the social exchange and rational choice perspectives are manifested more fully in market transactions than in any other kind of social formation. Socioeconomic classes emerge from inequalities in the resources, both material and nonmaterial, that individuals have at their disposal as they seek to satisfy their various interests through market transactions. The emergence and persistence of socioeconomic classes appear to be an inevitable outcome of the competitive struggle whereby individuals seek to satisfy their needs and interests in an environment of scarce resources. These conflicting interests are basic in the conflict theory perspective—one of the major macro theories to be previewed shortly.

The next five chapters focus explicitly on the macro level. Chapters 12 and 13 are devoted to functional theory, emphasizing how individuals' actions are structured in various social institutions to contribute to larger social outcomes that may go beyond their intentions. Within this framework, human behavior is seen as reflecting shared values and contributing to the maintenance of the overall society.

In contrast to the functional perspective, Chap. 14 will focus on conflict theory. The potential for conflict is seen as pervasive at all levels of the social world because of the differences in the interests of different individuals and groups. The effects of conflict in stimulating social change are heavily emphasized in conflict theory, as well as the way the disruptive effects of conflict can often be minimized through the development of procedures to regulate it. Chapter 15 will then deal with critical theory. This theory also emphasizes conflicting interests among different segments of society, with stability and social order explained by the way the dominant culture shapes people's consciousness to support the system. Raising people's consciousness regarding this process is seen as a necessary first step in moving toward the liberation of people from oppressive social structures.

The five chapters in Part III will cover some contemporary perspectives that reflect multiple levels of analysis. Chapter 16 will include important examples of feminist theory. The focus in feminist theory on patriarchal forms of male domination and female subordination shares many features of both conflict theory and critical theory. In addition, the emphasis on social definitions of gender roles draws heavily from symbolic interaction theory as well.

Chapter 17 will review structuration theory and systems theory. Structuration theory highlights the interdependence of agency and structure, with the routine practices of everyday life contributing to the maintenance (or transformation) of the structures in which they are involved. The overview of systems theory will emphasize how the dynamics of social systems reflect the changing relations and patterns of interdependence that make them up as well as how they can be distinguished from other systems with which they are related.

Chapter 18 will introduce the sociobiological perspective to show how social behavior and cultural patterns may be viewed as reflecting human beings' biological and genetic heritage. Chapter 19 will focus on the dynamics of cultural system, particularly beliefs and systems of knowledge, patterns of behavioral self-control, and moral codes. Chapter 20 will deal with several themes from postmodern theoretical perspectives, including the fragmentation of cultural meaning and skepticism regarding all forms of knowledge and systems of authority. The arbitrary and socially constructed nature of the social world as highlighted in postmodern perspectives contrasts sharply with the sociobiological emphasis on our underlying biological and genetic heritage. Finally, Chap. 21 will be devoted to a brief summary of the major theoretical perspectives that we have reviewed, highlighting once again the importance of multiple theories to advance our understanding of the multiple levels of our complex and multidimensional social world.

Any textbook author seeking to cover a field as broad and as fragmented as contemporary sociological theory can certainly be accused of omitting important scholars or theoretical schools, of overemphasizing certain perspectives and underemphasizing others, or perhaps even misinterpreting some of the key ideas of important theorists. This volume is no exception in that regard. The effort to incorporate these different theories in a single voume is intended to suggest that they may indeed be integrated so as to provide a more comprehensive picture of the social world than any one theory by itself. Fortunately, despite their primary focus on either the micro and macro level, most of the major theories to be covered in this volume can be expanded to other levels as well.

In addition to comparing and contrasting different specialized theories with one another, I also seek to relate key theoretical ideas to everyday life experiences. The questions for study and discussion at the end of each chapter are intended to stimulate additional reflection on some of the major concepts and ideas that are covered and their application to various aspects of the social world with which you are familiar. Readers of this volume are already highly knowledgeable and skilled participants in their own social world. This means it is not necessary to start from scratch. Despite the abstract nature of the major theoretical perspectives in our field, the ultimate test for any sociological theory is its power to expand our consciousness of all aspects of the social world and to provide new insights that go beyond our implicit everyday life understanding.

It is a challenging but rewarding adventure that can last throughout your life. Welcome to the adventure!

Doyle Paul Johnson

Acknowledgments

Despite the many hours an author spends alone with a project, writing a book is definitely not a solo performance. I express my deepest appreciation to several individuals who have assisted me at various stages in this project. Dick Welna provided a great deal of encouragement at the beginning and through the completion of the first draft of this manuscript. In addition, several anonymous reviewers provided critical reactions and suggestions to various parts of a much earlier version. Although I probably was unable to respond adequately to all of their insightful suggestions, their evaluations were nevertheless helpful in the revision process.

I am particularly indebted to David Knottnerus (Oklahoma State University) and Michael McMullen (University of Houston at Clear Lake) for their encouragement, support, and good advice, plus their evaluation of the prospectus and some of the chapters of this volume, as well as to Robert Liebman (Portland State University) and Bernard Phillips (organizer of the Sociological Imagination group), for the support and encouragement they have provided. I have also benefited from numerous discussions with my departmental colleagues at Texas Tech University, in particular, Charlotte Dunham, Yung-mei Tsai, Andreas Schneider, and Alden Roberts, as well as Julie Harms Cannon and Adam Rafalovich (who were formerly at Texas Tech University). Jane Winer, Dean of the College of Arts and Sciences at Texas Tech University, also provided encouragement throughout the time this project was in process. Despite the good suggestions and helpful advice I have received from these colleagues and many others, I am very much aware of the shortcomings and deficiencies of my efforts to cover a field that is as broad and diverse as that represented by the different theoretical perspectives represented herein. Certainly, none of the colleagues named above should be considered responsible in any way for the limitations of this project.

In addition to numerous colleagues in the field, it is appropriate, too, to express my thanks and appreciation to the numerous students in my course in contemporary sociological theory at Texas Tech University over the last several years. Their attentiveness and reactions to the key ideas and many of the examples herein have been helpful in stimulating my efforts to improve the overall organization of the material and its practical applications.

Special thanks are due to Marilyn Knutson for her diligent reading and her detailed and spirited editing of the next-to-last version of the entire manuscript. Her revision suggestions helped considerably with reducing redundancy, correcting and clarifying ambiguities, and improving the overall flow. I also express appreciation to Teresa Krauss and Katie Chabalko, Springer Publishers, for their enthusiastic support and encouragement of this project.

Other than the author, probably no one is more aware than an author's spouse of how time-consuming and distracting a book-writing project can be. From the very beginning, my wife Sharon graciously and patiently tolerated my preoccupation with this project, provided encouraging support in many different ways, and helped me during the various stages of the writing and revising process to keep the project in proper perspective.

Contents

Part I
Setting the Stage

Chapter 1
Introduction: From Implicit to Explicit Theories

The practical common sense we use in everyday life includes a good deal of implicit sociological theorizing. The purpose of this chapter is to move beyond these implicit theories. The different levels of the social world which will be discussed in this volume range from face-to-face encounters and personal relationships to the large-scale institutional patterns of society and long-range social trends. The goal of this process is to develop a distinctive sociological imagination.[1] To establish a foundation for achieving these goals, this chapter will focus on the following topics:

- Everyday life theories and facts
- Implicit versus explicit theories
- Multiple levels of social reality and contrasting theoretical perspectives
- Agency and structure
- National variations in the classical roots of sociological theory

Everyday Life Theories and Facts of Life

People who take great pride in their good common sense may never think of their underlying assumptions about social life as a social theory—or of themselves as social theorists. "Who needs theory? Just give me the facts!" For practical people, the facts are expected to speak for themselves. If the needed facts aren't available, we may need to fall back on a theory until the appropriate evidence is available. But facts do not speak for themselves. They must be interpreted. This interpretation always draws on taken-for-granted or implicit theoretical ideas that go beyond the facts and give them their meaning in some larger frame of reference. Some form of theory is needed to make sense of "mere facts."

---

[1] This term is the title of C. Wright Mills' 1959 book, *The Sociological Imagination*. In Mills' view, the sociological imagination is the ability to see the connections between individuals' personal troubles and larger structural patterns in the society. More recently, Bernard Phillips (2001) used Mill's concept of the sociological imagination to make the case for an integrated "web" approach that would focus explicitly on integrating the diverse subfields of sociological knowledge.

D.P. Johnson, *Contemporary Sociological Theory: An Integrated Multi-Level Approach.*

In ordinary conversations, for example, both parties must interpret what one another says or does in the light of what they already know from previous experience with one another. When misunderstandings occur, efforts must be made to try to explain or reinterpret what was said and done. This may lead both parties to redefine their implicit assumptions regarding their relationship. People also interpret whole categories of people and situations based on far less information than they may have about specific individuals with whom they may be involved. Their images and assumptions include implicit theoretical ideas about the attitudes and behaviors of different types of people and why they have the characteristics attributed to them. Perhaps the most obvious example is when people's implicit negative theories about others who are different are used to rationalize or justify their prejudices and patterns of discrimination.

Because everyday life theories are widely shared, taken for granted, and seldom questioned, many people never examine them objectively or critically. Such theories may work satisfactorily for most people most of the time, despite their limitations. But these limitations sometimes prevent people from seeing things in a helpful new light. They may sometimes be wrong or inappropriate, especially when applied to circumstances different from those where they were developed. Also, as the social world changes or becomes more complex, we may be challenged to confront and to question some of our implicit common sense ideas about the way things are, and why.

Implicit theoretical assumptions also underlie all of our efforts to diagnose and solve social problems. Such current issues as the threat of terrorism, the ever-changing role of our country in world affairs, the volatility of the stock market, the problem of youth violence in our society, political and corporate corruption, family disruption, and many other social problems often generate heated theoretical debate in both public and private life. For many of these issues, we may not have all the facts needed to provide adequate answers. Of course, the absence of facts does not dissuade some people from being convinced that they have the answer anyway. But whether backed up by relevant facts or not, our efforts to understand and deal with the social world, both in terms of questions raised and arguments offered, draw on various theoretical assumptions that go beyond the facts or sometimes are even inconsistent with them.

Even when a theoretical argument appears to be based on facts, this does not necessarily mean that the facts provide conclusive proof for the theory. People with different backgrounds and different theoretical assumptions often interpret the same facts differently—and both interpretations may seem on the surface to make sense. In some situations, the relevant facts are complex and not easily determined, and thus different interpretations may result from focusing on different sets of facts. Moreover, as more and more facts become available it becomes increasingly likely that any given theory will need to be revised to accommodate them, or perhaps rejected and eventually replaced by a better theory.

Human beings often struggle to make sense of facts that seem fragmentary, ambiguous, and conflicting. This struggle becomes readily apparent when we have to make choices that may have serious future consequences. These choices always rest on various assumptions about how present decisions and actions can influence future events, and such assumptions are theoretical in nature. We may follow a strategy of looking at present or past trends to make an educated guess about the future. But which present or past trends should we focus on as the key to the future? And of course, there is never any guarantee that the future will be like the past. But the key point is that some type of theoretical perspective, some interpretive framework, is involved in projecting the future on the basis of present or past trends. The development of one's sociological imagination involves moving from these implicit frameworks and theoretical assumptions to more explicit types of theoretical reflection and analysis.

Moving from Implicit to Explicit Theories[2]

The distinction between implicit and explicit theories helps us focus on the changing and fuzzy boundary between beliefs and ideas that we take for granted and those we are challenged to examine intellectually. Although many implicit assumptions always remain beneath the level of conscious reflection, people's consciousness may sometimes be raised so that implicit assumptions become explicit. Challenges to common sense assumptions come from several different sources. Increasing contact with societies with different cultures may lead to greater awareness of cultural diversity and alternative possibilities other people have found for a satisfying life. Rapid social change may trigger new ideas and strategies for coping with change, particularly when established beliefs and customs seem less relevant or become obsolete. Increased rates or new forms of deviance, or threats to the status quo, may stimulate efforts to try to justify existing customs and norms. Subordinate or oppressed groups may begin to question their position and to formulate ideas and ideologies that are critical of the existing distribution of power, privileges, and resources. Dominant groups may respond by developing opposing theories and ideologies in an effort to defend their dominant position. Experiences such as these may lead to increased awareness of our underlying theoretical assumptions and the need to question, challenge, or defend them.

In a stable and isolated social environment we might expect people to be less likely to think through the key underlying assumptions of their worldview or the theoretical implications of the customs and habits they routinely follow. Without being required to justify or defend traditional customs and beliefs, it does not occur to them to see the social reality in which they are embedded as an intellectual puzzle requiring explanation (Berger, 1963). Instead, there is an obvious and matter-of-fact quality to the social world that doesn't need to be justified. Why develop a theory to explain the obvious? Things are the way they are simply because that is the way the world is. But, as Berger pointed out, the taken-for-granted character of the

[2] This distinction between implicit and explicit theories is adapted from D. P. Johnson ([1981] 1986:6–11).

social world is more difficult to sustain in a pluralistic society, or one undergoing rapid change. When breakdowns or misunderstandings occur, when the meaning of events is not clear, or when shared expectations aren't fulfilled, people must face the challenge of working out some strategy for dealing with these ambiguous or unanticipated developments. In the process differences in implicit assumptions may be revealed and become explicit as topics for discussion, debate, and problem-solving.

In an environment of extensive subcultural pluralism or rapid social change, people's acceptance of the customs and beliefs of their family and local community is probably more likely to reflect a conscious choice than when alternatives are unavailable. We might expect that their choices will be heavily influenced by the reactions they anticipate from others as well as whether their own personal interests can be more fully met by such change. For example, when broadly established family patterns and gender roles are accepted unquestioningly, as they were for many people during the 1950s, it may never occur to young people that there are any feasible alternatives to getting married and establishing a traditional-type family. But in a society where traditional family forms and gender roles have undergone rapid change, people become more aware of alternatives, each with its own distinctive advantages and disadvantages. Although some continue to conform to the traditional expectations without consciously thinking through all the options, these alternatives are nevertheless available, and probably most people are generally aware that their choices could be different.

The experience of being in a marginal social position can also help stimulate conscious reflection on the social world. In a society with a high level of mobility, many people have probably found themselves in the position of being an outsider from time to time. The new member of a club or organization, or the new resident (or tourist) in a community, is likely to experience this sense of not really belonging until he or she learns the new customs, develops new social relationships, and eventually becomes an insider. But in the meantime the newcomer may initially perceive the beliefs and customs that insiders take for granted as strange and requiring explanation. Perhaps one of the most dramatic examples of being an outsider or feeling marginal is visiting another country with a different language and discovering through awkward experiences that even the most elementary types of communication are extremely difficult. In addition, even for long-time residents who are seen as fundamentally different in some way, or who see themselves as different, this experience of being an outsider who doesn't really belong may continue indefinitely. In either case marginal persons are less likely to have the same implicit understanding of the social world as insiders. Instead, their understanding will reflect their status as outsiders, which may lead them to develop insights that insiders lack.

Self-conscious reflection on the social world does not necessarily always require such experiences as rapid social change, subcultural diversity, or outsider status, however. Some who live in stable or sheltered environments do **not** maintain a nonreflective or noncritical attitude toward their social world. Traditional village communities of the past had their free-thinking skeptics and nonconformists who questioned what others took for granted. Young people often question established customs and beliefs. Their parents and others in older generations may become more reflective themselves in the process of trying to explain or defend (or perhaps modify) these customs and beliefs. On the other hand, persons who live in a rapidly changing social environment with numerous subcultural alternatives may fail to see their social milieu as a source of intellectual puzzles at all. They may simply go through life without ever reflecting seriously on anything more than simply how to cope from day to day with a world that doesn't always make sense, or that has become too confusing and unpredictable.

Rapid social change is almost always accompanied by strains, ambiguity, and inconsistencies of various kinds. These may be experienced as dilemmas or problems for which established traditions do not provide ready-made solutions. The search for solutions may involve questioning traditional assumptions and developing new norms. Alternatively, efforts may be made to defend traditional beliefs, perhaps by reinterpreting them to fit the new situation. Whether established norms are defended and reinterpreted, or rejected and replaced, social or cultural forms lose the obvious, matter-of-fact quality that individuals accept and follow automatically. Instead, traditional patterns of belief and behavior come to be recognized as needing revision in the light of new situations and new problems.

Increased awareness of cultural or subcultural diversity does not guarantee that people will try to understand or relate to those who are different. People may still regard their own particular social world and their own beliefs and customs as superior, or at least preferable for them, even after learning that these beliefs and customs are not necessarily natural for everybody. People vary considerably not only in their awareness of diversity but also in their tolerance or acceptance of those who are different. Probably most people tend to be ethnocentric to a certain degree. That is, at a deep (and implicit) level of consciousness they tend to see their own beliefs and customs as preferable to those of others. But one of the outcomes of developing a sociological imagination is that we learn to learn to grasp alternative forms of social life from the point of view of those who live them. Those who succeed in this effort will understand that the beliefs and lifestyles of those who may be different are just as natural and make just as much sense for them as ours do to us. In addition, we will also understand that our own beliefs and patterns of behavior may appear equally strange to those in a different social world. The result is that we become more aware of the arbitrary nature of our own beliefs and customs.

Differences in people's willingness and ability to examine their social world objectively and analytically cannot be accounted for solely in terms of their social environment, however. Regardless of the social environment, intellectual reflection on one's beliefs is promoted by the scientific attitude of curiosity and objectivity as applied to human behavior and society. Increased interest in the social sciences, such as sociology, may itself be stimulated by such experiences as are discussed above, but such education is itself likely to encourage a questioning and sometimes critical attitude toward social reality and an increased appreciation for a wide range of cultural alternatives. In this process social customs and beliefs may become relativized to a degree, and individuals become more consciously aware of alternatives.

The study of sociological theory helps us understand that our everyday social world is based on widely accepted conventions or definitions that indeed go beyond mere facts and that give them their meaning and significance.

Multiple Levels of Social Reality and Contrasting Theoretical Perspectives

Social scientists and other academicians are sometimes accused of living in an "ivory tower" separated from the real world of practical affairs. Like all other academic disciplines and specialized areas of activity, sociology has indeed developed its own specialized language and distinctive interpretive frameworks for helping us understand the social world. One of the major goals of sociological theory is to make explicit the implicit beliefs and assumptions that form the basis for people's social behavior and the social worlds they have established. But the sociologist's specialized knowledge will never be equivalent to the deep implicit understanding of the particular social settings shared by insiders in that setting. The important question is whether sociological analysis leads to new insights and increased understanding of one's own social world as well as social worlds other than one's own. Sociological theorists themselves do not all use the same language or theoretical framework. Some perspectives are more difficult than others to relate to everyday life, and some no doubt provide more enlightenment and better understanding than others. From the beginning, sociology has been characterized by disagreements over what are the most important questions that can help us better understand the most fundamental features of the social world. With the expansion of sociology as a major academic discipline, this internal diversity has increased, with various subfields developing their own distinctive perspectives (see Ritzer, 1975, 1981; Phillips, 2001).

One of the most important differences is the split between those who focus on micro-level social processes versus those who seek to understand macro-level structures. The micro-level focus emphasizes face-to-face interaction and personal relationships and how these encounters and relationships are related to people's identities, motivations, and behaviors. In contrast, the macro-level focus involves an effort to understand larger-scale social systems, including the overall society, its major institutions and how they are interrelated, its socioeconomic class structure, and its relations with other societies in our increasingly globalized world. Both are valid and important areas of sociological inquiry, in the same way that both microscopes and telescopes are useful for helping us see features of the natural or material world that we would not otherwise see.

Our different micro-level social worlds at the local level are definitely not insulated from the wider social environment, particularly in modern societies. Many types of complex linkages can be identified among the innumerable and complex micro-level social worlds in which the millions of people who make up the larger society are involved. Some of these linkages bind them together, willingly or not, in larger social systems, including the nation-state and beyond. As individuals, we are involved in social systems that extend far beyond our face-to-face relations through our roles as students, employees, or consumers, for example; as members of organizations like honor societies, fraternities, or sororities that are national in scope, or certainly as taxpayers and citizens. In our consumer role, for example, we may purchase products from countries around the world, without reflecting on how little we know about the micro-level social worlds of those involved in their production.

Despite the personal nature of our most important social bonds, we also sometimes feel an emotional connection to people in far-off places whose stories are portrayed by the mass media, reacting with pride, envy, anger, or sadness to actions done by or to people whose faces and names we see only on television. For example, who can forget the September 11, 2001, terrorist airplane hijackings that resulted in the collapse of the World Trade Center towers in New York City, the destruction of part of the Pentagon in Washington, D.C., and the crash of a fourth airplane in rural Pennsylvania that failed to reach its target because of the heroic actions of the airline passengers? The extensive and repeated portrayal of this tragic event by the mass media and the palpable emotions it still triggers dramatize the point that we are connected at an emotional level to a much larger social world than our own personal micro-level social relations. The same pattern of widely shared emotional reactions can also be triggered by news reports of human suffering around the world, whether caused by human beings' violence toward one another or by natural catastrophes.

In addition to our emotional reactions to specific news events, we may also have a profound sense that our lives are affected in fundamental ways by large-scale economic, political, social, and cultural forces that are beyond our control as individuals or even our knowledge. These macro-level social influences that touch our lives are not forces of nature, like the seasons, mountain ranges, or thunderstorms, but instead result from the decisions and actions of human beings—somewhere beyond our own range of vision or immediate personal concern. We may sometimes question whether anybody really is in charge of the large-scale social systems that shape our lives (including the nation-state). But we are nevertheless aware that our lives are affected in various ways by political and economic decisions made by key people in positions of power and influence with whom we have no personal involvement.

Whether our interests are in the intricacies of face-to-face interaction or large-scale institutional trends in the overall society, both micro and macro levels of analysis are equally important. And in between the micro and macro extremes are various intermediate or "meso" level structures or social formations through which micro-level processes of face-to-face social relations can be linked with the macro-level patterns of the overall society. Some basic types of meso-level social formations that will be discussed in this volume include communities, complex organizations, markets, and socioeconomic classes. Each of us can no doubt locate ourselves in such meso-level structures. They are grounded in our face-to-face relations but they also link us with a larger social world that extends beyond the horizons of our own personal experience.

From the beginning, sociology clearly has been concerned with the overall macro-level structure of the overall society. The interrelated patterns of behavior of individuals in their micro-level settings exhibit their own distinctive dynamics and are interesting to study in their own right, even though the actions of particular individuals may have only limited effects on the larger system. On the other hand, however, it is the complex aggregation, combination, and coordination of these micro-level patterns of action throughout society that constitute the macro-level social world. Social structures and systems do not even exist on their own, at either the micro or macro level, independently of the individuals whose actual social behavior helps to reproduce (or sometimes change) them. The question of how individuals' actions combine to generate wide-ranging macro-level effects, either intentionally or unintentionally, is one of the central questions addressed in sociological theory.

At the same time, the structures and patterns of the macro-level social world help constrain and shape our behavior through both the "meso" and the "micro" systems in which we are involved. This mutual interdependence of individuals' micro-level social actions and macro-level social structures is particularly important in analyzing **recurrent** or **general patterns** of behavior that are widespread throughout society. Such patterns can be analyzed independently of particular individuals in their local contexts. Even when macro-level patterns are not consciously recognized, the actions of individuals at the micro level nevertheless contribute to their reproduction, either intentionally or unintentionally.

For example, sociologists or social theorists may be interested in explaining how changing birth rates may be related to the state of the economy or general cultural attitudes toward children, even though individual decisions to have or not to have children will reflect personal choices that are not at all oriented consciously toward trends in birth rates or the overall state of the economy or the culture. Similarly, social theorists may seek to understand patterns of upward or downward socioeconomic mobility in a society without reference to particular individuals who are trying to "get ahead" or "get by" in terms of their own personal well-being. The difference between a focus on particular individuals in their local contexts and analysis of widespread patterns and trends of behavior within larger social systems can be likened to the contrast between a microscopic view of the social world versus a telescopic view.

From the standpoint of particular individuals in their local settings, the overall structures and dominant cultural patterns of a society may be taken as background or context, and their primary focus is the specific situation in which they find themselves. However, to understand society itself, sociological analysis at the macro level must focus on the major institutions of society as well as differences among people such as those based on social class, race/ethnicity, gender, or age. This means that our analyses of major institutional structures must be linked with an understanding of how individuals are stratified into various socioeconomic classes and numerous other categories that distinguish them from one another. Widespread inequalities among people in terms of basic life chances and well-being may be seen as inconsistent with widely acclaimed cultural ideals and moral values, and this discrepancy is often the source of individual frustration and alienation as well as an important area of sociological inquiry.

The different levels of the social world may be illustrated by a brief consideration of the educational establishment. The face-to-face relations between students and professor in a particular classroom clearly constitute a micro-level system within the university, but it also reflects the broad cultural values of academic achievement and intellectual development. In terms of structure, there is obviously a clear difference between the positions of professors and students in the university's hierarchy of authority, and the professor's ability to establish the agenda and assign grades is crucial in analyzing the specific dynamics of their relationship. If personal relationships should develop, they would exhibit their own unique trajectory, influenced by each person's specific background. But any particular class is part of the larger university system, which has its own complex division of labor as reflected in its various divisions and departments representing different academic disciplines, student support services, recruitment efforts, alumni relations, athletic programs, and financial affairs. The university itself is part of the public or private educational sector of the state and the nation. Moreover, colleges and universities have various types of relations with many other organizations as well, including accrediting agencies, legislative bodies, research funding agencies, athletic associations, corporate or individual donors, potential employers of graduates, and many others.

A specific university could be considered a relatively low-level meso structure, while all of the universities in a given state could be regarded as a higher-level meso-structure. For doing a sociological analysis at this level, the specific interaction patterns within a particular classroom would probably be overlooked. Of course, aggregate data such as average class size, student-to-teacher ratio, or proportions of social science majors could readily be obtained and used to do various types of analyses, such as changes over time or comparisons with other universities.

If we expand our view by moving from the state to the national level, all of the colleges and universities of all 50 states, public and private, including two-year community colleges, constitute the system of higher education. The concept of "system" or "institution" in this context obviously goes beyond any single organization. Colleges and universities in the United States are not organized as components of any single national system, even though public and private universities are regulated by state and/or regional accrediting agencies. But despite the lack of an overarching formal organizational structure, there are numerous similarities among colleges and universities throughout the country that contrast with colleges and universities in other countries.

To expand the telescopic view even further, the education "system" would also include the thousands of local elementary, junior, and senior high school systems throughout the country, most of which actually are governed at the local level but which have to comply with various guidelines from the state or national level. Moreover, the socialization and education process is not limited to the specialized "educational establishment." Families also engage in basic educational activities as parents try to teach their children and also serve as role models for them. So do day-care centers, boys' and girls' clubs, and religious groups. With this example, it is clear that there are alternative levels of analysis on which one may focus in analyzing society's "system" of education. Similar distinctions among alternative levels of analysis could be made with regard to other institutional structures in our society, including, for example, families, religion, businesses, government agencies, health care, and voluntary associations of all types.

The distinctions among micro, meso, and macro levels of analysis enable us to compare and contrast alternative theories in terms of the scope of their view of social reality. Theories vary in terms of whether their primary focus is more toward the micro or the macro end of the scale or somewhere in the middle. At the same time, however, all of the theories to be discussed in this volume can be elaborated and extended to other levels beyond their primary focus. A good theory can be expanded to enhance our awareness of how the different levels of the social world are interrelated. The ability to see sociologically significant connections between different levels of the social world increases our understanding and our consciousness beyond the implicit theories of everyday common sense.

Agency and Structure

The contrast between an overarching "social structure" that determines our behavior versus the ability of individuals to exercise their freedom in controlling their own actions goes back to the beginnings of sociology. In recent years, the concept of "agency" has been employed to emphasize the intentional and voluntary aspects of "social action" as individuals make choices, often in concert with others, from among the alternatives available to them. In contrast, those who focus on structure point out that these "choices" reflect structural constraints that limit individuals' options and freedom of action. Although the "structure" is obviously not a physical entity or object, it nevertheless has tangible effects on the distribution of material resources that individuals have available for meeting their needs or pursuing their personal goals. Structural influences are also reflected in the expectations of others as well as in one's own views of appropriate behavior that have been internalized in the socialization process and incorporated in the habitual routines of everyday life.

This emphasis on "agency" versus "structure" will be analyzed in more detail later on in connection with Anthony Giddens' (1984) "structuration theory." Mouzelis (1995) pointed out that the emphasis on agency has typically been associated with micro-level analysis, while the emphasis on structure has been associated with macro-level analysis. However, micro-level social behavior is also **structured** in the sense that it is not random but tends to follow (more or less) regular and often predictable patterns. Similarly, macro-level structures are not automatically self-sustaining, but require deliberate decisions and actions by individuals that reflect their particular choices and intentions. The decisions and actions of people as agents in key structural positions may have wide-ranging consequences and thus may appear to others as establishing external constraints beyond their control that limit the choices these others are able to make. Such processes, in which the decisions and actions of some limit and influence the decisions and actions of others, are highly amenable to macro-level, meso-level, and micro-level analysis.

Between the micro level of face-to-face personal relations and the institutional structures of society are such varied social formations as social networks, communities, formal organizations, social institutions, socioeconomic classes, and so on. Many of these meso-level social formations are represented in various specialized areas of sociological inquiry. Because the scope of sociological theory is so broad, covering all aspects of the social world, differences among scholars who focus on different levels or different aspects of our complex and multi-faceted social world should not be surprising.

The establishment of sociology as a discipline concerned with the structure of society itself (as opposed to individual behavior or interpersonal interaction at the micro level) was largely a European enterprise in the beginning, though the specific focus varied in different countries. In contrast, the earliest perspectives in American sociology tended to focus more on the micro level, though they were influenced from the beginning by the European pioneers. Eventually, the macro-focus became dominant in American sociology as well; however, the micro-level focus has consistently remained strong. The following section will highlight briefly the intellectual backgrounds that influenced the founding figures of the discipline.

National Variations in the Origins of Sociological Theory[3]

Clear contrasts can be identified among the classical-stage founders of sociology regarding the nature of sociology as a distinct field of study. These differences reflected variations in intellectual climate at the time, but comparable differences persist in contemporary sociology. One of the sharpest contrasts was between French positivism and German historicism. The positivist viewpoint was that human behavior is governed by universal natural laws that could be discovered through the same type of objective scientific investigation that is used in the other natural sciences. In contrast, German historicism involved the notion that the social world can best be understood in terms of the shared subjective meanings derived from the specific cultural traditions of a particular society rather than universal natural laws.

A third distinct emphasis can be identified in British social thought in which individuals' decisions and actions reflect primarily their own individual interests but also generate various social outcomes that go beyond individuals' intentions. Sociology in the United States was heavily influenced by all of these traditions.

[3]This brief survey of national variations in the classical roots of contemporary sociological theory is adapted from D. P. Johnson ([1981] 1986:22–27).

However, the early American social theorists added a strong pragmatic emphasis on social reforms intended to promote progress and improve individuals' well-being. To understand better the roots of sociology it is worth looking at these differences in more detail.

Postrevolutionary French Positivism

This perspective was reflected by Auguste Comte and his activist mentor St. Simon in the first half of the nineteenth century, and also by Émile Durkheim in the later part of the nineteenth and the early twentieth centuries. In this approach, all knowledge is based ultimately on sensory experiences or empirical data from the external world. This emphasis (which may seem to some today like noncontroversial common sense) represented a shift away from a worldview in which long-established traditions, many of which were grounded in religious beliefs, provided knowledge that was regarded as even more fundamental than knowledge of the material world based on sensory experience. In the perspective of positivism, traditional religious beliefs were regarded with skepticism as irrational and superstitious. Instead, valid knowledge was based on experience of the real (material) world, and scientific methods were needed to advance our understanding of it. Not only the world of nature, but also human behavior and society are governed by universal natural laws that can be discovered through scientific investigation. The results of such investigations can then used as a guide for establishing a more rational or enlightened society. In this way, social order and progress would be assured. The notion that sociologists would serve as counselors (or consultants) to political authorities was manifested in different ways by both Comte and Durkheim. Comte envisioned a dominant position for sociologists in the positivist industrial society of the future. Durkheim's vision was less grandiose, but he felt that sociological knowledge should contribute to a cohesive social order. Despite the changes in our contemporary understanding of science and knowledge systems, the contemporary vision of sociology as a discipline based on systematic empirical investigation reflects this tradition.

German Historicism

In contrast with the French positivist belief in universal natural laws that can be discovered through scientific methods, German social theorists saw a sharp distinction between the natural sciences and the social sciences. While natural laws determine events in the physical world, the social world is characterized by freedom and the ability of human beings to make choices that are not determined in a strong sense by natural laws. As biological organisms human beings are subject to the laws of nature, of course, but their social actions are not subject to the same kinds of constraints as biological or physical phenomena. Instead, human behavior must be explained in terms of its **meaning**, which means understanding individuals' subjective orientations and intentions. Beyond the individual level, the overall dynamics of a society must be understood from the perspective of its distinctive culture—its worldview, ideals, and values. Although insight into subjective meanings is not relevant for explaining the movements of physical objects, it is essential for understanding human behavior. For example, the action of a baseball player running around a baseball diamond after hitting a home run makes no sense except in terms of the subjectively shared rules and values of the game.

The goal of understanding the distinctive cultural "spirit" of a society as manifested in its culture and social institutions does not preclude comparative studies of different societies. However, such studies should not gloss over the differences between societies in the search for universal laws. Instead, comparative study should be oriented toward highlighting the significant cultural traditions that distinguish different societies, as well as how these different traditions are implemented in each society's social institutions and in individuals' actions. Such differences are inconsistent with the notion of universal deterministic laws governing social behavior.

Among the classical stage theorists both Karl Marx and Max Weber were heirs to the German historicist tradition. However, Marx ultimately rejected the emphasis on the deterministic influence of culture. In particular, he rejected Georg Wilhelm Friedrich Hegel's perspective on how the influence of cultural or spiritual ideals in society are gradually expanded through a long-term historical process involving the clash of opposing ideas. In Hegel's dialectical perspective, the dominant cultural ideas of each historical epoch are eventually contested; however, these contradictions are eventually resolved through a kind of reconciling synthesis, thereby setting the stage for the process to be repeated in the future. Marx applied this dialectical method to the clash of socioeconomic classes instead of ideas. He did, however, recognize the importance of the subjective consciousness shared among people (such as ideologies and class consciousness), and he emphasized that human beings' potential for cultural creativity could be developed more fully if people had the resources required to move beyond the challenges of mere physical survival. Weber was more systematic in his comparative studies of societies with different cultural traditions. His methodological strategies involved efforts to identify the unique cultural and institutional features of different societies while analyzing them in a comparative way. Some of the key ideas of both Marx and Weber will be elaborated more fully in Chap. 2. The emphasis of many contemporary sociologists on the importance of understanding subjective meaning and the dynamics of cultural systems can be seen as elaborating this early perspective.

English-Scottish Laissez-Faire Political Economy and British Utilitarianism

Classical economic theory and British utilitarianism emphasize that people make choices that are intended to promote their pleasure or profit and minimize pain or costs.

This highly individualistic focus contrasts with the German emphasis on how individuals' consciousness and motivations are shaped by deeply shared cultural patterns of a society as well as the French focus on the societal level of analysis. The most obvious application of this individualistic perspective is in the marketplace where individuals' decisions and action are guided by their own particular interests. The same principles underlie classical theories of crime and punishment in which it was believed that people can be deterred from crime if the pain of punishment outweighs the profit or pleasure to be derived from the crime.

When such theories are extended beyond the individual level to explain the overall organization of society, some form of a "social contract" assumption is involved. That is, human beings, acting out of their rational self-interest, voluntarily reach an agreement to restrict their autonomy, establish governments, surrender some of their "natural" rights, and obey rules that they develop to control their unbridled competition and conflict, insure social stability, and perhaps encourage various forms of cooperation. However, the long-term progress of society requires these controls to be limited. The classical economist Adam Smith described this paradox in which individuals' greed for personal gain becomes transformed, as though by the guidance of an invisible hand, into the welfare of society as a whole. This same perspective survives today in the form of ideological justification of the free enterprise system and opposition to excessive government interference in the private sector.

The once highly influential theory of social evolution that was developed later by Herbert Spencer involved many of these same assumptions. Spencer's overall goal was to show how the evolutionary process, biological as well as social, had involved gradual long-term growth in the size and complexity of various types of systems. This process was seen as being naturally progressive, based on the ongoing efforts of human beings to improve their individual well-being. This approach led Spencer to believe that the functions of government should be limited. In fact, he argued that as governments become stronger and more centralized, they tend to become more militaristic and thus detract from continued societal progress in enabling human beings to adapt better to their environment.

These ideas from Spencer played into the development of a "social Darwinist" perspective among several early American sociologists. This perspective provided ideological support to the growth of big business organizations, whose success was believed to "prove" their superior adaptive ability and their contribution to social progress. These implications were eventually rejected by social scientists, but the underlying focus on increasing growth in the size and complexity of societies (and other social systems) has been a major ingredient of the sociological image of long-range social change through a large part of the twentieth century. Moreover, the policy implications of this individualistic and utilitarian approach survive in the private enterprise arguments of conservative Republicans in our own time. The underlying principles of this approach are also reflected in the type of social exchange theory that was developed in sociology in the 1960s, as well as the more recent development of rational choice theory and its application to social organization.

All three of the intellectual sources described thus far—French positivism, German historicism, and British classical economics and utilitarianism—were incorporated into American sociology from the beginning, but with varying emphases over the years. In addition, the intellectual and social context of Italy is also relevant to note as background for the distinctive influence of Italian sociologist Vilfredo Pareto. The political environment of Italy was highly fragmented, and the idealistic notion that sociology could be relevant for guiding social reform or reorganization did not develop in Italy the way it did in France with Comte and Durkheim. Like Comte and Dukheim, however, Pareto was strongly committed to the scientific methods of positivism. In his perspective, the development of sociology as a scientific discipline would require exploring the underlying sentiments and characteristics of human nature that lie beneath the surface of the cultural variations as emphasized in German historicism. In addition to these distinctive European influences on the development of modern sociology, it should be noted that various forms of social theory and social thought can be identified in the non-Western world as well. Intellectual reflection about social life can also traced back to the ancient world, including the works of Plato and Aristotle. The following section will highlight the emergence of a distinctive American perspective from within the pragmatic tradition.

American Pragmatism and Micro-Level Interaction

American sociology today continues to reflect the European roots discussed above as well as contemporary contacts with scholars across the Atlantic. In the early years European theorists were introduced into the American sociological perspective by the pioneering "Chicago school" theorists, by Talcott Parsons, and by others. One distinctive American contribution to sociological theory was the symbolic interactionist perspective, which grew out of George Herbert Mead's "social behaviorism." This development provided the foundation for a form of social psychology that was different from that offered in psychology, and that focused primarily on the interrelated processes of interaction at the micro-level and subjective interpretation. In addition, the Chicago school in the first 20 to 30 years of the twentieth century included pioneering research in urban community studies, race and ethnic relations, deviant behavior, occupational behavior, and other substantive areas.

From the beginning, a large part of the American cultural mentality has been characterized in part by impatience with speculative ideas with no apparent practical value. Instead, ideas tended to be evaluated in terms of their usefulness in dealing with real-life problems. This emphasis was reflected in the educational reforms advocated by John Dewey, a leading pragmatist and central figure in the Chicago school.[4] Although Dewey is remembered today as a proponent of educational

[4] According to John Dewey's educational philosophy, formal academic learning should not be separated from everyday life problem solving. Thus, for example, the principles of democracy could be more effectively learned by participating in democratic decision making in the classroom than by memorizing the Declaration of Independence or other abstract principles.

reform, not as a pioneer in sociology, his pragmatic insights regarding the close link between thought processes, the growth of knowledge, and problem-solving action were shared by George Herbert Mead, his University of Chicago colleague. Mead analyzed in detail the way the human mind enables human beings to cope with problems they encounter by thinking through and anticipating the probable consequences of alternative lines of behavior without going through the sometimes risky process of trial and error. Moreover, unlike most other animals, human beings actually transform their environment in major ways as they adapt to it, as opposed to fitting into a natural ecological niche.

American sociology was also influenced from the beginning by the strong individualism of American culture, which was consistent with the individualism of British classical economics and utilitarianism described above, if not more so. From the beginning of the United States political system, individualistic values were promoted against the conflicting claims of a strong central government. However, this individualism could sometimes be modified by a surge of national solidarity and patriotism in the face of an external threat such as war, and it could also be undermined by an emphasis on group-based identities such as those involving race/ethnicity, social class, and gender. This emphasis on conformity could, in turn, eventually trigger critical concerns about the loss of individualism and various threats to its expression.

Given this individualism, it is not surprising that the American sociological pioneers would provide a micro-level view of social reality that focused heavily on relationships and transactions among more or less independent individuals as the foundation of the social structure. The image of social institutions grounded in long-term cultural traditions that are independent of individuals' intentions or decisions was far less prominent than the alternative picture of social groups as being established (or changed) by voluntary agreements negotiated among individual participants. A distinctive focus on large-scale social structures that are at least partially independent of individuals' motives and decisions was eventually developed in American sociology. But this more macro focus was initially influenced by exposure to the European pioneers.

The pragmatic emphasis in the American mentality was combined with an optimistic belief in progress. There were major differences, however, in whether or not deliberate or intentional social reform efforts were considered necessary to insure social progress. Chicago School theorists such as Mead and Dewey were in favor of reform efforts to cope with emerging social problems. Others associated with the Chicago School were concerned with specific social problems in poor inner-city neighborhoods, including crime and delinquency, unemployment, social disorganization, deleterious housing, and the challenge of assimilating immigrants into the mainstream of American society. Jane Addams was a key figure in the development of the social work profession because of her promotion of social reforms and her pioneering work in the settlement house movement in Chicago. But American reformers in general were not interested in total social reorganization as much as in ameliorative projects and programs directed toward specific problems.

Others, however, were influenced by Spencer's laissez-faire orientation as described earlier and feared that social reform efforts, especially when undertaken by government, would undermine long-term progress by interfering with the natural evolutionary process. This can be illustrated in the influential theoretical perspective of William Graham Sumner ([1906] 1979, 1934), who was doubtful that such reforms could be implemented successfully as planned, particularly if they are contrary to the folkways and norms that had gradually evolved as an integral part of a society's traditions. In addition, the strong individualistic emphasis of American culture tended to be resistant to government-sponsored reform efforts, and the expansive nature of the American economy for much of its history encouraged widespread beliefs that ample opportunities existed for individuals to improve their lot in life through their own personal efforts.

Summary

As an academic discipline, sociology represents a commitment to moving beyond the implicit taken-for-granted theories of everyday life in our efforts to increase our understanding of the social world. An important part of this enterprise is the development of explicit theories that can be used to help us explain how individuals' social behavior is influenced by their social environment. This environment can be viewed from a micro-level perspective that focuses on face-to-face relationships, a macro-level perspective devoted to the structure of the overall society, or a meso-level perspective that analyzes various social formations in between. At all of these levels, a major challenge is to analyze the interdependence of individual agency, as manifested in the specific dynamics of people's intentional actions in various social settings, and the structural patterns that may influence these actions—and also be influenced by them.

Contemporary theoretical perspectives reflect important ideas transplanted from Europe as well as their distinctive American roots. We looked briefly at the influences of French positivism, German historicism, British utilitarianism, and American pragmatism. As American sociology has become more and more fragmented into specialized areas of research, sociological theory has become a specialized area of its own but with a much wider domain, including both micro and macro levels of analysis. Moreover, much of the practical concern with solving social problems, as manifested in the early years of the Chicago School, has been institutionalized in the establishment of social work as a separate area of professional practice. This commitment to using sociological knowledge and research strategies in practical problem solving has also been expressed more recently in the emergence of applied sociology as a specialized field within the discipline.

For the most part sociology today gives top priority to scholarly inquiry and research rather than advocacy for social reform. But the ideal of using sociology to expand our understanding of the social world includes a deep concern to promote awareness of the problems many people face because of the way society is structured. Many sociologists are committed to showing how opportunities are limited and constrained through pervasive patterns of domination and subordination based on class, gender, race/ethnicity, sexual orientation, and other sources of diversity. Despite their differences probably most sociologists and social theorists would subscribe to C. Wright Mills' argument (either explicitly or implicitly) that the sociological imagination promotes an awareness of how the fortunes and misfortunes of individuals' lives are related to the dynamics of more macro structural and institutional processes. Much more than in Mills' time, these macro-level processes reach beyond our national borders to a global level.

Contemporary theory can be defined broadly to refer to the major schools of theory that have been influential since the middle of the twentieth century. Beginning approximately in the mid-to-late 1960s, fundamental changes in the field led to increased fragmentation among competing theoretical perspectives which continues to the present. A major goal in this volume will be to compare and contrast different theoretical perspectives in terms of the level of social reality on which they focused and the particular social processes that they emphasized. Most theories can be identified with a primary focus on either the micro level or the macro level, but most of these clearly move toward other levels as well. In addition, we will look explicitly at some major types of intermediate meso level social formations as well. By understanding clearly the differences in the level of social reality on which one may wish to focus, it is easier to identify the appropriate theory (or theories) for analyzing that particular level as well as compare and contrast different theories with one another. The result should be that we will be able to use the appropriate theory to expand our understanding of the specific area of the social world that we wish to analyze as well as its relations to other levels.

Questions for Study and Discussion

1. Recognizing the importance of the social environment in stimulating an intellectual interest in sociological inquiry, what were the specific influences in **your** life that led to your interest in sociology? In what ways have your implicit views regarding human behavior and society been modified or confirmed through your sociological study?
2. Identify some of the ways that your micro-level social world of relations with family and friends is influenced by macro-level structures or cultural influences of the wider environment?
3. What are the most important meso-level structures in which you are involved (school, work, voluntary organizations, and so on)? To what extent do you find that these structures determine your actions, as opposed to allowing you the freedom to make your own decisions on how to act and what goals to pursue?
4. In trying to explain why people behave as they do, how would you contrast the positivist viewpoint regarding universal laws that govern human behavior with the historicist viewpoint regarding the need to consider specific cultural traditions? Give an example of each of these types of explanation.

5. In considering the practical utility of sociological knowledge, what do you see as the most urgent contemporary social problems that sociologists should be investigating? Would the solution be likely to involve challenging, or trying to change, people's implicit assumptions about the way the social world works?

Chapter 2
Classical Stage European Sources of Sociological Theory

From the very beginning people have always been immersed in their social worlds and have influenced one another, both intentionally and unintentionally, in various ways, positive and negative. Their relationships, whether cooperative or competitive, long-term or short-term, have always involved common sense theoretical assumptions regarding why different people behave as they do and how they should adapt to one another or organize themselves for some common purpose. This applies to face-to-face relationships as well as larger social systems. Many of these implicit assumptions and beliefs, which may vary greatly in different societies or different groups within a society, tend to be passed along from generation to generation as parents socialize their children.

Although people have always speculated and theorized about human beings' behavior and the organization of their society, the scientific approach to social life as we understand it today did not develop until just a few hundred years ago. This chapter reviews this development briefly as a foundation for the more detailed discussion of contemporary theories in subsequent chapters. The general topics to be covered in this chapter include the following:

- Social and intellectual background—This section will highlight the growth of science and the transformation from traditional to modern society as helping stimulate the development of sociology. The contributions of Auguste Comte will be described briefly, plus the transition from the eighteenth century faith in reason to the nineteenth century rediscovery of the persistence of nonrational features of social life.
- Major European founders—This section will provide a highly selective review of the key contributions of Émile Durkheim, Karl Marx, Max Weber, and Georg Simmel to modern sociology.
- Other important classical-stage theorists—In this section, the contributions of several additional pioneering theorists will be highlighted, including Harriet Martineau, Alexis de Tocqueville, Vilfredo Pareto, Ferdinand Tönnies, and Marianna Weber.

D.P. Johnson, *Contemporary Sociological Theory: An Integrated Multi-Level Approach.*

Social and Intellectual Background

Auguste Comte has sometimes been called the "father of sociology," but the scientific approach he advocated was foreshadowed 500 years earlier by Ibn Khaldun, a solitary intellectual of the fourteenth century Arab world (see Chambliss, 1954:285–312). Khaldun's goal was to explain the historical process of the rise and fall of civilizations in terms of a pattern of recurring conflicts between tough nomadic desert tribes and sedentary-type societies with their love of luxuries and pleasure. He believed that the advanced civilizations that develop in densely settled communities are accompanied by a more centralized political authority system and by the gradual erosion of social cohesion within the population. As a result such societies become vulnerable to conquest by tough and highly disciplined nomadic peoples from the unsettled desert. Eventually, however, the hardy conquerors succumb to the temptations of the soft and refined lifestyle of the people they had conquered, and so the cycle is eventually repeated. Although this cyclical theory was based on Khaldun's observations of social trends in the Arabian desert, his goal was to develop a **general** model of the dynamics of society and the process of large-scale social change. His insights were neglected by European and American social theorists, however, perhaps partly because of the growing dominance of Western Europe over the Arab world in succeeding centuries.

A full understanding of why sociology emerged when it did would require detailed consideration of the convergence of the material, social, and intellectual transformations that had been occurring since before the eighteenth century. But it was Auguste Comte, writing in the first half of the nineteenth century, who coined the term "sociology" and whose ideas helped lay the foundation for the modern concept of sociology as a science.[1] In contrast to Khaldun's cyclical theory, Comte's (1858) model of long-range historical change was linear and reflected his goal of explaining both social stability and progress. His concept of sociology as the scientific study of the social world influenced Émile Durkheim half a century later and is still a basic tenet of the sociological perspective.

---

[1] Comte's first and major work, entitled *The Course of Positive Philosophy* and published between 1830 and 1842, set forth a vision for sociology that would not only explain the whole course of human beings' social and intellectual history but also provide a scientific basis for social reorganization. A summary of Comte's contributions to the establishment of sociology was previously published in Johnson ([1981] 1986:71–89). The first chapter of Lewis Coser's *Masters of Sociological Thought* (Coser, 1977:3–41) is devoted to Auguste Comte and provides a succinct overview of his major contributions, biographical details of his life, and background information regarding the social and intellectual context. Coser's book provides similar information for several other figures who are important for the development of sociology. See also Turner et al. (2002:7–33) for a additional information regarding Comte's major contributions and intellectual context.

Science, Social Evolution, and the Dream of a More Rational Society

The growth of the scientific mentality was a major stimulus for the birth of sociology. By the dawn of the nineteenth century, the scientific method had already made great advances in the physical sciences. In physics and astronomy it had been established that uniformities in the movements of physical objects, such as planets and falling rocks, could be explained by natural laws that could be discovered through scientific investigation. In biology much attention was given to classifying different species but a major breakthrough occurred with the 1859 publication of Charles Darwin's theory of biological evolution. By this time the notion of a long-term evolutionary process had already been used by numerous social theorists to try to explain the development of modern societies. Many of the new scientific discoveries led to conflict with traditional religious teachings, however, and many early social theorists believed that the influence of traditional religious teachings and practices would decline as scientific knowledge advanced.

The technological developments stimulated by the growth in scientific knowledge helped reinforce the validity of the scientific method. The employment of new production technologies in the emerging factory system and widespread migrations from rural to urban areas represented social changes leading to new kinds of socioeconomic class relations, new forms of exploitation, and numerous social problems. The goal of developing sociology as a scientific discipline resulted in large part from various efforts to understand these long-range and pervasive social transformations. The challenge was to explain the implications of the long-term transition from a rural and village-based agricultural society to an increasingly urban industrial social order. Of course, the stability and tranquility of traditional societies was sometimes overestimated. Nevertheless, it was the idealized image of the past that provided a basis of comparison with the strains and transformations of the unsettled and uncertain present. Despite the variations in different countries and at different times, all of the pioneering sociological theorists included an implicit (or explicit) dichotomy contrasting traditional with modern forms of society, plus models for explaining the transition from the former to the latter.

In addition to these internal transformations, Europeans had long been absorbing stories of social life and customs of people in nonindustrial or "pre-modern" societies in far-off places that had been brought back by traders, missionaries, and adventurers. To be sure, these contacts often involved efforts to dominate, colonize, and convert them. Nevertheless, this expanded knowledge led to speculation about cultural variations and about how societies might have evolved from pre-industrial and "primitive" forms to more advanced, complex, and urban-industrial types.

Most of the early sociologists dealt with the process of social evolution in various ways. One of the most notable was the British social theorist Herbert

Spencer.[2] He developed an elaborate theory of how societies had evolved over the centuries from simple, small-scale systems to complex, large-scale systems as a result of people's ongoing efforts to improve their overall well-being. This perspective has typically been regarded as highly individualistic. However, Spencer also noted that advances in moral sentiments accompanied the increased size and complexity of social systems. Given the importance of this evolutionary process in insuring social progress, it was important not to interfere with it, such as through excessive government regulation and control, for example. Of course, he regarded Great Britain (or modern European societies in general) as the most advanced in this long evolutionary process. This belief in evolutionary progress became highly influential in both England and America and influenced greatly the early development of American sociology.

In retrospect, we now understand that such ethnocentric attitudes of cultural superiority helped justify Western European colonialism. Despite Spencer's distrust of government interference in the natural evolutionary process, early social theorists recognized the increasing importance of the nation-state, particularly in international affairs but also in promoting internal social order. Colonial exploits were a major source of the material resources needed by developing nation-states to strengthen their control and expand international trade. As nation-states became stronger, the power and autonomy of local communities, villages, families, and other smaller-scale social units decreased. Combined with the changes brought about by increased mobility and urbanization, it seemed clear that traditional, localized small-scale social structures were being overshadowed by the expansion of larger-scale and more complex social structures, particularly nation-states.

Another important development that helped explain the nineteenth century rise of sociology as a scientific discipline was a wide-spread loss of faith in the optimistic eighteenth century "Enlightenment" belief in the power of reason to insure social progress through rational reorganization of society. This faith in the possibility of using reason to reorganize society had helped foster the critical social thought that led eventually to the French Revolution. Even the opening lines of our own Declaration of Independence ("We hold these truths to be self-evident…") reflect a faith in the ability to discover "self-evident" truths through the power of reason.

[2] Herbert Spencer (1820–1903) worked as a civil engineer in his early years but his father and grandfather were both teachers. His initial writings were as a journalist who was a strong advocate for individual rights. As he developed his expanding views, the books he wrote applied his general evolutionary perspective to human intelligence as well as the increasing size and complexity of social systems. Although he has not part of the academic establishment, his writings eventually became influential among leading intellectuals. His evolutionary perspective on societies as social systems was long considered crucial for the establishment of sociology as an academic discipline (Spencer, 1967). See Turner (1985) for a detailed summary of Spencer's theoretical perspective and Turner et al. (2002:43–101) and Coser (1977:88–127) for succinct overviews of Spencer's contributions and intellectual context.

We should remember in this context that the French Revolution, which was intended to establish a more rational society, occurred less than two decades after the American revolution. However, the strong faith in reason as the main source of knowledge of universal natural laws was severely shaken by the tumultuous social and political events of the nineteenth century. Thus the emergence of sociology occurred at a time when many intellectuals were becoming acutely aware of the persistence of the nonrational foundations of people's behavior and the traditions that help maintain social order.

Confronting the Nonrational Dimensions of Social Life

The establishment of sociology may perhaps be seen in part as a result of a struggle to understand, within a rational scientific perspective, the nonrational (or irrational) aspects of human behavior and of society itself. Auguste Comte's "positivist" approach to understanding society reveals this dilemma between reason and the nonrational. His pioneering theoretical perspective (which reflected the ideas of his one-time mentor, Henri St. Simon) involved the argument that the entire scope of human beings' intellectual history, and each of the various sciences in particular (physical and biological as well as social), had gone through three great stages—the "theological, the metaphysical, and the positive." Each stage had made an important contribution to progress, but was destined to be replaced by the next stage over the long course of human evolution. Since sociology was the last of the various sciences to reach the final "positive" stage, its "data" would include the advanced knowledge already acquired in all of the other sciences. This means that sociology would be able to provide the most comprehensive explanation of the scientific laws governing intellectual and social progress. Once discovered, these laws could (and should) be used as a basis for "positive" social reorganization (Coser, 1977:3–41; Johnson [1981] 1986:41–89).

Living some decades after the turbulence of the French Revolution, Comte was highly skeptical regarding eighteenth century Enlightenment philosophers' rationalistic faith and criticized their utopian (or "metaphysical") ideas for reorganizing society on the basis of reason alone. He believed that it was now time to move beyond this "metaphysical" stage and into the "positive" stage. Positivism would lead to an expansion of knowledge through empirical research rather than rational analysis alone, but it would also acknowledge that absolute truth or total knowledge is forever beyond human reach. At the same time, rather than disparage traditional beliefs as irrational (as Comte believed the eighteenth century Enlightenment philosophers had done), the positive approach would discover through scientific investigation the importance that particular traditions had played in the long course of social evolution, even though based on pre-scientific beliefs.

This "positive" approach would enable us to understand social order as well as the stages of progress in society. Social reform efforts must always work within the constraints of the currently existing beliefs and traditions as discovered through empirical investigation. Otherwise, these efforts run the risk of undermining social order instead of promoting progress. Despite his emphasis on systematic empirical research, Comte's own analysis was quite general and highly speculative and would not conform to contemporary standards of rigorous empirical research.

Comte later offered a rather elaborate social reorganization project of his own that he believed was consistent with the positivist approach. Briefly, his "research" convinced him that religion had played a major role in the past in promoting social solidarity, especially in the long "theological" stage of history. However, as the new age of positivism replaced religion, Comte feared that selfish individualism would increase as the moral codes previously promoted by religious beliefs were undermined. So, faced with the challenge of promoting altruism and social solidarity in the new positivist society of the future, Comte proposed a new religion—the religion of humanity (Comte, 1877). Sociologists would serve as the moral guardians of this new society, educating people regarding the need to conform to the requirements of the social order.

Comte's skepticism regarding the power of rational analysis to shape people's motivations, or to serve as the basis for a more enlightened social order, was widespread among nineteenth century intellectuals and is revealed in several of the classical stage sociological theories to be reviewed in this chapter. For example, the limitations of reason are reflected in Émile Durkheim's theory of the collective consciousness (or conscience) in which moral values are reinforced more through collective rituals than rational analysis. It is also reflected in Karl Marx's analysis of the "false consciousness" that he believed to be widespread in the working class and in Vilfredo Pareto's view that underlying sentiments are more important in motivating human behavior than the intellectual justifications people might offer to explain it. Max Weber emphasized the growth of rationality in modern society, but he painted a rather bleak picture of the stifling effects of highly rational forms of social organization in addition to emphasizing tradition and the emotional appeal of charismatic leaders.[3]

These considerations suggest that a scientific understanding of society must confront the nonrational foundations of people's behavior and society's traditions and the role these play in supporting the moral ideals underlying the social order.

---

[3]Of these early sociologists, the influence of Durkheim, Marx, and Weber are foundational for contemporary theory, as will be seen later in this chapter. Pareto's ideas will not be a major focus in this book, except as reflected in Parsons' early voluntaristic theory of social action. Freud's ideas will not be discussed in detail; however, it should be noted that Parsons incorporated certain aspects of Freud's theories regarding socialization in the development of his functional theory. Also, Norbert Elias (2000) used Freud's ideas in his analysis of the effects of the long-term historical "civilizing process" on individuals' personality formation. Elias's contributions to contemporary theory will be reviewed in Chapter 19.

Dominant Figures in the Establishment of Sociology

Émile Durkheim: Sociology as the Science of Social Integration[4]

Although Comte coined the term **sociology**, Émile Durkheim should be credited for getting it recognized as an academic discipline.[5] His style of analysis is closer to modern sociology than Comte's wide-ranging speculations. For example, he pioneered in the use of statistical methods to show that variations in suicide rates could be related to variations in the level of social integration (Durkheim [1897] 1966) Later in his career he also used qualitative ethnographic material in his analysis of how religious beliefs and rituals reinforce social bonds and moral solidarity in a pre-modern type of society (Durkheim [1915] 1965). Durkheim contrasted his emphasis on social facts with the highly individualistic evolutionary perspective developed earlier by British social theorist Herbert Spencer as briefly reviewed earlier. Instead of explaining the dynamics of society and social evolution in terms of individuals' previously existing self-interests, Durkheim emphasized that the formation of individuals and their interests is dependent on a pre-existing society. This means that society comes first, not individuals.

Durkheim ([1895] 1964) insisted that sociology as a discipline must focus on social facts, not psychological, biological, or other types of facts. Social facts are external to individuals, exert constraint over them, and are general throughout a society. Social integration is one of the principal social facts that he sought to explain by showing how its form and strength can be documented through specific empirical indicators that can be related to other social facts. The concept of social integration includes specific social attachments among individuals as well as the degree to which they share common sentiments and beliefs—or "collective consciousness". Both suicide rates and religious beliefs and practices also qualify as social facts in his terms, and both can be shown to be related to the level of social

[4] This brief description of Durkheim's contributions is adapted from a more extended overview in D. P. Johnson ([1981] 1986:160–201). See also Coser (1977:129–174) and Turner et al. (2002:307–378) for excellent summaries of Durkheim's contributions to contemporary sociology and his intellectual context, plus Steven Lukes (1973) for a thorough analysis of Durkheim's theoretical perspective.

[5] Durkheim was born in 1858 in a small Jewish enclave in France and died in 1917. His position at the University of Bordeaux in 1887 in pedagogy and social science reflected the first academic recognition of social science in the French university system. When he was promoted to full professor the name of his professorship was changed to science of education and sociology. Two years following his promotion Durkheim established the first scholarly journal devoted to sociology, *L'Anée Sociologique*.

integration in society.[6] Suicide rates tend to be lower in societies with optimal levels of social integration—neither too little nor too much. The data he analyzed showed that both single people and Protestants had higher suicide rates than married persons or Catholics, respectively, because in his view their level of social integration, was lower, as measured by their specific social attachments. Similarly, if the level of common sentiments and beliefs (or "collective consciousness") is low, the result is that individuals' desires and aspirations are not sufficiently constrained by regulative norms. This gives rise to a state of anomie, which can also result in high suicide rates. On the other hand, if the level of social integration and regulation are too high, individuals have an inadequate sense of their own individual autonomy and thus may be susceptible to social expectations that encourage suicide under some conditions, or that lead to extreme demoralization when they fail to fulfill social expectations. This form of suicide would apply, for example, to terrorists who sacrifice their own lives or to defeated military officers whose suicide rates tend to be higher than those of ordinary soldiers. In addition, a group may demand suicide in certain situations. These different conditions give rise to the distinctions Durkheim made between different types of suicide. Suicide that results from inadequate social attachments are classified as **egoistic** suicide, while those resulting from a weak collective consciousness are categorized as **anomic** suicide; both of these types can be seen as resulting from inadequate social integration and regulation. On the other hand, the type of suicide that results from excessive normative regulation is classified as **altruistic** suicide. Durkheim also briefly described a fourth type, **fatalistic** suicide, that can result from excessive social regulation that stifles individual freedom.

For Durkheim the key problem for modern society is to insure an optimal level of social integration by reinforcing adherence to a moral code that would be appropriate for a complex society with a highly developed division of labor and high levels of individualism. Early in his career, he contrasted modern with pre-modern types of social solidarity in terms of the difference between mechanical and organic social solidarity (Durkheim [1893] 1964). "Mechanical" solidarity was grounded in similarities among people, particularly in terms of shared beliefs and values or common membership in the same tribe or village. "Organic" solidarity, in contrast, reflects a higher and more complex division of labor, with solidarity based on increased levels of interdependence. In this type of situation people are often dissimilar, due to the occupational specialization resulting from the increased division of labor. Basically, the evolution from pre-modern to modern forms of society involved a decline in mechanical solidarity and an increase in organic solidarity. Mechanical solidarity decreases as people become more heterogeneous in terms of

[6] If only individual factors (such as depression, mental illness, economic misfortune, or whatever) were involved in suicide, this would not explain the patterns Durkheim described in which suicide rates differed among married people versus single people, for example, or Protestants versus Catholics in his society.

occupation and lifestyle. At the same time organic solidarity increases as a consequence of the higher interdependence resulting from the higher division of labor. This transformation leads to the expanded individualism of modern society as well as a decline in repressive laws and an increase in restitutive laws. Repressive laws are characteristic of a society with high mechanical solidarity that seeks to enforce high levels of conformity. Restitutive laws, in contrast, allow greater individualism and are intended to maintain the complex patterns of interdependence which are the foundation for organic solidarity.

Mechanical solidarity does not disappear in modern societies, but it is considerably weakened as a foundation for uniting the entire society. However, among different segments of society, such as religious groups, occupational groups, and social class groups, mechanical solidarity continues to be important. The challenge is for these intermediate-level groups to become aware of the organic interdependence of the whole society so they do not undermine the general welfare for the sake of their own narrow interests. This requires education in civic morality as well as a government that will demonstrate a concern for the whole society and promote an appropriate level of social and moral integration.

When Durkheim later turned his attention to religion, his focus shifted to the question of how external social facts become internalized within individuals' consciousness rather than remaining external to them. This means that society's control over individuals is exercised from within their subjective consciousness – or in other words, their **conscience**.[7] This collective consciousness (or conscience) is reinforced through participation in collective life, religious rituals in particular. Rituals generate shared emotional experiences that strengthen social solidarity as well as reinforce religious beliefs and moral codes. Durkheim suggested that the decline of traditional religion in modern societies may be seen as an indicator of a decline in social integration and solidarity.

Society's control does not eliminate individual freedom, however. In fact, deviant behavior occurs in all societies as an inevitable outcome of natural variations in people's interests and impulses. Although societies vary in their tolerance of deviance, all societies establish moral boundaries between acceptable and unacceptable behaviors. The punishment of those whose behaviors are beyond this range of tolerance helps reinforce the moral boundaries between right and wrong but does not eliminate deviance.

Durkheim recognized that social solidarity in modern societies could be threatened by anomie or class conflict. But, in the same spirit as Comte's positivism, Durkheim believed that sociological knowledge could benefit society by helping establish a new foundation for morality and social solidarity. His concern with questions of social solidarity, plus his emphasis on how individuals' consciousness, moral values, and behavior are shaped by the overpowering influence of the social

---

[7]The French term for conscience also refers to **consciousness** in the broad sense of overall patterns of thought, belief, and feelings as well as individuals' moral sense of right and wrong.

environment, became a major component of structural/functional theory developed by Talcott Parsons in the American sociology during the 1940s and 1950s. In addition to providing a clear alternative to Spencer's individualistic approach, Durkheim's approach also contrasted with the growing influence of Marx and the socialist theorists influenced by him.

Karl Marx: Human Needs, Class Conflict, and Social Change[8]

The work of Karl Marx actually precedes that of Durkheim.[9] The ideas Marx developed were intended to provide the theoretical rationale for a revolutionary transformation that would be even more radical than the French Revolution near the end of the preceding century (Marx and Engels [1848] in Tucker, ed., 1972:335–362). While the French Revolution had been directed toward replacing the traditional aristocratic type of society with a modern bourgeois social order, Marx believed that the next stage would involve an overthrow of this capitalist system by the newly enlightened and empowered proletarian class. To put this analysis in context, Marx argued that, except for the hypothetical earliest "communist" form of primitive societies, all known historical stages of the past inevitably involved antagonism between social classes, due to their opposing economic class interests. The economic resources human beings need for survival (the "means of production") have always been unequally distributed, giving rise to society's class structure and the oppression and exploitation of the "have-nots" by the "haves" (the owners of the "means of production").

This focus on antagonistic class relations illustrates Marx's strategy of using **dialectical analysis** to explore the contradictions built into the structure of society.

---

[8] This brief description of Marx's contributions is adapted from a more extended overview in D. P. Johnson ([1981] 1986:116–159). See also Coser (1977:43–87) and Turner et al. (2002:102–172) for excellent summaries of Marx's contributions to contemporary sociological theory and his intellectual context. For examples of more extended overviews, see Fromm (1961), Lefebvre (1969), McLellan (1971), and Elster (1886).

[9] Marx was born in 1818 in Trier, Germany, and died in 1883 in London. Like Durkheim he was Jewish, coming from a line of Jewish rabbis on both sides of the family, but his father led the family in converting to Lutheranism for the sake of his career. After training for an academic career, Karl Marx found himself without the necessary sponsorship when his mentor, Bruno Bauer, was dismissed for his leftist and antireligious views. As an alternative Marx embarked on a career in journalism with a liberal bourgeois German newspaper and began to advocate for the cause of peasants and the poor. He later went to Paris, where he met Friedrich Engels and became heavily involved in the socialist movement. Eventually he was expelled from Paris and, after additional moves on the Continent, by the early 1850s went into exile in London, where he and Engels had visited earlier and where he remained until his death. In his London years, Marx reduced his activist role and did his most elaborate analysis of the internal contradictions of the capitalist economic system.

This strategy had earlier been advocated by the German philosopher Georg Wilhelm Friedrich Hegel to analyze how cultural and intellectual progress results from the clash of opposing ideas. Influenced by the critical Young Hegelians, Marx turned Hegel's approach upside down by emphasizing that the contradictions and conflicts between opposing cultural ideas reflect real-life struggles between the opposing classes that hold these contradictory ideas. Through these conflicts society itself moves toward its next stage of development.

Whether the opposing interests of different social classes result in open conflict or not depends in part on specific historical conditions. When the ruling class is successful in promoting "false consciousness" within the subordinate class, the members of the subordinate class are unable to envision any realistic alternatives to the existing system, despite their exploitation. Instead, the alienation they experience gives rise to a sense of powerlessness to have any meaningful influence on the conditions of their lives. In fact, they are unable even to control the products of their own labor. During a crisis, however, the illusions created through false consciousness become more difficult to sustain. At such crucial periods of history (such as the 1840s in Europe) the subordinate (or working) class is better able to see through the illusions of the dominant ideologies and have their "class consciousness" increased, especially with appropriate ideological leadership. Marx sought to provide such enlightenment, especially during the 1840s, with the *Manifesto of the Communist Party*, written with his life-long friend and collaborator Friedrich Engels, published in 1848 (reprinted in Tucker, ed., 1972). His goal was to enable the members of the working class to overcome their alienation and enlist in the struggle to end their exploitation, advance their interests, and thereby transform society into its next historical stage.

The revolution Marx anticipated did not occur, however, and Marx eventually moved to London, where he spent the rest of his life. It was during his London years that he devoted himself to a comprehensive and systematic analysis of the basic economic dynamics of capitalism, leading ultimately to a 3-volume work, *Das Kapital*. Only the first volume was published (in 1867) before his death, however, with his rough drafts of the second and third volumes completed and published after his death in 1883 (see Marx, 1967).

Drawing on the perspective of dialectical analysis, Marx was convinced that the internal contradictions of capitalism would generate periodic crises that ultimately would lead to the revolution that he had earlier attempted actively to promote. He pointed out that with the development of modern capitalism, ownership and control of the means of production was becoming more and more concentrated in fewer and fewer hands. Since the material resources needed for survival are always in scarce supply, this increasing concentration of wealth and control over the means of production meant that the level of exploitation had to be increasing. The only feasible resolution would be a society-wide revolutionary struggle that would eliminate class-based divisions through the establishment of a socialist society with collective ownership of the means of production. This, he believed, would contrast with previous transitional stages that simply replaced one type of class-based society with a different system of class domination. Marx's utopian ideal was that with the overthrow of class domination, the expanded productive capacity provided through modern industrial technology could then be used to improve the standard of living for all members of society rather than to enrich individual capitalists. In this way, the internal contradictions that had always plagued class-based societies would be eliminated.

Marx's early work had already made a major impact in Europe by the time Durkheim developed his alternative vision of how the social problems of modern society could be resolved through sociological knowledge. Marx's ideas continued to influence socialist thought in Europe, however, and, perhaps more significantly, to serve as the ideological inspiration for communism in the Soviet Union—albeit in a restricted and distorted form that was by no means consistent with the humanistic idealism of his early years. Ironically, the Soviet Union's political leaders seemed to reflect Comte's overriding concern with maintaining social order more than Marx's professed goal of human liberation. In effect, as the Soviet Union developed, Marx served primarily as a symbol or icon used by Soviet political leaders in their long-term struggle against capitalism, and the project of ending exploitation and promoting human liberation was indefinitely deferred.

Marx's influence on sociology in America came much later than Durkheim's. Although Marxist-type economic analysis was known among American economists as an alternative to the classical and neo-classical economics developed in Great Britain, its influence on sociology was limited. During the long years of Cold War tensions between the United States and the Soviet Union, there was a deep-seated American bias against Marx, without much attention given to his economic and political thought by sociologists. But by the late 1960s, Marx's early humanistic writings (such as his *Economic and Philosophical Manuscripts*) became influential among some American sociologists who were involved in the development of a more critical "new left" perspective (see Marx, 1964). These developments reflected the social struggles and turbulence of that time and will be described in a subsequent chapter on critical theory.

Max Weber: Social Action as the Foundation of Society[10]

Max Weber did not deal with Durkheim's work, despite being his contemporary, but he was critical of Marx's one-sided emphasis on material forces and economic interests. Given the sharply different models of society offered by Durkheim and

[10]This brief description of Weber's contributions is adapted from a more extended overview in D. P. Johnson ([1981] 1986:202–245). See also Coser (1977:217–260) and Turner et al. (2002:173–250) for excellent brief summaries of Weber's contributions to contemporary sociological theory and their intellectual context. For examples of more extensive overviews of Weber's theoretical perspective, see Bendix (1962) and Randall Collins (1986).

Marx, we might question whether either view by itself is adequate. Everyday life observation suggests that social life includes both cooperative interdependence and solidarity on the one hand and exploitation and conflict on the other. Weber's contributions provide the potential for a more comprehensive analysis that can incorporate both of these competing perspectives.[11] His contributions are varied, covering such areas as the sociology of religion, bureaucratic organization, political and economic sociology, and social stratification. Weber emphasized individuals' subjectively meaningful social action as the most fundamental unit of social reality, but his substantive interests involved wide-ranging comparisons among different societies and long-range patterns of social change. His focus on subjective meaning clearly contrasts with Durkheim's initial focus on social facts external to the individual.

The structure of social systems, whether large or small, consists of nothing more than the set of interrelated probabilities that individuals will interact in ways that reflect the nature of their mutual subjective orientations toward one another. For example, an authority relationship exists when there is a high probability that one party believes he or she has the right to give orders, and the other party acquiesces to this right and complies. There may be unique or personal elements in participants' subjective orientations, but these may be ignored when attention is focused on the structure itself. This strategy is the basis for Weber's "ideal type" analysis—a methodological contribution for which Weber is widely recognized in contemporary sociology. An ideal type is an analytical or conceptual construct that highlights certain specific features of people's orientations and actions for purposes of analysis and comparison. For example, even though subordinates in an organization may vary greatly in terms of their personal attitudes toward their boss, the important point to note is the high probability that these subordinates will comply with their boss's orders.

Weber (1947:115–118) distinguished four "ideal types" of social action, reflecting differences in underlying subjective orientations. These include two types of rational action (instrumental versus value-oriented rationality) and two types of nonrational action (traditional and affective). Instrumental rationality involves conscious deliberation and explicit choice with regard to both ends and means; that is, a choice is consciously made from among alternative ends (or goals) and then the appropriate means are selected to achieve the end that has been chosen. Value-oriented rationality, in

---

[11] Max Weber was born in 1864 in Germany into an upper-middle-class Protestant bourgeois family and died in 1920. His father was politically active and had a very pragmatic orientation while his mother was pious and deeply religious. The differing orientations of his father and mother probably contributed to the inner tensions and conflicts that Max Weber experienced during part of his life. Max Weber's theoretical distinction between different types of social action may reflect the contrasting orientations of his parents. Weber studied at the University of Heidelberg and the University of Berlin, served for a time in the law courts, and eventually was appointed to a university teaching position at the University of Berlin. For biographical accounts of Weber's life, see Mitzman (1970) and Marianna Weber ([1926] 1975).

contrast, involves a subjective commitment to an end or goal that is not compared to alternative ends but instead is regarded as ultimate. For such actions the individual's rational choices are limited to selecting the appropriate means. In contrast to these types of rational action involving conscious deliberation and choice, traditional action is followed simply because it is consistent with well-established patterns or is habitual. Affective action expresses feelings or emotions (or affect) without conscious deliberation. All four of these are ideal types, of course; in real life, individuals' actions may reflect varying mixtures.

Weber's ([1930] 1996) analysis of the Protestant ethic and its effects on people's economic behavior, which was originally published in 1904–05 and was one of his earliest contributions to become widely known among American sociologists, fits the category of value-oriented rationality. Briefly, his argument was that Protestant religious beliefs shaped people's motivations in a way that contributed to the growth of capitalism. Specifically, the belief that eternal salvation is provided as a free gift to God's "elect" had the effect of bypassing the priesthood and sacraments of the institutional church. Instead, individuals could relate to God on their own, as implied in the Protestant notion of the "priesthood of all believers." The institutional church in Protestantism was no longer essential for salvation but served instead to strengthen believers' religious commitments. In this context, individuals had to rely primarily upon themselves and their own subjective faith to establish their moral worth and assurance of eternal salvation, though fellow believers in their religious community could provide guidance and reinforcement.

In addition, consistent with this downplaying of the institutional church, Protestants emphasized that all individuals (not just priests or members of religious orders) are expected to demonstrate their religious commitment in their everyday lives, especially in terms of fulfilling the duties of the secular occupations to which God had called them. As secular work thus became "sacralized," Protestantism contributed to the development of a strong work ethic. Diligent adherence to this work ethic could be seen as an indicator of one's moral worth, and the occupational success that was achieved could be regarded as a blessing from God that provided assurance of salvation in the hereafter.

Weber's interest in religion extended beyond Protestantism and included analyses of Hinduism in India (Weber [1916–1917] 1958), Confucianism in China (Weber [1916] 1951), and ancient Judaism (Weber [1917–1919] 1952). His basic argument was that these other religious orientations did not provide the moral incentive for breaking with tradition that could stimulate economic expansion. In this comparative perspective, it becomes clear that whether religion promotes economic change or reinforces tradition and economic stability depends in part on the nature of the religious beliefs themselves. In addition, Weber recognized that the social location and material interests of those who adhere to particular religious orientations are also relevant as well as the overall material conditions in the society. Protestantism was "inner-worldly" (not "other-worldly") and emphasized asceticism (i.e. deferred gratification, discipline, self-denial, and active engagement in the world), as opposed to mysticism. Other types of religious orientation, such as other-worldly mysticism, for instance, would not be expected to have such strong effects in stimulating economic innovation but would instead support the status quo by default.

Weber's view of the Protestant ethic as a stimulant for the expanding system of capitalism contrasts with Marx's view that religion leads to passive acceptance of the status quo. Of course, the meaning of the Protestant ethic no doubt differed for bourgeois capitalists and proletarian workers. Successful capitalist entrepreneurs could regard their success as a sign of God's blessing and, since the moral discipline associated with the work ethic discouraged idleness as well as the enjoyment of luxury, they could use their profits to expand their business. For workers, however, the moral discipline of the work ethic meant they should be diligent in performing their occupational tasks, regardless of how lowly they might be, which of course was a crucial contribution to the success of their capitalist employers as well as being essential for their own economic survival.

Weber also pointed out that the work ethic eventually became secularized, which meant that it no longer depended on religious concerns with glorifying or obeying God or salvation in the hereafter. This resulted in part from the way an increasingly affluent economy gradually undermined the ascetic lifestyle promoted in early Protestantism, and in part to the fact that regular work in an occupation became necessary for economic survival. Weber took religious motivations seriously but he did not assume that religious beliefs are always dominant in people's motivations. A devout Protestant entrepreneur might be motivated by religious concerns while a less devout Protestant capitalist may simply want to make money. Workers might feel they were fulfilling their religious duty in their work; they might hope to move up in the occupational hierarchy, or they might simply have no choice but to work in order to meet their material needs. Whether people are motivated primarily by their material (economic) interests or by ideal (religious) interests requires understanding their subjective orientations.

Individuals' actions, with their subjective orientations, are the basic building blocks of social structures of all types. Weber contrasted different forms of social organization ranging from social relationships to economic and political social orders, including bureaucratic organizations, in terms of the underlying subjective orientations of their participants. Bureaucratic organization represents the triumph of instrumental rationality as applied to social organization. Although the terms **bureaucracy** and **bureaucrat** have long been used in a negative way to describe excessive red tape and rigid adherence to rules and regulations, Weber's focus was on the way bureaucratic organizations are more efficient for large-scale and long-term administration than other forms of organization. Their **rational-legal** authority structures are based on formally enacted rules that define the duties associated with their various positions and the scope of officials' authority. This emphasis on formal and pragmatic rationality is intended to exclude both personal feelings and ultimate value considerations from the exercise of authority and the routine fulfillment of organizational responsibilities. When coupled with a secularized form of the work ethic, a bureaucratically-dominated society runs a serious risk of becoming a kind of dehumanized and controlling "iron cage" leading to widespread alienation.

Weber (1947:234–363) contrasted the rational-legal type of authority system as manifested in bureaucratic organizations with **traditional** and **charismatic** authority systems. A traditional authority system is based on people's acceptance of the traditions that define it. As developed in patrimonial systems, authority structures are basically extensions of family relationships, but they can be expanded through a wide range of personal ties involving various types of relationships of domination and subordination that eventually become traditionalized. In contrast, charismatic authority is based on people's beliefs in the extraordinary personal qualities of a particular leader, the inspiration such beliefs inspire, and the emotional bonds established between the leader and his or her disciples.

Authority systems of all types may be contrasted with **power** structures. Power involves the ability to carry out one's will despite opposition and does not necessarily rest on a belief in legitimacy. Authority is often backed up with power, of course, and people with high levels of power may attempt to promote acceptance of their domination as legitimate, thereby transforming power into authority. The concept of power can be related to Weber's three-dimensional model of social stratification. In contrast to Marx, Weber distinguished the power structure from the economic class structure. For Marx, those who control the means of production are also able to control the power structure of the political system as well. But for Weber, one's economic class and one's position in the hierarchy of political power are analytically distinct and may vary independently (although of course they may overlap).

A third basis for stratification in Weber's view involves hierarchies of prestige or honor that give rise to different status groups. This hierarchy depends on subjective standards of evaluation people use to establish high or low prestige. Status hierarchies may overlap with economic or political hierarchies but are analytically distinct. Criteria for prestige ranking include whatever characteristics are deemed important, including, for example, religion, lifestyle, ethnicity, age, education, or other criteria that can be used to make meaningful distinctions.

Weber's three-fold model of social stratification is one of his enduring contributions to contemporary sociology. Even when there is high overlap among these dimensions of stratification, their differences are important to note. When these dimensions are not consistent, people sometimes attempt to use their high rank on one dimension to attempt to improve their rank on the other(s). For example, wealthy people may make large financial donations to museums, universities, or other charitable causes in an effort to increase their prestige or honor. Or, people may use their economic resources to gain political power.

Despite Weber's focus on individuals' subjectively meaningful social action, many of his substantive analyses were at the macro-level. Between individuals' social actions and social systems of all types, there is the crucial process of **interaction** between or among people. This was the primary focus of Georg Simmel's strategy for sociological analysis.

Georg Simmel: Interaction Processes[12]

Georg Simmel identified sociology's task as identifying the **forms of interaction** whereby society itself is created.[13] These forms often include varying mixtures of both cooperation and conflict. In contrast to the **forms**, the **contents** of interaction consist of the particular needs or goals that people pursue through interaction (Simmel, 1950:40). In contrast to both Durkheim and Marx, much of Simmel's analysis was at the micro-level. Nevertheless, with Simmel's perspective we might regard the opposing approaches of Durkheim and Marx as providing limited, one-sided views.

Simmel did not provide a systematic theory of the forms of interaction, but he offered numerous examples of such forms, showing how they could be identified, subdivided, contrasted with one another, and manifested in various settings. In some cases, he extended his analysis from micro level examples to macro level manifestations of particular forms. More than any other classical theorist Georg Simmel insisted that society does not exist independently of the **process of interaction**. For example, superordination (or dominance) and subordination demonstrate reciprocity, despite the inequality of the relationship (for a discussion of various forms of subordination, see Simmel, 1950:179–303). Through participating in the interaction process, even subordinates may influence the nature of their relationship with their social superiors. Moreover, superordinates themselves are likely to take subordinates' anticipated reactions into consideration in some fashion, even if only to exercise control more effectively. Relations between superordinates and subordinates are obviously shot through with possibilities for conflict. In a hierarchical system, for example, subordinates may unite among themselves as they resist the demands of superordinates in an effort to protect their own interests. (This can be compared to the development of class consciousness in Marx's theory.)

As a basic form of interaction, conflict is often closely linked with cohesion (Simmel, 1955:13–123). When conflict erupts between groups, the solidarity within each group is likely to be strengthened. Even internal conflict may be related to solidarity, especially if the group is not engaged in external conflict. High solidarity

---

[12] This brief summary of Simmel's contributions is adapted from a more extended overview in D. P. Johnson ([1981] 1986:246–287). See also Coser (1977:177–215) and Turner et al. (2002:251–306) for excellent summaries of Simmel's contributions to contemporary sociological theory and their intellectual context. For additional reading, see Simmel (1950, including the Introduction by Kurt H. Wolff for an overview of Simmel's work), Spykmann (1964), and Coser (1965).

[13] Georg Simmel (1858–1918) was a contemporary of both Weber and Durkheim. He received his doctorate from the University of Berlin in 1881 where he began teaching in 1885. His university lectures were popular among Berlin's intellectual elite. In 1914 he left Berlin to accept a position at the University of Strasbourg but, unfortunately, academic life was soon disrupted by the outbreak of war. He was involved (along with Max Weber and Ferdinand Tönnies) in establishing the German Society for Sociology.

means that members have high expectations of one another, and these expectations may sometimes collide. Moreover, the emotional intensity of personal relationships in highly cohesive groups, plus the familiarity of members with one another, increase the odds that conflict will be more intense and personal than in less cohesive groups. Also, members of highly cohesive groups may sometimes feel the need to assert their autonomy to prevent being dominated by the group. In contrast, less cohesive groups may simply disband or fragment with the eruption of conflict. And if members are united more by pragmatic interests than emotional ties, conflict issues will be easier to negotiate through mutual compromise.

Just as cohesive relationships have the seeds of conflict, so also conflictual relationships may include potential sources of unification. With competition, the fact that both parties desire the same goal is actually a source of unity between them. Also, with both competition and conflict, rules are likely to be developed to regulate the conflict and establish its boundaries, and such rules provide a basis for at least a minimal level of unity. Sometimes, too, enemies eventually become allies, especially when both are threatened by a third party.

Despite Simmel's distinction between the forms of interaction and its contents, in some cases a form may serve as its own content. In competitive games, for example, participants are involved for the sake of the conflict itself, not for other purposes, such as economic gain, political power, or other interests. (This would probably not apply to professional sports, in which participants are presumably motivated by economic interests.) With **sociability** also, the interaction itself serves as its own content; people interact simply because of the pleasure it provides (Simmel, 1950:40–57). Sociable interaction at parties illustrates this form, provided participants do not have some ulterior motive, such as enhancing their reputation or establishing business or professional contacts. Such interaction contrasts with utilitarian forms of interaction that are intended to pursue personal goals or interests.

Simmel (1950:87–117) also showed how forms of interaction are affected by the numbers of people involved. His best known example contrasts a dyad versus a triad—a contrast that can easily be illustrated when a conversation between two persons is interrupted by the appearance of a third party (Simmel, 1950:118–144). Simmel suggested that a three-person encounter serves as a kind of microcosm of the larger social world. With only two persons, each can relate to the other as a unique person in a way that is not possible with three persons or in any larger system. With more than two persons, each party will need to consider what the others have in common, at least potentially. Even if a third party is silent, he or she still serves as an audience.

Simmel (1950:145–169) identified four third party roles that are impossible in two-person relationships. These include the roles of mediator, arbitrator, one who enjoys ("Tertius Gaudens"), and one who seeks to divide and conquer. Interestingly, all four of these roles involve conflict between two parties. The roles of mediator and arbitrator are widely understood, the main difference being that the mediator helps the two parties resolve their differences themselves, while the arbitrator actually makes the decision on how to resolve the conflict with the understanding that it will be accepted. The "Tertius Gaudens" role involves observing the conflict, perhaps for amusement but often to benefit from it. The "divide and conquer" role involves the third party in promoting conflict in order to benefit. Simmel showed how these roles apply at the macro level as well as in face-to-face relations. For example, consumers in a society play the "Tertius Gaudens" role as they benefit from the competition of sellers in the marketplace.

Simmel's analysis of the effects of numbers on forms of interaction can easily be extended with the addition of greater numbers of participants. For very small groups, the addition of just one more person is likely to influence the dynamics of the group. For example, adding a fourth person, and a fifth, and so on opens up new options not possible with smaller groups. Beyond a certain size threshold, the probability of subgroup formation increases. For an enduring group, definite changes in interaction patterns occur when a group becomes too large for all its members to meet together at one time or to know one another personally. If it becomes too large for face-to-face interaction, formal rules, designated leaders, delegation of authority and responsibilities, and strategies for collective decision making will be needed. (This explanation of how impersonal forms of organization result from an increase in a group's size might be compared with Weber's model of bureaucracy.)

Simmel (1955:125–195) contrasted modern and pre-modern types of society in terms of the nature of the linkage between individuals and the overall society. In pre-modern societies individuals tend to be absorbed in small-scale local groups or organizations with their whole identities or personalities, with their linkages to larger social organizations mediated through these groups. In contrast, in modern urban societies individuals are more likely to have limited (or segmental) involvement in a large variety of different social groups or organizations. Thus they are more likely than in pre-modern societies to be at the intersection of numerous overlapping social circles, corresponding to the various independent special-purpose groups in which they participate. Simmel believed that as the claims of individuals' various group memberships are limited in modern society, prospects for individual freedom are enhanced. On the other hand, as society becomes larger and more complex, it becomes more difficult for individuals to identify with the overall society or to feel that their participation is significant. This apparent diminishment of the individual is a potential source of alienation and feelings of powerlessness, which, ironically, increase at the same time that freedom from social constraints expands. Such are the dilemmas of modern society.

The impersonal nature of many transactions in modern society is reflected in our increased reliance on money. Simmel emphasized how money facilitates the expansion of exchange transactions beyond the level of personal reputations (Spykmann, 1964:215–253; Simmel, 1950:409–424). Reliance on money thus reflects the impersonality, the rationality, and the functional specificity of social encounters in modern society. People can participate in market transactions without any personal engagement with one another at all beyond the specific transaction at hand. Money also helps enhance individual freedom—at least for those with a sufficient supply of it. In this respect its sociological significance is somewhat similar to that of segmental involvement in multiple special-interest groups.

Despite his strong focus on micro-level interaction, Simmel's analysis of modern society is consistent with that of other nineteenth-century European theorists in portraying a long-term evolutionary transformation from small-scale, relatively simple, homogeneous types of society to large-scale, complex societies with much greater heterogeneity. His analysis is also consistent with the increasing importance of bureaucratic organization and market transactions in modern society.

Other Important Pioneers

In addition to Durkheim, Marx, Weber, and Simmel, there were others who were also recognized in previous years for contributing to the establishment of sociology. Still others have come to be recognized more recently. What is regarded as the essential "canon" of the founding period of sociology changes over the years, and one of the major concerns of many contemporaries is to be more inclusive in incorporating the voices of those not previously recognized. The following European figures are summarized in the order of their birth years.

Harriet Martineau: Discovering the Discrepancy Between Morals and Manners

Harriet Martineau (1802–1876), a contemporary of Auguste Comte, lived before sociology's establishment as a recognized discipline, but her strategies of social research and critical analysis anticipated later developments (see Lengermann and Niebrugge-Brantley, 1998:39–45). She was born in Norwich, England, a center of religious dissent from the established Church of England. She became well known and financially successful through her journalistic writings on political economy that helped popularize the ideas of classical British economists such as Adam Smith and David Ricardo, among others. She visited America and spent two years traveling throughout the country. Her books based on this experience demonstrated her distinctive style of critical and comparative analysis based on intensive participant observation (Martineau, 1836/1837, 1838b).

In their summary of the significant contributions of women sociologists between 1830 and 1930, Patricia Madoo Lengermann and Jill Niebrugge-Brantley (1998:23–45) make a persuasive case for including Harriet Martineau among the pioneer figures in sociological theory. For most of the second half of the twentieth century, Martineau was known among American sociologists primarily for her translation of Auguste Comte's work, but she condensed and edited it as well. Comte himself admired her translation and revision so much that he had it translated back into French (Lengermann and Niebrugge-Brantley, 1998:28). Martineau shared Comte's ideas regarding systematic empirical research as a basis for knowledge that could be used to promote continued progress. However, Martineau's primary commitment was with furthering human equality and happiness, in contrast to Comte's concern with preserving order while also promoting social and intellectual progress. In this spirit she strongly opposed slavery in the United States as well as the subordination of women in all societies. Martineau's method of participant observation research contrasts sharply with Comte's more detached style of analysis (Martineau, 1838a). Reflecting her travel experiences in America, she advocated a systematic and sympathetic form of research, based on conversations with a wide range of people, that would capture the details of their everyday lives. She was also interested in objective indicators of people's collective mentality and representative cultural patterns. Such indicators include not only the everyday customs that people followed in meeting their basic survival needs, but architectural styles, epitaphs on tombstones, music, and public gatherings.

Martineau's (1838a) research guidelines on observing manners and morals were published several decades before the publication of Durkheim's more frequently cited book, *The Rules of Sociological Method*. Her methodology differed sharply from Durkheim's by being grounded in intensive participant observation. This difference is reflected in contemporary sociology in the contrast between quantitative research designed to test general theoretical propositions and qualitative research that incorporates "thick" descriptions of the details of everyday life.

Martineau's focus on "morals" and "manners" made it possible for her to develop a critical analysis based on the discrepancies she observed between widely professed values and actual practices. She took American "morals" to be the ideals and beliefs regarding equality and democracy as expressed in documents such as the Declaration of Independence. These principles were consistent with eighteenth century Enlightenment ideals that formed part of Martineau's own intellectual background. But the "manners" she observed in everyday life often contradicted the moral values that were widely professed. These contradictions were particularly glaring with regard to the situations of slaves and of women, since neither slaves nor women were treated as equal to white males in America. Martineau pointed out that the everyday life treatment of both slaves and women was not consistent with one of the most basic principles of democracy—namely, that the laws governing people's behavior should be based on their consent.

Martineau's strong support for women's equality, plus her critique of everyday life experience, particularly domestic life, mark her as an early pioneer in the type of analysis promoted by many contemporary feminist scholars. Her goal of using knowledge gained through sociological research to promote social progress, equality, and human autonomy and well-being is consistent with contemporary critical and feminist theory. Although her critique of slavery would not apply in the United States today, her more general concern with problems of domination and subordination are still relevant with regard to women as well as other marginalized groups in society. On a more general level Martineau pointed out the negative effects of excessive economic competition in America, noting how it contributes to increasing levels of inequality in society, thereby reducing individuals' moral autonomy and increasing their anxiety.

Alexis de Tocqueville: An Analysis of American Democracy

Alexis de Tocqueville (1805–1859) was a French politician whose book, *Democracy in America* (Tocqueville, 1945), was also based on his visit to America in 1831. Although the American colonies and France had both experienced revolutions near the end of the previous century, the United States, unlike France, did not have the legacy of a long-established aristocratic social order or monarchy to be overthrown. This contrast with his own society probably increased de Tocqueville's fascination with the United States and the promise it held for fulfilling the dreams of liberty, fraternity, and equality that had inspired the French Revolution.

De Tocqueville admired American society greatly and believed that its democratic form of government was the wave of the future. At the same time, he cautioned that a democratic society was vulnerable to excessive individualism as well as to the development of strong social pressures for conformity that could stifle creativity and the rights of minorities or outsiders. He recognized that to be truly effective democracy depends on the widespread civic participation that he observed at the time in the United States. He felt that extensive citizen participation in various voluntary organizations, churches, and local government would help moderate excessive individualism, serve as an important mechanism for self-governance, and help prevent despotic rule by the central government. Despite the potential problems that he realized could develop with the American experiment in self-governance, de Tocqueville was generally quite optimistic about the relatively young United States of America.

Vilfredo Pareto: Logical Versus Nonlogical Action

Vilfredo Pareto (1848–1923), an Italian social theorist, became an economist and later a sociologist following his earlier training in the physical sciences and mathematics for a career as an engineer. (See Coser [1977:387–426] and Turner et al. [2002:379–433] for excellent brief summaries of Pareto's intellectual context and his contributions to sociological theory.) Despite the apparent rationality manifested in the cost/benefit analysis of economic action, Pareto ([1916] 1935) was convinced that a great deal of human behavior is nonlogical, based on sentiments rather than rational calculation. For example, even people's preferences as consumers are often likely to reflect traditions or social status considerations more than purely economic cost/benefit considerations.

Pareto viewed action as **logical** or rational to the extent that it reflects objective cause-and-effect relations that can be used to demonstrate its effectiveness in reaching desired ends. However, the explanations people offer for their actions are often outside the bounds of what can be evaluated as rational or irrational, logical or illogical. When actions are explained in terms that fail to meet logical or scientific standards, they should be considered **nonlogical**. For example, an engineer designing a bridge would engage in logical action if decisions on materials and techniques are based on scientific principles or past experience to insure that the bridge will not collapse. However, if the engineer were also to engage in a religious or magical ritual to insure safety in the construction process, this would be considered nonlogical because there is no scientific basis for claiming that the ritual reduces the chances of having accidents.

Pareto labeled the explanations people might offer for their actions as the **derivations**, while the real underlying reasons that motivate their behavior, which he termed the **residues**, reflect their underlying sentiments. The derivations are highly variable for different people, due to differences in their particular cultural or subcultural traditions. The residues are more constant, since the sentiments on which they are based may be considered part of human nature. This does not mean that people themselves are necessarily insincere or cynical in the "rational" explanations they offer. But they may be unaware of the influence of the residues. Pareto's distinction between underlying motives and sentiments and the explanations that people offer to explain their actions is regarded as one of the most distinctive insights he developed in his efforts to establish sociology as a scientific discipline.[14]

Pareto's theory of the "circulation of elites" has also been viewed among subsequent generations of theorists as an important model of the dynamics of political processes. Essentially, this model explains how society's political elites tend to alternate between liberal-type innovators and tradition-bound conservatives. These two "types" reflect different "residues" as defined above, with the liberals having a high concentration of the "new combinations" residue and the conservatives having a high concentration of the "persistence of aggregates" residue. The concept of "new combinations" suggests a willingness to try different kinds of policies and procedures (the liberal pattern), while the concept of "persistence of aggregates" implies a desire to maintain the status quo (the conservative pattern).

Pareto characterized those who give priority to "new combinations" as the foxes, while those who give priority to the "persistence of aggregates" are labeled as the lions. His cyclical model portrays a pattern in which the coercive control of lions alternates with the cunning guile of foxes in the political power structure of society. Once innovator-type leaders gain power through guile and fraud, there is a gradual shift to more conservative strategies and an increasingly strong appeal to tradition, reinforced by force if necessary. This can be seen as leading to a strengthened "law and order" strategy. Eventually, this reliance on tradition and force becomes excessively rigid and loses its effectiveness, at which point the conservatives become vulnerable to the machinations of rising innovative liberals whose cunning strategies ultimately overthrow the conservatives. The cycle is then repeated. In the long run there is equilibrium among all the various elements of society, including the political system,

[14] As we shall see in Chapter 12, Pareto's approach was analyzed in detail in Talcott Parsons' theory of social action as an example of a positivistic perspective that was overly deterministic and failed to give sufficient emphasis to the role of normative commitments that influence individuals' choices.

but it is a cyclical pattern rather than a static equilibrium. This cyclical model differs from the evolutionary models previously discussed in which social change is envisioned as a straight-line linear process. In contrast to Marx, the focus is more on political conflict than economic. Also unlike Marx, Pareto did not envision any ultimate resolution in a future utopian socialist society.

Ferdinand Tönnies: Contrasting Community and Society

Ferdinand Tönnies (1855–1936), a German sociologist, is most often remembered for his analysis of the contrast between **community** and **society**—terms which are translations of the title of his best-known work, *Gemeinschaft und Gesellschaft* (Tönnies [1887] 1963). (*Gesellschaft* may also be translated as *association*.) (These German words are sometimes used in English-language sociology textbooks and discourse as more or less technical terms for the different types of social order they represent.) Tönnies used these terms to deal with the typical nineteenth-century concern with the long-range development of modern society. The pre-modern *Gemeinshaftliche* (community-type) social order typically is small-scale, rural or village-based, and involves a strong emphasis on family ties and other types of personal social relations. Individualism is not highly developed. Religion and traditional customs and forms of morality have a strong unifying influence on people's worldviews and lifestyles. In contrast, the modern *Gesellschaftliche* (society-type or associational) social order is a larger-scale, more urbanized type of society. Although family and personal relations continue to exist, the overall system is characterized by the expansion of impersonal relations that are established for specific purposes (trade, commerce, political regulation). The influence of religion and traditional customs and moral standards decreases, and formally enacted law becomes relatively more important.

Tönnies considered these two types of social order to express two distinctively different types of will (or mentality), with the *Gemeinschaft* reflecting a **natural** will and the *Gesellschaft* a more **rational** will. The natural will is manifested in a social structure characterized by high organic unity, diffuse personal relationships, and behavior governed by strong traditions rather than being highly reflective or calculating. In contrast, the rational will is expressed in a social structure that has a more deliberately contrived character, and with a much greater proportion of specialized, segmental social relations intentionally established through formal contracts.

Marianne Weber: Exposing the Subordination of Women at Home and Work

Although long known in American sociology primarily as Max Weber's wife, Marianne Weber (1870–1954) was an influential and productive sociologist in her own right and deserves to be included among the founders of the field (Lengermann and Niebrugge-Brantley, 1998:193–214).[15] Her work centered largely on the subordinate status of women in the marriage relationship and in the larger society. This persistent subordination restricted women's opportunities to develop their full human potential and to contribute to society.

Marianne Weber's childhood was stressful. Her mother, whose grandfather was the brother of Max Weber's father, died when she was two years old. She eventually lived with her aunt on her mother's side for a time but eventually moved to the home of Max Weber, Sr. and his wife Helene, where she was attracted to her future husband, Max Weber, Jr. Following marriage she devoted herself to her own intellectual and academic pursuits and became involved with the emerging feminist movement in Germany. Husband Max Weber supported these efforts. However, Marianne Weber found herself in the position of supportive caregiver during her husband's severe depression that followed the death of his father. (The onset of Max Weber's depression had occurred shortly after a confrontation with his father over the way his father treated his mother.)

During Marianne Weber's life the issue of women's status and role in society had become a significant topic of discussion in Germany. Marianne Weber (here-after Weber in this section) was highly influential as a liberal feminist whose expertise was established by the publication (in 1907) of her book, *Marriage, Motherhood, and the Law* (Lengermann and Niebrugge-Brantley, 1998:197). She lectured widely on feminist issues and served for a time as president of the Federation of German Women's Organizations (Lengermann and Niebrugge-Brantley, 1998:201). In addition to her numerous writings on marriage and women's issues, she also wrote a biography of Max Weber ([1926] 1975) plus an autobiography of her own that was published in 1948.[16]

Marianna Weber's theoretical contributions went well beyond a simple critique of women's subordinate status in the home and in society, which was particularly pronounced in Germany at that time. She saw the marriage rules of society as the key to understanding the unequal relations between women and men. Despite women's subordinate status in marriage, Weber identified certain crucial historical developments that had helped moderate males' domination. For one thing, the development of the ideal of monogamy led to an increasing recognition of husbands' obligations and duties to their wives. Also, mothers shared authority over

[15] In addition to her own distinctive contributions to sociology, Marianna Weber organized many of Max Weber's unpublished manuscripts after his death and arranged for their publication.

[16] Regrettably, much of Marianna Weber's work has not yet been translated into English. Lengermann and Niebrugge-Brantley (1998:193) report that, except for the translated material they provide in their text/reader, the only work by Marianna Weber that has been translated into English is *Max Weber: A Biography* (Weber [1926] 1975). The works described in this section that have not been translated are not included in the list of references at the end of this book. Lengermann and Niebrugge-Brantley (1998:203–211) show how Marianne Weber's clear feminist focus contrasts with the perspectives of husband Max Weber as well as Georg Simmel.

young children with their husbands, and these shared parental roles reflected a pattern of partnership in the rearing of children. Moreover, the somewhat negative or ambivalent attitude of some in the early Christian church toward sexual activity carried the implication that the strong mutual intimacy of the marital bond should not be based on sex alone. In addition, just as Max Weber analyzed the importance of Protestantism for the rise of capitalism, so also Marianne Weber pointed out that Protestant beliefs in freedom of conscience and the equality of all human beings, both women and men, before God were inconsistent with all forms of domination. For Marianne Weber, domination undermines human autonomy and dignity.

Weber focused explicitly on the strains and dilemmas in marriage resulting from the conflicting dynamics of subordination versus intimacy. To put it succinctly, intimacy implies equality; therefore, domination undermines intimacy. Intimacy includes sexuality and eroticism, which Weber regarded as highly important for women as well as men. However, sexual intimacy alone is not sufficient to maintain a satisfying long-term marital relationship; emotional intimacy is also required, and this is difficult to achieve in relations involving domination of one party by the other.

Weber also described the personal humiliation that wives feel when they are totally dependent financially upon their husbands and so must justify requests for funds for household and personal expenses. To avoid such subordination would require women to have their own independent source of income. This means that women who contribute to their families, and to society, by maintaining a household deserve financial remuneration as well as those in paid employment outside the home, especially considering that men's accomplishments in public life are supported by their wives' contributions to the well-being of their families and the maintenance of their households. The logistics of how financial remuneration for household and family responsibilities should be worked out are difficult, especially in view of socioeconomic class disparities and other variations among different households. Even so, Weber suggested that arrangements should be made in the household budget for the wife to receive a specific sum of money on a regular basis for household maintenance plus funds for her own personal use.

In arguing for the importance of being provided funds for household responsibilities, Weber certainly did not intend to imply that women should be limited to the household or other traditional feminine spheres of activity. Instead, women should be equal to men in being able to develop their full human potential and to contribute to society in terms of their distinctive interests and abilities. Weber recognized that women themselves differ from one another, based in part on their social location and socioeconomic class position. The issues Weber identified are still urgent issues on the contemporary feminist agenda. These include the economic, domestic, and sexual dimensions of women's subordination, variations among women based on their different social locations, the crucial importance of pursuing the goal of gender equality, and the potential for women to expand their contributions in all areas of social life.

Summary

Although this book deals mostly with contemporary theories, the key ideas of the major founders of the field are important as a foundation. Each of the theorists whose major contributions were briefly reviewed in this chapter dealt with issues and questions of their own time. But their analyses also have relevance to our time, despite the wide-ranging social changes that have occurred over the course of the last century and the important advances made in the discipline since its early years. Specific features of the social and intellectual background that were relevant during the time of sociology's establishment include the rise of science, technological advances leading to the Industrial Revolution, the social transformations involved in the transition from "traditional" to "modern" society, the discovery of social and cultural variations among various non-European peoples, and a recognition of the persistent foundations of the nonrational dimension in social life.

We noted briefly Ibn Khaldun's cyclical theory of the rise and fall of city civilizations in the desert, Herbert Spencer's theory of the evolution of increasingly complex societies, and Auguste Comte's three-stage theory of social and intellectual progress. Of these three, Khaldun had no influence on the development of sociology in Europe; Comte's work had an important influence on Durkheim; and Spencer had an impact in the early years by providing the theoretical underpinning for an individualistic, *laissez-faire* evolutionary theory.

The pioneering scholars whose works have generally been considered the most important in recent years for establishing the foundations of the field are Émile Durkheim, Karl Marx, Max Weber, and Georg Simmel. Émile Durkheim reflects the influence of French positivism in seeking to establish sociology as an empirical science grounded on discoveries of important correlations among social facts. But he eventually went beyond this perspective in showing how the social order reflects a shared moral code that exists in people's subjective consciousness, not just as an external social fact. A large part of his theoretical analysis contrasted the moral consciousness of simple societies characterized by a low division of labor with that of modern societies in which a high level of interdependence, coupled with a high level of individualism, results from a greatly expanded division of labor.

Durkheim's theoretical perspective can be seen as an alternative to the critical conflict perspective of Karl Marx. Marx had rejected the strong emphasis of the determining influence of cultural ideas as reflected in German historicism. For him, the development of sociology required an analysis of how the actual material and social conditions of people's lives influenced their consciousness and behavior as well as their opportunities to develop their full human potential. With his focus on the economic class structure, he saw class divisions in modern society deepening as a result of the advancing centralization of the means of production and capitalists' expanding levels of exploitation of workers in their efforts to increase their profits. Although the capitalist system was subject to periodic crises, their resolution should not be expected to end the process of exploitation and class conflict until the capitalist system is eventually overthrown through revolutionary struggle.

Reflecting the influence of German historicism, Max Weber's work emphasized the importance of understanding cultural values that vary in different societies as they affect individuals' subjective consciousness and motivations. This was manifested in his analysis of the influence of the Protestant ethic on the development of capitalism, especially when compared with the economic influences of other religions. However, people's subjective interpretations of their values (religious and otherwise) will reflect their particular position in the social structure and the material and social interests associated with these positions. Like Marx, Weber recognized that people's social behavior is heavily influenced by their material and social environment, including not only their economic class position but their position in hierarchies of power as well as status and prestige. Weber analyzed modern bureaucratic organizations as structures of power and authority that are organized according to the logic of instrumental rationality, with concerns about ultimate values and underlying human needs subordinated to this constraining type of rule-governed rationality oriented toward pragmatic goals.

Simmel is unique among the four leading classical theorists in emphasizing the micro level. However, he moved back and forth between micro and macro levels, showing how similar types of social processes can be manifested at different levels. Although his intellectual environment was permeated by German historicism, his work dealt mainly with forms or patterns of interaction. Both social conflict and social cohesion can be regarded as basic forms of interaction in his perspective. This focus on both conflict and cohesion allows for incorporation of Durkheim's emphasis on interdependence and solidarity plus Marx's analysis of class conflict. Simmel also contrasted forms of interaction and patterns of individual involvement in small-scale social settings and those in larger social systems, and he emphasized how the latter are becoming more and more important in modern society.

None of the four leading classical theorists represent the British tradition as described in the last chapter. Instead, this British tradition served as a kind of foil for both Marx and Durkheim, as their perspectives were developed partly in opposition to its individualistic laissez-faire emphasis. Marx criticized economist Adam Smith by arguing that the unregulated market system did not promote the overall well-being of society but led instead to increasing levels of inequality and exploitation. Durkheim rejected the individualistic assumptions of sociologist Herbert Spencer and argued that individuals reflect the formative influence of society for their development as human beings. However, as we shall see in the next chapter, the individualistic implications of British social thought were highly compatible with the type of sociology that developed in America.

The remaining theorists reviewed in this chapter were also important for their contributions to the establishment of the sociological perspective, even though their long-term impact on contemporary sociology has not been emphasized as heavily as the impact of the four theorists identified above. Martineau pioneered in the development of participant observation ethnographic research that revealed clear discrepancies between cultural values and ideals (morals) and actual customs and practices (manners). De Tocqueville's analysis of democracy in America demonstrated how various voluntary groups (including churches) and local governments stimulated civic involvement and linked individual citizens to the larger social order. Pareto emphasized the importance of understanding the non-rational sentiments that motivate behavior as opposed to the rational explanations people may offer, and he incorporated this perspective in his model of the "circulation of elites" in which conservatives and innovative liberals tend to alternate in the political power structure. Tönnies' distinction between *Gemeinschaft* (community) and *Gesellschaft* (society) showed how people's natural social ties in traditional types of communities can be contrasted with the contractual nature of their relationships in formally established organizations in modern societies. And finally, Marianne Weber identified women's economic dependence on their husbands' as the primary source of their subordination in both their families and in the wider society—a pattern that she showed was in sharp conflict with the Protestant (and Christian) ideal of the equality of all people. American sociology was heavily influenced by these various European theorists but was distinctly different from any of them. We turn in the next chapter to the story of the development of American sociology, noting the influence of these European sources as appropriate.

Questions for Study and Discussion

1. Of all of the different theorists whose ideas have been reviewed in this chapter, which do you feel are most relevant in providing insights into the fundamental characteristics and major trends of contemporary society? Which are the least relevant? Explain your answers.
2. Explain how Durkheim's perspective on the increased division of labor in modern society can be compared and contrasted with Weber's analysis of bureaucratic organization and authority structures and with Tönnies' views regarding the growth in *Gesellschaft* types of structures.
3. Give an example of each of the two types of rational action identified by Weber—instrumental rationality and value-oriented rationality. How can these two types of rationality be related to the feminist issues identified by Marianna Weber and the moral challenges of a complex society as analyzed by Durkheim?
4. Explain how Simmel's analysis of the effects of numbers on forms of interaction can be used to explain changes in the social structure and personal relationships of people in small village-type communities versus large urban areas. How would these differences compare and contrast with Tönnies analysis of *Gemeinschaft* and *Gesellschaft?*
5. From the beginning sociology has reflected a concern with current social problems and moral challenges. Identify some major examples of the crucial moral challenges that can be identified in the works of Durkheim, Marx, Martineau, and Marianna Weber.

Chapter 3
Development of American Sociology: A Brief Historical Overview

The development of American sociology was heavily influenced by the European pioneers discussed in the last chapter, but it also reflected the distinctive historical background of the United States. Its foundations can be traced to the emergence of the Chicago School in the early decades of the twentieth century. The first professional sociology journal in the United States, the *American Journal of Sociology*, was established at the University of Chicago and today is one of the leading journals in the field. Chicago itself proved to be a kind of natural laboratory for qualitative, ethnographic-type research on urban social processes and problems.

Chicago School sociology represented the widespread American pragmatic and individualistic mentality in which knowledge is related to dealing with real-life problems and social reforms. This reform emphasis contrasted with the perspective of social Darwinism that was also influential at the time. Social Darwinism was based on the evolutionary theory of British theorist Herbert Spencer, in which social reform efforts were thought to interfere with the process whereby long-term evolutionary progress occurs through the struggle for survival and the survival of the fittest.

These opposing viewpoints can be illustrated in the contrasting perspectives of Lester Ward (1883) versus William Graham Sumner ([1906] 1979). Lester Ward, who in 1906 became the first president of the American Sociological Society (now the American Sociological Association), viewed the development of strategies to improve society as part of the evolutionary process, which to him was superior to the blind forces of nature in insuring long-range progress. In contrast, William Graham Sumner took a more *laissez-faire* approach in which efforts to implement social reforms were regarded as interfering with the natural process of evolution and were unlikely to be successful in the long run anyway, especially if they were counter to established customs and folkways.

By the time sociology reached its period of rapid expansion in the middle decades of the twentieth century a large part of the theoretical development in the field had shifted from the University of Chicago to Harvard University (under Talcott Parsons) and Columbia University (under Robert Merton). These developments will be reviewed and summarized in this chapter as indicated below.

- The Chicago School—represented by George Herbert Mead, Jane Addams, William I. Thomas, and Robert Ezra Park. Mead's ideas contributed to the

D.P. Johnson, *Contemporary Sociological Theory: An Integrated Multi-Level Approach.*

development of the micro-level perspective of symbolic interaction theory; Addams was devoted to using sociological knowledge in implementing social reforms; Thomas focused on the importance of social definitions in understanding behavior, and Park pioneered in the development of urban sociology through his ecological analyses of Chicago.

- Other noteworthy pioneers—represented by Charles Horton Cooley, W. E. B. Du Bois, and Charlotte Perkins Gilman. Cooley's perspective on the self-concept was also incorporated in symbolic interaction theory. Du Bois focused heavily on the distinct challenges faced by African Americans in coping with a racist society. Gilman provides an example of an early feminist critical perspective.
- Emergence of functional theory—manifested by Talcott Parsons through the major role he played during the middle part of the twentieth century with his elaborate structural/functional analysis of social systems. This development was preceded by the even more macro-level cultural analysis of Pitirim Sorokin. Robert Merton's "middle range" functional perspective provided an influential alternative to Parsons' perspective, while Lewis Coser developed a functionalist analysis of conflict. The functionalist perspective on macro-level social structures contrasts sharply with the more micro or local community focus of the Chicago School.
- Mid-century critics of functionalism—with the major alternative perspectives represented by Herbert Blumer (symbolic interaction theory), C. Wright Mills (critical theory), and George Homans (elementary exchange theory, later incorporated in rational choice theory).

Chicago School Beginnings: Social Interaction and Social Reform

Despite its American mentality, the Chicago School was influenced by various European theorists. This resulted partly from the pattern whereby young American scholars at that time would round out their education by study in Europe. Of the various classical European theorists, Simmel's influence was particularly noteworthy at Chicago, and his focus on micro-level social processes was highly compatible with the style of sociological analysis developed there.

George Herbert Mead and Social Behaviorism[1]

Of all the Chicago School theorists, George Herbert Mead was probably the most comprehensive and abstract. His contributions are important for analyzing the close

[1] This overview of Mead's contributions is adapted from D. P. Johnson ([1981] 1986:293–311). See also Coser (1977:333–355) and Turner et al. (2002:434–496) for excellent summaries of Mead's intellectual context and his contributions to contemporary sociology.

relationship between social interaction and subjective mental processes, as well as the way individuals' self-concepts link them with the life of the larger community or society.[2] Mead's perspective on how knowledge develops through the process of adaptation to the environment and problem solving provides a bridge between pragmatism and sociology. Mead referred to his perspective as **social behaviorism**, but many of his ideas were later incorporated in symbolic interaction theory. Mead's focus on interaction was similar to Simmel's, but Mead stressed more explicitly the way interaction is linked with subjective interpretation (the thinking process).

Mead's (1934) social behaviorism was intended as a critique of psychological behaviorism, which he considered incomplete for understanding both the social and the subjective dimensions of human behavior. For Mead, the simple stimulus-response model of behavioral psychology ignored the subjective process of interpretation whereby the meanings of environmental stimuli are established through interaction. This does not mean that stimulus-response patterns do not apply to human beings. But the intentional responses of human beings to their environment, and to one another, go beyond these automatic, nonreflective conditioned responses by incorporating the process of subjective interpretation that occurs between stimulus and response. Mead regarded the **mind** itself as the **thinking process** whereby human beings seek to make sense of their environment in the process of adapting to it.

Human beings' strategies of coping with their environment are interrelated and interdependent. Through communication and interaction people develop shared interpretations of their environment as they adjust to one another's expectations and behaviors. But communication is merely the overt or external aspect of the internal thinking process. Because Mead believed that psychological behaviorists neglected this social dimension, he referred to his position as **social** behaviorism.

In its simplest form communication may involve simply a "conversation of gestures." Gestures are seen as the first phase of an act, and they may trigger an adjustive response by others even before being completed. The initial phase thus comes to represent, or symbolize, the entire act. Mead's often-cited example is that of two dogs engaging in mutually threatening behavior (growling and baring teeth prior to actual attack). The significance of "gestures" is recognized by those who attempt to "read" people's "body language" for messages (feelings or intentions) that may or may not be intentional. When gestures are intentional, they serve as **symbols** for

---

[2] George Herbert Mead (1863–1931) was born in Massachusetts but moved with his family to Oberlin, Ohio, where his father (who had been a Congregational minister) was called to teach. Following his graduation from Oberlin College, Mead eventually enrolled at Harvard University and later went to Europe for additional study. He began his professional career at the University of Michigan, but after three years went with John Dewey to the University of Chicago, where both he and Dewey contributed to the development of pragmatic philosophy at the University of Chicago. He was also a friend and supporter of Jane Addams, the pioneering social worker and founder of Hull House.

completed acts (or associated feelings or plans). When meanings are understood by others in the same way, they thereby become **significant gestures** or **symbols**. For example, a clenched fist becomes a socially recognized symbol for anger or determination to win, even without any intention actually to engage in a physical attack. The transformation of a gesture to a symbol depends on the ability of human beings to become an object to themselves, which means they can understand their own behavior from the perspective of others. By using significant gestures or symbols, individuals can deliberately construct their behavior to call forth particular responses from others.

Communication among human beings relies heavily on **words**, which are linguistic symbols representing shared meanings. The use of vocal or written symbols contrasts sharply with physical gestures in that they can be experienced by the person using them in practically the same way that they are experienced by others (i.e., people can hear themselves talk, or read what they have written). This shared experience facilitates mutual understanding and enables people to cooperate with one another. Beyond this, human beings have the ability to create a symbolic world that is not limited to the immediate here and now of sensory experience or to particular material objects (or stimuli) in their environment. Instead, they can communicate about objects or actions that are far removed in time and space, or to ideas and concepts that have no physical existence in the material world at all. Human beings are thus able to construct a virtual world of cultural meanings based on nothing more than shared definitions, as opposed to the objective reality of the material world. Words can be used to represent abstract universal categories in which specific objects in the environment are seen merely as instances or examples of the abstract category in which they are classified. To illustrate, human beings are not required to point to specific objects such as chairs, trees, or whatever to communicate about them; instead, they can construct an abstract concept of chair as an object for sitting that can be distinguished from beds and tables, and these objects may be included in the general category of furniture that can be distinguished from other categories of objects.

A large part of the world that human beings experience is a socially constructed symbolic world that is based on shared definitions created and maintained through interaction. Thus the social world that human beings create includes not only physical or biological objects such as land, trees, furniture, tools, and other people; it also incorporates residential or commercial districts, parks and forest preserves, police districts and city boundaries. It also consists of traffic rules and legal codes, career paths and organizational structures, artistic styles and philosophical ideas, and its inhabitants include teachers, attorneys, politicians, military officers, musicians, business people, and students. In short, a large part of the world in which human beings live is a cultural world that they themselves have created. This symbolic cultural world is just as real in the subjective consciousness and in the social environment of human beings as the physical world.

The link between communication and subjective consciousness is so close in Mead's view that a large part of the subjective thinking process can be seen as an internal conversation with oneself. Individuals can easily make themselves aware of how they sometimes alternate between rehearsing what they anticipate saying or doing and what they expect the outcomes to be, including other people's reactions. This involves shifting back and forth between one's own perspectives and the imagined perspectives and anticipated responses of others. Individuals are often not consciously aware of this process, although in some crucial situations (such as an employment interview, for example) they may intentionally think through alternatives and rehearse what to say in advance. Everyday observation suggests that people vary a great deal in terms of how much they think before they speak, depending in large part on the particular situation they face.

A person's response to an environmental stimulus, or to another person, will depend on the particular need or impulse that is salient at the time. In general, individuals focus their attention on features of their environment that are relevant for satisfying their current impulses, or latent plans of action, while ignoring other aspects. The same stimulus may have different meanings for different persons, or for the same person at different times, depending on the specific needs or impulses that are salient at the time. When people are involved with one another in some fashion they typically may be expected to try to align or coordinate their perspectives and activities through the process of symbolic communication. In this process they may become aware of differences in goals or perspectives that may need to be resolved in some fashion in order to continue.

In line with his pragmatic philosophy, Mead emphasized that the active thinking process is often triggered by the appearance of a problem that blocks individuals' efforts to meet their needs or goals or satisfy their impulses. This blockage stimulates a covert mental process of constructing tentative solutions. The ability to think through alternative actions and to try to anticipate their probable consequences represents a major evolutionary advance that enables human beings to adapt to their environment in a less risky and more efficient way than through trial and error. Also, through the communication process (in education, in particular) the results of each generation's experience in dealing with the ongoing problems and challenges of life can be transmitted to the next generation, thereby avoiding the need for each new generation to start from scratch in learning through the process of trial and error how to deal with recurring problems or adapt to their environment.

One of the most important "objects" to be defined and interpreted is the identities and roles of the individuals involved in ongoing social relations. Mead emphasized the reciprocal interplay between the self as **acting subject** (the "I") and the self as **object**, as seen through the perspective of others (the "me"). The "I" is the nonreflective aspect of the self and consists of one's awareness of the actual behavioral responses he or she is making to the current situation as it is taking place. When an action is completed, however, the memory of it is incorporated in the reflexive "me" of the self-concept, along with the reactions of others. In this reflective process the individual evaluates the completed action from the standpoint of others as well as his or her own self-evaluation. If these results and reactions are not as anticipated, the "me" dimension of the self may be revised, and this revised self-concept will then be manifested in one's future actions.

A person's self-concept changes over time as a result of changes in the social groups in which one is involved and increased social maturity. Mead described the distinct stages through which children move in developing their identity. First is the **play** stage in which a child will "play at" some role. This begins the process whereby they learn to adopt the perspectives and attitudes of others. As they gain more social experience, the **game** stage emerges, which involves a higher level of social organization. In this stage children relate to one another in terms of the different roles they play in the activity in which they are involved. The third and final stage is when participants orient themselves toward abstract rules rather than specific individuals. When individuals evaluate their behavior in terms of impersonal rules, they are said to be taking the role of the "**generalized other**." Mead used the concept of the generalized other to move beyond the micro level and to discuss the expectations and standards of the overall community or society.

In Mead's view, the internal (or subjective) organization of individuals' definitions, attitudes, and self-concepts and the external organization of groups, social institutions, and society itself are interdependent, since both emerge through symbolic communication. Human beings are not biologically programmed with the responses needed for their survival, nor are they born with the ability to survive on their own. This means that the subjective process whereby they take the role of others and regulate their own behavior so as to fit within the framework of definitions and attitudes shared with others is essential for successful adaptation to their environment as well as for their ability to participate in organized social action. It is through this process that they eventually become functioning members of society.

Human intelligence itself emerges as individuals learn through experience how to adapt to their environment so as to meet their basic needs. This process involves the adoption of shared definitions and meanings developed through symbolic communication. In this way the emergence of human beings' intelligence helps insure their long-term evolutionary progress in learning how to adapt to a variety of specific environments. In addition, through the creation and manipulation of symbols, human beings are able to cooperate in transcending many of the limitations imposed by their biological nature or the physical environment. They can, for example, construct shelters to protect themselves from weather extremes so that they can inhabit areas that would otherwise be uninhabitable; they can overcome the limitations of physical distance by developing sophisticated transportation and communication technologies, and they can build machines to carry loads that would be humanly impossible to lift. These ideas reveal Mead's pragmatic mentality as well as his acceptance of an evolutionary model that envisioned continued human progress.

Mead's influence on American sociology is manifested primarily in the development of symbolic interaction theory, with its distinctive emphasis on micro-level processes of subjective interpretation and communication. Other early American sociologists whose ideas contributed to symbolic interaction theory will be reviewed later. But we turn in the next section to the contributions of Jane Addams, another member of the Chicago School and a strong advocate for social reform.

Jane Addams: Applying Sociology Through Social Work and Social Reform

Jane Addams (1860–1935) is best known as the founder of Hull House in Chicago, a settlement house for the poor that became an important center for various social services and reform efforts. As a pioneer in the settlement house movement and a strong advocate for helping the disprivileged and promoting social reform, Jane Addams was a major figure in the establishment of social work as a profession. But she was also involved with the early development of American sociology prior to the differentiation of social work as a separate profession (Lengermann and Niebrugge-Brantley, 1998:72–88; Elshtain, 2002). Although not a University of Chicago faculty member, she joined the American Sociological Society (now the American Sociological Association), conducted social research, and published in the *American Journal of Sociology*.

Jane Addams was born in a middle class family in Illinois. Her father served in the Illinois Legislature. Her mother died when she was young, and her father eventually remarried. Fulfilling her father's wishes, Jane Addams attended Rockford Female Seminary. After completing her schooling there, and after facing various family crises (including the death of her father) and a period of youthful indecision, she traveled to Europe twice, the first time with her stepmother. Her concern for the poor developed in part from her observations of the poor in London, with whom she contrasted her own comfortable lifestyle. On her second trip with college friends she observed a London settlement house and decided that she, too, should live among the poor and undertake such a project.

An isolated academic life without practical application would have been inconsistent with Jane Addams' ethical and moral commitments. She believed that being involved as a neighbor with the poor is essential for understanding their lives and generating the motivation to show concern for their welfare in practical ways (Addams [1902] 1920; see Elshtain, ed. [2002] for a representative sample of Addams' writings). She recognized the basic human potential for mutual kindness and believed that people are actually frustrated when they observe the discrepancy between the ethical and moral ideals they profess and the actual social conditions they observe in their community. However, when people's lives are isolated from one another, or are limited to their own families, they find it difficult to relate the abstract ethical and moral principles they profess to their everyday conduct in public life. Addams believed that the ideal for a democratic society based on the belief in equality would be for people to be concerned as naturally about members of their community as they are about members of their own family. In view of the poverty and related social problems that had developed as a consequence of industrialization, urbanization, and immigration, the challenge for modern society is to develop a "social morality" in which people will engage in collective action for the common good.

Addams proved to be effective in the fund-raising activities needed to accomplish her goal of establishing a settlement house. She and her college friend Ellen Gates Starr, who had gone with her on her second trip abroad, located a place for their settlement house in a poor neighborhood of immigrants. Its development was made possible through financial contributions Addams acquired, including significant amounts from wealthy women. Hull House was named after Charles Hull, the millionaire who originally owned the building. Addams' initial plan was to live as a neighbor among the poor residents who came to Hull House and help them by sharing her own culture with them. Soon, however, she came to appreciate their culture, along with the difficult challenges they faced because of poverty. The strategy she developed involved recruiting Hull House residents themselves to help provide social services and to work for social reforms to try to alleviate poverty. Hull House eventually became a major center for numerous education and reform efforts and social service outreach activities. Collaboration with Hull House residents even included a research project the residents wrote on the surrounding neighborhood (Residents of Hull-House–A Social Settlement, 1895), and Addams herself (1910, 1930) provided longitudinal accounts of the remarkable story of Hull House.

Addams believed that a settlement house could enable people to apply their ethical and moral principles by becoming involved in a practical way in helping to alleviate the sufferings of those victimized by the social problems of an industrial society. By actually living and working with the poor and disprivileged in their everyday lives as a neighbor, people can learn to show their concern for them in ways that do not undermine their dignity or autonomy as human beings. Such neighborly assistance contrasts with the approach used by "charity workers" who arrive from outside the local neighborhood. Despite their good intentions, they are likely to be perceived as condescending and controlling due to class-based differences in their life circumstances.

Addams was also a strong advocate for labor reforms that would improve wages, reduce working hours, and prevent the harsh exploitation of workers, particularly women and children. She even regarded the settlement house movement as a source of support for the labor movement. However, it was important for workers to move beyond competition with one another and learn to work together to achieve their common goals. Addams was hopeful that the long-range goals of the labor union movement would expand beyond the individualistic ethics expressed in class conflict so that both employers and workers could learn to cooperate for the common good.

With her high level of activity and visibility, Jane Addams' social network developed far beyond the University of Chicago. She became active in local government lobbying for social reform legislation. She was an advocate for the creation of the Cook County Juvenile Court, through which the legal distinction between juvenile delinquents and adult criminals was originally established. Her activism later expanded to the national level to include opposition to United States involvement in World War I, and she became president of the International Committee of Women for Permanent Peace. Although this activism in the peace movement was criticized, public opinion eventually changed, and in 1931 she was awarded the Nobel Peace Prize.

In Addams' ([1902] 1920) view, the ideals of our democratic society were undermined by the individualism of our culture, the capitalist organization of business, and the government's inability to move beyond the protection of individual rights to promote the welfare of all. The organization of industrial and business enterprises reflected the interests of capitalists as they competed for dominance. Workers were exploited in the process, resulting in extreme poverty, insecurity, and other social problems. The government was not organized to insure the public good in the fullest sense of this term. The democratic ideal of equality was undermined by the high priority given to the abstract ideal of individual rights. The overall outcome was that capitalist enterprises were unrestrained in their ability to exercise their "rights" even when this led to the unfair exploitation of workers. In this context the functions of government were limited to regulating and controlling those who were being exploited.

In the absence of a sense of responsibility for the collective good of all citizens, the situation in large cities like Chicago was ripe for corruption. Local politicians and law enforcement officials used their local contacts to provide favors and obtain support outside the framework of the law (Addams, 1905, 1907 [reprinted in Elshtain, ed., 2002:147–162]). The basic problem with both industry and government was an inability to move beyond an individualistic ethic toward a social ethic appropriate to a large and complex industrial society with high levels of interdependence.

The distinctive experiences and orientations of women offer a potential foundation for cultural and social structural transformation. Because of their traditional family responsibilities, women are accustomed to demonstrating their concern for others in the everyday context of family life. But their opportunities to contribute to the development of a social ethic in the wider society are limited if they are unable to move beyond the domestic sphere of their own families to participate more fully in the public sphere. Even for women who were employed, their major orientations reflected the dominant individualistic ethic of the competitive world outside the home environment. Also, many of the women employed in the industrial world were poor, young, exploited by low wages and long workdays, and naturally concerned primarily with their own survival. Thus it was important for Addams that women with a higher socioeconomic status should move beyond charity work among the poor on an individual basis by promoting greater concern for the larger public good and a more progressive social ethic. Jane Addams' vision of the potential for women to transform public life in ways that would reduce the harsh impact of domination, competition, and conflict mark her as having a distinctive feminist perspective on how women could play an active role in promoting the democratic ideal of equality.

W. I. Thomas and the "Definition of the Situation"[3]

Another key figure of the Chicago School, William I. Thomas (1863–1947), also contributed to the subsequent development of the symbolic interactionist perspective

[3]This description of Thomas's contributions is adapted from D. P. Johnson ([1981] 1986:317–319). See also Coser (1977:511–599) for an excellent summary of the contributions of W. I. Thomas and his collaborator Florian Znaniecki to contemporary sociological theory.

by emphasizing the need to understand people's shared subjective definitions.[4] Thomas is best known for pointing out how people's **definition of the situation** is likely to have definite social consequences. Like Mead, Thomas highlighted the point that human behavior is not simply an automatic reflexive response to environmental stimuli. Instead, as Thomas put it, "Preliminary to any self-determined act of behavior there is always a stage of examination and deliberation which we may call *the definition of the situation*." (Thomas, 1923:41–43) This idea gives rise to the oft-quoted Thomas theorem: "If men define situations as real they are real in their consequences." The same objective stimulus or environmental situation may elicit different reactions from different people, or even from the same person at different times, depending on their subjective definitions as applied to the situation at hand.

Individuals' definitions of their situations are always shaped by their sociocultural environment. Nevertheless, there may be tension or conflict between socially accepted definitions of the situation and individuals' own personal definitions. Individuals' personal definitions reflect their particular needs and desires at the moment, while standardized social definitions are based on shared values and purposes. Personal definitions consist of individuals' **attitudes** while shared cultural definitions refer to a group's **values**. Those who move from one subculture to another often find that the definitions learned earlier do not fit their new environment. This means that in order to adjust they must learn new customs and traditions—or new definitions.

This process of adjusting to a new subculture was demonstrated in the monumental and influential research project that Thomas did in collaboration with Florian Znaniecki in investigating the challenges faced by Polish immigrants in adjusting to their new American environment in Chicago (Thomas and Znaniecki, 1958). They contrasted individuals' personal subjective definitions with the objective cultural definitions as manifested in their social institutions. This project contributed significantly to the early study of ethnic subcultures and minority group relations, and it illustrates the way the sociologists of the early Chicago School focused their research on their own urban environment in their efforts to advance our sociological understanding of social processes and social problems.

Robert Ezra Park: Observing and Analyzing the Social Life of the City

The contributions of Robert Park (1864–1944) and his colleagues to the development of the Chicago School sociology extend beyond the level of symbolic interaction in

[4] William I. Thomas was born in Virginia but moved to Tennessee when still a child and later attended the University of Tennessee. After studying in Germany and then teaching for five years at Oberlin College, he enrolled at the University of Chicago, where he subsequently spent most of his career.

micro-level face-to-face relations and focus instead on the larger ecological and social organization of the urban environment (Chicago in particular).[5] In the analysis by Park and his colleagues (Park et al. [1925] 1967), the ecological structure of urban communities reveals patterns of interdependence that are based only in part on the shared definitions that emerge through symbolic interaction. The other part involves the effects of competitive struggles among human beings for survival and for dominance in their habitat.

In contrast to small-scale rural communities, social relations in an urban environment include complex forms of symbiotic interdependence as well as face-to-face symbolic interaction. These patterns of interdependence develop from the competition among different groups to adapt to their environment and establish themselves in the most favorable niche possible. The outcomes of these struggles can be seen in the ever-changing patterns of land use and residential settlement in urban communities. These symbiotic relations may be compared to the way other biological species adapt to each other's presence and activities in the habitat they share without intentional communication.

One important outcome of the competition and conflict among different ethnic groups in an urban area is manifested in ever-changing patterns of residential segregation. The typical pattern for recently arrived immigrants was to begin their new lives in America near the center of the city, where relatively low-cost housing could be obtained close to the available industrial-type jobs. Eventually, as members of the second and subsequent generations of these groups accumulated sufficient economic resources, they tended to move away from these congested neighborhoods to more expensive areas closer to the edge of the city. This was accompanied by gradual cultural assimilation as well. As members of a particular ethnic group moved out in this fashion, their place would be taken by a newer immigrant group, and the pattern would then be repeated.

This general model of how immigrant groups gradually become assimilated to the dominant culture was incorporated into a well-known textbook by Robert Park and Ernest W. Burgess ([1921] 1969) in which they proposed a four-fold typology of stages of intergroup relations that could be applied to the waves of immigrant groups that came to the United States. These stages were: competition, conflict, accommodation, and assimilation. Competition and conflict are manifested in the struggle for dominance within an ecological niche. Conflict is reduced as patterns of accommodation are developed, and assimilation essentially means that the boundaries between the groups have been eliminated.

Because of the strong belief in an open class structure in the United States, upward socioeconomc mobility and cultural assimilation were assumed to be virtually inevitable for immigrant groups, despite the fact that they started out at the bottom

---

[5]Robert Park was educated at Harvard and then continued his studies in Germany, where he attended lectures by Georg Simmel. Prior to his academic career he had worked as a journalist, and his journalistic interest in investigating various aspects of urban life carried over into his academic work. For a summary of the biographical details of Park's life and his major contributions to sociology, see Coser (1977:357–384).

of the socioeconomic hierarchy. However, as shown in subsequent developments, this general process whereby competition and conflict were eventually replaced by accommodation and assimilation failed to occur for African Americans who migrated in large numbers from rural communities in the South to industrial cities of the Northeast and Midwest in the decades following World War II. Instead, because of the stubborn persistence of racial prejudice and discrimination, African Americans found that opportunities for both economic advancement and residential relocation were blocked. The distinctive experiences of African Americans in the United States, both North and South, were eloquently portrayed by W. E. B. Du Bois, whose contributions to the development of sociology will be reviewed later in this chapter.

Other Significant Pioneers in Early American Sociology

The style of research and theory represented by the Chicago School in the early years of the twentieth century is still recognizable today, even though it has been widely diffused throughout American sociology. In addition to these Chicago School pioneers, there were many others who also contributed to the early development of American sociology. The following section will briefly present the theoretical ideas of three additional figures who demonstrate the diversity of the early years of the discipline in America.

Charles Horton Cooley: Primary Groups and the Looking-Glass Self[6]

Charles Horton Cooley (1864–1929) was born in Michigan and was associated with the University of Michigan for all of his professional life. Like Mead, his ideas also contributed to the development of symbolic interaction theory. His perspective on the relation between a person's self-concept and face-to-face interaction within primary groups is expressed in his frequently cited concept of the "looking glass self" (Cooley ([1902] 1964). This metaphor refers to the way one's identity is formed from the reflections one sees of oneself in the reactions of others. This concept is clearly parallel to Mead's insights regarding the social origins of one's self-concept. More than Mead, however, Cooley stressed the importance of our emotional reactions to these responses. When we perceive the reactions of others as indicating either approval or disapproval, we feel pride or shame as a result.

---

[6] This description of Cooley's perspective is adapted from D. P. Johnson ([1981] 1986:312–317). See also Coser (1977:305–330) for an excellent summary of Cooley's social and intellectual biography and his contributions to contemporary sociology.

Cooley ([1902] 1964) also pointed out that our identity may extend beyond ourselves to include our family, friends, and primary group relationships. To speak of "*my* family" or "*my* group" is to expand our sense of self to include these relationships. The groups with which we identify most strongly in this way are likely to be **primary groups**. Such groups differ from **secondary groups** in that they are characterized by intimate face-to-face relationships. It is through primary groups (especially the family) that individuals are bound together with a sense of unity and cohesiveness that finds expression in the mutual regard (or sympathy) they have for one another in their common life.

W. E. B. Du Bois: African Americans' Double Consciousness "Within the Veil"

As the influence of the Chicago School was expanding in the early decades of the twentieth century, William Edward Burghardt Du Bois emerged as an eloquent and persuasive critic of the pervasive and degrading "color line" which he identified as the central problem of twentieth century America (Du Bois [1903] 1999:5; see also Du Bois [1970]). W. E. B. Du Bois was born in Massachusetts in 1868 and earned baccalaureate degrees from both Fisk University and Harvard University. He also studied at the Friedrich Wilhelm University in Berlin. He received in Ph.D. from Harvard in 1895, the first African American to do so. His academic career in sociology included positions at Wilberforce University in Ohio, the University of Pennsylvania, and Atlanta University. At Atlanta University he was a professor of economics and history from 1897 to 1910 and chairman of the Sociology Department from 1934 to 1944. He participated in the founding of the National Association for the Advancement of Colored People (NAACP), in which he was active for many years, and was also a leader in the Pan-Africanism movement in the first several decades of the twentieth century. He moved to Ghana near the end of his life, where he died in 1963 (Du Bois, ([1903] 1999:365–371; see also Weinberg, 1970:xi–xvii).

When Du Bois moved south as a young man to attend Fisk University, he personally confronted the oppressive effects of racial prejudice, discrimination, and segregation to a far greater extent than he had in his growing up years in Massachusetts, where the proportion of African Americans was much smaller. It is important to note that this was long before passage of civil rights legislation, and Jim Crow laws actually provided legal support for what was in effect a rigid American caste system. With memories of the Civil War defeat still fresh throughout the South, African Americans were routinely subjected to systematic patterns of overt discrimination, oppression, and injustice that are difficult to imagine today.

W. E. B. Du Bois's contributions as a journalist went far beyond typical academic-type writing and included numerous magazine and newspaper articles as well as works of poetry and fiction. He devoted his life to exposing and criticizing the harsh realities of the underlying caste system of American society as manifested in deeply established patterns of degradation and discrimination that were directed against African Americans as second-class citizens in all areas of life. To enable African Americans to survive the cruel bigotry they experienced on a daily basis in a racist and oppressive society, Du Bois insisted that African Americans should seek to develop a strong sense of solidarity and should be willing to engage in collective action in the struggle for equality. He argued that a broad education was essential for promoting African Americans' awareness of Africans' distinctive contributions throughout world history, plus the contributions of African Americans to American culture in particular. He was critical of the inferior education African Americans received in segregated schools as well as the notion advanced by some that their education should be limited to vocational training oriented primarily to their economic needs (Du Bois, 2001). His passionate dream was for well educated African Americans to be able to draw on their distinctive historical backgrounds and experiences in enriching American life as an openly multicultural society. But Du Bois recognized that the prospects for this seemed quite bleak in his own time.

In *The Souls of Black Folk* (Du Bois [1903] 1999), one of his more frequently cited works among sociologists today, Du Bois describes how the rigid segregation and subordination of African Americans as a separate and subordinated caste profoundly affected their basic mentality and worldview, particularly their self-concept. In reviewing the history of the post-Civil War years, he demonstrated that the end of slavery failed to lead to the freedom and equality that were expected. Drawing on his own experience, he described how African Americans continued to be treated as inferior second-class citizens and subjected to deep-seated prejudice and harsh and pervasive forms of discrimination and oppression that in essence denied their basic humanity. Deprived of their basic rights and dignity as human beings, African Americans developed a kind of mental veil that sharply differentiated their consciousness, their self-concepts, and their ways of seeing the world from the mentality and worldview of whites. As Du Bois put it in his "Forethought" to *The Souls of Black Folk*, "Leaving, then, the world of the white man, I have stepped within the Veil, raising it so that you may view faintly its deeper recesses,—the meaning of its religion, the passion of its human sorrow, and the struggles of its greater souls." Du Bois ([1903] 1999:5).

This veil cannot succeed, of course, in insulating African Americans from the dominant culture of whites or enabling them to escape from it. In fact, understanding the dominant culture is essential for them to adapt and survive in the larger society, despite the constant humiliation they experience. Instead of escaping or denying the reality of the dominant culture, African Americans have developed a unique perspective on this dominant culture that is not available to those not behind the veil. Through this "second sight" African Americans are able to gain distinctive insights into the souls of white folk as well. This means they are also able to see the world from the perspective of the dominant culture of whites, but in a unique way because of their stigmatized second-class outsider status (Du Bois [1903] 1999:6). In their world behind the veil, African Americans struggle constantly to resist the denial of their basic humanity that they experience on a daily basis as they confront the dominant culture of the white world. Their basic worldview and identity reflect this struggle. The overriding challenge is to reject these negative dehumanizing evaluations and to engage in the struggle to achieve a sense of human dignity and competence that is denied them in the wider society.

This experience of living in two different worlds gives rise to the "double consciousness" that Du Bois described as characterizing the souls of African Americans. As he put it,

> "It is a peculiar sensation, this double-consciousness, this sense of always looking at one-self through the eyes of others, of measuring one's soul by the tape of a world that looks on in amused contempt and pity. One always feels his two-ness,—an American, a Negro; two souls, two thoughts, two unreconciled strivings; two warring ideals in one dark body, whose dogged strength alone keeps it from being torn asunder."
>
> (Du Bois [1903] 1999:11)

The most effective way for African Americans to achieve a sense of dignity, as individuals and as members of a stigmatized group, is to become aware of their unique cultural heritage, both in America and earlier in Africa, and their potential for expanding their contributions to America as a multicultural society. But the opportunities of African Americans to obtain the broad education that would prepare them for participating as equals in American society and contributing to its culture are systematically denied them. Without opportunities for education or for equal participation in American life, African Americans are unable to realize their potential, to achieve individual success, or to develop as leaders among their own people or in the larger society.

The outcome is an agonizing "no win" situation. African Americans are systematically denied access to the opportunities that majority group members have to demonstrate their abilities, develop their potential, and make their own valued contributions to American society—and then they are stigmatized as inferior and incompetent and thus incapable of contributing. Du Bois's critique of American society was based on his clear recognition that the problems African Americans experience are the result of the rigid two-caste structure of American society and the contradictions between the pervasive racist beliefs and practices that sustain this structure and the dominant American ideology of equality.

This analysis by Du Bois of the plight of African Americans, especially as it applied to those living in the South, helps explain why large numbers of African Americans began migrating from the rural South to cities in the North, often in search of industrial jobs, in the decades following the end of World War II. As mentioned earlier, however, even in the North, African Americans found they were unable to achieve the same level of economic success or cultural assimilation as immigrant groups from overseas had done earlier. The interrelated processes of socioeconomic and residential mobility and assimilation that Park described for the immigrant groups who had come to Chicago in earlier decades did not occur for African Americans, even though they were already American citizens. Instead, in cities throughout the country they were denied opportunities to move out of their segregated neighborhoods in the city because of the deep-seated patterns of racial prejudice and discrimination. Such patterns of residential segregation still persist, despite affirmative action legislation, and their consequences include continuing inferiority in educational opportunities, especially in large urban areas.

At the micro level, Du Bois's status description of African Americans' "double consciousness" adds an important component to Mead's and Cooley's insights regarding the way one's self-concept reflects the reactions of others. As we saw earlier, Cooley emphasized the feelings of either pride or shame that result from these reactions, plus the way individuals seek to adjust their behavior so as to elicit positive reactions that enhance their dignity and sense of belonging. But in the racist two-caste society described by Du Bois, any efforts African Americans might make to elicit more positive reactions from individuals representing the dominant white culture were automatically doomed to failure.

Nevertheless, the concept of the "double consciousness" also means that African Americans resist and reject the negative definitions they see portrayed in the reactions of those representing the majority culture. Despite their painful awareness of these negative definitions, African Americans actively struggle to resist them in their ongoing and often heroic efforts to achieve a sense of human dignity. It is in this context that Du Bois emphasized the importance of education in empowering African Americans to reject the negative stereotypes of the dominant culture. He believed that the human dignity of African Americans would be enhanced as they gained knowledge of their own historical and cultural heritage, both African and American, and the important long-term contributions Africans had made to world history and African Americans to American history. This insightful analysis demonstrates how one's self-concept may involve a large measure of resistance to the definitions imposed by others rather than acceptance and conformity, especially within the context of a minority group's subculture.

In the final analysis, Du Bois recognized that the concept of race is itself socially constructed, like one's own identity, through shared definitions. In a racist society the social construction and ongoing reinforcement of racial categories serve essentially to justify and legitimate the unequal distribution of power and privilege in society. Despite the extensive variations among the different immigrant groups who came to the United States, the cultural definitions that were developed regarding the meaning of being "white" resulted in the submergence of differences among different "white" people so they could be incorporated in a single "race" to be contrasted with "blacks." By the same token, differences among African American themselves, even including differences in actual skin color, were submerged as they were grouped together and treated in accordance with prevailing negative stereotypes that failed to acknowledge the variations among them in both background and ability. Du Bois's views on how the social construction of race supports the distribution of power and privilege in society is consistent with theoretical perspectives that have become highly influential in the last decades of the twentieth century (see, e.g., Rabaka [2007] regarding the relevance of Du Bois's work for the development of a distinctive contemporary Africana form of critical theory.)

Charlotte Perkins Gilman: Sexual Relations Related to Home and Work

Contemporary feminist theory builds on a strong feminist movement that goes back to the late nineteenth and the early twentieth centuries (and even earlier). Charlotte Perkins Gilman (1860–1935) was a feminist theorist who demonstrated the power of theoretical analysis in questioning and criticizing widespread implicit assumptions regarding "the way the world is." Her critique was intended to demonstrate how the taken-for-granted realities of everyday life are the source of numerous social problems and personal pain that people assume to be inevitable—but that she insisted could be changed (Lengermann and Niebrugge-Brantley, 1998:112–129).

It seems likely that Charlotte Perkins Gilman's unwillingness to fit into a patriarchal social world according to traditional expectations helped to shape and motivate her style of theoretical analysis. She was born into a New England family and experienced family crises early in life. Her father, who was related to the well-known Beecher family, deserted the family when Gilman was very young, and her mother conformed to the traditional role of sacrificing her life for her family. Charlotte Perkins Gilman married and the couple had a daughter, but Gilman found herself frustrated and unhappy with this traditional domestic lifestyle, probably because of the way it decreased her independence. She agreed to visit a doctor for treatment of her "nerves" but the doctor's advice to abandon her writing projects and devote herself to domestic life was exactly opposite to what Gilman wanted to do. Instead of following the doctor's advice, she wrote a book based her experience (Gilman ([1892] 1973).

Gilman eventually separated from her husband (and later divorced by mutual agreement) and moved to California with her daughter.[7] She eventually got married again, this time to a cousin, but managed to maintain the independence she craved. She soon was able to support herself by writing and publishing for a popular audience. With her reputation growing and her social network expanding, she became a popular and highly successful lecturer, speaking throughout the country on various progressive issues from the feminist perspective she was developing. She helped organize the California Woman's Congress which Jane Addams attended. Later she repeatedly visited Jane Addams and Hull House in Chicago, admiring the progressive ideas being discussed and implemented through the leadership of the women she met there (Deegan 1997:17).

Gilman's publications were varied and extensive and included essays, poetry, stories, and articles on feminism and various social issues.[8] Although she did not have an academic appointment she was a charter member of the American Sociological

[7] A supportive female friend there later married the husband she had divorced, with her support, following which her daughter went to live with her father. Of course, this aroused criticism.

[8] Gilman's series of feminist utopian stories, entitled *Herland* (Gilman, 1979) and *With Her in Ourland* (Gilman, 1997), appeared initially in *The Forerunner*, a monthly journal she published between 1909 and 1916.

Society (now the American Sociological Association) and wrote articles for the *American Journal of Sociology*. Gilman's influence in the women's movement was broader than sociology but her sociological analysis provided the basis for her strong advocacy of progressive (or radical) social reforms. Unfortunately, as male dominance in sociology became more firmly established, Gilman's work was neglected. In recent decades, however, interest in Gilman's work has been renewed, not only for her strong feminism but her comprehensive and systematic style of critical analysis.

A key argument in Gilman's (1904, 1911) perspective is that widespread patterns of male domination and female subordination reflect beliefs and assumptions about gender differences that are based mostly on social definitions. In contemporary terminology, gender roles are socially constructed in ways that exaggerate sexual differences and justify keeping women "in their place." Thus Gilman's work, like that of Du Bois, extends our awareness of the negative effects of socially constructed categories in limiting the opportunities of subordinate groups to develop their full human potential. This basic idea is consistent with the well-known principle articulated by W. I. Thomas that social definitions have real consequences.

Gilman's first and most comprehensive sociological work, *Women and Economics*, published initially in 1898, offered a distinct feminist orientation that can readily be related to the reformist perspective of her time (Gilman [1898] 1996).[9] The book was recognized at the time as an important statement on the role of women in society. It was reprinted several times and translated into several languages. The heart of Gilman's argument is that women's economic dependence on men led to an exaggeration of male-female differences. These socially defined differences resulted in distortion of their sexual relations and denied both women and men the opportunity to develop to their full potential as human beings.

It should be noted that the influence of Victorian culture in defining sharply different gender roles was much stronger at that time than today. Life for "respectable" married women was highly restrictive, and their options for high-level career success as single women on their own were extremely limited. Although women had been moving into employment outside the home, often in industrial jobs, their pay was low and working conditions extremely poor. Such employment resulted more often from economic necessity than a deliberate career choice.

Gilman pointed out that in no other species is the female so dependent on the male for her basic survival needs. This economic dependence reinforced male domination, undermined the human qualities women and men share as members of the same species, led to increased competitiveness among men, and limited women's opportunities to develop their potential in ways that went beyond their feminine and domestic roles. Moreover, to the extent that men are successful in their competitive struggle and thus able to fulfill their socially defined responsibilities to provide for

[9] The subtitle, "A Study of the Economic Relation Between Men and Women as a Factor in Social Evolution," puts her perspective in the context of the dominant evolutionary perspective of the time.

their families, they are thereby assumed to be entitled to consider their homes and families as their personal possessions. This entitlement was seen as justifying their status as "head of household" and their domination of their wives and children.

By focusing their social responsibilities so exclusively on their own families, men fail to develop a sense of the larger public good or to accept responsibility for the welfare of the community or the society as a whole. One consequence is that all of the major institutions of society—economic, political, and military—reflect exaggerated male patterns of aggressiveness, struggle, competition, conflict, and the relentless desire to dominate others. Public life thus becomes an arena of constant conflict and struggle that is impoverished by the exclusion of women, and also by the demand that men's primary social responsibilities are for their own families. This struggle for dominance even characterizes the educational system and childhood socialization patterns, as the task of education in both the home and the school is seen as subduing and controlling young people so they will be able to fit into this distorted system based on competition and domination (Gilman, 1900).

In the meantime family life itself suffers from various interrelated internal contradictions that result from merging the sexual relation of husbands and wives with their economic relation. The possibility for husbands and wives to have a mutually satisfying form of married love as autonomous human beings is undermined when the dynamics of sexual and emotional intimacy are contradicted by the hierarchical socioeconomic dynamics of domination and subordination. (These conflicting dynamics within the marital bond are consistent with Marianne Weber's analysis described in Chap. 2.) Women pay a heavier price than men in this situation because they, unlike men, are expected to sacrifice their basic human needs for autonomy for the sake of their families. There is no easy way out of this domestic trap for married women because of their economic dependence on their husbands. Men, in contrast, are able to retreat from their ongoing competitive struggles in public life into the security of their private family lives. But, the emotional isolation they experience in public life as a result of constant competition and conflict means that they must rely primarily on their wives for emotional support and self-validation. However, the ability of wives to provide such support, and of husbands to accept it, is contradicted by the dynamics of the power relation between them.

In making the argument for greater female autonomy, Gilman certainly does not mean to imply that women are generally unwilling to be nurturant, caring, and supportive of others. Indeed, she saw the propensity for nurturing and helping others as a general human characteristic shared by both women and men. For women, however, this propensity is undermined by their subordinate and dependent status, and by the way the nurturing role is confounded with household maintenance tasks. For men, this nurturing propensity is undermined by the excessive emphasis on conflict and domination outside the home and by the way this pattern of domination spills over into the home as well.

Another important human characteristic that men and women share is their capacity for self-development and self-fulfillment through work (Gilman, 1904). By working together human beings not only produce the resources they need for survival but also develop their sociable nature and demonstrate concern for their collective well-being. But despite this potential for self-fulfillment through satisfying work, Gilman acknowledged that people generally have a negative attitude toward work and often seek to avoid it as much as possible. Gilman explains this negative attitude as a byproduct of sexual and socioeconomic stratification in society. The outcome of this stratification system is that men are expected to give priority to trying to dominate others rather than actually working and producing themselves. Their subordinates, having failed to achieve a position of domination, have no choice but to work in order to survive. However, they also are unable to experience joy or fulfillment in their work because it does not reflect their own will but the will of their masters (employers and/or husbands). Moreover, workers in industrial jobs typically do not have the opportunity to express their autonomy through their work or to enjoy the fruits of their labor. The overall outcome of the way occupations are organized is that capitalist employers are able to enrich themselves through the labor of others who have no choice but to work for them in order to survive.

Gilman certainly recognized the importance of male-female differences, particularly in the reproductive process, as well as in their interests, natural talents, and predispositions. But her primary argument has to do with the way the differences between men and women are exaggerated through conventional social definitions of appropriate gender roles. Moreover, human nature itself tends to be defined in ways that exaggerate **male** characteristics as basic **human** characteristics, while women are typically defined primarily in terms of their sex as opposed to their basic human qualities. In contrast, the competitive activities in which men engage are seen as essential human characteristics. In developing her arguments, Gilman offers critiques of several popular stereotypes about male-female relations and about home and family life. She points out that women's economic dependence is not mitigated by the argument that their economic well-being is assured in exchange for their care of the household and family members. This exchange relation is not the same as a standard employment contract but instead reflects the husband's control over his wife and her obligations to be available to serve his needs (as well as the needs of other family members). Moreover, unlike a purely economic exchange, there is no correspondence between the amount of work a woman does (as mother or homemaker) and the benefits she receives. In fact, given the overall socioeconomic class structure of society, upper-class women who do the least work receive the most benefits, while lower-class women who do the most work receive the least.

In addition, even though women's long-term economic well-being depends on marriage (especially in Gilman's time), the rules and expectations for women with regard to marriage are obviously not the same as the rules governing economic relations. Instead, the rules of courtship for women reflected contradictory expectations, especially in the context of the times in which Gilman lived. On the one hand, women are expected to be somewhat passive and not too aggressive in pursuing marriage while at the same time following a strategy of displaying attractive feminine characteristics so as to try to be appealing in the marriage market.

To overcome the deficiencies of the hierarchical organization and social isolation of families in modern society, Gilman proposed that alternative household and family living arrangements should be considered. One possibility would be to expand or enlarge household units in ways that would more fully satisfy human beings' sociable nature, their interest in being engaged in fulfilling work, and their need for individual autonomy. Although these goals may themselves be somewhat contradictory, Gilman's key point was that the dominant family structure of her time provided neither men nor women with sufficient autonomy to achieve a satisfying personal balance among these different needs. Gilman's overall goal was to promote a better understanding of how social structures can be reformed to reduce the pain people experience in their personal lives that result from these structures and to address the social ills troubling society as a whole. She believed a critique of dominant beliefs and practices, even including the idealized image of marriage and family life, is an important first step in this process. With the liberation of women from their domestic confinement, the stage will be set for them to become more involved, along with men, in reform efforts to make a better society.

Gilman shared many of the racist ideas of the time—though one could argue that the spirit of her critical analysis is open to continuing change as society itself changes. In any case her focus was more on gender equality than racial equality. She believed that women's intimate connection with the basic life process of human reproduction provides the potential for them to resist the dominant patterns of individualistic competition and conflict and to promote more opportunities for expressing human beings' propensities for benevolence (which men also share). A crucial goal for a social reform should be a reduction in the level of all forms of inequality and the ongoing struggle for domination.

Development of Functional Theory for Analyzing Society's Institutional Structures

By the end of the 1930s, and even more over the next two decades, the dominance of the Chicago School began to be overshadowed by the growing influence of developments at Harvard University and later at Columbia University. Sociology at Harvard actually had its beginnings with the recruitment of Pitirim Sorokin in 1930. He founded the Sociology Department at Harvard University and recruited several faculty members who developed distinguished academic careers. One of them, Talcott Parsons, had just begun teaching in the Economics Department there. Parsons' eventual dominance of American sociological theory will be described shortly. But first, a brief overview of Sorokin's major theoretical contributions is in order.[10]

---

[10] Pitirim Sorokin was born in Russia in 1889 and educated at the University of St. Petersburg. He began his academic career at the University of St. Petersburg, but left Russia shortly after the outbreak of the Russian revolution. Eventually he arrived in the United States where he joined the faculty at the University of Minnesota and became known for his work on social mobility (Sorokin, 1927, 1959). Our focus here, however, will be on his theory of long-range cultural cycles (Sorokin, 1957). He died in 1968. For an overview of Sorokin's life and contributions to sociology, see Coser (1977:465–508). A more detailed biographical account of the development of Sorokin's intellectual orientation and changing status in American sociology is provided in Johnston (1995).

Sorokin's most noteworthy contribution to sociological theory was an analysis of major long-range historical cycles of cultural change. His approach was comparable in scope to such massive historical accounts as those of Arnold Toynbee and others who attempted to explain the dynamics of the rise and fall of total civilizations. Sorokin's goal was to document the long-range changes in the major worldviews that he felt had been dominant in the overall cultural mentality of the Western world over the centuries since Greco-Roman times (Sorokin, 1957; originally published as 4 volumes between 1937 and 1941). This project involved a century-by-century description of dominant patterns in cultural mentality as reflected in various artifacts of culture and dominant forms of social organization throughout the major cycles of Western history. He attempted to demonstrate long-term cyclical shifts between what he referred to as a "sensate" (or materialistic) cultural mentality and an "ideational" (or transcendental) mentality. In between these extremes there were intermediate mentalities or worldviews that could be distinguished by the level of integration of the opposing perspectives they incorporated. As evidence for this argument Sorokin pointed to shifts in the dominant themes that he saw manifested in cultural products such as architecture, art, works of philosophy, theories of law, and so on. To demonstrate the contemporary relevance of this perspective, Sorokin (1941) argued at the time (prior to the mid-twentieth century) that an increasingly sensate cultural mentality had been developing over the past several centuries in the Western world. He speculated that the Great Depression and the outbreak of World War II could be seen as the beginning of a major period of crisis that would be followed by a more idealistic or transcendental worldview.

The analysis was primarily at the cultural level, but Sorokin also attempted to show that these dominant worldviews were clearly reflected in the major social institutions of society (economic, political, religious, family, etc.) as well as in individuals' basic personality patterns. He theorized that the crisis of our (then) advanced sensate stage resulted from the long-term effects of this type of cultural mentality in eroding the shared beliefs and values that motivate people to transcend their narrow self-interests. This erosion results from the expansion of the underlying worldview and ultimate values implicit in the sensate cultural mentality.

Sorokin's cyclical theory of long-range cultural change has lost influence and is seldom cited by contemporary theorists today (Johnston, 1995). In fact, few sociologists attempt to theorize over such a vast domain of social reality, and most would be much more cautious in view of the difficulties of establishing such wide-ranging generalizations. Although the work of Talcott Parsons is also extremely wide-ranging, as we shall see, Parsons' primary focus was on the interdependence of the social institutions of modern society rather than analysis of long-range cycles of cultural change. Both Sorokin and Parsons emphasized the interdependence of culture, society, and personality but, despite their similarities, the basic focus and goals of the two theories are actually quite different, and Parsons' work, developed over the course of 30 years, is usually cited, analyzed, and criticized without reference to Sorokin. Moreover, Parsons accepted the dominant viewpoint of most of the classical sociological theorists in analyzing the long-range historical changes leading up to modern society in terms of a linear model, as opposed to Sorokin's cyclical model.[11]

Talcott Parsons and the Development of Structural/Functional Theory

The basic ideas of Parsons' theory will be discussed in more detail in Chap. 12, but our goal in this chapter is to put his theory in historical context and introduce its major themes. Since the 1950s Parsons has been best known as a strong proponent of functionalism—structural/functionalism in particular (e.g., Parsons, 1951). This involves an effort to explain the basic functional requirements and structural patterns to be found in all social systems, particularly the overall society. However, at the beginning of his career his goal was to develop a voluntaristic theory of social action that emphasized the shared values and norms that he believed are incorporated in people's subjective orientations (Parsons, 1937). Despite this emphasis on subjective orientations, however, he did not cite Mead, Thomas, or others in American sociology who emphasized the interpretive process whereby people develop shared "definitions of the situation," even though the underlying process is identical. His analysis drew instead on the perspectives of Durkheim, Weber, and Pareto, and the British economic theorist Alfred Marshall.

By the late 1940s and early 1950s, the emphasis in Parsons' work shifted from his earlier voluntaristic theory of social action to a functional analysis of social systems. The emphasis on shared values was retained, but the voluntary nature of social action seemed to be submerged by his attempt to explain how the various parts, or institutional subsystems, of society (or other social systems) are interrelated so as to contribute to the survival of the system and its long-term equilibrium.

Parsons' strong emphasis on social equilibrium, interdependence, shared values, and social order seemed to leave inadequate room for conflict and social change, particularly disruptive forms of change. Thus, even during the time of functionalism's greatest influence, it generated serious criticism and thereby probably helped stimulate the development of various alternative perspectives. Some of these alternatives were developed within the functionalist framework, even though they differed substantially from Parsons' perspective, while other alternatives were based on sharply contrasting theoretical assumptions. Some of these alternatives will be identified briefly in the following sections and discussed more fully in subsequent chapters.

[11] Sorokin's cyclical view can be contrasted with the linear view of most the classical-stage theorists who established the foundations of sociology. For a more extensive discussion of the contrast between cyclical versus linear models of social change as reflected in Sorokin and Auguste Comte's theory, see Johnson ([1981] 1986:77–111).

Alternative Perspectives Within Functionalism

Merton's Middle-Range Functionalism

Within the general framework of functionalism, Robert Merton, at Columbia University, was critical of Parsons' overly general and abstract "grand theory" and proposed the development of "middle-range" theories instead (Merton, 1968). In this way functional analysis would not be burdened by preconceived assumptions regarding specific functional requirements or specific structures that are essential for maintaining the society or other systems. In addition, Merton pointed out that some institutionalized patterns may be **dysfunctional** for society, or for some of its members. This more pluralistic approach became highly influential in American sociology as an alternative to Parsons' structural-functional perspective.

Coser's Conflict Functionalism

Lewis Coser (1956) used the dominant functionalist perspective of the time to analyze the functions of conflict. In contrast to Parsons' emphasis on shared values as a source of solidarity, Coser argued that conflict also often serves the function of increasing solidarity and cohesion within groups. His analysis drew heavily on Simmel's argument regarding the way cohesion and conflict are often intertwined in social life in various subtle ways. Coser's conflict theory will be reviewed more thoroughly in a subsequent chapter.

Alternatives to Functionalism

Blumer and Symbolic Interactionism

Drawing on Mead's term "social behaviorism," Herbert Blumer (1969) developed his distinctive micro-level version of "symbolic interaction" theory in opposition to macro-level structural theories such as Parsons' functionalism. Blumer argued that efforts to explain individuals' behavior in terms of broad macro-level structural concepts or functional requirements were too deterministic. He regarded the social world as a more fluid and open-ended process in which individuals engage in ongoing interaction and negotiation with one another as they interpret the various situations they face and collaborate in organizing their responses to these situations and to one another. The symbolic interactionist perspective continues today and will be reviewed in Chapter 5 as a major theory with a strong micro-level focus that offers an alternative to more deterministic macro level theories, including functionalism as well as macro-level conflict theories.

Mills and Critical Sociology

C. Wright Mills provided a radical and impassioned dissenting voice during the period of functionalism's dominance. In contrast to Parsons' focus on stability and social order, Mills (1959) insisted that sociology should promote a critical stance toward the existing social structure. He was a strong advocate for a developing a "sociological imagination" that would highlight the way individuals' personal troubles, when widespread among large segments of the population, can be shown to have their origins in the social structure. He argued that the structure of American society is governed by a "power elite" whose members see their own class interests as equivalent to the general welfare (Mills, 1956). In his critical perspective, individual needs should have priority rather than maintenance of the equilibrium of the social system. Mills' perspective will be reviewed in more detail in a subsequent chapter on critical theory. Mill's perspective will be reviewed in more detail in a subsequent chapter on critical theory.

Homans and Exchange Behaviorism

George Homans explicitly rejected Parsons' focus on the functional requirements of society. Instead, he advocated a strategy of **reductionism** in which human behavior is explained in terms of psychological principles at the individual level (Homans, [1961] 1974).[12] He drew explicitly on the stimulus-response model of behavioral psychology (which Mead had rejected) along with concepts from elementary economics to argue that human behavior is shaped by reinforcements and/or punishments and by cost/reward considerations. In essence, he proposed shifting the focus to the motivations and sentiments of human beings as such, as opposed to presumed needs of society or other social systems. Homans' exchange theory perspective will be reviewed in more detail in a subsequent chapter as part of the foundation for the contemporary rational choice perspective.

Summary

Our goal in this chapter was to review the historical development of American sociology from its beginnings in the Chicago School in the early decades of the twentieth century to the mid-century dominance of functionalism and the major alternatives to functionalism that were developed at the time. The Chicago School represented a distinctive style of sociological inquiry that is still recognized today, even though it is by no means confined to the University of Chicago.

A major contribution of the Chicago School to contemporary sociological theory was represented by the work of George Herbert Mead. His "social behaviorism" involved a micro-level focus on how people's adaptation to their environment reflected the interrelated processes of symbolic communication and subjective interpretation. Through this process people adjusted their own behavior in anticipation of

[12] This was the major theme in his American Sociological Association presidential address (Homans, 1964). We might assume that he would have included women too, but gender inclusive language was not yet in widespread use at the time.

the reactions of others. This focus on subjective interpretation was consistent with W. I. Thomas's emphasis on the importance of people's "definitions of the situation."

The Chicago School also included a strong pragmatic emphasis on social reform. This was manifested in Jane Addams' efforts to help the disprivileged on the neighborhood level through the settlement house she established and to organize them to work to improve their situation. Her career was devoted to advocating for social reforms on behalf of subordinated and disprivileged groups throughout society.

We also noted how Robert Ezra Park's ethnographic observations of Chicago promoted an understanding of the patterns of symbiotic interdependence that developed among groups as they competed to occupy the most advantageous niches possible in different areas of the city. This ecological analysis included studies of the changing distribution of different ethnic groups in different residential areas of the city.

In addition to the Chicago School, we also reviewed the early contributions of Charles Horton Cooley, W. E. B. Du Bois, and Charlotte Perkins Gilman. Cooley's notion of the "looking glass self" highlights the way other people's reactions determine individuals' feelings about themselves. He also emphasized the importance of primary groups for the formation of individuals' self-concepts.

Du Bois focused on the challenges faced by African American in a racist society in which they were systematically treated as second-class citizens. His notion of the "double consciousness" that African Americans experience "behind the veil" underscores their struggles to resist the negative stereotypes with which they are labeled by majority group members. In contrast to both Mead and Cooley, Du Bois's perspective demonstrates how minority group members struggle to resist and reject the images of themselves that they see reflected by majority group members. But he also emphasized the importance of a broad education for African Americans so they will develop an awareness of their distinctive cultural contributions to the world history of humanity and to American society in particular. Such an awareness will not only enhance their self-concepts but provide the potential for them to continue to make significant contributions within the context of America's pluralism.

We then looked at Charlotte Perkins Gilman's feminist perspective and the critical questions she raised regarding widely accepted social definitions of innate differences between women and men. She argued that such beliefs were largely a result of the way sexual relations between women and men were distorted by women's economic dependence on men. She was a strong proponent for reorganizing society to reduce male domination and excessive competition in public life and to empower women to fulfill their human potential as they contributed to society in ways that went beyond their subordinate domestic role.

Finally, we looked briefly at the development of functional theory, including Sorokin's theory of long-range cultural cycles and the structural-functional theory developed by Parsons in the middle decades of the twentieth century. Even during the time of functionalism's dominance there were alternative perspectives. Merton's "middle-range" functionalism and Coser's "conflict functionalism" were cited as alternatives within functionalism. Blumer's symbolic interaction theory, C. Wright Mill's critical theory, and George Homans' exchange behaviorism were identified as alternatives outside the functionalist framework. These perspectives have been elaborated over the last several decades, as we shall see in subsequent chapters.

But first, the next chapter will focus on some basic strategies of theory construction and theory formalization as a way to organize theoretical ideas so they can be used to guide research. We'll also look at the contrasting implicit images of the social world as reflected in different theoretical perspectives.

Questions for Study and Discussion

1. Using Mead's perspective on the self-concept, can you identify some examples of situations where the social expectations represented by the "generalized other" differ from the expectations of particular groups in which you or others are involved? From your own experiences of such situations, what type of communication might be expected when such discrepancies are identified?
2. Do you think Addams' notion that people should be concerned with the well-being of fellow members of their community in ways that are comparable to their concerns with their own family is realistic? Why or why not? How could communities be organized so that people would show greater concern for one another's welfare?
3. Drawing on Thomas's emphasis on the "definition of the situation" as well as Park's perspective on urban ecology, what differences would you expect between people who live in inner-city neighborhoods and those who live in outlying suburban areas with regard to their definitions of urban social problems such as traffic congestion, education, social services, crime, and so on?
4. To what extent do you think that Du Bois's concept of the "double consciousness" still applies to the experiences of African Americans today? How can this perspective be used to contrast African Americans who are extremely poor and live in segregated neighborhoods with the experiences of African Americans who have professional occupations and live in integrated neighborhoods? Could the same general perspective also be applied to other disprivileged or minority groups in our society? Explain.
5. Several early American sociologists, particularly those in the Chicago School, thought that sociology could be useful for dealing with various social problems. Of the various perspectives described in this chapter, which ones do you feel provide the best insights and most imaginative vision for making a better society? Explain.

Chapter 4
Formal Theory Construction: Developing Sociological Theory as Part of a Scientific Enterprise

As shown in the last two chapters, from the beginning several different approaches have been adopted to establish sociology as a scientific discipline. Should sociology be considered a science? If yes, what justifies this claim? And how does the knowledge it provides differ from our everyday life, common-sense knowledge as skilled participants in the social world?

This chapter demonstrates the major steps involved in theory construction as a formal part of a scientific enterprise. In doing so, we will see how sociological theories differ from the implicit theories of everyday life. One of the sharpest contrasts is whether the focus should be on discovering uniform relationships between objective social facts (as Durkheim insisted) or whether it must be concerned primarily with understanding subjective meanings which vary in different cultural contexts (as Weber argued).

Regardless of whether our focus is on objective facts or subjective meanings, the scientific method requires concepts and ideas to be established with sufficient clarity and precision that they can be used to guide research and evaluated in the light of research findings as well as everyday life experience. Since we are concerned in this book with already existing theories, our goal will not be to construct theories from scratch but to show how already existing theories can be formalized. Following are the specific points to be covered in this chapter:

- The challenge of linking theoretical analysis and empirical research
- Objective versus subjective dimensions of the social world
- Explanation through prediction versus interpretation "after the fact"
- Strategies for theory construction—This section (the heart of the chapter) emphasizes the importance of developing theories as explicitly and systematically as possible so they can be used to guide research. Special emphasis is given to the following:
  - Concepts, variables, and classification systems—The challenge is to identify and define concepts, variables, and categories as precisely as possible so that they can be clearly applied to specific features of the social world.
  - Propositions: statements of expected relationships among specific variables, and the conditions under which they are expected—This is the foundation for specific research hypotheses or questions.

D.P. Johnson, *Contemporary Sociological Theory: An Integrated Multi-Level Approach.*

- Explaining causes versus consequences
- The challenge of causal explanation
- Deductive versus inductive forms of research and theory development
- Multiple paradigms—This section highlights the variations among different theoretical schools in terms of underlying beliefs and assumptions.

Linking Theoretical Analysis and Empirical Research

Theorists often focus their attention on ideas expressed in texts by other theorists. At the same time, but along different tracks, researchers seek to contribute to the cumulative expansion of scientific knowledge in the field by devoting themselves to the collection and analysis of various types of empirical data. Although research projects are typically grounded in an appropriate theoretical framework, their results are often not clearly related to the kinds of general issues and questions that are the concern of theory specialists who focus on comprehensive and systematic theory development as such.

There are some areas where general theory and empirical research are closely related and show cumulative development of knowledge (see Knottnerus and Prendergast, 1994). But research projects often seem to move along independent specialty tracks that seem somewhat unrelated very clearly to the overall cumulative development of the field as a whole, despite the contributions they make to particular substantive areas. At the same time general sociological theory seems to move along its own specialized tracks, with theory specialists dealing primarily with basic questions regarding the fundamental nature of the social world and how we can best understand its essential properties and current trends in terms that often seem too abstract to guide research. One result of this lack of a clear linkage between general theoretical discourse on the one hand and basic research and data analysis on the other is the high level of fragmentation in the field, described by Bernard Phillips (2001) as a "tower of Babel" that makes overall progress in the discipline difficult to assess.

This fragmentation of sociology into highly specialized areas with their own particular theoretical perspectives, plus the insulation between general theoretical discourse and empirical research, is probably more characteristic of sociology in the United States than in Europe. Many European social theorists seem to regard sociology as being close to a philosophical form of discourse. Although deeply committed to understanding and explaining the social world, their style tends to involve philosophical reflection and critique as much as empirical investigation.

For theory to stimulate and guide research it is important to formulate key theoretical ideas in explicit propositional statements from which specific research questions and hypotheses can be derived. Among contemporary theorists, Jonathan Turner (1993, 2003; Turner, Beeghley, and Powers, 2002) has consistently devoted much of his work to formalizing the arguments of various theories in this way, both contemporary and classical. Before we identify the key strategies in theory construction or formalization, we need to confront the challenge of looking explicitly at both the objective and subjective dimensions of the social world. These dimensions are sometimes related to the general question of whether behavior is determined by factors beyond individuals' control (both external and internal), or whether it reflects primarily their conscious intentions and deliberate choices.

Objective Versus Subjective Dimensions of Social Reality

The assumption that cause and effect relations apply to human behavior in the same way they apply to the natural sciences seems to violate the cherished notion that human beings are free, within limits, to make choices. If behavior is determined by conditions over which individuals have no control, the notion of human freedom is undermined. One of the challenges in developing sociology as an objective scientific discipline is that the subjective mental processes leading to individuals' choices cannot be directly observed. If sociology is to be based on objective empirical data, like any other scientific discipline, internal subjective processes cannot be incorporated into a scientific theory unless manifested in measurable overt behavior. For those taking this **objectivist** position, sociology should resemble the natural sciences in being grounded in empirical data that would allow us to establish clear and uniform relations between external environmental conditions and the specific behaviors they stimulate. In contrast, **subjectivists** would insist that human behavior cannot be explained without understanding its subjective meaning. Different subjective meanings may result in different types of responses to the same environmental stimulus. This implies that sociology and other social or human sciences are different from the natural sciences. Failure to acknowledge this difference leads to a superficial analysis that ignores what is most distinctive about human behavior.

These contrasting positions were the topic of a noteworthy response by George Lundberg, a major representative of the objectivist position, in the late 1930s to Robert MacIver's example of the contrast between how one would explain a paper flying in the wind and a frightened man fleeing from a pursuing crowd.[1] In emphasizing the importance of subjective meaning (including attitudes and interests), MacIver pointed out that "[T]here is an essential difference, from the standpoint of causation, between a paper flying before the wind and a man flying from a pursuing crowd. The paper knows no fear and the wind no hate, but without fear and hate the man would not fly nor the crowd pursue" (MacIver, 1937:476–477). Lundberg, advocating for the similarity between the natural and social sciences, disagreed. He argued instead that there is no essential difference in the nature of the scientific explanation that could be offered to explain a paper flying in the wind and a man

[1] The debate between MacIver and Lundberg over the issue of subjectivism versus objectivism as described in this paragraph was previously published in D. P. Johnson ([1981] 1986:31–32).

running from a pursuing crowd. Rejecting the use of terms such as "fear" and "hate" as metaphysical and animistic, Lundberg (1939) insisted: "I merely point out that possibly I could analyze the situation in a frame of reference not involving the words 'fear' or 'hate' but in operationally defined terms of such character that all qualified observers would independently make the same analysis and predict the behavior under the given circumstances.... [T]he principle of parsimony requires that we seek to bring into the same framework the explanation of all flying objects." (Lundberg, 1939:13) The disagreement had to do with the priority to be given to objective measurement that could be applied to all cases of the phenomenon in question as opposed to subjective motivations and feelings which can vary greatly for different people in different situations. The position taken herein is that we must attend to both.

Social reality differs from the reality of the physical world. It is not part of the natural or physical environment but is socially constructed through symbolic communication and human action. The elusive, unobservable, and symbolic character of the shared subjective world in which human beings participate means that the challenge for understanding is greater. Both must be dealt with in sociological theory, even though measuring subjective processes and determining the nature of the relationship between the subjective meanings that influence people's choices and their objective behavior may not be easy.

In recent years questions have been raised about whether academic study in any scientific discipline can truly be objective. This skepticism is based on the notion that it is impossible for anyone—including scientists, especially social scientists—to transcend the cultural biases reflecting their particular location in the social structure.[2] This applies particularly to biases based on class, race, and gender. In the perspective of these critics, there is a political dimension to all types of knowledge claims, including science. The implication is that theories that become dominant reflect the political power of their adherents and promoters.

It may be impossible for any sociologist (or other scientists) to transcend completely the limitations and biases that result from his or her particular class, race, gender, and general social background. Despite the difficulties in doing so, it is important to evaluate our different theoretical perspectives critically in terms of how well they represent the social situations and life experiences of all the diverse groups of our society and around the world. This applies particularly those who are disprivileged and marginalized and whose views often tend not to be heard. If a theory is constructed in such a way that it leads to questions that can be explored with empirical data, limitations and biases can eventually be corrected as more information and new insights become available.

Developing a scientific discipline is not anyone's solo performance. It is a cumulative process in which many people are involved, with many different perspectives

[2] This critique of all forms of knowledge and discourse is a major theme in postmodern forms of analysis. This and other postmodern themes will be reviewed in more detail in Chapter 20.

to be heard. Through the process of dialogue and mutual criticism, biases and other deficiencies may be expected eventually to be exposed and corrected. Because these biases often reflect our own particular characteristics in terms of race, gender, social class, family background, sexual orientation, national origin, institutional training, and so on, it is particularly important to be open to alternative viewpoints representing as many different social backgrounds as possible. This openness to diversity implies that no single theoretical perspective can ever be accepted as providing a comprehensive explanation of all there is to know about social life.

Prediction versus Interpretation

The ideal for any scientific theory is to generate specific questions and hypotheses to guide research. Research findings are then used to evaluate the theory, leading to modification, refinement, elaboration, or even rejection of it. In the case of competing theories, we might anticipate that the evidence would allow us eventually to make a choice as to which is the better theory. If our explanations are valid, then we should be able to hypothesize that similar outcomes or events should occur in the future under similar conditions or, alternatively, that different outcomes should be expected under different conditions, with outcomes and conditions specified in advance in accordance with the theoretical ideas being evaluated. The ultimate test for a theory in this perspective is whether or not it leads to predictive hypotheses that can be tested through research.

In contrast to hypothesis testing, theories in sociology are often used to interpret and explain current trends or historical events and processes that have already occurred. Such theories may be useful in enabling us to understand and explain why certain things happened as they did, or why things are the way they are in social life. But for those who believe that successful prediction is the ultimate standard for evaluating a scientific theory, validation of a theory is not based primarily on interpreting or explaining past events (valuable though this may be) but on being able to predict outcomes that are likely to occur in the future under certain specified conditions. A large part of the challenge in anticipating future outcomes in social life is that it is usually impossible to control the conditions under which the predictions should be expected to be valid, or even to anticipate all the relevant details of future conditions.

The two goals of **interpreting** events that have already occurred and **predicting** future events are not limited to sociologists. Instead, the implicit theories of everyday life are used routinely both to make sense of past events and to formulate expectations for the future. For example, investors seek to interpret ongoing fluctuations in the stock market in their efforts to predict future trends as a basis for investment decisions. Efforts to explain past events may be illustrated when attorneys for both plaintiffs and defendants develop their competing arguments regarding the motives and the methods of why and how a particular crime was committed and who is guilty. Although everyday life explanations and predictions may not be as formal as those of academic sociologists, people routinely use implicit, common-sense theories in making plans that are based on their assumptions that future events are likely be influenced in foreseeable ways by certain past events (as they interpret them).

The goal of making predictions on the basis of abstract theoretical ideas is fraught with challenges, however. Too many unforeseen conditions may develop that are beyond the scope of the theory or the knowledge of the theorist. Unlike laboratory settings where conditions can be controlled, research in the real world is likely to require additional qualifying statements regarding the specific conditions that should hold for the predictive statement(s) to be relevant and valid. If known, such conditions can readily be incorporated into the theory in the form of "If... then" statements. But even with a good theory it is virtually impossible to anticipate all the conditions that may influence the eventual outcomes.

Strategies of Formal Theory Construction[3]

How do we begin to construct or formalize a sociological theory? What are the basic building blocks with which we start? What does the overall structure of a theory look like? How does it differ from abstract speculation or mere description of some general feature of social life? How does the formulation of scientific theory differ from philosophical arguments, historical analysis, or social criticism? How can theory be used to guide research? These are the sorts of questions to be addressed in this section.

In the late 1960s and 1970s several theorists proposed specific strategies of formal theory construction in sociology (e.g., Zetterberg, 1965; Stinchcomb, 1968; Blalock, 1969; Dubin, 1969; Gibbs, 1972; Hage, 1972; and Chafetz, 1978). By the late 1970s interest in theory construction seemed to decline. Explaining the reasons for the decline in theory construction and formalization is beyond our purpose here. For one thing, the skepticism described earlier regarding the notion of sociology as a science, and of science in all fields as the only valid form of knowledge, is inconsistent with the basic image of sociology as a scientific discipline that is implied in theory construction or formalization. Still another problem is the highly technical and abstract style sometimes used to present theoretical arguments in a concise and precise fashion. Finally, while proponents of formal theory emphasize the formulation of predictive hypotheses that are deduced from general principles, others opt for a more inductive strategy that involves interpretation of events as they unfold or after the fact.

[3] Some of the material in this section is adapted from D. P. Johnson ([1981] 1986:30–47).

The decline in formal theory construction was the topic of an American Sociological Association conference that was organized by Jerald Hage in 1990. The book developed from this conference included analyses of some of the conditions within the field and the larger environment that undermined the appeal of this style of theorizing, plus some strategies for renewing it as a way to promote cumulative progress in the field (Hage, 1994). A more recent book by Reynolds (2007) describes in detail the specific strategies involved in theory construction and offers examples of how several existing theories can be formalized. Most of these examples, however, are more limited in scope than the general theories that will be covered in this book.

The goal for theory construction or formalization is to develop a set of systematically stated, logically interrelated propositions from which specific research hypotheses can be derived and tested. Whether a deductive or inductive approach is used, the idea is to formulate explicit propositions that explain recurrent patterns that can be observed in the social world. Deductive strategies move "downward" from general principles to specific predictions, while the inductive style of theorizing involves working "upward" from particular observations or findings toward more general principles that can subsequently be tested in different settings. To put it as concisely as possible, a **proposition** is a statement that relates at least two variables. Typically, one variable is identified as independent and the other as dependent, although the relation may also be one of interdependence, especially if observed over time. And of course, either or both of these variables may be related to other variables that may be incorporated in additional propositional statements which modify or elaborate the original prediction. A theory, then, consists of a set of propositions that, ideally, are mutually consistent and logically related to one another, and that are intended to interpret, explain, or predict some phenomenon of interest.

Propositions may be contrasted with other types of theoretical statements. Some statements may consist of conceptual definitions, as suggested below, or may explain key distinctions between closely related concepts. Theoretical discourse may also include various arguments about the importance of a particular variable or social process. For example, statements about the importance of rituals in social life, or about variations in cohesion, domination, or alienation in social groups or in society, do not constitute a theory unless they are related to other concepts. These other concepts may include, for example, individuals' background characteristics, resource distribution, level of value consensus, group size, scope of shared experiences, or others.

Concepts and Variables

Knowing the names for things we encounter is an important first step in perceiving and understanding. This can be illustrated by the questions young children ask about the names for the objects they encounter in their environment. Their curiosity seems satisfied when parents simply supply the name. Similarly, when scientists discover some new phenomenon, whether an object in outer space or an archaeological fragment of bone, their initial challenge is to decide what it is. When people are introduced, the first information that is usually exchanged (after their names) is information about some aspect of their social identity, such as their occupation or where they are from—information that goes beyond the obvious fact that they are fellow human beings. In contrast to concepts that provide the names for objects or events, **variables** refer to characteristics or properties of some object or event that can take on different values in different cases. Variables enable us to establish categories for classifying different cases of the phenomena in question. For example, the concept of "group" refers to a set of individuals who have face-to-face relationships with each other and a shared identity as members. This simple definition enables us to distinguish **groups** from other types of social formations, such as social classes, bureaucratic organizations, crowds, audiences, publics, or populations, for example. Among different groups, however, there will be **variations** in characteristics such as size, cohesion, frequency of getting together, similarity of members, leadership, conflict, communication patterns, and so on. Such variations may be used to establish categories among different types. Groups may be classified in terms of size, purpose, membership criteria, level of cohesion or conflict, frequency of meetings, or other variables. The challenge in understanding the dynamics of a group is to explain and interpret these and other variations.

Concepts may also highlight certain aspects of the world that we may literally not have seen previously. In the social world, prejudice and discrimination, for example, may remain beneath the level of conscious awareness until recognized and named. Once identified, however, such patterns may then be detected in numerous types of social situations, subjected to criticism, and eventually changed. By formulating and applying concepts we actually create the world that we observe. This is especially true for concepts that do not refer to material objects but to patterns of relationship among objects or people. A social group, for instance, differs from a crowd of people waiting in an airport because of the interaction among its members. Large and complex social organizations are based on inferences regarding social relations that may be indirect instead of face to face. The concept of social class may or may not be reflected in people's subjective definitions (depending on their degree of "class consciousness"), but an observer can certainly draw inferences by noting the differences among people in terms of their control of resources, domination over others, and general lifestyle. At an even more abstract level, our inventory of concepts includes intangible notions such as justice, freedom, competition, honor, happiness, love, and so on that do not correspond in any simple way to material objects, but instead reflect shared social definitions involving subjective experiences and perceptions.

Many of the concepts used by sociologists are taken from everyday life language. This means it is important to cut through their vagueness, ambiguity, and multiple and shifting meanings to develop as clear and precise a definition as possible. Beyond this, it may be useful in developing a theory to elaborate the meaning and significance of a particular concept, to develop its practical and theoretical implications, to enumerate examples, to show it might be measured empirically, and so on.

Classification Systems

While concepts provide labels for objects or events, including people, variables are used to make distinctions among these objects, events, or people according to some characteristic or set of interrelated characteristics. When a particular variable or set of variables is used to compare and contrast different cases of a particular concept, the result is the establishment of a taxonomy or classification system. The categories of a classification system may be used to establish subtypes of individual cases on the basis of important distinctions among them. The development and refinement of classification systems, or taxonomies, is another important step in theory development. Through this process important variations are identified that can then be used in the development of propositions. Thus, for example, while all groups are similar in many ways, they also differ in important ways as well. A large part of theory development involves identifying important differences among various types of social formations or cultural patterns and exploring key distinctions within these broad categories. Contrasting social formations may include task versus sociable groups, for example, public versus private sector organizations, or democratic versus totalitarian societies. At the level of culture, categories may be developed to distinguish formal laws versus informal customs, or popular versus elite styles of artistic or musical expression.

Ideally, the categories of a classification system should be mutually exclusive and exhaustive. Being mutually exclusive means that the basis for distinguishing one category from another is sufficiently precise that any given case can fit into one and only one category. Being exhaustive means that the categories cover all cases of the phenomena in question; no cases are left unclassified. The catchall category "other" is sometimes used for cases that cannot be meaningfully classified. In the real world, we often encounter situations in which the boundaries between categories are fuzzy and thus are difficult to classify, particularly those that consist of social definitions. Some groups, for example, are highly sociable but also have tasks to perform. Some forms of music or other forms of culture may be distinguished by crossing the boundary between popular and elite tastes.

The variables used in classification systems may involve an underlying continuum or discrete categories. If they reflect an underlying continuum, decisions will need to be made as to where to draw the lines between different categories. At the individual level both age and income, for example, reflect an underlying continuum. For such variables we must decide the appropriate number of categories to establish and where the dividing lines should be. Should age, for example, be used simply to distinguish those 40 and over versus those under 40, or should each decade have its own category (i.e., 10 or under, 11–20, 21–30, and so on)? The answer may be arbitrary, reflecting the particular purpose at hand as well as the number of individuals to be classified. In the real world, the age categories used by public school boards, for example, will obviously be different from those used in developing senior citizens' social service programs.

In contrast to variables reflecting an underlying continuum, those based on discrete categories may at first seem easier to establish. The variable "sex" (in the biological sense) is usually represented by two discrete categories—"male" and "female"—though there are exceptions in which individuals are born with some of the biological characteristics of both sexes. In contrast to "sex" as a biological distinction, the concept of "gender" is generally regarded as socially constructed, especially by sociologists. Although gender is highly correlated with biological "sex," it also exhibits greater variation. The concept of **androgyny** was used by psychologist Sandra Bem (1974) to identify a pattern whereby some people exhibit behaviors that reflect either "masculine" or "feminine" characteristics in terms of cultural definitions, depending on the situation.[4] Our goal is this chapter is not to analyze different gender roles. However, the point to note is that even with categories that appear initially to be discrete, such as male and female, there is often a certain fuzziness that makes clear and unambiguous classification difficult and suggests the importance of noting distinctions within categories as well.

Classification systems in themselves do not constitute a formal theory, though they are important aspects of it. Similarly, showing that a particular case belongs in one category and not another is not the same as developing or testing a theory, even though both of these processes are important stages in the process (Zetterberg, 1965). The ultimate goal is to explain why social phenomena vary as they do. This involves formulating propositional statements that are intended to help explain such variations.

Propositions

If concepts, variables, and classifications systems are the building blocks of theory, the propositions developed from these building blocks are intended to try to explain and interpret the social world, and also to make predictions formulated as hypotheses to be tested through research. The standard format for expressing such relations is that the value of one variable will be related to, or influenced by, the value of a second variable. This means we seek to predict the value of the second variable by knowing the value of the first. The logical form of this statement can be simply expressed as follows: X→Y. The arrow refers simply to the expected direction of the relationship. The relation may be positive (as X increases Y will also increase)

[4]The feminist perspective Sandra Bem elaborated more recently emphasizes the way the dichotomous categories of masculinity and femininity are socially constructed and thus reflect cultural definitions (Bem, 1993).

or negative (as X increases Y will decrease). In this formulation, X is the independent variable, while Y is the dependent variable. In other words, the value of Y depends on the value of X.

When propositions are formulated in this way it may be tempting to assume that change in X **causes** change in Y. However, a correlation does not in itself prove a causal relation. Moreover, even if we have theoretical reasons to believe that a change in X causes a change in Y, additional questions can be raised as to why the variable X exhibits the value it does. This shift in focus means that X now becomes the dependent variable, and the search is then on for some other independent variable. The process can go indefinitely, but our concern here is simply to show the form and the logic of propositional-type statements. This logic may be demonstrated in practical everyday life questions. For example, why do some juveniles become delinquent? Why do some marriages end in divorce? Why do some students consistently get higher grades than others? Why do some business firms or voluntary organizations thrive and expand while others disintegrate and eventually disappear? Why do some people vote Democratic while others vote Republican—and why do some switch? Why do some societies (or communities or families) experience high levels of internal conflict? For all practical purposes, there is no end to such questions, and the tentative answers may be formulated as propositional statements.

When systems of classification are developed on the basis of more than one criterion, they imply certain relationships between or among the criteria used to distinguish them. For example, groups may be dichotomized simply as strong or weak, based on both their accomplishments and their cohesiveness. This would imply that a strong group will exhibit a positive relation between cohesion and accomplishment. Such assumptions may themselves be expressed in propositional-type statements. (The higher the cohesiveness, the higher the success in task accomplishment.) If it turns out that the criteria used to establish categories are sometimes unrelated to one another, this new information may lead to additional categories or subcategories. So, for example, groups that are successful in terms of task accomplishments may be subdivided according to whether their cohesion is low or high, or cohesive groups may be subdivided on the basis of their high or low level of task accomplishments. In this way the criteria for establishing categories are refined and made specific.

In many cases additional variables may be identified that are related either to the independent variable (X) or to the dependent variable (Y), thereby allowing elaboration of the theory. If we consider youth violence as an example, we might identify several potentially relevant variables. Is violence learned in the context of peer groups? Are parents to blame for being neglectful or abusive? Are violent youth more likely to come from poor or disorganized neighborhoods? Have they had frustrating experiences in school that lead them to become angry and violent? Does violence in the media or video games play a role? If all of these factors are involved, which are most important, and how are they related? Answers to these questions are crucial to anyone interested in developing policies or programs to prevent youth violence. A systematic theory could incorporate all of these variables in a series of propositional statements regarding the interrelations among these variables and how they interact in being related to youth violence.

One way to incorporate multiple factors into propositional statements is in the form of "If... then..." statements in which propositions are stated in such a way that they are expected to apply only under certain conditions. For example, **if** youth have parents who are highly neglectful or abusive, **then** exposure to mass media or video game violence will be more likely to be related to youth violence. On the other hand, if parents provide love, support, and guidance, we might speculate that media or video game violence would not stimulate imitative violence.

Propositional statements may also specify the time order in which different variables are expected to be relevant. For example, the negative influence of delinquent gang members may become relevant in stimulating violence only **after** a juvenile has experienced repeated school failure and frustration; prior to this critical level of frustration, delinquent peers may have no effect. Thus the school experience would not necessarily contribute directly to violent behavior, but it would contribute indirectly by increasing the chance that violent or delinquent peers will have an effect. On the other hand, frustration in school that is not accompanied by involvement with delinquent peers may lead instead to withdrawal, or perhaps to increased efforts to succeed in school.

Regardless of how convincing the argument or how persuasive the empirical evidence in support of a particular proposition might be, we can expect to find many exceptions in individual cases. For example, not all children whose parents are neglectful or abusive, or who experience high levels of school frustration, become violent. In contrast, some teenagers with devoted and loving parents who are successful in school may become violent. Many of the propositions in the social sciences reflect relationships that are not deterministic in a strong sense but instead probabilistic. The greater the number of appropriate variables that are identified, the higher the probability that predictions will be successful, but the lower the probability that any one variable by itself will explain a large proportion of the variation.

Causes and Consequences

The example of youth violence involved a **dependent** variable as the primary variable of interest. That is, we are seeking to identify variables that can help us explain and predict youth violence. These key variables are **independent** variables. Their influence may be direct or indirect, and they may operate in conjunction with one another or sequentially over time. But for our purposes, they are all independent because they are intended to account for the variations in the dependent variable that we wish to explain. However, it is also possible to begin with an **independent** variable as our primary variable of interest. Instead of asking what factors contribute to the differences in some dependent variables, the question is raised as to the **effects** or **consequences** of these variations on other variables. Schematically, this could be expressed as follows: X →?. In contrast, if the dependent variable is the primary variable on which we are focusing, the type of analysis could be symbolized as follows: ? →Y.

Beginning analysis with questions about the influence of an independent variable on one or more other variables is useful for framing questions regarding the social consequences of noteworthy changes. For example, we might want to explore the consequences of the feminist movement and changes in gender roles on various aspects of social life. How will such changes affect our personal lives or the overall level of civic involvement in society? As more women move into positions of power and influence, will national and corporate policies change? What will be the effects of feminism and changing gender roles on families and child care? Will boys and girls raised in households where fathers and mothers both have careers and share in child care and household maintenance differ from children in other families? What about leisure and lifestyle patterns? How are schools and child care affected?

Numerous other current social changes could be identified, the consequences of which would be interesting to try to predict. In terms of technological development, for example, what are the long-term effects of the widespread use of personal computers and access to the internet in homes, offices, and schools? This technology has obviously changed the nature of work in many settings. But are there additional effects on education, family life, religion, leisure patterns, and overall cultural worldview? How are our social relations affected by the ability to establish or maintain contact with one another via e-mail, chat rooms, and personal web pages? The same logic can be applied in attempting to assess the effects of specific one-time events as well. For example, the terrorist attacks on the World Trade Center on September 11, 2001, may be seen as a watershed event with multiple wide-ranging consequences that can be traced over the course of many years. The main point to note is that theory development may begin with efforts to identify the effects of changes in an independent variable as well as seeking to explain variations in some dependent variable.

Interdependent Relations

In some cases, deciding which variable is independent and which is dependent may be arbitrary. This would be true if the relationship is actually one of mutual interdependence, in which case each variable may be seen as both independent and dependent. This can be represented schematically as follows: X↔Y. Other variables may also be involved in such relationships, affecting either or both of the primary variables. One simple way to diagram such a relationship involving three variables is as follows: $X_1 \leftrightarrow Y \leftrightarrow Z \leftrightarrow X_2$, with X_1 representing a beginning time and X_2 a later time.

Social life offers numerous interesting examples of such interdependent relationships. The relationship described above between failure and frustration in school and involvement in delinquent peer groups is an example of a relationship that is probably interdependent. A one-time failure in school may have no noticeable effects immediately, but the relative appeal of a delinquent peer group may increase in comparison to school activities if such experiences are repeated. If involvement with delinquent peers occurs, this may then increase the chance for subsequent school failure, which leads to additional frustration, which then increases the appeal of the delinquent peer group even more, and so on. The development of a friendship or a relationship between lovers, or the gradual deterioration of a friendship or marriage, offer additional everyday life examples of such interdependent relationships. Friendship begins as each party expresses interest in the other, discloses limited information about himself or herself, perhaps offers some socioemotional support, and begins to look forward to spending time together. As they both respond to these self-disclosures and positive sentiments, the level of mutually rewarding interaction gradually increases.

On the other hand, the breakdown of a marriage or a close friendship reflects the opposite pattern. For some reason, perhaps minor oversights or disappointments, the level of positive interaction declines. Eventually, positive sentiments are outweighed by complaints and expressions of disappointment and frustration. These negative patterns, seemingly trivial at first, escalate until they reach a crisis or lead to apathy and withdrawal. As the popular image of the "straw that breaks the camel's back" suggests, a negative one-time event is not necessarily crucial by itself. It becomes crucial only in the context of a background of an escalating negative pattern of changes in the relationship. Negative relationships of this type may be referred to as a "vicious cycle," but the basic pattern revealed in cyclical relations of interdependence may be positive and beneficial as well. Several years ago Zetterberg (1965) described the gradual evolutionary nature of the process of incremental change in relationships of mutual interdependence as follows: "Thus, in an interdependent relation, a small increment in one variable results in a small increment in a second variable; then the increment in the second variable makes possible a further increment in the first variable which in turn affects the second one, and this process goes on until no more increments are possible." (Zetterberg, 1965:17)

Thresholds and Limits

The probability that two or more variables are related, or the strength of the relationships among these variables, may vary in different circumstances because of the initial differences in the values of one or more of these variables. That is, the expected relationship may occur only within a certain range of values of one or more variables but not above or below this range. Even if two variables are related, the magnitude of the relationship may change significantly once a threshold level is reached. As suggested in Gladwell's (2000) concept of the "tipping point," a slight change in a variable beyond a crucial threshold can sometimes trigger large-scale effects in one or more other variables. (This is the situation of the proverbial "straw that breaks the camel's back.") For example, slight increases in a community's crime rates will not necessarily trigger a significant shift in people's fears of being victimized or an increase in demands for better law enforcement or harsher punishment (except perhaps on the part of the victims). However, if crime rates continue to increase, particularly if they are publicized by the mass media, they may eventually reach a point where fears of being victimized are magnified through increased levels of local discussion of the growing crime wave, leading eventually to the mobilization of social pressures to hire more police officers or impose more severe punishments. The point at which a change in a given variable triggers a change in a second variable, or in the strength of its relationships to a second variable, may be considered a **threshold**. The threshold may vary in different settings or for different dependent variables. Slight increases in crime rates, for example, may trigger a greater concern and more organized action in rural communities than urban ones. Moreover, before reaching the level of stimulating a widespread sense of crisis, small increases in crime rates may trigger increases in residents' own protective measures (locking doors, installing security systems, talking with neighbors about the need to keep their eyes open for suspicious persons or activities) before it stimulates an organized social movement to expand the numbers of police officers in the community.

As the value of an independent variable continues to change (either increasing or decreasing), it may eventually reach a point at which it has no further influence on the dependent variables related to it (or at least some of these variables). If we look again at crime rates, regardless of how much these rates may soar, there is no doubt some upper limit beyond which a community would be unwilling to pay the increased taxes required to hire more police officers. This example illustrates the concept of **limits**—where continued change in an independent variable no longer has any significant effect on some dependent variable. With this example, it is, of course, an interesting question whether increasing the size of the police force actually results in a decrease in crime rates. Although this question cannot be pursued here, it may seem, on the one hand, that more police officers would result in more police surveillance and thus reduce crime rates. On the other hand, an increase in the number of police may lead to an increase in the number of arrests if more crimes are reported (due to increased community concern) and a greater proportion of them result in arrests, even if actual crime rates remain stable or even decrease.

Given the complex patterns of interdependence of numerous variables in social life, it should be easy to see that establishing definite causal relations is extremely difficult. Although social theorists and researchers may search diligently for strong relationships that are reasonably stable in a variety of circumstances, the search is often elusive. However, if relationships between certain variables are observed repeatedly in widely different contexts, this may strongly suggest the possibility of a causal relation between them, especially if supported by persuasive theoretical arguments. However, as will be shown in more detail in the following section, extreme caution is advisable in using correlations between variables to claim support for a causal relationship.

The Challenge of Causal Explanation

A major goal for sociologists is to formulate propositional statements that suggest insightful and important **causal** relations. However, neither theoretical plausibility nor empirical correlation can prove causality. In the discussion above we have attempted to avoid making causal statements, even though when we wish to explain the variation in Y, we really want to know how some other variable **causes** such variation. Causal statements are extremely difficult to prove, as many theorists and philosophers of science have pointed out. It is not sufficient to show that two variables are highly correlated, even in several different contexts, since correlation could result from the fact that both variables are each independently related to a third variable.

Moreover, the concept of "cause" itself has multiple meanings. Many centuries ago Aristotle distinguished between the idea of a cause that produces a subsequent effect versus a cause which is the purpose for which something exists (McKeon, ed., 1941:170–171 ff). The time order of the cause-effect sequence differs for these two meanings of cause. In the first case, the effect follows the cause in temporal sequence; the second case seems to imply that the cause somehow follows its effect. Although it is difficult to imagine a cause that actually **follows** its effects, this notion of cause does indeed make sense for goal-directed action. The **actual** achievement of a goal cannot cause the action that led to it, but the **desire** for it motivated the behavior that led to its achievement. Thus it is not the goal itself but the active pursuit of it that is the cause, and goal achievement is the outcome of this effort. For example, a good grade does not cause a student to study hard for an exam, but the desire for a good grade can be the cause motivating a student to study, especially if the professor has warned that it will be a difficult exam, even though the grade is not actually received until **after** the exam.

In everyday life (and in philosophical and theoretical discussions as well) we often think of **cause** as some factor or force that is instrumental in bringing about some event (or preventing its occurrence). However, as seen with several of the above examples, there are many events in social life that seem to reflect the influence of multiple factors, including human motives and desires, and this means that it is difficult to identify any single cause that can account for the outcome one wishes to explain. Instead, each of these factors becomes relevant only as part of a set of multiple factors, all of which are involved in producing the outcome—or at least increasing the probability of its occurrence. But each factor by itself may have no appreciable impact.

The challenges of identifying causes may also be related to the contrast philosophers make between **necessary** versus **sufficient** causes. Briefly, a necessary cause refers to a condition or factor that must occur for some other event to take place. However, the first event may occur without necessarily producing or influencing the second event. The first event is essential, but it does not by itself guarantee that the second event will occur. Thus, for example, gaining access to illegal drugs is a necessary condition for illegal drug use, but access by itself does not cause one to become a user. In contrast, a sufficient cause refers to an event that will inevitably guarantee the occurrence of a second event. However, the second event may also occur as a result of other factors as well; that is, even though the first event is sufficient, this does not mean it is necessary. Thus, for instance, getting shot in the head or the heart is usually a sufficient cause of death, but death may also result from many other causes as well.

If we apply these fundamental notions of causation to our earlier example of youth violence it becomes clear with some brief reflection that most of the factors identified as relevant (inadequate family background, frustrating school experiences, delinquent peers, TV or video game violence) are actually neither necessary nor sufficient to cause a juvenile to become violent or delinquent. To show that these are not necessary conditions, we need only to find cases of juveniles who become delinquent but whose parents are not guilty of neglect or abuse, who are not school failures or involved with delinquent peers, or who are not exposed to TV or video game violence. To show that parental neglect or abuse, school frustration or failure, or TV or video game violence are not sufficient conditions, we need only to find cases of juveniles who do **not** become violent or delinquent but whose parents are neglectful or abusive, who experience school frustration or failure, who associate with delinquent peers, and who are exposed to TV or video game violence.

Despite the fact that parental neglect or abuse, school frustration or failure, delinquent peers, and exposure to TV or video game violence are neither necessary nor sufficient to cause youth violence or delinquency, we may still feel convinced that these variables are somehow relevant. But despite the plausibility of such an argument, there are exceptions that don't hold up in real life in the way we would predict from our theory. We might still feel compelled by our theoretical arguments to include all of these variables in a "multicausal" model in which each of these variables, in combination with the others, increases the **probability** of youth violence or delinquency. But even with high probabilities, predictions may be in error in individual cases. That is, some youth may be "at risk" in terms of the various factors in our multicausal model and still not become violent or delinquent, or they may become violent and delinquent despite **not** being at risk in these ways. This example may serve to illustrate the difficulties of establishing strong causal relations.

Part of the difficulty in establishing strong causal relationships is our lack of knowledge of all the variables that are potentially relevant, and part of the difficulty may be lack of precision in measuring the key variables. Moreover, if human behavior truly reflects freedom of choice, this would suggest that it cannot be completely explained by deterministic forces that negate this freedom. But this argument regarding free will is impossible to settle unless we were far more certain than we are that all the critical variables have been identified and adequately measured. If it turns out that we are eventually able to identify the important variables that influence our choices, this knowledge may enable us to manipulate some of these variables. This means we could expand our freedom by moving it to a different level as we try to control the factors that influence our choices.

Theory: A Set of Propositions

So far we have identified concepts and variables, classification systems (or taxonomies), and propositions (statements of relations between variables) as the primary components of theory. In developing propositions, the challenge is to identify the important variables, determine which are independent, which are dependent, and which are interdependent, and decide whether the relationships among them are expected to be positive or negative. If one starts with a dependent variable (in an effort to understand or explain the variations it exhibits in different cases), the next step is to identify the independent variables that are believed to influence it. If one starts with an independent variable (in an effort to understand its consequences), then the next step is to identify the various dependent variables that are expected to be influenced by it. In both cases, further expansion of the theory may be done through identification of additional variables that are related to the initial variables, either directly or indirectly. Moreover, some of these additional variables may be related to one another in various ways, and these could also be incorporated.

With multiple variables some of the anticipated relationships are likely to be indirect rather than direct. This is especially likely with complex patterns of interdependence among different variables reflecting different levels of the social world (micro versus meso versus macro). The basic logical form of an indirect relation may be diagramed as follows: $X \rightarrow Y \rightarrow Z$, indicating that variable X has an indirect relation with variable Z through its influence on Y. This type of relationship would be manifested when some aspect of the social environment (X) exerts an influence on individuals at the social psychological level, perhaps in terms of attitudes or beliefs (Y), which then influences their behavior (Z). For example, we might theorize that school experiences of failure (X) lead to student frustration and hopelessness (Y) which then leads to delinquent or rebellious behavior (Z). Such behavior may then have feedback effects on the school environment (X). This could occur when social control efforts are increased, or when teachers give up on students who appear apathetic or rebellious. In short, indirect relationships are important to establish as well as direct relationships, especially among the different levels of the social world.

Despite the insights that well-formulated propositional statements may offer, they are often too abstract and too general for specific and clear-cut empirical research questions or hypotheses that capture their full meaning in a wide range or settings. Testing a theory or using it to guide research requires the development of more specific and detailed propositions from higher level, more abstract propositions. These lower-level, less abstract propositions may then serve as the basis for specific research questions or predictive hypotheses to be tested. This means that the abstract terms (the variables) in the propositional statements must be translated into empirical indicators that can be observed and measured. These indicators are then incorporated in hypotheses to be tested through research. If the results show these indicators to be related in the way predicted, this provides at least some degree of empirical support for the theoretical proposition.

The deductive form of theorizing described here is often associated with laboratory experiments or with survey research in which respondents' answers to interview or survey questions are taken as the indicators of the variables being measured. The results are analyzed through various statistical techniques to see whether the indicators of the key variables are related as predicted. However, the same logic can also be applied to individual case studies, to qualitative analysis of the results of participant observation research in particular settings, to documents and other cultural artifacts, or to historical events. Regardless of the specific form of data, the goal is to interpret the data as illustrative of theoretical concepts, to seek confirmation of the theoretical propositions that are tested, and to explore the relationships among variables that are incorporated in these propositions.

The strategy of using deductive theory for hypothesis testing may be contrasted with the inductive strategy that is often used in exploratory research. Inductive strategies of analysis are highly appropriate with qualitative participant observation or ethnographic research as well as with comparative and historical analysis. The purpose of such an approach is to enable researchers to make new discoveries or develop new theoretical insights based on the discovery of patterns revealed by the data, even though such patterns may not be anticipated or incorporated into a fully developed theory in advance of the data gathering process. This strategy is consistent with the notion of "grounded theory" as analyzed some years ago by Glaser and Strauss (1967; see also Strauss [1990]). It involves a deliberate intent to defer explicit or formal theorizing until data have been gathered and carefully considered with an open mind as a basis for identifying key variables and showing how they are related.

But even when researchers employ a "grounded theory" approach, they are still likely to have some implicit ideas and expectations in mind that lead them to focus on particular social processes and to raise certain kinds of questions rather than others. Understanding the basic strategy and techniques of theory construction is useful for enabling a qualitative or ethnographic researcher to identify the implicit theoretical framework that guides and orients the focus of observation and attention. As observational data from exploratory research projects are accumulated, the findings can then be formulated as propositional statements to be evaluated or tested in additional analyses of the data or in future research projects. As more data are accumulated, their theoretical implications may be further revised and elaborated.

The strategy of induction may also be used with quantitative techniques to explore possible new relationships, in addition to testing predictive hypotheses. Computerized packages for statistical analysis make it relatively easy to compute the strength of relationships among different variables or assess their significance in an exploratory fashion, even without specific predictions. Even though such "fishing expeditions" may be discounted by those who insist on the deductive strategy of developing specific hypotheses in advance from a well formulated theory, the discovery of unanticipated results through such exploratory quantitative research can provide new theoretical insights to be pursued in future projects.

A theoretical proposition that has been repeatedly confirmed in a variety of settings so that it is generally accepted as true could be considered a basic scientific **law**. Even so, there is always the possibility that disconfirming evidence will one day be discovered, and this may lead to efforts to specify the conditions in which the "law" does or does not apply. Even for law-like statements that have been strongly supported by various types of empirical data in a variety of settings, there is still a need to develop an explanation, even though tentative at first, of why the variables are related as they are. To demonstrate that a relationship exists in a variety of circumstances is not the same as explaining why it exists. Even so, when strong relationships are repeatedly observed in multiple settings, efforts may be made to subsume these relationships under even more abstract and general propositional statements. Statements that cannot themselves be tested but that serve as the foundation for propositional statements may be referred to as **axioms**. At the highest level of abstraction, such statements are not derived from other propositions. Such statements may be seen as providing an underlying foundation for theory development, with their persuasiveness based on widely shared experiences and underlying intellectual assumptions or presuppositions. We might refer to the highest-level theoretical statements that serve as the underlying assumptions or presuppositions that define the key characteristics of the subject to be investigated as **postulates**. It is at this level that differences among theorists become evident in terms of their underlying views and images of the social world. When these differences are not stated but remain implicit, the stage is set for conflict between proponents of different theoretical paradigms. We turn in the next section to a brief consideration of some of the long-standing conflicts among different paradigms in sociological theory.

The Challenge of Multiple Paradigms: Underlying Assumptions, Beliefs, and Values that Influence Theory Construction[5]

Why do some sociologists emphasize certain types of social processes or focus on certain concepts or variables while others focus on quite different processes and concepts? Why do different sociologists have such basic disagreements over the fundamental questions that should be asked in sociological analysis, or even the overall purposes and goals of sociology as a discipline? Exploring this issue would lead us to consider how sociologists' own beliefs and values are related to their underlying assumptions regarding the nature of the social world and the questions and issues that they believe should be the focus of attention. Unless formally stated, such assumptions may remain implicit, similar in some ways to the implicit assumptions of everyday life. Just as with implicit everyday life beliefs, these presuppositions may become explicit when challenged by others with a different set of assumptions or a different paradigm. Unless they explicitly acknowledge these differences in underlying presuppositions, theorists who

[5] Some of the material in this section is adapted from D. P. Johnson ([1981] 1986:47–54).

espouse different paradigms, or who start with opposing theoretical assumptions, may find themselves in conflict with one another, or they may simply talk past each other or ignore one another.

In a provocative and highly influential analysis of scientific revolutions written several years ago, Thomas Kuhn (1970) described the process where scientific paradigms that may be dominant for a time are eventually replaced by competing new paradigms (see also Masterman, pp. 48–89 in Lakatos and Musgrave, eds., 1970). As long as a dominant paradigm is widely accepted, scientific work moves forward in a routine way within its parameters without challenging it. Eventually, however, continued research often leads to the discovery of **anomalies** (negative cases) that cannot be explained within the framework of the dominant paradigm. As anomalies accumulate they become more and more difficult to ignore or dismiss. Eventually, the dominant paradigm is challenged and replaced by a new paradigm that, it is hoped, can explain the anomalies as well as the patterns previously explained by the older paradigm.

Kuhn emphasized that the competition between representatives of opposing paradigms is not carried out on a purely rational, scientific basis. Instead, there is also a political dimension to the conflict. This aspect reflects scientists' indoctrination during their training as well as their scholarly investments and commitments and their concerns for gaining prestige within the discipline. This suggests that we might expect older scientists and scholars who have invested a large part of their careers in working within a well-established paradigm to be more resistant than younger ones to a new paradigm. Younger scholars and researchers, in contrast, may regard promotion of a newer paradigm as offering more opportunities for rapid success than trying to compete with well-established authorities identified with the older paradigm. During the period when advocates for the competing paradigms are in conflict, loyalty to particular paradigms separates scientists into different scientific communities.

Several years ago, George Ritzer (1975), using Thomas Kuhn's paradigm concept, portrayed sociology as a multiple-paradigm science (see also Ritzer, 1981, 2000:496–498). This designation means that sociologists do **not** share the same underlying images or assumptions regarding their subject matter.[6] Instead, they have fundamental disagreements, with different sociologists raising different kinds of questions for analysis, emphasizing different types of concepts and social processes, and advocating different research strategies for advancing our knowledge. These include, for example, the contrasts between micro versus macro theories, the distinctions described earlier in this chapter between a focus on objective facts versus

[6] Of course, sociologists would all agree on the basic notion that our lives are profoundly affected by our social environment – but this obvious point is far too general to get us very far in understanding all of the crucial variations and fundamental dynamics we encounter in the social world.

subjective consciousness, and the deductive versus inductive strategies for linking theory and research.[7]

Beyond the general field of sociological theory, American sociology has witnessed a major proliferation of numerous special interest subfields that also helps account for the wide diversity of interests and approaches that exist within sociology. This is reflected in the fact that the major professional organization for sociologists in the United States—the American Sociological Association—has pursued a policy for the last several years of providing room for a large variety of different special interest subgroups (or sections), perhaps partly for political reasons, and this high level of fragmentation also no doubt helps perpetuate the multiple-paradigm nature of sociology.[8]

A useful distinction was made some years ago between an "establishment" type of sociology versus "critical" sociology. The former tends to focus on the status quo, seeking to explain why things are the way they are in social life, while the latter is oriented toward trying to understand how social structures can (and should) be changed so as to provide more opportunities for individual freedom and fulfillment. The contrast between these two orientations was particularly evident during the late 1960s and early 1970s, a time when major changes were taking place in American sociology as well as the wider society. Gouldner (1970), for example, developed a sharply critical analysis of the implicit conservative political and ideological orientation that he saw reflected in the dominant theoretical paradigms of the time. Friedrichs (1970) distinguished between "priestly" versus "prophetic" forms of sociology, with priestly sociology (represented largely by functional theory at the time) devoted primarily to explaining order and stability in society and prophetic sociology (represented largely by critical theory) committed to promoting social change.

The conflicts among advocates for different paradigms make it appear that there are profound disagreements regarding the fundamental nature of social reality and the type of research needed to advance our knowledge. However, another way to view these multiple paradigms is to regard them as alternative lenses through which we are able to view different aspects of the social world. We should expect the differences to be most sharply drawn when a scholar seeks to define his or her perspective in opposition to others with a different emphasis. As a paradigm is developed and its scope expanded to deal with more and more dimensions of the multifaceted nature of social reality, it may eventually incorporate aspects of the social world that are emphasized in other, competing paradigms. A significant feature of the major theories that have become most influential is that they are capable

---

[7] Ritzer (2000:362–365; 498–505) cross-classified the micro and macro levels of the social world with the objective versus the subjective dimensions of each level. The resulting set of four categories can be used to distinguish theories in terms of whether they focus primarily on micro-subjective, micro-objective, macro-subjective, or macro-objective levels or domains of social reality.

[8] For a perceptive analysis of this and other problems in the field, see Turner and Turner (1990).

of bridging alternative paradigms. As Ritzer put it, "*In fact, no aspect of social reality can be adequately explained without drawing on insights from all of the paradigms*" (Ritzer, 1975:211; emphasis in original).

In view of the complex and multidimensional nature of the social world, and the great variety of ways it can be viewed, it may be fortunate that sociology is a multiple-paradigm discipline. Far better it is to face the social world in all its multifaceted complexity than to close our eyes and minds by using a single theoretical framework that limits our ability to appreciate this complexity. For the foreseeable future, our best hope for expanding our knowledge and understanding is probably to use a variety of theoretical perspectives, as well as multiple types of research. At the same time we can also work toward integrating opposing theoretical paradigms into a more coherent and more comprehensive theoretical framework when this seems appropriate for reaching a fuller and more satisfying understanding of the social world.

Summary

The image of sociological theory developed in this chapter differs sharply from the notion of implicit theory discussed in the first chapter by providing an overview of formal theory construction as part of a scientific enterprise. Sociology and the other social sciences differ from the natural sciences in that explaining human behavior requires understanding its subjective meaning. The same type of behavior may have different meanings for different people, or even for the same person in different contexts. This need to go beyond overt behavior to deal with subjective meaning does not apply to the natural sciences.

In addition, human beings see themselves as making choices, as opposed to having their behavior determined by forces beyond their control. Even when we recognize the relevance of free will and choice in social life, this does not mean that social scientists are unable to identify important factors that are beyond individuals' knowledge or control and that may influence the choices they make. Gaining knowledge regarding these influences may increase the ability of human beings to bring some of these factors under partial human control.

The purpose of formal theory construction is to identify significant relationships among important and clearly defined variables. The most elementary building blocks of theory are concepts that provide the names for phenomena we wish to understand as well as identify the variations they exhibit. These variations provide the basis for classification. Theoretical work at this level involves establishing categories and identifying the criteria for making distinctions between or among them. The heart of a theory itself consists essentially of a set of propositional statements, each of which relates two or more variables. Such statements are intended to explain **why** a variation occurs in some dependent variable or to identify the **effects** of a change in some independent variable. This explanation may focus on individual behavior or on various types of social formations and social processes beyond the level of the individual. Relationships between variables may also be **interdependent**, indicating that both may be considered either independent or dependent, depending on the specific questions being addressed. Moreover, in some cases different variables may affect one another only with certain limits, as suggested by the concepts of thresholds and limits.

The ultimate goal for a theory is to develop predictive hypotheses that can be empirically tested through research. However, specific predictions indicating causal relations are difficult, due in part to inadequate knowledge regarding the nature of the relationship between particular variables and in part to the influence of other unidentified variables that may be involved. Most of the propositions constituting a theory in sociology are, in fact, statements of probable relationships as opposed to deterministic or strict causal ones. Despite the difficulties, a useful theory can serve as the basis for propositional statements that will reflect the complex and multidimensional nature of the social world, and that can be confirmed (or revised) through research in a variety of settings.

Like everyone else, sociologists also have their own biases and underlying assumptions about the social world. These assumptions include ideas regarding what issues and questions are important and what kinds of analyses are relevant for advancing our knowledge and perhaps thereby contributing to a better world. In contrast to the apparent consensus that often seems to prevail among natural scientists regarding the fundamental nature of their subject matter, sociology is fragmented among adherents of different underlying paradigms. One of the key distinctions among different theorists is whether they focus primarily on the micro level or macro level. Although most major theorists recognize and deal in some fashion with the interdependent nature of these different levels, many of them tend to emphasize one level or the other as primary. In the next several chapters of this book we shall use the distinction between the micro and macro levels as a strategy for classifying and discussing the various theories to be covered. The theories to be covered at each of these levels will be shown to have definite implications for other levels as well. In addition, we will also focus on selected social formations at the intermediate meso level, thereby offering another strategy for linking micro and macro levels of analysis.

Questions for Study and Discussion

1. Do you agree that our knowledge of social behavior can best be advanced by seeking to explain the variations among different people or in different situations? How does this contrast with the goal of discovering universal characteristics of human beings' behavior? How can the strategy of explaining variations lead to the discovery of uniform patterns that we might expect to find in a variety of situations? What would you identify as the most important universal features of human beings' behavior, and what do you see as the most challenging variations to be explained?

2. Drawing on mass media reports, identify a contemporary news story in which one or more tentative explanations are offered for some specific behavior or type of behavior (either individual or group) and formulate these explanations in propositional statements. What kinds of evidence would be needed to test these propositions? Do the explanations offered make reference to specific social influences? In what way?
3. How could the concept of threshold and limits be applied in an inductive way in explaining the development of "best friend" relationships, selection of an academic major, or career choice? What specific variables would you identify as crucial, and how would you determine when the threshold and the limit are reached?
4. What are some of the advantages and disadvantages of focusing attention primarily on people's observable behavior versus their subjective meanings? Identify an example of how the same behavior may have different meanings for different people, or how the same meaning may be expressed in different ways.
5. Contrast the way propositional statements can be developed and tested with statistical data from large numbers of people as well as from qualitative observational data.

Part II
Moving from Micro to Meso to Macro Levels

Chapter 5
Symbolic Interaction: Constructing the Social World–and its Participants' Identities

Anyone who watches small children playing is likely to be impressed by their ability to create a world of their own merely by definition—a world that includes distinctive make-believe identities that they express through their behavior, sometimes with the help of a few toys. This imaginary world is obviously fragile, easily disrupted by outside interference (such as parental interruption) or by disagreements that might break out within the group. The "real" world of adults is obviously more durable than the make-believe world of children and usually not quite as vulnerable to breakdowns. But the differences are not absolute. The adult world is also socially constructed, along with the identities and roles of its participants, and it is also subject to disruption and breakdown, often with much more serious consequences.

This chapter explores the process of how the social world is constructed and maintained through the perspective of symbolic interaction theory. Although symbolic interaction theory is often applied primarily to the micro level, the structuring of interdependent lines of behavior at the meso and macro levels also involves shared definitions developed through interaction. The overall culture of a society is the objective outcome of these shared social definitions whereby subjective meanings are created, often expressed in material artifacts of various types, and either sustained or transformed through interaction.

Our coverage of the symbolic interactionist perspective in this chapter will be organized around the following themes:

- Symbolic interaction as process versus structure—Herbert Blumer's emphasis on the fluid and ever-changing nature of the interaction process will be highlighted for its contrast with the traditional focus of sociologists on social structures. In addition, the development of a structural form of symbolic interaction will also be described.
- Roles and identities—This section will focus on individuals' self-concepts in relation to their various social roles in different social situations. The following perspectives will be highlighted:
    - Norbert Wiley's focus on an intentional, future-oriented aspect of one's identity that moves beyond a pattern reflecting past experiences
    - George McCall and J. L. Simmons' "role-identity" model for explaining both the stable aspects of one's identity as well as its changing aspects

- Social life as dramatic performance—This section will highlight Erving Goffman's dramaturgic focus on the strategies people use in staging their "presentation of self" in ways designed to gain social validation and to overcome the precariousness and uncertainty of the social world.
- Language and culture—This section moves toward the macro level by showing how the reality of the social world transcends individuals' subjective consciousness and micro-level interaction processes by being encoded in objective form in texts and other material artifacts that exist outside subjective consciousness.

Symbolic Interaction—Process Versus Structure[1]

Many of the core ideas of symbolic interaction theory are grounded in the pioneering work of George Herbert Mead, particularly his perspective regarding the close relationship between the mental processes whereby people make sense of their environment and their interaction with one another. This relationship is manifested in the patterns of collaboration among people as they seek to develop shared interpretations of the situations they face. It is also reflected in how one's self-concept develops through awareness of the perspectives of others. In addition, contemporary symbolic interaction theory draws on Charles Horton Cooley's analysis of how one's feelings about oneself (pride or shame, for example) reflect one's sensitivity to the positive or negative reactions of others, especially in primary group settings. This is consistent with his often-cited concept of the "looking-glass self." As explained in Chap. 3, however, W. E. B. Du Bois showed how the self-concepts developed by African Americans (and no doubt other members of disprivileged minority groups) reflect their ongoing struggles to resist the prejudice and discrimination they experience on a daily basis in interacting with majority group members. Even so, this resistance is reinforced through interaction in their primary groups settings. William I. Thomas's emphasis on the distinctive "definitions of the situation" that are shared among group members is also important in understanding how people interpret and respond to their environment and to one another.

Symbolic interaction theory is comparable in some ways to Georg Simmel's focus on the forms of **interaction**, as discussed in Chap. 2. But symbolic interaction theory goes deeper than Simmel's perspective in emphasizing the **symbolic** medium through which interaction takes place plus the subjective mental processes that accompany it. This focus on the **subjective** level may be compared to Weber's emphasis on understanding the subjective meanings of individuals' actions. But while Weber moved well beyond the level of individual actions and subjective meanings to deal with broad patterns of institutional and cultural change, many symbolic interactionists resemble Simmel in their strong micro-level focus.

[1] Some of this material on symbolic interaction is adapted from D. P. Johnson ([1981] 1986:319–322).

Human beings relate to one another and to their environment in terms of interdependent roles they create and sustain. At the center of this process are the self-concepts or identities of the individuals involved as they interact and adjust to one another in face-to-face encounters. Human beings are thus transformed into students and teachers, friends and lovers, husbands and wives, team players and college graduates, customers and sales people, celebrities and deviants, soldiers and social workers, lawyers and police officers, members and outsiders, and so on. Social definitions are crucial even for defining the meaning and social relevance of human beings' biological characteristics, such as sex, age, and weight, for example.

The socially contrived character of large-scale institutional structures may not be as obvious as in small group relationships or children's micro-level play worlds, but macro level social institutions are also socially constructed through widely shared subjective definitions that are developed and sustained through interaction. This implies that when subjective definitions and interpretations undergo widespread change, institutional transformation may occur, which then changes the context of subsequent interactions at the micro level.

The divisions between micro, meso, and macro levels of analysis are not rigid distinctions. From our various micro-level social circles, networks of social relations extend outward, thus providing an opening to meso and macro levels of the social world. The heritage we share as members of society also includes enduring cultural products and artifacts that have been constructed or reproduced by countless other people far beyond the range of our own limited social circles or personal knowledge. Our language obviously transcends our personal micro-level social settings, even though language is actually reproduced regularly in the context of face-to-face interaction as well as in mass media communication. Even our adaptation to the objective physical reality of the natural world (like the food we eat) is mediated through the symbols we use to define and interpret it. All symbolic interactionists emphasize the micro-level linkages between the subjective consciousness, interpersonal interaction, and identity formation, as well as the symbolic and socially constructed nature of the larger social world.

Symbolic interaction theory today differs from the pioneering "social behaviorism" emphasized by Mead in the early part of the twentieth century. As explained in Chap. 3, Mead had criticized the stimulus-response model in behavioral psychology. In contrast, symbolic interaction theory since the middle of the twentieth century, especially under the influence of Herbert Blumer, was in large part a critical reaction to macro level types of analysis, particularly as reflected in functional theory, and the strong emphasis on the notion that people's behavior is largely determined by social structures. For symbolic interaction theorists, the strong emphasis on culturally scripted norms and institutionalized roles was misplaced. This focus seemed to leave little room for individuals to make choices or to improvise as they interpret and adjust to the specific situations they face.

For symbolic interactionists social structures do not exist as an objective reality that is independent of the actions of its human participants. Instead, all aspects of the social world are negotiated, constructed, and reproduced (or sometimes transformed) through ongoing processes of interaction and subjective interpretation whereby people mutually shape one another's perceptions, definitions, and responses to their environment. Within this general framework, several different areas of emphasis can be identified within symbolic interaction theory. Over four decades ago, Manford Kuhn (1964) noted that the symbolic interactionist perspective serves as a general framework for role theory, reference group theory, analyses of social perception and person perception, self theory, and dramaturgic theory. Despite this diversity, contemporary symbolic interaction theory has continued to provide a distinct image of the nature of social reality, particularly with its strong micro-level focus, that sets it apart from other major theoretical perspectives. (For a useful collection of symbolic interactionist work that represents the early period as well as more contemporary contributions, see Herman and Reynolds, eds. [1994].)

Of the various versions of symbolic interactionism, Herbert Blumer's (1962) perspective expressed the strongest skepticism regarding macro-level theories such as functionalism. As he put it:

> By and large, of course, sociologists do not study human society in terms of its acting units, Instead, they are disposed to view human society in terms of structure or organization and to treat social action as an expression of such structure or organization. Thus, reliance is placed on such structural categories as social system, culture, norms, values, social stratification, status position, social roles and institutional organization.
>
> (Blumer, pp.188–189 in Rose, ed. 1962)

A student of Mead's, Blumer coined the term symbolic interaction and played a leading role in promoting Mead's strong emphasis on the interrelated processes of mutual role-taking, interaction, and subjective interpretation that occur as people adjust their actions to one another in dealing with the particular situations they face.

This emphasis on the need for people to improvise their responses to their environment and to one another seems to downplay the habits and memories that individuals bring to situations that they encounter over and over. It also seems to push the cultural and institutional "framework" that might influence their interpretations into the background. Even though social organization, culture, roles, and other structural features of the social world may not **determine** people's behavior in a strong sense, such features may nevertheless be taken into consideration, especially in familiar situations. When people repeatedly face similar types of situations, they may employ ready-made responses with only a minimal amount of negotiation or reflection. This does not mean that social organization **determines** people's behavior as an external force. It does suggest, however, that patterns of interaction and interpretation are not always as fluid as Blumer seems to suggest.

People do indeed sometimes face novel situations that are unstructured and ambiguous and so will need to make a conscious effort to make sense of them as they explore with one another how to cope. In other situations, they may each have their own distinctive ideas on how to respond and so will need to negotiate their differences. But in many routine situations they already share an implicit understanding of its salient features and know how to respond. This means that very little negotiation is required if any. Regardless of these variations, patterns of social organization, including written rules and established authority or power structures, are never automatically self-enforcing. Instead, these "structural" factors become relevant only to the extent that people remember them and decide how to apply them. Sometimes there may be discussion and debate regarding whether or how an established rule or custom should apply. If there are large differences in power and authority, the negotiation actually may be quite minimal, as those with relatively less power realize the futility of trying to get those with greater power to see things their way.

Blumer's emphasis on the uniqueness of people's responses to particular situations is consistent with qualitative or ethnographic types of research based on intensive participant observation (e.g., see Prus, 1996). Such research is limited in scope, however, since no researcher is able to monitor more than a limited number of specific situations with the required intensity. Such research is not necessarily designed to test general principles that are thought to apply throughout society. Instead, the goal is to portray "thick descriptions" that convey the rich texture of specific patterns in social life as they actually unfold in particular settings. Such projects may lead to the discovery of social processes that are repeated with sufficient frequency that they can tentatively be generalized to similar people or situations. But the "thicker" the description, the less the insights can reliably be generalized, despite superficial similarities.

By pushing social organization, culture, and similar concepts that transcend particular situations into the background, and by emphasizing the fluid and indeterminate nature of the immediate social world, Blumer's approach makes it difficult to establish principles of social behavior that apply across different situations or to move from the micro to the macro level. However, other symbolic interaction theorists give more emphasis to stable structural categories than Blumer did. These structural influences do not determine behavior from the outside, as external or objective forces, however; instead, they are encoded in individuals' subjective consciousness and shared memories and expectations. Although they may be interpreted to apply in unique ways in different situations, they are nevertheless reflected in participants' predispositions regarding how to respond to the specific situations they face.

The contrast between Blumer's view of the fluid and undetermined nature of the social world versus a more structural version of symbolic interaction theory can be illustrated through the process whereby individuals' self-concepts are developed, maintained, and changed. The relation between individuals' self-concepts or identities, their social roles, and the reactions of others can be traced back to the pioneering work of Mead and Cooley. Contemporary symbolic interactionist theory offers several different strategies for exploring how individuals' self-concepts or identities are expressed through the different roles they perform. The following section will deal in more detail with the relation between people's role performances and their identities.

Roles and Identities[2]

The concept of **role** links the individual's self-concept to the structured features of the social world. However, the way this concept is used varies in different versions of symbolic interaction theory (and also contrasts with macro-level theories). Blumer's image of the fluid and negotiated character of the social world implies that identities and social roles are not fixed but instead are largely improvised in each encounter as individuals seek to align their own self-concepts and intentions with the expectations of others. In contrast to Blumer, a more structural version of symbolic interaction theory puts greater emphasis on the standardized and routine expectations and behaviors of various roles. With this alternative focus social life is viewed as having a higher level of predictability than implied in Blumer's perspective, especially in routine situations. Although behavior is not **determined** by social roles, with no room for individual variations, this structural version is closer to the conventional forms of sociological analysis that Blumer criticized. While roles may not be scripted in detail, there are definite guidelines and expectations that people tend to follow.

People's self-concepts are multidimensional. They may reflect roles associated with various personal characteristics as well as with the social positions they occupy. These roles include, for example, those associated with gender, age, family status, occupation, race or ethnicity, residential location, leisure time pursuits, general lifestyle preferences, and so on. Such roles are likely to be partially structured by general cultural expectations as well as by specific expectations that develop among people who interact on a regular basis. Even so, there is room for considerable improvisation in most cases as individuals express their own unique individuality and seek to satisfy their current needs and concerns.[3]

A closely related issue is whether our self-concept remains fairly stable over time, once it has been formed, or whether it changes continuously from one situation to the next. If the self-concept is stable, an important question can be raised as to whether this results primarily from one's personal characteristics or from the stability in one's social position and social environment. Moreover, despite the fact that people may be similar in terms of personal characteristics and social

---

[2] The material in this section on Blumer's and Kuhn's contrasting versions of symbolic interaction theory, plus the material on McCall and Simmon's role identity model, is adapted from D. P. Johnson ([1981] 1986:319–324).

[3] This emphasis on the way individuals are involved actively in constructing their social roles as they express their identities contrasts with Mead's somewhat more passive view. Mead's explanation of how we move from the play stage to the game stage to the stage of the generalized other may be compared to Parsons' theory of how the socialization process leads individuals to introject or internalize the rules of the wider society, resulting in the formation of conscience and high levels of self-control. (Parsons' functional theory will be presented more fully in a subsequent chapter.)

positions, they nevertheless develop a sense of themselves as unique individuals, reflecting their distinct personal biography and experiences, and these unique features are likely to form the core of the stable components their self-concepts. But regardless of how stable our self-concept may be, we might expect that as we grow older and move through the predictable stages of the life cycle, significant changes are likely to occur, even if we retain the key defining aspects of earlier life experiences.

Blumer's image of the fluid and ever-changing nature of the social world became known as the "Chicago School." In contrast, a more stable image of the social world was reflected in Manford Kuhn's strategy for measuring the self-concept by asking respondents to complete 20 statements beginning with: "I am." (M. Kuhn and McPartland, 1954). This Twenty Statements Test (TST) would be meaningless if there were no stability in the self-concept from one situation to the next. To regard the self-concept as having some stability, however, does not mean that it never changes. But the key questions concern how and why some aspects of one's self-concept tend to change over time in response to new experiences, and why for some people such changes are more frequent or deeper than for others.

Kuhn's work contributed to the development of a more "structural" version of symbolic interaction theory, which was known initially as the "Iowa School" (see Vander Zanden [1984:13] for a brief description of the contrast between the Chicago and Iowa schools.) These place names are no longer accurate, inasmuch as representatives of both approaches can be found in various institutional locations. In fact, Sheldon Stryker, a major figure in the development of the structural version, has long been associated with Indiana University. In the structural version, the focus is on how people's expectations and behaviors are organized in terms of interrelated roles that tend to persist over time, especially in recurrent types of situations (Stryker, 1980). Roles are seen as the behavioral expectations associated with particular social positions (mother, son, friend, employee, customer, citizen, member, and so on), though actual role behavior reflects individuals' unique styles that may not necessarily conform completely to idealized expectations. The general perspective of role theory can be used to investigate how social roles are learned and incorporated in individuals' identities and how people are linked through their roles to various institutional structures. Some additional areas to be explored include role strain and role conflict, how deviant roles develop, and how roles may change over time (Ralph H. Turner, pp. 233–254 in Jonathan H. Turner, ed. 2001).

In addition, the affect control theory developed more recently by David Heise (also at Indiana University) provides a model that explains the strategies people use in attempting to insure consistency in their attitudes and sentiments toward one another (and other stimuli) in recurrent situations (Heise, 1979, 2007; see also Smith-Lovin and Heise, eds., 1988). Heise focused explicitly on people's perceptions of others in various social roles in terms of three specific dimensions: evaluation (good versus bad), potency (powerful versus powerless), and activity (active versus passive). In interacting with others people seek to control their own behavior and to interpret the behavior of others so as to confirm their already developed sentiments toward themselves and others with regard to these three dimensions. If this is not possible in a particular situation, adjustments may be needed in behavior or sentiments, including modification in their identity or the identities of others. In short, although people try to achieve consistency over time, changes occur as a result of behaviors that cannot be reconciled with established expectations.

The process whereby one's self-concept changes over time had earlier been suggested by Mead's distinction between the "I" and the "me" and the relation of these aspects of the self to past, present, and future behavior. The "I" is the self as acting subject in the present, while the "me" is the self as object to oneself. Mead recognized that present actions can be adjusted in the light of memories of past actions and the reactions of others, whether positive or negative. However, actions in the present are not always completely predictable, and novel aspects of one's behavior may lead to gradual modification of the "me." Mead's theory of how the self-concept changes did not deal in great detail with the future, except to acknowledge that the present is continually unfolding into the future (Mead, 1932). Although individuals' self-concepts undergo change as a result of the effects of their own novel behaviors and others' reactions, Mead did not explore how individuals may be proactive in intentionally changing or seeking to improve themselves. He recognized the importance of people's evaluations of expected future outcomes, but did not focus on people's effort to change themselves in accordance with their unique ideals and aspirations.

A useful elaboration of Mead's theory of the self-concept that includes a more explicit focus on the future is provided by Norbert Wiley's (1994) effort to integrate Mead's ideas with those of Mead's contemporary Charles Sanders Peirce, an important figure in American pragmatism. Our goal here is not to review Peirce's ideas but to show how Wiley's theoretical synthesis provides a more dynamic and intentional view of the self. This expanded view is critical for Wiley in evaluating contemporary developments in "identity politics" and also in sustaining a view of the individual that is compatible with a democratic society.[4] In contrast to Mead's portrayal of the "I" and "me" as aspects of the self, Wiley noted that Peirce's analysis revolved around the internal subjective dialogue that occurs between the "I" and the "you." The "you" in this model does not refer to another person but to one's own future behavior and its anticipated effects on one's identity. That is, the individual envisions his or her future behavior as well as his or her personal evaluation of it. Despite the use of the second person pronoun, the "you" refers to one's own future self. Of course, this may incorporate anticipations of others' reactions, just as Mead's "me" incorporates individuals' memories of the reactions of others. But while Mead's "me" incorporates the past reactions of others, the "you" in Peirce's theory includes one's own anticipated self-evaluations and their implication for

---

[4] George Herbert Mead also considered his perspective on the process of role taking and his concept of the "generalized other" to be compatible with a democratic society. His emphasis, however, was on the way one's self-concept is shaped and formed to fit the community's expectations as represented by the "generalized other."

one's identity. Just as individuals may try to predict others' future reactions, they may also anticipate how they will see themselves as they evaluate the effects of their own future actions on their identity.

Wiley (1994) proposed an integration of Mead and Peirce by combining Mead's "I" and "me" with Peirce's "I" and "you" so the result is a triad of "I-me-you." In this model, the "I" is the self in the present, the "me" is the self as past, and the "you" is the anticipated future self. Our present actions (the "I") may reflect the past (the "me"), but they may also be oriented toward a future self that is different from the past (the "you"). In practical terms, this seems to reduce the determining influence of the past on present behavior. Instead, present actions are directed intentionally toward an ideal future self that has not yet come into being. Like Scrooge in Charles Dickens' Christmas tale, we are not destined to continue to be what we were; instead, we can become active agents in constructing the self we want to become as we learn from the past and resolve to change.

Wiley distinguished between his triadic model of the self-concept and the notion of "identities" based on the various personal characteristics reflected in "identity politics." Identity politics involves efforts to mobilize individuals who are believed to have similar interests based on race, gender, sexual orientation, or other personal or demographic characteristics shared with others in order to achieve some goal. However, the actual self-concepts of those grouped together in this way are by no means identical. Nor are these characteristics necessarily salient for the core self-concepts of all of those who are so categorized. To regard people simply as members of a homogeneous category on the basis of objective social characteristics such as nationality, gender, race, ethnicity, sexual orientation, and so on represents a failure to recognize the uniqueness of each human being and the personal efforts individuals often make to establish their own distinctive individuality.

Wiley considered an adequate theory of the self-concept to be important for a democratic society. Such a theory goes beyond the characteristics shared with others in the same category (gender, age, race/ethnicity, etc.) in recognizing the unique identity, dignity, and worth of each individual person. Personal characteristics shared with others **may** become relevant for a person's identity or self-concept as alliances are established to pursue shared interests. But individuals involved in such mobilization still maintain their own individuality, and this unique identity may be more important for them than the characteristics they share with others.

In addition to objective personal characteristics that may be shared with others, it is important also to note that the specific manner whereby people perform their roles in various social positions (family member, friend, employee, student, neighbor, and so on) are also likely to constitute an important part of their self-concepts. In addition, people's self-concepts may include idealized notions about their basic character (honest, loving, hard-working, "people person," risk-taking, free spirit, conservative, outdoor person, connoisseur of fine food and wine, spiritual, leader or follower, and others). Such characteristics are not necessarily related directly to specific demographic characteristics or clearly defined social positions. People's identities may also incorporate personal tastes or lifestyle preferences, some of which may be related to family status, socioeconomic position, and so on.

Moreover, each person's identity will also reflect unique aspects of his or her particular biographical background and personal experiences.

People's self-concepts are thus multidimensional, incorporating a variety of self-identifying terms and associated images. Despite the similarities among people in terms of personal characteristics and social positions, the specific mix of roles and other aspects of self-identity will vary for different people, as well as their importance and the specific ways their roles are performed. In everyday life we recognize that some people give higher priority to their family roles than their occupational roles, for example, while for others the reverse seems true. All of the roles we play, and all the various characteristics that we use to define ourselves, can be seen as arrayed in a kind of hierarchy, ranging from central or highly important at the top to minor or rather peripheral at the bottom. People vary in terms of how stable this hierarchy is over time and in different situations. Although people's self-concepts or identities are likely to undergo some change as they move into new roles or into different social settings, people differ in terms of whether such changes in environment lead to fundamental transformations in the core areas of their self-concepts or whether the changes are more peripheral. In the area of religion, for example, some people may undergo a religious conversion experience that results in a drastic change in their self-concept, while others maintain the same general level of religious involvement or noninvolvement throughout their lives. This suggests that the "Chicago School" emphasis on change may be more relevant for some people while the "Iowa School" emphasis on stability may apply more clearly to others.

The "role identity" model developed by George McCall and J. L. Simmons ([1966] 1978) is useful for analyzing the structure of the self-concept and its stability and change over time. In their model role-identities are the idealized self-images individuals have as occupants of various social positions or as participants in various social relations. The overall configuration of role-identities makes up a major part of an individual's self-concepts. McCall and Simmons use the term **role prominence** to identify the long-term importance of a particular role-identity. The position of a particular role-identity in the overall prominence hierarchy reflects the individual's level of commitment to and investment in that identity, the gratifications it provides, the level of social support for it received from others, and the internal self-support one obtains for that identity. So, for example, if a person purchases a guitar, invests time and money in learning to play it, greatly enjoys playing, and ultimately performs so well that others enjoy listening, the role-identity of guitar player would probably become fairly high in that person's prominence hierarchy. If the person should eventually become a wealthy celebrity through concert performances, the musician identity may well become the most prominent or central role-identity in the entire hierarchy.

Role-identities are enacted through role performances, but the specific identity that an individual expresses will vary in different situations. In contrast to the relatively stable prominence hierarchy, an individual's role-identities can also be ranked in terms of a more temporary or situational **salience hierarchy**. The salience of an identity will be influenced by the particular situation in which the individual is involved. Obviously, persons cannot enact all of the role-identities at once, not even those most prominent. Instead, the role performed will reflect the opportunities and expectations associated with that situation. As situations change, the salience hierarchy changes accordingly. For example, the role-identity of gambler may be fairly low in the guitar player's prominence hierarchy. But if the guitar player visits Las Vegas with a gambling friend, the gambler identity may quickly be added to the salience hierarchy for the time being.

In addition to the nature of the situation itself, the salience of a particular role identity will also reflect individuals' current needs for the gratifications and social support that are usually received from performing a particular role. If an individual is deprived of a highly desired reward for a long time, the salience of the relevant role-identity will be higher than if the individual has recently received such a reward and is now satiated. A person who has just finished a meal is not likely to enact the role of culinary connoisseur. But assessing the level of deprivation or satiation may not be so easy for many social rewards. Just as many Americans seem never to have enough money, so also people's desires for social approval or prestige sometimes appear to be virtually insatiable. Fortunately, for most people there are many different ways to earn social approval.

In short, the prominence hierarchy refers to the more or less stable ranking of the role identities making up a person's self-concept, while the salience hierarchy refers to role identities that reflect one's needs at the moment and the opportunities and expectations presented by the current situation. Role performances in particular situations are influenced only in part by the idealized prominence hierarchy and in part by situational opportunities and constraints and specific needs at the moment.

McCall and Simmons emphasized the importance of our dependence on supportive reactions from others as well as self-support. But what happens when the reactions of others are less supportive than we feel we deserve (that is, low social support is not consistent with high self-support)? Overall, persons would probably have difficulty maintaining strong self-support in the long run if supportive reactions from others were never received. On the other hand, some individuals may be even more critical of themselves than others are. In either case, consistent lack of social or self support is likely to result in a long-term decline in the relative prominence of a given role-identity. Other options are also possible, however. People may choose different persons (or a different audience) with whom to enact a particular identity in the hope of receiving more supportive reactions. Or people may interpret (or misinterpret) the reactions of others so as to see themselves in a more positive light than intended by others. If negative reactions from others are impossible to misinterpret in a positive light or to ignore, these reactions may be rejected as coming from persons not competent to make a proper evaluation. Through subjective processes such as these, individuals are often able to sustain their idealized self-concept, despite lack of social support.

Our self-concepts influence our actions, our choice of interaction partners, and our interpretations of their reactions. Every action we perform may be seen as expressing some aspect of our self-concept, and every reaction of others has the potential for reinforcing or undermining it. We generally welcome opportunities to interact with others who provide social support, and we interpret their reactions so as to see ourselves in the most favorable light possible. At the same time, as our relationships and life experiences change, our self-concept changes accordingly. Moreover, our idealized self-concepts are not necessarily always positive or satisfying. Persons who are often criticized, or whose idealized self-concepts are unrealistically high, may see themselves in negative terms, even when they do receive social approval from others. For such persons the need to deal with constant criticism may lead to coping strategies that at least provide a sense of stability. When this pattern becomes well established, such persons may have difficulty in accepting or responding appropriately to positive feedback when it does occur.

This focus on the importance of our self-concept does not mean that individuals are necessarily always or consciously self-centered. Persons with high levels of empathy may often identify with the emotions or the needs of others rather than themselves. In symbolic interactionist terms, they are able to "take the role of the other." Moreover, people may become so thoroughly involved in some activity that they do not think consciously about the implications for their self-concepts or the reactions of others. As Mead pointed out, the behavior of the "I" is not necessarily simply an expression of the "me." Even so, when such activities have been completed, people are likely to reflect on their implications for their self-concepts. In McCall and Simmons' terms repeated successful performance of a highly salient role identity may elevate its rank in the prominence hierarchy.

Staging Performances: The Dramaturgic Approach to Interaction[5]

The way individuals' self-concepts are expressed in their behavior and interaction style is the major theme of Erving Goffman's (1959) dramaturgic perspective. (For a comprehensive overview of Goffman's sociological contributions, see Burns, 1992.) Using the language of the theater, Goffman described how individuals employ various strategies to try to create a good impression on others and thereby obtain social validation of their self-concepts. This approach reflects Shakespeare's insight that all the world is a stage and human beings merely players or performers, each with his or her entry onto the stage, a particular role to perform or character to portray and, finally, an exit. In their constant efforts to "put their best foot forward" individuals seek to control their appearance and the physical setting in which they perform, as well their actual behavior and accompanying gestures. For example, public speakers organize and rehearse their presentations in advance, and both musicians and athletes practice before their public performances. Similarly,

[5]This material on Erving Goffman's dramaturgic perspective is adapted from D. P. Johnson ([1981] 1986:325–334).

a married couple planning a party will make advance preparations to insure an appropriate supply of food and drink. During the party, they will mingle with their guests and attend to any mishaps that may occur without acting angry or frustrated. When the party is over and the guests have all gone, their demeanor will change as they begin cleaning up, putting leftovers in the refrigerator or throwing them away, and perhaps even talking about some of their guests in ways that they would not do if they were still present.

The deliberate staging and contrived character of events such as public performances or parties may seem obvious. However, all social occasions have this dramaturgic character. The effort to convey a good impression can easily be seen in many different types of settings. For example, students try to appear knowledgeable but nonchalant as they take part in class discussion; lawyers strive to exude confidence as they argue their cases in court, and employees make sure they look busy when their supervisor comes in. Individuals' general appearance and overall demeanor are also highly relevant for the identity they seek to project. They will thus attend to their appearance prior to a staging a performance (through personal grooming and selection of appropriate clothing) and will attempt to control various inappropriate mannerisms that might undermine the performance. Many people adhere to strict diets and regular exercise programs for health reasons, but such forms of discipline also help insure that their body image is consistent with the social identity they want to convey.

The physical setting where a role is performed may also be relevant. For example, a high-level corporate executive would expect to have a well-furnished private office, not a small cubicle among his or her subordinates. If the executive takes a prospective client or partner out for lunch, this would likely be at an establishment that caters to business executives and not at the local fast-food outlet where the high school crowd hangs out. The concern with the settings in which people perform their roles may be seen as reflecting their attempts to control the general social definition of the situation.

Goffman also pointed out the innumerable strategies people use to collaborate in protecting one another's various claims regarding the social reality they are attempting to stage or the identities they are trying to enact. Tact in interpersonal encounters is important because the contrived nature of the social reality people seek to create makes it fragile and vulnerable to disruption (Goffman, 1959:208–212). Sometimes, an individual may make a mistake in his or her performance that is impossible to ignore and, as a result, the impression being created cannot be sustained. For example, an outstanding athlete may accidentally trip over his or her own shoelace, or a guest at the dinner table may knock over a glass of red wine while making a dramatic gesture in the course of a lively conversation. In innumerable ways, individuals are vulnerable to the risks of losing face in their social relationships or having their performances discredited. However, since no one is immune to such threats, individuals often collaborate in overlooking errors so as to support one another's identity claims and the impressions they are attempting to convey. For persons in sociable or cooperative relations, elementary norms of tact and courtesy require us to try to overlook or cover for one another person's mistakes if possible, even when we have to adjust our own behavior accordingly.

On the other hand, in situations involving competition and conflict, individuals may deliberately try to discredit one another's performances. A political opponent, for example, will seek to expose an incumbent's failures. Sometimes, however, a person will prefer an opponent to be put in a position of **relative** inferiority as opposed to being totally discredited. An experienced tennis player, for example, will take greater pride in beating an outstanding opponent than in winning over an amateur. Another type of situation in which norms of tact may be suspended is when people know each other so well that they engage in humorous games of "give and take" in which they ritualistically "put one another down" or engage in some form of "one-upsmanship." Such games provide reassurance of the mutual trust they share, plus practice in recovering from threats to their self-concepts.

Teams and Audiences

Collaboration between persons in defining a situation or staging a performance is revealed in Goffman's analysis of teams and team performances (Goffman, 1959:77–105). A dramaturgic team is a group of persons who cooperate to stage the performance. To quote Goffman, "A team, then, may be defined as a set of individuals whose intimate cooperation is required if a given projected definition of the situation is to be maintained." (Goffman, 1959:104)

The dynamics of interaction within a dramaturgic team differ significantly from the patterns of interaction between team and audience. The audience is expected to accept the definitions of reality portrayed by the team, including the identities of those involved. However, team members will be aware of the contrived or staged nature of the reality being presented. Members of the team may need to cooperate in setting up the props (or at least they will know how they are set up deliberately to convey a particular impression). They may practice their "lines" with one another to determine their appropriateness, and they may invite critical evaluation by team members of the performances they plan to enact. This is often done in an informal fashion with a great deal of camaraderie. After all, team members do not have to worry about keeping up appearances in front of one another. In short, social relations within the team will be characterized by relatively low social distance because of the intimate familiarity that results from sharing insider secrets unknown to the audience.

Numerous examples could be cited to illustrate the dynamics of interaction within a team. A professor may describe some new classroom technique or explanation to a colleague to get his or her reaction prior to using it in the classroom. A corporation president may ask close associates to listen to a draft of a speech before delivering it before a meeting of the corporation stockholders. Ministers may joke with one another about how important it is to have an anthem or a time for silent meditation before the sermon to give them one last chance to go over their notes. Teachers or medical doctors will take care not to question their colleagues' professional judgment in a critical fashion in the company of students, patients, or other outsiders.

Related to the distinction between team members and audience is Goffman's contrast between "frontstage" and "backstage" regions (Goffman, 1959:106–140). The frontstage is wherever the audience is expected to be, while the backstage, where preparation and rehearsal take place, is typically off limits to the audience or other outsiders. In the backstage region team members can relax their concerns with appearances as they prepare for their frontstage performances. Practically every public establishment has an area designated "for employees only." Similarly, the bedrooms in most middle-class homes are not open to guests except by special invitation. Such invitations typically are seen as a signal to reduce social distance and to allow greater informal familiarity between host family and guests, thereby enhancing camaraderie and solidarity.

These distinctions depend on the specific circumstances, however. A backstage area may quickly become frontstage if an outsider intrudes, or it may become a frontstage for a different kind of performance. For example, the kitchen area of a restaurant would be backstage as far as the customers are concerned but, when a public health inspector makes an appearance, it may quickly be transformed to a frontstage region as the kitchen crew collaborates to insure the inspector that required sanitation standards are being followed. Or, the backstage area of a high school teachers' lounge will be off limits for students, and teachers will be free to relax and vent their frustrations in private. However, the lounge may become a frontstage area for the school administrators as they demonstrate to visitors or potential union organizers their concern for the comfort and well-being of the teaching staff.

The Precariousness of the Social World

Throughout his work, Goffman is sensitive to the difficulties people experience in maintaining desired appearances and impressions. These difficulties are compounded by the fact that people expect the social world not to be contrived or staged but "really real." Thus, for example, medical doctors are not supposed merely to **act** like doctors; they are expected actually to **be** doctors and to have the knowledge and skills that this implies. Similarly, worshipers in a religious service will expect their leaders actually to **feel** the religious sentiments they are expressing. At the same time, however, both physicians and religious leaders are highly skilled in the deliberate staging that is involved in their role performances, and they take care to guard against disruptions that would undermine them. Thus the experience of social reality will be different for the team staging its production than for the audience members for whom it is staged.

In many cases, the degree of success in having a particular definition of the situation or a particular identity accepted without question is directly proportional to the degree to which its contrived nature is concealed. Thus, for example, a host or hostess may wave off a compliment on the elaborate variety of food served to guests at a party by suggesting that it was really not out of the ordinary. Similarly, a golfer will take a stance and prepare to swing in a natural and easy style, even though this stance may have been privately practiced repeatedly. People giving public speeches often try to memorize their script as much as possible so that their talk will sound natural and their eye contact with the audience will not have to be interrupted by downward glances at their notes. In nationally televised addresses by the United States President, the "teleprompter" is placed so that it is concealed from the audience and the president appears to be looking directly at the audience even while referring to the prepared script.

Recognizing the socially constructed nature of social reality, Goffman's style of analysis emphasizes the tenuousness of the distinction between appearances and reality. In view of the socially constructed and therefore precarious nature of social reality, ambiguities, contradictions, threats of breakdown, and possibilities for deceit abound in the social world. In developing this point with reference to deliberate deceit, Goffman analyzes various discrepant roles, such as the informer, the shill, the spotter, the shopper, and the go-between (Goffman, 1959:141–166). To illustrate, the spy is an informer who gains access to a team's backstage region by pretending to be a team member, but whose real intention is to discredit its performance by sharing secrets obtained backstage with the audience. A shill is a dramaturgic team member who pretends to be part of the audience, perhaps "planted" for the purpose of leading the audience in applauding and otherwise expressing approval for the team's performance.

Another type of discrepancy occurs when an individual's or team member's actions or statements turn out to be inconsistent with the identities or definitions of the situation that are being projected. Many automobile accidents result from the mistakes of persons who insist they are always "excellent" drivers. Goffman discusses several types of communication that are "out of character." For example, a performer may become distracted and make a mistake. Or team members may need to engage in "stage talk" while the audience is present because of unforeseen problems that emerge during a performance. Or a team member may decide for some reason to project some personal identity that is not consistent with his or her role as a team member. When situations such as these occur, it is likely to distract from the image the team is trying to present of a natural and spontaneous performance.

Still another type of out-of-character communication occurs when team members make disparaging or otherwise inappropriate comments about the audience without being aware that someone from the audience is within hearing distance. For example, a group of students might make negative or mocking comments about a professor while in the local campus hangout, only to discover later that the professor is sitting nearby. Or a nurse's aide might complain to a nurse in very uncomplimentary terms about a patient's frequent complaints and demands, without realizing that the patient is awake and listening to every word. Such disparaging or cynical comments are sometimes due to team members' perception of the audience's lack of sophistication in evaluating a performance adequately.

Communication out of character need not disrupt or destroy a performance, however. Members of a team are often able to maintain their projected definition of the situation and to stage their performance successfully, even while they act toward one another in terms of a different reality. In other words, team members are involved with two different versions of reality simultaneously — one for the audience and another for fellow team members. This may involve the use of various subtle cues or special code words as team members interact with one another in ways that they believe will have no meaning to the audience. Such secret codes are common in retail establishments, for example, where salespersons collaborate in dealing with various types of customers, or in law enforcement where officers use special codes to communicate with headquarters regarding situations they encounter in the field.

Interaction Challenges of the Stigmatized

The difficulties of projecting a personally satisfying and socially acceptable identity are revealed dramatically in the challenges faced by persons who are stigmatized for some reason. As Goffman (1963) pointed out, a visible physical handicap is one of the main sources of stigma. Persons with obvious physical handicaps appear different to such a pronounced degree that others sometimes find it difficult to interact with them in such a way that the handicap itself does not become the focal point of the interaction. Physical handicaps are not the only source of stigma, however. People may be stigmatized by their reputation (e.g., convicted sex offender or former mental patient) or by other characteristics that have a denigrating effect. Whatever its source, those with a pervasive or obvious form of stigma have to deal with the way they are stereotyped by others as being incompetent (in general or in some specific fashion) unless they make it a point to establish their competence. Thus their first and probably most important challenge is to project an identity as a competent human being except for the specific limitations that may be imposed by the handicap itself.

Goffman (1961) also dealt extensively with the problems of persons in mental institutions. The ideology and organizational structure of mental hospitals are designed to reinforce the identities of their inmates as incompetent, unable to make basic decisions in their lives, not to be trusted, and perhaps even dangerous to others or to themselves. In contrast to this assumption of patients' incompetence, mental hospital staff see themselves as highly competent to evaluate properly the needs of patients, to control their lives so as to promote their improvement, and to evaluate their behaviors in an knowledgeable, objective, and benevolent way. Since the inmates themselves have little control over their environment or the decisions that affect their lives, their only alternative may be to appear to accept the negative definitions of self offered them by the staff. If the patient refuses to accept the staff diagnosis, the staff may conclude that the person is too ill to realize how serious the problem is and therefore really "belongs" in the institution. Successful adaptation and eventual release may thus require that patients collaborate with the staff in pretending to accept a negative identity and going through the process of trying to change themselves.

Although the difficulties of the physically handicapped, mental hospital patients, and others with stigmatizing characteristics highlight the challenges involved in gaining support for a satisfying self concept, even "normal" persons may also face challenges from time to time in gaining social support for the identities they seek to project. These problems are perhaps most acute for those whose identity includes some distinctive claim that sets them apart from the average person and requires differential (or deferential) treatment of some type. As every hero of the moment eventually discovers, one outstanding achievement does not guarantee a permanent identity as a hero. In contrast, those who are satisfied with being average persons must manage their behavior to guard against being singled out as strange or different. Regardless of the specific identity claims being made, the social realities people create are tenuous and fragile, continually subject to breakdown and requiring subsequent repair or renegotiation.

The Context of Interaction

People's actions are almost always subject to alternative interpretations or multiple meanings. Interpreting the meaning of activities or events is heavily influenced by the context within which they occur. There will necessarily be a physical dimension to the context, consisting of the specific space and time within which activities occur and the material artifacts which may be involved. In addition, there will be a social dimension, a set of conventional understandings whereby individuals who are involved in some collective undertaking will have an understanding what sort of undertaking it is. Goffman (1974) refers to these shared understandings that underlie the interpretive process as the "frame" within which social events take place.

The framing process may be illustrated by the example of a formal meeting, such as a session of Congress or a state's legislature, that is conducted according to standard parliamentary procedure. The opening statement of the chairperson, "The meeting will come to order," marks the beginning. From this point until the chairperson says "The meeting is adjourned," everything that is said will be considered part of the official meeting and duly recorded as such, unless the frame is broken for a recess or for some remarks that are "off the record." But even during the formal meeting some members may exhibit various "out of frame" behaviors, such as opening a soft drink or whispering to one another to make comments about the proceedings or to arrange for some future activity. These side involvements are not officially part of the meeting, even though they may be carried on within full view of everyone else while the meeting is in progress. Such side activities would be considered outside the frame and thus irrelevant for the official meeting.

In a "real" business meeting of a "real" organization, the official opening and closing statements of the chairperson mark the boundaries of the occasion. Informal conversations before, after, or even during the meeting are secondary to the main event and are not included in the official record (the minutes) of the meeting. But the words spoken to open and close the meeting officially rest on certain implicit understandings regarding the nature of the occasion. For a different occasion, these same words might be part of a different frame. For example, the words used in official proceedings (calling a meeting to order, hearing reports, making or amending motions for discussion and voting, and so on) could be used for the purpose of practice in a class in parliamentary procedure, as part of a comedy routine, as a portion of a dramatic play that includes such an activity, or as part of a narrative account to members who were absent of what happened at the "real" meeting. Thus the meaning of the words in defining the situation and marking its boundaries rests on the implicit understanding among participants regarding the context and the specific nature of the occasion.

The frame of a set of activities is not always as obvious as in the example of the formal meeting. There are occasions in which participants may be unsure as to exactly what is going on. Even though they see clearly the activities being performed, they do not know how such activities should be taken, and there may be some discrepancies in their understanding of what is going on. Such differences may or may not be known to the participants and may or may not be disruptive of the activities in process. Whether these differences are disruptive or not will depend on the nature of the activity and the importance of informed consensus regarding its meaning. For example, a casual conversation between a supervisor in a bureaucratic organization and a subordinate may be merely a means to fill some free time to the supervisor, while to the subordinate it may be a long-awaited opportunity to establish or strengthen a social contact with someone who may be able to help advance the subordinate's career. These differences in frame need not be disruptive, as long as both participants interact according to the general understandings that govern casual sociable conversations between supervisors and subordinates.

The frames within which activities occur are subject to transformation, either unintentionally or intentionally, in which case the activities performed will take on a totally new meaning. One delightful type of example is provided by puns, jokes, and other forms of humor. The person telling a joke seeks to lead the audience into implicit acceptance of one meaning of certain key words and then, at the punch line, the meaning changes radically, leading to a humorous reinterpretation of all that came before. Or, in the example of the official meeting previously discussed, the side conversation of two participants may result in loud, uncontrollable laughter that breaks up the meeting, or the chairperson may get a case of the hiccups and literally lose control of the meeting. These examples illustrate rapid transformations of the implicit frame that had given meaning to the activities, sometimes resulting in a different meaning being superimposed on the original meaning. Considerable effort may be required to overcome the disruption and restore the original frame.

In addition to inadvertent disruptions, deliberate efforts are sometimes made to mislead others as to the meaning of a particular set of activities. Such deceptions may be either malevolent or benevolent. A "con artist" illustrates a malevolent deception. The con artist attempts to get a victim to accept one interpretation of his or her "helpful" activities so as to gain the victim's trust; when this objective is achieved, the victim soon discovers that he or she has been "set up" or deceived.

An example is the case of the phony "bank examiner" who persuades a depositor to withdraw a large sum of money in order to try to catch a dishonest bank employee and then escapes with the money or subsequently uses the account number to make additional withdrawals. The contemporary internet version involves using an Web site that looks identical to a bank's official website to request verification of bank or credit card numbers which are then used to withdraw cash or make credit purchases. In contrast, the surprise family birthday party might be cited as an example of a benevolent deception. The "victim" is kept in the dark as to the nature of whatever preparations might be made on his or her behalf. Then, when all the guests jump out from behind the furniture and shout "Surprise!," the meaning of the family's secrecy and the evasive answers to the inquiries about what is going on become clear.

Goffman's focus is primarily on the micro level of the social world. His analysis is richly illustrated with interesting examples of the subtle dynamics of interaction in a variety of settings. However, he did not emphasize large-scale social institutions or the dynamics of social processes at the macro level. His study of the mental hospital is an exception and is his most systematic institutional analysis. In his final publication (published after his death), Goffman focused on the "interaction order" as it involved various types of face-to-face encounters in different social settings (Goffman, 1983).[6] Some of these forms of interaction are crucial in various institutional contexts. These include, for example, "processing encounters," in which clients or customers (or other "outsiders") are managed by organizational functionaries in an institutional setting. Another noteworthy example consists of platform performances and collective celebrations in which large numbers of people are brought together in an organizational setting for a collective activity with a common focus of attention. In both of the above settings, clear differences in power are likely to be reflected in the way such patterns of interaction are structured.

On an even more general level the micro level social processes emphasized in symbolic interaction theory can readily be related to the institutional or social structural level if we accept the symbolic interactionist notion of social institutions as shared definitions of situations and roles that are widely understood and accepted, and that have endured long enough to become more or less standardized. But, as individuals perform these standardized roles, they do so with their own distinctive style, reflecting their efforts to project their own unique identity through their role performances. It is through their individualized role performances that individuals' particular identities fit into a larger social structure that transcends specific individuals and particular situations.

The creation of a social world that transcends specific individuals in particular places and times depends heavily on a widely shared language. In view of the

[6] Goffman's article, "The Interaction Order" (1983), was written as his presidential address that was scheduled to be delivered at the 1982 meeting of the American Sociological Association. Unfortunately, his deteriorating health prevented him from doing so. He died of cancer in November, 1982.

emphasis of symbolic interaction theory on language and communication, the following section will examine in more detail the way language is used in constructing an objective social world that exists independently of **particular** individuals and their subjective interpretations, role performances, and social relations.

Language, Social Reality, and the Cultural World

To become competent participants in our social world, even at a minimal level during childhood, requires that we internalize the language and other features of that world. Although the capacity for language may be regarded as innate or part of human nature, people are not programmed with any particular language at birth. Instead, we confront it initially as existing outside ourselves as something that must be learned. As noted earlier, George Herbert Mead believed language developed from gestures, and that its development was crucial in human evolution for enabling us to cooperate in adapting to our environment and establishing human communities. Going far beyond gestures, language consists essentially of a vast array of symbols—spoken, written, or encoded in electronic media—that we use to convey information and meanings to one another in either a personal or impersonal form. More than this, language is the foundation for all aspects of cultural creation and its reproduction or transformation.

The linguistic symbols making up our language are essential for us to represent the external world to ourselves, reflect on it within our subjective consciousness, and communicate about it with others. However, the symbols we use to think and talk about objects and events in the external world are certainly not equivalent to that world. The world would continue to exist even if we did not have representations of it in our consciousness. Our representations, however, may vary depending on our particular interests. Physical objects such as trees, for example, may be defined and interpreted in different ways by biologists, people in the lumber industry, environmentalists, poets, and hikers seeking shade from the sun. The physical object is the same regardless of the words used to refer to it or the meanings conveyed by such words.

In the same way, our understanding of an action, such as pointing a finger at something or shaking hands, or utterances such as "That's good news" or "I agree" or "Why?" are limited without knowledge of the specific context in which such actions or utterances are made. The social reality that is constructed through words requires an awareness of context and associated implicit assumptions for us to establish meaning and reach intersubjective understanding. This implicit knowledge develops in large part through practical experience plus practice in using the language. The ability to reach mutual understanding through communication is much greater when people have a background of shared experience. The less their background is shared, the greater would be the need to communicate to reach mutual understanding.

The symbolic world we create through communication is in many ways an arbitrary and self-contained world. Although words may refer to objects in the environment, words have a kind of virtual reality of their own as well. To explain the meaning of words typically requires the use of still other words, even though the objective reality to which the words refer exists independently of the socially constructed linguistic world, no matter how elaborate or "realistic" the linguistic formulation of a definition may seem to be. This is true for material objects as well as social events. The "linguistic turn" that Richard Rorty (1967) identified several years ago in philosophy has also occurred in social and cultural theory in recent years to emphasize the arbitrary and self-contained nature of the symbolic world constructed through language. If pushed to its logical conclusion, this emphasis leads us to a profound skepticism that we can ever have objectively valid or accurate knowledge of "the world as it is." This is because all that we know of "the world as it is" is perceived through the linguistic framework we use to interpret it, and this framework is developed and sustained through communication. (For a balanced treatment of these and related issues, see Rorty [1989] and Zito [1984].)

The diversity of languages throughout the world demonstrates the arbitrary nature of linguistic codes. No single language can be said to be more natural or basic than any other language, nor can any particular language be proven to reflect better the "real" nature of the external world. Of course, the language developed within different environments may vary in ways that reflect the variety and complexity of these environments. So, for example, we would expect people in Canada to make more linguistic distinctions among different forms of snow than people living in southern California. Even so, the connection between words and objective reality is arbitrary, not intrinsic. In other words, there is no intrinsic connection between the sound of a word or the way it looks when written and the object or idea that the word represents. A couple of exceptions will confirm the basic point: the words "pop" or "buzz" may perhaps actually resemble some natural sound that they describe. But for the vast majority of words, the sound of the word, or its appearance when written, has a purely arbitrary relationship to the object, event, or idea for which it stands. The meanings of words are sustained solely through social convention, and the clarification of meanings, when needed, typically involves the use of more words.

It is impossible to escape the symbolic world we create through our words, arbitrary though our definitions and interpretations may be. Although it may sometimes be possible to convey the meaning of a word by actually pointing to the objects or events they represent, or by demonstrating the behavior being described, words are still needed to indicate the specific features or aspects of the object or event to which a particular word refers. Thus, for example, by pointing to a dog or a tree, a building, or the moon, one may intend to call attention to size, color, condition, relation to other objects, or one's response to it, and words are required to make this clear. Similarly, individuals may learn how to deal with various aspects of the environment simply by imitating one another's behavior without verbal communication. But if one wants to communicate a specific message through one's actions, it is often necessary to call attention to the features of behavior that are relevant. The socialization process often involves a deliberate strategy of "showing and telling."

In contrast to the symbolic world that is socially constructed, there is, of course, the natural or physical world to which we must adapt—the world of day and night, seasonal changes, rain and storms, forests, mountains, rivers, coastlines, plants and animals, and other objects in the environment. Our bodies are also part of the world of nature, and their material existence as biological organisms is independent of the symbolic meanings or identities with which we clothe them. Thus, regardless of our social environment or identities, we shiver in the cold, perspire in the heat, get hungry and tired, experience pleasure and satisfaction through eating and sexual activity, and eventually grow old (despite social definitions that encourage us to try to preserve our youth). Obviously, the natural world does not depend on our social definitions for its existence. Although the Genesis story of creation explains the natural world as coming into being through the word of God, the words of human beings do not have this kind of potency. The world of nature exists independently of our social definitions and interpretations, including our bodies as biological organisms. On the other hand, the sociocultural world is materialized and embodied through human beings' activities. All aspects of the social and cultural world, ranging from tools and material technology to art and architectural styles, are created by human beings and would not otherwise exist. Moreover, the social world is literally embodied in our actions. We employ our bodies to perform our various social roles while at the same time being constantly attentive to our needs as biological organisms.

Language is essential for enabling us to interpret and adapt to the natural world, even though the world of nature would continue to exist without our definitions and interpretations. However, the natural world has been coded and classified by human beings through cultural symbols that help organize their responses to it. More than this, the natural world has been transformed by human beings for their own use on a massive scale, with the result that a large part of the material environment to which we must adapt is a socially constructed, or "built," environment. Thus, for example, legal codes define what geographical areas may be used for residential, commercial, or industrial development, where the lines are drawn between a city and a neighboring suburban municipality, and what regions are to be preserved in their natural state as wilderness or national parks for tourists seeking an escape from the "built environment" of congested urban areas.

In his analysis of how the social world is constructed, John Searle (1995) emphasized the distinction between "brute reality" (the world as it actually is, independent of any social definitions) and socially constructed reality that is based on shared social definitions. Although we obviously live in the "brute reality" of the physical world, our relation to this world is mediated through the symbolic definitions and interpretations that we superimpose on it. This superimposition leads us to transform various features of the physical world as we adapt to it, with the result that we must then adapt to the brute material reality of our built environment.

The nonmaterial aspects of culture that human beings create through words or other symbols is also a real world that can be distinguished from the objective physical reality of the material world, whether natural or humanly constructed. In the final analysis, however, even this nonmaterial or purely symbolic world also rests on a foundation in the real material world of "brute reality." Abstract concepts such as love, justice, discrimination, or subordination, are manifested in actions and interactions that can be empirically observed in the actual behavior of human bodies as people adapt and respond to the physical movements of other human bodies and to the natural world. In addition, the meanings of such abstract concepts as these are represented as the actual sounds of spoken words or as written (or printed) marks on paper (or a computer screen) that are produced when people talk or write about such concepts.

Most symbolic interactionists focus heavily on face-to-face interaction, which obviously involves the use of language. But it should also be emphasized that face-to-face communication always takes place against the background of a wider cultural landscape, reflecting implicit definitions and assumptions that also are dependent on language, but that may not be shared equally throughout society. Many of the social definitions making up our social world are encoded in objective material forms, such as written texts (books, magazines, journals, correspondence, papers, computer codes) and various cultural artifacts of all types, including, for example, signs, paintings, statues, monuments, video or audio tapes, computer diskettes, statistical records in file cabinets, and so on. Such artifacts are meaningful and significant because of what they signify, not the material form on which they are encoded. But once materialized in some form, these artifacts of culture exist outside the realm of subjective consciousness. Moreover, people vary greatly in terms of the scope of their subjective awareness of the innumerable types of encoded meanings that are part of their environment, as well as their level of personal engagement with them. For example, they may be "tuned in" to certain types of music or popular literature but be unaware (or only vaguely aware) of other types in which they haven't developed an interest.

The meanings that texts or other cultural artifacts have for people from a different social world may be quite different from the meanings they represented for their creators or those to whom they were intentionally directed. Thus, for example, the writings of St. Paul, Thomas Jefferson, Karl Marx, Émile Durkheim, or Martin Luther King will be likely to have different meanings for these authors, the audiences to whom their writings were directed, other contemporaries at the time, and scholars today who seek to interpret their writings as part of some specific project of historical interpretation. For historical figures, the (then) future consequences of their messages could not have been foreseen by them, even though the long-term (and unintended) significance of such texts for contemporary life may be the primary meaning that our contemporaries today read into them.[7]

[7] Pursuing this line of analysis would lead us into the area of hermeneutics, which involves the effort to understand the meanings of texts (or other cultural products) in the light of their particular historical context and the subjective experiences of their authors at the time. For a thorough and highly influential explanation of the application of hermeneutic methods to the social sciences and the humanities, see Hans-Georg Gadamer (1989). Gadamer's hermeneutic approach contrasts with the approach of those who seek to apply the methods of the natural sciences to the social sciences. As Gadamer makes clear, the hermeneutic method is crucial for the interpretation of all type of cultural products, including art as well as written texts. For a shorter treatment of the hermeneutic approach, see Roy J. Howard (1982).

Texts endure as an objective reality that may continue to be relevant and perhaps regarded as classic when people are able to read new and contemporary meanings into them. Thus, for example, contemporary readings of well-known and frequently cited texts, such as the Bible, the Constitution of the United States, and Karl Marx and Friedrich Engels's *Communist Manifesto*, generate meanings that people sometimes apply to social life today that may differ in significant ways from the meanings originally intended. Recognition of the enduring objective reality of texts and other cultural artifacts makes us aware that the social reality human beings construct extends far beyond their limited social circles or face-to-face encounters—and even beyond the far-reaching networks of social interaction through which contemporary macro-level social institutions are sustained.

Despite the arbitrary nature of language systems as described above, the social reality constructed through language not only links micro, meso, and macro levels of analysis but also past, present, and future generations. As our understanding of the social world grows, we learn more and more about the contributions of our predecessors and their legacy to our generation, just as our own contributions to the social world will have an impact, for good or ill, on future generations yet unborn. This expanded view of our social world is a major emphasis in Alfred Schutz's (1967) phenomenological perspective, which will be reviewed in more detail in the next chapter.

Despite the importance of language, what we need to know to be able to participate successfully in social life goes far beyond language, however. Successful interpretation of the meanings encoded in spoken or written words requires awareness of the context as well as the dictionary definitions of the words used. This implicit understanding draws heavily on common-sense assumptions that are developed through shared experiences, often unintentionally. The perspectives of phenomenological sociology and ethnomethodology, which will also be reviewed in the next chapter, focus explicitly on the unspoken (or unwritten) and taken-for-granted implicit assumptions that underlie successful communication and participation in all forms of social life.

Summary

Symbolic interaction theory is grounded in the foundation provided by George Herbert Mead's social behaviorism as reviewed in Chap. 3. As developed by Herbert Blumer, symbolic interaction theory emphasizes the ongoing interpretive process whereby people develop shared definitions that enable them to cooperate in responding to the particular situations in which they participate. In this perspective cultural definitions and institutional structures do not determine people's behavior but instead provide very broad frameworks within which people must improvise a great deal. Blumer's notion of social processes represented a critical reaction to the kind of structural determinism he believed was promoted by other perspectives, functional theory in particular.

In contrast to Blumer's emphasis on the fluid and improvised character of the interpretations developed through ongoing interaction, a more structural version of symbolic interaction theory emphasized the continuities in people's interpretations and identities from one situation to the next. This structural version was represented by Manford Kuhn's effort to measure the self-concept as well as by the affect control theory that David Heise developed to explain the strategies people use to insure consistencies in their perceptions of one another in their various roles. We also reviewed Norbert Wiley's notion of how people's current behavior incorporates their vision of their own future identity—an important process in identity construction that must be balanced with the symbolic interactionist emphasis on the reactions of others.

A broader view that incorporates both the ever-changing situational aspects of one's self-concept (as emphasized by Blumer) and the more stable aspects (as represented by Kuhn) was provided in McCall and Simmons' "role-identity" model. Their model emphasized people's idealized images of themselves in various social roles. The concept of the "prominence hierarchy" refers to the relatively stable array of role identities making up one's self-concept. The structure of the prominence hierarchy is influenced by long-term investments and commitments as well as by social support and one's own internal self-support. In contrast, the "salience hierarchy" consists of the role identities expressed in particular situations that reflect specific needs and opportunities of the moment. Even the relatively stable prominence hierarchy may undergo change in the long-run, however.

Our focus on the self-concept was continued with a review of Erving Goffman's dramaturgic approach to analyzing interaction processes. His perspective pointed explicitly to the strategies individuals use in staging role performances that are intended to express the image of themselves they want to convey and have validated by others. Goffman's perspective suggests that one's basic character consists essentially of an ensemble of various fronts one is able successfully to enact in different situations.

Goffman also emphasized that even the most carefully planned role performances are vulnerable to disruptions or "loss of face." The challenges of obtaining validation for a socially desirable identity are particularly acute for those with various types of stigma, based either on reputation or physical appearance. But no one is insulated from the risk of having their role performances disrupted or their identity claims undermined or challenged. Even so, people generally adhere to basic norms of tact and courtesy in accepting one another's identity claims. This means they are willing to overlook minor mishaps that may threaten one another's performances or undermine the definitions of the situation that others seek to project. Their willingness to collaborate in sustaining a particular definition of the situation is based on an implicit framework of mutual understanding regarding the type of social occasion in which they are involved. In addition, recurrent forms of face-to-face interaction may be structured by particular organizational or institutional contexts. Goffman's focus, however, was mostly on face-to-face interaction, not the macro-level institutional context.

The social world that human beings have created clearly includes far more than role performances or face-to-face interaction. In fact, the entire macro level cultural world is the product of a vast network of ongoing processes of interaction and interpretation. The socially constructed world includes the nonmaterial world of symbolic meanings and the dominant worldview shared throughout society as well as the material artifacts through which these meanings are expressed in objective form. These artifacts range from art and buildings to texts and tools.

In considering this more macro level view we focused explicitly on the use of language to create enduring texts of various kinds that exist as an objective reality outside individual consciousness and that can be analyzed independently of the ever-changing world of subjective experiences. In contrast to this focus on overt forms of communication and objective texts, our next chapter will review the perspectives of phenomenological sociology and ethnomethodology. Phenomenological sociology emphasizes the level of subjective consciousness, while ethnomethodology focuses on the way people make sense of one another's practical everyday activities on the basis of implicitly understood shared understandings of what these activities mean.

Questions for Study and Discussion

1. In what circumstances would you would expect people's interaction patterns to be fluid and unstructured (as emphasized by Blumer) as opposed to more structured? Give an example of each of these types of situations from your own experiences or observations.
2. Social reality is created through people's social definitions. Give an example of how some aspect of social reality (the meaning of a particular event, for example, or a person's identity) can be changed through a change in social definitions.
3. Applying the symbolic interactionist perspective to the formation of your own self-concept, identify the aspects of your identity that are related to your various social positions or institutional roles, your personal relationships, and your unique personal characteristics. Which of these are most important to you? Why? Which ones provide you with the greatest level of social support? Which ones do you intend to try to change in the future?
4. Discuss the dilemma people sometimes feel between trying to make a good impression on others (as analyzed by Goffman) versus just "being themselves." Under what circumstances are people most likely to be consciously concerned with making a good impression? Can you tell when people you know are just trying to "put up a good front" that differs from the way they usually act? How do you respond?
5. Would you agree or disagree that the various symbolic meanings incorporated in the overall culture of our society provide a common background for interpreting world events and a sense of connection with others we do not know personally? Why or why not? Could these meanings be extended to give us a sense of global connection? Explain.

Chapter 6
Phenomenological Sociology and Ethnomethodology: The Everyday Life World of Common Sense

In contrast to the emphasis of symbolic interaction theory on language and overt communication, the theoretical perspectives to be examined in this chapter—phenomenological sociology and ethnomethodology—concentrate on implicit and taken-for-granted assumptions that simply "go without saying." Like symbolic interaction theory, these perspectives tend to focus on the micro level but their implications extend to the meso and macro levels as well.

The importance of implicitly shared perspectives can readily be appreciated when we consider that everyday life conversations are often fragmentary and ambiguous and require some minimal knowledge of the context to be understood. Interpreting the meaning of both words and actions requires implicit background knowledge acquired through shared experiences. If an outsider has difficulty in understanding due to limited experience, an insider may be expected to explain. This explanation will employ words, and the ability to understand these words in context may require additional background information.

This linkage between communication and implicit knowledge is the basis for the well-established teaching technique of moving from the known to the unknown—a process in which explicit verbal instruction builds on students' implicit (sometimes nonverbal) knowledge acquired through their personal experience. But experienced and knowledgeable participants in the social world are likely to find verbal explanations to be superfluous. Such knowledge does not need to be spelled out in detail except for newcomers who need to learn "the way things are" or "the way we do things" in order to participate. Indeed, experienced participants may have negative reactions toward those who insist in "explaining the obvious" to them as if they were naive newcomers.

Such issues are major themes in this chapter. The specific theoretical perspectives to be covered are the following:

- The phenomenological perspective in sociology as represented by Alfred Schutz—This perspective deals with implicit, taken-for-granted forms of knowledge that are widely accepted as everyday "common sense." This shared knowledge contrasts with the unique details of each individual's own personal subjective experience. In comparison to symbolic interaction theory, the emphasis is more on the relation between experience and consciousness than the relation between language and discourse.

- The ethnomethodological perspective as developed by Harold Garfinkel—This perspective examines the strategies people use to create a sense of order as they engage in the routine practices of everyday life. It also stresses the importance of implicit practical knowledge that enables individuals to make sense of one another's actions without extensive verbal explanation.
- The "social construction of reality" perspective as developed by Peter Berger and Thomas Luckmann—This phenomenological perspective is consistent with symbolic interactionism, but it deals more explicitly with how the larger institutional structures of society are grounded in the routine practices and interaction patterns through which individuals' subjective consciousness is formed.

Phenomenological Sociology: Alfred Schutz's Contributions

As a philosophical concept **phenomenology** can be traced back to the pioneering work of Immanuel Kant and the long-term philosophical problem of how our knowledge of the world is based on our limited perceptions of it as these are filtered through the implicit schemas already in our minds. In a general sense we understand that our perceptions do not necessarily correspond precisely to the way the world **really** is. In everyday life, we unconsciously make allowances for the fact that the sounds and sights that register on our ears and eyes will vary according to our distance from their source. Kant's position was that in the final analysis it is impossible to know the world as it really is, in itself. Instead, all we can know is based on our **perceptions** of the world as they are filtered through our senses and organized through our particular cognitive frameworks.

As applied to sociology this perspective reflects the notion that the way we see and interpret the world is based largely on the formative influence of our social environment. The cultural world into which we are born provides not only the language we use to communicate but also the perceptual categories and cognitive and interpretive frameworks through which we actually perceive and make sense of our world. At the micro level children learn early in life from their parents and other adults how to name and respond to the various objects they encounter in their environment. American children, for example, may have a pet **dog** while German children would have a ***hund***, but both would learn the appropriate name, and both would learn to distinguish their pet from similar but larger and more dangerous animals called **wolves** (in English) that they might see at a zoo.

The way we see the world will reflect not only the cognitive and interpretive framework of the overall culture but also the specific subcultural influences associated with our particular racial or ethnic identity group, gender, social class, and so on. Thus, for example, the implicit, common-sense knowledge that African Americans may have about police officers in their community will differ from the knowledge that whites have, reflecting differences in their experiences and their interpretive frameworks. (Police officers will have their own distinct perspectives too.) Similarly, women and men experience the world differently, and so might be expected to differ in how they would interpret the same event. The consciousness of each individual person will vary from that of anyone else, despite similarities in personal characteristics or social background.

The relationship between an individual's unique consciousness and the "intersubjective" or shared consciousness that develops among people who share the same social world was explored in detail by Alfred Schutz (1967; Wagner, 1970; Schutz and Luckmann, 1973). Alfred Schutz was born in Germany in 1899 but came to the United States in 1939 (as did many other intellectuals as the Nazis acquired political power), where he taught at the New School for Social Research. Schutz was influenced by the German philosopher Edmund Husserl, whose work dealt primarily with subjective consciousness at the individual level. Schutz borrowed extensively from Husserl in analyzing the complex relations between the stream of consciousness that accompanies our ongoing lived experience and the way subjective meanings are established through reflection and interaction.

Personal Versus Intersubjective Consciousness

In *The Phenomenology of the Social World* (1967), Schutz's point of departure was a critique of Max Weber's analysis of social action. He noted that establishing the subjective meaning of an individual's action is not as simple as Weber had suggested. This is because it is impossible for anyone (even a sociologist) to enter someone else's stream of consciousness and have an identical subjective experience, even when the other person is well known to the observer and the action is being observed as it actually takes place. Even when the other person's behavior is accompanied by observable facial indicators of subjective states (joy, satisfaction, frustration, anger, sadness, and so on), this information would be perceived through the observer's own perceptual and cognitive framework. Thus the observer's experience could not be identical with that of the person being observed. The difficulties are even greater if the observer is limited (as sociologists often are) to observing the effects of the action, or hearing an account thereof, after it has taken place, as opposed to observing it as it actually occurs.

Schutz pointed out that Weber did not indicate whether the subjective meaning applies during the time that an action is taking place or after it has been completed. These are not necessarily identical. Moreover, unless one's current behavior is part of some intentional project, it may not necessarily have a specific subjective meaning. Routine activities are sometimes performed in a nonreflexive or absent-minded way that do not necessarily register in a person's subjective consciousness or reflect any particular meaning. The subjective stream of consciousness that accompanies lived experience is often in a state of flux and not directly related to the activity in which an individual is currently involved. People's minds wander as they perform routine activities, or they may focus on some past experience or future project that is not directly related to their current activities. This does not mean that current activities are meaningless. But the meaning may be implicit and not part of an individual's conscious awareness at the moment. In driving a car, for example, people's conscious attention may be focused more on their conversation with their fellow-passenger or what they plan to do when they arrive at their destination than on the routines involved in operating their vehicle.

To identify the subjective meaning of a particular action is likely to involve a break in the stream of consciousness as we reflect and interpret it in an appropriate frame of reference. Moreover, the meaning that is given may vary, depending on the frame of reference being used, and this may be influenced by the audience being addressed. For example, a popular rock musician on tour may describe a performance as "another stop on the road," "doing a gig," "making music," "making money," "demonstrating artistic creativity," "giving the audience what they want," "spending too much time away from home," or in various other ways. The unspoken meanings implied by these different explanations are quite different, even though they all apply to the same action. Similarly, reading a textbook may be defined as expanding one's knowledge or fulfilling course requirements.

Schutz's argument that attribution of meaning is a reflective process after an action takes place does not mean that the anticipated meaning of some goal-directed action cannot be defined in advance. However, the ultimate meaning in this case is not the action itself but the goal that will have been accomplished. Achieving this goal may then turn out to be the means for some other project in a longer time frame. Actions may thus have multiple meanings, some of which may be linked sequentially. For example, a student studies for an exam in the hope of learning the material plus getting a good grade, but the good grade is an intermediate goal that serves as the means for the longer range goal of earning a degree. This, in turn, may be the means for an even more distant goal, such as getting into graduate school or starting a career. Although individuals certainly reflect on the long-range significance or meaning of their various activities and projects from time to time, such reflection involves a break in the ever-changing stream of conscious experiences that accompany their actual behavior.

The temporal dimension is important not only because of the way our self-concepts develop and change through time but also because our experiences and conscious attention undergo continuous change over time. The vividness of present experiences gradually fade into memory. Detailed memories of recent experiences gradually displace older, less detailed ones. At the same time past experiences may subsequently be reinterpreted in the light of new experiences. Thus our mistakes and disappointments may later be reinterpreted as valuable lessons that helped develop our present character. Even when the results of experiences from the distant past are forgotten, they nevertheless leave sedimentary traces that contribute to our becoming the unique individuals that we are. This ongoing flow of subjective experiences that make up our current stream of consciousness can be seen as continuum that can be traced back to the very beginning of our conscious life.

When we recognize the uniqueness of each individual's background experiences and the specific trajectory of his or her life course as reflected in character and memory, we can appreciate why it is quite impossible for anyone to enter the stream of consciousness of another person or to have exactly the same subjective experience.

People's subjective understanding of one another is always limited, despite the high level of empathy they may have or how close they may feel to one another, because the background experiences that color their interpretations of the present are unique. Even so, people nevertheless manage to achieve sufficient level of mutual understanding that they can adjust to one another's actions, cooperate and communicate with one another, share emotional experiences, and even gain limited insights into some aspects of one another's subjective thoughts and feelings. Through common experiences, shared "stocks of knowledge" are developed that enable people to reach a certain level of mutual understanding. A critically important component of this implicitly shared knowledge is the language we use in communicating our subjective thoughts, feelings, intentions, and experiences—as emphasized in symbolic interaction theory. This process contributes to the accumulation of shared, or intersubjective, "stocks of knowledge" that are eventually taken for granted without additional discussion.[1]

In seeking to understand one another's subjective meanings, we typically make the assumption that other people's subjective experiences are probably similar to what ours would be in similar circumstances. This would apply even in the absence of communication and would include others who do not even share the same language. Thus, for example, when we observe television news stories that portray grieving parents in another country whose loved ones have been killed as a result of war or terrorism, we are able to understand and sympathize, despite the fact that our stream of consciousness as we hear and watch the news cannot be identical to the stream of consciousness of those who just received the bad news and are overcome with grief.

Meanings, Motives, and Accounts

The concept of **motive** is often used, both in everyday life and in sociological analysis, to try to grasp the subjective meaning of another person's action. Schutz distinguished between two clearly different meanings of this concept: the "in order to" motive and the "because" motive. The "in order to" motive is future-oriented and involves explaining an action in terms of the goal or project for which it is being undertaken. In contrast, the "because" motive involves looking to the past to identify background experiences that contributed to the development of the action being analyzed. As Schutz put it, "The difference... between the two kinds of motive.... is that the in-order-to motive explains the act in terms of the project, while the genuine because-motive explains the project in terms of the actor's past experiences." (Schutz, 1967:91) His example is a murder explanation—a common challenge in

[1] The importance of the implicit "stocks of knowledge" that people employ as competent participants in various forms of social life is a major emphasis on Anthony Giddens' (1984) structuration theory—a theoretical orientation that will be pursued in more detail in Chap. 17. He contrasted this "practical" type of knowledge with "discursive" knowledge that involves verbal communication.

criminology and in actual crime investigations. An explanation using an "in-order-to" motive might be that the goal was to get the victim's money and then prevent the victim from contacting the police, while an explanation of the "because" type of motive might focus on the criminal's poverty, the prior influence of criminal companions, or inadequate socialization due to parental neglect. However, the murderer's conscious awareness at the time may have been focused on not getting caught while getting the money, as opposed to any consideration of background "because" influences. Subsequently, the action may be interpreted by the individual or by others in the light of earlier experiences which are seen after the act as a "because" explanation. If the alleged murderer subsequently makes reference to poverty, criminal peers, or other background factors in an effort to rationalize the murder, others are likely to be skeptical and to see this as an effort to shift blame when caught and questioned. With regard to the in-order-to motive, questions can be raised as to whether the murderer intended from the beginning to kill the victim, decided to do so on the spur of the moment to silence the victim, or did so accidentally when the robbery did not go as planned or the victim fought back. Such questions beg for additional analysis in providing an adequate account.

For some actions these two types of motives may seem more closely related than in the case of the two different explanations of murder. For example, a student studies hard **in order to** earn a high grade for the course. But the time and effort spent in preparing for the test may have resulted **because** the instructor indicated the test would be difficult and urged the students to study diligently. To push the explanation even further, the student may be committed to earning the highest grade possible **in order to** get into graduate school or qualify for a competitive scholarship. But these ambitious goals may also be explained **because** of his or her parents' strong emphasis on educational achievement or the student's own past experience in being rewarded for academic accomplishment. Both types of explanations could be offered, depending on the context. Such explanations may be incorporated in the **accounts** people are sometimes expected to provide of their own behavior. (The concept of accounts will be examined in more detail in connection with the ethnomethodological perspective.) At the same time observers (or social scientists) may be able to identify possible motives of which individuals are unaware.

The question of motivations and other aspects of subjective meaning are often of interest to other parties. In addition to trying to understand or account for our own behavior, people frequently make attributions regarding the motives of others, despite the difficulties involved in understanding what goes on in anyone else's subjective consciousness. In addition to simple curiosity, we may have practical reasons for wanting to understand how to motivate people, perhaps because of an interest in influencing their behavior. In any case, whether the motivations we attribute are consistent with the conscious motivations of the person whose behavior we are trying to understand or predict is always an empirical question that may be difficult to answer.

Different people have varying (and sometimes conflicting) interests in explaining their own motives or the motives of others. In the case of an accused murderer brought to trial, for example, efforts to provide explanations (including both **in-order-to** and **because** motives) will likely differ for the individual accused, the arresting officer, the state's attorney, the defense attorney, the victim's family, and the alleged perpetrator's own family. All of these parties are likely to have definite opinions about the motives and the state of mind of the murderer, even though none of them actually witnessed the murder or could know exactly what the alleged perpetrator's state of mind was at the time. Even when an individual is being observed in the actual performance of an action, the observer's ability to understand the action is limited, since the observer's ongoing stream of consciousness while viewing the action will differ from that of the actor performing it.

Mutual Understanding in Personal Versus Impersonal Relations

Despite the difficulties in reaching mutual understanding, the language people use to attribute motives and other kinds of subjective experiences (intentions, feelings, goals, wishes) makes it possible to develop a common frame of reference through which a certain level of mutual understanding may be possible, even if limited and "through a glass darkly." But despite its opaque nature, people's ability to understand one another through the intersubjective consciousness they share is indeed sufficient for them to be able to influence one another (even though the influence sometimes turns out not to be exactly as intended), to make ongoing adjustments to one another's behavior, and sometimes even to glimpse at least part of what is going on in one another's minds.

Schutz (1967:163–172) identified the highest level of mutual understanding as a "thou" orientation. This occurs in face-to-face relationships when the parties involved intentionally seek to "tune in" and share one another's subjective thoughts and feelings. Such relationships are the type Cooley referred to as "primary group" relations. When people share this kind of mutual orientation, they form a "we-relationship" which can be contrasted with the less personal orientations involved in "they-relationships." In face-to-face relationships people are able to gain a level of mutual understanding of one another's subjective experiences that is much greater than in more impersonal relations. They can literally "read" one another's faces, which are highly expressive of their current subjective states, as well as communicate their thoughts and feelings—which, of course, may or may not always be consistent with their facial expressions. This face-reading process can occur in any kind of face-to-face encounter, but the details will be much more extensive in primary group relations as well as the background experiences that may help each party to account for the thoughts and feelings that they attribute to one another.

But even in the close encounter of a "we relationship," the ongoing subjective streams of consciousness of the parties involved will not be identical. When I experience myself speaking to you, I cannot have the same experience as you have in listening to me. Nevertheless, even though mutual understanding of one another's subjective experiences is always limited, it is greater in close personal relationships than in other types. However, when participants in a "we-relationship" go their separate ways, their mutual awareness of one another's subjective experiences and states of consciousness is broken, and all that remains are the memories—until they meet again. Although their memories may overlap considerably, they will not be identical. If their subsequent communication are by telephone, letter, or e-mail, the immediacy of face-to-face encounters cannot be duplicated. And shared memories inevitably fade over time unless renewed by additional face-to-face contacts.

In contrast to "we-relationships" with mutual "thou" orientations, Schutz's concept of "they-relationships" describes encounters in which individuals' orientations toward one another are more limited or impersonal (Schutz, 1967:176–186). In such secondary relationships people may be in one another's presence, read one another's facial expressions, and actually influence one another, but they do not relate to one another as unique persons. Instead, they relate in terms of general roles associated with their positions in the social structure. Examples include the relation between a movie-goer and ticket taker, or a store clerk and customer, or a flight attendant and an airline passenger. These are extreme examples of impersonal relations with minimal levels of verbal communication. In between the extremes, relationships vary greatly in terms of how much individuals actually seek to understand one another as individual persons in their encounters with one another, or how much eye contact they regard as appropriate.

Moreover, relationships may change over time from "they-relationships" to "we-relationships" and then back again. For example, students and professors initially see one another in rather impersonal terms, but over the course of a semester personal relationships sometimes develop. Such relationships usually end when the course is over, and the students and the professor will thereafter see one another as "former professors" and "former students." In a successful employment interview, however, the relationship may change during the course of the interview from an impersonal encounter to a relationship that both parties anticipate will probably be longer-lasting and perhaps somewhat more personal, though within limits. The same pattern of ebb and flow may also be seen in long-term relationships between couples who divorce, neighbors who move, attorneys and their clients, co-workers, ex-lovers, former "best friends" whose lives move in different directions, and casual acquaintances whose paths eventually diverge.

The detailed mutual understanding that develops in "we-relationships" is not generalizable to the larger social world. Despite the similarities in best friend, lover, and family relationships everywhere, people generally see their relationships with their own friends and families as distinctive and unique. In contrast, knowledge based on "they-relationships" is more general and more generalizable. For example, experiences with various professors or students, physicians or patients, social workers or clients, fellow members of one's religious group, store clerks, airline flight attendants, and persons in other roles provide knowledge regarding how people in general will behave in such positions. However, detailed personal knowledge of the individuals performing these various roles is often lacking.

Contemporaries, Predecessors, and Successors

If we move beyond the range of our own personal experiences in both personal and impersonal encounters, a comprehensive description of the social world would also include all of our contemporaries throughout our society and beyond—plus our predecessors from previous generations and our successors in future generations (Schutz, 1967:139–150; 207–214). All of these "others" are relevant for a phenomenological analysis because they are included in our subjective awareness of the social world as well as the intersubjective understanding we share with others.

Our knowledge of particular persons beyond our own social circle is likely to be based on reputation and thus limited to second-hand reports by people we know (whose information may also be second-hand) or by the news media. Or, we may be aware of many people we don't know personally through their cultural products that become part of the public domain (movies, songs, books, articles), or in some cases we may view their television performances. Beyond the range of this indirect knowledge about particular individuals, our mental images of our contemporaries are limited to impersonal and anonymous "ideal types" whose roles are associated with the various positions that make up our society (Schutz, 1967:181–207). Thus, for example, we have a general awareness that individuals throughout the country are involved in performing roles in their local contexts as school teachers, parents, students, police officers, physicians, city officials, building contractors, bureaucratic administrators, bank officials, political leaders, baby sitters, store clerks, newspaper and television reporters and editors, social workers and their clients—the list could go on and on. We may know in general terms what these various roles involve, and we often make various assumptions about the types of people who perform them, even though they are far beyond the range of our own personal experience.

The social world of our intersubjective awareness also includes a general awareness of past generations. Specific knowledge of the past varies greatly for different people. Many people have heard tales of late great grandparents or even earlier ancestors from their parents or grandparents or done their own "family tree" research. Probably most Americans also are aware of the historic roles played by George Washington, Thomas Jefferson, Abraham Lincoln, Thomas Edison, Henry Ford, Franklin D. Roosevelt, Elvis Presley, and Martin Luther King, for example. Beyond this, people can identify various historical ideal-type figures such as pilgrims, settlers, pioneers, inventors, writers, leaders of historic social movements, Civil War soldiers, former presidents, and so on.

Many of our predecessors have left an enduring legacy of various works that they themselves produced, ranging from famous paintings such as the Mona Lisa to the plays of Shakespeare, the music of J. S. Bach, the writings of Thomas Jefferson, and the innumerable tools and other artifacts preserved in museums. All of these cultural products "carry" or symbolize objective meaning which at one level we can understand in our own subjective consciousness. With a vivid historical imagination we might even be able to imagine some aspects of the life experiences of past generations. Obviously, however, we cannot experience the subjective stream of consciousness of these historical figures as they were involved in the creation of the enduring cultural products we now observe. We may make inferences regarding their motivations, both "in-order-to" motives and "because" motives, but such inferences may or may not be "on target." Highly knowledgeable historians may even disagree among themselves on such issues, even while admiring and appreciating their long-term significance.

In contrast to the world of our predecessors, which is now closed and unchangeable, and the world of our contemporaries, which is partially open and contingent on choices not yet made and circumstances not yet determined, the world of our successors is one about which our subjective understanding is obviously limited. We know in general terms that our generation and all our contemporaries will eventually be replaced by future generations, and we tend also to assume that our successors will probably be like us in many ways, but no doubt different in other ways. Yet, the world of the future is open and unknown. Unlike the past, it is not yet determined, even though we may anticipate the continuation of present trends. But the unknown possibilities that lie beyond the range of our vision make the world of future generations appear to us as a realm of freedom and unrealized (and perhaps unlimited) potential—or otherwise (Schutz, 1967:214).

People vary greatly in terms of their conscious concerns for the needs of future generations and their sense of commitment to them. Political leaders promote policies that they claim will preserve and protect the environment or Social Security for future generations. But rhetorical references such as these are not the same as knowledge about the actual life experiences of future generations. Moreover, our concerns for the future are always constrained by the need to deal with the problems and challenges of the present. Although we know that the world of future generations will be affected by the legacy we leave, for good or for ill, our ability to predict the long-range impact of our own actions is limited.

Phenomenological Perspective on Sociological Knowledge

A final important point from Schutz's (1967) phenomenological perspective has to do with the nature of sociological knowledge. Schutz recognized the limitations that sociologists, like all other people, face in achieving the in-depth understanding of other people's subjective consciousness that is possible in genuine "we-relationships" where participants share mutual "thou" orientations. This insight seems inconsistent with the optimistic expectations regarding the possibilities for deepening our sociological understanding through participant observation research leading to ethnographic "thick descriptions" of the ways of life among particular people in their local setting. This type of qualitative research is often promoted by symbolic interactionists as being able to provide in-depth insights that cannot be captured through the more impersonal strategy of survey research. Although ethnographic research may indeed reveal interesting details that might be missed in survey research, it is important to recognize that the understanding researchers may gain regarding social processes they observe and document is likely to differ from insiders' own collective self-understanding. In fact, insiders themselves may be expected to vary in terms of their understanding of themselves.

When sociologists are involved in a participant observation or ethnographic research project, their research interests and motivations may be expected to be quite different from those of the people they observe, and this will color the level and type of mutual understanding that they develop. At the same time, researchers cannot avoid observing and participating as fellow human beings, and thus their perceptions will reflect their own cognitive frameworks as shaped by their particular background. With survey research data that are not based on direct observation, the difficulties of inferring particular details of individuals' subjective consciousness or experiences are even greater.

Since it is not possible to achieve complete in-depth understanding of other people's subjective consciousness, Schutz (1967:215–250) proposed that sociological knowledge should be based on the ideal-type form of understanding, as opposed to assuming that the details of the subjective consciousness of particular individuals can be accurately grasped. This strategy is, of course, consistent with Max Weber's "ideal-type" method, but Schutz went beyond Weber in explaining why this approach is necessary and appropriate for sociological analysis. Sociological knowledge for Schutz does **not** consist primarily in the details of a particular social situation or the specific subjective experiences or meanings of the participants involved. Instead of "thick descriptions" of specific individuals, their relationships, and their unique social worlds, the goal of sociological research and analysis should be to identify patterns of action and relationships that can be associated with general social types.

The ideal-type method used by sociologists is not the same as the generalizations used in everyday life, since the ideal types identified by sociologists will reflect their own intellectual interests and theoretical frameworks. Some aspects of individuals' subjective consciousness may indeed become relevant, particularly when expressed in an objective form that may influence others, but a particular sociologist's focus on other people's subjective consciousness will reflect his or her own distinctive interests and theoretical orientation. This means that the sociologist's subjective interpretation of an individual's action will by no means be the same as that individual's own subjective interpretation. Moreover, sociologists with different theoretical orientations are likely to vary in their interpretations.

Despite Schutz's emphasis on the uniqueness of each individual's subjective consciousness, his argument regarding the ideal-type nature of sociological knowledge is important for the accumulation of knowledge that can be generalized beyond the level of specific individuals and their unique subjective consciousness. At the same time, it recognizes that sociologists' efforts to interpret people's consciousness reflect their own particular interests and personal biases. The next perspective to be reviewed focuses even more on overt behavior than subjective consciousness as such.

Ethnomethodology

Despite the uniqueness of each individual's subjective consciousness, when people participate in the same social world they develop shared perspectives that enable them to adjust to one another appropriately. Through their shared or intersubjective consciousness, they are usually able to interpret one another's behaviors reasonably well and to respond appropriately, even without overt discourse regarding meanings and motives. When breakdowns or misunderstandings occur, participants typically are able to repair the breakdown and restore the normal flow of activity. This emphasis on implicitly shared understandings might suggest that the need for explicit discussion or explanation signals a breakdown or misunderstanding that must be repaired if the collective activity is to continue. Ethnomethodology is a distinctive type of sociological analysis that focuses on how people manage to make sense of one another's actions (at least most of the time) and adjust their own behavior appropriately without the need for explicit explanations. This process employs implicitly understood frames of reference as highlighted in the phenomenological perspective. The term **ethnomethodology** literally means the "methods of people"—and it refers to the methods people use in creating and sustaining a subjective sense of the orderliness of the social world. Like Blumer's symbolic interactionist perspective, ethnomethodology can be contrasted with macro level perspectives that treat the social structure as external to, or as existing independently of, the deliberate actions of the participants whose actions constitute it.

Harold Garfinkel (1967), who contributed to the founding of ethnomethodology, drew heavily on the phenomenological perspective in emphasizing the implicit common sense "stocks of knowledge" that people routinely use in the ordinary practices of everyday life. He was critical of the notion that institutional structures exist on their own, determining people's behavior independently of their interpretations and intentions. Of course, individuals themselves may influence one another's behavior through the use of positive or negative sanctions or through persuasive forms of interaction. The key point, however, is that the orderliness and interdependence of people's actions and relationships are not produced by an external structure that exists independently of the actions of its participants. Instead, social order is the outcome of members' skilled accomplishments as competent participants in the social world. Although the influence of some participants may carry more weight than others, it is through their own intentional and collaborative actions that they are able to create and sustain a sense of external order.

The successful construction of the social world through people's interdependent actions is an ongoing process that is grounded in their shared interpretive frameworks and implicit common-sense assumptions, including their beliefs and assumptions regarding the orderliness of the social world and its structural framework. Acting on the basis of these implicit beliefs and assumptions, people's actions and relations with one another actually create (and reproduce) the external orderliness and the structural properties whereby such beliefs are sustained. The basic theoretical question, then, has to do with the practical methods people use to establish and maintain this sense of structured order, especially since a great deal of the common sense knowledge that is used in this process is implicit and simply taken for granted.

To take an obvious example, it is not necessary for people sharing the same language to negotiate about which language to use; they simply know. Anyone who has traveled in other countries with a different language can appreciate the challenges experienced from the lack of this elementary knowledge. Another common example is the implicit turn-taking rule in conversations, especially among people who are roughly equal in status. This refers to the expectation that people will take turns in contributing to a conversation, as opposed to talking non-stop on the one hand or remaining silent on the other. People also have an implicit understanding of the nonverbal reactions that are felt and displayed (often unconsciously) in facial expressions. This leads them to adjust their contributions to a conversation appropriately when their partners seem to be experiencing confusion, disagreement, anger, boredom, sadness, joy, surprise, or other emotions. Such adjustment is likely to be particularly noticeable when these emotional reactions appear to be strong and overwhelming.

Reliance on implicit knowledge also applies to the larger world beyond face-to-face or personal relations. Thus we expect people in the United States to drive on the right hand side of the street (but not in England). In institutional contexts, we expect the people with whom we interact in various establishments such as restaurants, supermarkets, and university offices, for example, to perform the usual functions associated with these positions, even though we do not know them personally or by name. If we give a clerk at the counter in a fast-food restaurant a \$10.00 bill to pay for our \$5.65 meal, we anticipate getting \$4.35 back in change, and we both understand that no tip is needed. This is part of the common-sense implicit knowledge that we employ without thinking and without negotiating the terms of the exchange in advance.

Reciprocity of Perspectives

In both personal and impersonal relationships, our heavy reliance on implicit assumptions involves the notion of the **reciprocity of perspectives** (Cicourel, 1973:34–35; 52–53). This means simply that people make mutual assumptions that they would experience a particular situation in essentially the same as that of other people in the same situation for all practical purposes. The details of individuals' subjective consciousness are not identical, of course; however, their perceptions and interpretations overlap sufficiently for them to understand how others are likely to experience the particular situation in which they are involved and to anticipate one another's behaviors with enough accuracy to adjust appropriately.

We make such common-sense assumptions without even thinking about it, and this reciprocity of perspectives enables us usually to accomplish the routine business of everyday life without great difficulty. Thus, with the example of the fast-food meal again, we know the procedures involved in ordering our meal at the counter in a fast-food restaurant like McDonalds and so do not go sit at a table and wait for someone to come and take our order. As another example, in a large city's subway system, an observer can readily distinguish the regular riders and the tourists. Those who use the subway to commute to work every day follow their habitual routine without even thinking as they purchase their card or token, insert it at the turnstile, and then wait at the appropriate place on the platform. Visitors, in contrast, can readily be spotted as they study the posted instructions in detail to try to figure out how the system works.

The reciprocity of perspectives is learned, often unconsciously, through actual experience as a participant in the social world. Much of this practical knowledge is based on informal observation of others and trial and error rather than on formal instruction. Based on their shared experiences, people with similar backgrounds tend to make certain assumptions about one another, and the fact that they are usually correct in anticipating one another's actions and responses helps insure the taken-for-granted orderliness of the social world. If these assumptions turn out to be incorrect, participants will then need to adjust their perspectives in order to restore orderliness as they coordinate their actions in adapting to the situation they face.

Even among people with roughly similar backgrounds, or who know one another well, maintaining reciprocity of perspectives and the orderliness of social life can be a challenge. Maintaining a sense of order is always contingent on people's less-than-perfect abilities to interpret and predict one another's responses. When serious misunderstandings and breakdowns occur frequently, or if they persist despite people's attempts to repair them, the social world is likely to appear disorganized and unpredictable, at least in part. In extreme cases people's actions and responses literally make no sense. In such situations people experience a sense of discomfort and frustration and are unsure of what to do or how to respond. Faced with uncertainty, their attention shifts from simply "going with the flow" to attempting to figure out what is happening so that they can attempt to restore a sense of order. Everyday life is filled with numerous distractions and lapses in routines, such as unexplained flight delays, automobile accidents, unexpected phone calls or visits to our home by salespeople, accidentally bumping into someone in the hallway, or simple misunderstandings among friends about being too busy to talk at the moment or when to meet for lunch. Misunderstandings and breakdowns provide an occasion actually to observe and analyze the methods used to re-establish order. Sometimes this occurs when individuals offer explanations of their puzzling behavior, either by way of apology or justification, before they attempt to realign their actions.

One strategy that Garfinkel and other ethnomethodologists proposed for demonstrating how order is restored is through the use of **breaching experiments**. This involves a deliberate effort to violate expectations or to disrupt some social occasion so as to analyze the interaction and behavior patterns whereby individuals attempt to make sense of the situation and restore order. Such a disruption may be as simple as questioning implicit assumptions. A simple type of breaching experiment is to pretend not to understand the common sense meaning of a statement. For example, if a person describes having a flat tire, the experimenter then says, "What do you mean by a flat tire?" (Garfinkel, 1967:42). We can easily imagine that if the experimenter persists in "misunderstanding" or argues that the tire is flat only on the bottom, the likely reaction will be an irritated response such as "You know what I mean." Persistent questioning or refusal to understand the common-sense meaning of statements inevitably leads to frustration. The other party's response may be to dismiss the question as crazy—unless a "reasonable" explanation is eventually provided.

Another type of breaching example is to behave deliberately in an inappropriate way so as to observe people's reactions, such as trying to bargain with a cashier at an American supermarket check-out counter over the price of some item. Such behavior is clearly inappropriate in the local Wal-Mart, but it would be quite appropriate with a street vendor in a Mexican village or a homeowner at a suburban garage sale. Still another breaching experiment reported by Garfinkel (1967:47–49) was for students to act like strangers or guests when going home to visit their parents—asking permission to check the refrigerator for some food, for example, or wondering where to sleep. It is not difficult to imagine parents' response to such behavior, or to visualize how these reactions will change when an explanation is offered that the strange behavior was part of a sociological experiment.

In most of the typical or routine situations of everyday life, people manage to relate to one another appropriately and adapt to their environment without being expected to negotiate or explain every specific detail of their activities. But sometimes there is breakdown, confusion, or misunderstanding. When this happens, people must realign their perspectives in their efforts to establish (or re-establish) at least a minimal degree of mutual understanding and order. One important strategy for doing this is simply to provide an **account** for one's actions—that is, to explain one's intentions and motives or give some type of rationale—or to request an account from the other party.[2]

In theory, people are generally expected at all times to be able to provide some type of account or explanation of their actions if necessary; this is what it means for actions to be purposeful or meaningful, or to "make sense." In routine situations such accounts are unnecessary because the meaning is implicitly understood. However, accounts are more likely to be expected—and given—when people deviate, either accidentally or intentionally, from commonly understood expectations. When a person makes an error, he or she may apologize and explain what was intended. Or, if a person deliberately engages in some novel form of behavior, he or she may feel that some justification is needed, particularly if an adjustment is required on the part of other people. If an explanation is not offered, observers may ask for one.

When people offer explanations of their actions they sometimes make reference to their motives, particularly the "in-order-to" type as explained by Schutz. In other words, individuals explain the goals they hope to accomplish. Or, they may explain

[2] This notion of being able to "account" for one's actions is an important aspect of Giddens' (1984) concept of agency in his structuration theory. For Giddens, the term refers to the ability of individuals to "rationalize," or give appropriate reasons for, their actions if asked for an explanation. (Giddens' perspective on the reciprocal interdependence of agency and structure will be explained more fully in Chap. 17.)

how they expect others to respond. "Because" motives may also be used, especially if a person wants to deflect blame for inappropriate behavior. (e.g., "The devil made me do it.") In general, however, "because" motives may be used to suggest that present behavior is consistent with past behavior or reflects the individual's identity or the type of person he or she is (or wants to be). Or, explanations may refer to specific expectations of others even when such expectations deviate from established routines. ("This is different from what I usually do in this situation, but it is what I thought you wanted.") But a deviation need not necessarily be explained. Instead individuals simply assume that others will believe there must be a good reason for it and will not question it. Whether or not explicit accounts are expected or provided, there may be significant discrepancies in people's understanding of the same event of which they may or may not be consciously aware. If they are aware but the discrepancies are not seen as relevant to the situation at hand or do not disrupt the flow of activity, participants simply overlook them or let them pass.

In contrast to minor disruptions and misunderstandings that may be repaired through an explanation or simply overlooked, there are occasions where more elaborate accounts and justifications are needed, especially if a person is trying to influence others to change their behavior in a major way, or to persuade them to accept a change in her or his own behavior. For example, someone who experiences a religious conversion, or who gets involved in social movements or political activities designed to promote change, may develop elaborate justifications for such behavior which he or she is eager to share with anyone who will listen. Such justifications may include reference to the core of one's own identity (plus appeals to the core identities of others one is trying to influence) or to widely shared values. Thus, for example, people on both sides of the abortion controversy will seek to defend their position in terms of the need to "take a stand" for sacred or ultimate values in which they believe deeply, whether these be "pro-life" values or "pro-choice" values.

Context and Meaning

Whether explicit accounts or justifications are provided or not, the meaning or significance of any action depends on its being interpreted in a larger context or framework of meaning. Garfinkel (1967:76–79) used the concept of the "documentary method" to refer to the way in which actions may be seen as reflecting or referring implicitly to—or documenting—this larger and usually implicit frame of reference. Thus, for example, an action such as lifting weights or engaging in aerobic exercises would hardly seem to make any sense except as related to a whole complex set of beliefs and strategies involving efforts to keep in "good" physical condition, control one's weight, prepare for competitive sports, preserve one's youthful appearance, or fulfill someone else's expectations. The specific action is thus made meaningful as a kind of "documentation" of this larger set of definitions, beliefs, goals, or purposes, as well as reflecting the weight lifter's own personal identity.

Similarly, encounters between social workers or attorneys and clients, for example, or police officers and suspects, medical doctors and patients, or teenagers and their parents are interpreted by both parties in the relationship in terms of broader implicit frameworks of meaning. In such situations, these meanings may not be the same because of the difference in the roles of each party and the specific personal interests they have. Each will interpret and adapt to the expected behavior of the other in terms that are relevant to his or her own goals and interests. In this way a specific encounter can be seen as reflecting participants' orientations to a larger institutional framework of meaning, even though their perceptions of this institutional framework are by no means the same.

Garfinkel emphasized that people must continuously interpret and reinterpret everyday life events as they seek to make sense of them. One unusual experiment he reported involved having undergraduates talk with a "counselor" about a personal problem to get some advice (Garfinkel, 1967:76–103). Briefly, the subjects were to explain their problem and then ask questions to which a simple "yes" or "no" answer could be given. They were allowed ten questions. After each question they could reflect on the "counselor's" response to the previous question in formulating their next question. Unknown to the subjects, the responses of the "counselor" were evenly and randomly divided between "yes" or "no" answers in advance. Garfinkel's findings revealed clearly that subjects managed to make sense of the random "yes" or "no" responses, incorporating them into their own developing interpretation of how the counselor's "advice" was relevant in helping them deal with the personal problem they presented. In some cases, students admitted to being puzzled by the "counselor's" advice, but they attributed this to the counselor's lack of knowledge of some of the particulars of their situation and anticipated that their puzzlement would be resolved as the session continued. In other words, they "made sense" of what were literally random "yes" or "no" responses to their questions. Later, when told the nature of the experiment, they reinterpreted the session in ways that validated their earlier skepticism and frustration. Despite their lack of knowledge of what was really going on, the subjects assumed that they and the "counselor" were operating from a common frame of reference, and they "made sense" of the "counselor's" random responses in terms of this assumption. The basic point about "real life" that this experiment reveals is that people's need to "make sense" of what is going on in the social world leads them to make assumptions about one another that are sufficient for their purposes at hand but not necessarily accurate.

The importance of the larger context can be seen even in the course of a casual conversation at the micro level. The specific meanings of the messages exchanged in the conversation are not entirely self-contained, nor does any given statement necessarily carry the same meaning in different situations. This applies particularly to "indexical" words which require knowledge of the specific context for their meaning (Garfinkel, 1967:4–7). Perhaps the most obvious type of example of an indexical expression is the first person personal pronoun ("I"), which necessarily varies for every individual who uses it. Similarly, what I mean by "now" as I write this sentence will differ from your "now" when you read it. So, for example, a written statement such as "The weather today is no good to do what we planned" could be seen as laden with indexical expressions, since the meaning of "weather," "today," "we," and "what we planned" cannot be understood without knowledge of the larger context. Indexical expressions such as these can be contrasted with more objective statements which can be generalized beyond a specific context. For example, a statement such as "It is usually warmer when the sun is shining than when it is cloudy" is an objective statement that can be generalized. But even the implied meaning of an objective statement like this vary in different contexts, depending in part on the season and whether some type of outdoor activity is being considered.

A great deal of communication is not very explicit, particularly verbal communication. Instead, there are often incomplete sentences or ideas, sudden shifts in topics, vague and indirect references, and often extensive use of fill-ins such as "you know," "etc.," "like," and "so on." Although a grammarian would find ample reason to criticize everyday speech, people engaged in a conversation typically have no trouble filling in as necessary to make sense of what is being said—or to ask for clarification when needed. In some cases, however, the meaning of an event or a statement is not immediately clear. We may sometimes question the meaning immediately ("What do you mean by that?" or "I wonder what that means."). Or we may wait for the meaning to become clear as the conversation or activity develops. Or we may need to reinterpret statements or actions when subsequent developments make it clear that our original interpretation was incorrect. The reliance on implicit background knowledge in interpreting the ambiguous and fragmentary nature of verbal statements demonstrates how the major focus of ethmethodology may be seen as complementing the symbolic interactionist focus on overt communication. So, for example, a person going for a work-out at the gym after work or school may mention casually that it is time to "go work up a sweat," and people would probably understand that the person is going to the gym to exercise.

Since at least the early 1970s, "conversation analysis" has become a specialized area of inquiry that has stimulated research in both institutional and noninstitutional settings. This involves an extremely micro-level exploration of the flow of conversational encounters in which expressions like "uh oh," "hmmm," huh," "you know," "etc.", pauses, laughter, body language and eye contact, interruptions, and overlapping talk are recorded and analyzed (e.g., see Button and Lee, eds. 1987; Psathas, 1995). The goal of such research is to document how conversations are actually accomplished. Despite the clear micro-level focus, the challenge of understanding how order is achieved in face-to-face conversations can be seen in some ways as being parallel to the more macro-level process of how the social order of society is maintained. Without some implicit consensus on how the flow of talk should be managed, it is clear that a sense of social order (or orderliness) would be difficult to sustain.

One of the basic implicit rules governing conversations, particularly among those who are roughly equal in status, is the rule regarding turn-taking. Up to a point, however, acceptable departures from this rule are allowed, especially for individuals with a story to tell. The shift between routine turn-taking in a small group setting and storytelling is typically accomplished without explicit verbal negotiation as the story-teller increases voice volume and expands the range of eye contact, and as others turn their faces and their attention toward the story teller and maintain their silence. However, the story-teller sometimes fails to capture everyone's attention, or the story fails to hold their interest. This failure is likely to be signaled when someone interrupts. The interruption may be ignored, as listeners increase the intensity of their focus on the story-teller, or it may lead to negative sanctions ("Stop interrupting."). Alternatively, the attention of some may shift to the interrupter, in which case the original story may be truncated or perhaps continued with a subgroup. (For an analysis of how interruptions in conversations are handled through the techniques of conversational analysis, see Schegloff, pp. 287–321 in J. H. Turner, ed. 2001) But despite the contingencies and the open-ended nature of the process, participants nevertheless manage to make the micro-level adjustments that enable them to sustain their interaction and make sense of what is going on. This will continue until they decide to disband, a process that may be instigated when one or more participants signals a tentative intention to withdraw (looking at watch, stepping back) and then initiates departure rituals ("Time to go now; see you next time."), others follow, and they then go their separate ways.

The interpretive process may continue after an encounter or event has ended, sometimes in one's own personal reflections and sometimes in conjunction with others. In some cases participants' interpretations may be revised in the light of subsequent developments that in retrospect are seen as relevant. This ongoing process of interpretation and (reinterpretation) may also involve relating micro-level events and encounters to larger-scale social processes. A more macro level phenomenological perspective is provided in Berger and Luckmann's model of the "social construction of reality" that we shall examine in the next section.

The Social Construction of Reality: Berger and Luckmann

Peter Berger and Thomas Luckmann (1966) provide the theoretical underpinning for the phenomenological approach known as the "social construction of reality." Their analysis moves beyond Schutz's perspective on consciousness and Garfinkel's focus on everyday life routines at the micro level in that it deals more explicitly with the macro-level institutional structures of society. Berger and Luckmann did not focus primarily on the interaction process itself at the micro level as is done in symbolic interaction theory. However, their perspective incorporates the basic insights of symbolic interaction theory in their analysis of the interrelations between subjective consciousness and the everyday life practices and patterns of communication whereby cultural meanings are sustained. But while symbolic interaction theory emphasizes the relation between micro level interaction and the formation of individuals' consciousness, Berger and Luckmann emphasize how the formation of individuals' consciousness and worldviews, plus their sense of psychological security, are related to macro-level cultural meaning systems as these are reflected in society's major institutional structures.

Macro-level institutional structures are sustained and reproduced through the routine practices of everyday life whereby they acquire their objective and common sense status. At the level of consciousness, the stability of these larger institutional patterns helps provide a subjective sense of security and meaning by providing implicit support for the dominant cultural worldview shared throughout the society. However, in a complex, highly differentiated, and rapidly changing society, there is a risk that these structures may lose their obvious and matter-of-fact quality and reflect inconsistent and conflicting worldviews. When the major institutional structures of society fail to reinforce one another, the result, in Berger and Luckmann's view, can be an erosion of the implicitly accepted subjective understandings of "the way the world is." This inconsistency and uncertainty may lead to an increase in people's sense of psychological insecurity and anxiety.

Mutual Interdependence of Social Institutions and Subjective Consciousness

There are three principle concepts that Berger and Luckmann (1966) used to analyze the mutual relationships between human action, social institutions, and subjective consciousness: **externalization**, **objectification**, and **internalization**. **Externalization** refers to the ongoing human activity through which the material and cultural conditions of the social world are actually created and reproduced. These activities range from the production of tools, technology, and other material artifacts to the development of laws, morals, science, and various belief systems in the nonmaterial realm. Social structures of all types, ranging from friendships and family groups to neighborhoods, formal organizations, and large-scale institutional patterns, emerge from the process of interaction whereby people develop shared definitions of the material, social, and symbolic world they share and develop stable patterns of interdependent relations with one another based on these definitions. This process of externalization might readily be compared to Marx's image of human beings as being continually involved in the production (and reproduction) of the material and social conditions of their lives, as opposed to simply fitting passively into an ecological niche in the natural world. The concept of externalization emphasizes the intentional and sometimes creative aspects of human beings' actions whereby the cultural underpinnings of the social world and the institutional structures of society come into being and are continually reproduced (or sometimes transformed).

Once established, the products of human beings' creative actions appear to them to be a part of the external world, existing independently of their personal actions or subjective definitions. Berger and Luckmann refer to this as the process of **objectification**. The objective or external nature of the social world is clearly evident with various artifacts of material culture, including tools, art, buildings, highways, and the entire "built environment" which seems sometimes to eclipse the "natural environment," especially in large cities. Even so, the meaning of the various artifacts of material culture, plus the knowledge needed to make use or make sense of them, rest on shared definitions developed and sustained through interaction. This external objective world also includes all the diverse areas of nonmaterial culture as well, including beliefs, values, rules, norms, and customs. To take a simple example, in working toward a baccalaureate degree, students must comply with the graduation requirements indicated in the university's catalog and abide by the official rules of the university. These rules were not established by the students themselves, and they exist outside their subjective consciousness; nevertheless they were created and are enforced by other human beings in their roles as agents for the university. Although rules of all types are created (and changed) by human beings, they also exist as an objective reality which people are expected to follow, whether they agree with them or not. Informal customs likewise are experienced initially as an external reality. Even though not officially required, individuals often choose to follow them in order to fit into an already established social world. There is considerable variation in the influence different people have in creating the social reality—the rules and customs—that others are expected to follow. Rule making and rule enforcing are often specialized activities that help define the essential features of the social world for everyone else.

After being created, however, the social world becomes more than an external reality. Instead, people actually internalize large parts of it in their subjective consciousness through the socialization process. This process of **internalization**, the third of the three major concepts in Berger and Luckmann's perspective, occurs as people are socialized into their culture or subculture and thus develop a basic understanding of "the way things are" and "the way things should be." When the process is successful, these understandings become deeply embedded in people's subjective consciousness and are eventually taken for granted and accepted as everyday common sense. This process of internalization begins right after birth and eventually includes not only the general culture and worldview shared throughout society but also the common sense customs and particular viewpoints reflected in the various subcultures associated with different social classes, racial/ethnic groups, regions, groups, and institutional settings. Despite intense socialization efforts, however, no one internalizes the total culture, and there are variations in how deeply different aspects of it become internalized. But at the highest level of generality, the symbolic universe of meaning (or overarching worldview) that human beings create and reproduce provides a sense of subjective order and meaningfulness to individuals' lives. Through internalizing these beliefs and assumptions, individuals gain assurance that the routine activities and experiences of their everyday lives not only "make sense" but are "real" and provide a sense of purpose, significance, and personal fulfillment.

The three interrelated processes of externalization, objectivication, and internalization form the heart of Berger and Luckmann's "social construction of reality" perspective. Overall, these processes portray a reciprocal relationship between individuals and society. Individuals create society (through externalization) but the objective social reality that is created then shapes individuals' development (through internalization) and insures that their actions will continue to reproduce the external social world. It is through interaction among people who share the same cultural worldview that the social world is continually reproduced (or sometimes transformed) and reinforced in people's consciousness. The importance of interaction for sustaining the social world applies clearly to nonmaterial aspects of culture such as basic worldviews, religious beliefs, knowledge, customs, morals, and so on. Artifacts of material culture (such as art, texts, buildings, and tools) obviously do not require interaction for them to exist in a purely physical sense, but their meanings could not be maintained without interaction. Cultural remains such as "dead languages" or artifacts in museums have a quite different meaning for those who encounter them today than they did to those who produced them or used them originally in the normal course of their everyday lives.

At one level, people certainly understand that the social world and cultural products of all kinds result from their own intentional and sometimes creative activities. They know that it is through their actions that marriages are performed or terminated, voluntary organizations supported, goods and services produced and purchased, classes conducted, projects completed, business enterprises incorporated, government agencies established, laws passed, artistic works created, religious beliefs reinforced and celebrated, and scientific discoveries made. However, people are not necessarily aware that the taken-for-granted worldview that underlies such actions and makes them possible and meaningful also depends on nothing more than shared social definitions. Instead, people tend to believe that our worldview must correspond to the way things **really** are, in an objective sense, grounded in the nature of ultimate reality—as opposed to being socially constructed and reflecting mere social definitions.

Because the social world is constructed and maintained through human beings' actions and interaction, it is inherently precarious, subject to all the contingencies and risks that attend human activities. Peter Berger (1964) used the concept of the "sacred canopy" to describe how shared religious beliefs provide a system of ultimate meaning that anchors our basic worldview and explains and legitimates our social world and our individual lives in ways that make our underlying beliefs and values seem to be independent of mere human definitions. Such beliefs may refer to an ultimate reality that is transcendent and independent of the ever-changing material world. Or, the material world itself may be seen as ultimate reality. The widespread contemporary belief in science, for example, as knowledge about the way the world **really** is, independent of our social definitions, exemplifies this pattern. The main point is that our beliefs in the objective reality of our ultimate worldview helps compensate for the precariousness and contingency of mere social definitions. Such beliefs provide security and stability to our understanding of the social order, as well as a sense of purpose and ultimate meaning to our individual lives.

At the macro level, the various institutional structures of society (economic, political, religious, educational, family) may be seen as potential sources of support for the overall worldview shared by the members of society. For large-scale social institutions, the implicit beliefs and meanings that support them are often objectified in material artifacts such as buildings and other forms of symbolic representation (flags, uniforms, trademarks, and insignia of various types). But the fundamental reality of institutional structures is that they consist of complex patterns of interdependent actions and networks of interaction that enable members of society to order their lives in ways that are meaningful and sensible for them. Moreover, in a society with a high level of institutional and cultural integration, the dominant institutions are able to serve as "plausibility structures" that reinforce the underlying worldview that supports and legitimates them. But with the emergence of modern society, this high level of integration between major institutional structures and the dominant cultural worldview that supports them becomes more and more difficult to sustain.

Cultural Homelessness in the Modern and Late Modern World

Analyzing the interdependence between the institutional structures of society and the underlying cultural worldview that supports them is a major emphasis of Berger and Luckmann's social construction of reality perspective. Societies differ in terms of the degree to which their various institutional structures are consistent in supporting the plausibility of the particular beliefs that make up their particular worldview or reinforcing the customs that reflect such beliefs. In relatively simple (or pre-modern) societies with high levels of cultural homogeneity, the major social structures may indeed provide such support. But with the advance of modernity, societies become more and more complex, due in part to the high level of differentiation among different social institutions and in part to increasing subcultural pluralism. The result of these institutional and cultural transformations is that the overarching worldview that may earlier have provided a sense of ultimate meaning and significance becomes fragmented and thus loses its obvious, taken-for-granted quality. Different segments of society and different institutions gradually develop their own distinct beliefs and customs, leading to inconsistency or even conflict in the larger society instead of mutual reinforcement. The process is one that sociologists have analyzed in various ways from the very beginning of the discipline.

From this perspective we would conclude that modern or late modern societies face distinct challenges in maintaining the subjective plausibility of their underlying worldviews that less complex and more homogeneous societies did not have to face. Of course, traditional societies were not really as simple or homogeneous as they have sometimes been portrayed in the contrast with modern societies. But their stability was often greater, and their level of complexity less than modern society. In any case, a potential consequence of high levels of institutional differentiation and subcultural pluralism is a deterioration of the implicitly accepted worldview that earlier may have been shared throughout society. Instead, there is increased potential for cultural conflict, as groups and organizations with different fundamental beliefs about the way the world "is" or "should be" battle to undermine one another's legitimacy and establish their own dominance.

An advanced stage of this process of subcultural fragmentation has been reflected in recent years in the notion of a "culture war" to depict the conflict between cultural progressives and conservatives (Hunter, 1991). Although the concept of "war" may be overstated when applied at the "grass roots" level (in contrast to the leaders of the opposing sides), an example of cultural fragmentation and conflict can be seen in the debates in our society over abortion, prayer and sex education in public schools, evolutionary theory, and the definition of marriage.

Such debates reflect fundamental differences in underlying beliefs and ultimate values that relate to basic "meaning of life" issues. Although subcultural conflicts may ebb and flow over time, in a pluralistic (and individualistic) society, even a broad consensus on societal values and goals is often difficult to sustain.

Another possible consequence of the lack of consensus in basic beliefs and values resulting from the deterioration of an overarching worldview is the growth of anomie. In the literal sense, this term refers to feelings of normative uncertainty, meaninglessness, and skepticism regarding ultimate values. People find themselves caught between inconsistent and conflicting claims regarding the basic meaning and purpose of life. In effect, this fragmentation of worldviews and ultimate meaning systems has the potential to undermine the legitimacy and plausibility of any of them. As a result, people may experience ambivalence, insecurity, and anxiety. Peter Berger and his colleagues (Berger et al., 1973) used the concept of the "homeless mind" to describe this high potential for anomie in modern society. On the other hand, despite the fragmentation of the cultural world at large, at the psychological level some individuals may respond to the cultural ambiguities and confusion of the wider society by withdrawing into a homogeneous subcultural enclave that will reinforce their particular beliefs and thereby provide them a sense of psychological and moral security in their own particular social world that is somewhat insulated from the ambiguities and conflicts of the wider society. Others may respond by seeking to promote change in the larger society so it will better reflect their own particular values and beliefs.

It is, of course, an empirical question as to whether a high level of subcultural pluralism leads to widespread anomie, anxiety, or meaninglessness, or whether it leads instead to cultural or subcultural conflict between "cultural warriors" who are strong proponents of opposing worldviews. A third possibility is for individuals to embrace the freedom to develop their own individualized ultimate meaning systems, thereby demonstrating a high level of psychological and moral autonomy, despite the lack of unambiguous social support. If this pattern is widespread, the result could be a high level of subcultural pluralism without extensive contact between those representing different subcultural orientations. In any case the underlying plausibility of a consensual worldview is undermined. Instead of experiencing the psychological security of any type of overarching "sacred canopy," individuals instead are expected to make up their own minds with regard to alternative worldviews and ultimate meaning systems. They also have the option of identifying with the subcultural cognitive and moral community of their choice (if any) in gaining support for their own particular vision of the ultimate meaning and purpose of life. These options for dealing with cultural fragmentation will be explored more fully in Chap. 20 in connection with postmodern types of theory.

Summary

The three theoretical perspectives reviewed in this chapter differ in their specific focus but are generally consistent in underlying assumptions. In all of these theories the social world is seen as consisting of human beings' actions and interactions and their outcomes. All of them are also concerned with the relationship between individuals' subjective consciousness and the social world in which they participate, and all emphasize the importance of the ongoing activities of human beings in sustaining and reinforcing all aspects of the social world.

Of these three perspectives the phenomenological approach represented by Alfred Schutz concentrates most heavily on subjective consciousness at the individual level. Each individual's stream of consciousness is emphasized as being unique, reflecting each person's own distinctive past and present experiences. At the same time, however, people who live in the same type of environment, share similar experiences, and interact with one another develop intersubjective (or shared) forms of consciousness. Despite the overlap this involves, shared experiences are not identical for the parties involved. The greatest degree of mutual sharing is with persons with whom one has a personal relationship.

Beyond the level of personal relationships, our knowledge of others is in the form of social types or public persona rather than through awareness of their specific subjective experiences. The importance of intersubjective consciousness for social life is revealed in the common sense "stocks of knowledge" that are widely shared throughout society and that exist at a deeper level than expressed through language. These stocks of knowledge provide the foundation for people to understand and adjust to one another and to cooperate in various joint actions. In the process of communication, implicitly shared stocks of knowledge provide the background or context in terms of which people are able to interpret one another's discourse as well as their actions.

The ethnomethodological perspective as developed by Garfinkel is based on phenomenological sociology but deals more with the actual everyday life practices that enable people to sustain a sense of the orderliness of social life. The focus is on the way people make sense of one another's everyday life practices on the basis of implicitly shared understandings (or stocks of knowledge) of the way the world is and how it is organized. As people routinely conform to the routines of social life, the resulting continuity of the social world provides a sense of security and stability. This often occurs without discussion or discourse simply because it fits the mutually understood expectations of all involved. When disruptions occur people seek to restore a sense of order through seeking or offering explanations and adjusting or realigning their actions. But even when people seek to repair a disruption or improve their mutual understanding thorough communication, their ability to understand one another is likely to depend on the specific context and implicit background knowledge.

Finally, the "social construction of reality" perspective developed by Peter Berger and Thomas Luckmann shows how the phenomenological emphasis on our subjective sense of the ultimate meaningfulness of the world is reinforced by the institutional structures of society. At the same time these institutional structures are themselves sustained and reproduced through everyday life patterns of action and interaction. The routine practices of everyday life reflect and reinforce the underlying beliefs and values that provide meaning and purpose to our individual and collective lives. Berger and Luckmann do not emphasize the subtle dynamics of interaction at the micro level as much as symbolic interactionists typically do. Nor do they emphasize how people seek to make sense of one another's behavior in particular situations as much as ethnomethodologists do. But they do highlight the point that people's subjective consciousness mirrors the cultural worldview that is shared in the wider society and expressed in various ways in its institutional structures. In addition, Berger emphasized the importance of people's efforts to anchor their cultural worldview in an ultimate meaning system that is seen as independent of the humanly constructed social world. The overall emphasis of Berger and Luckmann's "social construction of reality" was centered on the interdependent relationship between subjective consciousness and institutional structures—a perspective that helps bridge the micro and macro levels of the social world.

Like symbolic interaction theory, the ideas of phenomenological sociology and ethnomethodology are foundational for all levels of social reality: micro, meso, and macro. The next three chapters will show how micro level social processes lead to the emergence of meso and macro level social formations. The micro level processes to be discussed in the next chapter do not emphasize subjective consciousness as much as symbolic interactionism or the theories covered in this chapter. Instead, as we shall see, they focus on how people's behavior and social relationships can be explained in terms of their efforts to satisfy their needs and achieve their individual goals.

Questions for Study and Discussion

1. Describe a typical situation in which you might be asked to provide an account of some intentional action that you perform that is different from your usual routine. How would your explanation differ for members of your family, your close friends, or casual acquaintances you don't know very well? Would you be more likely to focus on the situation in which you were involved or your own subjective motives or identity?
2. "Actions speak louder than words." Discuss the implications of this statement in the light of the emphasis of phenomenological sociology and ethnomethodology on implicitly shared stocks of knowledge that are used to interpret people's actions. What are some examples of how people's actions convey messages without words?
3. Explain how the legacy of predecessors may sometimes be used to explain traditional beliefs and practices or to try to influence people's current or future behavior in our society, or in some social setting in which you are involved (family, school, fraternity or sorority, religious group, or some other setting). Also, what do you anticipate will be the legacy of your own generation to future members? In what ways (if any) are the present activities of people with whom you are familiar oriented toward future members?
4. Can you identify some naturally occurring disruptions or misunderstandings that could be considered comparable to breaching experiments? Drawing on your own experience or observations, describe this situation and the efforts that were

made (if any) to correct the misunderstandings and deal with the disruption so as to restore a sense of order.

5. Do you agree or disagree with the diagnosis of our society as characterized by high levels of cultural fragmentation and conflict? Why or why not? Can you identify particular institutions or areas of culture that seem to be based on fundamentally different worldviews (such as science and religion, for example, education and entertainment, or economic and politics)? Explain.

Chapter 7
Social Exchange and Rational Choice at the Micro Level: Looking Out for #1

In everyday life we clearly understand the contrast between market transactions at the shopping mall or an automobile dealership and our personal relationships with family members, friends, and lovers. In market transactions our goal is to get the best deal for ourselves, without being obligated to show concern for the personal welfare of the person with whom we happen to be doing business. In contrast, our relationships with family members, friends, and lovers reflect our emotional attachments to one another. This means we are expected to consider their wishes and needs as well as our own, and we are confident they would do the same for us.

But personal relationships, like market transactions, can also be viewed in terms of costs and rewards. Being involved in family relationships or spending time with close friends or lovers is intrinsically rewarding. But there are certain costs to consider as well, even though they may not always be experienced as costs. At the very least, there are the costs of time, energy, and alternative activities that may be foregone, plus the obligation to provide help to our family and friends when they need it. Even though friends and family members may feel it is not appropriate to "keep score," their mutual sharing and caring is probably expected to be balanced over time. If costs and rewards should seem to either party to be unevenly distributed, this may lead to feelings of resentment or conflict that may eventually undermine the relationship.

The perspective of exchange and rational choice theory involves looking at all social relations—friendships and other personal relations as well as one-time market transactions and long-term formal contracts—in terms of costs and rewards, both material and nonmaterial. As with symbolic interaction theory, analysis begins at the micro level. However, micro-level exchanges may be seen as the foundation for meso and macro level structures. Regardless of the level, social exchanges of all types reflect individuals' efforts to meet their own personal needs and interests through the choices they make, including material as well as nonmaterial social and emotional needs. Even when their actions are consciously oriented toward the wishes or welfare of others, the focus in both social exchange and rational choice theory is on the benefits received in return.

D.P. Johnson, *Contemporary Sociological Theory: An Integrated Multi-Level Approach.*

This chapter will deal with social exchange theory and its elaboration and eventual transformation into (or absorption by) rational choice theory. Despite the high overlap between these perspectives, "rational choice" theory suggests an even more individualistic model of social behavior than "exchange" theory. The major topics of this chapter are as follows:

- Historical differences between individualistic and collectivist theories of social exchange—This section draws on Peter Ekeh's analysis of these contrasting models that were implicit in some of the early classical-stage theories.
- Application of behavioral psychology to social exchanges—George Homans' individualistic explanation of "elementary" (or face-to-face) behavior will be reviewed as the beginning of modern exchange theory.
- Emergence of power structures from imbalanced exchanges—This section will review Peter Blau's perspective on how imbalanced exchanges give rise to power and dependency relations which provide the foundation for macro-level structures in which exchange patterns are institutionalized.
- Individual interests as the foundation for normative conformity and group solidarity—This section will use Michael Hechter's rational choice perspective to explain how individuals seek to satisfy various personal interests through involvement in different types of groups and conformity to their norms.
- Development of normative systems to regulate exchange transactions—This section introduces James Coleman's systematic explanation of how the exchange transactions that individuals develop in pursuit of their personal interests are regulated by norms and laws based on social consensus regarding individuals' rights and responsibilities.
- The challenge of irrational consequences of "rational" action—This section examines Raymond Boudon's explanation of how action that appears to be rational at the individual level may generate unintended irrational consequences, particularly when the benefits being sought are contingent on the actions of others.

As contemporary rational choice theory has been elaborated from the earlier ideas of exchange theory, the individualistic assumptions of these perspectives have been expanded to incorporate the notion that individuals' personal interests may be modified through their participation in a network of social relations and organizational involvements. But even though their interests are shaped by this social environment, rational choice theory in American sociology seems to emphasize individual interests more than shared values or normative commitments or widespread concerns for the common good. In the following section, this highly individualistic model will be contrasted briefly with a more collectivist version of exchange theory that was implicit in some of the earlier, classical-stage theories.

Historical Background: Individualistic Versus Collectivist Theories of Social Exchange[1]

Long before the development of the current exchange and rational choice theory perspectives, the social exchange process had been analyzed by earlier theorists from within an individualistic, utilitarian (or rational choice) perspective. For example, the classical British economist Adam Smith emphasized the benefits of market exchanges in promoting the overall welfare of society. As noted earlier, the policy implication of this view is that government regulation of the market system should be minimal. Smith also recognized that people's basic selfishness could be restrained somewhat by shared moral sentiments, although individual interests were given priority in his analysis. According to the closely related utilitarian perspective, a basic law of human nature is that people always seek to avoid pain (or reduce costs) and maximize pleasure (or other rewards). This image of human nature is reflected in the view that the overall organization of society itself is based on a contractual agreement that was negotiated in the beginning to accomplish goals that could not be achieved satisfactorily through individual effort or independent market transactions.

This individualistic emphasis can be contrasted with a more "collectivist" version of exchange theory. Although Durkheim is not generally considered an exchange theorist, a significant expansion of exchange networks in modern society is certainly implied in his analysis of the increased interdependence that results from the elaboration of the division of labor. In his view, the increased individualism that results from this process is a reflection of the greater social heterogeneity resulting from occupational specialization and a more complex division of labor. However, people's growing dependence on one another for meeting their various needs promotes a greater level of "organic solidarity" that is based on exchange transactions and that partially replaces the "mechanical solidarity" of simpler and more segmented societies with less interdependence.

The individualistic and collectivist versions were contrasted in Peter Ekeh's (1975) analysis of the "two traditions" in exchange theory. Ekeh drew on French anthropologist Levi-Strauss's analysis of the custom whereby marriages were arranged through exchange transactions among different clans in primitive societies. Working in the tradition established by Durkheim, Levi-Strauss attempted to show how the exchange of marriage partners contributed to social cohesion among the clans involved. His theoretical argument distinguished between **restricted** versus **generalized** exchanges. The restricted pattern involved direct exchanges. In generalized exchange, in contrast, members of a triad or larger group receive benefits from a partner other than the one to whom

[1] This description of the contrast between individualistic and collectivist theories of social exchange is adapted from in D. P. Johnson ([1981] 1986:344–346).

they give benefits. Thus the interchange is does not involve direct mutual reciprocity. The restricted exchange involves the pattern A↔B, C↔D,..., n↔n, while the generalized exchange is based on the pattern A→B→C→D→A... → n→A. In Ekeh's argument the restricted pattern will reflect a concern with balance or equity. Exchange partners may be involved personally with one another, but each transaction is relatively self-sufficient, and there is no overall integration of these limited transactions within a larger network of relationships. Such exchange patterns would seem consistent with a structure of relatively self-sufficient families, tribes, or local communities. Within these relatively self-contained social circles, social exchanges would be extensive, but exchanges between different social circles would be minimal.

Generalized exchange, in contrast, involves a larger network of transactions, many of which are indirect. There is less emphasis on personal negotiation of exchange terms. Instead, individuals are oriented more toward the overall system and the rewards received from participation in it. In such a system, each party is expected to make contributions that benefit others without expecting an immediate benefit in return. This means that members must have a relatively high level of trust that others will discharge their obligations, even without receiving immediate benefits in return. All members benefit, but without individual negotiation or immediate payment. Ekeh suggests that the generalized pattern should be associated with a higher level of moral development than the restricted pattern. Members are expected to fulfill their obligations without concern for their own interests (in the short run), and to trust that others will do likewise. The underlying image of this generalized pattern differs from the individualistic implications of market transactions as highlighted in classical economic thought and British utilitarianism. Moreover, the form of the exchange is not a matter for individuals to decide on their own. Instead, exchange patterns are institutionalized and legitimated by a moral code that transcends individuals' utilitarian interests. This pattern contrasts with economic market exchanges which individuals negotiate on their own, and which are expected to be governed by self-interests.

To illustrate how the debate regarding these contrasting perspectives has continued, George Homans' early exchange theory was developed in opposition to the collectivist orientation of Levi-Strauss's analysis of marriage and kinship patterns (Homans and Schneider, 1955). In contrast to Levi-Strauss's focus on the functional need of society for social solidarity, Homans insisted that these practices should be understood in terms of already-existing emotional attachments between the families involved. The individualistic pattern is also reflected in John Thibaut and Harold Kelley's (1959) analysis of the particular configuration of social relations that develop in group settings. In their model, these relations can be explained in terms of individuals' calculations of anticipated costs and rewards. They argued that individuals will focus on one-on-one relations if they anticipate greater rewards than could be obtained by including additional parties. On the other hand, if they see an opportunity to increase their total rewards (minus whatever costs may be involved) by expanding the scope of interaction to include others, they will attempt to do so. Of course, their success will be contingent on the expectations of these other parties that their rewards will also be greater than with alternative patterns in which they may become involved. Such patterns can readily be observed in the mingling of participants in unstructured social gatherings.

A Behavioral Approach to Elementary Exchanges: Contributions by George C. Homans[2]

The strategy of explaining customs and social institutions in terms of their contributions to the needs of society characterized functional theory during the time that it dominated American sociology in the mid-twentieth century.[3] In criticizing this view Homans insisted that behavior must be explained in terms of the motives and sentiments of human beings, not the needs or functional requirements of society. The exchange theory that he developed was targeted explicitly against Talcott Parsons' analysis of how individuals' actions contribute to the fulfillment of the functional needs of society.[4]

Behavioral Dynamics of Groups

Although Homans' micro-level exchange theory reflected his rejection of functionalism, he actually had used a type of functional approach in his earlier analysis of the dynamics of small groups (Homans, 1950). Briefly, his argument was that these dynamics can be portrayed by three basic concepts: (1) activities, (2) interaction, and (3) sentiments. These are interrelated so that if one changes, the others are likely to change as well. This basic notion of how different components of social systems are linked together in relations of mutual interdependence was also a key characteristic of functional theory. In addition, he pointed out that some activities,

---

[2] This overview of Homans' exchange theory perspective is adapted from D. P. Johnson ([1981] 1986:347–358).

[3] Functional theory involves a strong focus on institutional structures at the macro level, as opposed to the social psychological dynamics of face-to-face relations or the dynamics of small groups. We will deal in more detail with alternative versions of functional theory in Chaps. 12 and 13.

[4] For an interesting explanation of the development of Homans' thinking along this line, see his Autobiographical Introduction in Homans (1962:1–49, especially pp. 22–35). George Homans (1910–1989) was educated at Harvard University and spent most of his professional life there. Many of the basic ideas of his exchange theory were foreshadowed in his criticism of Levi-Strauss's functional analysis of primitive societies' marriage customs (see Homans and Schneider ([1955]).

interactions, and sentiments are imposed on the group from its environment, or are required for its survival. Homans referred to these requirements as the external system. This notion of survival requirements is also comparable to a functionalist analysis. The internal system, in contrast, consists of activities, interactions, and sentiments that are elaborated beyond survival requirements. Thus, for example, the external system for members of a work group would include formal job requirements and organizational rules and regulations. But beyond these requirements, members often elaborate or expand their activities, interactions, and sentiments in various informal ways. For example, members of a work group may become close friends and go drinking after work or bowling together on weekends.

Moreover, the external and internal systems are also linked so if a change occurs in one system, it will be likely to produce change in the other. For example, if job assignments in a work group change so that members are more scattered, opportunities for interaction will decrease, and their sentiments toward one another may decrease in intensity as a result. Or, change may originate in the internal system. For example, a group of junior high students may collaborate in resisting classroom routines (an internal change), resulting in closer supervision or more restrictive rules (external system change).

The exchange theory Homans later developed is more individualistic than his analysis of group dynamics. It explicitly employed a reductionist strategy of explaining social processes in terms of the principles of behavioral psychology.

Psychological Foundations of Social Relations

In contrast to the inductive approach of symbolic interaction theory, Homans' ([1961] 1974) goal was to develop a deductive theory. His intention was to formulate a set of basic principles from which hypotheses about social behavior could be logically derived. By focusing explicitly on **elementary** social behavior, Homans limited himself primarily to face-to-face interaction in which social exchanges are direct, not indirect (restricted instead of generalized in Levi-Strauss's terminology). Homans drew heavily on the basic principle from behavioral psychology that human behavior is shaped through reinforcement and punishment. He reviewed psychologist B. F. Skinner's operant conditioning laboratory experiments in which pigeons were taught to peck a target "in exchange" for food, or to avoid a target so as not to receive an electric shock. Homans extrapolated from these findings to point out how human beings provide positive or negative reinforcements of various types to one another as they interact, thereby mutually shaping one another's behavior.

Homans also incorporated several concepts and principles from elementary economics. In particular, he used such concepts as costs, rewards, investments, and profits in an attempt to shows that people seek to "profit" as much as possible, given their preferences, through their social exchanges as well as through economic market transactions. Although he did not intend to explain why individuals have the particular goals or preferences they do, much of his analysis makes reference to highly general reinforcers like social approval, which, like money, can be used to reinforce a wide variety of behaviors.

The economic concept of reward is, of course, parallel to the psychological concept of reinforcement, while the economic concept of cost is parallel to the psychological concept of punishment. However, there are some important differences between the implications of the operant conditioning model drawn from behavioral psychology and the economic model in terms of their underlying assumptions. Behavioral psychology focuses on the here and now or on past reinforcement instead of the future, with individuals' behavior explained in terms of current stimuli and comparison of current with past reinforcement experiences. In contrast, economics reflects a more explicit orientation toward the future, with present decisions made in anticipation of future rewards. In addition, unlike the economic model, the emphasis of operant conditioning model at the time did not deal explicitly with covert or subjective processes, such as the subjective weighing of alternatives or the making of choices based on predictions of future outcomes. The two perspectives are not contradictory, despite the difference in focus, since expectations for the future typically reflect past experiences. Moreover, individuals may differ in terms of whether they usually give priority to immediate reinforcement or to long-range profits. Contemporary rational choice theory draws much more explicitly on economics, partly because of its focus on explicit decision-making based on expectations regarding future outcomes.

Additional key concepts in Homans' exchange theory include deprivation and satiation, investment, and distributive justice. Obviously, deprivation and satiation are themselves inversely related. Investments consist of personal resources that may be relevant to a particular exchange but are not actually expended (as costs would be). Age, for example, could be considered an investment in some situations, as could seniority in an organizational setting, or expertise in a professional context. In general, people's profits (i.e., rewards minus costs) are expected to be higher if their investments are higher. For example, long-time employees are typically seen as entitled to more pay than newcomers.

The concept of distributive justice refers to individuals' judgments regarding the fairness of the way costs and rewards are distributed. Other things being equal (including investments), individuals generally expect that if their costs are high, their rewards should also be high. If investments are not equal, distributive justice requires that those whose investments are higher should enjoy higher profits (i.e., a more favorable cost-reward ratio), just as those who incur greater costs are expected to reap higher rewards.

How do individuals evaluate whether or not a particular exchange is fair? Part of the answer is their own past experience. Individuals generally expect to do at least as well in future exchanges as they have in the past—or even better if their investments increase. If a person receives less, this reduction will be seen as unfair. This would account for the extreme difficulty any business firm would face in lowering wages and salaries, despite the fact such reductions might be necessary in a declining market to protect existing jobs. The same general standard of evaluation would hold for social exchanges as well. Thus a husband or wife might complain that "You do not love me like you used to" if the other partner seems to be even slightly less responsive or appreciative. And best friends are likely to be sensitive to any suggestion that they are reluctant to continue spending so much time together or doing favors for one another.

People's standards of fairness are also based on comparison of their own outcomes with the outcomes of others who are similar. Specific comparisons may vary for different individuals or groups. Characteristics such as age, expertise, occupational responsibilities and authority, and seniority are common bases for comparison. Whatever the basis, individuals expect rough equality in the payoffs (or reward/cost outcomes) received by others who are similar. Thus a person would feel it is unfair to be paid less than another who is performing a similar job and is identical in training and seniority. Again, the same general principle would apply in social exchanges, even though determination of precise levels of cost and reward on an objective basis would normally be more difficult than for economic exchanges.

These various concepts are incorporated into a set of basic propositions that form the heart of Homans' exchange theory. These propositions focus on (1) the likelihood that an individual will enact a particular behavior, (2) how he or she reacts to the consequences of that behavior, and (3) the process of choice between alternative behaviors (Homans [1961] 1974:15–50). Briefly, the likelihood of a particular behavior increases in direct proportion to the frequency with which that behavior has been rewarded in the past, the value of the reward received, and the similarity of the present situation to past situations in which the behavior in question was rewarded. On the other hand, the likelihood of a particular behavior will be decreased by high cost (relative to reward) and by satiation.

The relevance of satiation is obvious with respect to physiological needs such as food; with social rewards like social approval, it may not be so obvious. The desire for some types of rewards seems to be elastic (to use a concept from economics); that is, people seem never to be satiated completely. Both social approval and money may have this characteristic for many people. Even so, those who receive a large amount of social approval, or money, may find that other kinds of rewards become relatively more important in the short run. For example, even when persons may get paid more by working more hours, they would not be willing to spend all their waking hours at work. Or, with nonmaterial rewards, many students will slack off somewhat from their studies after they receive high grades at the end of an academic term and will try to "catch up" on social activities. In contrast to satiation, the effects of deprivation increase the longer the time period since a particular reward was received. The higher the deprivation, the higher the value of a particular reward, and the greater the likelihood that an effort will be made to obtain it.

An individual's reaction to the rewards received for a particular behavior will be influenced by a comparison of these rewards with those anticipated. This comparison involves the idea of distributive justice, as discussed earlier. If individuals receive less than anticipated, or if they received unexpected punishment, they are likely to become angry and perhaps engage in aggressive behavior. In contrast, if they fare better than expected, they will be pleased and will be likely to provide approval to their exchange partner(s) (Homans [1961] 1974:37–40). People's choices regarding which line of behavior to enact or what reward to seek will reflect their assessment of the value of the rewards to be received (given their particular preferences), the contrasting effects of deprivation and satiation, and their estimate of the chances of receiving that reward. Individuals sometimes will choose a less rewarding line of action when the reward is more certain than a potentially more rewarding alternative for which the rewarding outcome is less certain. ("A bird in the hand is worth two in the bush.") Moreover, we should recognize that our ability to predict outcomes successfully is always limited.

Applications of Exchange Theory to Elementary Social Behavior

Homans uses the exchange theory perspective to analyze numerous sociological concepts, such as social rank, normative conformity versus innovation, influence, esteem, status, and authority. Findings from various empirical studies are used to support his basic propositions. For example, one's social influence reflects his or her ability to reward another for compliance. One highly general reward is social approval, or expressions of positive sentiment toward the other person. Other things being equal, people who like one another, and who share positive sentiments toward one another, are more likely to be able to influence one another than if they do not. Moreover, groups in which all the members like one another (or have high solidarity) should show high rates of conformity to group norms, since such conformity is rewarded by the approval of fellow members. By the same token, groups that are low in social cohesion, or exchanges of positive sentiments, should show lower rates of conformity to group norms. Low levels of cohesion and conformity are more likely in groups whose members have numerous alternative sources of social approval outside the group. With these outside sources of approval and perhaps other rewards as well, the cost of conformity within the group increases (since costs include alternatives foregone by a particular choice) and, as a result, individuals feel less need to conform.

Some groups exhibit high levels of competition and conflict instead of cohesion. If rewards cannot be shared and are in scarce supply, or if they cannot be apportioned in accordance with individual costs incurred, the result may be competition or conflict instead of cooperation, since cooperation is likely to involve higher costs than individuals feel are justified by the rewards they receive. In contrast, cooperative behavior may be expected when rewards are greater or costs lower than would be possible through individualistic or competitive activity. The rewards need not necessarily be shared equally, particularly if investments are unequal; the only requirement is that each person's reward/cost ratio be more favorable than it would be through individualistic or competitive activity.

Individuals in cooperative groups exchange social approval as they contribute to group goals. However, social approval is neither very scarce nor very costly for others to provide. For this reason individuals whose contributions are extremely valuable but are in scarce supply will be rewarded with esteem, or a higher-than-average level of social approval. (This point will be elaborated in more detail in the discussion of Blau's social exchange theory.) To some extent, individuals grant esteem to others whose activities are considered valuable, even though they may not benefit personally from these activities. This would indicate a general acceptance of standards of distributive justice, plus, perhaps, the anticipation of possible future benefits. Also, individuals sometimes interact with others they do not like if the costs of avoidance are great enough. However, such costs are offset by the benefits obtained from membership in a group, despite the lack of a favorable reward/cost outcome with certain members. Many examples could be noted; an employee may intensely dislike a boss but continue to interact simply because another job cannot readily be found with all the benefits of the present one. In such a situation, the individual's choice is simply the lesser of two evils.

When individuals make choices from among alternative interaction partners, are they more likely to interact with others who are similar to them in terms of status, or are they likely to choose others who are higher or lower? This will depend in large part on the types of rewards available from these different sources, and also on whether the group is a task or sociable group. When people in sociable groups are roughly equal they can provide social support for one another with neither party enduring the cost of subordination. In contrast, interaction with a higher-status person involves the cost of being subordinate. At the same time the higher-status person risks possible loss of status from associating with a lower-status person, a cost which must be balanced against the deference likely to be received from the lower-status person in exchange. On the other hand, persons who are roughly equal in status may avoid one another if they are competing for dominance and instead seek the support of lower status persons to support their claims of superiority. And low-status persons (for whom the risk of status loss would be minimal) may seek to enhance their status by being associated with someone of higher status.

In task groups we should expect relatively more interaction between persons at different status levels. For one thing, lower-status persons may be able to benefit from the higher-status person's task-related knowledge or experience. But the higher-status person may prefer to provide such knowledge to the entire group, since this is less costly than dealing individually with lower-status persons on an individual basis. Also, in many cases the lower-status person probably would experience less subordination as part of a group receiving benefits from the higher-status person than by soliciting help on an individual basis. In the final analysis the collective rewards of task accomplishment should be expected to offset the costs involved for all parties; otherwise, the group may be expected to disband or perhaps change to a sociable group instead.

Status itself is a multidimensional concept. Some of the characteristics that may influence a person's rank or esteem are ascribed, such as family, racial/ethnic background, age, and gender. Other characteristics are achieved, such as educational attainment, knowledge, or physical skills. Some aspects of status may be relevant as investments in an exchange transaction. But whether ascribed or achieved, when several such characteristics are considered, interesting questions can be raised regarding the effects of these different indicators of status in establishing a person's overall rank. If they are not congruent, which characteristics are most important in establishing one's overall rank? Equally important, how does status consistency or inconsistency influence a person's style of interaction and the reactions of others? One of the main effects of status incongruence is to reduce an individual's level of security or certitude in social relations. There is uncertainty as to whether others will focus on the low-status characteristic or the high-status characteristic. Since status incongruence produces social insecurity, it could be considered a cost (or liability), and efforts to reduce incongruence would, if successful, be rewarding, especially if the low-status characteristics are elevated to match the high-status characteristics. In the short run, such efforts may be reflected in a style of presentation of self so that high-status instead of low-status indicators are emphasized. Such efforts may readily be related to Goffman's dramaturgic perspective on "presentation of self" as discussed in Chap. 5. In the long run, the desire to reduce status incongruence may even lead to efforts to change the basis for evaluation of a person's rank. For example, the women's movement represents an effort to eliminate sex or gender as a basis for differential job assignments, pay, and promotion.

In the last chapter of *Social Behavior: Its Elementary Forms*, Homans contrasted his focus on elementary, or subinstitutional, social behavior with institutional behavior (Homans [1961] 1974). In general, institutional behavior is more complex, with many exchanges being indirect instead of direct. It also involves greater usage of general reinforcers (such as money) that may subsequently be exchanged for other desired rewards. But social institutions never persist of their own built-in dynamic independently of elementary social exchange processes. If conformity to widespread institutional norms should become less rewarding or more costly, deviance rates are likely to increase and, ultimately, institutional patterns themselves may be changed. The next section will deal with the emergence of power structures as an important step in establishing a foundation for the emergence of macro-level institutional structures.

Elementary Social Exchanges and the Emergence of Power Structures: Peter Blau's Micro-Level Exchange Theory[5]

In contrast to Homans' emphasis on psychological processes, Peter Blau focused instead on the structure of the associations that result from people's exchange transactions. While Homans used a **reductionist** strategy by drawing on elementary psychological principles to explain social behavior, Blau's goal was to show that basic exchange processes generate **emergent** phenomena in the form of more complex structures that are based on imbalanced exchanges. Blau's theory thus provides

[5] Blau's exchange theory as summarized in this section was previously published in D. P. Johnson ([1981] 1986:362–372).

a transition from the micro to the macro level, even though our goal in this chapter is limited to his micro-level analysis.[6]

Peter Blau's 1964 book, *Exchange and Power in Social Life,* provides his most systematic exposition of exchange theory. One of his major goals was to show how imbalances in exchange transactions give rise to differences in status and power, with power structures providing the foundation for larger (meso or macro) level structures. Blau (1955) had previously anticipated some of the basic principles of his approach in his case study of informal power and status that developed among agents in a bureaucratic organization. Briefly, as experienced personnel shared their expertise with less experienced colleagues, they developed high informal rank in the group, in effect exchanging their knowledge for status. Chapter 9 will deal in more detail with Blau's model of how macro structures emerge from power and dependency relations in imbalanced exchanges. Our primary concern in this chapter is more at the micro level, where rewards tied to particular personal relationships will be contrasted with impersonal rewards that are independent of such relations. This corresponds roughly to the difference between social versus economic exchanges.

At the micro level, Blau's exchange theory was intended to apply to behaviors that people undertake in anticipation of rewarding reactions from others, and that do not continue in the absence of such rewarding responses (Blau, 1964:6). Like Homans, Blau emphasized social approval as a general reward. Even "altruistic" behavior can be motivated in part by the expectation of receiving gratitude and social approval, but engaging in such behavior may mean that the individual must transcend personal interests in order to show concern for the needs of others. Blau (1964:78–86) even applied his exchange theory perspective to the relationships of lovers, clearly demonstrating the importance of emotional bonds that lead individuals to identify strongly with one another and to exchange a variety of rewards, particularly socioemotional. Material items such as gifts that lovers might exchange are important not for their practical utility or economic worth, but as symbolic expressions of their mutual emotional attachment. The contrast between relationships of this type and economic exchanges that take place in the impersonal market are reflected in Blau's distinction between intrinsic and extrinsic rewards.

[6] Peter Blau (1918–2002) was born in Austria but came to America after the outbreak of World War II. He received his graduate training in sociology at Columbia University. He held various academic posts, including Cornell University, the University of Chicago, and Columbia. He was president of the American Sociological Association in 1972–73. In addition to his theoretical contributions, he did extensive research in the areas of organizational sociology and occupational mobility. In the area of theory, his focus shifted from the strong social psychological emphasis of the exchange theory perspective reviewed in this chapter to a more structural approach that will be reviewed in Chap. 9.

Intrinsic Versus Extrinsic Rewards

All social relations can be distinguished on the basis of whether the rewards exchanged are intrinsic or extrinsic, or some mixture of both (Blau, 1964:33–50). Intrinsic rewards are derived from the relationship itself, like the relationship between lovers mentioned in the previous section. In contrast, extrinsic relationships serve as a means for some other reward instead of being rewarding in their own right. This means the reward may readily be detached from the specific relationship and obtained from any exchange partner. Economic transactions in the marketplace provide clear examples where the exchanges involve extrinsic rewards. Although this distinction parallels the contrast between social versus economic relations, many social exchanges involve varying mixtures of both intrinsic and extrinsic rewards.

Exchanges of intrinsic versus extrinsic rewards can be contrasted in several ways. For one thing social relations involving intrinsic rewards are expected not to involve deliberate negotiation and bargaining in the same sense that economic transactions are. Indeed, the authenticity of the rewards given and received depends on their **not** being consciously negotiated or transparently revealing selfish interests. Lovers or close friends who "keep score" on the frequency or value of favors they exchange demonstrate thereby a lack of the intrinsic emotional commitment on which such relationships depend. Even for casual acquaintances, the value of social approval or other nonmaterial rewards is discounted if it is seen as an inducement to gain some favor. The ulterior motive behind such approval undermines its sincerity and thus its value as a reward.

The intrinsically rewarding social bonds of a close friendship and impersonal economic transactions in the market are extreme cases. Many relationships reflect varying and sometimes changing mixtures of intrinsic and extrinsic rewards. For example, a group of co-workers or professional colleagues may develop strong friendships with one another, even as they recognize that these relationships may enhance their professional careers in various ways. Or, a person might attempt to relate to a higher-status person partly because of intrinsic rewards and partly because of the anticipation of extrinsic benefits, such as enhancement of one's own status. A person who has recently lost status may be dismayed when former friends and associates begin to drift away. On the other hand, it is commonly recognized that only when one is "down" does one discover who one's true friends are. Probably most relationships have varying combinations of different types of rewards.

The initial stages of many social relationships often involve comparisons among alternative potential exchange partners, indicating that the rewards sought are not yet intrinsically linked with any one particular partner. Prior to the intense and highly personal emotional attachment leading to marriage, for example, both parties may assess and compare alternative potential marital partners. Once committed to a relationship, however, comparisons are regarded as highly inappropriate—though the pattern of divorce and remarriage shows that consideration of alternatives is always a possibility.

As personal relationships develop, rewards that may initially have been extrinsic are gradually transformed into intrinsic rewards as they come to be associated with a particular partner. As more and more rewards of various kinds are exchanged, particularly emotional rewards, mutual attachment grows. Thus the relationship takes on a special and unique character that is valued for its own sake, and that makes comparison with alternative partners difficult if not impossible and inappropriate. This means that the value of the goods or services that might be exchanged, or the rewarding character of an activity that is shared—whether going to the movies, watching sunsets, or exchanging gifts—is not based on economic value but the fact that it is shared with a particular person.

The transformation of relationships from extrinsic attraction (involving comparison) to intrinsic attraction (in which comparison is not appropriate) would apply most clearly to relationships in which there is freedom to choose from among alternative partners. Children in a family, for example, are not in a position to make a choice among alternative sets of parents. On the other hand, even in this example, most parents probably hope that their children will eventually love and appreciate them for their own sake and not because of what they do for their children. And children often learn that a sincere display of intrinsic attachment and appreciation can be effective in securing some extrinsic favor from their parents.

Dilemmas of Attraction

People generally are attracted initially to one another because of the rewards they anticipate receiving. The strategy of seeking to impress others as a potentially rewarding exchange partner is common in both economic and social exchanges. With extrinsic market exchanges, merchants' advertising campaigns are clearly intended to attract potential customers because of the greater value they claim to offer for the price than their competitors. With intrinsic exchanges the process is less blatant and more subtle, but the basic dynamics are the same. A man or woman who is attracted to a potential dating partner, for example, will attempt in various ways to impress the other party with attractive qualities that he or she is willing to share. Similarly, persons involved in a developing friendship will offer one another intangible rewards of various kinds, such as emotional support and acceptance of one another's unique identity claims.

However, the characteristics that make a person highly attractive (the ability to supply relatively high rewards) may lead potential exchange partners to be reluctant to try to initiate a relationship because of the high costs that they fear may be required, including the costs of dependency and subordination (Blau, 1964:43–50). To overcome this potentially inhibiting effect of being highly **impressive** and therefore costly, a person wishing to attract exchange partners must also show a willingness to provide rewards at relatively low cost. This involves being **approachable** as well as impressive. To do this, individuals with impressive personal qualities or other resources (skills, experience, knowledge, social contacts, attractive personality, money) may sometimes engage in self-deprecating behavior that demonstrates that he or she is really no different from anyone else. Political candidates, for example, often stress their similarity to average citizens or to particular constituents at a political rally. At a local public hearing that I attended, the mayor's soothing response to a citizen who confessed to being nervous in speaking in public to the mayor and city council was a reassuring statement, "It's just us; do not worry." And in some social settings students may sometimes downplay their high grades, or financially successful business persons may emphasize that they had to work hard for it just like everyone else.

Once relationships are established, the parties involved are likely to attempt to maintain an appropriate balance in terms of the rewards and costs that are exchanged, in the long run if not the short run. This concern with balance reflects the widely understood "norm of reciprocity" (Gouldner, 1960). Simply stated, this means that favors received should be reciprocated. For ongoing relations this reciprocation may not necessarily be immediate. Except for an immediate expression of gratitude, an appropriate time lag between receiving a favor and reciprocating with an equally valuable favor can serve as an inducement for both parties to maintain their relationship. The one who provided the favor can thus be assured of an eventual return on the "investment," while the recipient will avoid the negative reputation of not returning favors. What happens when relationships become imbalanced will be addressed in the next section.

How Power Structures Develop from Imbalanced Exchanges

Overall balance in the transactions between exchange partners helps preserve a state of equality between them. In many cases, however, differences in the needs and/or resources of exchange partners result in obvious imbalances (Blau, 1964:25–31). A person who supplies benefits that others cannot reciprocate is in a position to expect (or require) some form of compliance with his or her influence attempts in exchange. In other words, power differences emerge from imbalanced exchanges. This is one of the central themes of Blau's exchange theory and provides the transition between micro level exchange processes and macro level structures.

To understand how power differences emerge, let us imagine that a person (A) desires or needs certain rewards or benefits that are available from another person (B), but has no resources to offer in exchange. Person A may try to persuade B to provide the favor without reciprocation, except perhaps for an expression of appreciation and gratitude plus assurances that the favor will be returned in the future if possible. ("I would appreciate it if you would do this for me. I won't forget it, and I'll help you in the future when you need it.") One such transaction would probably not lead to significant power differences, but it would create a tacit acknowledgment of indebtedness. If A were to continue receiving such rewards from B without being able to reciprocate, the same level of appreciation and assurances of future payback may eventually be inadequate as an inducement for B to continue providing such benefits, partly due to B's increasing costs and partly to B's satiation with A's gratitude. Although A may attempt to increase the value of the gratitude offered in return by embellishing it in various ways ("I really do appreciate this—you'll never know how much"), the underlying inequality in the exchange leads eventually to the emergence of status differences. In other words, those who use their resources to provide benefits that the recipients cannot reciprocate acquire increased status (or esteem) from recipients' appreciative and deferential responses. If recipients should become dependent on such benefits and unwilling or unable to do without, this dependency in itself would indicate lower status in the relationship and is actually part of the cost of continuing to receive the benefits.

If this one-way transfer of benefits leading to dependency continues, the stage is set for the status differences to evolve into a differentiation of **power** (Blau, 1964:115–142). This occurs when the high esteem enjoyed by a generous patron becomes inadequate as an inducement to continue providing benefits on a unilateral basis. For the dependent recipient, the only recourse may be to offer compliance in exchange. ("If you will continue to provide benefits, I'll comply with your requests [demands] in the future.") Or, indeed, the high-status patron may make the benefits contingent on such compliance. ("I'll continue to do this for you, but this is what I expect in return.") Of course, strategies for communicating this expectation will vary for different types of relationships. Depending on the nature of the relationship, these understandings may be stated explicitly, or they may be expressed in general terms. The extent of compliance that is expected will depend on the value of the rewards received. If major benefits are performed unilaterally on a continuous or repeated basis, the dependent partner's indebtedness may become so great that ongoing compliance is required to establish balance and maintain the exchange pattern. In this way, continuing power differences emerge from imbalanced exchanges.

The relationship between power and dependency is clearly revealed in relationships where people start out on an unequal basis, due to obvious differences in the resources they possess. For example, an employment contract is essentially a formalized agreement that employers will provide wages or salaries to their employees on a regular basis in exchange for their ongoing job performance. But the employer and the employee are likely to be quite unequal in terms of the resources they bring to the table, especially if the employee is just getting started in his or her career. The result, as anyone who has ever been employed knows, is that ongoing compliance is required in exchange for a regular paycheck.

Acquiring Power or Avoiding Subordination Through Strategic Exchanges

Blau's analysis of how power structures develop from imbalanced exchanges drew on Richard Emerson's (1962) analysis of the inverse relationship between power and dependency. To put Emerson's argument briefly, the power of one individual

(A) over another (B) is proportional to the dependence of B on A. Understanding this basic relationship provides a key for developing strategies for either acquiring power or avoiding dependency and subordination. One strategy for attempting to acquire power is to provide others with overwhelming benefits that they cannot reciprocate (Blau, 1964:106–112). Although costly for the benefactor, such a strategy leads eventually to status and power differences among persons who may appear initially to be on roughly equal footing.

Numerous illustrations could be cited to illustrate this process. For example, when parents provide their young adult offspring with abundant material resources that cannot be reciprocated (tuition payments and ample spending money while in college, a new car, a down payment or furniture for a new home), they no doubt expect their offspring to show their appreciation by taking their ideas and advice seriously. Or when grandparents provide lavish gifts to a young couple with a new baby that the couple cannot reciprocate, they probably have an implicit expectation of influencing how the couple fulfills their parental role or schedules visits with them. In public life, when wealthy business people contribute to charities, they can anticipate earning the gratitude of recipients as well as the rewards of public esteem or status. The promises that political candidates make to lower taxes or to provide more benefits to the public (or to the interest group being addressed) than their opponents also illustrates how the process works. Also, as many people no doubt suspect, there is a risk that the public welfare may be undermined when political leaders do special favors for large contributors that fulfill their implicitly understood obligations to them. Finally, in another context, as Blau (1955) showed in his analysis of informal bureaucratic practices, agents with superior experience or expertise achieved high informal rank and power by providing consultation services (i.e., help with difficult tasks) to less experienced colleagues.

Practical understanding of the relation between imbalanced exchanges and the emergence of power structures may also lead people to develop strategies to avoid being subordinated or indebted in their social relations. Individuals may simply refuse to accept goods or services that cannot be appropriately reciprocated. The poor but proud person who declines to request or accept help from family and friends, the politician who refuses excessively large contributions, the newly married couple who do not accept generous offers of financial help from their parents, or nonconformists who are unconcerned with the approval or disapproval of their peers demonstrate the pattern of maintaining independence through avoidance of imbalanced exchanges that would lead to subordination or dependency and indebtedness.

This strategy of doing without a particular reward is one of four different strategies that Blau (1964:118–125), following Emerson (1962), identified for avoiding indebtedness and subordination. Another alternative is to acquire resources that can be used to offer reciprocal rewards of equal value. This would lead to a relationship of mutual dependence or interdependence instead of a one-way dependency relationship. Still another strategy is to find an alternative source with whom reciprocal interdependence can be established. A final strategy is the use of force (as in break-ins or robberies). However, this strategy is likely to be both costly and risky, and is normally not acceptable because of legal or moral constraints. When individuals are unable or unwilling to adopt at least one of these strategies, their only alternative may be to accept a subordinate status in a dependency relation with someone who will provide the benefits they need in exchange for compliance (as routinely done in employment situations).

As noted earlier, the development of power structures in exchange relations provides a bridge between micro and macro levels of analysis. The process whereby power structures establish a foundation for larger-scale meso or macro level structures will be described in more detail in the next chapter. But in the next section we will draw on Michel Hechter's explanation of group solidarity to look more closely at the way individual interests lead them to incur the costs of participation in various types of groups. As we shall see, the challenge is to insure that the rewards members receive for contributing to the group's success are linked to their contributions.

Individual Interests and Group Dynamics

In everyday life people often face the challenge of trying to balance their own interests with the obligations they have to one another and to the various social groups to which they belong. Such obligations are linked in the perspective of exchange theory to benefits received in return. The potential for conflict is built into the structure of most relationships because of the interests of all parties in minimizing costs and maximizing rewards. This applies both to market exchanges and to the emotional exchanges that occur among friends and family members. The tension between social obligations and personal preferences is probably greater in groups involved in tasks which are not intrinsically enjoyable and rewards not received immediately. In groups or organizations where the required activities are intrinsically enjoyable, or where rewards are closely linked to participation or are received immediately, the tension between obligations and desires may not be quite so great. For example, when a group of friends get together to play golf, have a party, or go out to eat, the activity they share is intrinsically rewarding as well as the emotional support they provide one another. There are costs nevertheless, including, for example, the time, energy, and money that are spent as well as alternatives that are foregone, but they may not be experienced as burdensome because of the enjoyable nature of the activity itself and the sociable interaction with friends that it provides.

In contrast to intrinsically rewarding voluntary activities, probably few people would show up for work each day without getting paid. Even though people may enjoy their work, they often feel their pay is too low for the contributions they make, but they continue anyway because of their dependence on this pay for their economic survival. In voluntary organizations like religious groups, for example, leaders often struggle to motivate members to make the contributions needed to sustain the organization, even though the activities may be intrinsically enjoyable for those participating. This is consistent with the experience people sometimes have when they are reluctant to participate in some social event (due to the anticipated costs) but afterward are glad they did (since it proved to be rewarding after all). In such situations, the challenge is to be willing to incur the cost before receiving the reward, sometimes without knowing in advance what the extent or value of the reward will be.

The challenge of linking contributions and rewards is highlighted in Michael Hechter's (1987:125–128) useful distinction between "compensatory groups" and "obligatory groups." Participants in compensatory groups are expected to fulfill obligations that may not necessarily be intrinsically rewarding. Thus some form of compensation is required to motivate their contributions. Employment in an organization where we are paid to do perform tasks that are not intrinsically rewarding is perhaps the clearest example. There is a natural conflict of interests between employees and employers, however. The interests of employees is in maximizing their compensation and minimizing the cost of their contributions (time spent or the amount of work they are required to do), while the interests of their employers is just the opposite. The challenge for employers is to devise strategies to monitor performance and administer sanctions (positive or negative) in an effort to elicit a sufficiently high level of contributions. From an employer's point of view, the costs of such monitoring and sanctioning strategies must be evaluated in relation to the higher levels of production that they stimulate.

In contrast, obligatory groups are those in which the benefits produced are immanent; that is, they are linked directly with membership in the group. This contrasts with benefits like monetary compensation, which has value regardless of its source.[7] Just as with compensatory groups, members may be tempted to try to get by with the lowest possible level of contributions necessary to maintain their membership and their access to the benefits it provides. Thus the challenge for obligatory groups is to minimize members' free-riding. Hechter argued that to try to avoid free-riding, obligatory groups tend to emphasize the need for members to accept their responsibilities to the group without insisting on short-term payoffs in direct proportion to contributions made. In many cases, too, it may be difficult to allocate rewards in exact proportion to members' costs, especially for intangible rewards. In religious or sociable groups, for example, it is the collective participation in shared activities that is rewarding, and it would be impossible to divide this reward in accordance with the cost each participant incurs. Indeed, participation may be seen as both a cost (because of the time spent and alternatives foregone) and a reward (because of the intrinsic enjoyment provided). In the final analysis, the threat of expulsion is the ultimate sanction that can be used to induce at least minimal contributions from those who value the benefits of membership.

---

[7] This notion of immanent rewards may be compared to Peter Blau's notion of intrinsic rewards (in contrast to extrinsic ones) in which the value of the reward is linked to the person from whom it is received. However, the obligations required for receiving immanent rewards are not necessarily intrinsically enjoyable—though of course they may be.

To motivate members to contribute beyond the minimal level to avoid expulsion, obligatory groups may develop strategies for rewarding high levels of contributions by providing high levels of approval or prestige. For example, those who attend services of their religious group regularly, perform voluntary services in its programs, and make above-average financial contributions earn more prestige than those who rarely attend or who make minimal contributions. Some voluntary or social service organizations stage elaborate rituals to recognize and honor those with outstanding contributions. Probably most of us want to be respected for "carrying our weight" (or perhaps a little more) as long as the costs for doing so are not excessive. We may even value the extra approval (or esteem) that we receive for doing more than our share. But for loyal participants, the mutual social approval and emotional support that are exchanged help promote a sense of belonging and social solidarity that stimulates their willingness to incur the personal costs that are involved in contributing to the welfare of the group and the achievement of its goals.

The dilemmas involved in participation in sociable groups or voluntary organizations like religious groups in the United States illustrate some distinctive characteristics of obligatory groups. Some of the contributions members make through their participation seems virtually equivalent to the benefits they receive. The "goods" produced by their contributions are intended for "internal consumption," as it were, as opposed to being produced for outside exchanges in an impersonal market. Although there are costs involved in attending and participating (in addition to financial contributions that may be expected), these costs are intrinsically related to the benefits and cannot be clearly separated. Even so, some members may seek to free ride by avoiding (or minimizing) their contributions while sharing in the rewards of group membership. Leaders of voluntary organizations face a constant challenge in promoting continued or increased contributions while also seeking to make programs and activities more intrinsically rewarding.

Many groups and organizations combine characteristics of compensatory groups and obligatory groups. Even in compensatory groups, the rewards of seniority or personal relationships, for example, may be tied to a particular group and cannot readily be transferred from one organization to another. Likewise, the socioemotional satisfaction individuals receive as a respected member of a particular group is likely to be linked to specific relationships with fellow members, and this would apply to both compensatory and obligatory groups. In addition, in both types of groups efforts may be made to organize tasks so as to minimize the burdens they impose on their members. If the activity is intrinsically enjoyable (and thus rewarding to perform), this would provide additional motivation, despite blurring the distinction between cost and reward.

In addition to being dependent on their members' contributions, all groups also depend on conditions in the wider social environment. These include the availability of resources that can be obtained through alternative exchange transactions, plus a minimal level of security and trust that other people's behavior will conform to widely accepted expectations consistent with a minimal level of social order. The next section will introduce James Coleman's rational choice perspective on how social consensus is developed with regard to individual rights and responsibilities that go beyond specific exchange transactions. His analysis shows how exchange transactions are governed by various rules, both formal and informal, that are designed to regulate them and minimize their negative consequences for others. The following section will be limited primarily to the micro level. Chapter 9 will then portray Coleman's rational choice explanation of meso and macro level structures.

Individual Interests, Rights, and Resources: James Coleman's Perspective on Exchanges Between Rational Actors

The behaviors and exchange patterns that develop from people's rational choices always take place in a wider social environment. Included in this environment are widely shared social definitions of individuals' rights and normative expectations that govern and regulate many aspects of their behavior, including the types of exchange transactions they are allowed to develop. This larger environment was a major concern in James Coleman's (1990) rational choice theory, as presented in his book, *Foundations of Social Theory*, published some 26 years after Peter Blau's primary book on exchange theory. Coleman's intention was to develop the rational choice perspective into a systematic and comprehensive perspective that would explain social behavior ranging from micro level exchange transactions to normative and legal systems and the establishment of "corporate actors" at the macro level.[8]

The scope of Coleman's theory contrasts sharply with Homans' focus on "elementary" face-to-face social behavior. Also, in contrast to Blau's account of how macro structures "emerged" from micro-level exchanges, Coleman (1990) sought to demonstrate how macro (or meso) level structures (including governments, economic enterprises, and other purposive organizations) are intentionally constructed to pursue goals that can better be achieved collectively than individually and that go beyond particular exchanges transactions. These structures, and the normative patterns that support them, plus the various strategies developed for their enforcement, constitute a major part of the social environment that influences and regulates the way particular exchange transactions are developed.

Long before he developed his systematic rational choice perspective, James Coleman was widely known among educational policy makers for the "Coleman Report," based on his 1965 U. S. Office of Education research project (Coleman et al.,

[8] James Coleman received his PhD in 1955 from Columbia University and spent a large part of his professional life at the University of Chicago, where he was associated with the National Opinion Research Center. He was president of the American Sociological Association in 1991–92. His contributions to sociology cover a wide range of areas, including research methods, adolescent life and development, education, minority relations, and social policy. He died in 1995, just 5 years after the publication of his comprehensive and systematic rational choice theory.

1966). This influential report, based on a survey of a national sample of over 600,000 school children from over 4000 schools, showed that the academic achievement of minority children and children from lower socioeconomic backgrounds was higher when they attended school with classmates from more privileged backgrounds with higher levels of academic performance. This discovery of the importance of the social context of peers for educational achievement was subsequently used to justify the policy of busing to achieve racial integration and equality of educational opportunity.[9] The "Coleman Report" also emphasized the critical importance of family background and community context for educational achievement.

In expanding the individualistic rational choice perspective to the meso and macro levels of analysis, Coleman argued that macro-level social changes always require explanation at the level of individuals. Starting with a basic assertion of the rational choice perspective, Coleman explained: "Actors have a single principle of action, that of acting so as to maximize their realization of interests." (Coleman, 1990:37) However, individuals cannot be considered in isolation from the already existing social environment—an environment previously created through human beings' actions and therefore reflecting the results of innumerable rational choice decisions previously made by other people.

In making his case Coleman pointed out that as human beings pursue their individual interests and goals, they are almost always dependent on resources or events controlled by others. Fortunately, however, they also control resources and the potential for creating events in which other persons may have interests. The resources and events that individuals control provide the basis for initiating exchanges. Exchange transactions are established when each party has less interest in certain resources or events that he or she controls than in resources or events that are controlled by one or more other parties. Essentially, the exchange process involves giving up control over resources of our own in which we have less interest in return for gaining control over resources controlled by others in which we have a greater interest. We might assume that we naturally have interests in maintaining control over our own resources and actions. However, whenever we make a purchase, this indicates that our interest in keeping our money is less than our interest in the product or service that we purchase.

The process can also be illustrated with nonmaterial resources, as illustrated by the development of legislative coalitions. Although members of legislative bodies are each entitled to one vote, some issues will be more important to them (and their constituents) than others. Thus, for example, a member of Congress from a large city like New York may care deeply about a bill that deals with urban transportation issues, but have no real interest in another bill that affects, say, Texas ranchers, while the opposite may well be true for a member from rural

[9] This finding regarding peer effects was consistent with his earlier analysis of the importance of adolescents' peer group subcultures in influencing academic orientation and achievement (see Coleman, 1961).

Texas. For both members, the rational strategy would be to form a coalition in which the New Yorker agrees to vote for (or against) the bill affecting Texas ranchers in exchange for the Texan's vote for (or against) the bill dealing with urban transportation issues. They are both thereby exchanging a resource in which they have minimal interest for a resource controlled by the other in which they have a greater interest.

People vary greatly in terms of the resources they control, but one resource that all individuals control is their own behavior. The power to employ our own actions in exchange transactions (and the right to do so within the socially established normative and legal framework) can readily be illustrated in any employment contract. People give up the right to control their behavior to their employer (for certain time periods and certain defined activities) in exchange for money. Then, when they spend their money for groceries, a place to live, travel, entertainment, or whatever, they give up the right to control their money in exchange for control (for consumption) of the goods and services that they purchase.

The fact that people have the power to control their own behavior does not mean that they have the right to engage in any behavior they please. As Coleman pointed out (and most people recognize), people do not have the right to smoke in a non-smoking area, for example, or to drive the wrong way on a one-way street. Nor do people in modern societies have the right to sell themselves as slaves or to enter a contract that would enslave others. But rights vary in different societies, and a major part of the normative structure or legal system of any society includes limitations on individuals' rights to do as they please with resources, including their own behavior, that they themselves control.

The norms people develop may be **proscriptive**, limiting individuals' rights to engage in certain types of actions, or **prescriptive**, requiring individuals to perform certain types of actions (Coleman, 1990:246–249). Regardless of the nature of the norm, the emergence of social consensus regarding norms means in effect that we collectively establish certain rights that involve controlling other people's actions while other individuals also have rights to control our actions. In other words, members of society agree to abide by certain restrictions on their rights to act, and to accept obligations to act in certain ways, in exchange for similar restrictions and obligations imposed on others. The process of generating such consensus may involve appeals to moral values and the collective welfare or to individuals' personal interests, but it is essentially a political process. This emphasis on social consensus and contractual agreements for establishing rights contrasts with the arguments of social philosophers who insist on inalienable natural rights. "Natural rights" are seen in Coleman's perspective as reflecting a form of social consensus that is sufficiently widespread and long-standing to appear to be "natural."

Norms are never automatically self-enforcing. Instead, their enforcement requires some form of monitoring or surveillance plus the right to impose sanctions for nonconformity. In small-scale social systems with a rich network of social relations and high levels of mutual surveillance, informal social controls, like expressions of approval or disapproval, may suffice to enforce reasonably high conformity with widely accepted norms. In contrast, large-scale systems require formal authority systems and social control agencies that are authorized to administer sanctions. (The creation of agencies to enforce legally encoded norms will be discussed in more detail in Chap. 9.) Whether surveillance and sanctions are formal or informal, there are costs associated with enforcing norms, and these costs must be evaluated in relation to the benefits that result. In any case, the development of a normative and legal framework that regulates our behavior may be expected to influence the cost/reward calculations of persons entering particular exchange transactions. For example, an employer's hiring decisions must conform to minimum wage and affirmative action legislation or major negative consequences could result. In family contexts, external sanctions may be invoked to insure that parents care for their children or to prevent spouse abuse.

People have multiple interests, of course, and the ongoing challenge individuals face is to apportion their limited resources (time, energy, money, etc.) in ways that provide optimal satisfaction of a wide range of interests. This requires choices. A major collective dilemma for the members of society has to do with how much freedom individuals should retain to use their resources in pursuit of their own interests, as opposed to giving up certain resources (taxes, charitable contributions, voluntary social services) for the collective welfare. The tensions people experience in deciding how to allocate their scarce resources in pursuing a variety of sometimes conflicting goals seems to be an inevitable feature of the human condition that makes rational decision making difficult. Moreover, the ability of people to make rational decisions in pursuit of their own interests (as well as collective interests) is limited by their inability to anticipate the relevant actions of others or the consequences of their own actions. In the following section, we shall deal with some of the conflicts, dilemmas, and uncertainties that people face as they pursue their individual interests, especially when others are likewise attempting to maximize their interests.

The Risk of Perverse Effects

The concept of perverse effects refers to unintended outcomes of people's actions that turn out to be more costly or less beneficial than alternative actions would have been (Boudon, 1982). Ironically, this is a common occurrence that results from the rational choices individuals make in seeking the best possible reward/cost outcome in pursuing their interests. The problem is that the anticipated rewarding outcomes are often contingent on the actions or responses of others. Even though the actions of others are not known in advance, people generally assume that they will also act in terms of their self-interests, and so they plan their own strategies accordingly. But when all participants act rationally to maximize their own interests, the combined effects of their actions may be less beneficial, or less rational, than if they had opted for some alternative course of action. For example, from the narrow and short-term standpoint of individuals' own personal interests, one might be tempted to free-ride as much as possible, provided negative sanctions can be avoided. In this way one could benefit from the contributions of others without incurring the costs of making contributions in return. However, if everyone were to adopt this strategy, no contributions will be made, collective goals will not be achieved, and no benefits would be available for anyone. To prevent this negative outcome, procedures are established to insure that people pay their "fair share" for benefits received and that the negative sanctions for free-riders are more costly than the benefits they could otherwise receive from the free-riding strategy. Even so, theft from retail establishments, plus failure to attend meetings of voluntary organizations, provide illustrations of the appeal of free-riding and the limits of social control.

This free-rider illustration demonstrates in a blatant way the irrational or negative outcomes that can result from individuals' "rational choice" decisions to give priority to their own personal interests instead of fulfilling their social obligations or paying their fair share. In other words, actions that appear "rational" at the individual level generate **less** benefits than some alternative action that initially appears more costly and thus less "rational." This paradoxical result occurs when the aggregation of individuals' apparently "rational" actions generates unintended consequences that turn out to be irrational, either in terms of their self-interests or the collective welfare. In a similar way, irrational effects may result when the satisfaction of short-range needs undermines long-range goals, an outcome that may occur at either the individual or the collective level.

To the extent that the potential problem of perverse effects is recognized, people may develop norms that restrict or regulate their freedom to satisfy their immediate individual preferences. Justification for such norms is provided through arguments regarding individuals' own long-range interests or the greater public good. But from the individual's own perspective, particularly in the short run, such norms may appear to be more costly than beneficial. Ironically, however, normative regulations that appear irrational from a short-term or individualistic perspective may be rational in a longer-term or larger perspective. All share in the benefits of actions that contribute to the public welfare, despite the reluctance that individuals may feel in incurring costs that they may feel are greater than the benefits they will receive personally, especially in the short run.

The law of perverse effects is clearly illustrated in the well-known Prisoner's Dilemma game as described by Boudon (1982:79–80). In this game two persons must each decide whether or not to confess to a crime they committed, but neither knows what the other will do. The game is set up so that if both individuals confess both will get 5 years in jail; if neither confesses both of them will get 2 years, but if one confesses and the other does not, the confessor will go free while the non-confessor will be sentenced to 10 years imprisonment. Since neither knows whether the other party will confess or not, the rational choice for both would be to confess and to hope the other will not confess. But if both make this rational choice, the 5 years in jail both would receive would be preferable to the 10-year sentence the non-confessor would receive if the other confesses. Both could have come out better if neither confessed, with only 2 years imprisonment each. Thus when both parties do what appears to be most rational for themselves by confessing, the 5-year outcome both will receive is longer than the 2 years both would have received if neither had confessed.

Comparable rational choice dilemmas could be identified in other games as well as in real life. In basketball, for example, the player who is determined to establish a strong individual record by always going to the basket to try to score may end up actually scoring less (because of the opposing team's defensive strategies), plus contribute to the team's defeat. Real life choices are of course more complicated, with more choices and larger numbers of participants. Moreover, the problem in real life goes beyond lack of knowledge regarding the decisions or actions of others. After all, we can usually plan our own actions on the basis of the assumption that other people will act in their own self-interest. But even when these assumptions are correct, the combined effects of the rational actions of many people may include unanticipated negative consequences and/or fewer benefits than anticipated. For example, if everyone in a large city tries to avoid rush hour traffic by leaving home or work early, the result is early rush hour traffic.

Another example of a perverse outcome resulting from the aggregation of individuals' "rational" decisions was illustrated in Boudon's (1982:80–104) analysis of the choices made by French students as to whether to enroll in a longer-term advanced higher education program or shorter-term technical or vocational education. The shorter-term option had been established in the late 1960s, partly because the labor market was not able to absorb the increasing numbers of higher education graduates at a level commensurate with their education. However, students continued to prefer the longer-term university education, despite the advantages of the shorter-term option and the oversupply of graduates from the longer-term system for the labor market. In making their decision, it appeared that each student anticipated being an exception by obtaining one of the increasingly scarce high-paying jobs requiring the longer-term education. But because of the large the number who made this apparently "rational" decision, the probability that any one of them would succeed was decreased.

The same sort of perverse effect outcome is evident in the job market for PhD graduates in many fields in the United States as well. As many university departments have in the past sought to enhance their reputation by expanding their graduate program enrollments and producing ever increasing numbers of PhD graduates, they contributed to the oversupply of PhDs in some areas in the labor market. This decreased the probability that graduates in these fields would be able to obtain the traditional career goal of an academic appointment. Perverse effects can also be identified in the education system in the social processes that contribute to "grade inflation." Naturally, it is in students' interests to obtain high grades. However, as more and more students figure out how to succeed in this effort, the result is a decline in the value of grades as a reliable indicator of above-average achievement. To put it bluntly, there is nothing special about grades of A or B when almost everyone earns them.

The key point to note is that perverse effects are the ironic result of the combined effects of "rational" actions that individuals undertake in pursuit of their own self-interests. (For a more elaborate analysis with numerous historical examples, see Boudon, 1979). It is precisely this individualistic type of action that characterizes market systems. In fact, in market economies the dynamics of currency inflation, recession, or high unemployment can be seen as perverse effects of the aggregation of innumerable actions that appear rational from the standpoint of individuals' self-interests and perhaps the collective welfare as well. On a much broader scale the contemporary problem of global warming, as documented in the film, "An Inconvenient Truth" (starring Al Gore), can be regarded as a perverse long-term outcome of the technological and industrial progress associated with the development of modern society.

As unanticipated and unintended perverse effects accumulate, they may eventually be impossible to ignore. Once recognized as social problems, various strategies may be devised to try to prevent, minimize, or eliminate them. One strategy is to develop formal or informal alternatives to individualistic decision-making. For example, if participants in a prisoners' dilemma game were allowed to communicate with one another, they could collaborate in developing a more rational strategy than what they would choose on their own, and over time they would learn the benefits of mutual trust. When we learn through experience what to expect from one another, we are able to make a more informed and thus more rational decision. The potential benefits that may result when people deal with others they know and trust helps explain the efforts they often make to maintain their social networks. In contrast to the trust that often develops in personal relations, transactions among people who do not know one another personally often require a formal agreement or contract backed up by legal sanctions to insure their ability to predict one another's future behavior and thereby be assured of a mutually satisfactory exchange.

The next chapter will provide a fuller analysis of different types of social networks. In addition to viewing networks solely in terms of individuals' self-interests, we will also focus on processes by which some network relations evolve to incorporate socioemotional bonds whereby individuals' personal interests expand to embrace the interests of others.

Summary

The primary goal of this chapter has been to focus on the process whereby individuals seek to advance their interests, both material and nonmaterial, through the exchange process. Exchange patterns may be contrasted in terms of whether they are direct or indirect. Direct exchanges tend to reflect a strong individualistic orientation in which participants develop the terms of exchange on their own. Indirect exchanges are more likely to reflect a collectivist orientation in which the benefits received and the obligations incurred are linked to membership in some social group. American exchange theory reflects primarily the individualistic view, beginning with George Homans' effort to explain elementary (face-to-face) behavior in terms of principles taken from behavioral psychology and economics. Homans' initial concern was to show that people's behavior reflects their own needs and motives as human beings, not the needs of society or other social systems as implied in functional theory. People's behaviors are shaped through the reinforcements or punishments (such as approval or disapproval) they provide one another. Relationships tend to persist when the rewards people receive (minus the costs) are greater than those that could be obtained elsewhere, though the specific terms reflect variations in investments as well as the effects of deprivation and satiation.

We looked next at Peter Blau's exchange theory, which focuses heavily on how imbalanced exchanges give rise to status differences and the emergence of power structures. At the micro level his distinction between intrinsic and extrinsic exchanges corresponds roughly to the differences between social versus economic exchanges. Intrinsic exchanges reflect mutual emotional attachments and are common among persons who are roughly equal in status. Extrinsic exchanges in contrast, do not involve emotional attachments. When people are unequal in terms of their resources relevant to the exchange, the resulting imbalance generates power and dependency relations. The emergence of power differences provides the foundation for macro structures and collective action—a process to be described more fully in Chap. 9.

The basic ideas of exchange theory were eventually incorporated into the contemporary perspective of rational choice theory. Individuals' rational choice efforts to minimize costs and maximize rewards means there is a fundamental conflict of interest built into all exchange transactions. Hechter's analysis contrasts the way these dynamics are manifested in compensatory versus obligatory groups. In compensatory groups some form of payment is needed because individuals' interests are not intrinsically linked with achievement of the group's goals. With obligatory groups, in contrast, members are expected to contribute because they all benefit through membership in the group and accomplishment of the group's goals.

The individualistic orientation of the social exchange and rational choice perspectives was further developed in James Coleman's explanation of how the exchange process is initiated when people have less interests in resources that they control, including their own behavior, than they do in resources controlled by others. However, exchange transactions are regulated by normative systems that limit and constrain individuals' rights to do as they please with the resources that they control, including (again) their own behavior. Such regulations reflect a consensus that certain behaviors should be either prohibited or prescribed, regardless of individuals' short-term preferences, for the sake of long-term benefits or the public good. With high levels of normative consensus, people restrict their rights to do as they please in satisfying their personal needs and preferences. They thereby avoid the negative sanctions prescribed for noncompliance, but they also benefit from the conformity of others. Chapter 9 will focus more heavily on macro level applications of Coleman's rational choice perspective as applied to the formation of corporate actors and the production of public goods.

People's ability to make rational choices is always limited by their lack of knowledge regarding all of the outcomes of their own behavior, especially when these outcomes are contingent on the outcomes of the actions of others of which they may be unaware. One of the effects of incomplete knowledge was illustrated in Boudon's analysis of the perverse effects that may occur when individuals' "rational" actions lead to irrational outcomes, both individually and collectively.

This was illustrated in the Prisoner's Dilemma game, but the basic process can be illustrated in many real-life contexts. The establishment of social networks of various types may help reduce the perverse effects of individualistic decision making by promoting increased awareness of one another's actions and their consequences. In addition, mutual trust often develops as individuals cooperate in achieving both individual and collective goals. In some cases, too, socioemotional bonds may be formed which lead people to be concerned with the interests and welfare of others as well as their own. In future chapters we shall look at how varying combinations of rational self-interest and socioemotional attachments give rise to contrasting types of social structures.

Questions for Study and Discussion

1. Do you agree or disagree that the concepts of investments, costs, rewards, and profits are useful in explaining people's level of satisfaction or dissatisfaction with their various social relationships? Explain. To what extent do people evaluate (or discuss) their various relationships in terms of the rewards they provide to one another? What strategies might they use if one party believes that another party is being unfair?
2. Which of your important current relationships involve power and dependency relations? Explain. Are you in a position of power or dependency in these relationships? How do these relationships compare and contrast with relationships where there is greater equality in terms of costs and rewards (material or nonmaterial)? Do you generally prefer to engage in sociable interaction with others who are roughly similar to you in terms of overall status, or with those who are higher or lower? Why?
3. Discuss the free-riding problem from a rational choice perspective and identify some strategies used by different types of orgnizations to minimize it. In thinking of this issue, consider costs and rewards in compensatory-types of organizations as well as obligatory and voluntary organizations.
4. Identify some examples of how exchange transactions (both economic and social) are regulated by the normative, moral, or legal framework of the larger society. From a rational choice perspective, what are the conditions that help explain whether individuals will comply with these regulations or violate them?
5. Explain why rational action sometimes turns out to be irrational, both for the individual involved and for others as well. What are some examples of these irrational outcomes and how do they develop?

Chapter 8
Networking and Belonging: Opportunity Structures, Rational Choice Exchanges, and the Sociology of Emotions

Exchange theory emphasizes that our various social relations reflect choices we make to try to satisfy our own needs and wants, both material and nonmaterial. In market transactions for material goods, it is appropriate to give priority to our own personal interests without regard to social ties or emotional considerations for the other party. Also, in making a decision as to which of two or more job offers to accept, for example, the pay is a major consideration, along with the nature of the job, which we evaluate in terms of our own personal preferences. Once we accept a job, we are then "out of the market"—at least until we consider changing jobs.

The "market" perspective may also be used when persons seek new friends after moving to a new community, when they evaluate potential marriage partners, or when they reflect on which of their acquaintances they would like to know better, or otherwise. Once relationships are formed, however, they lead to the formation of socioemotional bonds and patterns of mutual identification, and their dynamics then differ from pure market transactions. Individual interests are likely to be modified by shared concerns and diffuse obligations that cannot be defined in terms of narrow self-interests and impersonal market dynamics. In personal relations individuals not only engage in mutually rewarding emotional exchanges, but they actually experience one another's rewards and costs—their pleasures and pains—as their own. In this way personal needs and interests are expanded to include the needs and interests of others.

In between impersonal market transactions and personal relationships, many relationships involve a combination of different types of rewards. In a pure market system the resources people control, whether material, social, intellectual, emotional, or any other type, are not linked to any particular exchange partner but are available for using in any way individuals might choose. Their available choices, however, reflect the opportunities provided by their specific location in the social structure. In particular, their social location helps determine the range of their contacts and whether the people they encounter are likely to be similar or different in terms of various personal and social characteristics.

This chapter will build on the perspective of social exchange and rational choice theory but will balance its individualistic assumptions by incorporating ideas from two other areas of analysis: opportunity structures for different types of social contacts and relationships and the sociology of emotions. Following are the specific topics to be covered:

D.P. Johnson, *Contemporary Sociological Theory: An Integrated Multi-Level Approach.*

- Individual characteristics and opportunity structures—This section will review Peter Blau's structural theory of inequality and heterogeneity in order to show how opportunities vary in different segments of society for establishing social contacts or relationship with persons who are similar or different. As we shall see, Blau's structural theory provides a distinct alternative to his earlier social exchange theory.
- Social networks—The goal in this section is to show how the social exchange process gives rise to networks of relations with distinctive structural characteristics that can be analyzed independently of the particular social relations that make them up.
- Sociology of emotions—This section will show how socioemotional bonds lead individuals to identify with the welfare of others as well as their own needs and interests. Key ideas of David Kemper, Diane Rothbard Margolis, Thomas Scheff, and others will be reviewed to highlight the emotional aspects of personal relationships, reflecting people's efforts to meet their needs for belonging and acceptance. In addition, Arlie Russell Hochschild's analysis of airline flight attendants will serve as one example, among others, of how emotions are managed in organizational and institutional settings.
- Virtual social networks—In this final section, we will consider the sociological significance of new electronic forms of communication for market transactions, networking, and personal relationships, drawing on Manuel Castells' concept of the rapidly expanding "network society."

Opportunities and Limitations: Peter Blau's Structural Approach

As shown in the last chapter, Peter Blau's exchange theory emphasized that people's social exchanges reflect their assessments of the outcomes of the alternatives available to them. However, people do not have unlimited choices. We do not choose our parents, for example, and usually not our neighbors and co-workers, even though we may experience many different types of costs and rewards in all of these relationships. Moreover, the family into which we are born determines our socioeconomic class and the type of community in which we grow up. In our mobile society, we may eventually move to a different community and perhaps experience socioeconomic mobility in the process. But throughout our lives the specific circumstances of our background and present environment help to shape and limit our opportunities for developing relationships with different types of people.

The structural theory developed by Peter Blau (1977; see also Blau, 2001) can be used to explain both the opportunities and the constraints we have for associating with various types of people. This perspective begins by identifying the criteria used to differentiate people into different categories and positions, as opposed to the interactional dynamics of the exchange process itself. Blau's structural theory represents a clear shift away from the social psychological level as reflected in his earlier exchange theory.

Blau starts with the notion that people can be categorized in terms of both **nominal** and **graduated** parameters. **Nominal** parameters distinguish people into clearly distinct groups or categories, but with no rank ordering of the categories. **Graduated** parameters, in contrast, distinguish people in terms of higher or lower rank on various characteristics, but without sharp breaks between discrete categories. The **heterogeneity** of a society is based on the number of nominal categories used to classify people. Examples of such characteristics include ethnic background, religious identification, occupation, gender, and residential community. Graduated parameters, in contrast, include characteristics such as height, age, years of school, income, or other characteristics which allow for "more" or "less" ranking.[1] Such characteristics provide the basis for **inequality** in society, including in particular people's differential positions in the socioeconomic class structure. Both nominal and graduate parameters may overlap or crisscross in many different ways, giving rise to an objective set of social positions that may be defined in terms of multiple criteria.

A society or any other social formation can be described in terms of its **heterogeneity** and **inequality**. By implication, both types of parameters are measures of the extent of differentiation in society. These distinctions are useful in explaining our chances for encountering or associating with different types of people and establishing relations with them. As suggested by the everyday life observation that "birds of a feather flock together," people generally tend to develop personal relations with others who are similar to them in terms of both nominal and graduated characteristics. This may be due partly to choice and partly to circumstance. When interaction occurs among individuals who differ in important characteristics, the dynamics are likely to be different than when they are similar. All else being equal, we would expect mutual attraction, social bonding, and a sense of cohesion to be more common among persons who are similar in terms of group membership and status. This tendency for people to interact with others who are similar would give rise to a segmented type of social structure with limited interaction across the boundaries of different groups or status levels and thus low levels of integration of the overall society. On the other hand, even in a highly differentiated society, when there is extensive association between members of different nominal groups or status levels, this may be seen as an indicator of a higher level of social integration of the overall society than if these different groups are insulated from one another.

Despite the simplicity of Blau's basic structural concepts, real life distinctions are often blurred. This is due in part to the fuzziness of the boundaries between categories and also to the way different characteristics may overlap and crisscross one another in various ways. For example, although biological sex may seem to be a fairly clear-cut nominal parameter in most cases, socially constructed gender roles vary widely. Race and ethnicity are socially constructed categories that gloss over

[1] The contrast between nominal and graduated parameters is comparable to the distinction between nominal versus ordinal or interval levels of measurement in statistics.

the biological similarities among all peoples, and intermarriage among different groups in multiracial or multiethnic societies results in an obvious blurring of boundaries. Even so, such distinctions are often defined as socially important and are associated with variations in prestige, opportunities, and power in multi-racial and multi-ethnic societies.

Individuals are sometimes similar on several important characteristics. For example, people who live in the same neighborhood may belong to the same ethnic group, have the same general occupational prestige and religious orientation, identify with the same political party, and share the same values and lifestyle. This indicates a high level of **consolidation** among these various characteristics. On the other hand, instead of being correlated these characteristics may intersect and crisscross in various ways. Thus, for example, in some neighborhoods, residents vary in terms of race and ethnicity, religious affiliation, occupational prestige, family structure, and lifestyle. This indicates a high level of **intersection** among these different parameters.

High levels of **intersection** mean that any two people may be similar in some characteristics but different in others. Thus, for example, ethnic groups include people with different religious affiliations, occupations, residential locations, and so on. Similarly, a religious group may include people who vary in terms of ethnicity, education, occupation, residence, and family status. With high intersection and multiple criteria of classification, the odds are increased that people will be differentiated in multiple ways in terms of their particular configuration of nominal and graduated characteristics. The result is an increase in the complexity of the social structure, which Blau believed has the potential to help promote social integration.

In contrast, high **consolidation** means that the various dimensions that define individuals' structural positions are highly correlated, with different distinctions superimposed on one another so that people who are similar on one important characteristic are likely to be similar on others as well. Other things being equal, with high consolidation we should expect ingroup relations to be stronger than relations between groups, due to the fact that these various structural parameters provide multiple potential sources of cohesion that unite members of the ingroup and distinguish them from other groups.

Blau's distinction between intersection and consolidation is similar to Simmel's (1955) contrast in the early years of sociology between crosscutting versus overlapping group memberships. Like Simmel, Blau also pointed out that high levels of intersection require individuals to balance the conflicting claims of different groups, and this may limit their opportunity to become absorbed in highly cohesive groups that are insulated from one another. Even in differentiated societies with relatively high levels of intersection and integration, there may still be considerable consolidation in terms of several crucial distinctions in some segments of society. Thus some occupations are dominated by men while others are dominated by women—despite the increase in recent years in the numbers of women in occupations formerly filled only by men. In addition, patterns of racial segregation are still clearly evident in many communities and most churches. Despite the progress blacks have made in moving into occupations from which they had been excluded in the past, their overall distribution in terms of the various criteria of socioeconomic status still puts them at a lower average level than whites.

Consolidation of different dimensions is especially notable for the multiple graduated parameters that define people's socioeconomic positions. Individuals with high-prestige occupations typically have higher incomes, more power or authority, higher levels of education, more expensive lifestyles, and larger homes as well. But the overlap is not perfect. For example, a person may have administrative authority over several subordinates in a government agency but have far less wealth than a celebrity figure or a successful real estate entrepreneur who has no formal authority over others. Or, public school teachers or clergy persons may have more education but less income than many successful business owners.

In general, the chances people have for encountering or associating with different types of people is influenced by the level of heterogeneity and inequality in society and the distribution of people among various groups and status hierarchies. If minority group members, for example, were randomly distributed throughout the society, both majority and minority group members would be less likely to encounter minority group members than majority group members simply on the basis of the greater numbers of majority group members. But of course, the distribution is not random. Minority group members are often insulated in their own neighborhoods, and this increases their chances of encountering fellow minority group members and decreases their chances of encountering majority group members. The same logic would apply to relations among members of a community's small elite class versus a large middle or working class. Opportunities for members of the middle or working class to interact with elites is limited in part by the smaller size of the elite class and in part by their separation of members of the elite class in their own neighborhoods. Moreover, encounters are more likely to occur between persons who are adjacent to one another in a status hierarchy than between those who are more distant. Thus elites would be more likely to have contacts with middle class persons than with those in the working or lower class. And working class persons are more likely to encounter those in lower middle class occupations than those in upper middle class occupations.

Although heterogeneity tends to create social divisions and barriers to interaction, Blau pointed out that high heterogeneity also has the paradoxical effect of increasing the chances of intergroup association. This is due to the simple fact that high heterogeneity reduces the likely proportion in any one category. Thus the odds are increased of encountering others who are different, other things being equal. Similarly, when multiple status hierarchies intersect with one another (as opposed to being consolidated), this increases the likelihood that individuals will encounter or associate with others who are similar in some ways but different in others. The general effect of intersecting status hierarchies is to reduce overall status differences. On the other hand, if members of different groups are insulated from one another through residential segregation or other barriers, this would counter the effect of high heterogeneity.

Real life examples can readily be cited to illustrate how Blau's concept of social structure affects the chances for different types of people to encounter or associate with one another. In the area of race relations, for example, because blacks are a much lower percentage of the population in northwestern states such as Idaho than in southern states like Georgia, both blacks and whites are more likely to encounter whites than blacks in Idaho. As the percentage of minority group members increases, the chances that majority group members will encounter them increases. However, this effect is often offset by segregation. Thus in large cities the percentage of blacks is high enough for patterns of neighborhood segregation to develop that limit opportunities for chance encounters between blacks and whites.

Blau's model can also be applied to the effects of increasing numbers of women in positions previously dominated by men. When women began to make progress in shattering the glass ceiling that excluded them from top positions in the corporate world, the professions, and government, their opportunities to associate with women colleagues at the same level were extremely limited. The same was true for men's opportunities to interact with women in elite positions. These structural conditions made it likely that women would be seen as "tokens" and treated differently. A study by Kantor (1977) examines the experience of women and men in corporate life and described the problems that women experience as a result of their significantly lower numbers in high-level positions. But as the proportion of women expands, their "token" status eventually fades, and opportunities for both women and men to interact as colleagues (or competitors) will increase.

Within the overall context of the structural conditions analyzed by Blau, there is a large element of chance in terms of the specific people who cross our paths and with whom we have the opportunity to initiate social relations. Inevitably, some of our encounters are likely to be more rewarding than others, and different types of people turn out to be relevant for providing different types of rewards. Thus we are more likely to exchange emotional support with others who are similar to us in terms of power, status, and group membership. In contrast, persons who are higher or lower in terms of power or status, or who differ in terms of the nominal groups to which they belong, may provide other kinds of rewards, including, for example, new opportunities and experiences and potential access to different social networks. Theodore Kemper (1978) analyzed in detail how differentials in the power and status that people attribute to one another in their encounters affect their level of satisfaction as well as their anticipations of the outcomes of future encounters. All else being equal, we might exact that interaction among persons who see themselves as roughly equal would be less guarded and more likely to develop into a close personal relationship.

As emphasized in Homans' exchange theory, individuals tend to repeat behaviors that provide the best overall reward/cost outcomes, thereby giving rise to enduring social relations. All of these various relationships constitute identifiable networks. As social networks are stabilized, specific channels emerge through which costs and rewards flow as people repeat satisfying exchange transactions over and over again. But despite the general stability that often characterizes network structures, changes occur over time as a result of changes in people's social locations as well as their periodic assessment of the costs and benefits they receive in comparison to other alternatives that become available.

Many repetitive exchanges no doubt reflect habits that people develop. However, the persistence of habits can be explained in the rational choice perspective in terms of avoiding the costs of spending time, emotional energy, and other resources in exploring other alternatives and facing the risk that new choices may be less rewarding than the old ones. Although habits and routines are changed from time to time, probably most people tend to maintain relationships in which they have learned to trust one another and that they find rewarding. Some of these may involve close friendships or alliances while others are more casual acquaintances or occasional contacts. Both types may change over time, becoming more or less intense, sometimes intentionally and sometimes as a result of other circumstances in people's lives. We turn next to an analysis of the various types of relationships that make up our social networks and how these networks themselves may vary.

Networks, Groups, and Personal Relationships

Social networks and relationships emerge from repeated exchange patterns (Emerson, pp. 58–87 in J. Berger, M. Zelditch, and B. Anderson, eds., 1972). The social ties they reflect may provide the foundation for additional types of exchanges whereby varying levels and types of social bonding sometimes occur. At one extreme are casual acquaintances with whom we have fairly weak bonds, perhaps rare or occasional interaction, and only mild emotional involvement. At the other extreme, some relationships involve frequent (even daily) interaction and strong positive emotional ties. Some relationships may involve negative emotions, in which case the persistence of the relationship at some level would suggest that there are other, perhaps extrinsic-type rewards that are involved in the exchange or major costs in terminating it.

Regardless of whether the relationships in people's social networks are intense or more casual, or their exchanges frequent or infrequent, such ties can be seen as a kind of resource, a form of social capital, that may be useful to the people involved as they pursue their individual interests. In everyday language, it is often important to know the "right" people to achieve the best outcomes for oneself. Individuals in our network can link us to other networks, serve as important sources of information, and provide numerous other benefits, in addition to providing validation for our self-identities and some level of emotional support.

Network Analysis

Once social networks emerge, their characteristics can be analyzed at their own level, independently of the cost/reward considerations of the individuals involved in them. This strategy was pioneered by Moreno's (1934) strategy of showing how the basic features of individuals' direct and indirect social contacts could be portrayed in terms of a sociometric diagram. A more recent technical analysis is provided in Burt's (1982) effort to show how network properties are linked to social structure. Such an analysis goes beyond Blau's focus on objective similarities and differences among people, but it is consistent with the goal of providing a structural explanation for people's social relations. Network analysis deals explicitly with the structure of the various associations people develop, analyzing their shape, the characteristics of the various positions within them, how they may vary, and the way different networks may be linked.

At the individual level, people can be distinguished according to whether their position in a particular network is central or peripheral. Another distinction is whether most of their social network contacts are in their own local community or ingroup or are more widespread—sometimes described as the contrast between "locals" and "cosmopolitans." Related to this is the difference between those whose relationships are mostly with others like themselves (in terms of occupation, residential neighborhood, religion, age, gender, and other characteristics) and those whose who have a wide range of contacts with different types of people in diverse social settings. In addition, networks can be compared and contrasted in terms of characteristics such as size, the nature and strength of the ties among participants, the ratio of direct to indirect linkages, and the proportion of participants with outside ties of various types. Analyses of network structures and the various positions within it do not require detailed explanations of the specific reward/cost calculations that motivate people's involvement in particular networks and relationships.

A crucial characteristic of networks is the degree to which the members are mutually connected in some fashion. At one extreme, individual A may have ties with individuals B, C, D, and E, but these latter four have no direct ties among themselves. At the other extreme, all five members may be connected directly, indicating a high level of density. In between these extremes there may be various other combinations. These combinations may shift according to the occasion and the specific interests of those involved. Thus, for example, B, C, and D may get together regularly to engage in certain activities, while A, C, D, and E get together less frequently for other types of activities. Network configurations expand as individuals introduce acquaintances to one another or contract as they lose touch.

A dense network is necessary for group formation, but it does not necessarily constitute a social group in the full sense of the term. For A, B, C, D, and E to form a group, it would be necessary not only that all members be connected as individuals but that they be involved in interaction as a distinct collectivity. This means they must be aware of the mutual relationships they share, and each must identify with all of the others not just as individuals but as fellow members of their group. It does not mean they must be in regularly scheduled contact, or that every single member must be present each time some of them get together. But if a member is absent, the others will recognize that one of their members is not there. With networks that do not form actual groups, in contrast, participants may be unaware of the full range of social ties they share and thus have no sense of a collective identity, or they may be familiar with one another's reputation and perhaps some of the relationships other members have with one another but without necessarily having their own connection. In everyday life probably most people recognize the difference between loose and unstructured forms of "networking" versus "belonging" to particular groups with a distinct identity and high levels of mutual identification of members with one another.[2]

The probability that individuals who are connected indirectly through various network ties will actually encounter one another is likely to be influenced in part by chance and the routine trajectories they follow in their particular social worlds. But social exchange and rational choice theory would suggest that whether individuals who encounter one another by chance will actually develop social relations will depend upon their assessment of potential reward/cost outcomes. In a heterogeneous network with various forms of inequality, we might expect that some relationships will be balanced through reciprocal interdependence and some imbalanced in terms of power/dependency relations (Cook et al., 1983). Whether a group is formed from interconnected network ties will likewise depend upon whether the rewards that are anticipated through forming a group are greater than the rewards they could each achieve through the individual relationships that some of them have with one another. As implied in Thibaut and Kelley's (1959) perspective, individuals compare the reward/cost outcome involved in interacting with one another as individuals, as opposed to developing a group out of some of their network ties. For a network to be transformed into a group, it would be necessary for its members to become aware of their various ties and the interests they share that could be advanced collectively. This process would probably require some leadership initiative to handle the necessary logistics to form a group (establishing a time and meeting place, for example), but whether this is successful will depend on the assessments of others in the network as to the benefits they would receive.

Between the extremes of loose connections versus cohesive groups, networks may be characterized by varying proportions of both direct and indirect relationships. For example, A may be connected directly to all four of the others in a network (B, C, D, and E), while B and C know one another, plus A, but have no ties with D and E. Similarly, D and E may have ties with one another, plus A, but not with B and C. In this type of network, A would serve as a bridge, linking the two dyads consisting of B and C on the one hand and D and E on the other. These variations could be extended to larger networks as well, but the underlying analysis would be the same. In any case the resulting network structure will reflect both the opportunities and the reward/cost assessments of all involved.

[2] This concept of a group differs from Blau's definition as described above in his structural theory. Blau defined a group in terms of objective nominal categories that are used to establish distinctions between people, whether or not they are connected through interaction. However, Blau's theory makes it clear that being in the same nominal category tends to increase the odds of association, all else being equal.

Exchange Processes in Networks, Groups, and Personal Relationships

Mapping network structures can be contrasted with the more social psychological analysis of individuals' reward/cost considerations. Even so, inferences can readily be drawn regarding the social psychological dynamics that occur within networks, particularly when we take into consideration the power differentials resulting from variations in resources (Cook et al., 1983). For example, participants in dense networks whose resources are roughly equal will typically find it easier to develop strong social bonds and a sense of group identity than participants in networks with fewer mutual interconnections, less similarities, or great disparities in resources. Moreover, participants in networks that are dense and relatively closed are likely to see their social ties in these networks as important to their self-concept and the satisfaction of various emotional needs, such as the need for belonging. In addition, frequent or highly intense involvement in such a network means that less time and energy are available for maintaining social ties in other networks.

On the other hand, persons in more marginal positions in a particular network (or group) may be expected to derive less emotional rewards from it, to be less bound by its norms, and to regard it as less important for their identity. Some marginal members may also be involved in other networks. To the extent that individuals maintain ties with multiple networks, the intensity of their involvement in any one network will probably be less, due simply to limitations of time, energy, and other resources. As Blau emphasized in his structural theory, persons who have even limited involvement in several different networks may serve as a bridge or link between these networks. The contrast between the bonding and the bridging functions of different types of network involvement is highlighted in Robert Putnam's (2000:22–24) analysis of how network ties serve as the foundation for the development of the social capital that promotes people's willingness to be involved in voluntary activities promoting the public welfare.[3]

In a frequently cited analysis of the "strength of weak ties," Granovetter (1973) emphasized the importance of such bridging or linking positions in a large and heterogeneous society. Through "weak ties" in multiple networks people are linked together in larger, more encompassing, and more complex social structures than would otherwise be possible. But persons in marginal positions in multiple networks may be faced with the challenge of balancing conflicting claims and loyalties. At the same time, they are more likely to be able to maintain a higher level of detachment and independence than those with strong ingroup ties and limited involvement in multiple networks. In addition to promoting integration and interdependence in large and complex social structures, weak ties may be important at the individual level in providing access to valued information, opportunities, and other resources that can be used in other exchange transactions. For example, the social ties that

---

[3] The concept of social capital will be developed more fully in the following chapter.

students establish with their professors may be useful in gaining information about colleagues in a graduate program they are considering or job openings. Or, individuals who want to change jobs may learn about new job openings through network contacts in other organizations.

As we shift from impersonal markets to network contacts to personal relationships and groups, there are corresponding shifts in the nature of the costs and rewards involved. In impersonal market transactions individuals are expected to attempt to satisfy their individual needs and wants, with no personal obligations to their exchange partners other than to abide by the general norms and laws governing market transactions. At the other extreme, the development of personal relationships reduces individuals' independence and produces greater identification with their exchange partners or with groups to which they belong, plus corresponding obligations. Although individuals may benefit personally from these social relations, their own interests are tied closely to the welfare of others, and they develop varying levels of emotional identification with them. As described by Cooley and by Schutz, the individual's "I" has been merged with the "we" in the relationship or the group.

The level of cohesiveness in personal relationships and groups varies greatly. In general, social networks may be classified between the extremes of impersonal markets and cohesive groups. In a large and complex society with high mobility and numerous crisscrossing and overlapping group memberships, we would expect a large proportion of network contacts to be low-intensity, where contacts may be incidental and serve mainly to reaffirm the social tie and share news regarding common interests, but with no other rewards exchanged. ("Give me a call when you are in town and we'll talk.") Even indirect ties can be recognized and reaffirmed through occasional contacts such as these. ("How are Betty and John? Tell them Hi for me.") Network ties that are maintained (or renewed) through occasional contacts are common when people's opportunities for interaction are truncated because of geographical mobility or multiple obligations in different social circles. Even so, these low-intensity network ties may readily be utilized as individuals seek to satisfy their interests. Thus, for example, we are likely to go back to the same dentist if we are satisfied; if not, we may solicit advice from friends or co-workers. Or students may ask professors they know for advice about various graduate schools, reference letters, or information about employment opportunities. Or a person may ask a co-worker or some casual acquaintance for the name of the attorney or accountant he or she used rather than search the internet or the yellow pages of the phone book.

Within networks where there is ample opportunity for interaction, we would expect cohesion or solidarity to be greater if members are similar in terms of personal characteristics, trust one another, exchange emotional support, and validate and support one another's core identities. Being a part of a relationship or a group with high solidarity is likely also to be a major component of participants' identities and may help motivate frequent interaction. Social exchanges between close friends contrast with more casual network exchanges not only because of the greater intensity of emotional bonds on which they are based but also the way this changes the nature of the exchanges that occur. This distinction corresponds to Cooley's distinction between primary and secondary groups. As Homans pointed out in his exchange theory, people who interact frequently often (but not always) develop positive sentiments of mutual liking. Blau also distinguished between the exchange of extrinsic rewards in impersonal market-type transactions from the exchange of intrinsic rewards involving mutual emotional attachments. Molm and her colleagues also highlighted the process whereby emotional bonds develop from repeated exchanges that both parties regard as highly satisfying (Molm et al., 2000), and Lawler and Yoon (1996, 1998, 2000) pointed out the way emotional ties produce commitment to particular exchange partners and promote group cohesion.

All such relationships may change over time. Network contacts sometimes develop out of impersonal market transactions, and close friendships may evolve from network contacts. Alternatively, the emotional intensity of friendships may deteriorate for various reasons, or positive ties may be replaced by negative feelings if either or both parties should betray their mutual trust or if costs should escalate above the value of the rewards received. Even so, former friends may continue to be part of one another's social network. Network ties may also dissipate when individuals simply lose touch with one another. The next section will focus more explicitly on the emotional dynamics of exchanges that occur in personal relationships.

Social Bonding and the Sociology of Emotions

The sociological study of emotions has expanded greatly in recent years. Such a focus is appropriate because of the importance of emotions in all aspects of our everyday life experience. Some type of affect or feeling is a ubiquitous component of our subjective consciousness, even when it may be in the background. Emotional bonds and exchanges are clearly important in the ongoing dynamics of close personal relationships and cohesive primary groups. Even the impersonal or secondary encounters of the market and in formal organizational settings can be characterized in terms of the level of positive or negative emotional arousal that they stimulate and that influence their dynamics. The management of one's emotions in various relationships and contexts requires self-awareness as well as empathy and sensitivity to others.[4] A large part of the emotional tone that characterizes all types of relationships has to do with the degree of people's willingness or unwillingness to accept one another's perceived "definitions of the situation" and the identities they seek to project in the manner analyzed by Goffman. As pointed out by Mitchell (1978), the concerns people have regarding their reactions to one another reflect underlying social bonds that are not adequately reflected in the calculating individualism emphasized in exchange theory. The importance of these bonds can be seen in people's efforts make to a good impression on others through the strategies of presentation of self emphasized by Goffman, as well as in their willingness, usually, to

[4] For a practical discussion of how people can learn to manage their emotions see Goleman (1995).

understand and accept one another's claims regarding their identities and their understanding of the situation they face. In addition, the widely shared implicit knowledge that is emphasized in the ethnomethodological perspective also points to a foundation of underlying social bonds that exist at a deeper level than the individualistic calculating orientation of the exchange theory perspective.

The term **emotion** is rather amorphous and can have different implications in different contexts. In everyday life the term often refers to specific forms of arousal with commonly understood labels (love, pride, shame, anger, jealousy, envy, joy, happiness, and many others). Some other term, such as affect or feeling, may then be needed to label the more inchoate and ill-defined subjective states that we experience as an ever-present feature of our subjective consciousness. All of these subjective feeling states can readily be distinguished as highly positive, mildly positive, highly negative, or mildly negative. Despite their personal and subjective character, emotions are socially constructed and reflect varying levels of sensitivity to the social setting and the expectations of others. In some settings, such as funerals or weddings, it is difficult to be present without being drawn into the collective emotional experience. Both emotional arousal and the labeling and expression of emotional states reflect socially defined expectations that are implicitly understood.

Some level of emotional arousal is likely to be involved in all types of encounters and social relations, whether intended or not. As noted earlier, Kemper (1978) showed how emotional responses are influenced by status and power considerations. He focused heavily on people's evaluations of their own perceived status and power relative to that of others as well as their attributions of power and status to others. For example, although adequate power in a relationship provides a feeling of security, excessive use of one's own power in a relationship can trigger feelings of guilt and anxiety, while inadequate power results in feelings of inadequacy and vulnerability. Regarding status, when a person sees his or her behavior as indicating less competence than expected on the basis of his or her status in the eyes of others, the emotional outcome is likely to be a sense of shame, while if others fail to attribute the deserved level of status, the result is anger (Kemper, 1978:47–71).

Both rational choice theory and the sociology of emotions are useful for understanding different aspects of social relations. Despite the popular contrast people often make between being rational versus being emotional, rational choice and exchange theories allow ample room for analysis of emotional costs and rewards. However, the development of strong socioemotional bonds in close personal relationships often seems to overshadow the individualistic assumptions of the rational choice perspective. In contrast to impersonal market transactions, in our close personal relationships the emotional ties that bind us together have the potential to override (though not eliminate) or to combine with our narrow individualistic interests. While people certainly find such relationships personally rewarding, they also are likely to develop genuine concerns for one another's well-being in ways that appear to go beyond the individualistic assumptions of rational choice theory. Even the self-concepts of those involved in close personal relationships are modified to incorporate their mutual identification with one another and their attachment to the relationship.

With high levels of mutual identification, friends, lovers, and family members are emotionally attuned to one another, empathize with one another, and readily experience one another's pleasures and pains as their own. We are rewarded vicariously when the needs of our families and close friends are satisfied or when they receive rewards that give them pleasure. Thus we are motivated to engage in behaviors that will be rewarding to them, even when it may be costly to us personally or detract from the rewards we would otherwise experience. "It is more blessed to give than to receive"—especially to those to whom we feel strongly attached and who reward us with their gratitude, acceptance, and support. In the context of family life, for example, parents make sacrifices for their children, while adult children may devote themselves to caring for aging parents despite the costs involved. Although self-sacrificing behavior may be motivated in part by the desire to avoid social disapproval, sincere concern for the well-being of others is also part of the picture. On the other hand, tensions and conflicts among individuals in close personal relations may be fueled by emotions that go well beyond rational calculation of costs and benefits. Intense emotional experiences and expressions are a major source of the tensions and divisions among people involved in personal relations as well as a major aspect of the social bonds that unite them. In contrast to the rational choice emphasis on calculations of individual costs and benefits, the sociology of emotions sheds a somewhat different light on both the positive and the negative dynamics of social relations.

Beyond the level of personal relationships, emotional commitments may include identification with larger groups, even including individuals with whom one has no personal relationship, and sometimes extending to the general welfare of society or all of humanity. When this occurs, it may motivate behavior that transcends or goes beyond individuals' own personal interests for the sake of others. Saintly individuals like the late Mother Teresa, for example, intentionally devote a large part of their lives to sacrificing their own interests for the sake of others in need. While Mother Teresa clearly illustrates a rare form of altruistic saintliness, everyday life includes numerous examples of people who devote time, energy, and money to various voluntary organizations because of their idealistic commitments to causes greater than their own narrow self-interests.

Rational choice theorists may focus on the personal rewards of sainthood or altruism, such as the gratitude of recipients and the acclaim of others. But this emphasis on individual payoffs seems to miss the point regarding the subjective motivations expressed in saintly or altruistic behavior. Despite the emphasis of rational choice theorists on self-interest in motivating people's behavior, individuals sometimes seem inspired to give higher priority to conforming to their moral ideals and fulfilling their obligations to others than earning benefits for themselves, including the gratitude of recipients or celebrity status (D. P. Johnson, 2003). On a more mundane level, a large part of the drama of social life involves seeking to balance our own needs with our obligations to collaborate with others in meeting their needs as well as our own. Selfish behavior would no doubt be even more blatant if we had no concern with the potential disapproval of others. Moreover, positive or negative reactions seem to carry more weight for our self-esteem when they are from people with whom we have strong emotional ties.

Our emotions are probably never completely "switched off." Even in casual encounters with minimal levels of arousal, subtle signals of approval or disapproval are likely to have some effects on our emotions and self-esteem, leading us to feel either more positive about ourselves or more negative. In his analysis of interaction ritual chains, Randall Collins (1981, 2004) pointed out that the positive or negative emotional arousal that results from any encounter lingers for a time and may influence subsequent encounters in a positive or negative way. We recognize these carry-forward effects in everyday life, such as, for example, when anger aroused at work is carried home and leads to negative family encounters. Even when the feelings aroused are mild and not even consciously recognized, their effect is still likely to carry forward to the next encounter, especially if it occurs soon afterward, and to influence its initial stages. The emotional aspects of all types of social relations are important to consider along with individuals' rational calculation of costs and rewards.

Gender Differences in Emotional Bonding Versus Pursuit of Self-Interests

People differ greatly in terms of how sensitive they are to the positive or negative reactions of others. They also vary in terms of how individualistic and independent they are, as opposed to identifying with the needs and feelings of others. Such contrasts are often linked specifically to sex and gender roles. Sociologists generally emphasize that many of the differences that are often considered to be natural or based on our biological characteristics as human beings are socially constructed. Our concern in this section is not primarily with whether these gender differences are due primarily to biology or to social influences.[5] In any case, it should be pointed out that there are major variations within socially constructed gender categories as well.

Carol Gilligan's (1982) analysis of gender differences emphasizes the contrasting socialization experiences of girls and boys, beginning in the earliest years of their lives, that shape their fundamental character development and identity. Her portrayal of gender roles is consistent with everyday life experience; girls develop a stronger orientation toward cooperative social relationships and greater sensitivity to their emotional dynamics, while boys learn to be more independent and assertive and to think in terms of abstract principles as opposed to being sensitive to feelings. An explanation of these gender differences is provided in Nancy Chodorow's (1978) analysis of the typical pattern whereby mothers encourage their sons from the earliest years of their lives to differentiate themselves from her in their growing up years and learn to be independent, while daughters are encouraged to identify with their mothers. Thus mothers reproduce the sensitive, nurturing, and self-giving patterns of the role of motherhood in their daughters, and these patterns then carry over into the daughter's social relationships. This contrasts sharply with the way mothers

[5] In Chap. 18, we will look at gender differences from the contrasting perspective of sociobiology.

encourage their sons to learn to stand up for themselves and be independent. Fathers, of course, tend to concur with these patterns. These differences in the way girls and boys are socialized, beginning in the earliest years of their lives, are reflected in the adult roles of both women and men as they follow the gender scripts they have internalized and that seem to reflect "natural" differences between them.

These culturally defined gender roles were clearly evident in the United States in the 1950s, when it seemed only "natural" that women would give priority to nurturing and providing emotional support for their families while men would devote themselves to competitive career pursuits outside the home. Such patterns also prevailed in earlier periods as well, as indicated by Charlotte Perkins Gilman's critique of the social expectations imposed on both women and men in the early decades of the twentieth century (as reviewed in Chapter 3). As more women have moved into professional and executive careers in recent years, some have suggested that women would bring their own distinctive style into their occupational careers, reflecting a greater concern for the emotional dynamics of relationships and a less authoritarian and more collaborative style of leadership.

Socially constructed gender differences in the dynamics of exchange transactions were incorporated in Diane Rothbard Margolis's (1998) analysis of contrasting types of self-concepts. In her view the self-concept reflected in exchange theory tends to be a male image that emphasizes independence and one's own self-interests. She contrasts this "exchanger self" with an "obligated self" in which higher priority is given to the needs and well-being of others, particularly those with whom one shares emotional bonds.[6] Her description of the obligated self portrays the traditional role of women, who are socialized to be sensitive to others and to sacrifice their own personal needs and goals for the sake of their families or others with whom they are involved.

Both the "exchanger" self and the "obligated" self can be seen as limiting individual development if pushed to the extreme without being balanced by the other type. Excessive and one-sided emphasis on the obligated self involves the risk that a person may become so highly absorbed in close-knit social bonds and the obligations they entail that she or he is unable to establish a sense of individual autonomy. In contrast, the exchanger self risks emotional isolation, due to the difficulty of maintaining meaningful social bonds while giving top priority to the individualistic pursuit of one's own interests.

Margolis also identified a third type of self-concept: a "cosmic self." Persons who give priority to this orientation devote themselves to actions or experiences that are intended to link them with a larger reality than that represented by their narrow self-interests or the specific social relationships in which they may be

[6] It is interesting to compare Margolis's (1998) view of the exchanger self versus the obligated self with Hechter's analysis, reviewed earlier, of the difference between compensatory versus obligatory groups. The basic contrast is consistent, although Margolis deals more with the social psychological level. Briefly, the exchanger self Margolis identified would be consistent with the pattern for Hechter's compensatory groups, while Margolis's obligated self would of course fit Hechter's obligatory group category.

involved. The cosmic orientation clearly allows for a high level of autonomy, but one's autonomous actions are oriented toward deep and meaningful connections outside of oneself. Such connections may involve a sense of identification with the natural world, a transcendental realm, or all of humanity, and they may be expressed in the kind of love for others that goes beyond one's own particular ingroups. The cosmic self ideal may be manifested through artistic work that is done without regard to utilitarian pay-offs, through the efforts of mystics who seek to cultivate a sense of union with a transcendent world or divine being, or through moral commitments to humanitarian efforts to improve the welfare of others such as disprivileged groups. Margolis also described a "reciprocating self" which avoids the extremes of both the exchanger self and the obligated self and achieves balance between one's self-interests and one's obligations to others.

For both men and women, an optimal level of emotional well-being seems to require balance between the need for personal autonomy and the need for social bonds. This is likely to mean facing the dilemma of balancing one's own personal interests with concerns for the welfare of others. Deficiencies in one's ability to form or maintain social bonds can lead to feelings of isolation and loneliness, while excessive preoccupation with one's own needs results in a lack of sensitivity to the needs of others. In extreme cases, inability to relate to others may be manifested in a sociopathic personality pattern involving an inadequate or undeveloped conscience and resulting lack of self-control. Such individuals are so preoccupied with their own needs and impulses that they are unable to identify with others or to evaluate their own behavior from the perspective of others. This means that they are immune to the informal social control expressed through others' approval or disapproval. Lacking the ability to identify with the needs and feelings of others, and with informal social controls neutralized, such individuals may seek to manipulate others to satisfy their own needs, or they may strike out in violence against those perceived as frustrating their needs and impulses.

At the other extreme, social bonds may be so tight that individuals fail to develop an adequate level of personal autonomy or to give sufficient priority to their own needs, emotional or otherwise. Instead, their identity is engulfed by the social relationships in which they are involved. Their personal interests and goals are absorbed by the needs of others, and they become dependent on these others to bolster an inadequately developed self-concept or to compensate for their own lack of personal autonomy. Such individuals are vulnerable to being manipulated and abused by others who seek only to satisfy their own needs. Perhaps the most dysfunctional combination is when a person who is insensitive to the needs of others develops a relationship with someone whose inadequate sense of personal autonomy leads to emotional dependence on the other party's approval to maintain a fragile sense of self-esteem.

The need for balance between personal autonomy and social bonds is reflected explicitly in Thomas Scheff's (1997) analysis of the role of emotions in social relationships. Scheff emphasizes the role of shame and anger in signaling threats or disruptions to the interdependence and mutual attachments that are the foundation of balanced social bonds. Secure social bonds require emotional attunement that leads to mutual understanding of one another's feelings, thoughts, and needs, but without sacrificing personal autonomy. Secure bonds involve reciprocal interdependence, with the needs of both (or all) parties acknowledged and respected. Such bonds generate feelings of pride which reinforce the relationship.

Extreme levels of both independence and dependence undermine the balance of reciprocal interdependence in a relationship. As Scheff put it, "Threats to a secure bond can come in two different formats; either the bond is too loose or too tight. Relationships in which the bond is too loose are isolated: there is mutual misunderstanding or failure to understand, or mutual rejection. Relationships in which the bond is too tight are engulfed: at least one of the parties in the relationship, say the subordinate, understands and embraces the standpoint of the other at the expense of the subordinate's own beliefs, values or feelings. The other is accepted by rejecting parts of one's self. In engulfed families, a child can only be 'good' by blind obedience and conformity, by relinquishing its curiosity, intuition, or feelings" (Scheff, 1997:77).

Scheff does not limit himself to family relations at the micro level. Instead, in the "part/whole" type of analysis that he advocates, the smallest unit of analysis, such as a family conversation at the breakfast table, can be regarded as integrally related to the overall level of social integration or anomie that exists in society as a whole. In the final analysis the integration of the overall society is based on the emotional solidarity that is embedded in the various micro-level relationships that make it up.

Both isolation and engulfment involve alienation and threats to the social bond. Isolation involves alienation of people from one another, while engulfment involves alienation from one's self. In either case, the result is a rupture in the solidarity of the social bond, leading to feelings of shame. In Scheff's perspective shame can be seen as an introjected form of social disapproval which is transformed into self-disapproval. This negative emotional experience results from individuals' failures to meet the expectations of others as well as their own self-expectations (which are, of course, based on the expectations of others). Failure to meet expectations may lead to social disapproval, or to anticipations of such disapproval, or it may trigger the disapproving internal voice of one's conscience, which reflects the standards internalized from prior socialization.

Shame is crucial, in Scheff's perspective, in reflecting the dynamics of social bonds. The effects of shame vary in terms of whether or not the shame is acknowledged, as well as whether it results from isolation or engulfment. If the source of shame is acknowledged, it is possible for the threat to solidarity it represents to be repaired. Acknowledgment of one's failure and the resulting disapproval of others provides an important opening for renegotiating expectations, or for an apology and forgiveness. The result is that the bond is repaired and the value of the relationship to the parties involved is reaffirmed. If shame is left unacknowledged it can lead to a vicious cycle of emotional responses which makes repairing the social bond more and more difficult. There are two such cycles Scheff identifies, one resulting from excessive isolation, the other from excessive engulfment. The cycle resulting from excessive isolation is a shame $\rightarrow$ anger sequence, while that resulting from engulfment leads to even deeper levels of shame (a shame $\rightarrow$ shame sequence).

With the shame → anger cycle, the individual denies or represses the shame, refusing to accept blame for his or her shortcomings. Instead, he or she strikes out in anger at others, particularly at those who indicate disapproval, who attempt to control the inappropriate behavior, or who may be blamed for the failure. When the anger is expressed in antisocial or violent behavior, it is likely to trigger additional social disapproval, which leads to even more intense anger and antisocial behavior, and then stronger disapproval, and so on, in a vicious cycle type of process. In contrast, individuals caught up in the shame → shame cycle respond to initial feelings of shame through additional denial of their own feelings, needs, and interests, even stronger identification with the other(s) in their social relationships, and deeper levels of engulfment. In this way, a series of otherwise minor failures leads to general feelings of inferiority. As the cycle continues, increased levels of shame lead to additional engulfment and denial of one's own needs, which erodes one's personal autonomy and sense of self-worth even more, and so on. Thus the shame deepens, along with one's self-esteem and sense of autonomy, also in a vicious cycle process.

One outcome of the shame → shame pattern is vulnerability to being manipulated by others for their own purposes, especially others who are insensitive because of the excessively high priority they give to their own needs and impulses. This process can be observed in marital relationships, for example, in which husbands are abusive to their wives. In such relationships the hostility of an emotionally isolated husband whose shame is transformed to anger reinforces the low self-esteem of his engulfed wife. The result is that the wife becomes even more subservient as she tries harder and harder to satisfy her husband's seemingly insatiable emotional needs for self-validation. Another example of a vicious cycle is provided by those who seek to bolster their inadequate self-esteem through identification with a charismatic leader whose excessive need for power may also reflect an effort to compensate for low self-esteem. When followers lack an adequate sense of personal autonomy or self-esteem, their blind compliance may serve to bolster the leader's inadequate self-concept (see D. P. Johnson, 1979).

Scheff points out that gender differences in socialization experiences tend to result in a higher incidence of isolation for men and engulfment for women. This is consistent with Margolis's distinction between men's exchanger self and women's obligated self. Scheff's analysis, however, points more explicitly to the dynamics of the dysfunctional consequences that result from extreme individualism on the one hand or engulfment on the other. He also emphasizes the importance of balance between these extremes for maintaining secure social bonds in which both interdependence and autonomy are acknowledged and validated.

On an even broader level, Scheff's "part/whole" analysis points explicitly to the way that problems of isolation or engulfment may develop in people's involvements with social organizations of various types as well as the overall society itself. Members of society who lack meaningful social ties, such as old people who live alone, are vulnerable to loneliness as a result of their social isolation. Of course, at the social psychological level it is an empirical question whether or not living alone gives rise to subjective feelings of loneliness, or whether individuals may experience loneliness even when they are not actually isolated (see D. P. Johnson and L. C. Mullins, 1987). On the other hand, people may avoid isolation and loneliness by identifying so strongly with some group or organization to which they belong, or with the overall society itself, that they fail to develop a sense of personal autonomy. In Scheff's terms, they are engulfed and thereby alienated from themselves.

The perspective of the sociology of emotions leads us to modify some of the highly individualistic assumptions of social exchange and rational choice theory. To experience the deeply satisfying socioemotional rewards of their various social relationships requires that individuals moderate the pursuit of their own self-interests, identify with the needs and interests of others, and sometimes put their social obligations ahead of their own personal needs and goals. In emphasizing the emotional dynamics of social relations, both Margolis and Scheff highlight some aspects of social relationships that seem to be downplayed (though not denied) in the individualistic rational choice version of social exchange theory.

Beyond the level of personal relationships, individuals are sometimes expected to display or project certain types of emotions as part of the obligations of their social roles in larger institutional or organizational structures. Such expectations are common in many occupational roles, particularly those involving public contact. In such roles, it is generally understood that in exchange for financial compensation, individuals must agree to manage and control the emotional dynamics of their relationships with customers, clients, colleagues, supervisors, and others, sometimes without regard to the nature of the responses they receive in return. The next section will explore the implications of such expectations.

Emotional Labor in Organizational Settings

Arlie Hochschild's (1983) analysis of the roles of flight attendants illustrates the process of the "commercialization of human feeling" whereby emotional displays are expected to conform to the policies and rules of the airline industry. Her analysis demonstrates an aspect of the relationship between emotions and organizational involvement that goes well beyond the dynamics of personal relationships discussed in the preceding section. As she showed in detail, the feelings and emotional displays of flight attendants clearly reflected institutional pressures and demands. Flight attendants were expected by the airline management to learn to handle the challenges they faced in managing their feelings so as to project a helpful, cheerful, and confident attitude that would elicit and reinforce positive relations with all types of passengers, including those who may have negative attitudes. The organizational goal, of course, is to promote positive public relations among passengers. Airline officials are concerned to promote positive feelings as much as possible, minimize the hassles of complaints, increase the chances of repeat business, and thereby insure continued profits.

As the major point of contact with customers, flight attendants are trained to manage the emotional tone of their relations with passengers so as to encourage their confidence and loyalty and to accept on-board rules and regulations in a positive way. This involves learning the "feeling rules" that will insure that their emotional displays will appear natural and sincere. The process illustrates the deployment of deliberate strategies for "presentation of self" that Goffman analyzed. For flight attendants, however, the self to be presented was expected to be an "organizational self" representing their airline as opposed to their personal character or identity. Nevertheless, Hochschild showed that women flight attendants were expected to relate to passengers in ways that are consistent with general cultural definitions (or stereotypes) of their gender role. Like women in general, flight attendants are expected to perform the kind of "emotional labor" that reflects attentiveness and deference to the needs and well-being of others—the pattern described by Margolis as the "obligated self" that is so central in the social definitions of women's roles. But there are some dimensions of women's flight attendant roles that reflect tensions and ambiguities when compared to other "female" occupations. As Hochschild explains, ".... flight attendants mingle with people who expect them to *enact* two leading roles of Womanhood: the loving wife and mother (serving food, tending the needs of others) and the glamorous 'career woman' (dressed to be seen, in contact with strange men, professional and controlled in manner, and literally very far from home.)" (Hochschild, 1983:175, italics in original)

Hochschild described in fascinating detail the dynamics of the emotional displays that occur between flight attendants and passengers in various situations and the numerous practical strategies flight attendants employ to help them maintain their confident and helpful demeanor and friendly smiles, even when dealing with irate or troublesome passengers. They learned, for example, to distance themselves emotionally from difficult or disrespectful passengers by developing hypothetical explanations of these passengers' behavior (such as personal problems at home or work) that enabled them to avoid taking these negative responses personally. When passengers' complaints concerned such hassles as delayed flights, for example, flight attendants attempted to maintain positive relations by demonstrating sincere sympathy and assuring passengers that these problems were beyond their control. In contrast to female flight attendants, male flight attendants are more likely to be seen as authority figures—both by the flight attendants and by passengers. In fact, in dealing with difficult passengers female flight attendants sometimes enlisted a male colleague for support as a more persuasive authority figure, despite the fact that this strategy seems to undercut the feminist goal of recognizing women's strength and promoting gender equality.

Hochschild's analysis suggests that a certain degree of exploitation is involved in the "commercialization of feeling" that occurs as flight attendants engage in the emotional labor expected of them. This process can be seen as potentially going much deeper into flight attendants' self-identities than the exploitation of factory workers that Marx had analyzed at a much earlier stage of modern industrial society. It is difficult to sustain feigned feelings for a lengthy period of time, and the ability of others to see through the pretension would render such displays less effective anyway. Thus the real demand for flight attendants is not merely that they **display** the kind of emotions expected by management but actually **feel** them. It was only by learning these feeling rules that the emotions they were expected to display would be seen as sincere and effective.

Hoschschild drew on Goffman's dramaturgic perspective to discuss the tension that sometimes exists between the way flight attendants **really feel** and the feelings they are **expected to display** as they perform their organizational role. When flight attendants learn to feel the emotions they are required to express, this demonstrates their success in "deep acting" as they perform their role. That is, they learn how to manage their feelings so that the emotional displays they enact in performing their role are consistent with the way they really do feel. This type of deep acting can be contrasted with "surface acting" in which the emotions displayed are not consistent with the emotions really felt. With surface acting there may be a certain level of tension between the impression one is trying to create and one's real feelings, plus the risk of not appearing sincere.

Goffman had pointed out that people feel a moral obligation to be sincere in their dealings with people so as to avoid accusations of hypocrisy or dishonesty. Thus the challenge the flight attendants faced was to manage their emotional lives and even their identities in such a way that they could be effective in conveying the expected emotions in a sincere manner. Of course, it seems plausible that flight attendants would probably prefer to be cheerful and positive rather than surly and negative, regardless of company policy, simply because it makes their work situation more pleasant and is more likely to elicit rewarding responses from passengers. But the demands of the business did not give them a choice; instead, displaying the expected emotions with sincerity was essentially a job requirement. Even so, in their interaction with one another, flight attendants learned to manage their emotional lives through various strategies of expressing some personal distance from the enforced helpful cheerfulness of their organizational roles, as well as to provide emotional support to one another in coping with the various stresses they faced in their jobs.

At the opposite end of the scale from flight attendants are those whose occupational roles require a certain level of aggressiveness in interpersonal encounters. Hochschild (1983:137–147) contrasted flight attendants with bill collectors to underscore her central argument regarding the importance of feeling rules in occupational settings. While flight attendants are expected to be attentive to passengers' needs in ways that enhance their self-esteem, the more unpleasant task of bill collectors is to make demands on the debtors they contact to pay their debts. This involves efforts to deflate their self-esteem in such a way that the only way they can maintain their dignity and restore their self-esteem is to clear their accounts. Emotional labor is required for bill collectors as well as flight attendants—though it is obviously a different type. The challenge for the bill collector is to generate and convey the type of assertive or threatening feelings that will insure that their demands for payment are taken seriously.

For flight attendants, bill collectors, and other roles involving public contact, the expected emotional displays involve encounters with strangers. Flight attendants are not personal friends with the passengers on board, and bill collectors have no personal basis for feeling aggressive or hostile toward the debtors from whom they are trying to collect. When passengers or debtors respond as expected, this no doubt helps reinforce the emotions displayed toward them and so makes the encounter feel natural rather than contrived. Even so, the impersonal nature of the encounter puts pressure on both the flight attendants and the bill collectors to carry the burden of the emotional labor that is required for them to perform their roles in a convincing and natural way.

The challenge of managing and displaying one's feelings so as to promote positive encounters with strangers applies also to many other occupations that involve extensive public contact, such as retail sales, for example. The emotional labor associated with impersonal relationships in public settings may be contrasted with the emotional involvement of individuals who are **expected** to establish some type of personal relationship with others as part of their organizational or occupational roles. Examples include teachers, psychiatrists, attorneys, clergy, social workers, counselors, family therapists, real estate salespersons, and occupational or professional roles that involve personal interaction with students, patients, clients, members, customers, and associates. In many ways the emotional labor that is involved is probably even more intense than that required for the role performances of airline flight attendants. This is especially so when the persons with whom these relations must be established are resistant or unable to respond in ways that reinforce or reward the occupational professional's emotional displays. Both teachers and social workers, for example, sometimes encounter resistance on the part of those they are expected to help.

Professionals in occupational roles that require the development of personal relationships with clients may sometimes identify sincerely with the needs of their clients and derive a sense of personal satisfaction from working with them. The effect of this identification is to reinforce the emotional involvement that is expected and to validate their professional identities. This would probably be more likely for professionals who are expected to give priority to their clients than for salespersons or others who are expected to look out primarily for their own interests or the interests of their employers. Of course, professionals are also concerned with their own interests as well, as one might infer by the financial rewards earned by many medical doctors and attorneys, for example. In fact, a frequent criticism of physicians is their lack of an appropriate "bedside manner." Although physicians' responses to such criticism no doubt varies, their training leads them to focus primarily on patients' physical needs rather than their emotional needs, and they learn that this focus on physical needs may require a certain degree of emotional detachment.

A different type of situation is presented by human service professionals who deal with needy or emotionally vulnerable clients. Such professionals must be trained to be on guard against allowing a dependency relationship to develop because of the emotional rewards that may be received from being needed. Regardless of the nature of the client's need or the "bond" that may develop between a client and human service professional, the professional is expected to adhere to professional ethical codes and organizational regulations to avoid inappropriate emotional entanglement. Thus the emotional labor that is required involves establishing an optimum balance between responsiveness to the client's needs and emotional reactions and maintenance of an appropriate level of emotional distance.

For all relationships, the perspectives on emotions reviewed above indicate the need for balance between one's own individual needs, interests, and goals and the obligations one has to others. Whether personal or institutional, the emotional exchanges involved in these various relationships can provide a highly satisfying sense of belonging as well as enhancement and reinforcement of the self-esteem of those involved. In addition, such exchanges also contribute to valuable social outcomes in the lives of others that transcend one's narrow interests.

Our options for maintaining various kinds of relationships with others and for meeting our own needs have undergone a great deal of change in the last few decades as result of major innovations in information and communication technology. We turn in the final section of this chapter to a brief consideration of the fascinating issue of how our modes of connecting and belonging are being transformed through the current continuing revolution in information and communication technology.

Cyberspace Markets, Networks, and Personal Relationships

For increasing numbers of people, the dynamics of market transactions, network contacts, and personal relationships have changed significantly as a result of the proliferation of "hi-tech" electronic forms of communication made possible by the widespread use of personal computers and the internet. The internet has already proved itself as an effective and efficient medium for comparison shopping and impersonal marketing transactions (as well as for fraud and identity theft). It also provides the basic technology for maintaining network ties, both far and near, or to develop new ones, much more easily and efficiently than personal visits, "snail mail," or telephone. Through e-mail, chat rooms, personal or family Web pages, blogs, and the like, personal relations may also be maintained, or new ones formed, that transcend the traditional limitations of space and time.

It is also possible to experiment with new strategies for electronic "presentation of self" that enable a person to project an identity that differs significantly from his or her local or "real" identity. Unlike one's local identity, the identity that one chooses to project on the internet is not necessarily grounded in bodily characteristics, face-to-face relationships, and personal reputation—though one may incorporate these personal characteristics by including photos and disclosing valid information about oneself as one may choose. In any case, the increasingly widespread use of the internet in establishing or maintaining social contacts demonstrates the appeal of the "virtual world" that people are able to construct as an alternative to the "real world" and its space and time constraints.

More research is needed in this rapidly changing area to help us understand how the internet and electronic forms of communication are transforming network contacts and personal relations. For example, is the internet used more to maintain existing relationships or to establish new network ties? To what extent are internet-based social ties replacing social ties involving physical co-presence and eyeball-to-eyeball contact or real time voice communication via telephone? It seems likely that people will feel a need to supplement virtual electronic encounters with personal contacts in relationships that include valued emotional exchanges. Facial expressions and direct eye-to-eye contact are crucial for conveying emotions, to say nothing of the role of bodily touch in intimate relations. Although emotional exchanges utilizing "emoticons" may help in conveying feelings through the internet, it seems doubtful that such virtual exchanges can be as rich or as emotionally satisfying as the complex array of emotional exchanges that are possible face-to-face. But for more "extrinsic" types of contacts between acquaintances with "weak ties," the internet is proving to be an important tool for maintaining such ties. It seems plausible that some weak ties may be strengthened because of the ease and speed of electronic communication.

Future investigations of the social effects of the internet will no doubt show additional long-term transformations in social relations of all kinds, including markets and organizations as well as personal relations. Manuel Castells (1996) has explored the implications of electronic network technology in the creation of a "network society." Such a society clearly is not limited to local or even national boundaries but is world-wide in its scope. In addition to the new venue the internet provides for impersonal marketing transactions, organizational dynamics are also undergoing change as a result of arrangements being made for employees to work at home and to maintain contact with the office electronically. With widespread "home work" we might anticipate that the informal organizational culture that has traditionally been sustained through face-to-face contacts among colleagues at work will be modified or replaced by new forms of sociable contacts. For those who perform a large proportion of their occupational tasks at home, it also seems plausible that a increased proportion of their reduced time at the office will involve forms of interaction that function primarily to sustain socioemotional bonds rather than to accomplish tasks.

Questions regarding the geometric shape of internet networks, their size and density, also need to be explored. Are electronic networks similar to networks based on face-to-face contact, or more traditional forms of personal contact at a distance such as telephones and "snail mail?" Given the rapid growth and largely unregulated nature of internet contacts, it would seem that network structures and boundaries would be more difficult to identify or to diagram than those based on face-to-face contacts. We also do not know how common it is (or will be) for individuals to serve a bridging function that links different internet-based networks on either a personal or institutional level.

Even if several friends or associates arrange to be logged in simultaneously to engage in "real time" conversation in a designated "chat room," it is difficult to sense whether an electronic conversation can duplicate the kinds of intensive socioemotional exchanges that occur in a group whose members are physically in one another's presence and can establish eye contact and observe one another's gestures and facial expressions. Although this limitation may be partially overcome by computer monitor-mounted cameras, research is needed to show how such communication compares and contrasts with actual face-to-face communication as well as with electronic communication without cameras. Such research may be expected to become obsolete rather rapidly in view of the expansive growth and the volatile nature of the virtual social world of electronic media.

The rational choice perspective would suggest that internet-based markets and social networks can be analyzed in terms of the same individualistic reward/cost considerations as markets, networks, and organizations based on more traditional types of social contacts. Since market transactions are intended to meet individualistic needs without any emotional involvement, the internet may be seen as encouraging increased rationality by expanding people's ability to research alternatives and find the best deal. Unlike groups, neither markets nor networks involve a sense of a collective identity—even though, as we have seen, dense networks may be the basis for the emergence of social groups in which members do indeed develop a collective identity.

For personal relations, however, their overall dynamics may be expected to be transformed in various ways as electronic encounters displace or supplement personal contacts. The challenges of maintaining group cohesion through electronic media are probably even greater because of the difficulties of attending to several others in multiple contexts simultaneously. In any case, people may eventually discover that there are limits to how much satisfaction they will experience in their social lives if their socioemotional bonds decline as a result of increasing reliance on electronic forms of communication to sustain personal relationships.

Summary

This chapter contrasted exchange transactions that result from individualistic rational choice-type decisions with those involving some form of socioemotional attachment through which people identify one another's interests as their own. For the latter type, the relative strength or salience of each party's own personal interests versus his or her level of socioemotional bonding with others varies greatly in different types of relationships. As we move from the impersonal market relationships to social networks to cohesive groups and close personal relations, the individualistic calculation of personal benefits is likely to be modified as individuals take one another's needs and feelings into consideration in ways that transcend their own narrow self-interests.

Opportunities to develop relationships with different types of people vary greatly in different social settings. Blau's structural theory was reviewed to emphasize the importance of similarities and differences among people in the formation of social relations. People tend to initiate encounters with others who are similar to themselves to meet their socioemotional needs. In populations with a great deal of crosscutting forms of diversity, the chances are greater that relationships will be formed across these barriers than in more homogeneous populations. Moreover, interactions among people who are different from one another are crucial for both individual and collective goals as well as for promoting social integration and cohesion in a complex, pluralistic society.

Within the framework of the opportunities and constraints that are available, the encounters people have with one another give rise to various forms of social networks. Network ties vary greatly in terms of frequency and duration of contact as well as the nature of the exchange transactions they involve. In general, network ties are stronger and more likely to endure when they are mutually rewarding in terms of socioemotional exchanges. But network ties may also be utilized for various other types of exchanges as well, including exchanges of information, mutual assistance of various types, introductions to people in other networks, and material resources.

In addition to reward and cost considerations, the structure of networks can be analyzed and different networks compared and contrasted in terms of their size, density, relations to different networks, and other characteristics. Similarly, positions within networks can be compared and contrasted in terms of how central or peripheral they are and whether or not they are linked to other networks. Strong ties in dense networks are characteristic of cohesive groups with intensive socioemotional attachments that lead to clear distinctions between insiders and outsiders. On the other hand, individuals with weak ties to multiple groups are in a structural position to link different groups together and thus facilitate social integration in a complex and heterogeneous society.

Obviously, not all network ties evolve into close personal relationships. Nevertheless, there is the potential for at least a minimal emotional component in all interpersonal encounters. For relationships in which there are significant emotional exchanges, the sociology of emotions provides a perspective that offers important insights into the dynamics of the process that leads individuals to identify with the needs and interests of others as well as their own. People vary in terms of the priority they give to their own personal interests as opposed to being willing to make sacrifices for the sake of others. We considered the ways in which men and women often differ in this respect, due largely to the way traditional gender roles have been socially constructed. Although women have generally been expected to be more attuned to the emotional dynamics of relationships and men to be more independent, there are large differences within gender categories. There are also significant variations in different situations, such as business or professional versus family or close friend relationships. Diane Margolis's distinction between the "exchanger self" and the "obligated self" helps highlight these differences and points to the need for balance. In addition, Thomas Scheff's perspective on shame and anger cycles also pointed to the need for balance between autonomy and emotional attunement in relationships of mutual interdependence.

Emotional displays and exchanges are often expected even in impersonal contacts as part of one's organizational obligations. We reviewed Arlie Russell Hochschild's detailed analysis of the "emotional labor" expected of airline flight attendants, which she contrasted with the emotional displays required of bill collectors. In contrast to the emotional aspects of these impersonal relations, we also discussed the importance of the emotional exchanges that occur in other occupational settings, including the social relations of professionals with those they serve and how these differ from the transactions of business representatives with customers.

The final topic in this chapter, noted briefly, had to do with the rapidly changing dynamics of what Manuel Castells referred to as the "network society." Electronic communication may be expected to have major sociological effects on various types of relationships, including impersonal market transactions, network contacts, organizational communication, and even personal relations among family and friends. More research is needed to assess the impact of electronic communication on various types of social exchanges, particularly those involving socioemotional bonds, and how they are combined in various ways with more traditional forms of communication.

For both individual and collective needs and goals, there are limits to what can be accomplished through impersonal markets, social networks, and personal relationships. To overcome these limitations social organizations of various types are established to provide more reliable and better reward/cost outcomes than would be possible in a market system or through unorganized networks. The dynamics of how meso and macro level organizational structures are established will be explored more fully in the next chapter.

Questions for Study and Discussion

1. How do the characteristics of residential neighborhoods or occupational positions vary with regard to the opportunities they provide for meeting a wide variety of different types of people? Based on your own experience or your observations of others, would you agree or disagree that people tend to form closer relations with others who are similar, even when they have the opportunity to relate to a wider range of people? Why?
2. Compare and contrast "bonding" and "bridging" network ties with respect to providing a sense of belonging and promoting integration in a society with a great deal of diversity. How might a person's identity be affected by these different types of network ties?
3. Explain how various types of emotions (both positive and negative) can lead individuals to fulfill their various social obligations or move beyond their own personal interests to show concern for the welfare of others? Can these contrasting types of emotional arousal be analyzed in cost/reward terms? To what extent do you believe these emotions are self-generated versus being aroused by the reactions of others?
4. Identify some examples of the emotional tone that is expected in various occupational or institutional settings? What kinds of responses might be expected when inappropriate emotions are expressed? How are emotions in a person's occupation affected by material rewards as well as by the responses they receive from other people (colleagues, supervisors, subordinates, clients, and others)?
5. Discuss some of the effects of electronic communication (e-mail, for example), on the scope of people's networks, the emotional intensity of their relationships, or the frequency of their contacts, both personal and impersonal. How have your own network ties been influenced by electronic communication media? Explain.

Chapter 9
From Micro-Level Exchanges to Meso- and Macro-Level Structures

Everyday life observation suggests that some people are known for being a good "team player" and showing concern for the welfare of others while others are concerned only to satisfy their own needs and interests without being aware of how their actions might affect others. Probably most of us experience conflict from time to time between fulfilling our obligations to others and doing what we really want to do for ourselves. When such conflicts occur, what is the most rational thing to do? From the perspective of rational choice theory, we would almost always be expected to give priority to our own self-interests. Our social obligations would have high priority when we anticipate that the reward/cost outcome will be in our favor.

As noted in previous chapters, rewards and costs may be either material or nonmaterial and may include social approval or disapproval plus positive or negative emotional arousal. These outcomes have implications for our identities, either supporting or failing to support our idealized self-concepts. Moreover, as noted in the last chapter, both material and nonmaterial exchanges may be balanced or imbalanced, with imbalanced exchanges giving rise to differences in power and dependency as well as differences in levels of independence versus engulfment.

This chapter builds on the foundation previously established by drawing on Peter Blau's and James Coleman's perspectives for linking micro-level exchange processes with macro-level organizational and institutional structures. In Blau's perspective, inequalities in power that emerge from imbalanced exchanges serve as the bridge for macro structures. In Coleman's perspective, meso or macro level corporate actors are intentionally created to achieve goals that are difficult or impossible for individuals to accomplish on their own or through market transactions. For both theorists, the development of meso or macro structures has a major influence on the terms of exchange that individuals are able to establish at the micro level.

The specific topics to be covered are as follows.

- Emergence of macro structures from imbalanced exchanges—This section will present Blau's analysis of how the power and dependency relations that emerge from imbalanced exchanges provide the basis for collective action. The following points suggest the key processes that are involved.

- Emergence of status and power differences through competition at the micro level
- Stabilization of power structures through norms and values
- Transition from power structures to meso and macro structures
- Legitimation versus opposition of power structures
- The institutionalization process in macro structures

- Normative conformity, social capital, and corporate actors—This section is based on James Coleman's rational choice analysis of how individual interests are reflected in normative conformity, social capital, and corporate actors. The major points to be developed are as follows.

  - Normative and legal regulation of people's behavior
  - Promoting normative conformity and deterring deviance
  - Social capital and public goods
  - Authority relations of principals and agents
  - Corporate actors versus natural persons

Emergence of Macro Structures from Imbalanced Exchanges[1]

In Peter Blau's perspective differences in status and power develop from imbalanced exchanges. Power structures provide the foundation for the formation of groups and larger organizations. To trace the dynamics of this process, let us imagine a newly formed task group in which members seem initially to be roughly equal in terms of status and power, but successful task accomplishment will result in rewards for all. Initially there is no structure or organization, and participants may not even know one another very well. What will happen?

Micro-Level Competition for Status and Power

If we assume that the participants in our hypothetical newly formed group are willing to participate in the hope of receiving benefits, we might imagine that their initial interaction will involve mutual introductions and random small talk as they engage one another in exploratory conversations. In this process, some may indicate various resources they have that could be useful while others will offer ideas and suggestions to be considered. Some of them may eventually have to compete to gain the attention of others. Their goal at this stage is simply to be heard.

[1] This summary of Blau's model of how macro structures develop from imbalanced exchange transactions is adapted from D. P. Johnson ([1981] 1986:372–379).

To get the attention of others, they will need to convince them that their ideas and suggestions will lead to a better outcome than the competing ideas and suggestions that may be offered by others. Others may simply listen and evaluate the alternatives proposed. As conversation proceeds, some participants may offer support, modifications, or criticisms of the ideas and suggestions that others propose. In essence, as described in Chap. 7, participants attempt (with varying degrees of success) to be impressive (offering ideas they hope others will accept as valuable and helpful) or approachable (listening attentively or supporting the ideas of others), or they may alternate between these strategies (Blau, 1964:125–132).

Out of this exploratory conversation, let us imagine that the group manages to organize itself. (In reality, of course, groups may fail to reach this stage.) This will involve a shift in communication toward those whose ideas and suggestions seem most convincing for leading to the best reward/cost outcome in terms of task accomplishment. Competition may intensify as potential leaders compete for dominance in having their ideas accepted. Others may compete for respect or for recognition and acceptance, especially by those emerging as dominant. Let us imagine that one person eventually convinces most of the others that his or her ideas or other resources will result in the most rewarding outcome for all. This person becomes dominant as others defer and express their willingness to have their behavior influenced by his or her ideas and suggestions. This hypothetical example portrays the way power and leadership are earned by providing convincing assurances of beneficial outcomes for potential followers.

If the group is successful in accomplishing its task and thereby gaining rewards for its members, this success will itself reinforce the leader's position. Members' initial compliance will have been rewarded, which will strengthen the leader's basis for expecting continued compliance in the future. If the rewards can be distributed among group members (such as material or financial rewards), the emergent leader may assume the responsibility for doing so, thereby reinforcing his or her power. As all politicians understand, providing benefits to constituents is one of the best strategies to insure their loyalty. If the rewards cannot be divided (such as the emotional rewards of membership or successful task accomplishment, for example), the collective enjoyment of such rewards is still likely to reinforce the leader's power, especially if the leader provides additional rewards by showing public appreciation to members for their contributions.

This model of how leadership structures emerge is perhaps most evident in groups in which the members expect their involvement to be rewarding (or withdrawal costly). But if members do not share a commitment to the group's goals, or if they choose to use one of the previously described strategies for avoiding indebtedness and dependency relations, this particular model would not apply in the same way. It also would not apply if the leader fails to maintain a pattern of fairness in distributing rewards or making demands on group members. Everyday life offers numerous examples of groups in which members are not strongly committed to shared goals, would-be leaders are unable to generate the support or trust that would sustain their leadership, or an established leader begins to take unfair advantage of members.

Stabilization of Power Structures Through Norms and Values

If an acknowledged leader is perceived as fair, norms and values are likely eventually to emerge whereby the leader's power is stabilized and reinforced by being transformed into legitimate authority (Blau, 1964:199–233). This means that the leader will be seen as having the **right** to expect compliance from subordinates. To the extent that members accept the existing distribution of power and authority, and are also satisfied with the rewards they receive, they may augment the leader's authority by rewarding one another with social approval for their compliance with the leader (or by showing disapproval for noncompliance). This is especially likely if the values and norms that develop are consistent with members' own personal values and identities.

In the final analysis, acceptance of an authority structure rests on favorable reward/cost outcomes for members (along with their expectations of future benefits). However, the specific terms of the exchange do not have to be negotiated from scratch with each transaction when these terms are normatively defined and legitimated in terms of shared values. In some cases compliance might be expected even in the absence of short-term benefits in exchange for a continued share in long-range benefits. In other words, the relationship moves beyond a "tit-for-tat" situation in which each specific transaction must be balanced and toward a longer-term perspective in which short-term imbalances are expected eventually to be balanced. In a work situation, for example, people fulfill the requirements of their jobs each day, even though they do not get paid until the end of the week or the month.

These internal group process do not occur in a vacuum, however. The development of values and norms that legitimate a group's power and leadership structure is likely to reflect the influence of the surrounding cultural and institutional context in which many of the relevant norms and values will have already been internalized through the socialization process. For example, the norm of reciprocity predisposes people to be prepared to engage in the give and take of exchange transactions by returning favors granted by others; the norm does not have to be created from scratch by each group.[2] Similarly, people who enjoy the benefits of membership in a group are expected to follow the widely established cultural norm of doing their "fair share" for the good of the group.

When the overall reward/cost outcomes are perceived by all parties as fair, both leaders and subordinates will have an interest in stabilizing their relationship through legitimating values and norms instead of relying solely on short-run cost/reward balance in their exchange transactions. By holding legitimate authority, the leader is protected from the necessity of continually having to negotiate or provide

[2] These common sense understandings that underlie the negotiation of the terms of exchange and the emergence of stable exchange patterns include the kind of implicitly shared knowledge emphasized in phenomenological sociology.

short-term payoffs to members to maintain their dependency and indebtedness. At the same time subordinates are protected from excessive demands that a domineering or exploitative leader might impose or from an arbitrary reduction in rewards on which subordinates have become dependent. Legitimation of a leadership structure enables a group to move toward long-range goals that are intended to provide eventual benefits to all, even when this involves short-term sacrifices. A leader whose authority is reinforced by the group's values and norms will be able to persuade members to incur the necessary costs in striving for such long-range goals without any immediate payoff except the internal satisfaction and social approval that results from normative conformity—plus the hope of future rewards. In addition, if members have an intrinsic commitment to the group's activities or goals, or the ideals and values they represent, this provides an additional source of rewards.

Sometimes, however, the legitimacy of a particular authority structure breaks down, either because of changes in the exchange process itself or changes in people's preferences and expectations. Leaders, for example, may seek to increase their compliance demands (such as when governments raise taxes, for example) or reduce the rewards for compliance (such as reductions in pay). Alternatively, members may reduce their level of compliance (by cheating on their taxes, for example, or reducing their level of job performance). When perceptions of a leader's unfairness emerge among subordinates, the stage is set for the development of opposition movements, and such movements sometimes succeed in overthrowing established power and authority structures and establishing new ones. This process will be analyzed in more detail later in this chapter.

From Power Structures to Meso and Macro Structures

The emergence of power and authority structures enables leaders to control and coordinate the actions of subordinates in developing a collective line of action. The extent of this control will reflect the degree of dependency among group members, the value of the rewards they anticipate from the group's collective action, and their commitment to the group's legitimating values and norms. In some cases this collective action may be oriented primarily toward goals set by the leader, with members being compensated for their contributions. Alternatively, goals may be based on group members' consensus, with the expectation that all will share the rewards of goal accomplishment. In either case, the challenge for the leader is to coordinate members' actions so that they fit together in a collective line of action. This means it is the group, not its constituent members, that becomes the interacting unit, and members may be seen as acting on behalf of the group or its leader.

Many examples may be cited where it is the group, not the individual, that is the appropriate unit involved in some line of action. For example, even though the individual players in a football game may strive for outstanding individual performances, the overall project is that of the team. Or, when labor union officials decide to go on strike, or to accept a contract offer and go back to work, their members' actions should be understood as part of the union's overall line of action. Members do not decide as individuals whether to strike or go back to work (unless organizational discipline has broken down), though of course they may vote in order to establish the collective decision that they agree to follow. The same occurs in military parades or battlefield campaigns, where individual soldiers act as part of their unit and not on their own behalf.

Is a leadership structure necessary for a group line of action? Or could a collective line of action be developed by persons who are equals, with no power and dependency relations? In order for coordinated action to emerge spontaneously, it would be necessary for all the parties involved to perceive that their personal goals could best be advanced through collaborative action. There would also have to be agreement on what this action is and what the contributions of each party should be—without being directed by anyone with authority. For long term projects of any type, reliance on the spontaneous organization is a precarious strategy. Even if the members agree on the goal, there may be disagreement on strategies to use in accomplishing it or on the contributions each member should make. These difficulties can be overcome by the emergence of a clear leadership or authority structure. In an athletic context, for example, even though all members may want to win, a coach or team leader is still needed to coordinate the actions of individual team members to achieve the highest possible level of effectiveness.

A group organized to act as a collective unit is able to initiate interaction with other groups that are also organized as collective units. Whether this occurs will depend initially on network ties between members of different groups. Both individuals and groups vary in terms of their network linkages. When network ties exist (or can be established) between groups, the development of exchange relationships will depend on the reward/cost outcomes expected for the groups involved. But this evaluation of alternatives and potential outcomes will involve the group itself as a collective unit rather than the individual members acting on their own behalf. This does not mean that individuals do not also seek to benefit personally through such exchanges. But individuals' decisions and actions are part of the group's line of action.

The process whereby power and authority structures provide the possibility for collective action is essentially the foundation for meso and macro level organizations and institutional structures. Macro structures may be regarded as consisting of relationships among groups (or organizations) while micro structures consist only of individuals. For our purposes, micro structures involve face-to-face relations while meso structures include both direct and indirect relations that develop in between the micro level and the macro structures of the overall society.[3] However, meso and macro level groups and organizations have no independent existence and

[3]George Homans' ([1961] 1974) analysis of "elementary social behavior" that was reviewed in an earlier chapter was focused primarily at the micro level.

cannot act except through their members. Thus the actions of individual members should be seen as contributing to, or helping to constitute, part of the collective line of action of these larger structures. Moreover, regardless of its size, once an organization is established, its collective action may be continued despite turnover in the group's membership.

The exchange patterns that develop among different groups and organizations are parallel in many respects to the same processes that occur among individuals. Particular transactions may be either balanced or imbalanced, with results that are comparable to those at the individual level. If balanced, relations of reciprocal interdependence will be established. If exchanges are imbalanced, differentiation of status and power will emerge at the group level. If a group achieves dominance through relations with one or more groups that become dependent, the stage is set for a possible higher-level combination of groups. That is, the dominant group (or its leader or representatives) can organize subordinate groups into an even larger group or organization to engage in some collective or joint line of action. When this happens, it is then the larger conglomerate organization that becomes the acting unit and the subordinate groups or organizations become its constituent parts.

As groups increase in size, whether through adding more individuals or absorbing other groups, various patterns of internal exchange are likely to develop that lead to internal subgroup formation. This process is likely to lead to additional differentiation of status and power. These internal process may be expected to reflect in part the division of labor developed within the organization and its elaboration of power and authority structures. But additional subgroup exchanges may develop over and above those that are involved in the division of labor and the official authority structure (Homans, 1950; Blau, 1955). These internal relationships may include various socioemotional exchanges or informal forms of collaboration. They may also include participants' efforts to compensate for—or resist—the demands imposed by those in authority or the pressures that may develop in pursuing the organization's goals.

Internal subgroups may sometimes become sufficiently organized on their own, independent of the larger organization of which they are a part, to form their own network contacts and to engage in exchange transactions with other individuals or groups either inside or outside the organization. These external contacts and exchanges may involve, for example, subgroups (or individuals) in other associations that are similar in status or organizational function. For example, labor unions and professional associations transcend the particular organizational boundaries where workers and professionals are employed. When relationships are developed between similar subgroups in different organizations, the stage is set for the emergence of new overlapping or intersecting groups or associations for pursuing distinct goals that may differ from the organizational goals where their members are employed.

The general image of a large, complex society implied in Blau's model is that of an elaborate network of associations that are involved in numerous kinds of exchange transactions, some direct and many indirect, within and across various organizational boundaries. Many of these exchanges, both within and between different groups and associations, reflect varying degrees of imbalance and consequent relations of power and dependency. The magnitude and complexity of the exchange networks within and between the numerous large-scale organizations of a large urban-industrial society practically defy description. Huge complex bureaucratic organizations dominate almost all institutional sectors of society, and many of them are linked in various kinds of interorganizational relationships. A comprehensive picture of the overall structure of society would include groups and organizations that are made up not only of individuals but also of other groups and organizations, myriad subgroupings, both formal and informal, various interest groups within practically all large organizations, organizations that overlap and crosscut other organizations at various hierarchical levels, and networks of social relations that link different organizations or their subgroups. Modern society is honeycombed with innumerable overlapping and interpenetrating groups and associations of various types. To the extent that these various social formations (or subgroups within them) are capable of collective action, they rest on underlying exchange processes, particularly imbalanced exchanges through which power and dependency relations develop.

Legitimation Versus Opposition of Power Structures

The legitimation of power structures through values and norms does not guarantee that members will continue indefinitely to be totally satisfied with the existing distribution of costs and rewards. Power structures are frequently resisted and sometimes overthrown and replaced. This is true both in small-scale groups and large-scale complex associations as well as in the overall society. In the long run, the legitimacy of structures of power and authority rests on reward/cost outcomes that are widely perceived as fair. But if conditions should change, the stage is set for the formation of an opposition movement and, in an extreme case, the overthrow of the existing power structure (Blau, 1964:224–252).

There are numerous processes that could adversely affect reward/cost outcomes for subordinates and lead to dissatisfaction. For example, authority figures may begin to take advantage of subordinates' dependency by increasing the demands made on them, which they would see as unfair. Or, even if demands remain stable, the reward/cost ratio may become relatively less attractive as members become satiated with the rewards they receive. (This is probably less likely for employees who are dependent on the financial compensation they receive for their livelihood, but could readily apply to members of voluntary organizations.) Or members may become aware of other groups in which reward/cost outcomes are more favorable, so feel disadvantaged by comparison. Power and authority structures are inherently precarious and potentially unstable. Despite shared values and norms, members' continuing commitment rests in the long run on favorable reward/cost outcomes.

Dissatisfaction with existing reward/cost outcomes does not guarantee that an opposition movement will be developed or the power structure overthrown. People may fear that efforts to promote change would be unsuccessful, and that the negative consequences of failure would be even worse than putting up with the existing situation. Even if an opposition movement is formed, some dissatisfied members may be reluctant to participate because they see such a struggle as risky and futile. Some dissatisfied members may simply leave the group and join alternative groups with a more favorable reward/cost outcome. (People may leave their current employment, for example, to take a better-paying job.) Or, a leader may take advantage of his or her power to insure that members do not have the opportunity to organize themselves, in which case members' efforts to do so are likely to be seen as involving unacceptably high costs.

The relationship between legitimation mechanisms and opposition mechanisms can be seen as one of more or less continuous dialectical conflict (Blau, 1964:312–338). The emergence of strong authority structures invariably creates the conditions for the formation of opposition movements. For one thing, the authority structure rests, as we have seen, on resources the leader controls that can be used to reward subordinates for their compliance. But, to the extent that a leader is able to increase the resources at his or her disposal, he or she is likely to arouse dissatisfaction on the part of subordinates who would like to see these resources distributed more generously. Thus, for example, the loss of legitimacy of the Communist Party in Russia and other countries of the former Soviet Union in the late 1980s reflected in part the widespread resentment of the affluence that high-level Communist Party officials enjoyed at a time when the emerging market system left many people without the basic economic survival guarantees to which they had become accustomed.

The social dynamics involved in opposition movements are similar to those described earlier in connection with the emergence of power structures from imbalanced exchanges. That is, those who are dissatisfied and desire change will begin to interact and to evaluate and debate alternative goals and strategies, seek to mobilize support, and so on. Out of this preliminary process a leader may eventually emerge by convincing others that his or her ideas will prove more effective (or rewarding) than the competing ideas that may be offered by others. Imbalanced exchanges will develop if the emergent opposition leader is able to create dependencies and obligations on the part of fellow members to insure their participation despite the risks and sacrifices that may be involved. Wide variations may emerge in the specific goals of opposition movements. These can include changes in the distribution of costs and rewards, replacing current authority figures, or revolutionary overthrow of the existing structure and establishment of a new system. If the opposition movement is successful in redressing grievances or implementing change, this will reinforce the opposition leader's position and may lead to continued mobilization to pursue additional goals. On the other hand, if an opposition movement is unable to get organized by generating a leadership structure or consensus on strategies, those who are dissatisfied will find they are unable to act consistently as a unit. The refusal of totalitarian governments to tolerate the organization of opposition parties reflects their awareness that unorganized opposition is not very effective.

Thus the success of dissatisfied subordinates in opposing or replacing the existing power structure depends on the emergence of its own leadership structure.

The effectiveness of opposition leaders will depend on the development of consensus regarding specific goals and strategies and the mobilization of individuals' commitments to incur the costs that are involved in pursuing these goals through collective action. In addition, just as the existing authority structure is stabilized by legitimating values and norms, so also the opposition movement may be reinforced by the development of opposition ideals. This opposition ideology is particularly important for neutralizing the conservative influence of legitimating values and norms. Some of those participating in the opposition movement may have previously internalized the legitimating values and norms and therefore feel ambivalent about participating in the movement. An opposition ideology, however, can assure participants that their struggles are not undertaken for narrow, selfish interests but are consistent with high moral principles, superior to those being practiced by the current regime, and that their success will lead to greater benefits for all. Thus, for example, many participants in the American civil rights movement attempted to justify their demonstrations to promote integration and justice in terms of traditional Judeo-Christian teachings that were not adequately implemented in our society. By claiming the moral "high road," participants and leaders were able to criticize those who failed to join the struggle as accepting an unjust system. Even when an opposition movement is not completely successful, it may still stimulate reform and lead to improved reward/cost outcomes for subordinates (Blau, 1964:301–309).

Appeals to abstract values and norms, both to support existing authority structures and to mobilize support for opposition movements, are usually much more fully developed in larger and more complex systems. Such processes are not as critical in small-scale systems because of the opportunity for immediate and direct negotiation of costs and rewards. Large-scale systems, in contrast, are more likely to involve multiple and complex series of indirect exchanges between individuals or groups who are not in direct contact with one other. Thus internalization of the appropriate values and norms becomes more crucial for shaping behavior and interaction patterns, as opposed to relying on ad hoc agreements. In the following section, reliance on values and norms will be seen as a major feature of large-scale institutional structures.

Institutionalization in Macro-Structures

Even though large-scale associations emerge from elementary exchange processes, their emergent properties or characteristics sometimes seem to outweigh the dynamics of the small-scale processes of direct exchange transactions. Extensive reliance on appeals to abstract values and norms is one of these emergent characteristics. Other important aspects of large-scale structures and institutional processes include a significant increase in the proportion of indirect exchanges compared to direct exchanges, the maintenance of exchange patterns over multiple generations, and support of these patterns by dominant groups in society. As noted earlier, commitment to widely shared abstract values and norms helps insure conforming behavior, even in the absence of specific payoffs in the short run, except perhaps the rewards of social approval.

Both **legitimating** values and **opposition** values are integral to the culture of large, complex democratic societies. In fact, the widespread acceptance and implementation of democratic values may be seen as the long-term outcome of successful historical struggles to insure that government rests on the consent of the governed. In contrast to values that support existing institutional structures, opposition values often develop within the context of social movements that develop outside established structures. However, in a complex democratic society, even opposition values are more or less permanently institutionalized, as opposed to emerging outside the realm of political discourse and debate or in an unorganized and ad hoc fashion in response to particular grievances. At the societal level the two-party political system in the United States allows for the permanent institutionalization of opposition values. In societies with more than two political parties, opposition to the current regime is often less effective because of its fragmentation.

Blau also distinguished between **particularistic** and **universalistic** values in providing a foundation for different types of exchange relationships.[4] Particularistic values apply to distinct categories of people. Such values help promote solidarity among people who share particular characteristics, including race or ethnicity, for example, gender, age, religion, occupation, lifestyle preferences, family status, and residential location. Universalistic values, in contrast, apply to all people throughout society, regardless of such differences. Universalistic values are important in Blau's perspective for mediating complex networks of indirect exchanges between persons who are dissimilar. They are crucial for binding together diverse types of people in a complex and pluralistic society and promoting general ideological consensus and legal equality. Laws prohibiting racial discrimination, for example, reflect universalistic-type values, thereby helping to insure fairness and equity in exchange transactions between persons in different racial categories. Such values should be expected to increase in importance as the division of labor expands, since growth in the division of labor itself promotes heterogeneity.

In our age of increasing globalization, the implications of universalistic values may be expanded to transcend national boundaries. The widespread concern with human rights, for example, is intended to appeal to a common humanity that is shared by all human beings everywhere, regardless of nationality or cultural background. The struggle to implement such values is intended to protect individuals from being exploited in their exchange transactions with those who are more powerful and who control the resources on which disprivileged persons depend for their survival. Despite the abstract appeal of such values and their obvious relevance in our

---

[4] Both of these types of values were also basic in Parsons' functional analysis, as we shall see in a subsequent chapter. This distinction between particularistic values that unite people who are homogeneous and universalistic values that unite heterogeneous people may be compared with Durkheim's dichotomy (reviewed earlier) between mechanical versus organic solidarity.

age of increasing globalization, such values are far from being institutionalized on a global basis.

In a summarizing these different types of values Blau described "particularistic values as media of solidarity, universalistic values as media of exchange and differentiation, legitimating values as media of organization, and opposition ideals as media of reorganization." (Blau, 1964:265)

Another important contrast between micro level exchange processes and macro structures is that the ratio of indirect to direct exchanges increases significantly in large and complex exchange networks. In many cases the complex chains of exchange transactions through which costs and rewards flow may be difficult to trace. Individuals become dependent on a lengthy series of indirect transactions among innumerable others who may be widely separated in time and space and who do not even have personal knowledge of one another. Such chains of interdependence might be identified by tracing the flow of money or material resources. Values and norms are particularly important for these complex networks of indirect exchanges, partly because of the need for trust in highly interdependent impersonal transactions and partly because of the wide disparity in the resources of the various exchange partners.[5]

When the exchange patterns of a complex society are supported by widely shared values, we can say that these patterns are institutionalized. In addition to this subjective dimension of institutionalization, there is also an objective dimension. Exchange patterns that have become well established, and that are repeated over the course of many generations, develop an objective reality that is independent of the particular individuals who become involved in them. Members of each new generation obviously do not start from scratch in determining the exchange relationships in which they will be involved. Instead, they are socialized to participate in them as established procedures that are expected to be followed. Thus, for example, when children begin their formal education in kindergarten or the first grade, they obviously are not given the opportunity to calculate the personal benefits of going to school, or to negotiate the terms of exchange that are involved. If the socialization process is effective, new members also internalize the supporting values and norms so that conformity becomes rewarding, both intrinsically and extrinsically.

In addition, in large-scale systems such as total societies the maintenance of established exchange processes is also dependent on the support of dominant groups. Such groups will be likely to have a strong interest in preserving the structure of the exchange patterns that protect their dominant position. Thus their power to control resources and exert influence on less dominant groups is used to reinforce the established institutional patterns which support their dominance. As a result, the options available to subordinate groups to negotiate more favorable terms of exchange are limited, sometimes severely. In extreme situations subordinate groups may be faced

[5] As noted in Chap. 7, Ekeh (1975) also emphasized the way in which commitments to moral values became relatively more important in indirect exchange patterns than in restricted patterns of direct exchange.

with the simple option of complying with the demands of more powerful groups or not surviving. However, as noted earlier, opposition movements may sometimes be developed that seek to improve the welfare of subordinate groups.

The institutionalization process that Blau describes in large and complex macro structures like total societies contrasts sharply with the micro-level (subinstitutional) exchange transactions analyzed by Homans as discussed in a previous chapter. The social world that Blau's theory portrays consists of complex networks of numerous types of exchange transactions, both direct and indirect. Blau's emphasis on values and norms is comparable in some ways to functional theory, though Blau focused more explicitly on the reward/cost considerations that underlie shared values and norms. In addition, his emphasis on the differential distribution of resources whereby dominant groups maintain their dominance is a major focus of conflict theory. Both functional theory and conflict theory will be discussed in more detail in subsequent chapters.

In the next section of this chapter we will look at James Coleman's elaboration of his rational choice theory beyond micro-level exchange transactions to explain how larger-scale patterns, including formal organizations ("corporate actors"), enable people to pursue collective goals that are beyond their ability to accomplish on their own or through market-type exchanges.

Social Capital and Corporate Actors from a Rational Choice Perspective

The well-known words of the United States Declaration of Independence explicitly state the rationale for the organization of governments: to secure the "inalienable rights" of individuals to "life, liberty, and the pursuit of happiness." Unlike individuals, the government is **not** seen as being endowed by the Creator with rights or interests of its own; its rights and responsibilities are established through social consensus in order to secure individuals' rights.

The basic idea that organizations are established to fulfill individuals' purposes and goals can be applied to all types of deliberately established formal organizations. This does not mean, however, that all organizations are designed to secure their members' basic "inalienable rights." In contrast to the governments of the United States and other **democratic** societies, business organizations are established to enable their founders to make profits. But to make profits, they must recruit employees and provide them with inducements (wages or salaries) to motivate them to contribute to the goal of making profits. In the voluntary sector, organizations are established to enable people to pursue various collective goals more effectively than any one person could do alone. The notion that establishing a formal social organization may be the most rational strategy for pursuing individual interests and goals (some of which are shared with others) is fundamental in Coleman's model of "corporate actors" (Coleman, 1990, especially Parts III and IV)

Coleman's perspective is similar to Blau's in linking micro and macro levels of analysis on the foundation of individuals' utilitarian interests, but his emphasis was somewhat different. Blau had attempted to show how macro structures "emerged" from micro-level social processes, exhibited properties that distinguished them from micro-level exchanges, and eventually became institutionalized. In contrast, Coleman's concern was to explain how macro (or impersonal meso) level structures ("corporate actors") are deliberately constructed and institutionalized when individuals determine that their individual interests and goals can be achieved more effectively (or at lower cost) through collective or organized action than through their individual efforts. These goals may include controlling the behavior of other people who are not even initially involved as participants in the exchange process. This purpose of controlling people's behavior is to avoid undesirable social consequences that might result from their actions, as well as to promote or require actions that contribute to the public welfare.

Normative and Legal Regulation of People's Behavior

Despite the strong individualistic emphasis of rational choice theory, an adequate understanding of our interests requires us to consider the potential actions of others and their consequences. For example, we want to live in safe neighborhoods, and we do not want anyone to "borrow" our car or our class notes without permission. In addition to being protected from criminal behavior, we also do not want to be victimized by careless drivers, air pollution caused by industrial plants, or unsafe food and water. We also believe that others should pay their fair share of taxes and fulfill their various civic responsibilities as citizens. These considerations suggest that our individual interests include controlling the behavior of others in various ways. As we saw in Chap. 7 in the case of the Prisoner's Dilemma game, our ability to satisfy our interests and achieve our goals is heavily contingent on the actions of others. The concept of **negative externalities** refers to the negative consequences of people's behavior for the interests and goals of others, whether intentional or not, and whether they are in direct contact with one another or not. **Positive externalities**, in contrast, are beneficial consequences that result from the behaviors of others. As we shall see later, controlling behavior that generates externalities is closely associated with the maintenance of individual rights and promoting the public welfare as well.

Widespread consensus regarding behaviors that should be controlled or regulated in some fashion provides the foundation for the development of norms and laws. In some cases, a consensus develops that certain behaviors should be **prohibited** because of their negative consequences for others. In other cases, certain behaviors may be **required** because of their contribution to the general welfare. Although conformity to norms and laws always involves controlling behavior, and so may be costly (to us as well as others), the costs of such control are seen as less than the costs of leaving such behavior uncontrolled. Thus, for example, we accept the need to abide by traffic rules when we drive our vehicles and to pay our taxes to maintain our highways and other public goods because we realize that the public benefits outweigh the costs—and as individuals we share in these benefits. Moreover, it would not be feasible to try to preserve public order or provide public goods through exchange patterns that individuals negotiate with one another on their own.

This general perspective is consistent with the contract theory of society developed by Thomas Hobbes in the seventeenth century. Although Hobbes' theory was intended to explain how anarchy and unregulated conflict are avoided, the behaviors subject to regulation and control in a modern society are actually far more extensive than simply the prohibition of mutual plundering, pillaging, and killing. The overall political organization of a society—the establishment of government itself and its various social control agencies—thus illustrates the basic principle in Coleman's theory that formal organizations are established to accomplish goals that cannot be accomplished (or accomplished as effectively) by individuals acting on their own, or by relying solely on ad hoc individually negotiated exchange transactions.

Norms and laws establish rights for people to control one another's behavior, but they are never automatically self-enforcing. Instead, their enforcement requires the use of power, and there are costs involved in the mobilization and exercise of power. It is customary to distinguish informal and formal methods of social control. Compliance with widely accepted norms relies heavily on informal social control, while formal laws that regulate behavior crucial to the public welfare are enforced through specialized social control agencies. In both cases, members of the public who benefit from such controls may be said to have rights that extend to other people's behavior.

Informal social control involves widespread participation by the public at large in monitoring one another's behavior and administering informal sanctions, such as social approval or disapproval. Such informal controls are likely to rest in large part on moral codes that strongly encourage individuals to consider their own behavior from the point of view of others who are likely to be affected by it. This ideal is expressed in the "Golden Rule" appeal that individuals should treat others as they wish to be treated themselves. Among individuals who have been well socialized, conformity to such moral codes may be self-reinforcing in that it helps make individuals feel good about themselves, despite the costs involved. But self-control and informal social control are not always adequate, especially where conformity is essential for the public welfare. In such cases, it is crucial that the negative sanctions outweigh the benefits individuals might receive through such behavior. Thus the stage is set for the development of formal social control organizations and agencies as manifested, for example, by law enforcement and criminal justice systems.

The fact that people would agree to give up certain rights to control their own behavior (and also to control the behavior of others) might initially appear puzzling from a utilitarian, rational choice perspective. However, such restrictions make sense when a social consensus develops regarding the need to prevent behavior that results in "negative externalities" that are socially disruptive or harmful, or that undermine the rights of others in ways that are regarded as socially unacceptable. Thus, for example, we have the right not to have to suffer the negative consequences of other people's behavior, even when these consequences may be inadvertent, just as they have rights not to suffer the negative consequences of our own behavior, even when such behavior may be rational from our point of view for satisfying our needs.

As noted in our discussion of Coleman's explanation of norms in Chap. 7, individual rights are limited not only by **proscriptive** norms and laws forbidding certain types of actions but also by **prescriptive** norms and/or laws that create obligations to perform certain types of action. In general, it is more difficult to enforce a prescriptive obligation than a restrictive prohibition. Probably any elementary teacher understands that it is easier to restrict a child with behavior problems to a "time-out" area than to force the child to complete his or her reading and writing assignments when the child refuses to do so. In general, prescriptive norms can probably be enforced more effectively through positive sanctions for compliance than through negative sanctions for noncompliance. Thus, for example, we are compensated financially when we fulfill the duties of our occupation, but no one pays us when we refrain from stealing. The obligation to pay our taxes is enforced by the threat of negative sanctions, of course, but the mechanisms for doing so are often linked with other economic transactions and so are not really voluntary (income tax withholding, for example, or sales taxes).

In modern democratic societies, basic rights have expanded as societies have moved toward a "welfare state" model and an expanded definition of the public welfare. The rights of employees to a minimum wage and the rights of consumers to be assured of safe food and automobiles illustrate this process. Moreover, the anti-smoking movement of recent years provides a specific example of how social definitions of rights can change dramatically over the course of a few years. Difficult decisions are often required to achieve a socially acceptable balance between different types of rights and responsibilities. For example, legislation to limit environmental pollution from industrial activities must be evaluated against the economic benefits provided by such activities. If industries are required to incur the costs of installing pollution controls, such costs will no doubt to be passed along to the consumers. If these industries respond by relocating to a less regulated environment in another country, this would mean loss of the public benefits they generate (such as jobs and taxes). In addition, such relocation would simply shift the "negative externalities" to populations that are more vulnerable and unable to resist. Clearly, the challenge of balancing conflicting rights and interests is not an easy task in evaluating alternative policies for promoting the public welfare.

It is interesting to contrast Coleman's perspective on how norms emerge with that of Peter Blau. As noted earlier, in Blau's theory norms and values are developed to stabilize rewarding exchange relations or to challenge authorities perceived as unfair. Coleman, in contrast, emphasizes the process whereby norms are developed to control the actions of **other** people—that is, people with whom one is not necessarily involved in an exchange relation. As Coleman explained, "… [T]he genesis of a norm is based in externalities of an action which cannot be overcome by simple transactions that would put control of the action in the hands of those experiencing the externalities." (Coleman, 1990:251) Both Blau's and Coleman's explanations of how norms are established are valid but for different types of situations.

Promoting Normative Conformity and Deterring Deviance

A major reason that norms and laws are not automatically self-enforcing is that compliance involves costs that may outweigh immediate short-term rewards. This means that costs for noncompliance must be established that will outweigh the rewards to be gained. But in addition to the cost/reward considerations reflected in individuals' decisions regarding their own compliance, there are also costs for others who are involved in monitoring people's behavior to detect noncompliance and administering negative sanctions to violators. These costs must also be weighed against the benefits of insuring other people's normative conformity.

When there is a high level of social support for a norm, plus widespread willingness to use informal controls to enforce it (through social approval or disapproval, for example), the cost of enforcement is widely distributed among all who presumably benefit from others' compliance. Such informal enforcement is more likely when people feel a sense of civic responsibility for the public welfare. This sense of civic responsibility is likely to be nourished when there are rich networks of social relations that lead people to be concerned with one another's needs and interests as well as their own. In Coleman's terms such networks constitute a form of **social capital** that can be utilized to mobilize people to work together for the achievement of collective goals and promotion of the general welfare. But when the level of social capital is low or informal social controls are ineffective, enforcement depends heavily on resources allocated to specialized social control agents. This, in turn, will also reflect public sentiments regarding the costs and benefits of enforcement. These sentiments will be based on public perceptions regarding the relative importance of conformity versus the harm that would result from widespread nonconformity. Such evaluations always involve comparisons to various other public needs and concerns for which resources may be needed. And public needs of all type are always also evaluated in the light of people's desire to maintain as much individual freedom to control their own resources as much as possible. (Politicians usually cannot expect to be elected if they promise higher taxes, regardless of the benefits that may be promised.)

Levels of conformity may be expected to be higher if individuals find conformity to be rewarding in terms of their own personal interests. Obviously, for example, it is more rewarding for nonsmokers to adhere to nonsmoking norms than for smokers. Norms that are consistent with individuals' own interests are described by Coleman as **conjoint** norms. In contrast, **disjoint** norms are those in which the conforming action is not consistent with the individual's own personal interests. Although individuals may conform to obtain social approval or to avoid negative sanctions, the conforming behavior itself is not sufficiently rewarding in itself to outweigh the costs. Thus sanctions are needed to insure conformity

Levels of conformity are also higher among people who actually internalize a norm, perhaps incorporating it into their self-concepts along with appropriate justifying rationalizations or values. The result of internalization is a change in individuals' interests so that they derive internal psychological or emotional rewards from conformity, in addition to whatever other rewards might be earned. To the extent that norms are internalized, external monitoring and negative sanctions are not needed to insure conformity. Instead, individuals control their behavior voluntarily. This suggests that it is in the interest of socialization and social control agents to promote high levels of internalization because this reduces the costs involved in monitoring behavior and administering sanctions to insure compliance. But efforts to promote internalization also involve costs, particularly in terms of the expenditures of time, emotional energy, and other resources in establishing socioemotional bonds with the person being socialized, plus the opportunity costs of alternatives forfeited by the socializing agent. However, the establishment of a close relationship with a person being socialized not only helps promote internalization but may also be highly rewarding to the socializing agent as well, as many parents and teachers could testify. But within the framework of rational choice theory these rewards must be evaluated in the light of costs incurred. To experience such rewards would require a level of socioemotional attunement and bonding that in some contexts would seem somewhat inconsistent with the individualistic assumptions of rational choice theory.

Individuals vary (as do societies and subcultures within them) in terms of the priority given to individual needs and goals as opposed to maintaining and strengthening socioemotional bonds in families and other close relationships. This variation may be related to the use of informal versus formal social control strategies. In American society, for example, it seems plausible to argue that the costs of relying on the police to control youthful crime and violence could be reduced if more resources were spent in insuring that children have emotionally close relationships with parents and other desirable adult role models. When parents are successful in having relationships with their children that promote their normative conformity, such relationships may be seen as a form of social capital existing within the family. But the development of such social capital requires the expenditure of time and emotional energy that parents could otherwise use in pursuing their own personal goals.

When members of a close-knit local community support and reinforce families through their social network contacts, informal surveillance, and appropriate expressions of approval or disapproval, this indicates a high level of social capital at the community level. This social capital may also be expressed in the willingness of community members to participate in various activities that benefit the young people in the community, such as providing adult supervision for Little League baseball or boys' or girls' clubs, plus other activities that promote the general welfare. Without the willingness of community members to be involved in their community in ways that encourage normative conformity, the need for formal social control mechanisms may be expected to increase. In the next section we will look at Coleman's explanation of how social capital is related to the provision of various public goods.

Social Capital and Public Goods

As suggested earlier, individuals' actions may sometimes generate positive externalities; that is they benefit others as well as the individuals who perform such actions. For example, the existence of strong social ties among members of cohesive social groups increases the odds that they will be aware when one of their members experiences a family crisis or economic setback, and their mutual concern for one another may lead them to work out a strategy to render aid. As another example, community members who watch out for one another's children in their neighborhood thereby help promote community safety and solidarity, from which these children and their parents benefit. Similarly, homeowners who keep their houses in good repair contribute to the attractiveness of the neighborhood and the resale value of their homes, from which all residents benefit.

But there are many aspects of the public welfare for which individual rewards are inadequate to offset the personal costs required, or that are impractical to provide through informal cooperation or individually negotiated exchange transactions. If widespread social consensus develops regarding the need to control people's behavior in ways that will promote the general welfare, norms or rules may be developed to require or prohibit behaviors to meet these needs, even though such behaviors may not necessarily be consistent with individuals' narrow self-interests. Thus, for example, communities may establish zoning regulations requiring conformity to certain standards regarding building construction and property upkeep. Or, they may vote to raise taxes to provide community recreation programs for adolescents during the summer or to expand the level of law enforcement in areas that have recently experienced increased levels of crime.

Coleman also emphasized the importance of prescriptive norms in connection with the need to obtain material resources to provide public goods such as streets and highways, public schools, police protection, parks, and facilities such as community libraries, for example. Despite the obvious benefits to all citizens that such public goods provide, it is typically not in any single individual's interest to incur the cost of providing them. For one thing, the costs would be far too great. In addition, such goods are often not divisible; that is, it would be difficult for a collective project to be developed in which individuals could extract their personal share of benefits in proportion to their personal costs. (Toll roads or usage fees for public goods are exceptions.) If members of a community (or a state or a society) agree to finance such public goods through taxes, the result is that each person pays a relatively small amount of the total cost while all have the potential to benefit. But this means that enforcement mechanisms must be established so that the costs of non-payment outweigh the cost of payment.

Many instances could be cited of political conflicts that revolve around whether the benefits received by all segments of a community are proportional to the taxes they pay. Paying increased taxes to support a new football stadium, for example, may be resisted on the grounds that the primary beneficiaries will be the wealthy team owners, not the taxpayers, especially those unable to afford the price of tickets. In some cases, inadequate public services may stimulate individuals to compensate through actions they undertake on their own or through voluntary associations. For example, if crime rates rise, individuals may invest in alarm systems for their homes, establish neighborhood watch associations, or move into gated communities and pay dues for the additional security they provide. The dynamics of exchange patterns and conformity are somewhat different in voluntary organizations, like religious groups in the United States, for example. The norms in voluntary organizations certainly encourage all members to make contributions (of time, money, energy, and other resources) from which all may benefit. But in contrast to involuntary taxes, members of voluntary organizations may opt to leave if the costs turn out to be too great for the benefits received.

Whenever people cooperate to achieve shared goals, whether in organizational or community settings, social capital emerges as one of the potentially important byproducts (or positive externalities) of their cooperation. When people are strangers to one another, they are usually not very likely to cooperate in achieving collective goals over and above what they are required to do as individuals (like obeying the law and paying their taxes). But once social relations are developed, these network ties may serve as a foundation for various additional forms of collective action. Whether these social relations are established initially to pursue specific goals or simply for sociability, they may subsequently be mobilized to advance participants' shared interests and promote the public welfare. This was illustrated in the analysis by Coleman and his colleagues of how community context and parental involvement in the school system have positive effects on students' academic achievement (Coleman et al., 1966). In the next section we will examine the way corporate actors may be formally established when informal forms of cooperative behavior are inadequate for achieving collective goals.

Establishment of Corporate Actors and Authority Relations

For satisfying many individual and collective interests in our modern complex society, it is obvious that reliance on the social capital represented by informal social relations is not sufficient. Instead, there is a need for formal organizations to be created to achieve goals that would be more difficult (or costly) if not impossible to do otherwise. Coleman refers to such formal organizations as "corporate actors." Corporate actors vary greatly in terms of whether their primary goals involve the individual interests of a founder or group of founding partners, the members themselves as voluntary participants, or the public welfare of all citizens living in a politically organized geographical area.[6] To establish or maintain corporate actors requires that individuals agree to transfer certain rights, resources, and responsibilities to them. But for corporate actors actually to act, individuals must be designated as their agents who have access to organizational resources to accomplish the goals they are established to accomplish. These resources may be material or financial resources, or they may include authority to direct the behavior of others (subordinates) in performing their organizational roles. Coleman's perspective regarding the hierarchical authority structure of corporate actors is consistent with Blau's notion of the need for power and/or authority structures for accomplishing collective goals.

As noted in Chap. 7, individuals have the power to control their own behavior in many areas of their lives, even though their rights to do so are limited by norms and laws. Individuals also have the right to transfer control of their behavior in certain areas to some other party. This right to give up control over one's own actions to someone else is the foundation for all authority structures. This probably occurs most commonly in an employment context, but it also occurs in voluntary organizations as well (though typically to a lesser degree). In essence, employees, rank-and-file members, or other types of participants surrender the right to control their own actions in their organizational roles in exchange for benefits they expect to receive as individuals or as members of some constituency. This means that the authority figure to whom control is granted in an organizational context has the right to control subordinates' actions in certain specifically defined ways for achieving organizational goals.

The distinction Coleman made between simple and complex exchange transactions can be applied to authority relations. In a simple exchange system there is a direct exchange between two persons, while a complex system involves third parties. In a simple authority system, an individual agrees to give up the right to control certain aspects of his or her behavior to another person in exchange for return benefits from that person. In a complex system, in contrast, an individual transfers these rights of control in exchange for benefits to be received from a third party in a system of indirect exchanges. Similarly, when an authority figure is given the right to control a subordinate's behavior, this right of control may then be transferred to a third party. Thus, for example, an owner of a business firm may hire an employee and then transfer the right to control that employee's behavior to an assistant or a lower-level supervisor. It is these complex types of social relations that provide the basis for social organizations with a complex division of labor. Such hierarchical structures have been the focus of sociological analysis since Weber's ideal-type description of bureaucratic organizations.

---

[6] In Chap. 10 we will look at how Peter Blau and Richard Scott (1962) distinguished among different types of organizations based on who is the primary beneficiary of the organization's goal achievement.

Coleman emphasized that the identity of a "corporate actor" is distinct from the identities of its members as "natural persons." Some form of constitution may be developed to establish a corporate actor, plus explicit rules that define the rights and duties associated with the various positions that make it up. A corporate actor is thus able to persist through time despite turnover of its personnel. The recruitment of new members is based on their acceptance of an agreement that their actions in their organizational roles, their relations with one another, and perhaps even their transactions outside the organization will be governed by its authority structure. Their behavior in their organizational role is expected to serve the interests of the organization, as opposed to their own individual interests—although, of course, they are likely to receive some form of compensation in return or to benefit from the organization's accomplishments.

Despite the fact that members of an organization agree to be bound by its rules and to comply with its designated authorities, this definitely does not mean that they are powerless to try to change the terms of their membership so as give greater priority to their own personal interests and goals. In fact, members may develop informal subgroups, or even organize themselves formally, to challenge or change existing rules or the way authority is exercised. This is consistent with Blau's portrayal of the emergence of opposition movements. The persistent tension that often exists between individuals' needs and interests and organizational obligations is a major feature of all bureaucratic organizations and a topic for numerous types of sociological analysis (for example, see Mintzberg, 1983).

In analyzing authority structures and corporate actors, Coleman distinguished between **principals** and **agents**. The principal is the one whose interests have priority while the agent is expected to act in terms of the principal's interests. Thus an authority figure would be the principal while the subordinate is the agent of the principal. At another level, however, the authority figure is an agent of the corporate actor (the organization itself). In fact, employees at all levels are agents while the corporate actor itself (the organization) is the principal. In a self-governing association in which all members benefit from achievement of the organization's goals, participants may be seen either as principals (and thus as beneficiaries of the collective action) or as agents (who act on behalf of the organization); it depends on the specific role they are playing. In a corporation with stockholders, even the members of top-level management would be agents and the stockholders would be the principals. Of course, top-level managers (and personnel lower in the hierarchy as well) may also be stockholders—and as such they also are principals (along with all other stockholders) as well as agents (unlike other stockholders).

Persons in positions of authority in bureaucratic organizations may thus be seen as being principals themselves, directing the activities of subordinates, or agents of the organization, bound by its rules and committed to its goals. If the organization is a public agency or government body in a democratic society, the public at large would be the principal, and the organization itself would be the agent. But whether the corporate actor is a private or public agency, its authority figures are well aware of the temptation for subordinates to devise ways to put their own interests first or to resist having their actions controlled. Thus they will need to develop strategies to monitor and control their subordinates' actions. Coleman discusses various strategies that principals may devise to try to police agents' behavior or to implement quality control inspections of the results (or products) of agents' actions. All such strategies of surveillance and control involve cost/reward considerations on the part of principals or authority figures that must be considered in addition to the cost/reward considerations involved in compensating their agents and subordinates for their contributions.

The nature and scope of the challenge of controlling behavior in organizational contexts will vary for different types of organizations and different types of tasks. In organizations with paid employees, it will obviously be in a principal's interest to recruit persons with a strong work ethic whose training and basic values are consistent with the type of work expected. If employees have an intrinsic commitment to the type of work they are recruited to perform, or find it enjoyable and satisfying, the need for supervision should be less than for those without such motivations. Of course, even the most idealistic professionals (teachers, social workers, and clergy) who claim to enjoy their work and find it intrinsically satisfying are not expected to perform their jobs day after day without being compensated. Even so, the internal commitments to the task at hand or internal enjoyment of it help reduce the need for supervision.

In addition to careful selection of well-motivated agents in the recruitment process, strategies may be devised to promote internalization of norms and values that will lead agents to identify with their principal's interests as their own. One strategy for doing this is through procedures whereby the benefits agents receive are linked to their performance of actions advancing the principal's interests. This pattern is manifested in compensation policies whereby employees are paid according to the quantity or quality of their performance, or are allowed to share in a company's profits. Another strategy involves the staging of organizational rituals in which outstanding performances are recognized and celebrated.

In contrast to organizations where people are compensated by wages or salaries, voluntary or mutual-benefit organizations presumably attract members who share similar interests, goals, and values. This means that regardless of their position in the authority structure, they may be expected to have intrinsic motivations to pursue the collective goals. Coleman used the concepts of **conjoint** versus **disjoint** authority structures to distinguish those in which principals and agents have the same interests versus those where they do not. (This is comparable to his distinction discussed earlier between conjoint and disjoint norms.) Having similar goals in a conjoint authority structure does not necessarily mean that no supervision is necessary, however. There is always the potential for conflict regarding the responsibilities each party is expected to undertake in pursuit of these goals. In addition, participants may disagree regarding the best strategies to use in reaching organizational goals. Some members may also be tempted to try to free-ride, since it would be in their personal interest to share the collective benefits without incurring the costs of producing them. These considerations indicate the need for some form of authority structure to insure the coordination of individuals' actions.

In a democratic organization or society, the identification of principles and agents is not equivalent to its authority structure. Instead, those in positions of authority actually are the agents of the membership of the organization or of society as a whole. The challenge in this case is to devise strategies to prevent leaders from giving priority to their own interests, such as maintaining themselves in power, for example, or enriching themselves beyond the level to which they are entitled. The interests of leaders in maintaining their power leads to the type of pattern that Robert Michels ([1915] 1949) described in his well-known analysis of the "iron law of oligarchy." For the overall society, such constitutional provisions as periodic voting and the separation of powers (such as between legislative, executive, and judicial branches of government) are intended to help insure that leaders do not abuse their power and authority for the sake of their own interests. In addition, having a political system with two or more political parties, freedom for the formation of opposition movements, and independent mass media that serve a watchdog function are also important in reducing the opportunity and the temptation for political authorities to abuse their power.

The challenge for devising strategies to preserve democracy is usually greater for the overall society than for voluntary organizations. The authority structure of the state extends to all who live within its boundaries and is backed up by the threat of coercive power. Moreover, many citizens feel relatively powerless in influencing government policies, as suggested by their failure to vote because they feel it will make no appreciable difference in their lives anyway. When this occurs on a wide scale, it contributes to the erosion of democracy. With an apathetic public, political authorities may be even more tempted to give priority to their own interests rather than the public welfare. When this leads to collaboration with influential private interest groups that seek to influence government policies, there is a risk that the public welfare may be sacrificed to unofficial alliances between such special interest groups and government authorities of which the public at large may be unaware.

On the other hand, in many voluntary organizations, it may be relatively easy for members to exercise the option of leaving if the leaders' actions fail to satisfy their interests, or if they feel the benefits are not worth the costs. Members may simply quit participating or decide not to renew their membership. Of course, the costs of exit are obviously greater in some organizations than others. Being a member and making contributions to labor unions, for example, may be required in certain industries for continued employment. In view of the resources controlled by labor union leaders and the dependence of members on the jobs where union membership may be required, the challenge of maintaining internal democracy may be expected to be particularly great. Long before Coleman's rational choice perspective, Lipset et al. (1956) identified some of the conditions that enhance democracy (or prevent oligarchic control) in labor unions. Briefly, democratic control is more likely to be maintained when workers have extensive social contacts with one another, not only at work but in their communities as well. This emphasis on social relationships in the community is another illustration of the importance of social capital. In general, however, one of the negative consequences of heavy reliance on corporate actors is the erosion of social capital based on informal network ties. This next section will elaborate this point.

Corporate Actors Versus Natural Persons

Government bodies, business enterprises, labor unions, professional associations, voluntary organizations, and other types of formal organizations are all examples of what Coleman refers to as corporate actors. They are established, as noted earlier, to accomplish goals that cannot be accomplished (or accomplished as effectively) by "natural persons." By their nature corporate actors pursue specific and limited goals. Nevertheless, through their agents they may wield a great deal of power, due to the rights transferred to them by large numbers of people and the extensive resources that many of them control. Coleman's analysis of modern society emphasized the pattern whereby responsibility for more and more aspects of social life has in fact been transferred from individuals as natural persons to corporate actors (Coleman, 1982). As a result of this process, the "social capital" created through the elementary and primordial social relations of "natural persons" are vulnerable to erosion as corporate actors gradually become more and more dominant. In Coleman's terms, as the power and scope of corporate actors has expanded, the power and rights of individuals as "natural persons" and the scope of their action has been reduced accordingly. The result is the emergence of an "asymmetric" society.

This pattern can readily be illustrated in many areas of social life, including, for example, child care and socialization of the young. Prior to the establishment of the public school system in modern societies, it was the parents who had the right and the primary responsibility to control their children and socialize them for adult life. Their socializing activities might have been supplemented by extended family members as well as by other adults, reflecting the relatively high level of social capital in the community. But with the development of the public school system and compulsory school attendance, a large part of these parental rights were reallocated to school systems, which are intentionally constructed corporate actors. In more recent years other types of specialized agencies, such as day care centers, provide various forms of child care and socializing experiences for young people. In this process the rights of parents have been undermined, as well as the social capital that develops as parents establish social relations with one another to provide mutual support and reinforcement in caring for their children.

With this increasing reliance on specialized corporate actors to meet the educational, social, and other needs of young people, the effort to retain (or regain) parental rights requires that parents themselves get involved in various special-purpose organizations (such as parent-teacher associations, for example). In recent years, too, some parents have resisted the erosion of their parental rights by home schooling their children. Coleman certainly did not advocate eliminating public schools or other beneficial special purpose organizations (or corporate actors). In fact, a great deal of his research and consulting work was intended to strengthen the role of public schools in promoting equality of educational opportunity throughout our society.

On a broader level, the scope of special purpose corporate actors is always limited to the goals for which they were established. Their high level of specialization creates an environment in which tensions and conflicts are likely to develop among competing organizations and institutional structures. In the meantime, high reliance on these specialized corporate actors undermines the social capital that might otherwise enable people to cooperate in dealing with issues and problems as "natural persons" in a holistic way. Such cooperation would no doubt give people a sense of empowerment as they exercise responsibility for their collective welfare. As implied in Coleman's own research, special purpose organizations like schools are likely to be more effective if they are able to draw upon the rich reservoir of social capital that can be found in the informal social relations of cohesive and well integrated communities.

Overall, Coleman's analysis emphasized how corporate actors enable us to accomplish various goals beyond what would be possible in an unregulated market where individuals' exchange transactions are intended solely to satisfy their own self-interests. However, his analysis of the "asymmetric" society demonstrates the perverse effects that may result when individuals rely too heavily on corporate actors to solve social problems and promote the public welfare. These effects include a decline in individual freedom and a sense of personal responsibility for the common good. The challenge this analysis suggests is to work toward an optimal balance between freedom for individuals to pursue their own interests and responsibility for cooperating in the achievement of collective goals. To achieve a sense of personal autonomy and empowerment, it is important for this cooperation to include informal social relations between individuals as natural persons as well as participation in formal organizations,

To sum up, Coleman's overall contributions range from people's efforts to satisfy their personal needs and interests to the establishment of complex organizations for pursuing goals that cannot be achieved (or achieved as effectively) through individual effort or independent market transactions. In between, he applies his perspective to numerous aspects of the social world, including authority relations, trust among participants in cohesive networks, the development of norms for controlling behavior, the potential benefits of social capital, the production of public goods, and the emergence of collective behavior. Micro-level processes involving individuals' social actions and exchange transactions are shaped by the already established macro-level social environment but can, in turn, have an impact on that environment. Not only does Coleman link micro and macro levels, but his analysis of corporate actors provides an important theoretical perspective for analyzing complex organizations of all types, both public and private.

Summary

The primary goal in this chapter has been to explain the emergence of macro structures from elementary exchange transactions. In doing so we have drawn on Peter Blau's exchange theory and James Coleman's rational choice theory. Despite the differences in their specific focus, these two perspectives are similar in explaining how formal organizations are developed from individuals' efforts to satisfy their individual interests. The rational choice foundations of this perspective are consistent with the notion that such organizations develop from efforts to meet needs or pursue goals, both individual and collective, that are difficult or impossible for individuals to do on their own.

Blau's basic argument was that power structures develop from imbalanced exchanges, and that their emergence provides the foundation for macro structures such as complex organizations. When people have resources that enable them to acquire power by providing unilateral benefits, this creates the conditions whereby they are able to organize the recipients of such benefits for some form of collective action in exchange for continued benefits. To the extent that participants regard such exchanges as fair, values and norms emerge that help stabilize and legitimate them. However, opposition values and norms may develop if people perceive the terms of exchange as unfair or believe they can change these terms for their own benefit.

With the macro level expansion in the size of organizations that is made possible through the development of widespread and complex networks of power and dependency relations, the proportion of indirect exchanges expands significantly as compared to micro level exchanges. These widespread patterns of exchange can be said to be institutionalized when they are legitimated by widely accepted values and norms, when they endure beyond one generation, and when they are supported by the dominant groups of society and reinforced by the coercive power of the state. The institutionalization of stable and complex exchange patterns limits the ability of people to start "from scratch" in negotiating the terms of the exchange transactions they establish in pursuing their individual interests.

In contrast to the major focus of exchange theory, Coleman dealt explicitly with how people deal with the consequences of one another's actions in ways that go beyond the particular exchange transactions in which they are involved. Specifically, his explanation of the development and enforcement of norms emphasized the interests people have in regulating the behavior of others, even in the absence of any specific exchange relationship with them. These interests include preventing or controlling the negative consequences of others' behavior, as well as in promoting behavior with positive social consequences. This explanation of norms contrasts with Blau's emphasis on the notion that norms emerge among exchange partners themselves in an effort to maintain mutually advantageous patterns of exchange.

Building on his exchange and rational choice theory Coleman explained how "corporate actors" are established to accomplish goals that individuals would not be able to accomplish on their own or through individually negotiated exchange transactions. These may be collective goals that extend beyond the organization's boundaries. Such goals include the establishment of norms or legal codes that restrict other people's behavior to prevent undesirable social consequences, or that require behaviors that contribute to the social welfare or help provide public goods of various kinds. Or they may be individual goals, such as a business entrepreneur's goal of earning money, when this goal can only be achieved by recruiting others and compensating them for their contributions. Or, the goals may involve providing benefits for members of the organization or satisfying needs for social services or public benefits that are not being adequately addressed otherwise.

With the establishment of organizations as corporate actors, individuals must be designated to act as agents for the organization. The actions of these agents are expected to reflect the interests and goals of the organization itself, not their own individual interests and goals. But of course, individuals are always concerned with their own interests as individuals, even within organizational contexts. Thus the challenge is to devise strategies whereby the accomplishment of organizational goals is linked to the individual benefits provided to its agents. Even so, organizational life is often permeated by tensions between individuals' own personal interests and their obligations as organizational agents.

Coleman's analysis of corporate actors provided the background for his analysis of our modern "asymmetric society" in which individuals have given up many of their individual rights and responsibilities as "natural persons" to various "corporate actors." One unfortunate consequence of this development is a decline in individuals' sense of personal autonomy and empowerment. This, in turn, contributes to the erosion of the "social capital" that might otherwise emerge from a rich network of informal social relations and lead individuals to accept personal responsibility for their collective welfare.

As discussed in the last chapter, the dynamics of relationships involving socioemotional bonds may be contrasted with the individualistic assumptions of the rational choice perspective. When individuals enter into exchange transactions with one another, either on their own behalf or as members or agents of an organization, the stage is set for the emergence of various socioemotional bonds which may change the dynamics of the relationship and even the personal needs and interests of the exchange partners. The next chapter will contrast formal organizations with communities in terms of the contrasting dynamics of self-interests versus concern for others and the public welfare.

Questions for Study and Discussion

1. Do you agree or disagree with the argument from Blau's theory in this chapter that the emergence of power structures is necessary for a group of people to engage in collective action as a coordinated unit? Why or why not? Under what conditions do you think it might be possible for people who are equals to work together to accomplish some goal, either long-term or short-term? Select a group or organization in which you are involved and describe the rewards and costs that are exchanged between leaders (or authority figures) and subordinates (or followers).
2. Explain how values and norms can substitute for individually negotiated exchange transactions in governing people's behavior. For the overall society, or for some organization in which you are involved, how would you describe the overall balance between legitimating values and opposition values? How do

these values compare and contrast with universalistic versus particularistic values? How might the universalistic/particularistic distinction be applied to the difference between authority figures and their subordinates?

3. Although most people tend to conform to widespread normative patterns most of the time, deviant behavior is also common in our society. What are some examples of normative patterns that you find intrinsically rewarding, and what are some that you would prefer to ignore? For the latter, what types of negative consequences would you anticipate from failing to comply (guilty conscience, social disapproval, formal punishment)?
4. What is mean by the concept of "social capital," and how can this concept be related to people's identity as well as their "bonding" and "bridging" social network ties?
5. Do you agree or disagree with Coleman's diagnosis of the effects of extensive reliance on "corporate actors" in reducing individuals' power as "natural persons?" Why or why not? Do corporate actors contribute to the erosion of informal social capital? In what way? How could new forms of social capital be developed through the formation of voluntary organizations for dealing with social problems? Explain.

Chapter 10
Meso-Level Structures: Communities and Organizations

According to the widely acclaimed book by Robert Putnam, *Bowling Alone* (2000), the deterioration of social bonds in recent years has led to a decline in people's civic mindedness and participation in voluntary organizations. This decline may be attributed to the high level of individualism of our culture as well as the pattern of frequent mobility that seems to discourage people from putting down roots in their local community. The overall result is deterioration of the "social capital" that is based on durable social connections plus widespread reluctance to get involved in showing concern for our neighbors and the larger public welfare.

Putnam's contemporary diagnosis, like that of other social critics who worry about the contemporary decline in our sense of community, can be contrasted with French sociologist Alexis de Tocqueville's description of the United States in the early years of the nineteenth century. As described in Chap. 2, de Tocqueville noted that American citizens were connected in numerous types of social organizations in their local communities through their municipal governments, local churches, and various voluntary associations that were established to achieve collective goals. Despite the individualism of our society even then, de Tocqueville was impressed with the way American democracy seemed grounded in high levels of neighborliness and mutual helpfulness at the local community level, plus a widely shared sense of civic responsibility and participation.

Since de Tocqueville made his observations nearly two centuries ago, American society has become larger and more complex, and impersonal relationships have expanded tremendously in many areas of social life. Although informal neighborliness still exists in many communities throughout the country there are also many neighborhoods where neighbors hardly know one another. As suggested in Coleman's analysis of our "asymmetric" society (discussed in the last chapter), we rely heavily on "corporate actors" to meet various collective needs instead of the informal forms of social capital that emerge from people's sociable relations as "natural persons."

This chapter deals explicitly with communities versus organizations as meso-level social formations. The concept of community involves a subjective emotional sense of being linked with others on the basis of similar values, interests, or experiences. Organizations, in contrast, are formally constructed to achieve goals that individuals are unable or unwilling to try to achieve on their own. From the perspective of the last two chapters, organizations are seen as reflecting rational choice considerations

D.P. Johnson, *Contemporary Sociological Theory: An Integrated Multi-Level Approach.*

while communities are based on shared emotional identification that provides a sense of belonging.

The following topics and themes will be explored:

- Communities—The concept may refer either to actual relationships among people or to an abstract cultural ideal. In either case a sense of community emerges from similarities and shared interests. Our discussion will focus explicitly on the following:
  - Geographical communities;
  - Ecological interdependence and community formation in urban areas;
  - Communities of shared interests and values.
- Formal organizations—Such social formations are intentionally established to pursue various goals. (The definition is essentially the same as for James Coleman's concept of "corporate actors.") The following aspects of formal organizations will be discussed:
  - Beneficiaries of organizational goals—based on an organizational typology developed by Peter Blau and Richard Scott.
  - Organizational control and compliance structures—based on Amatai Etzioni's comparative perspective.
  - Bureaucrats versus professionals in organizational settings—a distinction that is related to issues of organizational identification and control.
  - Organizations as open systems—Dealing with Issues of Boundary Maintenance, Input/output Transactions, Internal Interdependence, and Interorganizational Relations.

Communities may be based on geographical proximity (such as residential neighborhoods), but other sources for a sense of belonging may also be identified. Communities of all types vary in terms of whether or not they are formally organized to accomplish collective goals. Even when a small town, for example, is formally "organized" through its municipal government, most residents may be passive participants, even though they may identify strongly with their community at an emotional level. However, if a small town or residential neighborhood were to face some type of threat, this may trigger explicit efforts tqo "get organized" and "do something" about it. When this occurs, the resulting social relations often give rise to a strengthened sense of community. In Coleman's terms, such mobilization generates social capital. And the feeling the members should "get organized" may actually lead to the establishment of a formal organization.

The distinction that Tönnies ([1887] 1963) made in an earlier stage of sociology between *Gemeinschaft* (community) and *Gesellschaft* (society) highlights the contrast between communities and formal organizations. Although *Gesellschaft* is typi cally translated "society" it can also be translated as "association," and Tönnies emphasized the notion of a deliberately established social system that is based on the "rational will." The *Gemeinschaft* (or community), in contrast, reflects a more spontaneous type of social formation based on "natural will" and subjective emotional feelings.

Communities: Actual, Potential, and Ideal

The concept of community often goes far beyond relationships based on face-to-face interaction. Perceptions of similar experiences and interests provide a potential basis for personal bonds, but the sense of belonging or connection may extend beyond those with whom one has developed such bonds. Even so, we would expect that overall solidarity would be significantly related to the strength of the social ties among members as well as their shared sense of identification with the overall community. The highest level of solidarity and identification might be expected in communities with extensive social relations that are limited mostly to fellow members. Thus members of a residential community, a religious organization, a local social club or professional organization, or any other type of group will exhibit higher cohesion if their close relationships are mostly with one another. The emotional cohesiveness of communities might be compared to that of small groups in this regard. Even though no single group includes the entire community, there may be considerable overlap among various groups in the community which helps promote a high level of community identification. In contrast to face-to-face relations, community identification may also be nourished by shared lifestyle experiences, awareness of networks of indirect social connections, and mass media portrayals of people and events with which members may identify (see Calhoun, pp. 95–121 in Bourdieu and Coleman, eds., 1991). This sense of belonging may be partially independent of actual social relations with fellow members—although claims of belonging or emotional identification may seem rather vacuous in the absence of any such relations.

In everyday life we often think of communities as based on geography, neighborhoods in particular, even though the social relations among neighbors may be minimal. Geographical communities vary greatly in terms of how well members know one another and in the "community spirit" they exhibit. In contrast to the geographically defined nature of residential communities, members of a religious group, for example, may feel an abstract sense of oneness with all who share the same religious identity throughout the society or even the entire world. The concept of community is sometimes used to invoke an abstract ideal of solidarity among people who share certain characteristics and interests that are important for their identities, and that they believe distinguish them from those who do not "belong." The fact that community identification often involves distinctions between insiders and outsiders can be seen as a challenge for those who seek to develop a more inclusive sense of community. Even when individuals define their community in open and inclusive terms, there are still likely to be boundaries between open-minded "people like us" who share this inclusive definition and those who would prefer to be more exclusive.

Political leaders may refer to an entire nation-state as a community, thereby hoping to invoke a sense of emotional cohesion and solidarity at the national level—as well as support for their leadership and policies (Anderson, 1991).[1] For large and heterogeneous societies like the United States, an inclusive sense of community is difficult to develop, especially when the culture is fragmented into numerous subcultures and dominated by a high level of individualism. Political strategies to promote national solidarity are often criticized for giving higher priority to the interests of the dominant segments of society than to policies that will promote the highest possible level of inclusiveness of all the divergent groups making up the society. Unfortunately, a widely shared sense of community at the national level often tends to remain latent unless aroused by dramatic tragedies. Such arousal was manifested in the weeks and months following the September 11, 2001, terrorist actions resulting in the destruction of the World Trade Center by two hijacked airplanes, extensive damage to the Pentagon by a third airplane, and the crash of a fourth airplane in a Pennsylvania field following the heroic struggle of the passengers on board. On a more positive and less dramatic note, a sense of national solidarity is aroused through annual July 4 celebrations in communities throughout the country as well as by noteworthy events such as outstanding Olympic performances by American athletes. In any case, the important point to note is that the concept of community may refer to abstract ideals and goals of solidarity as well as to actual social relations among members.

Within a society any of the characteristics that differentiate people from one another that Blau (1977) identified in his structural theory as "nominal" and "graduated" parameters may be potentially relevant for providing a sense of community as well as for the initiation and development of personal relationships (see Chap. 8 for an overview of Blau's [1977] structural theory). Whether based on subjective ideals or actual social relations, such communities reflect the type of values that Blau had earlier referred to in his exchange theory as "particularistic" values. For example, senior citizens or teenagers, African Americans or Native Americans, atheists or Christians, police officers or computer software developers, baseball fans or golfers, musicians and artists and their admirers, members of professional and occupational groups, pacifists and war veterans—all of these examples illustrate the wide range of characteristics that may be relevant as the foundation for developing a sense of community and making distinctions between insiders and outsiders.

Because they are based on emotional bonds, the dynamics of communities differ from formal organizations. Under certain circumstances formal organizations may be established among members of a community to promote shared interests or goals. Thus, for example, residential communities form neighborhood improvement associations and crime watch programs, and organizations such as the National Organization of Women and the National Association of Retired Persons are intended to promote the interests of women and retired persons, respectively.

[1] Benedict Anderson (1991) used the concept of "imagined communities" to develop a broad comparative and historical analysis of nationalism and the efforts on the part of political leaders of developing nation-states to establish a sense of national consciousness and shared identity.

Moreover, a sense of community may also develop within organizational settings as members develop socioemotional bonds, a sense of a shared identity, common values, and overlapping interests that go beyond their formal organizational relationship. But the formation of bonds that reinforce emotional solidarity may sometimes be in tension with the need for rational strategies of cooperation that are needed to pursue collective goals.

Geographical Communities

Residential location is probably the most widely recognized of all the criteria that can serve as the foundation for a sense of community. But in contrast to traditional rural or small town communities, the dynamics of urban areas are often seen as undermining community ties and fostering high levels of anonymity and social isolation. This perspective was developed by Louis Wirth (1938), an early Chicago school urban sociologist who built on Georg Simmel's perspective in describing the social psychological consequences of urban life. Wirth's analysis is consistent with that of other classical and contemporary sociologists with regard to the effects of urbanization in eroding the social bonds necessary for community solidarity and fostering a high level of individualism. At the same time, these sociologists recognized how city life expands opportunities and frees individuals from the social pressures of the close-knit villages and rural communities of the past.

Although residential proximity may not be sufficient in itself to create a dense network of social bonds, it often provides a potential basis for social encounters that result in a sense of community. Even though neighbors may not know one another's names, they may still recognize one another and exchange brief greetings if they encounter one another in the neighborhood or at the local grocery store or laundromat. Beyond this, they actually have many shared interests, such as preventing crime and preserving neighborhood stability, even though these interests may not be highly salient to them most of the time and may not lead to interaction. In addition, neighborhood residents may identify emotionally with their neighborhood because of its appealing amenities, and they may assume others do likewise even without extensive personal relations with one another.

The lack of strong social relations among community residents may be explained in part by the fact that local formal organizations, such as police departments or zoning boards, eliminate the need for residents to worry about crime or undesirable land use patterns. In other words, they do not need to get involved as individuals in developing strategies from scratch to protect their collective interests. Also, in contrast to the greater isolation of rural communities of the past, local communities in modern society are linked in multiple ways to a much larger social world, and their members' occupational and voluntary activities may take them out of their local community much of the time. Moreover, the overall welfare of local communities is influenced by national and global processes over which local community control is limited (e. g., see Vidich and Bensman, 1960; Abrahamson, 2004). Indeed, even in coping with local problems, they may require assistance from state or federal government agencies, and any local actions they initiate may need to conform to external governmental guidelines and regulations.

Even so, community mobilization around shared interests may be aroused by local crises or threats. We would anticipate that a community's response would be more rapid and perhaps more effective if there is already a reservoir of social capital, as manifested in ongoing social relations among its members. In addition, the mobilization process itself is likely to generate an increase in social capital that continues even after the threat is gone. A city-wide sense of solidarity sometimes develops beyond the local neighborhood level, even in large cities, when there are major threats and crises. As suggested earlier, this was evident in New York City following the destruction of the World Trade Center on September 11, 2001. In addition, despite the limited number of personal relationships, city-wide activities and events may provide a focus that promotes community identification. Large cities may have their local festivals, such as New Orleans' Mardi Gras, for example, and local professional sports teams may provide an additional stimulus for city-wide solidarity that radiates outward to include the entire region. A positive sense of identification may also be reinforced by local amenities that residents believe set them apart from other communities.

The focus on community as grounded in shared definitions and socioemotional bonds is consistent with the symbolic interactionist perspective. But even when identification with one's residential community or social ties with one's neighbors are minimal or nonexistent, ecological communities may nevertheless be identified from the symbiotic relationships that emerge from the way people adapt to their local environment. A significant part of this environment includes the effects of one another's presence and actions, both intended and unintended. Strictly speaking, ecological communities do not necessarily require symbolic interaction or socioemotional bonding, although human communities often involve varying combinations of both symbiotic and symbolic interdependence. An ecological approach based on symbiotic relations was developed by Robert E. Park and his colleagues in Chicago, as pointed out briefly in Chap. 3. The analysis by Park and his colleagues will be reviewed briefly in the next section, along with some brief highlights of significant changes in the dynamics of urban areas that have occurred more recently.

Ecology and Community in Urban Environments

Symbiotic forms of interdependence give rise to ecological communities in which the focus of analysis is on how different individuals (and different species) adapt to their environment and to one another and how their activities affect the habitat they share. In contrast to the symbolic interactionist emphasis on communication and shared subjective definitions, ecological communities are based on patterns of competition and interdependence that emerge without conscious design. Such effects may be positive or negative with regard to resources and obstacles that are available for different categories of individuals and groups to survive and satisfy their needs and interests.

Because the urban environment is largely a built environment, many of its most noticeable physical characteristics (buildings, monuments, streets, landscaping) are obviously the result of the actions of individuals with whom current residents may have no personal relations at all. These physical features include the legacy of previous generations. Current inhabitants also affect one another's environment just by their presence and the effects of their various activities, both intended and unintended, even in the absence of socioemotional ties or symbolic communication. This may be illustrated by the way automobile commuters in large cities adjust their daily commuting schedules to allow for heavy rush-hour traffic.

Patterns of mutual adaptation vary greatly, ranging from unintended mutual support to competition for scarce resources. Out of these interrelated processes, distinct ecological niches develop in which different types of activities or different types of people are concentrated. When these specialized activities are mutually supportive, they give rise to a stable equilibrium. But as individuals and groups constantly seek to improve their position, this equilibrium is frequently disrupted as activities in different niches undermine or compete with one another. This disruption may eventually be followed by a new equilibrium. The dynamics of such mutually interrelated processes may readily be illustrated by the displacement of many types of Main Street stores in small towns across the country in recent years by gigantic Wal-Mart superstores located near the intersection of major highways at the edge of town. Some of these superstores eventually attract additional business establishments like gas stations, fast food restaurants, and smaller retail establishments that are intended to benefit from the increased traffic in the area.

Although people are likely to identify most closely with their own residential neighborhoods (even when they may not know their neighbors), metropolitan communities obviously include many specialized nonresidential areas, including, for example, business or commercial zones, manufacturing and warehousing areas, government or corporate headquarters, leisure and recreation attractions, educational and cultural sites, medical and human services centers, transportation and other infrastructure facilities, and so on. Residential areas themselves tend to be differentiated among different types of people, based largely on their residents' socioeconomic class position and lifestyle preferences.

This ecological view of specialized zones was explored in detail within the early Chicago school of American sociology, largely through the influence of Robert E. Park and his colleagues (Park, 1952; Park et al. [1925] 1967). A former newspaperman, Park was a keen observer of his own urban environment and the dynamic interdependence between the natural "biotic" order and the socially constructed "cultural" order. As he put it in describing the complex "web of life" in human communities, "There is a symbiotic society based on competition and a cultural society based on communication and consensus. As a matter of fact the two societies are merely different aspects of one society, which, in the vicissitudes and changes to which they are subject remain, nevertheless, in some sort of mutual dependence each upon the other" (Park, 1952:157).

In the pioneering work of Ernest Burgess, (pp. 47–62 in Park et al., [1925] 1967), the urban area of Chicago during that time period could be represented as a series of concentric ecological zones that radiated outward from the central business district. Located around the downtown area, with its high concentration of corporate and government offices and extensive retail commercial activity, was an industrial zone with various manufacturing and warehousing establishments. This was ringed mostly by low-cost and deteriorating transient housing which was vulnerable to being replaced as the manufacturing zone expanded. Surrounding this "transitional" residential zone was a more stable area of working people's homes. As one moved further and further away from the central city, one moved through a series of residential zones of larger and more expensive homes. This pattern is clearly visible in Chicago from the windows of commuter trains as one travels north, west, or south toward the suburbs from the downtown area near Lake Michigan on the east.

The overall ecological structure of the city develops through a process of ongoing competitive struggle as various individuals and groups seek the most advantageous location or niche possible in their struggle for survival and security. As changes occur in the resources of different groups, their strategies of adaptation and their ecological location relative to one another may shift. Over time modifications occur in land-use patterns reflecting the twin processes of invasion and succession. Invasion refers to the influx of new types of people or different functional activities into a particular area. Succession refers to the resulting change in the characteristics of an ecological zone or niche as the previous inhabitants or types of activities are displaced.

Downtown areas with high concentrations of business and commercial activity have historically tended to develop at the hub of transportation networks. In Chicago, for example, the convergence of several rail lines from throughout the American heartland, plus proximity to inland water transport on Lake Michigan, were crucial. In addition, the construction of the elevated light rail line around the central part of the city (the "Loop") provided a physical and symbolic focus for downtown business and commercial development. High land prices and the heavy concentration of business and commercial activities made downtown areas unsuitable for residential development, particularly for families with children. This concentric zone pattern varies in different cities, and the basic pattern has been modified in recent years as many businesses have moved out of central city areas to major interstate highway interchanges or near airports. The result in some cases is that downtown areas have been allowed to deteriorate or eventually be replaced by other land use patterns, including specialized types of residential development and tourist attractions, for example.

In sharp contrast to the transient housing that Burgess (pp. 47–62 in Park et al., [1925] 1967) described in the zone of transition adjacent to industrial areas, many urban areas also include well-established zones of high-density elite residential enclaves in expensive urban neighborhoods that are fairly close to the downtown area and are thus attractive for their proximity to urban amenities. An example of such a zone is Chicago's "Gold Coast," which is located a short distance north of the Loop close to Lake Michigan, and which appeals to high-income people who prefer a downtown residential location rather than the distant suburbs. This same basic pattern of land use specialization that Burgess described in Chicago applies as well to other American cities, though the specific configuration of land use patterns varies in different cities.

In addition to the transitions in land use patterns in various ecological zones, there were also transitions in the ethnic and later the racial characteristics of the residents of different neighborhoods. When Park, Burgess, and McKenzie ([1925] 1967) and their colleagues did their research, the effects of earlier widespread immigration were still evident in Chicago and other large industrial cities of the Midwest and the Northeast. As explained in Chap. 3, new immigrants tended to start out in the cheapest housing they could find in the zones of transition that were close to working class jobs in the industrial plants in the area. However, as they (or their children or grandchildren) gradually moved up in the socioeconomic class structure and became more assimilated to American culture, they tended to move into the next zone of more stable working class homes, and later to even more desirable neighborhoods out toward the edge of the city or into the suburbs. As immigrants (or their children) moved out, they would be followed by the next group of immigrants, and the cycle would be repeated.

As noted earlier, this pattern did not occur for African Americans who migrated to Chicago and other large cities in the North from the rural areas of the southern United States during and especially after World War II. This was due to the pervasive patterns of prejudice and discrimination that blocked African Americans from achieving the same level of occupational success and upward socioeconomic mobility that immigrant groups from abroad had earlier achieved. With discrimination in housing added to educational and occupational discrimination, African Americans were restricted to segregated neighborhoods in most cities in the United States. This pattern of racial segregation is still evident in many urban areas, despite the gains made since the Civil Rights legislation of the 1960s and subsequent years.

The shape of cities has changed considerably over the years since the pioneering work of Burgess, Park, and their Chicago School colleagues.[2] Even at that time, the concentric zone model did not apply to other American cities in exactly the way Burgess and his colleagues applied it to Chicago. Some large cities had secondary nuclei of industrial or commercial developments that developed in outlying areas. But despite these variations, the development of most of the large industrial cities of the Northeast and Midwest reflected their heavy reliance on rail transport. In the years following World War II, however, and especially during and after the1950s, the suburbanization process expanded greatly. This was related to the long-term economic prosperity of that time period, the high priority given to conventional

[2] For an overview of some major historical transformations of cities and changes in sociological approaches to them, see Padilla, ed. (2006).

forms of family life, the development of techniques for mass producing more or less standardized single-family housing, and increased reliance on automobiles instead of trains, light rail streetcars, and busses. The tremendous expansion of automobile traffic has contributed to high levels of traffic congestion, plus changes in land use patterns to provide for traffic and parking in downtown areas. Cities like Los Angeles and Atlanta, for example, that achieved significant growth after the widespread shift to automobiles clearly differ from the older pre-automobile cities of the Midwest and Northeast in more clearly reflecting the need to accommodate automobile traffic. Even when efforts are made to reduce traffic congestion by constructing new mass transportation systems, people nevertheless persist in exhibiting a strong preference for automobiles.

In focusing on residential communities in urban areas, the essential point to note is that the overall distribution of the population in different types of communities reflects a competitive process that results from people's efforts to obtain the most desirable residential location for themselves that they can afford. The overall result of this sorting and selecting process is that residential neighborhoods are stratified by economic class as well as by ethnicity and race. This is evident in the clearly visible indicators of socioeconomic class distinctions that can readily be observed in different residential neighborhoods. There is also a clear relationship between the socioeconomic class level of an area and various indicators of social problems, such as crime and delinquency rates. Also, although older ethnic neighborhoods can still be identified in many urban areas, they are not as sharply defined as they once were. However, newer ethnic communities have developed in recent years with the influx of immigrants from southeast Asia and from Puerto Rico and Mexico, and in many ways they tend to exhibit the same general patterns of residential concentration as the older southern and eastern European ethnic communities.

At the ecological level, patterns of symbiotic interdependence are associated with the emergence of specialized ecological niches in which different groups adapt to the surrounding population without necessarily being based on consciously developed overall plans. Thus, for example, a high concentration of office jobs in downtown areas creates a niche in which Starbuck's coffee shops or restaurants specializing in lunch-type fare can flourish—even though there may be no communication at all between corporate officials and restaurant owners about their particular functions in the niches they occupy. Similarly, commercial retail establishments benefit from being located in areas where major transportation lines intersect and generate high concentrations of people on a regular basis. In working class neighborhoods, small-scale establishments such as corner bars survive through local residents' repeat business, while suburban areas with young families provide an environment in which retail stores specializing in children's clothes or toys, obstetricians, and child-care centers can prosper.

For many cities, the construction of urban segments of the interstate highway system has had effects that are similar in some ways to railroads in earlier years in attracting industrial and commercial development and contributing to other changes in ecology and land use patterns. The expanded highway system also facilitates increased use of trucks for long-range transport of goods. In addition, increased reliance on air transport in more recent years has stimulated extensive commercial development around many major airports. The mobility patterns made possible by automobiles and airplanes, plus the need for large amounts of land devoted to streets and highways, parking spaces, and airports means that industrial and commercial development is more dispersed than in older cities that developed when rail transport was dominant.

While the extension of limited access interstate and other major highways into the heart of downtown areas makes it easier, theoretically, for people to drive downtown for work, shopping, and entertainment, the resulting increase in traffic congestion and the scarcity of parking space often tend to discourage such trips. At the same time, the automobile also resulted in more extensive residential dispersion of people than train travel. The network of streets and roads is far more extensive than rail lines, and people's strong preference for cars has led to continued expansion of the highway and suburban street network, plus the suburbanization of large open country areas adjacent to large cities. Eventually, of course, business and commercial enterprises also continued to expand greatly in suburban areas, taking advantage of the increased population and providing more convenient locations for shopping and employment than the central city. Such developments are particularly notable along interstate arteries and adjacent to major interchanges. The result is that shopping malls located near major highway interchanges around the edge of the city, plus other businesses they attract, have replaced central-city shopping for a large proportion of the population (see Garreau, 1991).

People's efforts to escape the increasing congestion of downtown areas have resulted in a kind of vacuum in the central part of many cities as the major focal point for extensive public contact. The result is that many downtown areas seem to have lost some aspects of their dominance as a symbolic center for community identification in the overall ecological structure of the city. In addition, the social psychological effects of extensive reliance on automobiles have no doubt also contributed to the decline of human contact in public places and erosion of a sense of community. Automobile transportation tends to isolate people from one another more than public transit, as well as contribute significantly to urban (and suburban) sprawl and population dispersion. Opportunities for encountering different types of people in highly variegated public spaces have thus been truncated and replaced by the kind of encounters experienced in the homogeneous and artificial environment of shopping malls.

Although it is beyond our purpose here to describe these urban dynamics in detail, it is noteworthy that many cities have taken steps to attempt to reverse the long-term decline of their central city areas. These efforts include promotion of downtown upscale housing (often designed to appeal to single young people who work downtown), establishment of major convention centers and adjacent hotels, redevelopment of certain areas as "oldtown" tourist attractions, construction of major league sports facilities, and cleaning up adjacent "skid row" slum areas. Efforts such as these demonstrate the ongoing dynamic quality of urban life and the continuing importance of the downtown area as a potential focal point for community identification and a major source of the symbolic identity of metropolitan areas.

The distinctive character and dynamics of large industrial cities in the United States must be seen in the light of American history, particularly the history of immigration from other countries. Patterns of growth of many major cities of the world outside North America are clearly different from those in the United States. Our goal here is not to compare American cities with cities in other countries. However, such a comparison would demonstrate some of the limitations of the Chicago school perspective and the importance of the American experience in explaining the distinctive dynamics of American cities, particularly with regard to the development of distinct ethnic and racial enclaves. Patterns of urban development in other countries should not be expected to follow the same pattern. In large South American cities, such as Rio de Janeiro, for example, patterns of residential development are opposite to those of American cities in terms of the socioeconomic class structure of inner-city versus outlying residential communities. Wealthy or affluent people live downtown while the poor tend to live in substandard housing without basic amenities at the perimeter of the city. Explaining such differences is beyond our scope in this chapter, however.

It should be emphasized that the meaning of the city as a community varies greatly, depending on the context. The city as a whole certainly provides a potential basis for residents' identification, regardless of the particular neighborhood where they live. At one level, perhaps this identification may be stronger if the city is widely recognized for its distinctive physical or cultural amenities, or if it is home to a major league sports team (especially a winning team). But even when people identify emotionally with the city as their community, the sheer size of a city (or even a medium-size town) makes it impossible for them to have meaningful social relationships with more than a tiny proportion of fellow residents. In contrast to this abstract form of identification with the larger community, the residential neighborhoods that honeycomb the greater metropolitan area provide possibilities for a different, more tangible, and more localized form of community identification. This more localized form of community may be expected to be stronger when it is reinforced by primary group relations with neighbors.

The extent to which neighborly relationships are actually developed is, of course, an empirical question. With the availability of television and now home computers, plus the widespread use of air conditioning in the summer, many families tend to remain indoors rather than mingle with neighbors outdoors. Moreover, for many people it is easier to establish socioemotional bonds with colleagues at work than with their neighbors. This applies to women as well as men as more and more women have moved into long-term careers. Although the dynamics of the organizations where people are employed are clearly different from the dynamics of the neighborhoods where they live, the potential for primary group relations at work is clearly relevant for giving both women and men a sense of community belonging and meeting their socioemotional needs for being connected. On the other hand, however, neighborhood relations often do develop in some residential communities, perhaps particularly among those who feel they have a long-term stake in their neighborhood as homeowners. These relations may be based on such activities as attendance at Little League baseball games at the local park or school, for example, sponsorship of neighborhood crime watch programs, participation in community-wide events such as July 4 parades, or even brief chats between neighbors who happen to encounter one another outside or at the grocery store. This sense of community contrasts sharply with the frequently-noted impersonality and anonymity of modern urbanized forms of life. But even when social relations among neighbors is limited or nonexistent, people may still identify emotionally with their community, and this probably increases the longer they are there.

Communities of Shared Interests and Values and Socioemotional Bonds

Perhaps the most widespread alternative to residential location as the source of a sense of community belonging in the United States is religion. In the case of Catholics in ethnic communities, the territorial organization of Catholic parishes may sometimes coincide closely with these communities. This was particularly so for Irish Catholics and for Catholics from southern and eastern European countries shortly after their immigration to America. Jewish synagogues may also serve as the symbolic center of community life in areas with a high Jewish concentration. But with the Protestant pattern of denominational pluralism, the sense of community based on religious identification is more likely to involve shared beliefs, traditions, and lifestyle preferences than ethnicity. There are exceptions, however, as illustrated by the development of German and Swedish Lutheran communities in towns and cities scattered throughout the upper Midwest, particularly in the years immediately following their immigration. These various ethnic communities may still be identified, although the salience of ethnicity is far less today than in earlier years for the groups identified above. In any case, the teachings of all the major religious groups emphasize their particular "community of faith" at the same time that their idealistic teachings also embrace a broader or universal human community.

A sense of community identification may be based on other types of shared interests as well. People may refer in general terms to broadly defined communities such as the business community, the arts community, the education community, the sports community, and so on. Such references imply a sense of shared values and interests and common bonds that are obviously more abstract than those of residential communities. Although the degree to which people actually identify with such communities is an empirical question, we should expect their identification to be stronger if it is rooted in intensive social relations. The organizations where people are employed may also serve as the foundation for developing a sense of community, as well as unions or professional organizations. When this occurs, the result we might expect is a sense of belonging that may influence members' orientations and encourage various forms of involvement that sometimes contributes to one another's welfare as well as serving one's own personal interests.

In the absence of strong identification or mutually supportive social relations, the concept of a community is often used as a kind of ideal image that is invoked as an antidote to the negative consequences of excessive individualism or group conflict. As such, it implies an appeal to people to act in ways that will promote concern for the general welfare. Political leaders at all levels, from city mayors to United States presidents, often invoke such an ideal in the hope of promoting unity or generating political support. National political leaders may refer to the overall society as a community in an effort to persuade citizens to transcend their narrow interests and commit themselves to the general welfare of society (or to support their particular policies, which they may believe amounts to the same thing). For a large, complex, and heterogeneous society, however, the level of cohesion that is often idealized, or sought by political leaders, often seems to develop most readily in times of major conflict with other societies, such as during a war that is widely supported. Otherwise, identification with the interests of particular groups seems to take priority over the general welfare.

Moreover, as Nisbet (1953) argued over 50 years ago in his analysis of the "quest for community," it is difficult to achieve community solidarity through political appeals or strategies. The dynamics of the political arena reflect the struggles of various groups to promote their individual or group interests. Although workable compromises may emerge, this outcome is not the same as the community cohesiveness that emerges from socioemotional bonds. A genuine sense of community transcends individual or partisan interests and reflects shared interests and mutual concern for the general welfare.

There is probably a widespread and highly idealized feeling that a stronger sense of community solidarity at some level is preferable to the rampant individualism that many see as characterizing our society. Robert Bellah and his colleagues (Bellah et al., 1985) documented this concern and described the difficulties people have in engaging in the kind of moral discourse that will help them transcend their isolation and narrow interests to discover the greater fulfillment that derives from being connected to a community and committed to the welfare of all its members. This "quest for community" is also reflected in Etzioni's (1993) "communitarian" perspective, with its emphasis on the need for people to accept their mutual responsibilities to one another as well as insist on their individual rights. This concern for a stronger sense of community is clearly oriented toward transcending the differences among people that have often been the primary basis for community formation. People who actually live in communities with a high level of racial/ethnic and multicultural heterogeneity sometimes develop a great deal of pride in their inclusive sense of community and their appreciation for the diversity they experience on a daily basis. Ironically, however, as noted earlier, those who identify with a highly inclusive and heterogeneous community may be tempted to draw the line between themselves and others who have a more restrictive or particularistic sense of community.

Whatever the basis for community identification may be, the resulting sense of belonging may be expected to be incorporated at some level in members' identities. When this occurs, the mutual concern they demonstrate for their collective welfare may be expected to lead to an emotionally satisfying sense of personal fulfillment that reinforces their identity and status in the community. Even though they may earn social approval and respect from fellow-members in return, obtaining such rewards is not necessarily their primary motivation.

Concern for the general welfare is an important component of the concept of civil society, the contemporary importance of which at the societal level has recently been analyzed in detail by Jeffrey Alexander (2006). The concept of civil society involves more than giving lip service to abstract democratic or patriotic ideals, or an ephemeral arousal of collective emotions during times of national grief or celebration. A robust civil society involves the capacity to mobilize for effective collective action and widespread engagement in activities that promote the public welfare. This often involves the establishment of formal organizations, particularly in the voluntary sector. But whether organizations are established to pursue the general welfare, individual interests, or the interests of particular groups, the dynamics of formal organizations differ significantly from the dynamics of communities and primary group relations. We turn in the next section to the characteristics of formal organizations.

Formal Organizations and Individual Versus Collective Goals

Informal social relations and community spirit do not automatically translate into coordinated actions for achieving collective goals or promoting the general welfare. Some type of organization is required to mobilize people and coordinate their activities. Formal organizations can be distinguished from communities in that they are established for the explicit purpose of coordinating people's actions to achieve goals that would be difficult or impossible for individuals to achieve on their own.[3]

The foundation of formal organizations in micro-level processes of rational choice and social exchange was discussed in Chap. 9. Sociological analyses of formal organizations can be traced back to the early years of sociology with Max Weber's detailed analysis of the characteristics of bureaucratic organizations.[4] In addition, we looked earlier at Peter Blau's explanation of how organized collective action depends on the emergence of power structures from imbalanced exchanges, and how power structures may be transformed into structures of legitimate authority

[3] This orientation toward specific goals also distinguishes social organizations from other types of social formations, including markets and socioeconomic classes, which are the social formations to be discussed in the next chapter.

[4] These include formal rules, a hierarchy of authority, an explicit division of labor, and assignment of organizational tasks to occupants of various offices who are recruited on the basis of technical expertise and whose long-term career commitment is sustained by regular compensation and the prospect of promotion to higher levels (Weber, 1947:329–341).

through the development of shared values and norms. We also reviewed James Coleman's rational choice analysis of people's willingness to transfer their individual rights and responsibilities as "natural persons" to "corporate actors" to accomplish various collective goals.

Numerous variations can be identified in the types of transactions that occur between individuals and formal organizations. In their occupations, for example, individuals exchange their labor power, time, and job-related skills and expertise for pay. Their compensation is a personal benefit, of course, but receiving it does not necessarily mean they identify subjectively with the overall goals of the organization. Instead, their personal goals are more likely to reflect a concern for fair financial compensation. Some people may also contribute time and money to their religious group or to a charitable social service organization, thereby demonstrating their moral commitments or fulfilling their social obligations. Organizations vary in terms of whether members must be compensated for the contributions they make to goals that do not necessarily benefit them directly, or whether they benefit directly from achievement of collective goals.[5] Organizations also vary in terms of members' level of emotional identification with the organization, its fellow members, and the values the organization represents.

Individuals also engage in numerous transactions with organizations to which they do not belong, and to which they may not feel any moral or emotional connection at all. Perhaps the most obvious example is their transactions as customers with various retail establishments. Such transactions reflect their individual rational choice considerations without any emotional or moral identification with the organization or personal ties with its members. Individuals often have little choice with regard to the transactions in which they are involved. For example, they contribute to their local or state government when they pay a sales tax at a retail establishment, even though this payment does not necessarily reflect their personal decision or involve any personal contact or negotiation with the taxing authorities. But when seen in a different institutional context, however, the collection of taxes reflects political policies influenced by citizens' votes, and persons who pay sales taxes in one context may have a limited and indirect voice in a different context in influencing the amount of tax they pay. In considering different types of formal organizations, it is important to distinguish those oriented toward individual goals that are pursued through economic transactions in a market system versus those oriented toward collective goals that involve a political process.

Despite the pervasiveness of many types of large-scale formal organizations in all aspects of our lives, their continued existence is never automatic. Instead, they depend on individuals' ongoing contributions of resources such as time, energy, labor power, ideas, or money, either eagerly or reluctantly. These contributions may be seen as the costs incurred in exchange for the benefits received, whether individual or collective. Individual benefits would include, for example, financial rewards, a sense of

[5]This point draws from Michel Hechter's (1987) contrast between compensatory and obligatory groups, as discussed in Chap. 7.

belonging and status, enjoyment of shared activities, an opportunity to exert power, fulfillment of moral ideals, or perhaps simply avoidance of negative sanctions. Collective benefits vary greatly but may include various public goods plus the maintenance of social order and promotion of the general welfare. This distinction between individual and collective benefits is an important basis for distinguishing public versus private organizations.

Primary Beneficiaries of Organizational Goals

Many different strategies can be used to analyze the structure and dynamics of formal organizations. But since organizations are established to achieve specific goals, one useful way to distinguish them is in terms of the primary beneficiaries of these goals. Several years ago, Peter Blau and Richard Scott (1962:43) developed a typology of organizations based on their prime beneficiaries. These are: (1) mutual benefit associations (with the organization's membership as the prime beneficiary), (2) business enterprises (where the owners are the major beneficiaries), (3) service organizations (with various client groups as principal beneficiaries), and (4) commonweal organizations (with the public at large as the intended beneficiary). In addition to the prime beneficiary there may be secondary beneficiaries as well. These would include the paid employees in any type of organization.

These different types of formal organizations vary in their internal and external dynamics and the specific challenges they face. As analyzed by Blau and Scott, the challenge for mutual benefit organizations is to prevent members from receiving benefits without making their fair share of contributions—in other words, to prevent free-riding. Business enterprises obviously have to provide incentives to employees whose personal interests may not necessarily include an intrinsic commitment to the goals of the owner(s). In fact, employees' goal of maximizing wages or salaries is in direct conflict with the owners' goals of maximizing profits. For service organizations the challenge is to insure that service providers give priority to clients' needs instead of their own, often in a context where maintenance of organizational routines and following rules seem paramount. The challenge for commonweal organizations is to insure that serving public needs is not sacrificed for the sake of organizational survival or personal career goals.

Regardless of who the primary beneficiaries are, a major goal for members who are paid for their contributions is to maximize their compensation and other benefits. Whether members are paid or not, they are likely to be interested in having satisfying social contacts, earning recognition and prestige, and perhaps receiving other intangible benefits as well. Moreover, due to their own interests, different individuals or groups may develop their own particular ideas of what the organization's goals should be, and their efforts may lead to modification of the original goals. In a large organization with a complex division of labor, members of different departments and divisions and different hierarchical levels may disagree and compete with one another in attempting to shape the organization's goals, and perhaps to increase their own benefits in the process. Thus, despite the primary focus on explicit goals and clearly defined prime beneficiaries, the actual dynamics of organizations reveal complex political processes in which various constituent groups seek to shape the organization's goals for their own benefit.

Organizational Control and Compliance Structures

Because of the importance of issues of coordination and control in formal organizations, another important basis for distinguishing different categories of organizations is the type of control utilized to insure compliance with organizational rules and expectations. A useful typology based on an organization's "compliance structure" was developed several years ago by Amatai Etzioni (1961). The concept of compliance structure refers to the type of power used to control subordinates plus the orientation of subordinates to the exercise of power.

Essentially, Etzioni identified three basic types of power structures: coercive, remunerative, and normative. Coercive power involves physical force (or threats of such force) and may be illustrated by the social organization of prisons, for example. Remunerative power refers to the ability to provide rewards such as wages or salaries, as illustrated by business firms or other organizations with paid employees. It is this type of power that seems most consistent with Blau's exchange theory of how power structures are based on imbalanced exchanges. Finally, normative power involves the use of symbolic rewards in seeking to promote subordinates' identification and commitment because of the intrinsic value of the organization and the worthiness of its goals. Religious organizations, especially those that rely on voluntary membership in a pluralistic society, illustrate this type of power structure.

Subordinates' orientations toward the exercise of power include the following: alienative (strong negative orientation), moral (a strong positive orientation), and an intermediate calculating orientation that may shift back and forth between positive or negative depending on the balance between costs and rewards. These different orientations tend to be linked to power structures in predictable ways; that is, coercive power is associated with an alienative orientation, remunerative power with a calculating orientation, and normative power with a moral orientation.[6]

Compliance structures may be mixed and may vary for different levels within organizations. The sharpest contrasts are at the lower levels, while normative power becomes relatively more important at higher hierarchical levels where members are more likely to identify with the goals of the organization. Thus, for example, the guards and higher authorities in a prison may identify strongly with "law and order" type values, defining their job in normative terms as promoting public safety and

[6]The contrast between coercive power and normative power may be compared to the opposing ideas of functional theory versus conflict theory as applied to the overall society. These theories will be covered in more detail in subsequent chapters.

giving prisoners what they deserve, while inmates are obviously controlled by coercive power. Some organizations may have "dual compliance" structures. For example, military units emphasize patriotic ideals (normative power), but coercive power can be used as a last resort if necessary. Business firms that rely primarily on remunerative power may nevertheless seek to promote normative commitments to the organization. Normative power may be expected to be dominant in voluntary organizations, but participants may also benefit by the useful social contacts they develop.

Etzioni's focus is **power** structures, not structures of **authority**. As emphasized in Weber's analysis, authority structures are based on subordinates' acceptance of the legitimacy of the power structure. Such beliefs seem to imply a form of normative orientation. But this does not necessarily mean that subordinates have a strong moral commitment to the organization or its goals. On the other hand, commitment to the moral values represented by an organization does not necessarily imply belief in the legitimacy of its current power structure. Whether or not members' acceptance of the legitimacy of the current power structure and their commitment to the moral ideals and values of the organization are correlated is an empirical question.

Persons in positions of power and authority often attempt to increase subordinates' emotional identification with the organization and their roles within it as well as its goals and current authority structure. In organizations with paid employees, this may include attractive incentive packages (good pay and benefits, job security, promotion prospects, positive social environment) that are designed to promote commitment by satisfying participants' individual interests. Efforts to promote commitment may also focus on informal social relationships within work groups, job characteristics, or the overall organizational culture. A major emphasis of the "human relations" approach that was popular in organizational analysis and management practices in the 1950s and 1960s reflected strategies to encourage positive informal social relations that would provide socioemotional rewards. A focus on job characteristics can be illustrated by "job enlargement" programs designed to expand or redesign job responsibilities so that they will be intrinsically more satisfying and provide a sense of accomplishment and fulfillment. Efforts to manage the organization's culture may be illustrated by the staging of rituals designed to celebrate and reinforce outstanding achievements and to generate emotional enthusiasm for the organization's mission and goals.[7]

Bureaucrats Versus Professionals in Organizational Settings

The ongoing challenge of linking individual motivation with organizational goals can no doubt be met more easily if those recruited already have high levels of commitment to the tasks they are expected to perform or the overall mission of the

[7] Randall Collins (1975:286–347) analyzed many of these various organizational processes from a conflict theory perspective. His theory will be examined more fully in Chap. 14.

organization—especially when they get paid. There are major differences between professional and nonprofessional personnel in this regard. In general, professionals are expected to be committed to goals that transcend their narrow self-interests. These may be linked in various ways to organizational goals, but they may also be partially independent. Thus the type of control used in professional service occupations such as education, social work, medicine, and law, for example, may be contrasted in several ways with the hierarchical control that is standard in bureaucratic organizations.

Professionals are expected to be self-controlled, or controlled by their professional peers, rather than by a bureaucratic hierarchy. Professional occupations are by definition based on mastery of an appropriate body of theoretical knowledge and practical expertise, usually acquired through extensive advanced formal education, plus adherence to strict standards of professional ethics. Professionals also have their own associations to protect and promote their interests, insure compliance with their values and normative standards, and reinforce their identity. In some cases, professional values may lead to tension and conflict with bureaucratic rules or authority figures, especially in service organizations when organizational rules sometimes seem to conflict with the needs of the people served (students, clients, and patients, for example).

Different types of organizations reveal various combinations of both bureaucratic versus professional control. Although bureaucratic structures may be designed to protect professional autonomy (such as through norms of academic freedom for faculty members, for example), it is not unusual for professionals to resent or to resist the "bureaucracy." In some situations professionals' knowledge and expertise provide a basis of authority that gives them considerable influence over administrators or managers who may rank higher in the organization's hierarchy of authority. They may also establish their own professional practice organizations to provide their services to the public (medical clinics, law firms, and accounting groups, for example). In such organizations, professional norms are expected to have priority over bureaucratic control.

Formal Organizations as Open Systems

For any organization, the accomplishment of its mission and the management of its various environmental transactions are reflected in its internal division of labor. Organizations also depend on various types of contributions (inputs) from the environment, including both material and human resources. The open systems perspective focuses attention on internal patterns of interdependence among the different parts of the organization as well as on its environmental transactions. This section will focus on the importance of organizational variations in both internal and external relations.

Within an organization it is important to consider how tight or how loose are the linkages among the various tasks different people perform—or, in other words, their degree of interdependence. Social systems of all types are considered to be much more "loosely coupled" than mechanical or biological systems.[8] But the nature of the interdependence among the various tasks or positions in an organization is highly variable, ranging from the tight coordination required for critical surgical procedures, for example, to the much looser connections among agents in a real estate office.

Also, through transactions with other organizations or individuals in its environment, an organization's outputs are exchanged for the inputs needed for the organization to survive and accomplish its goals. The environmental transactions of business firms, for example, may be illustrated by the process whereby they procure raw materials and tools for manufacturing products which are then sold in the market in exchange for financial resources that are used to obtain more raw materials and also to pay their employees to continue producing and selling more products. Schools, in contrast, provide educated graduates as their output but receive financial inputs from tax dollars and/or tuition plus inputs of new students from families in the general population. The permeability of organizational boundaries varies greatly, ranging from the highly restricted boundaries of a maximum security prison, for example, to the open boundaries of a shopping mall or retail "superstore."

Variations in Interdependence

The degree to which activities must be coordinated to accomplish the organization's mission, or even to survive, differs among different organizations, and even within organizations among different subunits. Some examples will make this clear. Military units, whether in combat or in a military parade, exhibit high levels of interdependence, or "tight coupling." Participants in a parade are required to coordinate their steps and the movements of their arms with great precision. The same pattern of tight coupling can also be seen among musicians in a symphony orchestra when they are performing. "Loose coupling," in contrast, may be demonstrated by the relatively low levels of coordination that are involved in most academic departments, where each faculty member has his or her own particular teaching schedule and research program. Similarly, accountants or attorneys who may be members of the same firm have their own clients and thus would be likely to exhibit a pattern of relatively loose coupling.

[8] Walter Buckley (1967) viewed social systems of all types as open systems with highly varied patterns of interdependence that tend over time to become more elaborate. Buckley's systems perspective will be reviewed more fully in Chap. 17.

In general, the higher the level of interdependence in an organization, the lower the level of autonomy of its individual participants. High interdependence (tight coupling) requires individuals to coordinate their activities to insure that they act as a unit. On the other hand, with low interdependence (loose coupling), there is more room for individual discretion and perhaps greater variation in how tasks are performed. This was the major theme in Gouldner's (1959) argument that reciprocity (or interdependence) among the component parts of a system is inversely related to the autonomy of these parts. (At the lowest level of analysis the "parts" of an organization are the individuals who perform their organizational roles.) One of the advantages of "loose coupling" is that it allows flexibility to participants to deal with changing conditions. This flexibility can also be beneficial in helping satisfy individuals' psychological need for autonomy. However, tight coupling is sometimes necessary to coordinate activities involved in complex tasks requiring precise timing.

The optimum balance between interdependence and autonomy (or an optimal level of "coupling") depends in large part on the nature of the tasks and the way the organization is structured. For example, in a hospital setting, physicians generally have high levels of autonomy plus high levels of intrinsic commitment as professionals. Their linkage to the hospital's organizational routines may in fact be rather loose (which may be a source of patient complaints), as their primary orientation is to their profession and, ideally, to their patients. But during the course of a risky and complicated surgical procedure, the team of surgeons, anesthesiologists, and nurses is tightly coupled as each member of the team performs his or her specialized role in a highly coordinated fashion. In the meantime, the ongoing day-by-day maintenance of hospital routines depends on the coordinated contributions of many others, with varying degrees of coupling or interdependence.

Variations in Boundary Permeability

Organizations also vary in terms of how open or permeable they are to environmental influences as well as the nature of the specific input/output transactions that occur across their boundaries. Such differences may be illustrated by comparing and contrasting a retail store's openness to walk-in customers, a university's orientation of incoming freshmen, a religious group's procedures for incorporating new members, and a business firm's strategy for training new employees.

Organizational boundaries are both physical and symbolic, but the two dimensions do not necessarily overlap. Like families, formal organizations also have their physical domiciles. The permeability of their boundaries can readily be observed in terms of how easy it is for their own members or members of the public to enter their physical space. Retail shopping outlets or shopping malls, for example, have high permeability and depend heavily on a steady stream of customers (and "window shoppers") from the outside. In contrast, many industrial plants have fences around their property and a gate at the entrance, where employees are required to show identification and others are denied entry unless they get a visitor's pass. In the aftermath of terrorist attacks such as the bombing of the federal building in Oklahoma City, many government agencies require all visitors to go through a security checkpoint just inside the building before they are allowed to proceed. Similarly, boundaries within airports have been made less permeable to prevent terrorism since September 11, 2001, despite the frustrations experienced by passengers as a result.

Formal organizations of all types distinguish insiders from outsiders, and special procedures are usually employed to incorporate new members and assign them to appropriate positions. Criteria for membership may vary between being rather lenient or very strict. The same is true for different positions within the organization. For example, occupations vary in terms of the level of education or experience that are required, with such criteria related both to the nature of the job and its level in the hierarchy of authority. Strict criteria are exemplified in many government jobs that require new employees to obtain security clearance. Voluntary organizations likewise vary; some have specific membership requirements, such as high membership fees or strict eligibility standards, while others are open to any who wish to join and pay nominal annual dues. Religious organizations in the United States, for example, vary greatly in terms of the particular beliefs and standards of behavior they expect of their members, with the result that some groups are easier to join or more open than others.

Once potential recruits decide to join an organization, they may be required to undergo various forms of socialization before becoming full-fledged members. Many organizations may also have special rituals or ceremonies to induct new members and celebrate their status as members. Through such strategies, organizations seek to insure new members' emotional identification with the organization and its goals as well as its rules and procedures. At the same time, processes such as these help to maintain the traditions and the character of the organization, and they reinforce the boundaries between insiders and outsiders.

In organizations that are involved in "processing" people on a long-term basis, a special "intermediate" or temporary type of membership category may be assigned to those being processed. Perhaps the most common example would be students and their membership status in schools. Are students actually members of their elementary or high school, or the college or university they attend? In one sense, of course they are. Moreover, by being incorporated to the fullest extent possible consistent with their temporary student status, they are encouraged to develop a sense of belonging that enhances their loyalty and their acceptance of the school's educational objectives as well as its rules and authority structure. But at the same time, students are not long-term members in the sense that teachers and staff are, and their influence on long-term organizational policy is limited. Despite the obvious differences in their goals, this same general type of limited and temporary membership exists also with prisoners, hospital patients, and clients of residential "therapeutic communities."

Organizational Relations

A large part of the environment of any formal organization consists of other formal organizations, and many of the transactions that occur across an organization's boundaries are with other organizations. For example, organizations engage in selling and buying transactions and, as is the case with individuals, such transactions reflect the efforts of each party to secure the greatest benefits possible for the least cost. In addition, like individual exchange relationships, the repetition of such transactions may give rise to more or less stable relationships between suppliers and customers. The development of ongoing relationships provides predictability to transactions and often costs less in the long run than relying on open market transactions. These considerations give rise to the notion of interorganizational network ties that develop through the contacts that agents of different organizations establish with one another. Moreover, unlike natural persons, corporate actors may actually buy one another, with the (usually) larger buying organization absorbing the smaller organization into its structure. Understanding the development of interorganizational network ties, their effects on the overall society, and the dynamics of changes in interorganizational relations over time are major areas of investigation in contemporary organizational analysis (see Scott, 2003).

Organizations also compete with one another for public support or acceptance, customers or members, and financial resources. This clearly applies to business firms as they compete for customers. But the process of competition extends also to other types of organizations. For example, public social service agencies, public schools, and law enforcement agencies compete for state or federal funding, with each type of organization seeking to show that its needs are greater than those of the others. With government agencies, the process of competition involves political pressures rather than market dynamics. Among voluntary organizations, the process may be less intense but still exists. Thus religious groups and private sector social service agencies are involved in covert (or perhaps overt) competition over charitable contributions and other forms of support, even though they may not see themselves in this way.

Despite such competition, organizations often collaborate in joint projects to improve their collective welfare or accomplish shared goals. Business firms make use of network ties among their various agents to form coalitions or alliances that may attempt to influence legislation or public opinion. Within the public sector, the "war on drugs" and homeland security illustrate a pattern of cooperation in the public sector between federal and local law enforcement agencies. Such cooperation may be combined with various forms of competition as well. Or, various enterprises with common interests may establish new organizations that include their constituent organizations as members—in other words, an organization of organizations—to work collectively on general goals they share or on particular projects. For example, many mainstream religious groups in the United States are members of the National Council of Churches. It should also be pointed out that collaboration between organizations may not necessarily always be in the public interest.

Thus, for example, dominant business firms that provide essential goods and services are prohibited by government regulations from collaborating to engage in "price fixing" agreements. Also, when government regulatory agencies develop network ties with the private organizations that they are expected to regulate, there is the potential for corruption if these ties become too cozy.

The relations among the different organizations in the environment was the major focus of analysis in Howard Aldrich's (1979) ecological perspective on interorganizational relations. Using an evolutionary model, Aldrich emphasized the process of competitive struggle for survival or dominance as organizations adapt to their environment and seek to improve their position within it. Some fail in the struggle to adapt while others expand, displacing their competitors and becoming dominant. Still others may find a particular niche in the overall organizational environment, where they are able to maintain stability. Thus, for example, small locally owned Main Street hardware and grocery stores have been displaced on a large scale by gigantic discount chains such as Wal-Mart. But the increased traffic generated by Wal-Mart may provide a nearby profitable niche for gas stations, fast food restaurants, or other small business establishments. In addition, long established and dominant airlines have proven to be vulnerable to low-cost upstarts such as Jet Blue or Southwest Airlines in a deregulated competitive environment. And in another area, new opportunities have developed in the organizational environment for child care centers, since more and more women maintain their career involvements after the birth of a child.

Essentially, Aldrich's evolutionary ecological perspective is comparable in some ways to the Social Darwinism of the early years of the century as applied to populations of organizations. Once organizations are able to succeed in becoming a dominant and significant part of the organizational landscape, they can be said to be institutionalized in the society. But even if they become firmly institutionalized, this does not guarantee their long-term survival. In a social world characterized by constant competition, the relative position of all organizations may be expected to change as a result of their efforts to adapt to changes in the material and nonmaterial resources—or their failure to adapt successfully. These dynamics of the organizational landscape should always be seen as reflecting individuals' ongoing efforts to pursue their various interests, both individual and collective. They also serve in a major way to help determine the nature and character of the linkages between individuals and the overall society.

Summary

Communities and organizations were seen in this chapter as contrasting types of meso level social formations. As discussed in the last chapter, a significant part of the dynamics of formal organizations can be understood from the standpoint of rational choice theory. In contrast, communities are based on emotional identification with others who are seen as having similar characteristics or interests, or who share common values or life experiences. Thus the perspective of the sociology of emotions is useful for exploring this shared sense of community belonging and its effects on individuals' orientations and identities.

Although community identification is likely to be nourished and strengthened by actual socioemotional bonds among its members, people may identify with abstract or ideal communities that would include members far beyond their own personal relationships or network contacts. Unlike a formal organization, however, with its clearly established boundaries and specific goals to be pursued through various types of rational choice exchange transactions, the notion of a community reflects people's abstract ideals regarding the socioemotional bonds they share, including actual as well as potential relationships. These sentiments may be grounded in clear distinctions between insiders and outsiders that are based on shared characteristics or experiences. On the other hand, in an abstract sense, the concept of community may include the entire society or even all of humanity—in which case the outsiders might be those who do not share this inclusive sense of community.

Our discussion of community focused heavily on residential location. Even in the absence of extensive social relations, people often identify with their neighborhood or hometown as their community. But geographical communities are also based on impersonal and objective ecological processes, including competition over desirable locations, adaptation to local environments, creation of specialized niches, patterns of dominance and displacement, and processes of invasion and succession. The multifaceted patterns of interdependence that develop among the different groups and activities in a particular area make up an ecological community that is based on patterns of symbiotic interdependence. Such patterns may be identified even in the absence of social relations or emotional identification. The early development of the Chicago school of urban sociology demonstrated how geographical communities can be analyzed in terms of both symbolic interaction and symbiotic interdependence. The contributions of Park and his Chicago school colleagues highlighted the interdependence among different ecological areas of the city, the variety of activities and lifestyles supported in these different zones, and the dynamic processes whereby these patterns change over time.

The character of urban communities has changed greatly over the years, particularly with the expansion of the use of automobiles and the suburbanization process, followed by deterioration of downtown areas and subsequent efforts to promote their redevelopment in various ways. But through all these changes, the geographical location of people's residences provides a potential foundation for a sense of community identification as well as the formation of actual social ties. In addition to residential location, a sense of community may also develop from shared interests and values, similar occupational or professional positions, racial or ethnic identification, religious group membership, leisure and lifestyle activities, and so on.

Whether members of communities act in concert or not (beyond the level of personal relationships) will depend in large part on whether or not they establish formal organizations to promote their collective interests. Since formal organizations are established to achieve specific goals, they can be compared and contrasted by identifying the primary beneficiaries of these goals. Based on Blau and Scott's typology, we distinguished mutual benefit, business, service, and commonweal organizations.

In addition, given the frequent tension between individual interests and organizational goals, formal organizations can also be analyzed in terms of the strategies used to insure compliance with organizational rules and increase commitment to organizational goals. Etzioni's analysis of compliance structures was reviewed to compare and contrast the use of remunerative rewards (wages and salaries), moral appeals, or the threat of coercion in insuring that individuals fulfill the requirements of their organizational roles. We also looked briefly at the differences between bureaucratic type control through organizational hierarchies and rules versus professionals' collective self-control in terms of shared values and norms.

Since formal organizations are designed as systems of cooperative interdependence, their internal processes can clearly be analyzed in terms of the specific patterns of interdependence they exhibit. In general, the need for precise conformity to clearly defined organizational roles is greater if activities are "tightly coupled," thereby creating high levels of interdependence. In contrast, "loosely coupled" systems with low levels of interdependence allow greater variability, more opportunities for assertion of individual autonomy, and greater flexibility for participants to respond to changing conditions they face.

Formal organizations are open systems, with ongoing interchanges of various types with their environment, including other organizations. Relations among organizations as corporate actors can be analyzed in terms of the same processes that apply to relations among individuals. Organizations thus compete with one another, engage in exchange transactions with one another, and sometimes form alliances. The competition and conflict in which they engage may lead to relations of domination and subordination. Formal organizations make up a large part of the meso-level social world, and their transactions often dwarf the activities of individual persons acting on their own. Indeed, for all who earn their living through employment in some organizational setting, a large part of their lives involves fulfilling their obligations as agents for the organizations where they are employed.

Variations in the value of the resources different people bring to their market transactions and social relations in all types of settings are inevitably reflected in multifaceted systems of social stratification. However, the effects of pure market system in reinforcing and sometimes magnifying inequality and socioeconomic class distinctions may be reduced through the social formations discussion in this chapter: communities and organizations. A strong community orientation may lead to a sense of responsibility for the welfare of others, particularly those in one's social network, and the emergence of norms that limit the most extreme forms of market exploitation. In addition, formal governmental organizations are involved in regulating market competition and redistributing financial resources. Private voluntary sector organizations may also be involved in various forms of redistribution of material resources through their social service programs. The next chapter will look more explicitly at markets and socioeconomic classes as additional meso-level social formations whereby individuals are linked to the larger society.

Questions for Study and Discussion

1. What do you think are the most important characteristics of residential neighborhoods that contribute to a strong sense of community spirit? Is this more likely to be expressed through personal relationships residents have with one another or by public events in the community? To what extent is it possible for people's occupations to support or undermine their identification with their residential community? Explain and illustrate with experiences you have had (or observed) in your hometown or other communities where you have lived.
2. Do you agree or disagree that identifying with abstract communities without personal ties with at least some members can provide a sense of belonging or concern with the general welfare? Why or why not? Based on your own experiences, are there abstract communities with which you identify that may include but also go beyond your actual social relations with fellow members?
3. Explain how different types organizational structures can provide a basis for the development of a sense of community among its members or employees or satisfy individuals' needs for belonging. What advantages and disadvantages do you see in having most of your important social ties (outside your family) with colleagues at work.
4. Using Blau and Scott's "prime beneficiary" distinction and Etzioni's "compliance structure" distinction, what types of organizations are likely to generate the highest level of emotional identification with the organization and the greatest level of commitment to organizational goals?
5. Select two different types of organizations and explain in detail the nature of its input/output transactions with the environment PLUS the degree of internal interdependence required to be effective in reaching its goals. Also, to what extent does this internal interdependence reduce individuals' sense of autonomy in being able to perform their roles in their way? To what extent to you prefer to work as a member of a close-knit team as opposed to working independently?

Chapter 11
Meso-Level Structures: Markets and Socioeconomic Classes

In many of our everyday economic transactions, we have little say in setting the terms of the exchange. We may "shop around" to try to get the best deal, especially for major transactions like buying a new car or accepting a new job, and we may sometimes be able to negotiate the terms within fairly narrow limits. But in many cases, the terms are set by corporate actors with resources far greater than their customers or employees. With unequal exchange partners, those with fewer resources may have no alternative but to accept the terms offered or do without.

Economic exchanges involving material resources in an impersonal market differ sharply from social exchanges of nonmaterial resources in personal or primary group relationships. These resources include emotional support, mutual understanding, useful social contacts, or helpful information. When used in social exchanges, such resources may be categorized as emotional capital, social capital, or cultural capital. These intangible forms of capital are sometimes used to enhance one's financial capital. As suggested in our earlier discussion of network theory, knowing the right people (social capital) can be useful in learning of attractive job openings that provide material resources. Being a college graduate, or "credentialed" with appropriate knowledge and skills (cultural capital), is crucial when competing for financially rewarding careers.[1] And the ability to relate positively to people ("good people skills") can be seen as a type of social or emotional capital that is useful in maintaining or extending one's social contacts.

As is the case with resources used in material exchanges, people are not necessarily equal in terms of nonmaterial resources. Some people are more interesting or enjoyable companions than others or provide more positive emotional reinforcement in interpersonal encounters. Others have higher levels of expertise or experience and are able to offer better advice in solving problems or coping with new situations. Still others have more network contacts or better interpersonal "people skills." Exchanges between people who are roughly equal in terms of resources may be expected to differ

[1] These different types of capital will be discussed in more detail later in this chapter, along with our review of the perspectives on class cultures developed by Randall Collins and Pierre Bourdieu. See Stewart (1997) for an overview of the crucial importance of knowledge in today's "information society" and the role of "knowledge workers."

from those in which there is great disparity, regardless of the nature of the resource. This is true for social relations as much as for economic transactions.

This chapter looks at markets, both economic and social, as well as the socioeconomic classes that emerge from inequalities in material resources. The primary topics to be covered are as follows:

- Markets and individual interests versus the welfare of others—The following themes will be addressed under this heading:
  - Equality versus inequality in exchange transactions
  - Market regulation—responses to inequalities and instabilities
  - Economic versus socioemotional markets
- Socioeconomic classes in the stratification system of society—This section will deal with the following themes:
  - The primacy of economic resources in a multidimensional stratification system
  - The class structure of American society—Erik Olin Wright's analysis of control over the means of production and of the people involved in the relations of production
  - The interdependent relations of income, education, occupation, status, lifestyle, and interpersonal relations—Randall Collins' multidimensional perspective on conflict and social stratification
  - Reproduction of class cultures—This section will review Pierre Bourdieu's analysis of how class cultures are reproduced as people make use of their material and nonmaterial resources to respond to the constraints, expectations, and opportunities of their class positions.

As emphasized in Marxist theory, the economic dimension can be seen as the foundation for understanding class relations. Material resources are crucial in gaining access to other types of resources and are highly correlated with people's overall worldviews and lifestyles. Other dimensions of stratification may be distinguished from the economic dimension and exhibit their own dynamics, as indicated in Weber's distinctions between economic class position, status, and power as discussed earlier. One's worldview and lifestyle are closely related to status group membership as well as economic resources. Power is a key aspect of the position one occupies in formal organizations. All three dimensions tend to be highly correlated, even though they are conceptually and analytically distinct. In addition to Weber's distinctions, the parameters analyzed in Peter Blau's (1977) structural theory of heterogeneity and inequality are often correlated with both economic class and power.[2] For example, young people usually have fewer economic resources (separate from their family) and less power than middle-age adults. Gender likewise has long been associated with differences in power, status, and economic resources, as emphasized in feminist

---

[2] Blau's (1977) structural theory, which was reviewed in Chap. 8, emphasizes the importance of the objective distinctions among people in terms of nominal or graduated parameters that give rise to subgroup formation and social ranking.

theories. Because of these differences in economic class, status group membership, and power, people often do not participate in market systems as equals.

Markets and Individual Versus Collective Interests

Unlike communities or formal organizations, pure market systems do not involve emotional bonds or collective goals. Instead, markets emerge as individuals and organizations (as corporate actors) pursue their own interests through exchange transactions. Despite the individualistic image of human nature that is reflected in market transactions, personal needs and interests are in fact shaped by the social and cultural environment, just as the opportunities and resources to satisfy them reflect one's position in the social structure. Even in satisfying basic physiological needs such as for food and shelter, people are influenced by their particular culture. Societies vary in terms of emphasizing individual autonomy versus social obligations that bind individuals to their families, communities, and overall society as the primary source of their social identity. Even in the United States, the individualistic emphasis of the culture changes over time. But in other societies, the high level of independence that Americans take for granted would be unthinkable. For example, young people would not even consider leaving their families and home communities to establish their lives elsewhere. Although the rational choice perspective clearly applies to market transactions, rational choice theorists do not seek to explain why people have the particular preferences or values they do. In other words, the focus of rational choice theory is not why people might desire a particular product or service but how they can get the best deal in obtaining such a product or service.

Opposing views regarding the effects of markets for the general welfare can be traced back to the classical economist Adam Smith versus Karl Marx. In Smith's perspective, the general welfare can be advanced most effectively by minimizing traditional constraints on people's behavior so they can be free to pursue their own individual interests. However, he also believed that widely shared moral sentiments would moderate people's selfish interests with concerns for the common good. In contrast to this optimism, Marx insisted that capitalism tends to destroy the communal social bonds that tie people of different social ranks together and replaces them with a narrow (individualistic) "cash nexus." Within capitalism, human labor itself had become a commodity for sale, thereby helping to bring about higher levels of exploitation than in more traditional societies. In addition, Marx's distinction between "use value" versus "exchange value" highlighted the pattern whereby the "means of production" (land and tools) were shifted under capitalism from producing for one's own use (or for use by one's family and local community) to producing for impersonal market exchanges.

As capitalism has evolved since Marx's time, the range of products and services offered for sale in the market has expanded far beyond anyone's expectations, reaching explosive proportions in the "consumer society" of today. This expanding scale of consumption has been insightfully diagnosed by George Ritzer (1999) as an effort to provide enchantment in a disenchanted world and as "luxury fever" in Robert H. Frank's (1999) book by that name. Among large segments of the middle class, everyday life routines make use of such "commodified" services as food preparation (in both restaurants and supermarkets), children's day care (important for dual-career families), and even walking for exercise (on health club treadmills).

Consistent with its emphasis on the ideal of individual freedom, American culture includes a strong faith in the market system for the production and distribution of goods and services. The ideal for many is a "free market"—that is, one in which individuals are able to pursue their interests without being constrained by traditional community or family norms or governmental regulation. In this context, it is perhaps not surprising that the individualistic assumptions of rational choice theory seem so plausible.

Economic Market Instability and Government Regulation

In a hypothetical pure (or free) market, no one is in charge of the overall system. Instead, markets emerge as a byproduct of the various exchanges whereby individuals seek to satisfy their interests. **If** material or financial resources were distributed equally, it seems plausible to argue that the welfare of trading partners would improve as a result of the transactions they voluntarily negotiate. Neither party would have an advantage over the other, and the resulting relationship would reflect mutual interdependence rather than a one-way dependency relationship. Since society consists of the individuals who make it up, it is easy to see the appeal of an argument that equates the overall welfare of society with the aggregate welfare of its members. However, individuals are not equal in terms of their resources. Participants in the market include corporate actors with resources and power far greater than those of most individual persons. The large discrepancies between the "haves" and the "have nots" enable those with more abundant resources to control the terms of the exchange to their advantage. This leads to imbalanced exchanges, one-way dependency, and the possibility of exchanges that many would see as unfair. As suggested in Marx's analysis, "negotiations" between capitalist employers who own the means of production and workers with no resources except their labor power readily lead to exploitation.

Despite widespread American faith in the free enterprise market system, the United States economy today is too heavily regulated by government to be considered a truly free market, even though the scope of regulations may be less than in other societies. Government regulations and programs that restrict people's freedom are justified in terms of the general welfare. Such regulations are represented in minimum wage legislation, for example, tax policies, and public agencies that oversee conformity to rules developed to insure public health and safety. Some regulative programs are designed to moderate the negative effects of economic cycles that market systems seem to develop. Other programs provide social services to meet the basic security needs of those whose resources are insufficient for them compete on an equal footing in a pure market system. Part of the government's regulatory role is to protect individuals from being exploited by powerful corporate actors in the market system. In this process governmental corporate actors also develop their own interests plus acquire a great deal of power. In addition to the restrictions on individual freedom represented by government regulations, religious and moral leaders, plus critical social theorists, may invoke cultural ideals and values that encourage people to transcend their "narrow self-interests" by contributing to the public welfare or providing material assistance to those in need. Charitable contributions themselves could be considered as being outside the range of pure market transactions—even though such generosity, like other forms of altruistic behavior, may be rewarded with social approval.

Societies vary greatly in terms of their level of inequality. Excessive inequality may be considered undesirable for both political and moral reasons. From a political point of view, people who feel exploited are likely to resist pressures for normative conformity, perhaps commit crimes to satisfy their needs, and feel alienated from the current power structure. Also, among the more well-to-do segments of the population, there may be a negative moral reaction to the suffering of the "have-nots" that is reflected in efforts to implement some form of resource redistribution to satisfy cultural ideals of fairness and justice. This may involve support for government programs that reduce inequality and provide social services to people in need, or at least tacit acquiescence to the existence of such programs. The scope of the government's involvement in this area is subject to ongoing debate between those who believe government should do more versus those who believe it is probably already doing too much.

Another problem in relying on the "invisible hand" of the market to insure the public welfare is that markets tend over time to become unstable. This is shown in the historical pattern whereby periods of economic recession or depression alternate with periods of prosperity and expansion. These cycles suggest that a stable equilibrium is difficult to sustain through reliance on market mechanisms alone. The most extreme fluctuations of economic cycles have been moderated considerably throughout the second half of the twentieth century through countercyclical strategies implemented by government. These strategies include various fiscal policies, such as controlling money supply, modifying tax rates, establishing Federal Reserve interest rates, and so on. But despite policies to reduce inequality or stabilize the market, it is clear that distinct socioeconomic classes and economic uncertainties persist, despite widespread acceptance of the abstract cultural ideal of equality.

Economic Versus Socioemotional Markets

The concept of markets can be also be applied to social and emotional exchanges. The determination of fairness is sometimes more difficult in socioemotional exchanges because of the lack of an objective measure of value, comparable to money, that can be used in computing costs and rewards. In addition, the distinction between costs and rewards is sometimes difficult to establish. Although exchange and rational choice theorists may consider the time and emotional energy that friends and lovers "spend" with one another as costs (along with alternatives that are foregone), the parties involved consider their time and activities together as rewarding, not costly. Also in contrast to economic markets, the inequality and instability that may sometimes develop are matters for individuals to resolve on their own, or through their micro-level social networks, as opposed to macro-level policies or programs. Moreover, as noted earlier socioemotional exchanges are experienced as unique and cannot readily be duplicated in other relationships. By the same token, it is also difficult for any outsider to regulate their emotional tone or the nature of the socioemotional exchanges that occur within them.

Another contrast to economic markets for material resources is that the rewards in socioemotional exchanges are not necessarily zero-sum; that is, a net gain for one party does not necessarily mean a net loss for the other. When individuals provide one another with acceptance, emotional support, social approval, advice, friendship, and love, they do not deprive themselves of these resources for future exchanges. In addition to stimulating a rewarding response from the other party, such actions are also likely to be intrinsically rewarding, not costly. They may reinforce one's self-concept, enhance one's own self-esteem, and increase one's ability to offer such rewards graciously in the future, thereby increasing their value, independently of what the other offers in return. Similarly, to share one's knowledge with someone who seeks advice does not deplete the mentor's knowledge but actually helps reinforce it. Thus it is possible for the parties involved in exchanges of nonmaterial rewards to "eat their cake and have it too."

For social or socioemotional exchanges the difficulties in defining the meaning of costs versus rewards, or identifying scarcity versus abundance, imply that their dynamics differ in crucial ways from economic exchanges and thus may be seen as outside the realm of economic calculation. As noted earlier, Blau (1964) pointed out that the value of rewards in social exchanges reflects the mutual attachment of the exchange partners to one another. From the sociology of emotions perspective discussed in Chap. 8, they identify with one another's needs and welfare and experience one another's costs and rewards as their own. The socioemotional dynamics of attachment and commitment thus make the individualistic assumptions of the market and the notion of economic calculation less salient and appropriate. Instead, through the process of emotional attunement and mutual identification, each party's needs and interests are shaped and expanded by the needs and interests of the other. In Cooley's terms, the individual "I" is merged with the "we" of our relationship.

Nevertheless, all of our relationships may be evaluated from time to time in cost/benefit terms. Despite the contrast with economic exchanges, it is sometimes appropriate to view social exchanges in terms of a market model where individuals assess their alternatives in the light of their own needs and interests. This market model is appropriate, for example, when individuals are away from their homes and families for some reason, leading them to become lonely and seek companionship—a phenomenon which helps explain some of the dynamics observed in college and university dormitories, hotel bars, or cocktail lounges. When people move to a new community, they are likely to find themselves "in the market," as it were, for new friends or sociable relations with other residents. When young people evaluate their various heterosexual friendships in the hope of eventually finding someone to marry, they can be said to be in the "marriage market." The same process may apply following a divorce or the death of spouse. Personal needs and goals are clearly relevant in such circumstances as individuals consciously consider their options.

As with material interests, individuals often have conflicting needs, such as needs for personal autonomy as well as for intimacy and closeness. Close personal relationships are sometimes vulnerable to becoming unstable and precarious as a result of tensions between exchange partners' different needs and interests, plus differences in their level of attachment. If one party's need for intimacy leads to efforts to strengthen their sense of togetherness, this may threaten the other party's need for autonomy. When the other party tries to pull back to preserve or restore autonomy, the first party is motivated to try even harder to move closer. This leads the other party to withdraw even more, thereby stimulating the first party to try even harder to move closer, thereby escalating the tensions and conflict in a vicious cycle process. In highly intimate long-term relations such as marriage, such processes may be described by the metaphor of a dance in which couples move back and forth, sometimes in different directions or at a different pace, between togetherness and separation—and in this dance frustrations and disappointments are bound to arise if the underlying needs and feelings of each party are not mutually aligned. If a mutually satisfying balance cannot be established, the eventual outcome is that one party may decide to terminate the relationship in an effort to establish (or re-establish) his or her autonomy, or the other party may break it off due to feelings of being unloved and betrayed. The need for balance between too much independence versus too much dependence is comparable to Scheff's (1997) analysis, reviewed in Chap. 8, of avoiding the extremes of isolation versus engulfment.

Even when levels of mutual commitment and emotional attunement are high, individuals are usually sensitive to whether or not their socioemotional needs are being met and so may monitor their relationships from time to time. If they feel that their personal needs are not being met, they may reevaluate their relationships and perhaps consider other options. Thus many marriages end in divorce—since the late 1970s about 50%—despite the ideals of mutual devotion and commitment expressed in wedding vows. Later, when a divorced woman or man begins "circulating" once again in the hope of finding a new partner, we might say that she or he is now back in the market—comparable perhaps in some ways to being back on the job market after a job doesn't work out.

Change occurs constantly in all types of relationships and social formations as individuals back and forth across the boundaries of markets and other types of social formations. Underlying the dynamics of such changes are individuals' efforts to deal with their own sometimes conflicting and ambiguous needs and interests along with their various obligations and the needs of others with which they may be concerned. These tensions and conflicts are played out differently in economic versus socioemotional exchanges and in different types of social settings. The interlocking and interpenetrating nature of different types of social formations can readily be illustrated in our occupational experiences. Our employment is important primarily because of economic rewards (consistent with a market model), but it may offer nonmaterial benefits as well, including feelings of accomplishment, socioemotional rewards from friendships formed at work, perhaps a sense of belonging to a larger community, and being able to help other people or contribute to society. When individuals enter the "job market," even though financial compensation is likely to be a high priority, they also may be expected to try to satisfy these other interests as well. Even when people are not completely satisfied with their jobs, they may be reluctant to reenter the "job market" unless the frustrations of their present job rise significantly above what they consider tolerable for the rewards received—and their eventual decision to make a move may be triggered by learning of an appealing alternative through their social network contacts.

Socioeconomic Classes

Like the notion of "community as ideal" discussed in the last chapter, equality is a cultural ideal that differs sharply from social reality.[3] Moreover, in the absence of political or moral constraints, inequalities in economic resources often seem to expand over time in market systems. (For a highly readable description of the tendency of markets to generate increasing levels of inequality, see Frank and Cook [1995].) Socioeconomic classes develop as individuals and groups struggle to survive, to improve their well-being, and to achieve their various goals. This struggle involves competition and conflict over scarce resources, including both material and symbolic resources. Many material resources are always in scarce supply relative to demand, even with the increases in production made possible through modern technology. With symbolic resources, competition and conflict involve social definitions concerning the way personal characteristics, lifestyle practices, or other differences are evaluated in terms of status or prestige. Individuals also vary in terms of resources such as knowledge or other forms of cultural capital, emotional energy, and social network contacts. All of these resources may be relevant to the bargaining power individuals have in their exchange transactions, and the overall outcome of their transactions may include various forms of power/dependency relations.

Economic Resources as the Foundation for Socioeconomic Stratification

At least three fundamental questions may be raised regarding people's socioeconomic class position. First, **how much** money do they earn (their income)? Second, **how** do they earn it (their occupation)? Third, **how do they spend** their money

[3] The assertion in the United States Declaration of Independence that "all men are created equal" (or all human beings–to use more inclusive language) was obviously inconsistent with the existence of slavery in the southern colonies and the lack of opportunity for women to vote at the time.

(their lifestyle and consumption patterns)? The answers to these questions are highly interrelated, but the first one is crucial. This emphasis on material or economic resources is consistent with a Marxist analysis of social stratification. Education is also crucial in modern society because it provides the credentials and cultural capital required for many types of careers and thus influences the amount of money individuals can earn. Education is also relevant for developing distinctive cultural tastes which may be reflected in one's lifestyle and which leads to variations among people as "higher" or "lower" in social ranking.

Other dimensions of social rank could be identified, but income, occupation, education, and lifestyle are crucial. Weber's distinctions among economic class position, status group membership, and location in hierarchies of power and authority are useful in helping us analyze both occupation and lifestyle as distinct dimensions of socioeconomic class position. As noted earlier, status group membership reflects subjective criteria of honor or prestige (a cultural dimension). Both economic class position and status group membership can be contrasted with one's placement in hierarchies of power and authority (a political dimension), and such hierarchies are crucial in formal organizations where people perform their occupational roles.

Capitalism in modern and postmodern societies differs in many ways from the capitalism of Marx's time. Two of the most crucial differences are the expansion of large-scale corporate capitalism and the development of a large middle class.[4] The dominance of corporate capitalism over smaller-scale entrepreneurial capitalism is somewhat parallel to Marx's predictions regarding the centralization of capital. However, Marx did not distinguish between ownership (through stock) and actual management of capitalist enterprises, especially when ownership is widely disbursed among numerous stockholders throughout the society. Also, the expansion of large-scale corporate capitalism involves the proliferation of middle-level occupations that provide sufficient income to allow a level of consumption far greater than was possible for the members of the working class in Marx's time. In addition, a large number of working class individuals have also been able to move into the middle class in terms of income—a development resulting in large part from the successful struggles of the labor union movement in many key industries.

Moreover, the expansion and ongoing operation of capitalism depends not only on the production of commodities and services to be offered for sale in the market (the supply side), but also on the ability of people to purchase such commodities or services and the motivation to do so (the demand side). The growth of a relatively affluent middle class provides a pool of potential consumers to sustain and expand the demand side. The saturation of our popular culture with advertising is intended to encourage higher and higher levels of consumption as the key to living a good life,

---

[4] Ralf Dahrendorf (1959) analyzed the dominance of "organized capitalism" as a distinctive feature of modern society that distinguishes it from the earlier forms of capitalism in Marx's time. Dahrendorf's analysis of modern industrial society will be reviewed in Chap. 14 in connection with conflict theory.

enhancing one's identity, and being seen as successful. In analyses at both the micro and meso levels, consumption patterns are a major component of people's lifestyles and one of the more visible indicators of their socioeconomic class position. We turn in the next section to a brief overview of the socioeconomic class structure of American society.

Economic Classes in American Society

Income, occupation, and education are widely used in research projects as indicators of socioeconomic class position. These variables tend to be correlated with one another, but the correlation is not perfect. At the highest level, chief executive officers (CEOs) of large corporations are at the top of the hierarchy of authority in their corporations, and the huge incomes they enjoy enable them to sustain luxurious lifestyles with expensive homes in exclusive and prestigious neighborhoods. Professional athletes, rock stars, and television and movie celebrities may also have huge incomes and luxurious lifestyles but little formal power in the areas of economic production or political influence. However, celebrity status may give some of them the potential for both economic power and political influence. The cases of Ronald Reagan, the actor who became governor of California and later United States president, and of Arnold Schwarzenegger, who became governor of California, illustrate the way celebrity status and financial wealth can be transformed into political power, especially when combined with other appealing personal characteristics. Moreover, despite their high overall rank in the socioeconomic class structure, the educational level of corporate executives and celebrities may sometimes be lower than the educational level of university professors and other professionals who earn only a small fraction of their incomes.

At the other end of the scale are the poor and disadvantaged who are low in terms of all of the standard criteria of socioeconomic class position. These include, for example, many female-headed households with young children who live in poor neighborhoods. With little education, they may work at minimum-wage jobs without long-term job security or prospects for advancement. Still others are unable to find steady work or are unable to work and thus have no choice but to rely on the meager resources provided through welfare programs. Migrant farm workers are in a particularly vulnerable position in terms of basic economic resources and security.

Between these extremes is the large middle class, with its wide range of income levels, occupations, and educational backgrounds, and with considerable heterogeneity in the specific nature of the overlap between these different indicators of socioeconomic class position. Analysis of the distinctions between the lower-middle class and the upper-middle class would reveal notable differences in lifestyle and level of consumption as well as economic security and prospects for future advancement. For example, construction or factory workers with strong unions may earn sufficient income to have reasonably affluent lifestyles (though not equal to those in higher-level managerial or professional positions), but their lifestyles are likely to differ from those in lower or middle level administrative, technical, or professional positions. Supervisory or managerial personnel in business corporations participate at some level in direct control of the "means of production," but this control may be limited to insuring that their subordinates perform their jobs according to rules and policies transmitted from higher levels in the hierarchy.

A large proportion of the population in all socioeconomic class levels are not at all involved with the means of material production (as emphasized by Marx) but instead work at jobs that involve services. Of course, the notion of production could be expanded to include intangibles such as emotional production, leisure production, education production, and so on.[5] This shift from material to nonmaterial production reflects the growth of the service sector of the economy, as described in Daniel Bell's (1973) analysis of the transition from an industrial to a "postindustrial" society. In addition, with the tremendous expansion in the regulatory and social welfare functions of government at all levels, employment in government jobs, like that in private industry, represents a wide range of income, prestige, and authority. In general, the highest paid government jobs provide less total income than the highest paid jobs in the private sector, but job security is often somewhat higher.

Drawing on the Marxist perspective Erik Olin Wright (1979) analyzed the class structure of American society by focusing on (1) control over the means of production and (2) control over people. (See Wright [1997] for an analysis of the importance of class beyond the United States.) Control of the means of production does not necessarily mean 100% ownership, especially when ownership of corporate resources is widely dispersed among thousands of stockholders. Some stockholders, however, own sufficiently large shares to be able to exert ultimate control over the means of production, even though they may not necessarily be involved in day-by-day management. These major stockholders are considered by Wright to be part of the top bourgeois class because of their potential power to influence basic decisions with regard to the means of production. In addition to these major stockholders, top corporate executives are also members of the dominant bourgeois class because of their authority positions at the top of the corporate hierarchy. Many of them may also be major stockholders as well. In the broadest sense of the term, these top executives play a key role in making or influencing strategic decisions regarding investments and capital accumulation as well as actually managing the ongoing operations of the corporate enterprises that make up a large part of the economic system of the society. They thereby exert a high level of control over the material means of production as well as the labor power of employees at all levels below them in the hierarchy of authority.

At the other end of the scale, the proletariat (or working class) do not own or control the means of production (financial capital or actual tools) and must sell their labor power to earn their livelihood (just as Marx described). Some of them may

---

[5] Marx recognized the importance of the process whereby labor power itself is reproduced in the context of family life, with the unpaid labor of women contributing disproportionately to this process.

have a certain amount of autonomy or discretion in the work process, but they are nevertheless expected to follow the orders of their supervisors, who serve essentially as a channel for those at higher levels in the authority structure.

In between these extremes, Wright identified the petty bourgeois class, whose members control investments and capital accumulation on a limited scale. This class would include owners of small-scale businesses who own material "means of production" sufficient to earn their living, but whose scale of operations is too small to hire employees.

Wright (1979:42) estimates that no more than one to two percent of those who are employed are members of the true bourgeois class—that is, they both own and control the means of production. At the other extreme, he estimates that the proletariat (or working class) makes up approximately half of those involved in the labor force. Members of this class do not own or control the means of production, nor do they control the labor power of others. Wright classified the remainder of the labor force as being in "contradictory" class positions. This contradiction does not refer to conflict with other classes (though there may be conflict) but to the internal structural contradictions of these class positions. Like income, position in a hierarchy of authority involves a rank order with multiple levels. Middle-level personnel provide a clear illustration of the contradictory nature of their socioeconomic class position. Those in such positions have partial or minimal control over the means of production or over the labor power of others, but they are also subject to the control of others or to conditions of work over which they have minimal control. One's position relative to others in such a hierarchy may be regarded as a kind of indicator of the extent of control over the "means of production" and over the "labor power" of others. Depending on the size of the hierarchy, there are major differences between those near the top and those near the bottom in the degree to which they control the means of production and the labor power of others, as well as in their income and occupational prestige.

Wright groups top managers who are just below chief executive officers, middle managers, and "technocrats" together in the top half of the hierarchy (just below the very top bourgeois class). "Bottom managers," foremen, and line supervisors are grouped together in the bottom half, just above the proletariat (or working class). Wright estimates that the top group in these categories includes 12% of the work force, while the bottom group includes 18 to 23% (Wright, 1979:42).

Wright also considers small employers, semiautonomous employees, and members of the petty bourgeois class to be in contradictory class locations. Small employers are comparable to the petty bourgeois class in being able to control their own behavior, but they are also similar to the bourgeois class in controlling the behavior of others, though on a much smaller scale. Members of both the small employer class and the petty bourgeois class have limited resources that they control, and their operations are overshadowed by large corporations. Semiautonomous employees are also somewhat comparable to the petty bourgeois class in that they are able to control their own behavior more than the working class, but within limits.

According to Wright's estimates, small employers make up six to seven percent of those involved in economic activity; semiautonomous employees make up five to eleven percent, and the petty bourgeois class makes up just under five percent. When these categories are combined with the middle levels of corporate business and government hierarchies, the total percentage that Wright estimates are in "contradictory" class positions would perhaps be a little over half of all who are in the work force or involved with productive economic activity. Moreover, consistent with his Marxist-type analysis, the proletariat (or working class) makes up the largest single group, while the tiny percentage that make up the true bourgeois class clearly reflects a high concentration of control over the basic means of production.

Wright's portrayal of the class structure in the United States differs from those who emphasize the importance of the large middle class for reducing inequality. This is because his analysis is based explicitly on the Marxist definition of social class as based on one's position with regard to the means and the social relations of production rather than income or lifestyle variables. With a broad definition of the middle class, a large percentage of those in Wright's contradictory class positions could be considered middle class in terms of income, as well as the better paid and more secure members of the working class, even though their power and resources are far less than those of the socioeconomic elites making up Wright's top "bourgeois" class.

For those employed in the middle levels of organizational hierarchies, a comfortable and reasonably secure level of income is important for encouraging a sense of having a stake in the system and thereby helping to insure acceptance of its legitimacy. However, it is important to note that this security has been undermined in recent years as a result of widespread corporate downsizing. In addition, the economic well-being and security of the working class has been undermined significantly in the American economy by the relocation of many working class jobs to countries with lower wages. These recent developments suggest increasing levels of vulnerability and strain for all except those in the elite bourgeois class. In a Marxist-type analysis this vulnerability can be seen as yet another of the periodic crises to which capitalism is vulnerable. These current strains in the capitalist system differ from earlier stages, however, in terms of being part of a more highly developed global system.

Education, Socioeconomic Status Groups, and Lifestyle

Education is a key aspect of one's socioeconomic class position in modern society. In his analysis of the "credential society," Randall Collins (1979) highlighted education as the "ticket" certifying eligibility for more and more types of occupational careers and the income and status associated with them. In fact, one of the defining characteristics of professionals is their acquisition of advanced theoretical knowledge and highly specialized expertise that is available only through formal education.[6] This

[6] As explained in the last chapter, professional groups' efforts to control their own activities can be contrasted with the bureaucratic model of hierarchical control.

clearly applies to professional occupations that typically require graduate degrees for certification or licensure, such as physicians, lawyers, engineers, teachers, and social workers, for example. At a lower level in the stratification hierarchy, vocational education is intended to provide technical knowledge and skills, as opposed to more advanced theoretical knowledge. Graduates of vocational education programs are certified as competent for less prestigious occupational careers for which such practical training is deemed sufficient.

For many occupational positions, educational requirements may be less specific or extensive. The knowledge acquired by graduates of general liberal arts programs may be less relevant than training and skills acquired on the job. Even so, a baccalaureate degree in any field often serves as a kind of "certificate" that a job applicant has acquired broad analytical and communication skills, is capable of learning to deal with complex situations, has demonstrated the kind of personal dedication that will be required for occupational success, and has learned to exhibit appropriate levels of deference to those with authority. Moreover, educational experiences broaden one's intellectual perspective. In this sense formal education may be seen as providing a general reservoir of "cultural capital" that may become relevant in different ways in various occupational and lifestyle contexts.

Despite the crucial importance of education, other criteria may also be relevant for status distinctions among different subgroups. These may include demographic characteristics such as generational cohort and gender, or race and ethnicity. In local communities distinctions between long-time residents versus newcomers may be important. In a society with religious pluralism, members of different religious groups tend to see their group as distinctive and perhaps superior to others. Even among devotees of leisure pursuits such as baseball and classical music, knowledge regarding performers and their achievements or personal contacts with them may be a source of prestige.

Historically, the trend in modern society has been to emphasize **achievement** rather than **ascription** as the primary basis for status distinctions. This transition is related to the ideal of equality, which involves evaluating and ranking people on the basis of accomplishments rather than personal characteristics such as gender, race, or ethnicity, for example. With the implementation of the achievement pattern, one's eligibility for prestigious, high-paying jobs is based on education and/or experience, not race, gender, or the type of family into which one is born. This emphasis on ability and achievement as the basis for social ranking has not occurred automatically, despite the obvious unfairness of relegating whole segments of the population to second class citizenship on the basis of ascribed personal characteristics with which they were born. Understandably, those with high-status ascribed characteristics often resist efforts to change discriminatory rules and customs. Nevertheless, due to the moral arguments and political pressures generated by the civil rights movements and the women's movement, significant progress has been made in reducing the use of race and gender to justify limiting access to opportunities for educational and occupational achievement.

Age, on the other hand, is an ascriptive characteristic that is still relevant in many areas of social life. Adults usually rank higher than teenagers regardless of gender.

Adolescents, in turn, may develop their own generational ranking system in which adults are regarded as out of date or incapable of understanding the younger generation—although high rank in the adolescent peer group subculture does not translate into being socially dominant in the larger society. In any case, teenagers eventually become adults so their age status is not permanent. However, generational cohort experiences may continue to be relevant, as is evident in the distinctive status of the World War II generation (especially veterans) as well as those involved in the Vietnam war era of the 1960s, either as veterans or anti-war protesters.

Differences in lifestyles, subcultural tastes, and leisure preferences may also be relevant for one's status in various prestige hierarchies, with distinctions made between opera and classical music lovers and those who prefer country and western music, for example, or between members of golf clubs and bowling leagues. People may regard their own particular subcultural and lifestyle preferences as superior to those of other groups. Or, they may simply show a preference for relating to others with similar tastes and lifestyles as "our kind of people" but without necessarily viewing others as inferior or superior. Still others may learn to appreciate a wide range of subcultural tastes and take pride in being able to relate to a variety of people representing diverse subcultural backgrounds. Such diversity should be expected in a pluralistic society where people are free to make their own choices regarding leisure and lifestyle preferences.

Occupational Authority Structures and Socioeconomic Class Cultures

The income, power, and authority associated with one's occupation is perhaps the most crucial dimension of economic class and status group membership. Occupation is also related to one's social relations, lifestyle, and basic identity. In Randall Collins' (1975) perspective, individuals' position in the hierarchy of authority at their place of employment is the most crucial component of their class position.[7] Of course, some individuals are self-employed, and some of the organizations where people work may lack a well-developed hierarchy. But for those employed in bureaucratic organizations, Collins regards their position in the hierarchy of authority as the most important influence on their general subjective outlook on the social world—or "class consciousness"—as well as their lifestyle and basic orientation in relating to people. Authority relations boil down essentially to the experience of giving or taking orders in face-to-face relationships. As Collins puts it, "Undoubtedly, the most crucial difference among work situations is the power relations involved (the ways that men [and women] give or take orders). Occupational classes are essentially power classes within the realm of work." (Collins, 1975:62)

[7]Collins' (1975) conflict theory perspective will be examined in more detail in a subsequent chapter. Collins is a leading contemporary theorist whose work covers a wide range of sociological analysis, much of it devoted to showing the micro level foundations of macro level social processes.

Patterns of dominance and submission are symbolized by rituals that authority figures and their subordinates employ in their face-to-face interaction. Such rituals illustrate the types of social processes analyzed by Goffman (as reviewed in Chap. 5), in which individuals attempt to control the impressions they make on others as they attempt to gain social validation for the identity they seek to project. These problems of self-validation differ for persons in authority positions versus those in subordinate positions. At all levels, people seek to make the best impression they can, given the material and social situation in which they find themselves.

In general, three broad categories of occupational groups may be distinguished in Collins' perspective. At the top of the hierarchy are authority figures who give orders to many but take orders from few or none. In the middle level are those who give orders to some but take orders from others. (These positions might be compared to Wright's "contradictory" class positions.) In large bureaucratic organizations this middle level is extremely broad, with gradations from upper middle management (near the top) to lower level supervisory positions (near the bottom). The lowest occupational class at the bottom of the hierarchy consists of subordinates who simply comply with the orders they receive, as opposed to delegating them to others at a lower level. Collins' focus on authority relations would not apply to independent entrepreneurs with no employees, or to those whose income is not based on being employed in a formal organization with a hierarchical authority structure.

Collins emphasizes that the micro-level patterns of interaction between those who give and take orders reflect and reinforce the stratification system through various rituals expressing dominance or deference. Those in positions of control are naturally concerned with subordinates' adherence to rituals that will respect and preserve their dominance and perhaps strengthen subordinates' emotional attachment to the existing social order and its authority figures. On an even broader level, outside the context of the organizations where people are employed, deference rituals would include expressions of patriotic commitment to the symbolic representations of society itself, such as the custom of standing during recitation of the pledge of allegiance to the flag or the singing of the national anthem, or when the judge enters a courtroom. Such rituals can also be illustrated by the use of titles of deferential respect when addressing one's superiors ("Yes, Sir," "No, Sir," "Dr.", "Your Honor"), as well as the custom whereby military personnel salute their superiors. The performance of rituals such as these helps to dramatize and thereby reinforce the legitimacy of the existing distribution of power and authority.

In contrast to the expectations of authority figures, individuals in subordinate positions will develop styles of interaction that express their emotional detachment from the power structure and dramatize their efforts to maintain or enhance their independence and autonomy as much as possible. Of course, their resources for controlling the definitions of the situation are less than those of high-level authority figures, and they may feel they have no choice but to be deferential and submissive in their encounters with authorities. But this does not mean they are emotionally committed to the existing social order, even though they may perform their jobs adequately and demonstrate at least minimal outward respect for their superiors. But when they are not in the presence of authority figures, their behavior with one another may reflect considerable role distance, or detachment and lack of commitment. This is often reflected in negative references and derogatory "nicknames" they may use to refer to those higher up in the authority structure. It also leads to strategies to maximize their individual autonomy in the course of performing organizational roles.

An employee's position in the organizational hierarchy is also related to involvement in internal and external communication networks. Those at the top tend to be more centrally located in the organization's communication network, and to have more social contacts outside the organization. These network contacts may facilitate their ability to obtain and control organizational resources, some of which may be used to enhance their influence over their subordinates. Those at or near the top are also more likely to be in a position to speak or act on behalf of the organization in their outside contacts, while those in intermediate positions may represent their subordinates with persons higher in the hierarchy. In contrast, those at the bottom tend to have a more limited range of social contacts and to be located at the periphery of the organizational communication network. This may help to account for their less cosmopolitan orientation.

Still another difference between people in different occupational classes is the physical nature of the occupational tasks they perform. Those at lower levels not only earn less money but are obliged to perform the dirtiest, most unpleasant, or riskiest tasks. This may lead them to take pride in their toughness and their ability to perform such jobs, and they may enjoy a great deal of camaraderie as they engage in put-downs of their superiors with their desk jobs. At the same time, many of them would be happy to be promoted to such jobs. They also are more likely to respect supervisors who have come up through the ranks and thus had the same type of real-life practical experiences that they themselves have.

Collins argues that the nature of one's occupational position, particularly the experience of giving or receiving orders, carries over in a significant way into other aspects of life, including one's subjective worldview and degree of attachment to the existing social order, one's lifestyle, and the general tone and demeanor expressed in interactional encounters. Those in the highest positions of authority are accustomed to receiving deference and thus tend to be proud, self-assured, and domineering. Such persons may also insist on ritualistic formalities, especially in their relations with subordinates, since such formalities dramatize their dominant position. In contrast, the occupational experiences of those at the lowest level give rise to a distinctive working-class culture. Collins describes this culture as "localistic, cynical, and oriented toward the immediate present." (Collins, 1975:71) Working-class persons usually have little stake in the maintenance of the existing authority structure and so do not feel a strong attachment to the moral ideas that legitimate it or the ritual formalities that dramatize it. They may exhibit the appropriate respect to their superiors when necessary, but such deferential rituals do not necessarily carry a strong emotional commitment. Their socioemotional needs are likely to be met with others at the same occupational level. The alienation of working-class persons from the existing social order and its established power structure will be diminished to the extent that working-class persons anticipate being able to improve their material well-being or achieve upward mobility.

The lifestyles and subjective orientations of those in the middle levels of power will reflect how close to the top or bottom they are. In general, those in the upper middle levels will exhibit patterns similar to those in the top levels, although to a lesser degree. The sharpest break is between the bottom level and the lower middle level, particularly first-line supervisors just above the bottom. Those in the lower middle level have at least a minimal stake in the existing social structure in that their status is higher than that of the subordinates they supervise. However, their stake may be tenuous. This leads them to be highly moralistic, emphasizing the importance of self-discipline and hard work, especially in their efforts to control the behavior of their subordinates. These first-line or lower level supervisors may also hope that their successful job performance will enable them to move up in the hierarchy—or at least to hold onto the low level of authority they have attained. The ascetic lifestyle and moralistic orientation of this class are consistent with Weber's analysis of the Protestant work ethic.

Collins also described the close relationship that exists between people's occupation and their status group memberships outside the work place. In addition to social contacts at work, individuals develop social relations in the communities where they live, the religious groups and voluntary associations to which they belong, their social clubs and friendship networks, and so on. These nonoccupational relations are likely to be heavily influenced by the nature of their occupational position and the level of economic resources it provides. Specifically, individuals' income determines the type of community where they can afford housing, with the result that neighbors in residential communities are likely to have similar income levels. To a considerable degree, individuals' social relations off the job reflect their voluntary choices, but their options will be influenced by their socioeconomic class position.

In Collins' perspective, individuals' social relations outside of their occupational involvements will always reflect their efforts to maintain or improve their subjective status as much as possible. Through rituals of mutual deference, friends and acquaintances who are roughly equal in status provide support for one another's identities, lifestyles, and viewpoints. In contrast, interaction with higher status persons would involve the cost of expressing deference and thereby being reminded of one's own lower status. Such costs must be balanced against the possible enhancement of one's own status that may result from associating with higher-status persons. On the other hand, close relations with lower status persons could be seen as a potential threat to one's own status, since people tend to be evaluated by the company they keep. This risk must be balanced against the rewards to be gained by the deference provided by these lower-status associates. Overall, an individual's status is always relative to the status of his or her associates, and individuals may be seen as always having some awareness of how their relations with others may reinforce or undermine their own status.

Since individuals are concerned to enhance their status as much as possible, they will seek to stage their behavior and self-presentations in such a way that others will recognize their distinctive status claims. Consistent with Goffman's dramaturgic perspective, this staging may involve displays of material resources that symbolize superior status, demonstrations of extraordinary knowledge or skill, conversational references to personal involvement in networks of high-status persons, or the use of other resources to support one's claims. Groups in which individuals' resources are about equal may alternate between the use of rituals that symbolize fraternal equality and those that symbolize nonthreatening status competition. Playful or ritualistic games among colleagues or close friends that involve "putting down" one another or "one-upmanship" may be seen as tentative probes of the resilience of one another's status or identity claims without contesting their underlying equality.

The extent to which one's close friends and associates are equal or unequal in status is obviously an important empirical question. We might anticipate that camaraderie would be higher and social distance lower among persons who are roughly equal in status. For one thing, people who are similar in occupation and income probably have more in common than they do with those who are much higher or much lower in the status hierarchy. Even so, in some social circles, individuals take pride in overlooking status inequalities and being open to people who vary in terms of education, occupation, income and lifestyle. In such groups, high status would be earned by those who are able to relate easily to people in diverse status groups, while individuals who are less flexible or versatile who have lower status.

Status groups themselves are not necessarily egalitarian. Although all who share a similar status may seek to distinguish themselves as superior to others, such groups have their own internal differences of resources, power, and prestige. Members of particular religious groups, for example, may feel a sense of superiority to those in other groups or those with no religious group involvement. But within such groups, there are status differences between the professional clergy, persons in lay leadership positions, regular attendees who may also be major financial supporters, and marginal members who rarely attend or contribute. The African American community also has its internal distinctions between leaders and major spokespersons versus the rank and file. Groups of teenagers have their own multiple criteria for ranking one another. For both formal and informal groups, individuals are highly sensitive to their own position and rank in the group and may be expected to deploy the resources at their disposal to maintain or enhance their status as much as possible.

The interaction patterns and lifestyles of different socioeconomic classes and status groups that Collins describes suggest that people tend to invest considerable effort in strategies to try to enhance or improve their positions in these hierarchies. Such patterns are common in a country such as the United States in which widely shared cultural definitions support the idea that the class structure is open and fluid and people believe that they can improve their overall standing in the system. On the other hand, some of the most fundamental aspects of people's behavior often tend to reinforce their class position. This is a major emphasis in French sociologist Pierre Bourdieu's analysis of class cultures.

Reproduction of Class Cultures: Material Conditions and Symbolic Definitions

Pierre Bourdieu's perspective has become highly influential among American theorists. (For an overview of Bourdieu's perspective, see David Swartz ([1997]). Bourdieu's concept of the "habitus" is the key to his explanation of how class cultures are maintained and reproduced, typically without conscious intent (Bourdieu [1980] 1990:52–65). The **habitus** consists essentially of the objective material and social conditions in which people find themselves as these conditions are incorporated into their implicit subjective perceptions of their environment and influence their predispositions regarding appropriate ways to adapt. This perspective may be compared with the phenomenological emphasis on the implicitly accepted and taken-for-granted subjective assumptions people share regarding the social world as discussed in Chap. 6. For Bourdieu, this concept is important because it provides the link between the objective social world and people's subjective perceptions and behavioral dispositions.

Bourdieu's concept of **habitus** can be contrasted with his concept of **field**, which consists of the totality of the networks and patterns of social relations associated with a particular area of social life (Swartz, 1997:95–142). Fields include the various social institutions of society, but the concept is used to refer more broadly to all of the different social settings in which mutual influence, competition, and conflict may occur—even when such processes are not encapsulated within definite institutional structures or specific behavioral predispositions. Examples include areas of social life such as the artistic, the education, the entertainment, or the scientific fields. While specific institutional structures may be identified within these fields, each field is broader in scope than the structures it includes. Within all fields, individuals' behavior involves an ongoing process of competition and conflict as they use their resources to pursue their various interests in ways that reflect their standing in the social order. This competitive struggle does not usually lead to changes in the class structure, at least not in the short run. Instead, people adapt to the realities of the situation in which they find themselves. This process tends to reproduce the overall cultural patterns that reinforce the class structure.

The resources involved in people's efforts to adapt to their class-based situation include not only material or economic capital (as emphasized by Marx and Marxist theorists), but nonmaterial cultural and social forms of capital as well. Cultural capital includes knowledge of all types, including discursive and technical knowledge acquired through formal education as well as implicit knowledge and skills gained through practical experience. Cultural resources also include verbal abilities, manners and styles of speech and behavior, and aesthetic tastes, much of which depends on one's socialization experiences in the family. Social resources include one's various social relations and network ties. ("Knowing the 'right' people" may be as important as "what one knows.")

Material resources are a crucial dimension of one's socioeconomic class standing, but a great deal of the struggle in which people engage involves conflicts over cultural definitions rather than material resources as such. Regardless of the economic resources people may possess, the key to understanding their status competition is to focus on their efforts to establish symbolic superiority over other groups whose cultural resources, lifestyles, and tastes differ. Thus, for example, **economic** elites and **cultural** elites may disagree over their evaluation of the status implications of abundant financial resources versus distinctive cultural tastes and consumption patterns. Those with "elite" or highly refined cultural tastes may see themselves as superior to those whose status is based primarily on extravagant material consumption. In both cases, however, their choices do not involve basic economic necessities or survival issues but instead reflect distinctive status claims. Lifestyle and consumption patterns are evaluated more for their symbolic status value than for their practical utilitarian or survival value.[8]

At the other end of the socioeconomic hierarchy, lower or working class individuals develop preferences for practical goods and services reflecting their concerns with economic survival and security. By making a virtue out of economic necessity, they thereby establish their own distinctive status claims. Although they may certainly be desirous of having more money for the economic security it would provide, their cultural or lifestyle tastes lead them to regard the cultural tastes and consumption patterns of those at higher levels as unnecessary, pretentious, and not relevant for "our kind of people." Those in the middle will have more options to make choices that distinguish themselves from others, especially those they regard as lower in the status hierarchy, but, depending on how low or high they are, their choices will of course be more limited than those in the top levels.

Even when people do not see any realistic prospects for improving their position in the stratification system, they still seek to maintain the distinction between "our kind of people" and others who are regarded as inferior on some cultural dimension (Swartz, 1997:143–188). In Bourdieu's (1984) perspective, cultural comparisons always involve evaluative dichotomies in which people distinguish between superior and inferior lifestyles and cultural tastes.[9] These distinctions may be revealed in the contrast between those with elite cultural tastes versus those who are satisfied with the artifacts and experiences of mass culture. Thus the symbolic meanings associated with original paintings can be contrasted with the symbolic meanings of reproductions, for example. Similar distinctions can be made with regard to preferences for classical versus popular music, or elite vacation destinations or leisure activities versus those with mass appeal. (Each of these dichotomies may be further subdivided, of course.) In addition, people also make distinctions among themselves in terms

[8]This contrast between economic class position and status group membership can be traced back to Max Weber's theory of stratification as discussed earlier.

[9]Bourdieu's analysis of this tendency of people to make dichotomous distinctions reflects a pattern that can be traced back to Durkheim's distinction between the "sacred" and the "profane" in his perspective on the sociology of religion. This same emphasis on dichotomous distinctions is also manifested in Mary Douglas's (1966) analysis of culture.

of the nature and range of their social networks, particularly in terms of whether they are primarily local or more cosmopolitan.

The dynamics of class relations include not only subjective perceptions of superiority and inferiority but also objective differences in power. Such differences are expressed in actual patterns of domination and submission in various institutional settings as well as in less structured areas of social life (Bourdieu [1980] 1990:135–141). This illustrates the way class relations include both a subjective and objective dimension. Bourdieu insists, however, that objective differences in power reflect much more than differential control of material or economic resources or overt domination. Cultural domination does not necessarily involve exerting direct control over other people's behavior in the strong or coercive sense of the term. Instead, there is a "softer" form of "symbolic" domination that is manifested in widely understood expectations and obligations that people have toward others who are similar to themselves, or who are higher or lower in the status hierarchy. These expectations involve norms of honor and social obligations that vary for different status hierarchies. Conformity to these expectations for the sake of one's self-respect or social standing helps in a major way to reinforce the existing status hierarchies (Bourdieu [1980] 1990:122–134).

This pattern of symbolic domination can clearly be contrasted with controlling access to material resources or actual coercion (Bourdieu [1980] 1990:112–121). High ranking individuals with abundant material resources are sometimes expected to convert such resources to symbolic capital through various forms of benevolence, either private or public, whereby their elites status and cultural dominance are maintained.[10] In the United States, for example, wealthy business entrepreneurs and entertainment celebrities may earn considerable status and symbolic power by orchestrating highly publicized charitable contributions to various worthy causes, while failure to do so may lead to loss of status. While such benevolence may reinforce or enhance the perceived superiority and social influence of elites, it does not involve overt domination or authoritative control over the recipients of their benevolence.

Despite Bourdieu's strong emphasis on the cultural dimension of opposing class dynamics, it should also be emphasized that economic resources provide the necessary foundation for all types of cultural distinctions. Moreover, it is probably easier in most cases to transform economic resources into cultural or social resources than to convert cultural or social resources into economic resources. Intellectual elites in liberal arts areas, such as English literature, philosophy, or history, for example, may find it impossible to use their knowledge to acquire great wealth. On the other hand, wealthy individuals can invest in the acquisition of cultural capital through education, either formally or informally. If they are beyond the stage in life where

[10] These patterns may be analyzed as micro-level strategies for status enhancement as suggested by Collins, or as efforts to acquire power through creating dependency relations as suggested by Blau and Emerson (as discussed earlier). Bourdieu's model is somewhat more macro than Blau's, but the general strategy of acquiring or maintaining distinctions in terms of status or power through imbalanced exchanges is somewhat similar.

it would be seen as appropriate to go back to school themselves, they can make financial contributions to a college or university, through which they can develop a social network and earn prestige in the higher education field. They also, of course, have the resources to buy books, visit museums, travel, attend cultural events, or develop social relations with intellectual, artistic, or scientific elites and thereby share in their status.

Perhaps the most widespread pattern of using economic capital to acquire cultural capital is when young people invest money to pursue a higher education degree as preparation for what they hope will be a fulfilling and high-paying career. Upper class families can afford to send their offspring to expensive and prestigious universities, thereby promoting the intergenerational transmission of elite status. By way of contrast, those in the middle class in the United States are more likely to attend less expensive state-supported universities, and many of them (especially those from the lower middle class) will need to be employed while in school and perhaps take out long-term student loans. Their hope, of course, is that the cultural capital they acquire through higher education can eventually lead to a career with a payoff in economic capital, which they may hope can then be converted to additional status.

Higher education has traditionally been much less likely for working or lower class individuals, and these class differences still persist. In the United States, however, widespread social encouragement and financial assistance may be provided to promising young people who demonstrate high potential for future achievement through success in their high school studies. Informal mentorship of poor but "promising" students by perceptive high school teachers may play an important role in young people's decisions to apply for college or university admission—and to seek financial assistance as well.

Bourdieu (like Collins) treats educational credentials as a crucial form of cultural capital in modern society. Not only does a baccalaureate or graduate degree certify people for entering various technical and professional careers; it also promotes general awareness and increased intellectual sophistication in areas such as art, science, literature, and other areas of culture. It also increases proficiency in verbal, quantitative, and analytical abilities, interpersonal skills, self-discipline, aesthetic tastes, and many other areas. There are important differences, of course, in different areas of study with regard to the career paths to which they lead. Training for high-status professions such as law and medicine can be contrasted with general education in the liberal arts and sciences, and both of these can be contrasted with vocational education for a skilled trade.

In contrast to the widespread American belief in formal education as a stimulus for upward socioeconomic mobility, Bourdieu's analysis shows that the educational establishment actually plays a major role in reproducing the social class structure, reinforcing patterns of inequality in contemporary society, and also introducing its own internal stratification system (Bourdieu and Passeron, 1979; see also Swartz, 1997). One of the major reasons for this is that the culture represented by the higher education field is largely consistent with the culture of the dominant social classes in society. Thus it is natural that those who enter higher education from the dominant classes would be better prepared to be successful than those who do not share the same culture. In addition to reinforcing the socioeconomic class structure, colleges and universities also have their own internal stratification system. This is reflected not only in the authority structure and differential distribution of prestige among faculty, but also in the way students themselves are ranked in terms of academic performance and extracurricular activities.

The objective habitus (the material and social conditions) of individuals in different social classes shapes their subjective dispositions and expectations regarding higher education. Individuals in lower or working class settings generally are less likely than those in the middle or upper classes to see higher education as a realistic option for them to consider, or to envision being successful in the education field. Their habitus is shaped by the distinctive subculture of their class, which is transmitted in their family setting. From their earliest years in elementary school, many working or lower class students are likely to have experienced the daily frustrations of school routines and of sometimes seeing the class culture of their own families and communities denigrated as inferior. The typical response to such frustration and failure is psychological or emotional withdrawal or overt resistance and rebellion. This triggers the predictable social control reactions of teachers and school authorities, which leads to additional withdrawal and rebellion and continued failure. In this way a kind of "vicious cycle" develops in which students' own behavior (withdrawal or rebellion) helps to reproduce the conditions that make it difficult or impossible for them to succeed. The pattern illustrates Bourdieu's basic argument: the way people adapt to their material and social environment unwittingly reinforces their class culture and thus their socioeconomic position in society.

There are exceptions to this pattern, but those from lower socioeconomic class levels who do manage to enroll in higher education are likely to discover that they face great obstacles because of the limitations of their cultural background—in addition to the financial pressures they may experience. College or university students from middle (and especially lower-middle) class backgrounds may also face similar challenges, depending on how much convergence there is between their cultural background and the culture they encounter in the college or university setting. Among students whose families have middle-class incomes, we might expect that those with college-educated parents would fare better than those whose parents who did not attend college. In addition, even when students from culturally limited backgrounds succeed in their formal academic studies, they may lack the informal experiences that increase their cultural awareness and worldly knowledge, and that enable them to feel and act at ease among the cultural elites they may encounter or relate to them as equals.

The challenges and demands of higher education may sometimes trigger reactions that serve inadvertently to reproduce the distinctive class cultures that students bring with them from their family and community backgrounds. The attitudes and orientations of students from lower and working class backgrounds (and perhaps those from lower-middle class backgrounds whose parents did not attend college) are likely to contrast sharply with the orientations and expectations they encounter in the higher education field. The differences are manifested in such areas as attitudes toward academic study and intellectual life, for example, standards of emotional control and communication styles, and lifestyle and aesthetic preferences. The formal and informal cultural patterns of the education field differ from the cultural patterns of the social world to which they are accustomed, and the emotional and behavior reactions to these differences make it a difficult and challenging task to be successful in the education or academic field.

Of course, the responses of young people to their experiences in the education field differ from the strategies adults use in trying to maintain their dignity and self-respect as they deal with the sometimes harsh realities of their lives. But the basic point in Bourdieu's analysis is that the "logic" of the everyday practices of people in different social classes reflects a high level of correspondence between the objective conditions of their habitus (or situation) and their subjective dispositions to act in ways that they see as appropriate in the light of these conditions. At the same time, these normal everyday practices of coping and adapting thereby help reproduce the habitus, thus insuring that such practices will continue. To the extent that conscious choice is involved at all, the choice is for people to do what they feel is necessary or appropriate in the situation in which they find themselves.

This same logic applies to all levels of the socioeconomic class structure. Persons in middle or upper class positions also face various social expectations associated with their class position. Conformity to these expectations may be regarded as obligatory, as opposed to being a personal choice. At the very least they are expected to maintain a style of life and patterns of consumption that are regarded as appropriate for their elite status. Beyond this there may be specific social obligations that must be fulfilled. For example, the leading citizens in a community may feel they have no choice but to play a leadership role in their community's annual United Way campaign and to make a substantial financial contribution to set a good example. Compliance with such obligations no doubt reflects their feeling (which others share) that they should "give something back" to their community in consideration of their success and their standing in the community. On a smaller scale, people may feel obligated to make a contribution to the annual Christmas/Hanukkah or New Year's party at their place of employment, or to purchase a gift for a couple getting married in order to avoid the stigma that would result from their refusal to do so.

These various expectations and obligations reflect the objective structural conditions of the habitus, but they also are incorporated in the subjective definitions that influence individuals' decisions regarding how to deal with the social situations they face. An individual's "voluntary" acceptance of the obligations associated with his or her social position helps to reinforce his or her status, while refusing to do so is not seen as a realistic option and would certainly involve the risk of diminished status. Moreover, the choices of any particular individual are not unique but are in large part consistent with the choices made by others in similar social positions who share the same habitus.

Bourdieu's emphasis on the objective conditions of the habitus seems to imply that socioeconomic class positions and status group subcultures are highly persistent and that individual mobility is difficult and unlikely. This is due to the high correlation between objective class-based conditions and subjective predispositions learned in the socialization process. Although some limited mobility in economic position or cultural status may be possible, and although changes may occur in the long run, the dominant picture that emerges is that major short-term change is unlikely. As people adapt to the realities of their situation, the choices they make seem like the only practical option available for them to maintain their current standing in the socioeconomic hierarchy. These choices reflect the subjective dispositions associated with their particular habitus. In other words, it is the life they know. As a result their behaviors tend to reproduce the very conditions that reinforce the subjective expectations associated with their positions.

This perspective helps us understand the difficulties of initiating changes in subjective predispositions (attitudes and motivations) that would promote upward mobility or stimulate changes in the class structure leading to greater levels of equality. This point is important to keep in mind in evaluating the challenges and difficulties of "remedial" programs in the education system that are intended to overcome family background disadvantages and provide the cultural capital needed for academic success. Although some may succeed, the high correlation between class-based cultural distinctions, differences in power and influence, and the distribution of material resources make major changes in the class structure extremely difficult.

Despite Bourdieu's emphasis on the way class cultures tend to be reproduced over time, there are variations among different societies, different groups, and different historical periods within a society in terms of how fluid or open the boundaries between socioeconomic classes are, and how much socioeconomic mobility is possible—or believed to be possible. It is always an empirical question as to whether people's class-related behavioral practices reflect a pattern of more or less automatic adaptation to the objective realities of their situation or conscious selection of strategies from among alternative options that may lead to upward socioeconomic mobility. An equally important question is the extent to which individuals are given encouragement and opportunities to improve their economic or cultural position, and how such mobility affects the overall distribution of resources, status, and power. Options always seem to be limited, especially for those at the lowest levels of the socioeconomic hierarchy. Although exceptions sometimes occur, it is rare for persons to move from near the bottom of the socioeconomic hierarchy to near the top. Some professional athletic stars, entertainment celebrities, and lottery ticket winners may be catapulted to high-level positions in terms of economic resources, but these cases are exceptional and do not guarantee entry into the cultural elite. Even when class cultures appear to be somewhat fluid and open, the typical pattern is a limited move to the next rung or two on the socioeconomic ladder, which is usually a long way from the top. Overall, Bourdieu's analysis emphasized the tendency for socioeconomic class cultures to be reproduced as individuals adapt to the material conditions and the cultural definitions they encounter in their social environment.

Summary

This chapter began with an overview of the dynamics of markets. Since market transactions reflect individuals' efforts to pursue their own interests, the individualistic assumptions of rational choice theory are more relevant to markets than to communities or organizations. However, the exchange of nonmaterial social rewards, particularly emotional support, leads to the formation of personal relationships based on socioemotional attachments, which may reduce (but not eliminate) the salience of the highly individualistic assumptions of an impersonal market model. In pursuing their individual interests, individuals use not only material resources, but emotional, social, and cultural resources as well. Moreover, the rewards they seek include material benefits as well as nonmaterial rewards such as emotional support and validation for their self-concepts plus various forms of social and cultural capital.

The dynamics of impersonal market systems in which material resources are exchanged clearly differ from social exchanges involving nonmaterial symbolic or emotional rewards. In both cases, however, markets tend to become unstable. In the economic realm, levels of inequality tend to increase in a pure market situation; in other words, the rich become richer and the poor become poorer. Efforts to regulate the economy to promote stability or reduce inequality are major responsibilities of government, but the degree of regulation is always a matter of ideological debate, reflecting the conflicting interests of different groups. In social relations involving socioemotional bonds, instability may result from inconsistent expectations, including the tendency for people in relationships to move back and forth between autonomy versus intimacy in ways that may not necessarily match one another.

Inequalities in material resources give rise to distinct socioeconomic classes with their distinctive class cultures and lifestyles. We reviewed Erik Olin Wright's application of Marxist class distinctions to the American socioeconomic class structure. His analysis focused on ownership and control of the means of production through the corporate hierarchies of capitalist enterprises. Between the elites who have major ownership and control of these corporate structures and the working class at the bottom, a large proportion of the middle class are in contradictory class positions. These contradictory positions are manifested in the intermediate levels of authority in corporate hierarchies as well as by small-scale self-employed entrepreneurs.

Individuals' occupational positions in organized hierarchies of authority was also a major focus in Randall Collins' conflict theory perspective. For Collins, people's experiences of giving and taking orders in their occupational settings are crucial in determining their styles of relating to others and their identities. For most people their occupation is the primary source of their financial resources, and differences in occupation and income are highly correlated with variations in overall status, range and type of social relations, and lifestyle. Education is important in Collins' analysis primarily because of the way educational credentials are used to certify that people have acquired the knowledge and expertise they need for their occupational careers. Education also provides cultural capital that may be relevant in people's social relations and lifestyle choices. In developing his overall conflict theory, Collins emphasized the various micro-level strategies whereby individuals seek to use their cultural capital, social networks, and economic resources to maintain or improve their socioeconomic class or status group position.

In contrast to Collins' focus on intentional strategies for trying to improve one's overall position in the stratification system, Bourdieu emphasized that individuals' objective socioeconomic class locations give rise to implicitly accepted subjective predispositions leading to behaviors that unintentionally reproduce the material and cultural distinctions among different socioeconomic classes. His concept of the habitus was intended to portray the objective conditions associated with different class positions and the way these conditions influence people's worldview and strategies of adapting to their environment. The high correspondence between objective conditions and subjective behavioral predispositions contributes to a high degree of stability in the socioeconomic class structure and class relations. This emphasis on class reproduction is a major emphasis of Bourdieu's analysis of the educational establishment.

Is social stratification of people into different socioeconomic classes inevitable or necessary? Or could societies be reorganized so all are equal—or at least so that the level of inequality is reduced? The theoretical perspectives to be discussed in the following chapters—alternative forms of functional theory versus conflict and critical theoretical perspectives—offer contrasting perspectives in response to such questions.

Questions for Study and Discussion

1. Describe some of the ways that individuals move into or out of the "market" for socioemotional or nonmaterial rewards of various types? To what extent do people's existing relationships and social obligations undermine the likelihood of their being "in the market" for increasing the personal rewards they receive from such relationships? What are some of the rational choice considerations that lead them to continue in relationships in which costs have increased and rewards decreased?
2. Other than material or financial resources, what do you consider to be the most important criteria for a person's position in the overall socioeconomic class structure of society? Do these depend on material or financial resources? In what way? What are some examples of groups where other types of resources are important for a person's rank in the group?
3. Do you agree or disagree with the argument that socioeconomic class position is based primarily on a person's relations to the means of production and hierarchies of authority in productive enterprises? Why or why not? What other significant sources would you identify for determining people's position in the socioeconomic class structure?
4. Discuss the relationship between education and socioeconomic class position. Do you think that education in this country promotes upward socioeconomic mobility or reproduces existing socioeconomic class positions? What evidence would you need to support either of these arguments? Have you found your own orientations changed or reinforced through your educational experience? In what ways?
5. In middle-class occupational settings, how would you expect the relationships of people to differ according to whether they involve persons who are roughly equal to themselves or persons who are higher or lower in the socioeconomic class system or hierarchy of authority? Do you think people are conscious of these differences? How might these relationships be managed to promote a person's own upward socioeconomic mobility?

Chapter 12
Integration and Social Order at the Macro Level: Parsons' Structural-Functional Perspective[1]

On November 19, 1863, President Abraham Lincoln's Gettysburg address described the United States Civil War as a test of whether a "new nation, conceived in liberty and dedicated to the proposition that all men are created equal" would "long endure." There is no guarantee that any society or nation will "long endure." But for people living in a well-established society, its survival and stability are likely to be taken for granted and not seen as problematic unless threatened by a more powerful enemy. We should recognize, however, that the relative position of any society is dependent on several factors, both internal and external, that determine its relative strength or weakness as well as its long-term survival prospects. Historian Paul Kennedy's (1987) analysis of the rise and fall of the great powers has shown that no power can take its continued dominance for granted.

Understanding the requirements for the survival of a society and other social systems is a major feature of functional theory. Fundamental questions regarding how individuals are socialized to become contributing members of society, and how its different "parts" (or social institutions) fit together to insure its survival and maintain social order, are crucial in functional analysis. This societal focus is implicit in many public policy discussions concerning the long-range consequences of alternative policy decisions. Political leaders often engage in passionate debate regarding their contrasting visions of what is good for society and the welfare of its members. Individuals may be asked to sacrifice their own welfare for the good of society, as members of the armed forces do routinely when in combat. As expressed in the challenging words of President John F. Kennedy's inaugural address, "Ask not what your country can do for you, but what you can do for your country." The implication is that the well-being and even the survival of society are dependent on its members' willingness to make their contributions.

For modern sociology, functional theory was developed most systematically by Talcott Parsons, along with numerous colleagues. Although Parsons' earliest contribution was an attempt to integrate previous perspectives into a comprehensive theory of social action, he is best remembered for his structural/functional analysis of the overall society. In this perspective, the focus is on how individuals' actions are organized through their roles in social institutions in ways that contribute to

[1] A large portion of the material in this chapter is adapted from D. P. Johnson ([1981] 1986:328–428).

society's basic functional requirements. Although functional theory is usually seen as most relevant for a macro-level analysis of society itself, the strategy of functional analysis can be applied to any social system, including those at the micro and meso levels. Following a brief introductory section, the major themes from Parsons' structural-functional framework to be discussed in this chapter are as follows:

- Voluntaristic theory of social action—Parsons argued that human behavior involves choices people make, but these choices are regulated by shared values and norms.
- The pattern variables—This refers to a series of specific choices individuals make within the normative guidelines of their society with regard to their orientations toward others as well as the priority they are expected to give to their own interests versus their normative obligations.
- The strategy of structural-functional analysis—This section, sometimes considered the heart of Parsons' theory, will deal with how the major institutional structures of society fit together in fulfilling its functional requirements. Parsons' AGIL model, which is perhaps his most enduring legacy to contemporary theory, will be seen as applicable to other social system as well as the overall society.
- Hierarchy of cultural control—Social systems are shown in this section to be linked to the culture, personality patterns, and the behavioral organism as analytically distinct systems. Cultural values and norms are seen as controlling the dynamics of social systems and personality formation, but this control operates within the constraints and conditions established by the lower level systems in the hierarchy.
- Structural differentiation and evolutionary change—Despite his strong emphasis on stability and social order, Parsons also used his perspective to analyze the evolutionary changes leading to modern society.
- The ultimate meaning of human life—This section reflects Parsons' efforts to provide a comprehensive analysis of the "human condition" that incorporates the level of ultimate or transcendent meanings (as expressed in religious beliefs and symbols, for example) as well as the material environment and biological characteristics of human beings.

From Social Action to Social Systems: Introducing Parsons' Structural/Functional Theory

Throughout his career Talcott Parsons looked at the social world from a very broad perspective. In addition to the social system, the personality system, the cultural system, and the behavioral organism are also included in his overall theory, even though they are analytically distinct. But despite his primary focus on social structures and systems for most of his career, his underlying image of social systems is that, in the final analysis, they consist of individuals' actions. For this reason we will look at Parsons' early social action theory as background for his functional analysis of social systems.

By way of a brief biographical background, Talcott Parsons (1902–1979) was the son of a Congregational minister.[2] Following his undergraduate major in biology at Amherst College and an early interest in medicine, he shifted to social thought and economics during his graduate study at the London School of Economics. After a year in London, he went to Heidelberg, Germany, where he became acquainted with German sociology, particularly the work of Weber and Marx. Weber's influence was the stronger of the two, and Parsons would later introduce Weber to American sociology and incorporate many of his ideas into his own theoretical perspective. In 1927, Parsons was awarded a doctorate from the University of Heidelberg. His dissertation dealt with the ideas of Max Weber, Werner Sombart, and Karl Marx on capitalism. Except for teaching one year at Amherst prior to completion of his doctoral work, Parsons' professional career was spent at Harvard University. He first taught economics but soon became a charter member of Harvard's Sociology Department, where he later organized the interdisciplinary Department of Social Relations and was its first chairperson. Parsons' involvement in such a broadly defined group may have been influential in his long-term goal of developing a comprehensive theory ranging from individuals' social actions to large-scale social systems at the societal level, as opposed to a more narrowly focused perspective.

As noted in Chap. 3, Parsons had enormous influence in American sociology in the 1950s and early 1960s when functionalism was dominant. Many of the students he helped train became leading representatives of American sociology who expanded and developed the functional approach. Sociologists with alternative or opposing orientations could not ignore his dominating influence, and opposing theories were probably sharpened in the confrontation with functionalism. Although Parsons is best remembered for his macro-level functionalist approach, his earliest work was comparable to Weber in its focus on individual action as the basic unit of sociological analysis.[3] Ironically, however, there is little continuity between Parsons' work and that of earlier American sociologists such as Mead and Cooley. His education in England and Germany probably accounts for the fact that his point of departure was European social thought. Moreover, his abstract and comprehensive style resembles the European approach more than the more micro-level and individualistic approach and the strong empirical bent of American sociology.[4]

The influence of Parsons on American sociology declined significantly in the late 1960s and early 1970s, but many of the fundamental theoretical concepts and

---

[2] These biographical highlights and intellectual influences on Parsons are drawn mostly from Devereux, Jr., (pp. 1–63, especially pp. 3–7 in Black, ed. (1961). For an autobiographical statement, see Parsons (1970).

[3] Some sociologists identified a sharp break between Parsons' early social action theory and his later structural-functional analysis of social systems (see, for example, Scott, [1963]).

[4] Parsons described himself as an "incurable theorist." (See the dedication page in Parsons' book, *The Social System*, [Parsons, 1951]). He did engage in interpretation of various current social issues, however, such as the medical profession (Parsons, 1951:428–479), the McCarthy era in American politics (Parsons, 1961b:226–247), and American universities (Parsons and Platt, 1973). Even these substantive areas are analyzed in an abstract, speculative style instead of being grounded in systematically gathered empirical data.

issues he addressed have been revisited and reformulated so as to incorporate more recent theoretical development and to be more clearly relevant in analyzing contemporary social trends (see Fox et al., 2005). In this chapter, however, our focus will be primarily on Parsons' perspective as developed at the time. The continuing relevance of functional theory for contemporary sociology is also revealed in the development of neofunctionalism the 1980s—a development that will be described more fully in the next chapter.

The Voluntaristic Theory of Social Action

Parsons' (1937) early theory of social action was based on an intensive critical analysis of the works of Alfred Marshall, Vilfredo Pareto, Émile Durkheim, and Max Weber—all early theorists from across the Atlantic. His major argument was that these theorists converged, despite different starting points, in pointing to the essential elements of a voluntaristic theory of social action. Parsons regarded his contribution as identifying these crucial elements and integrating them in a more general and systematic perspective. In pursuing this goal, he made extensive use of the means-ends framework. His analysis was complex, but the basic ideas are consistent with our common sense and everyday experience. In its barest essentials, his argument is that all social action has the following characteristics:

1. it is goal directed (or has an **end**);
2. it takes place in a situation that provides **means** individuals can use to achieve their goal, plus **conditions** the actor cannot change, and
3. it is **normatively regulated** with respect to the choice of both ends and means.

In effect, Parsons' analysis was intended as a comprehensive synthesis of the opposing viewpoints of positivism and idealism.[5] Although positivism itself is not a unified theoretical or philosophical position, the point to note is that it involves a deterministic model of human behavior. In Parsons' terms, this implied that behavior could be adequately explained as being determined by either the situation or the underlying characteristics of human nature. This emphasis ignored the role of individual choice, as well as the normative orientation that governed and regulated individuals' choices with regard to the means employed and the ends or goals that are sought.

---

[5] For a concise overview of the schools of thought that Parsons attempted to integrate in his voluntaristic theory, see Devereux (pp. 1–63, especially pp. 7–20 in Black, ed., 1961). The discussion that follows differs from Devereux's, however. Devereux distinguished (1) utilitarianism and economic theory, (2) positivism, and (3) idealism. The discussion that follows is based on Parsons' treatment of utilitarianism as one branch of positivism which he contrasted with an "antiintellectual" branch. Of the four theorists analyzed, Marshall, Pareto, and Durkheim start from a positivist position, while Weber starts from the general context of German historicism and idealism. In each case, however, Parsons contends that these theorists each moved toward a recognition of the validity of the opposing position.

Parsons distinguished between a utilitarian branch of positivism and an "antiintellectual" branch. In the utilitarian branch, represented by British economist Alfred Marshall, individuals consciously adapt to the environment in their efforts to meet their individual needs. In the antiintellectual branch, individuals are influenced by conditions of which they may not be consciously aware. These include underlying sentiments that motivate their actions as suggested in Pareto's early theory (see Chap. 2). Durkheim also started from a positivist foundation in Parsons' view. This was manifested in his emphasis on the external reality of social facts which he developed in opposition to the individualistic approach of utilitarianism. Later, however, Durkheim moved toward a position of sociological idealism in showing how individuals internalize collective representations (ideas, beliefs, values, and normative patterns) in their subjective consciousness.[6]

In contrast to positivism, idealism emphasized the normative orientation that governs individuals' choices. Its major shortcoming in Parsons' view was that it did not deal adequately with the constraining effects of the environment or with the limitations and predispositions of human beings' biological characteristics. Cultural values do not implement themselves automatically; instead, human energy must be expended in confronting and overcoming obstacles and in making use of material resources in an effort to achieve them or have them manifested in their individual and collective lives.

Of the four theorists Parsons analyzed, it was Weber, in Parsons' view, who demonstrated most systematically that cultural values and norms can be incorporated in a comprehensive model of social action that also recognizes the importance of material conditions and the social environment. Both emphases—the subjective normative orientation and the objective situational context—are crucial for a general theory of action. The normative orientation gives direction to individuals' choices of means and ends, while the situational context provides opportunities and sets constraints for individuals' actions. The basic argument in Parsons' voluntaristic theory of social action is that individuals make choices, but their choices are normatively regulated with regard to the goals individuals pursue and the means they employ to reach these goals.

The Pattern Variables: Variations in Subjective Orientations

Parsons' voluntaristic theory of social action, as described above, is crucial as a starting point, but the ultimate goal is to explain the variations in people's subjective orientations through which their goal-directed behavior is normatively regulated.[7]

---

[6] Parsons' emphasis on widely shared values and norms may be compared with Mead's emphasis on the way in which individuals evaluate their actions in terms of the shared perspectives and standards of the wider community, which he referred to as the "generalized other."

[7] This strategy of identifying key variations was a major emphasis in the "theory construction" approach described in Chap. 4.

To this end it is important to establish criteria for distinguishing different types of subjective normative orientations. To what extent do these orientations vary in different situations? In collaboration with Edward A. Shils and other colleagues, Parsons dealt with these questions in a 1951 book, *Toward a General Theory of Action*, in which categories were developed for distinguishing different types of subjective orientations (Parsons and Shils, eds., 1951). The question of how individuals' orientations and resulting actions fit together in a social system was addressed more fully in Parsons' book entitled *The Social System* (1951). The **pattern variables** were the most general and influential of these classification systems, although their long-term influence is not as great as Parsons' strategy for functional analysis of social systems (to be described shortly).

The pattern variables were intended to refer simultaneously to the motivational orientations plus the value orientations involved in social action (Parsons and Shils, 1951:58–60). The concept of motivation refers to a person's desire to maximize gratifications and minimize deprivations, including the goal of balancing immediate needs with long-range goals (which often requires deferring gratification).[8] The value orientation refers to the normative standards that govern an individual's choices and priorities with respect to different needs and goals.[9] These pattern variables help insure mutually compatible orientations among people as they interact. Essentially, they represent five dichotomous choices that must be made, explicitly or implicitly, in relating to another person in any social situation. They are as follows:[10]

1. Affectivity versus affective neutrality
2. Self-orientation versus collectivity orientation
3. Universalism versus particularism
4. Ascription versus achievement
5. Specificity versus diffuseness

Affectivity versus Affective Neutrality—This is the dilemma of whether or not to seek or expect emotional gratification through a particular action or relationship. The affective side means that individuals are oriented toward becoming emotionally involved with one another, such as expressing affection or otherwise providing gratification of one another's emotional needs. Relations between lovers or family members illustrate this choice. In contrast, neutrality means that individuals avoid emotional involvement or immediate gratification. The relationship between a doctor and patient or between a social worker and client would illustrate this pattern.

---

[8] This notion of a gratification/deprivation balance is consistent with the basic principles of social exchange and rational choice theory, except that Parsons' underlying assumptions regarding social action are less individualistic. In contrast to social exchange and rational choice theory, Parsons explains individuals' goals and strategies for achieving them in terms of widely shared cultural influences.

[9] This contrast between motivational orientation and value orientation may be seen as related to the legacy of the utilitarian tradition and the idealistic tradition, respectively.

[10] These choices are listed here in the order in which they appeared in Parsons and Shils, eds., 1951:77.

Self-orientation versus Collectivity Orientation—This dilemma involves the question of which party's interests has priority. A self-orientation means that the individual's own personal interests are expected to have priority, while a collectivity orientation would indicate that one is obligated to give priority to the needs or interests of others, or of the collectivity as a whole. Market transactions as described in the last chapter are expected to be governed by a self-orientation. In contrast, family relations, relations between close friends, or relations in a church congregation are expected to reflect a collectivity orientation, sometimes governed by shared moral values requiring the sacrifice of individual interests.[11]

Universalism versus Particularism—This variable concerns the scope of the normative standards governing a social relationship. The universalistic pattern involves standards that apply to all others who can be classified together in terms of impersonally defined categories. In American society, the ideal of the equality of all citizens under the law, plus laws prohibiting racial discrimination in education, employment, and housing, are examples of universalistic norms. In contrast, the particularistic pattern involves standards based on specific relationships or specific characteristics people may share. Norms that apply only to one's family, for example, to persons in the same ethnic or racial group, or to others in one's own age category would be particularistic.

Ascription versus Achievement (or *Quality versus Performance*)—Parsons contrasted this variable (plus the following one) with the preceding three in that this variable (plus the following one) concern individuals' **perceptions of others** instead of their own **personal orientation**. Ascription involves evaluating others in terms of who they are, while achievement is based on their accomplishments or capabilities. Ascriptive characteristics may include one's family background, for example, as well as gender, racial or ethnic background, or physical characteristics. In contrast, the achievement pattern may be illustrated by policies requiring career promotions to be based on merit, for example, as well as the use of objective measures (such as test scores) in determining college admission or graduation.

Specificity versus Diffuseness—This variable deals with the scope of an individual's obligations toward another person. If mutual obligations are narrow and precisely defined (such as formal contractual relations, for example), the pattern would be one of specificity. In contrast, if there is a wide range of gratifications that are exchanged, the pattern would be one of diffuseness. The distinction can readily be understood if we consider how obligations and expectations are negotiated. In a relationship characterized by specificity, the burden of proof would be on the person making a demand on the other party to justify that demand; in contrast, with a pattern of diffuseness, the burden of proof would be on the person on whom a demand is made to explain if this expectation cannot be met.

---

[11] This contrast is parallel to the contrast Margolis (1998) identified between the "exchanger self" and the "obligated self" that was discussed in Chap. 8.

The pattern variables can readily be related to Tönnies' well-known distinction between *Gemeinschaft* and *Gesellschaft* types of social relations, perhaps even being seen as basic dimensions of Tönnies' typology. The pattern variable choices associated with Tönnies' dichotomy are as follows.

Gemeinschaft	Gesellschaft
Affectivity	Affective neutrality
Collectivity orientation	Self orientation
Particularism	Universalism
Ascription	Achievement
Diffuseness	Specificity

However, Parsons insisted that the pattern variables are analytically distinct and may vary independently. In other words, there is no logical necessity why they should always cluster in the manner suggested in Tönnies' dichotomy, although some combinations are clearly more common than others. Even so, treating these different dimensions as analytically independent makes some interesting comparisons possible. For example, relations between clerks and customers in a large supermarket and between welfare workers and clients would both be *Gesellschaft*-type relations. However, supermarket relations reflect a self-orientation, while the welfare worker is expected to give priority to the needs of the client, not personal interests. Thus the pattern variables provide tools for analysis of social relations that are intermediate between the extreme *Gemeinschaft* and *Gesellschaft* types.

Parsons suggested that the pattern variables can also be used to distinguish the value systems of entire societies (Parsons and Shils, eds., 1951:184–185; Parsons, 1951:180–200). Thus the dominant value system of American society corresponds to the universalistic achievement pattern. In contrast, he suggested that the universalistic ascriptive pattern could be illustrated by pre-Nazi Germany, with its historic strong emphasis on status, its authoritarian tendencies, and its stress on collective political action to promote the dominance of its national culture. The particularistic achievement pattern fits the classical Chinese value system according to Parsons. This accounts for the strong emphasis on family and community ties and the priority given to traditional values. The particularistic ascription pattern corresponds roughly to the Spanish-American value system. Again, there is a strong emphasis on the family network, with activities that express socioemotional bonds given high priority. It should be kept in mind that the use of abstract categories to classify entire societies overstates the differences among them as well as fails to consider important internal variations. Moreover, the emergence of a global culture, which will be highlighted in more detail in Chap. 20, should be expected to decrease the differences among societies.

By providing a set of categories for classifying subjective orientations, the pattern variables thus represent an advance beyond Parsons' earlier analysis of the general characteristics of voluntaristic social action. The next step, then, would be to try to explain why the pattern variables assume the values that they do in different situations. This leads eventually to Parsons' analysis of the how individuals' orientations are related to the dynamics of social systems in fulfilling their functional requirements, particularly those of the overall society.

The Strategy of Structural–Functional Analysis

All social relationships involve mutual orientations of two or more persons toward one another, and these orientations can be classified in terms of the pattern variables. Although their actions are goal-oriented, reflecting their concerns with their overall gratification/deprivation balance, Parsons' goal is to emphasize that the specific manner in which goals are pursued and gratification is sought will be governed by the normative standards and value orientations of the overall culture. Also, in addition to satisfying individual needs and interests, additional requirements must be fulfilled for social relationships and systems to endure—and this is the specific emphasis of functional theory. Such requirements include, for example, maintaining compatible mutual orientations (not only in terms of general cultural values and norms but also in terms of specific role expectations) and developing ways to resolve conflicts. This applies to all social systems, from the simplest dyadic relationship to a complex society.

By the early 1950s, Parsons gave higher priority to the functional requirements of society (and other social systems) than to the categorization of individuals' orientations in terms of his pattern variables. Since social systems are made up of individuals, one underlying requirement is to insure that the basic needs of their members are met and that their motivations are linked to their roles in the system. However, the functional requirements of social systems are not the same as the needs and goals of individuals. Parsons' social system focus gave rise to an in-depth analysis of the social structures (or subsystems) through which the functional requirements of social systems (including the overall society in particular) are met. Although the pattern variables were no longer the primary focus of attention, they can be used to categorize and analyze the basic structures of the social relations through which these functional requirements are met. An early formulation of this structural-functional approach was provided in Parsons' (1951) book, *The Social System* (see also Parsons, 1949:212–237).

The transition from individuals' actions to social structures requires clarification of some additional concepts. A"**role**" refers to patterns of action that are expected by virtue of a being in a particular relationship or occupying a particular position or status. Actions that an individual is expected to perform are the responsibilities of a role; the actions or responses expected of others constitute its rights. The concept of role is linked with the concept of status, which in this usage refers to a person's position in a relationship or social system, not to prestige. Roles (or status-roles) are the most elementary units of social structure and, in Parsons' terms, are "the primary mechanisms through which the essential functional prerequisites of the system are met." (Parsons, 1951:115)

Roles are organized into larger units referred to as "institutions." The concept of **institution** in this context does not refer to a particular organization, but to a set of roles and normative patterns that are relevant to a particular functional problem. Parsons used "**collectivity**" to refer to a specific social organization. Thus, for example, in contrast to a particular business firm, the economy as an institution consists of a whole set of institutionalized patterns such as private property, occupational choice, the monetary and credit system, contractual relationships, bureaucratic forms of organization, and the like. As Parsons explains the distinction, "A collectivity is a system of concretely interactive specific roles. An institution on the other hand is a complex of patterned elements in role-expectations which may apply to an indefinite number of collectivities." (Parsons, 1951:115)

Functional Requirements and Institutional Structures of Societies

A major goal of Parsons' functional analysis was to explain the mechanisms that produce congruence between individuals' motives and needs, specific role expectations, and shared cultural values. The concepts of **internalization** and **institutionalization** are used to describe the processes involved. Internalization is the process whereby cultural value orientations and role expectations are incorporated into the personality system through socialization. As Parsons explained, "It is only by virtue of internalization of institutionalized values that a genuine motivational integration of behavior in the social structure takes place, that the 'deeper' layers of motivation become harnessed to the fulfillment of role-expectations." (Parsons, 1951:42)

While internalization refers to the personality system, institutionalization refers to the social system. When internalized normative commitments lead to actions that fulfill the expectations of others and elicit their approval, they can be said to be institutionalized. As Parsons noted, "In so far as… conformity with a value-orientation standard meets both these criteria, that is, from the point of view of any given actor in the system, it is both a mode of the fulfillment of his own need-dispositions and a condition of 'optimizing' the reactions of other significant actors, that standard will be said to be 'institutionalized.' " (Parsons, 1951:38)

In addition to the need for congruence between the personality system, social system, and cultural system, additional functional requirements can be identified within each of these systems. At the level of the individual personality, there is a need to maintain at least minimal equilibrium between competing needs and motives. Similarly, the pattern of role expectations in the social system must be compatible with minimal needs for order and integration. In addition, mechanisms are needed to solve the recurrent problems of allocation of material resources, rewards, authority, and power, and for integrating and coordinating the actions of various individuals into a system. At the level of the cultural system there is the need to insure a minimal degree of consistency or symbolic congruence in values and cognitive orientations.[12]

Parsons' emphasis on congruence and consistency has been subjected to much criticism. Gideon Sjoberg (pp. 339–345 in Demerath and Peterson, eds., 1967), for

[12] Dealing with inconsistencies at the cultural level is a major focus of Margaret Archer's (1988) more recent perspective on cultural elaboration and change. Archer's perspective on culture will be reviewed in more detail in Chap. 19.

example, suggested that social systems may have contradictory functional requirements involving inconsistent values. To illustrate, a social system may place a high value on equality at the same time that it also places a high value on providing rewards consistent with individuals' accomplishment when levels of achievement clearly differ among different people. Both of these values may be important but for different functional requirements. Sjoberg suggests that a dialectical type of analysis can help direct attention to such internal strains and conflicts.

Since functional analysis can be applied to different groups and organizations within society, strains and conflicts may be expected as these groups and organizations seek to fulfill their own functional requirements, sometimes in competition with one another and with the overall society's functional requirements. This means that mechanisms for resolving conflicts must be considered. Moreover, socialization is never so complete that individuals' needs and motives always correspond 100% with the role requirements and value orientations of the society. Because of the strains and tensions that exist between social expectations and individuals' needs and impulses, mechanisms of social control are needed to deal with deviant or rebellious behavior when it occurs (Parsons, 1951:249–325). Parsons' functional analysis grows out of his analysis of the "human condition" and the need for people to cooperate in adapting to their environment in order to survive. To meet the basic needs of society the following specific types of structures should be expected to be found in some form in any society. (The following discussion of these structures is drawn from Parsons, 1951:153–167.)

Kinship Structures—concerned with the regulation of sexual expression plus the care and training of the young. Since infants and young children are unable to survive on their own for several years after birth, their ability to function as members of society requires extensive socialization. In modern societies socialization also occurs within the specialized educational establishment.

Instrumental Achievement Structures and Stratification—needed to channel individuals' motivational energy to accomplish tasks necessary for maintaining the overall welfare of society in accordance with its shared values. To motivate the actions needed, rewards are provided in proportion to members' contributions. In this way the stratification system is linked with instrumental achievement. In America (and other modem societies), it is through the occupational structure that instrumental achievement activities are organized. The distribution of money, prestige, and power are coupled closely with the occupational structure within the economic system and other institutions as well. This explanation of stratification has been criticized as justifying inequality and reflecting an unrealistic view of which contributions to society are most valuable or essential. For example, are the contributions of top athletic stars more valuable than the contributions of school teachers? The dynamics of market systems and socioeconomic class structures, as discussed in the last chapter, may be more crucial than the functional importance of a particular role in explaining social and economic inequalities.

Territoriality, Force, and the Integration of the Power System—the need for some form of territorial organization for controlling internal conflict, developing policies for relating to other societies, and territorial defense. This means that all societies must have some form of political organization and systems for internal and external defense (law enforcement and military organizations).

Religion and Value Integration—the requirement to define cultural values and reinforce commitment to them. Religion has traditionally provided the overarching cultural worldview that gives ultimate significance to the society's shared value system. Even when traditional religions undergo change or deterioration, it is important for societies to develop some type of shared values and ultimate meaning system and to reinforce people's commitments to these shared orientations. This applies particularly to those involving basic moral codes that govern individuals' transactions and relations with one another.

In line with the differences in the contributions that various structures make in fulfilling these requirements, there will be corresponding variations in the pattern variables manifested in them. For example, kinship systems will be characterized by affectivity, particularism, ascription, diffuseness, and a collectivity orientation. Instrumental achievement structures in modern societies, in contrast, are more likely to reflect affective neutrality, universalism, achievement, specificity, and a self-orientation. However, the extent to which these variables are involved in instrumental achievement will be heavily influenced by the degree to which instrumental achievement is structurally segregated from the kinship system. If instrumental achievement is carried out within the context of the kinship system (as in many primitive societies or in a family business enterprise in contemporary society), these patterns are likely to be undermined by the conflicting dynamics of kinship ties.

The AGIL Framework

Parsons and his colleagues gradually expanded the strategy of functional analysis to other types of social systems, including dyadic relations, small groups, families, and complex organizations. This modified form is more systematic in identifying functional requirements of all types of social systems and also more abstract in analyzing the dynamic interrelations between the component parts (or subsystems) of the system in question. This revised version is referred to as the AGIL model; the acronym refers to generic requirements faced by all types of social systems. These expanded requirements are as follows:

A—Adaptation to the environment: transforming the material environment to meet needs and to cope with environmental conditions that cannot be changed.

G—Goal attainment: deciding on collective goals (not individual goals) and mobilizing resources to achieve them.

I—Integration: coordinating the actions of the various "parts" of the system, including individual members and other subsystems.

L—Latent pattern maintenance: maintaining and reinforcing commitments to underlying cultural values and motivation to conform.

The expansion of Parsons' functionalist perspective was related to his collaboration with Robert F. Bales, a Harvard colleague who analyzed the way small task groups in a laboratory setting usually went through a series of predictable phases during the course of a typical meeting. These phases were divided into two broad areas: the **instrumental task** area—adaptation and goal attainment—and the **socioemotional** area—integration and latent pattern maintenance (Parsons et al., 1953:112)[13] Despite the obvious differences between Bales' laboratory task groups and the overall society, Parsons and his colleagues suggested that the phases of Bales' small groups could be explained in the same way as the institutional structures of the overall society. In other words, the basic institutions of society and the phases observed in these small laboratory groups could both be seen as fulfilling their underlying functional requirements as social systems (Parsons et al., 1953).

This AGIL framework is used in most of Parsons' subsequent writings (e.g., Parsons, pp. 30–79 in Parsons et al., eds., 1961). Along with the pattern variables, it was highly influential at the time and continues to be regarded as the most distinctive feature of his structural/functional theory. However, the specific meaning of each of the functional requirements denoted in the AGIL model may vary for different types of social systems. These requirements are further elaborated below and also related to Parsons' earlier voluntaristic theory of social action.

Adaptation—All social systems must cope with their physical and social environment. For small groups, the environment would include the larger institutional setting, and for total societies it would include other societies plus the physical or geographical setting. Two dimensions of this requirement may be distinguished. First, there must be "an accommodation of the system to inflexible 'reality demands' " imposed by the environment (or, to use Parsons' earlier terminology, to the "conditions" of action). Second, there may be some type of "active transformation of the situation external to the system." (Parsons et al., 1953:183) This involves utilizing resources available in the environment as the "means" for accomplishing some goal. However, any particular set of means (or resources) may be used for a variety of goals; thus the procurement of means and the accomplishment of goals are analytically distinct. (In everyday life, deciding on strategies to try to earn money is not the same as deciding how to spend it.)

Goal Attainment—This requirement grows out of Parsons' contention that action is goal directed. In this context, the concern is **not** limited to personal goals but also includes the collective goals individuals share as members of the system. Actual goal achievement represents a kind of intrinsically gratifying culmination of action following the preparatory adaptive activity (such as procuring resources). In the mean/ends framework, goal achievement is the end, while the earlier adaptive activity is the means for achievement (Parsons et al., 1953:184, see also p. 88). At

---

[13] These general areas were further subdivided into numerous specific categories that could be used to classify each member's utterances, both positive and negative. For our purposes it is not necessary to discuss the details of these categories or the specific sequence of stages that were observed.

both the individual and the social system levels, there are numerous, sometimes conflicting goals that might be desired. Thus the goal attainment functional requirement will involve making decisions regarding the priority of different goals. For social systems this is essentially a political process.

Integration—To function effectively, social systems must have some solidarity among the individuals involved, and their activities must be coordinated in some fashion for maintaining social order and achieving other desired outcomes, both individual and collective. The integrative problem refers to the need for appropriate socioemotional attachments and willingness to cooperate in coordinating their interdependent and mutually supportive lines of action. Socioemotional bonds must not be wholly contingent on personal benefits received; otherwise, social solidarity and willingness to cooperate would be much more precarious, since they would be based on individuals' personal self-interests, which often leads to conflict.[14]

Latent Pattern Maintenance—The concept of latency suggests a suspension of interaction. Members of any social system are subject to fatigue and satiation as well as the demands of other social systems (or subsystems) in which they may be involved. Therefore, all social systems must provide periods when members are temporarily relieved of the obligations of their roles in the system. During this period of latency, however, their commitment to the system must be maintained and sometimes reinforced. In some cases special mechanisms may be developed to help restore motivational energy and to renew or reinforce commitment to shared cultural values and norms. For large-scale systems, such as total societies, this may take the form of collective rituals such as holiday celebrations like Thanksgiving or July 4 celebrations. For smaller systems, other types of rituals may be followed, such as birthday celebrations, for example. Such rituals also help to reinforce members' socioemotional bonds and shared moral values, thereby reinforcing their underlying motivational commitments.[15]

It is usually not possible to give priority to all four functional requirements simultaneously. In small groups, the dynamics of sequential phases make it possible to shift from one requirement to another. Thus the adaptive requirement of obtaining necessary resources and information occurs **prior** to concentrating on goal accomplishment. The focus on goals typically requires deferring gratification and postponing concerns with emotional solidarity. Goal accomplishment is often then followed by an emphasis on socioemotional integration and solidarity. For the overall society and other large-scale complex systems, these requirements are allocated to distinct functional subsystems (Parsons and Smelser, 1956). This means that the major institutions of society may be analyzed in terms of their specialized contributions to these functional requirements.

In collaboration with Neil J. Smelser, Parsons used this framework in an intensive analysis of the economic system, including its internal processes as well as

[14] This emphasis clearly differs from the underlying assumptions of the rational choice perspective.

[15] The function of collective rituals in reinforcing commitment to shared values and normative patterns was central in Durkheim's analysis of religion.

the differentiation of the economy from other institutions (Parsons and Smelser, 1956). This long-term differentiation process involved the shift from household to factory production in the early stages of the development of the industrial capitalist economy. In this perspective the economy is viewed as the institution with primary responsibility for fulfilling the **adaptive** functional requirement for the society (Parsons, 1961a; Parsons and Smelser, 1956:20). It is through the economy that raw materials are transformed into resources that can be used for a variety of personal and collective goals, including, for example, meeting individuals' basic biological needs as behavioral organisms (food, shelter, security, and so on).

Similarly, the goal attainment process involves the polity, or political system. The overall goals of society must be distinguished in this framework from individuals' personal goals or the goals of particular organizations within society. Individuals' goals relate to societal goals primarily through their citizenship role. For large-scale and complex societies, however, major decisions regarding societal goals are influenced as much by influential collectivities, such as political parties and various interest groups, as by individual citizens. Large-scale private organizations (corporate actors) may also exert influence on collective goals—sometimes in inappropriate ways that benefit themselves more than the public welfare. Ultimate authority (and power) for mobilizing resources to achieve societal goals is a major responsibility of the various levels of government. In a democratic society, establishing goal priorities is a complex process that involves the political strategies of struggle and conflict, negotiation and compromise.

The functional requirement of integration does not correspond to any specific institutional structure as clearly as adaptation and goal attainment. Integration refers to the need for sufficient solidarity to insure that members are willing to cooperate and try to avoid disruptive conflict as they coordinate and align their actions. Although conflict can never be eliminated, when it occurs it must be carried out within some form of regulatory framework and not be allowed to degenerate into anarchy. The legal system and social control processes deal specifically with the integrative problem, especially when deviance or other breakdowns occur (Parsons, 1961a:40). On a more positive note, all of the normative patterns that encourage and reinforce norms of mutual respect, tact, and courtesy in interpersonal relationships contribute to social integration. Religious institutions contribute to this function by strengthening general ideals for social life, including concerns for the welfare of others that helps restrain egoistic impulses. Even though people may often fail to live up to the moral ideals their religion promotes, many of these ideals (such as the Golden Rule) are reinforced regularly through religious rituals designed to strengthen people's shared beliefs and moral commitments (Parsons, 1961a:40–41).

The latent pattern maintenance function also is related to promotion and reinforcement of commitment to moral values as expressed in the ideals of how people are expected to relate to one another. Another important aspect of this function involves efforts to deal with fundamental questions regarding the ultimate meaning and purpose of life and insuring that social processes are in place to reinforce the basic cultural worldview shared by members of society. As with the integrative problem, several institutional structures are involved with this function. The religious institution is highly relevant because of its promotion and reinforcement of ultimate values, moral codes, and meaning systems. The educational system also contributes in a major way to latent pattern maintenance by helping to socialize the "new recruits" of each new generation through transmitting the basic cultural patterns that are needed to participate in social life and to prepare to be able to contribute to society as they meet their individual needs and goals. Families are also involved as they socialize their children in the implicitly understood and commonly accepted rules and patterns of social life.

The family is also crucial with respect to the specific notion of latency. Individuals' participation in society through their occupational roles is typically suspended or "deactivated" within the context of the family. Tensions and fatigue that are built up in the process of fulfilling occupational obligations are alleviated by rest and relaxation at home at the end of the day, on weekends, and during vacations when occupational roles are latent. Through such "tension management," motivational energy is replenished for eventual resumption of occupational (or other societal) tasks. At the same time, however, the family is also a system in its own right and therefore has its own functional requirements, including adaptive and goal attainment tasks.

Figure 12.1 (below) summarizes the way the four major functional requirements in Parsons' AGIL model are fulfilled through the major institutional structures of society. Despite the emphasis on institutional specialization in Parsons' AGIL model, the linkages between institutional structures and functional requirements often seem fuzzy in the real world. In reality, any social structure may contribute at some level to the fulfillment of any of the functional requirements. For example, even though business corporations are primarily part of the economy and contribute to the adaptation requirement, they may also influence the political process of defining societal goals. This would occur, for example, when manufacturers of military supplies seek to increase the priority given to national defense, as suggested by the idea of the "military-industrial" complex.[16] It also occurs when large

Adaptation (Economy)	Goal Attainment (Polity)
Integration (Law enforcement and social control; Religion, Families)	Latent Pattern Maintenance (Religion, Education, Families)

Fig. 12.1 Functional Requirements and Social Institutions

[16] The ability of large corporations to have "too much" influence on political decisions in ways that undermine the overall welfare of society is recognized as a major problem in democratic societies.

corporations seek to influence legislation that can affect their interests (either appropriately or inappropriately). Similarly, government itself engages in various types of economic activity, such as contracting with private business firms to construct and maintain highways and other infrastructure facilities and providing economic resources to individuals in need through various social welfare programs. Also, even though families are involved primarily in latent pattern maintenance subsystem and integration, they also perform economic functions (such as purchasing goods for consumption) and political functions (participating as citizens through paying taxes and voting).

Subsystem (Institutional) Interchanges

The dynamics of social systems can be analyzed in terms of input and output transactions among their different subsystems and with the environment. The transactions across subsystem boundaries employ generalized symbolic media of exchange (Parsons in Parsons et al., 1953:31–62). Perhaps the most common and easily understood example of such a medium of exchange is money. The significance of money obviously is not its intrinsic or physical worth but its symbolic representation of economic value and its use in facilitating market transactions. In analyzing the relationships between the economy and other institutional subsystems of society, Parsons and Smelser (1956) developed the idea of a double interchange across subsystem boundaries. The process can be illustrated in the relations between families (as part of the latent pattern maintenance subsystem) and the economy (adaptive subsystem). In the first exchange, household members contribute to the economic system through their occupational roles in exchange for financial compensation. The money earned is then used in a second type of exchange with other economic structures, particularly retail establishments, to obtain goods and services to maintain their household and meet its members' needs.

To parallel money as a medium of exchange in the economy, Parsons (1969:352–404) suggested that power serves as the general medium of exchange in the goal attainment subsystem. Power resembles money in many ways. It can be transferred from one person or unit to another (as suggested in our Chap. 9 review of Coleman's perspective on the delegation of authority), and it can be used for a variety of collective purposes. Also, as we know from Blau's analysis of imbalanced exchanges, the emergence of power structures can be crucial in achieving collective goals.

Although the notion of distinct exchange media is not as fully developed for the other two functional subsystems, Parsons (1969:405–438) suggested that influence (as opposed to power) may be seen as a general medium of exchange that is relevant to the integrative subsystem, and that value commitments are generalized media of exchange for the latent pattern maintenance system (Parsons, 1969:439–472). Influence is often linked with social approval as a general medium of exchange that can be used to reinforce a variety of behaviors. The expectation of receiving social approval (or avoiding disapproval) often underlies people's ability to exert influence on one another. A social system in which people are able to influence one another in multiple and mutually beneficial ways in exchange for social approval would thereby demonstrate high a level of solidarity or social integration.

Similarly, value commitments may be linked with the concept of prestige. Individuals who are above average in terms of achievement, or in their level of conformity to shared norms and values, are rewarded with prestige, which can be regarded as a higher-than-average level of approval and respect. In contrast to social approval, prestige cannot be shared equally without undermining its meaning. Even so, the recognition that people often receive for their outstanding achievements may be expected to help reinforce the commitments of others to the underlying values that these exemplary achievements represent. Indeed, the celebration of noteworthy accomplishments often provides opportunities for ritualistic reaffirmation of shared values. Everyday examples include selection of superior students for the honor roll, awards of military honors to those who exhibited courage in the face of danger, and choosing the "most valuable player" after an athletic victory. Prestige can thus be considered a generalized medium of exchange for rewarding important above-average or outstanding role performances.

The concepts of functional requirements and subsystem interchanges can be applied at different levels, depending on the focus of analysis. To illustrate, within the economy interchanges can be identified between different sectors, such as between banking and manufacturing. Or, within a particular firm, interchanges can be identified between different divisions or departments or between hierarchical levels. At the lowest level, such interchanges take the form of exchange transactions between performers of particular roles as they act as agents for the groups or organizations that make up the institutional structures of society, or some segment thereof, in which they are involved.

Specifying levels of analysis is important because all of the organizations and groups that make up society can be viewed as systems in their own right, with their own specific AGIL requirements. Moreover, participants in these various subsystems and sub-subsystems are likely to have vested interests in their own particular function. This point is important in responding to critics who claim that Parsons limited his analysis to harmonious cooperation reflecting high levels of value consensus. Recognition of multiple functional requirements among different systems and subsystems opens the possibility of conflict among groups or organizations whose functions differ. All of the interrelated processes whereby different subsystems of society try to satisfy their particular functional requirements suggest an image of social systems as being highly complex, with multiple and sometimes conflicting dynamics among different levels and different subsystems. Theoretically, the process of identifying various levels of systems, subsystems, and sub-subsystems could be extended from the major institutional structures of society to the micro level of face-to-face relations. For practical purposes, however, it is usually sufficient to identify three levels: (1) the primary system of reference; (2) the larger system of which it is a part; and (3) the primary subsystems of which it is composed.

Hierarchy of Cultural Control

In addition to their internal interchanges, social systems are involved with interchanges with their environment. The environment of social systems includes not only the material or physical environment, but also the personality systems of members, the cultural system, and even the behavioral organisms of participants (Parsons, 1961a:36; 1966:10–16). The behavioral organism is considered part of the environment because the basic constituent units of social systems are not individual bodies as such but patterns of social actions that are organized through the institutionalized roles associated with different social positions. Individuals' bodies are linked to social systems through their role performances. As far as any particular social system is concerned, even the roles that individuals have in other systems are part of the environment. For example, the family roles of a business firm's employees would be part of the firm's environment, as well as the biological characteristics and personality patterns that are not relevant to employees' occupational roles.

The cultural system is also considered part of the environment in an analytical sense. Culture is an extremely broad concept that includes various forms of knowledge, art, beliefs, ideals, values, norms, customs, techniques, tools, and many other material and nonmaterial products that people construct and use as members of society. However, the degree to which cultural patterns are employed in people's behavior, or institutionalized in the social system, is always a matter of degree. For example, abstract cultural ideals regarding equality are inconsistent with the actual socioeconomic class structure, even though appeals to such ideals may be made to try to inspire efforts to reduce the level of inequality. Although Parsons' primary focus was the social system, he also highlighted its dynamic relations to culture, personality patterns, and the behavioral organism as analytically distinct systems.

Consistent with his 1937 voluntaristic theory of action, Parsons' AGIL perspective on social systems emphasized that shared values and norms are crucial in regulating and controlling people's social behavior. After 1961 he treated the relationships among all the different systems of action identified above in terms of a cybernetic "hierarchy of control." This control involves a flow of information from the cultural system to the social system to the personality system to the behavioral organism (Parsons, 1961a:37–38; 1966:10–16). This influence from the cultural system involves primarily the latent pattern maintenance function of the social system, though cultural inputs of various types (knowledge, techniques, beliefs, values, norms, etc.) are also employed in regulating the fulfillment of all of the other functional requirements of the social system as well. The energy required for action flows in a reverse direction, deriving ultimately from the capabilities and potentialities of the behavioral organism. The need for human beings to deal with the physical environment as biological organisms involves the adaptive function of social systems. These relationships can be expressed in the hierarchical arrangement diagramed on p. 328. (Fig. 12.2).

Culture provides the basic orientation that guides behavior, but this control must always be exerted within the constraints of the lower-level systems. At a mundane level, in an athletic contest like basketball, for example, the cultural values and norms require players to position themselves to take shots and hit baskets to earn

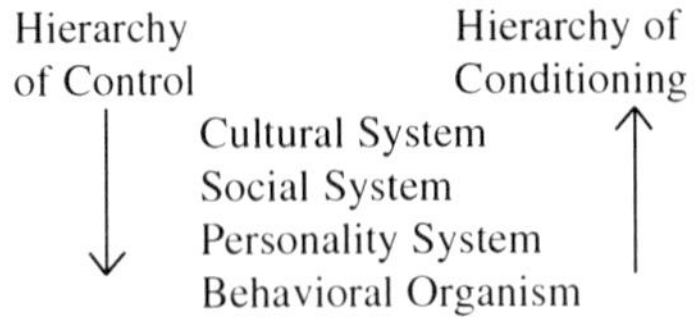

Fig. 12.2 Relations among the Four Different Systems of Action (Adapted from Parsons, 1966, Table 1, p. 28)

points, but these efforts frequently fail, due either to mistakes or to the opposing team's defense. Also, in every game one team must lose, despite the cultural goal of winning—though both losers and winners are expected to conform to the cultural ideals of good sportsmanship. On a more general level, the abstract cultural ideal of equality is inconsistent with the pattern of distributing rewards in proportion to the value of individuals' contributions or accomplishments. In Parsons' theory, distributing rewards in proportion to achievements is important for reinforcing people's motivation to perform their institutional roles, despite the inequality that results. Similarly, the abstract cultural ideal of a close-knit, *Gemeinschaft*-type community is limited in large-scale systems by the scarcity of time and energy that would be needed to establish and maintain the innumerable socioemotional bonds that would be required. Although people's general orientations may indeed be shaped in a general way by the abstract cultural values and ideals they have internalized, the implementation of these values and ideals is limited by the constraints of multiple lower-level systems in which different people's definitions of appropriate behavior and the requirements that must be fulfilled are often in conflict.

Structural Differentiation in the Evolution of Modern Society

Because of its high level of generality, the AGIL model can readily be used to compare different types of systems or different stages in the history of a society. A key issue in such an analysis is the extent of structural differentiation among the different units (or subsystems) that are involved in performing all of the various tasks that are relevant to the fulfillment of the four primary functional requirements discussed above. With low differentiation, a limited number of structures fulfill multiple functions. In pre-industrial societies, the extended family had primary responsibilities for economic production, social welfare, some aspects of defense and social control, performance of religious rituals, and education of the young. All of these required functions were thus performed in a single type of structural unit, or perhaps a limited number of relatively simple units. In modern urban-industrial societies, however, these functions are performed by different institutions. This means that they exhibit a high degree of structural differentiation (Parsons, 1961a:44–60; 1966:18–25). This process is related to the expansion in the division of labor as analyzed by Durkheim, the long-term outcome of which is increased complexity and institutional specialization.

Historically, the process of differentiation has involved the removal of various functions from the family institution to more specialized institutions. Some examples include the transfer of productive functions to specialized economic structures (such as business firms and factories), plus the assignment of many aspects of the socialization and education process to the specialized structures of formal education. This process has left the family as a more specialized institution, with its major remaining contributions including socialization of the young (a responsibility shared with schools), provision of sexual gratification, and fulfillment of tension release and socioemotional support (Parsons and Bales, 1955; see also Burgess et al. [1963] for a similar analysis).

Another important example of differentiation is the structural separation of religion from the state (as expressed in the United States Constitution and the Bill of Rights). This means that the political organization of society is no longer fused with the maintenance of ultimate value commitments as defined by dominant religious traditions. These value orientations still serve as an important source of legitimacy for the political system and sometimes exert major influence on societal goals. However, structural differentiation means that the political establishment is more "on its own." Value commitments and religious beliefs do not "automatically" translate into support for the existing political structures or policies. It also means that universalistic religions that transcend political boundaries are better able to promote the idea of a universal moral community that includes all people, regardless of their nationality.

Differentiation between religion and politics also means that religion has the potential autonomy to stand on its own in criticizing political policies. This implies a structural source for potential tension between the religious institution and the political establishment. The result in some cases is that abstract religious values can employed as a catalyst for social and political change. However, if such efforts lead to imposition of specific religious norms, of the acquisition of political power by religious authorities, the result would be a reduction in the differentiation between religion and politics. For example, contemporary Islamic societies in the Middle East in which religious leaders also function as political leaders reveal a low level of differentiation between religion and politics.[17]

On another level of analysis, the concept of differentiation was used in Parsons and Bales' (1955) analysis of the internal structure of families in modern societies. Their perspective reflected the historical context of the time, but is less relevant to contemporary dual career families. The focus of their analysis was that the father's role and the mother's role in the socialization of children and the maintenance of the household had become more differentiated, with the father specializing in the

---

[17] Although much less extreme, part of the dynamic of contemporary religious fundamentalism in the United States can be seen as an effort to use the political process to inject specific religious beliefs and norms into political decisions enforced by law.

instrumental task area and the mother in the socioemotional area. In contrast to the historical period in which Parsons and his collaborators did their analysis, the ideal for many people today is for husbands and wives to share in all aspects of family life, with both having careers and earning an income and both involved in household maintenance and child care. Such a process represents a reversal of the process of differentiation.

The process of structural differentiation was a key element in Parsons' perspective on long-range social change at least since his 1956 book with Neil Smelser, *Economy and Society*. His analysis of the process of differentiation is consistent with the image of long-range historical change reflected in classical theorists such as Durkheim, with his focus on the expansion in the division of labor. Additional contemporary examples of this process can be seen in the proliferation of different medical specialties and in the development of specialized areas of scholarly research in different academic disciplines. However, instead of seeing differentiation as an inevitable linear process, probably a better strategy is to see it as an optional pattern that may expand in some areas for a time but may sometimes be reversed. Under some circumstances, functions may be combined that had previously been separated. For example, business firms that adopt "family friendly" policies by having day-care facilities on the premises may be seen as undermining the differentiation between business and childhood socialization. Similarly, employees who utilize new electronic communication technology to work at home are reversing the long-term differentiation between work and home. Within the economic system, the expansion of business enterprises through corporate mergers reverses the pattern of increasing differentiation by bringing disparate enterprises together into a single corporate structure, though the resulting internal divisions of such conglomerate structures may continue to be highly differentiated and retain considerable autonomy. In academic life, the development of interdisciplinary areas of study may be seen as going counter to the long-term trend of increasing specialization and fragmentation.

Despite Parsons' analysis of the evolutionary process of differentiation, his emphasis on social order and equilibrium led to much criticism that he neglected to deal adequately with the topic of social change. Perhaps partly in response, Parsons eventually began to focus more explicitly on long-range social change (Parsons, 1964, 1966). The result was a modern evolutionary theory that incorporated themes developed earlier by Spencer (increased heterogeneity of social structure), Durkheim (increased specialization and growth in organic solidarity), and Weber (increased rationality as reflected in bureaucratization). The long-term process of structural differentiation was seen as having been facilitated and supported by a series of "evolutionary universals" that include: (1) emergence of a stratification system distinct from kinship; (2) cultural legitimation of emergent political structure; (3) bureaucratic organization; (4) a money system and impersonal market network; (5) universalistic norms; and (6) patterns of democratic association (Parsons, 1964). Although we will not analyze these processes in detail, they were important for the long-range course of social evolution in Parsons' view because they enhanced the overall adaptive capacity of society.

Parsons later developed a set of four "developmental processes" that were linked with the four functional requirements specified in the AGIL model (Parsons, 1971:11). These processes, and their linkages with the AGIL model, are as follows:

Adaptive upgrading: Adaptation.
Differentiation: Goal attainment.
Inclusion: Integration.
Value generalization: Latent pattern maintenance.

The process of adaptive upgrading involves the increased efficiency and productivity that is made possible in the economic system (and other systems as well) through specialization and technological development. The process of differentiation is linked with goal attainment, though it is not limited to the political system (which is the primary societal institution involved in goal attainment). Differentiation can, of course, be applied to political structures, both in terms of their differentiation from other institutions and in terms of their internal differentiation (such as the separation of legislative, executive, and judicial functions of government). On a more general level, however, differentiation is associated with goal attainment through the establishment of specialized collectivities (organizations) oriented toward a variety of collective goals (Parsons, 1961b:16–58, especially p. 18).[18] The process of inclusion helps prevent differentiation from leading to fragmentation. Of special significance in this regard is the organization of society on a democratic basis. The notion that government is expected to represent the interests of all members and all segments of society is seen as enhancing loyalty to the "societal community" as such, independently of other loyalties based on ascriptive bonds (race, ethnicity, and local communities) or other associational involvements. Finally, the developmental process of value generalization refers to the tendency for shared values to become more abstract as differentiation increases. Simple societies with a low differentiation may be united by specific normative patterns shared by the entire society. But in a highly differentiated society, specific normative behaviors vary in different institutional settings. Thus the values that are shared must become more abstract and general so as to be relevant for a great variety of normative patterns in different institutional contexts.

Parsons applied his evolutionary model primarily to the long-range historical development of modern Western societies. He began with "primitive" societies and then dealt with the "historic" intermediate empires of China, India, the Islamic empires, and the Roman empire. Israel and Greece were treated as "seed-bed" societies because of the crucial cultural innovations they produced that later contributed to evolutionary developments in other societies. This evolutionary process culminates in modern urban-industrial capitalistic democracies, with the United

[18] Parsons' focus on formal organizations as being oriented explicitly toward some form of goal achievement is consistent with Coleman's analysis of corporate actors as discussed in Chap. 10.

States identified, in 1971, as the "lead" society in this process (Parsons, 1971:114).[19] Parsons' glowing description of the United States in this context seemed strangely inconsistent with social and political developments of the late 1960s and early 1970s. In 1968, only 3 years before the publication of Parsons' "lead society" designation, Democratic candidate Robert Kennedy was assassinated, violence broke out between anti-Vietnam war demonstrators and the police at the Democratic National Convention in Chicago, and former Alabama Governor George Wallace (known for his opposition to racial desegregation) ran for president as a third party candidate. In Parsons' long-range evolutionary perspective, perhaps these events could be seen as short-term anomalies.

Parsons has frequently been criticized for neglecting social conflict and change. Perhaps his critics were reacting in part to the conservative ideological implications of his analysis (for example, see Gouldner, 1970). As will be shown in our later discussion of critical theory, arguments could certainly be made for an alternative and less benign interpretation. And despite Parsons' preoccupation with explaining social order, his evolutionary theory also dealt explicitly with social change. However, the crucial role of conflict in stimulating change is neglected. Also, as noted earlier, all of the institutional structures that make up society may be seen as systems in their own right, each with its functional requirements in an environment where resources are scarce and competition and conflict are part of the picture as much as value consensus and harmonious cooperation.

The basic argument in Parsons' perspective is not that societies can eliminate conflict, but that the social order requires conflict to be carried out within a framework of values and both legal regulations and informal norms that prevent it from being overly destructive to the social order. Even when there is widespread consensus regarding general values, disagreements often develop over the question of how these values should actually be implemented. This would suggest that despite the lack of a strong emphasis on conflict in Parsons' overall perspective, conflict can nevertheless be incorporated into his functional theory. In fact, as illustrated by the United States civil rights movement, conflict may sometimes stimulate the type of social change that leads to greater institutionalization of widely professed values.

Human beings' efforts to align their behavior and their social life with transcendental cultural values and abstract normative ideals illustrate the importance of the analytical distinction between the social system and the cultural system. Such idealistic efforts must always work within the parameters of the biological characteristics of human nature, however, and the dependence of human organisms on the

[19] Parsons wrote: "The United States' new type of societal community, more than any other single factor, justifies our assigning it the lead in the latest phase of modernization. We have suggested that it synthesizes to a high degree the equality of opportunity stressed in socialism. It presupposes a market system, a strong legal order relatively independent of government, and a 'nation-state' emancipated from specific religious and ethnic control. The educational revolution has been considered as a crucial innovation, especially with regard to the emphasis on the associational patterns, as well as on the openness of opportunity. Above all, American society has gone farther than any comparable large-scale society in its dissociation from the older ascriptive inequalities and the institutionalization of a basically egalitarian pattern." (Parsons, 1971:114)

material and energy resources provided by the physical environment. We look briefly in the next section at the perspective Parsons developed regarding the way human beings' social actions reflect the biological conditions of their existence as well as the transcendental world of ultimate reality.

Human Life, Social Action, and Ultimate Reality

Throughout his career, Talcott Parsons' work reflects a commitment to developing a comprehensive and systematic analytical framework within which different levels of social reality can be classified and their interrelations explored. Near the end of his career he expanded his basic framework even further to cover virtually the entire universe, ranging from the "Physico-Chemical System" of the material world to the "Telic System" of transcendental meaning at the level of what might be considered ultimate reality (Parsons, 1978:352–433). This expansion was the topic of the final chapter of Parsons' last book, entitled *Action Theory and the Human Condition* and published in 1978, just one year before his death. In this enlarged perspective, the action system itself becomes only one of four different systems; the others include the telic system, the physico-chemical system, and the human organic system (the latter corresponding to the behavioral organism in his earlier framework). The relations between these systems and the AGIL framework are as follows (Parsons, 1978:361–367):

Adaptation: physico-chemical system
Goal attainment: human organic system
Integration: action system
Latent pattern maintenance: telic system

A large part of his analysis is devoted to developing analytical subdivisions within these systems and explaining their various input and output transactions with one another and within their various subsystems. The survival of the human organism requires input/output exchanges with the physical environment (eating and drinking and eliminating human waste), while the development of the human personality involves incorporating cultural orientations regarding the ultimate meaning of life and death provided from the transcendent realm of the telic system. For both levels (physical survival and ultimate meaning), individuals are immersed in a social world consisting of symbolic meanings that are reflected in their actions and interactions. Parsons even discussed the basic senses involved in perception, plus the parts of the human body involved in sensory pleasure, biological survival, and reproduction, through his AGIL framework (Parsons, 1978:414–433).

Except for this last chapter, Parsons' final book is based largely on previous publications. Since religion deals explicitly with issues and questions related to the ultimate meaning of life, it is interesting to note that Parsons devotes a large part of his sociological analysis of religion to interpreting various religious beliefs of the Judeo-Christian heritage as symbolic portrayals of the underlying biological conditions of human existence. In a chapter (with co-authors Renée C. Fox and Victor M. Lidz) entitled "The 'Gift of Life' and Its Reciprocation," the biblical story of Adam and Eve is interpreted as symbolic of the close connection between death and sexual reproduction (Parsons, 1978:267–270). The expulsion of Adam and Eve from the Garden of Eden for eating the forbidden fruit was closely linked to their awareness that they would eventually die, as well as the initiation of their sexual union leading to offspring. Part of the human condition is awareness of the "knowledge of good and evil" (which implies the ability to make choices, unlike nonhuman animals), but the expulsion from Eden meant that human creatures would not live forever and thus be like God. Part of the knowledge the couple gained could also have been the knowledge of their own future death—a form of knowledge that (as far as we know) differentiates human beings from nonhuman species. But despite this knowledge of their own individual mortality, they also are aware that human life will continue in their offspring. In the meantime, human beings have no choice but to engage as biological organisms in the ongoing struggle for survival—thereby facing the always challenging functional problem of adaptation—even as they struggle also to achieve a sense of meaning and significance through their spiritual connection to ultimate reality. To complement this picture of constant toil and eventual death, the Christian belief system regarding the incarnation of the creator God in human flesh (through Jesus Christ) can be seen as a symbolic representation of how the ultimate reality of the divine world (or telic system) is infused into the mundane and precarious world of organic and social life, thereby giving human life transcendent meaning.

Parsons' analysis of how religious beliefs symbolized the human condition was limited to the Judeo-Christian tradition (Parsons, 1978:264–322). His interpretations are highly speculative and clearly have theological and philosophical implications that seem far removed from most forms of sociological analysis.[20] Nevertheless, these interpretations illustrate a strategy for cultural analysis that takes the content and underlying symbolic meanings of religious beliefs seriously. In other religious traditions as well, specific beliefs and practices could presumably be analyzed in terms of how they seek to relate the ultimate (telic) or transcendental meaning of the human condition to human beings' basic biological conditions. By relating religious beliefs to the biological conditions of human life—birth, death, productive labor, and reproduction—Parsons demonstrates that the relation between culture and biology consists of far more than the mundane pragmatic process whereby human beings simply adapt as biological organisms to their material and social environment.

Parsons also pointed out the importance of sex and age as biological variables that provide an important part of the basic foundation for understanding the human condition as well as for establishing various patterns of social organization. The

---

[20] It should be noted that Parsons' interpretation of these various religious beliefs does not focus on their literal truth value. Instead, the goal is to show how these beliefs may be seen as highly symbolic representations of the conditions of human existence, particularly with regard to issues of life and death.

biological differentiation between males and females is obviously important for reproducing the next generation, while age is related to the trajectory of human beings' biological development over the life course. Both processes—sexual reproduction and biological growth and development (and eventual death)—are fundamental life processes that humans share with other species and which do not depend for their reality on social definitions, even though these processes are subject to highly elaborate social interpretations and cultural meanings. Parsons also highlighted Freud's perspective regarding the way individuals learn to manage their biological energy and natural impulses in the process of becoming socialized, plus the largely unconscious influence of human beings' genetic code on the underlying characteristics of human nature (Parsons, 1978:411, n.122). The relevance of the genetic code in understanding human behavior will be discussed in a subsequent chapter on sociobiology.

Summary

This chapter summarized the contributions of Talcott Parsons, at one time the leading representative of structural/functional theory in American sociology. Parsons' earliest work was devoted to developing a voluntaristic model of social action. His goal was to reconcile the opposing views of positivism (including both utilitarianism and an "antiintellectual" branch reflecting the nonrational foundations of social action) and idealism, based on his synthesis of the theories of Alfred Marshall, Vilfredo Pareto, Émile Durkheim, and Max Weber. His fundamental argument was that people make choices, and that the social actions resulting from these choices are both goal oriented and normatively regulated. Also, the environment within which action takes place includes resources used for goal attainment plus conditions to which individuals must adapt.

Alternative orientations toward goals and norms were incorporated in a set of five pattern variables that describe some fundamental choices individuals must make, either implicitly or explicitly, in any social relation. These choices may be seen as elaborating the distinctions implicit in the *Gemeinschaft-Gesellschaft* dichotomy, or the primary group-secondary group dichotomy. The pattern variables can be applied to specific role expectations that are institutionalized in the social system. These expectations reflect the socialization process as this process influences people's motives and needs as well as their shared value orientations.

The next general area of concern was to specify the basic functional requirements of society and to determine how these requirements are met through various institutional structures. The major institutions of society, such as the economy, the polity, family, and religion, are each seen as contributing to the fundamental requirements that must be fulfilled for a society to survive. These include producing and distributing the resources needed for individuals' survival, settling conflicts and deciding on collective goals, socialization of the young, and reinforcing commitments to shared values. The development of the AGIL model expanded the scope of functional analysis by showing how all social systems, ranging from the micro to the macro level, must face the functional requirements of adapting to the environment, deciding on system goals and mobilizing resources for their attainment, integrating individuals through socioemotional bonds and social control mechanisms, and developing and reinforcing underlying cultural values and norms. Social systems are seen as being under the control of cultural values and norms, with the basic energy manifested in action supplied by the behavioral organism and expressed in social roles that are organized within various institutional structures to contribute to the fulfillment of society's functional requirements.

Eventually, Parsons shifted his attention from the structures involved in fulfilling the functional requirements for maintaining social order to an evolutionary model that focused heavily on the process of structural differentiation and related processes of long-range social change. Overall, however, Parsons' structural/functional model of society has generally been regarded as focusing much more heavily on social order and stability than social change. Also, as Parsons' critics have noted, his image of the dynamics of society seems to downplay the pervasiveness and the inevitability of conflict. Thus the stage was set for the emergence of conflict theory as an opposing theoretical perspective.

Near the end of his life Parsons expanded his theoretical framework in an effort to provide an even more comprehensive analysis of the underlying features of the "human condition." In this framework all human action is seen as grounded in the fundamental material conditions of life as well as being oriented toward the level of ultimate or transcendent meaning. The need to deal with the material conditions of life led to a more explicit concern with human beings' underlying biological characteristics. Also, his focus on ultimate meaning systems involved a much stronger concentration on the cultural level than his earlier analysis of social systems. Much of this cultural analysis involved showing how various religious beliefs reflect human beings' biological characteristics, including the basic conditions of life, death, work, and reproduction.

Parsons' image of the harmonious nature of society, plus his style of developing theory on a grand scale, was criticized at the time by Robert Merton, who was influenced by Parsons but advocated a more modest style of functional analysis that would be developed through middle-range theories that were to be less abstract than proposed by Parsons. Although functionalist theory declined significantly in the late 1960s and early 1970s, by the 1980s functionalist-type theories experienced a revival with the development of neofunctionalism. Merton's middle-range functionalism and the new perspectives of neofunctionalism will be presented in the next chapter.

Questions for Study and Discussion

1. Would you agree or disagree with the argument in Parsons' theory that social order requires a high level of correspondence between individuals' motives and needs, other people's role expectations, and widely shared cultural values? Why

or why not? Can you identify situations where this applies (i.e., people are clearly motivated to do what others expect them to do in terms of complying with widely shared cultural values)? On the other hand, can you identify situations where people's motives and other people's expectations are inconsistent—and/or where both may be inconsistent with cultural values? Explain.

2. Discuss the challenges of modern family life (or some other social system with which you are familiar) in terms of the AGIL model. In addition, how might the opposing pairs of pattern variables both be relevant in different types of situations? (For example, in what situations are family members expected to be concerned about their own personal needs as well as the needs of their family)?
3. Drawing on Parsons' analytical distinction between social and cultural systems, explain how specific cultural ideals and values can be used to criticize existing arrangements in the society and to legitimate or justify pressures for such change.
4. Compare Parsons' concept of integration with the concept of social capital as discussed in Chapter 9. In what ways does the challenge of integration apply to all institutional areas of social life (as opposed to being limited to specialized institutions)?
5. Explain how Parson's AGIL framework can be used to analyze key problem areas in American society (such as the threat of terrorism, for example, poverty, immigration policy, moral conflicts, or others that you identify as important).

Chapter 13
Middle-Range Functionalism and Neofunctionalism

No social system is automatically self-sustaining, including society. And no individual's actions within a social system are without consequences for others, whether positive or negative. In everyday life, anyone who has taken on leadership responsibilities in a voluntary organization has to think in terms of motivating its members to do their part to contribute to the organization's survival and success. Even for purely sociable events like a party, it would be highly embarrassing to have things ready and no one shows up—or to have them come and behave in ways that are inappropriate and disruptive. For work groups in organizational settings, employers and supervisors are well aware of the need to motivate members to perform their tasks in a coordinated and cooperative manner. They also are likely to be concerned with preventing behavior that would be disruptive or would undermine the group or prevent it from reaching its goals.

As people participate in various types of collective activities, at least some of their actions may be seen as contributing to the maintenance of the system in which they are involved, enhancing its solidarity and welfare, reinforcing its values, and promoting its progress toward whatever goals it may be pursuing. Many of these positive types of actions are the result of people's intentions as they work together to promote the general welfare while also seeking to satisfy their individual needs and interests. On the other hand, it sometimes happens that people's actions generate negative consequences for others. Such consequences may be unintentional or, in the case of conflict between individuals or groups, they may be intentional. For some actions it is difficult to evaluate whether the positive consequences outweigh the negative consequences and to assess how these different types of consequences are distributed among different groups or different segments of society.

This focus on the consequences of people's actions for the various social systems in which they are involved illustrates a form of functional analysis that is less elaborate than Parsons' abstract model of how individuals' actions in their various roles contribute to society's functional requirements. Although all actions have various consequences, it is always an empirical question as to whether these are beneficial or harmful, and to whom. Some consequences may contribute to the system's functional requirements or the welfare of its members (or some of them). Others may be harmful or disruptive. Functional analysis is not limited to explaining a stable social order but can be expanded to deal with all of the various ways in which the social consequences of our behavior affect other people and the various social systems in which we are involved, whether intended or unintended, beneficial or disruptive.

This chapter moves beyond the dominant image in Parsons' theory of a stable social order characterized by a shared value system that promotes harmonious interdependence. By modifying functional analysis through the perspectives to be reviewed in this chapter, we will see how the social consequences of people's behavior vary greatly for different participants and systems. In addition, although cultural ideals and values may be important in efforts to sustain the social order, they are inadequate by themselves in explaining the dynamics of people's social actions. People's motivations also reflect their interests, and their actions always involve a subjective assessment of how the relevant values and norms apply (or don't apply) to their particular situation. The specific theoretical perspectives to be covered in this chapter are as follows:

- Robert K. Merton's strategy for "middle-range" functional analysis—As explained in Chapter 3, Merton was critical of Parsons' overly abstract "grand" theory, even when functionalism was still dominant. Instead of making claims about functional requirements, his alternative focus involved exploring how individuals' actions contribute to social outcomes that may or may not be consciously intended, both functional and dysfunctional.
- Emergence of the "neofunctional" perspective—Following the decline of functionalism in the late 1960s and early 1970s, functionalism experienced a revival in the 1980s with the development of neofunctionalism. Although the earlier dominance of functional theory was not restored, neofunctionalism is an important contemporary perspective, particularly as represented by the contributions of American sociologist Jeffrey Alexander and German sociologist Richard Münch.
  - Jeffrey Alexander's multidimensional analysis of the interdependent dynamics of social action and order—Alexander emphasizes the challenge of explaining social order, but social processes promoting social order through normative commitments must be balanced by explicit recognition of conflicting interests, environmental conditions and constraints, and the unforeseen contingencies individuals face in dealing with the particular situations in which they find themselves.
  - Richard Münch's multidimensional analysis of social action—As we shall see Münch used Parsons' AGIL perspective to analyze the dynamics of social action in terms of symbolic complexity at the level of meaning and contingency at the level of individuals' choices. His perspective indicates that all actions can be analyzed in terms of their economic, political, socioemotional, and value orientational dimensions.

Robert Merton and Middle-Range Functionalism[1]

During the years that Parsons worked diligently at building his theory, most American sociologists pursued less elaborate goals in linking specific theoretical developments with empirical research. Despite Parsons' influence, the general categories he developed were too abstract to lead clearly to specific research hypotheses, and his substantive analyses seemed to imply support for the status quo, especially when viewed in hindsight. Robert K. Merton was one of many leading mid-twentieth century sociologists who was critical of Parsons' abstract style of theorizing. He was one of Parsons' earliest students at Harvard University, where in 1936 he received his PhD Since the early 1940s Merton was on the faculty of Columbia University, where he collaborated extensively with Paul K. Lazarsfeld in numerous research projects. He died in 2003.

Overall, Merton's work shows a greater sensitivity to the dynamic interrelations between empirical research and theoretical reflection. On the theoretical side, he advocated a "middle-range" approach that provided a clear alternative to Parsons' strategy of trying to explain all aspects of social reality, including the entire society, in terms of a single comprehensive theoretical model. Merton's major argument, developed in Part I of his well known book, *Social Theory and Social Structure* (Merton, 1968), was that more progress could be made by concentrating on "theories of the middle range" instead of grand theories, at least at the then-current stage of maturity of the discipline.

Middle-Range Functional Analysis

Robert Merton defined middle-range theories as –

> ... theories that lie between the minor but necessary working hypotheses that evolve in abundance during day-to-day research and the all-inclusive systematic efforts to develop a unified theory that will explain *all* of the observed uniformities of social behavior, social organization and social change.
>
> Middle-range theory is principally used in sociology to guide empirical inquiry. It is intermediate to general theories of social systems which are too remote from particular classes of social behavior, organization and change to account for what is observed and to those detailed orderly descriptions of particulars that are not generalized at all
>
> (Merton, 1968:39; emphasis added).

Although Merton believed that the functionalist perspective could serve as a useful starting point and a general guide, the specific theories developed from this orientation should be able to stand on their own merits, supported by appropriate empirical

[1] This description of Merton's "middle-range" functionalist perspective is adapted from D. P. Johnson ([1981] 1986:428–439).

data and guiding additional research. The goal is to be able to explain uniformities in relationships among variables in different social contexts.

Merton insisted on distinguishing individuals' subjective motives or intentions from the objective social outcomes that flow from their actions. Whether or not these objective consequences enhance a social system's ability to survive is independent of subjective motives and purposes. Parsons also had recognized that individuals' motives are expected to reflect their own subjective orientations, as opposed to the functional requirements of society. In some situations, these orientations may involve giving priority to their own needs and interests. However, Parsons' emphasis on the congruence between individual need-dispositions that develop through the socialization process and the role requirements of society (or other social systems) led in effect to a blurring of the distinction between subjective motives and objective social consequences. For example, given the mortality of human life, the long-term survival of society requires that its members by replaced through reproduction. Although people may reproduce and care for their children for a variety of personal reasons, their conscious motivations to do so probably do not include the long-range survival of society. Whether babies are born as a result of individuals' deliberate decisions to have children or are unplanned is itself an empirical question. But whatever their subjective personal motives may be, the objective outcome for society is the replenishment of its population.

The importance of unintended consequences can also be illustrated in the area of religious rituals. Individuals probably do not consider how rituals contribute to fulfilling the latent pattern maintenance function (to use Parsons' term) or enhancing social solidarity; instead, their motives may involve fulfilling their religious duties, honoring God, attaining salvation or peace of mind, or perhaps simply conforming to established customs. Of course, professional religious leaders are no doubt aware of how religious rituals increase social cohesion and other positive emotions, since they are involved in planning and orchestrating them. Although other people may also be aware of how participation with fellow believers in religious rituals helps reinforce their beliefs and moral commitments, it is an empirical question as to whether this actually motivates such participation or is a beneficial side effect. The distinction between subjective motives and objective social functions can be represented follows: Motive→Action→Function

This distinction is reflected in Merton's contrast between manifest functions and latent functions. To quote, "Manifest functions are those objective consequences contributing to the adjustment or adaptation of the system which are intended and recognized by participants in the system; latent functions, correlatively, [are] those which are neither intended nor recognized." (Merton, 1968:105) Moreover, Merton warned, the outcomes of people's actions may sometimes be dysfunctional or "lessen the adaptation or adjustment of the system." (Merton, 1968:105) Still a third alternative is that outcomes may be irrelevant as far as the survival or well-being of the system is concerned; in other words, they are nonfunctional, even though the behaviors contributing to these nonfunctional outcomes may meet individuals' personal needs or be maintained out of habit. In developing this paradigm

Merton introduced several qualifications and exceptions to some of the implicit assumptions that seemed to underlie the functionalist perspective.

Analysis of both functions and dysfunctions may involve either a short-term or long-term time frame. Although some actions may have short-term dysfunctional consequences, in other cases it may be a long time before dysfunctional consequences accumulate to the point where they are apparent or begin to undermine the system in a noticeable way. For example, some of the long-range dysfunctions of technological progress include increased pollution of the environment, depletion of natural resources, increased risk of nuclear accidents, and the threat of global warming. Questions regarding whether the social consequences of a given action are functional or dysfunctional, and in what time frame, are always empirical questions that cannot be settled by abstract a priori assumptions.

Actions may also have multiple consequences for the numerous social systems in which they are embedded. These consequences must be identified and evaluated in terms of their functional significance for each system in which they are involved. The need to identify multiple outcomes is especially crucial in stratified and pluralistic societies in which actions that are beneficial for one group or segment of society may be harmful to other groups or segments of society. For example, installation of computerized robots in factory production or automated record systems in offices is no doubt functional for reducing labor costs and thus enhancing the profits of the owners, but these actions are dysfunctional for employees who lose their jobs. Similarly, labor strikes that result in high wage settlements are presumably functional for labor unions and the workers they represent, but dysfunctional for stockholders and consumers. Contemporary airport security procedures may be functional in terms of reducing the risk of terrorism and providing employment for security personnel, but dysfunctional in terms of increasing the routine hassles of air travel and reducing individual freedom.

Similar questions regarding multiple and inconsistent consequences can be raised with regard to the functions of religion in society. Following Durkheim, Parsons had emphasized religion as a major source of value consensus and social integration. However, the unifying effects of religion may not apply to societies that are sharply divided along religious lines. In such situations, religion may undermine the overall solidarity of society and reinforce conflict instead. This is especially likely if the religious disagreements are superimposed on economic or political conflict, as manifested, for example, in the long-term opposition between Protestants and Catholics in northern Ireland. In such situations, it seems that the greater the salience of religion, and the stronger the solidarity within a religious in-group, the greater the tension and the conflict with other religious groups in society. The United States has also had its share of religious conflict. However, the historic pattern of separation of church and state, coupled with constitutional guarantees of freedom of religion, plus the high level of religious pluralism that eventually developed in the United States, has meant that it has not been feasible in the long run for any single religious group to try to subdue all of the others to establish its dominance. Moreover, conflict may be minimized if different religious groups share the same fundamental beliefs and values. At the time Parsons' functionalist theory was dominant, the American pattern of denominational pluralism was seen as resting on a foundation of widely shared Judeo-Christian beliefs and values that supported a broad American "civil religion" and made it possible to develop extensive cooperative or ecumenical relations. However, with the distinctiveness of different religious groups undermined in this way, there is a risk that members' commitment to their own particular religious group could decline, which could prove to be dysfunctional as far as religious groups themselves are concerned.

Although it might be argued that some "functional requirements" apply to society as a whole, Merton was far more cautious than Parsons in making any claims of being able to identify such requirements. In addition, the examples of multiple and contradictory consequences for different segments of society and different socioeconomic class levels are so numerous and pervasive that an analysis that is limited to functional requirements for the overall society as a single system begins to look quite limited and rather tenuous as an adequate model for how social systems work. Merton acknowledged that there must be a net balance of functions over dysfunctions for a system to survive. However, this does not mean that survival depends on some specific set of institutional patterns. Whatever the survival requirements may be, a variety of ways could be developed for these requirements to be fulfilled, just as there are numerous types of family forms, economic arrangements, political structures, and religious orientations in different societies.

This point is related to Merton's concept of functional alternatives (or substitutes). No structure should be assumed at the outset to be indispensable. Alternative structures might be able to satisfy the same requirement just as effectively. For example, although religion may be important for promoting value consensus and social solidarity, it should also be recognized this same positive outcome might also occur through secular value systems such as nationalism or democracy, or through conflict with other societies. The specific functions of any institution may or may not be fulfilled as effectively in alternative ways, but the issue requires empirical investigation.

Latent Dysfunctions, Social Problems, and Social Change

In Merton's perspective, functional analysis is definitely not limited to stability and social order. Institutional patterns may survive for reasons other than their contribution to the overall functional requirements of society, including the vested interests of influential or powerful groups in society. Or they may reflect the persistence of traditions and habits. At the societal level the ritualistic exchange of gifts and greetings during the Christmas/Hanukkah and New Year season may be explained in part as a well-established tradition, even though it may also include both functional and dysfunctional consequences. For example, increased consumer spending on gifts helps boost the economy, but some individuals may experience the strain of increased debt as a result. Everyday life routines such as evening television viewing or internet browsing might persist simply as habits, even though a sociological analysis could identify both functional and dysfunctional consequences of such patterns (such as beneficial individual relaxation versus decrease in family communication and solidarity, for example). If dysfunctional outcomes outweigh the positive functions, the adaptability of the overall system could be decreased, despite the benefits that may occur in the short run for particular groups.

The distinction between functional and dysfunctional consequences is useful when considered together with the distinction between manifest and latent functions. Numerous instances could be cited in which the manifest functions of some pattern of action or some institutional structure are intended to benefit the system (or a specific segment thereof), but unanticipated negative consequences emerge as an unfortunate byproduct, either for the same system or for some other related system. This notion of unintended negative consequences for others may be compared to the notion of "negative externalities" as identified in Coleman's rational choice theory (discussed in Chap. 9).

Dysfunctional patterns may sometimes persist because their negative consequences are not (yet) recognized. However, when these latent dysfunctional consequences accumulate over time, they may eventually become manifest in people's consciousness as social problems about which people believe something should be done. Merton's concept of dysfunction is thus useful in developing a "functional" analysis of social problems and social change. For example, the problems of widespread environmental pollution or the risk of global warming as byproducts of industrial activity were not recognized in the early stages of industrial development, but are now seen by some groups as urgent problems requiring attention.

One consequence of efforts to deal with dysfunctions that become manifest is the establishment of regulations or programs leading to changes in people's behavior and perhaps some form of structural change. Many government agencies and programs can be seen as efforts to deal with the accumulations of dysfunctions that could no longer be ignored and so eventually were defined as social problems demanding some type of organized response. But these efforts to deal with newly recognized problems may eventually generate their own dysfunctional consequences, which may eventually stimulate additional structural change, and so on indefinitely. Moreover, the proliferation of complex government regulations and overlapping government agencies may generate additional dysfunctions in the form of decreased freedom, heavy financial cost, inhibition of individual initiative, and the like.

Numerous examples of unintended dysfunctions could be cited. For instance, although legislation to increase the minimum wage is intended to benefit those at the bottom of the occupational hierarchy, an unanticipated byproduct of such legislation is that unemployment rates for the minimum wage segment of the labor market are likely to increase. This would result when employers increase their level of automation or decrease their level of services in order to avoid the increased labor costs. If investment in automated equipment increases, this may then generate positive consequences through expanded employment opportunities in a different (and probably higher paid) sector of the labor market, leading eventually to increases in productivity. Whether the positive consequences of higher minimum wages outweigh the negative consequences of higher unemployment on a long-term basis is a matter for systematic investigation and careful evaluation.

Focusing attention on the unanticipated dysfunctional consequences of social actions highlights a paradoxical dimension of social life that is often associated more with dialectical analysis than functional analysis (Schneider, 1975). The paradox involves the contradiction between subjective intentions and objective social consequences. This process is similar in some ways to the "perverse effects" that Boudon (1982) analyzed in the rational choice framework. As Boudon showed, individuals sometimes fail to achieve the positive outcomes they anticipate, even when their actions reflect their efforts to make rational choices, because they do not foresee how the rational choices that others make will have effects that combine with the outcomes of their own rational choices in generating widespread negative consequences for all. Boudon's focus was individual outcomes rather than the overall welfare of the system, but of course the two levels are related.

Our emphasis so far has been on the unintended or latent dysfunctions or negative consequences resulting from human actions. However, the unintended byproducts may include benefits as well. For example, if members of a neighborhood get to know one another at their children's Little League baseball games or community youth programs, this is likely to generate social capital which may subsequently lead to cooperative efforts to implement community improvement programs or deal with local problems that had previously been tolerated because no one was willing to get involved. The same positive outcome of increased social capital may also occur when members of the community are stimulated initially to cooperate by the need to deal with the appearance of local crises, such as a surge in unemployment or crime rates or increased traffic congestion. As people sometimes observe in everyday life, good outcomes can result from bad situations. On a broader level, the basic institutional structure of society and underlying patterns of social order can be seen in large part as latent outcomes of actions that are typically oriented toward more limited and personal ends. The advantage of functional analysis is that it looks beyond the motivations and intentions of individuals' actions and focuses instead on the social consequences of these actions, particularly when combined with similar actions of others on a widespread basis. The interdependence among the actions of large numbers of people throughout society means that the outcomes of their actions may extend outward in unforeseen ways, affecting the lives of other people in both positive and negative ways as well as the overall welfare of society.

Merton's strategy for functional analysis underscores the notion that individuals' subjective orientations and conscious motives or intentions provide a limited picture of the dynamics of our social world. Human beings' actions usually have far-reaching and long-lasting social consequences for their social world of which they may be unaware, some of which may undermine their goals as well as have negative consequences for others or for the larger social system. These unintended and unanticipated effects become part of the environment to which they and others must subsequently adapt. The basic image of social life that emerges is that we experience ourselves living in a world that is beyond our control, with a design that is not of our own choosing, even though this world is actually one that we ourselves have created through our actions.

To sum up, Merton's "paradigm" for functional analysis involves investigating the consequences of recurrent or institutionalized patterns of action, whether consciously intended or not, and evaluating them in terms of whether they are functional, dysfunctional, or nonfunctional for the various systems in which they are embedded. Such consequences may be functional for some segments of society or some institutional structures but dysfunctional or nonfunctional for others. In addition, even though current institutional structures may be beneficial for the survival and overall welfare of society, this does not necessarily mean that these particular structures are therefore indispensable. There is always the possibility of functional alternatives that would lead to consequences which are equally positive or even better. Moreover, when we extend our analysis to look at the process whereby some latent dysfunctions eventually become manifest and are defined as social problems, the stage is set for exploring a major source of ongoing social change.

Examples of Middle-Range Functional Theories

Overall, Merton's work was not intended to provide a comprehensive explanation of individuals' social behavior or the overall society. Instead, he focused on specific and limited problems. Most of the chapters of *Social Theory and Social Structure* (Merton, 1968) are devoted to a series of middle-range theories on a variety of specific topics. These theories stand on their own, however, without making extensive use of the terminology of functional analysis and without being clearly related to one another. Some of these middle-range theories are reviewed briefly below.

Social Structure and Anomie

Merton's theory of anomie and its effects in motivating deviant behavior is probably his most frequently cited middle-range theory (Merton, 1968:185–248). His basic contention is that various forms of deviant behavior in American society result from a discrepancy for some segments of the population between the material and occupational success goals that our culture emphasizes and the institutional means that are provided for achieving these goals. The American emphasis on equality and achievement (Parsons' universalistic achievement pattern) encourages all members of society to aspire to high levels of occupational and financial success, regardless of their social and economic class background. The stories of poor immigrants who gradually moved up the socioeconomic ladder in the American "land of opportunity" and the heroic status of successful "self-made" entrepreneurs express such ideals. But despite these culturally prescribed ambitions, opportunities for success are not equally distributed. Some segments of the population do not have access to the legitimate means for achieving these ends in culturally approved ways and so experience the frustrations of anomie. This discrepancy between goals and means is thus dysfunctional for those segments of the population that have internalized the culturally prescribed goals but lack the opportunities to achieve them through legitimate means. The result is often some form of deviant behavior.

Whether all forms of deviant behavior are dysfunctional for society is a separate question, however. Merton's theory has been widely used to explain crime and delinquency, in which case it is generally assumed that deviance is dysfunctional for society (and certainly for victims). However, some forms of deviant behavior, such as inventing a new product or providing a new kind of service, may be functional for society (or segments thereof) as well as for the innovative deviant. In addition, deviance may stimulate various forms of social change designed to improve the distribution of opportunities for success. However, it is beyond our purpose here to explore these issues regarding the various consequences of negative versus positive forms of deviance.

The Bureaucratic Personality

Merton's analysis of the bureaucratic personality is another example of a counterproductive or dysfunctional consequence (Merton, 1968:249–261). As sociologists have recognized since Weber, bureaucratic organizations rely heavily on conformity to established rules and procedures to insure the positive functions of continuity, reliability, and coordination in accomplishing their goals. However, Merton pointed out that this heavy reliance on rules may also be dysfunctional because it leads bureaucratic officials to emphasize conformity to the rules as an end in itself. The result is that these officials lose their capacity to adapt to new situations. In some cases, rigid adherence to rules may actually undermine the achievement of organizational goals, particularly when new situations develop that the rules are not designed to cover and the organizational culture fostered by the rules discourages flexibility and innovation. Whether conformity to established rules is functional or dysfunctional depends on the circumstances. In public organizations, often it is the clients who bear the brunt of bureaucratic rigidity as they encounter the unwillingness of bureaucratic officials to modify rules and regulations to fit individual needs.

Reference Group Theory

Still another example of a middle-range theory that draws on the strategy of functional analysis is reference group theory (Merton, 1968:279–334 [in collaboration with Alice Rossi]; 335–440). Reference groups are the groups with which an individual identifies as a basis for self evaluation, comparison, and normative guidance. The idea that individuals' self concepts and attitudes are derived from the group(s) with which they identify is consistent with Mead's concept of the "generalized other."

Also, the insight that individuals' level of satisfaction with their current situation is based on comparisons with others is used in exchange theory to explain how people evaluate their reward/cost outcomes and either maintain or change their relationships. Merton pointed out that individuals are sometimes oriented toward the standards and normative patterns of groups to which they do not currently belong. This sometimes helps to account for deviance from the normative patterns of groups to which they do belong. Although this may undermine solidarity and thus be dysfunctional for a particular group, it may be quite functional in an open society in encouraging people to devote themselves to the kind of effort that will lead to upward socioeconomic mobility. When individuals identify with a group that they expect to join someday, their eventual transition to the new group may be facilitated by their prior identification with it. Thus this process is functional by encouraging and promoting anticipatory socialization (Merton, 1968:316–329).

These examples illustrate Merton's strategy for developing "middle-range" theories. Additional areas represented in *Social Theory and Social Structure* (Merton, 1968) include the contrast between "local influentials" and "cosmopolitan influentials" (pp. 441–474), the "self-fulfilling prophecy"—particularly as applied to ingroup and outgroup relations (pp. 475–490), the effects of the Puritan ethic in promoting scientific inquiry (pp. 628–660), and audience responses to mass media propaganda, which sometimes includes an unintended "boomerang" effect (pp. 563–582). Middle-range theories are difficult to summarize because, by definition and design, they are developed to stand on their own, as opposed to fitting into a more comprehensive theoretical framework. However, Merton has had a major long-term impact on American sociology, not only in the area of theory but numerous other substantive areas as well (see Lewis A. Coser, ed. [1975]). His strategy for developing "middle-range" theories draws on findings from several research projects. His analyses demonstrate the value of his strategy for highlighting the social (and sometimes psychological) consequences (or functions) of various behavior patterns, particularly those that are unintended and/or dysfunctional, to which individuals must subsequently adapt.

From Functionalism to Neofunctionalism

The decline in functional theory that occurred by the late 1960s corresponded with several interrelated changes in American society. The Vietnam war and the anti-war movement, along with the growing influence of the civil rights movement, made Parsons' image of widespread value consensus underlying and supporting the major institutional structures through which social equilibrium is maintained much less tenable. At the same time the growing popularity of neo-Marxist perspectives, particularly the early philosophical and humanistic writings of Marx, attracted considerable attention, and critical forms of theory became much more popular, particularly at the macro level. As noted in Chap. 3, even before these developments C. Wright Mills had been sharply critical of Parsons' focus on society's functional requirements. He insisted that sociologists should focus instead on explaining how existing social structures create personal troubles for people as they are dominated and exploited by them in various ways.

On another front, the symbolic interactionist perspective (as reviewed in Chap. 5) had also long provided an alternative to functionalism. In contrast to the emphasis on functional requirements and culturally prescribed roles, symbolic interaction emphasized instead the ongoing micro-level interaction processes whereby individuals actively collaborate in constructing and reproducing (or sometimes modifying) their social worlds, expressing their distinctive identities in this process as much as standardized social roles. This applied particularly to Blumer's "Chicago School" version of symbolic interaction theory. In addition, social exchange theory was launched by George Homans (as noted in Chap. 7) as an explicit rejection of functionalist explanations of behavior in favor of micro-level psychological explanations. These criticisms were directed more to Parsons' structural-functional theory than to Merton's middle-range functional perspective. At the same time, Merton's distinctive strategy for functional analysis demonstrated that it could be used to analyze dysfunctions, conflict, and social change as readily as to portray a social order based on the assumption of value consensus and functional integration.

The decade of the 1970s was largely a time of theoretical fragmentation in American sociological theory. No single theory became dominant as a replacement for functionalism. In the following decades, however, a number of theorists devoted considerable attention to trying to integrate micro and macro levels of analysis, or to theories focusing on human agency versus those focusing on social structure (see, for example, Fielding, ed. [1988] and Mouzelis [1995]). This fragmentation continues to the present, even though considerable progress has been made within several different theoretical traditions. And by the early 1980s, functionalism staged a comeback in the form of what was termed "neofunctionalism." Major contributors to this development include Jeffrey Alexander (1998) in the United States and Richard Münch (1994a, 1994b, 1994c) in Germany. Both theorists provided critiques of Talcott Parsons' works, but their perspectives incorporated many of his most important ideas in ways that were intended to avoid its shortcomings and promote theoretical integration with opposing perspectives.

Social Action and Social Order: Jeffrey Alexander's Multidimensional Perspective

In sharp contrast to Merton's advocacy of middle-range theories, Jeffrey Alexander (1982a) shifted the focus of attention to an even more abstract level. In his view many of the conflicts between different theories result from inconsistencies and contradictions in implicit underlying assumptions that may not be explicitly acknowledged. This lack of attention to underlying theoretical presuppositions that cannot be tested directly is no doubt related to the strong empirical focus of American sociology. However, the failure to focus on these implicit assumptions makes it appear that theorists working at different levels of analysis or different types of social processes have fundamentally different images or perspectives on the nature of the social world. This is reflected in the way sociology is characterized by multiple paradigms as discussed in Chap. 4.

Alexander argues for a "postpositivist" theoretical logic that would focus on underlying presuppositions that are even more general and abstract than those incorporated in most other theoretical perspectives.[2] In his view, it is just as important to make underlying theoretical presuppositions explicit as to generate specific propositions for research. Only by shifting to the most general and abstract level is it possible to have a coherent theoretical perspective that can incorporate the opposing but partial viewpoints of less abstract theories with their more limited views on the social world.

Social Action and Social Order: Environmental Versus Normative Influences

At the most general level possible, all sociological theories have to deal with fundamental issues and questions regarding both **human action** and **social order**. These concepts may appear to parallel the micro/macro distinction, but they are not equivalent. Both human action and social order are involved at both the micro and macro levels and at all levels in between. Moreover, neither of these concepts should be regarded as more fundamental than the other in principle, nor should either of them be reduced to (or explained in terms of) the other. Both are essential for sociological analysis, and each is inevitably linked with the other. Of course, at a lower level of generality, or in doing empirical research, one may choose to focus on the dynamics of social action or on the structured properties of the social order. Moreover, from the standpoint of any particular individual born into a society at a specific moment in time, the social order clearly is already in place—representing the outcomes of the actions of preceding generations of individuals. It is not up to each generation to start from scratch in establishing the social order, even though their actions will eventually contribute to its reproduction (or perhaps its transformation).

Theories that concentrate on **action** can be distinguished between (a) those that regard action as determined by objective external conditions versus (b) those emphasizing a voluntaristic view that action results from individuals' subjective choices and intentions. This dilemma can be compared to the long-lasting philosophical

[2] Alexander's approach contrasts sharply with the strategy of theory construction described in Chap. 4, in which conceptual schemes, definitions, classification systems, propositional statements, and laws are intended to "mirror" or represent the empirical social world as closely as possible. In the perspective of this book, both strategies are appropriate, despite their limitations. Theoretical analysis always has empirical implications, even though different interpretations of empirical data may make it impossible to prove (or disprove) a particular theoretical orientation. This is why it is important to become aware of the underlying assumptions reflected in different theoretical paradigms, even though such assumptions cannot be tested directly.

debate between determinism versus free will, as well as Parsons' distinction in his voluntaristic theory of social action between positivism and idealism. Theorists who focus on external conditions may emphasize either material constraints or social influences, but the possibility for individual choice is minimized or in effect neutralized. In contrast, those who emphasize voluntary choice tend to emphasize subjective ideals and normative commitments, as opposed to the external factors that limit and constrain people's choices.

Alexander regards individual choice in the rational choice perspective as more of a reflection of the reality of the situation people face than a genuinely voluntary choice. In effect, people's rational choices are largely determined by the resources and obstacles of the environment to which they must adapt. Although their choices reflect their particular goals, there is no explanation in rational choice theory of why people pursue the particular goals that they do—a limitation that rational choice theorists themselves acknowledge. Instead, within the rational choice perspective people's preferences regarding their goals are taken as given and left unexplained, and the focus of attention is on making the most rational or effective decision possible (given the available information) in confronting the obstacles of their environment and mobilizing the necessary resources for achieving their goals. The ultimate source of explanation thus becomes the environment to which individuals adapt as they assess its opportunities and constraints and seek to satisfy their needs and interests.

In effect, then, Alexander proposes that the underlying presupposition of rationality reduces the question of the "ends" of action to a question regarding "means." As he put it,

> The central question that every social theory addresses in defining the nature of action is whether or not–or to what degree–action is rational.......... [T]o presuppose that action is instrumentally rational is to assume that action is guided by ends of pure efficiency. In terms of the more differentiated terminology of goals and norms, it assumes that goals are calculated to achieve broader normative purposes in the most efficient manner possible, given the constraining external conditions. Because any relation of goals to norms that is not efficiently rational is disregarded, goals can be viewed as performing a function similar to means. Ideally oriented goals, are, in effect, reduced to materially oriented means, and more general norms as such become irrelevant: action is viewed as a continuous effort at economizing, calculating, and, indeed, "rationalizing."
>
> (Alexander, 1982a:72–73)

In other words, questions regarding ultimate goals cannot be answered from within the rational choice perspective. Instead, the answer must draw on theoretical presuppositions that stress the subjective nonrational foundations of social actions. These nonrational foundations may include people's ideals and values, or normative commitments—which was a major emphasis in Parsons' theory. People would thus be seen as engaging in conforming behavior, or perhaps even altruistic or self-sacrificing behavior on occasion, because they believe this is the right thing to do to express their moral commitments, as opposed to anticipating personal benefits from such action. Or, the nonrational foundations may be more affective or emotional in nature, reflecting or expressing their feelings. Behavior that is emotionally expressive may or may not be consistent with moral ideals, but it clearly contrasts with calculative rational choice considerations. The importance of socioemotional bonds and emotional exchanges was a major focus of the perspective of the sociology of emotions as discussed earlier.

Alexander's basic argument is that an adequate multidimensional theoretical framework for analyzing social action must reflect subjective intentions as well as objective conditions, including both the material and the social environment. Moreover, subjective intentions regarding ultimate goals and values tend to reflect moral commitments and emotions as well as instrumental rational choice calculation. Theorists err, in Alexander's critique, when they take any one of these elements of action as primary and attempt to conflate or combine other dimensions with the one selected as primary. Theories that seek to explain social order in terms of presuppositions regarding social action (whether based on the assumption of rationality or on the assumption of a nonrational normative or emotional foundation) conflate action and order, in effect blurring the distinctions between them. The strategy of trying to explain social order in terms of presuppositions that apply to individual action is to treat the social order as a residual category that can be reduced to the dynamics of action.[3]

In contrast to theories that focus on action, other theories are devoted primarily to the challenge of explaining social **order**. This problem is analytically separate from questions regarding social action but is of equal importance. Theories that focus on social order may also be dichotomized in terms of whether they treat the social order as reflecting objective or external constraints or subjective internal commitments. This contrast turns out to be parallel to the contrast between rational choice theory and theories that emphasize nonrational normative commitments at the level of social action. Social order is explained as emerging from and being sustained (or changed) through individuals' actions. The question, however, is whether the voluntary character of action is adequately preserved in theoretical analyses of social order.

Alexander argues that rationalist explanations represent a "coercive" form of social order that in effect denies individual choice. Consistent with rational choice theory, the establishment and maintenance of social order involves a system of positive and negative sanctions that shape individuals' actions to fulfill social obligations that sustain the social order (and, of course, to refrain from behavior that disrupts it). This means, in effect, that individuals' actions reflect their adaptation to these external sanctions rather than their voluntary choices. In contrast, those who emphasize voluntaristic normative conformity for explaining social order preserve the process of individual choice involved in social action, but the focus on voluntarism tends to overstate the scope of individuals' free will. This point can be compared with the emphasis in symbolic interaction theory on the ongoing interpretative process whereby individuals are seen as always facing the need to

---

[3] Alexander's argument clearly contrasts with George Homans' explicit reductionist strategy as discussed in connection with his elementary exchange theory perspective. It also goes against the strong individualistic implications of the rational choice perspective.

negotiate their responses to the particular situations they confront. This perspective allows for a high level of voluntarism in explaining people's actions but downplays the constraining influence of their already structured social environment.[4] The challenge is to explain the **collective** character of normative standards at the same time that **individual choice** in interpreting and applying norms in particular situations is preserved. Both dimensions are equally important.

At the level of general presuppositions with which he deals, Alexander regards the question of order itself is more basic for sociological analysis than the question of how a particular type of social order is created and sustained. At this level of abstraction, it is not necessary to choose between external control (whether negative constraints or positive inducements) versus internal moral commitments. Instead, at this abstract theoretical level, both sources of order are equally important. At the empirical level, in contrast, different social systems may be compared in terms of the extent to which their social order reflects objective external controls versus subjective internal commitments.

This dual focus is parallel in some ways to the contrast between organizations and communities as discussed in an earlier chapter. Despite the wide range of empirical variations, organizations and communities may be distinguished in part in terms of the dichotomy between participants' individualistic rational choice calculations and their socioemotional identification with others or the community in general. Formal organizations are likely to reflect individual self-interests, although this may be modified when individuals identify emotionally with an organization to which they belong or develop a subjective moral commitment to its goals. In contrast, cohesive communities are more likely to be characterized by the mutual subjective commitments of members to one another and to their community and its welfare and moral values. The distinction between rational self-interest and normative commitments is also reflected in the pattern variables in Parsons' perspective in which different types of role expectations are contrasted in terms of whether personal self-interests or obligations to the collectivity have priority.

The type of general theoretical framework that Alexander proposes would provide room for a balanced analysis of the objective constraints and conditions in which individuals act as well as their voluntary subjective choices. Moreover, these choices would incorporate individuals' rational analysis of their situation in pursuing their various goals as well as their normative commitments and emotional ties. It would also make allowances for the contingent character of people's actions as emphasized in the micro-level perspectives of symbolic interaction theory and ethnomethodology. This means it would modify the highly structured and overly determined view of people's behavior that seems implied in Parsons' perspective by providing considerably more theoretical space for individual improvisation and for the need to make adjustments to unforeseen disruptions. In Alexander's multidimensional

[4] As explained in Chap. 5, this would apply more to Herbert Blumer's ("Chicago School") version of symbolic interaction theory than to the structural forms of symbolic interaction represented by Manford Kuhn, Sheldon Stryker, and David Heise.

perspective, the situational contingencies and decision-making processes involved in individual action should be seen as reciprocally related to, but analytically independent of, the conditioning and constraining effects of the social order.

Despite Alexander's plea to deal explicitly with both action and order, he gives priority to order (though this does not require that any specific type of order be specified). He explained:

> If theory is individualistic, the problem of order becomes a residual category. One must therefore discount individualism as a viable option for a truly social theory–despite the fact that it often reveals fundamentally important aspects of actual empirical processes. One is left with two sets of fundamental presuppositional dichotomies: social theory can be normative or instrumental [or rational] in its approach to action, and it can conceptualize the collective arrangement of this action in an internal or external manner.
>
> (Alexander, 1982a:123).

The "internal" manner of explaining social order can incorporate normative commitments or socioemotional ties, while the "external" manner involves controls exerted through positive or negative sanctions that in effect deny the analytical independence of voluntaristic choice. Alexander's concern with the problem of order based on normative commitments is also reflected in his subsequent focus on the challenges of understanding the nature of "civil society"—a concept that in some ways resembles Parsons' notion of the "societal community" (Alexander, 1998:210–233).

In more recent work Alexander (2003) shifted his focus more explicitly to the cultural level of analysis. Cultural systems exhibit their own structure and dynamics that can be analyzed independently of their linkage to the social structure. Various aspects of culture (moral codes, religious doctrines, scientific theories) are sometimes the primary focus of social action as people seek to refine, elaborate, or criticize their ideas and beliefs in these areas. Alexander insists that the "strong program" in cultural analysis that he advocates would employ the techniques of hermeneutic interpretation to understand cultural meanings. Analysis of fundamental meanings would involve an elaboration of binary oppositions, such as sacred versus profane (to draw on a basic distinction in Durkheim's sociology of religion), good versus evil, and so on. Some binary oppositions may refer to such features of social life as the distinction between ingroup versus outgroup, or democracy versus authoritarianism. But the meanings referenced by such codes can be read as self-contained texts at their own level, regardless of how they might be implicated in the structure of social systems. These meanings are not limited to actual written "texts" of course, but can also be expressed in various other cultural artifacts as well. Alexander's perspective on cultural sociology will be reviewed more fully in Chap. 19 in our discussion of various cultural-level theories.

Alexander's Critique of Earlier Theories

Alexander's general strategy is similar in some ways to that of Talcott Parsons over half a century earlier but it avoids the strong emphasis on value consensus and social equilibrium that many of Parsons' critics found objectionable. Specifically, his multidimensional framework provides the basis for his intensive critical analysis of the works of Marx, Durkheim, Weber, and Parsons himself. His project, entitled *Theoretical Logic in Sociology*, includes four volumes. The first volume presents his basic multidimensional framework as summarized above. Volume two analyzes the works of Marx and Durkheim (Alexander, 1982b). Volume three is devoted to Weber (Alexander, 1983a). The fourth volume deals with the work of Talcott Parsons (Alexander, 1983b). Space limitations prevent a thorough review of Alexander's insightful analyses of these theorists' works. For all four theorists, however, the theoretical logic presented in his first volume is used to highlight crucial ambiguities, dilemmas, and shortcomings that limit the scope of their works. Specifically, none of them developed the kind of abstract or comprehensive framework that Alexander felt would be necessary to deal with the contrasting dimensions of both action and order that he identified. Alexander's goal is to incorporate the perspectives of these theorists in a more comprehensive theoretical framework that explicitly identifies the underlying presuppositions that distinguish them.

Alexander saw Marx's theory as emphasizing primarily the external environment, particularly the economic class structure and the differential distribution of material resources—which, of course, Marx saw as moving toward an extreme level of inequality under capitalism.[5] In addition, Alexander also shows that Marx's concept of *Praxis* allows for the possibility of voluntarism and choice. This concept involves the notion of human action guided by enlightened self-interest. Marx believed that such action would occur when the development of class consciousness leads the oppressed and exploited classes of society to resist their subordination and work for the revolutionary overthrow of capitalism and the formation of a new type of social order. Thus, despite Marx's overall determinism, Alexander shows that Marx's notion of *Praxis* provides an opening for the voluntaristic dimension.

Marx's emphasis on the environment contrasts with Durkheim's focus on shared normative commitments. Consistent with Parsons, however, Alexander also pointed to certain inconsistencies and ambiguities in Durkheim's work. Early in his career Durkheim had emphasized objective social facts in order to contrast his approach with the individualistic assumptions of British utilitarianism. However, the constraining effects of social facts were simply added to the constraints of the material environment in undermining the voluntaristic dimension of action. Later in his career, however, Durkheim shifted to the subjective level as he sought to explain how moral ideals are internalized in individuals' consciousness in the form of religious beliefs reinforced by rituals. However, the voluntaristic dimension of action continued to be downplayed as individuals' "voluntary" choices turned out to mirror the culture and normative patterns that were reinforced through the group's rituals. In

[5]Parsons did not deal with Marx (who had not yet become influential in the mainstream of American sociology), but his analysis of Pareto involved a critique of determinism that can be compared with Alexander's critique of the determinism implicit in Marx. Of course, Marx and Pareto reflect very different forms of determinism; as noted earlier, Pareto had focused on underlying sentiments, rather than the external environment, while Marx focused on material resources and their differential distribution in the class structure.

short, Alexander felt that Durkheim, like Marx, failed to achieve an appropriate balance in dealing with the multidimensional nature of social action.

Among the classical stage theorists, Alexander (like Parsons) considers Weber to have come the closest to synthesizing in a balanced way the opposing implications of materialism versus idealism, or determinism versus voluntarism.[6] Weber's concept of instrumental rationality is largely consistent with utilitarianism and rational choice theory in emphasizing adaptation to the external environment, while his concept of value-oriented rationality allows for voluntary normative commitments. Weber's analysis of social structures, such as bureaucratic organizations, social classes, and status groups, clearly reflects the influence of the external social environment on human behavior. However, his analysis of charismatic social movements demonstrates the possibility of innovative value-oriented or emotion-driven action that breaks out of the constraining influence of the current social environment. It is always an empirical question whether individuals give priority to their material interests or to their ideals and values, and the answer to this question can no doubt be related to how much their behavior reflects structural conditions or voluntary choice. Although Weber's perspective allows more room for voluntarism than Durkheim's emphasis on collective consciousness, Alexander considers Weber's work inadequate for explaining which of the opposing dimensions will be manifested in particular situations. Partly as a result, theorists since Weber have tended to focus either on Weber's idealistic (or voluntaristic) emphasis (as Parsons did, for example) or his emphasis on the external social structure in ways that sometimes seem parallel to Marxist forms of analysis.

In Alexander's view, Parsons also ultimately failed to achieve the synthesis he sought between idealism (and voluntarism) on the one hand and environmental determinism (material and social) on the other. Voluntary choice is not eliminated, but the voluntaristic focus of Parsons' early theory of social action was diminished as he later shifted his attention to the functional requirements of social systems. Moreover, it turns out that individuals' choices mirror the shared norms and values they have internalized and reflect their conformity to the culturally mandated requirements of their various social roles. Although some individuals may deviate in disruptive ways that produce strains in the social system, the effect of such deviance is to trigger social control mechanisms that are intended to restore their willingness to conform and thereby reinforce the social order. Thus the two processes of socialization and social control reduce the analytical significance of people's voluntaristic choices. Implicit in this type of analysis is a kind of justification of social processes that maintain the equilibrium of society and provide ideological support for the status quo.

Despite Alexander's determination to develop a comprehensive theoretical framework that would avoid the shortcomings of Parsons' theory, the similarities between his basic theoretical strategy of analysis and Parsons' early voluntaristic theory of social action are striking. Both wanted to establish a comprehensive

---

[6] See also D. P. Johnson ([1981] 1986:202–245]) for a more extended discussion of how Weber's work can be analyzed in a way that incorporates the opposing perspectives of Marx and Durkheim.

theoretical framework that could encompass the contradictions within and between the theories they analyzed. Both emphasized the need for dealing with the rational and the nonrational aspects of human behavior, and both used the means-end schema for analyzing individuals' goal-oriented behavior. Both also stressed the voluntaristic aspects of behavior plus the external conditions that both influence and limit people's choices. Finally, both insisted that sociological analysis must concentrate on the broader social order, and that an adequate theory of social order must incorporate normative commitments that transcend individual interests.

In the perspective on "cultural sociology" that Alexander (2003, especially pp. 15–16) later developed, he showed how that the reinforcement of society's normative patterns is sometimes played out in dramatic symbolic struggles between good and evil when major normative violations lead to a heightened level of determination to restore the moral order by purging the contaminating effects of such violations. These efforts sometimes culminate in dramatic ritualistic reaffirmations of the moral code. Although it is important to understand the cultural meanings underlying such processes on their own terms, at the cultural level of analysis, actions that are undertaken in the cultural realm often have definite implications for the social structure as well. For example, Alexander's analysis of the Watergate crisis that occurred in the United States in the 1970s during Richard Nixon's presidency demonstrated the way the cultural-level struggle between social definitions of good and evil resulted in specific political changes, including, for example, Nixon's resignation and the elevation of Vice President Gerald Ford to the presidency (Alexander, 2003:155–177).

Overall, Alexander's multidimensional theoretical logic incorporates conflicting but equally valid dimensions of social life—the contingent aspect of individuals' actions and the persistence of social order, voluntary choices and the conditioning and constraining influences of the social environment, shared moral values and emotional bonds plus individual interests. His theory is sufficiently general and abstract that it can be applied to any of the specific levels of social reality that have been identified in this volume: micro, meso, and macro. But the application of his perspective to people's actual behavior in real-life social settings would require shifting to a lower level of abstraction. It would also involve identifying in more detail how each of the dimensions he identified are manifested in different types of behavior and different social formations. One possibility for doing this would be to compare and contrast the social behaviors manifested in the meso-level social formations identified in Chaps. 10 and 11—communities, organizations, markets, and socioeconomic classes—in terms of the dimensions Alexander identified.

The next "neofunctional" theory to be examined—that of the German sociologist Richard Münch—uses Parsons' AGIL model to analyze different dimensions of social action as well as to classify and analyze alternative theoretical traditions. Like Alexander, Münch argued for a multidimensional framework. However, a large part of his focus was on action itself rather than the social order, and this focus was used to contrast different theories in terms of the specific dimensions of action which they emphasized.

Contrasting Dimensions of Action in Richard Münch's Neofunctional Perspective

To develop his multidimensional framework Münch (1994a:1–12) proposed that the four functional requirements of social systems represented by Parsons' AGIL model can be seen as reflecting different aspects or dimensions that can be identified to varying degrees in all forms or types of social action. Although Münch focused on social action, the distinctions he makes could also be used in analyzing different types of social systems. Following our review of Münch's explanation of these dimensions we will look at how he used Parsons' AGIL model to classify different theoretical perspectives.

AGIL Dimensions of Action

As explained earlier, Parsons' AGIL model specified the fundamental functional requirements faced by all social systems. These requirements are listed below:

A–Adaptation: The need to adapt to the environment so as to meet basic survival needs.
G–Goal attainment: The need for some type of agreement regarding collective goals and for the mobilization of resources to be employed in trying to achieve them.
I–Integration: The need to insure at least minimal solidarity, to coordinate individuals' interdependent activities, and to deal with deviations that occur.
L–Latent pattern maintenance: The need to establish and reinforce shared values and norms among the members of society (or other social systems), restoring motivational commitment through various rituals and through periods of latency.

In contrast to Parsons, Münch does not emphasize institutional (or subsystem) structures. Instead, he regards all four of Parsons' functional requirements as fundamental dimensions of a theoretical action space that can be used to compare and contrast different types of actions in various contexts. Any particular action may be analyzed in these terms. The priorities of these different dimensions may, of course, vary in different institutional structures (systems or subsystems) or different situations. But all four dimensions may be identified in some form in all types of social action. To develop this multidimensional model, Münch proposes an even more abstract conceptual framework that involves two crosscutting dimensions: (1) symbolic complexity and (2) contingency (Münch, 1994a:9). **Symbolic complexity** refers to the total number of alternative meanings that individuals could theoretically employ in interpreting, or making sense of, various aspects of their environment. This can range from high to low complexity. Similarly, **contingency** refers to the number of possible responses whereby individuals conceivably could respond or adapt to their environment (as they interpret its meanings); it also can be seen as a continuum ranging from high to low. By crosscutting **complexity** and **contingency** Münch creates four different theoretical categories, which he suggests can be related to the contrasting dimensions of action represented by the AGIL framework. These categories are explained below

1. The combination of high complexity and high contingency reflects the functional requirement of **adaptation**, which Münch regards as the "economics" of social action.
2. The high complexity/low contingency combination concerns the functional requirement of **goal attainment**. This aspect involves the "politics" of social action.
3. The combination of low complexity and low contingency is manifested in action involved with the functional requirement of **integration**. Münch suggests that this dimension deals with the "structure" of social action, particularly as this involves emotional solidarity or community cohesion.
4. The combination of low complexity and high contingency involves the function of **latent pattern maintenance**. Münch labels this dimension the "symbolics" of social action, and its primary focus is basic values and moral commitments.

Münch's strategy for linking the concepts of complexity and contingency to Parsons' AGIL model are rather abstract and perhaps not immediately obvious. To understand the argument, let us begin with the "economics" of action (high complexity and high contingency), involving adaptation to the environment. The material environment can be seen as providing a wide array of multiple resources that could theoretically serve as the means for many different purposes. This total array of resources reflects the complexity of the environment, and the high contingency of this dimension indicates the immense variety of uses (or goals) for which these resources may be deployed.

This contingency is reduced as we move into the arena of the "politics" of action, involving goal attainment. Once decisions are made (either individually or collectively) regarding specific goals to be pursued, this in effect reduces the contingency of action by reducing the range of alternatives to consider (although, of course, decisions regarding goals may be reversed or revised for various reasons). Once a goal is selected, other options are thereby eliminated. The next set of decisions, then, has to do with obtaining and utilizing the resources (or means) needed for goal attainment. Money, for example, can be used for a wide variety of goods and services; however, once a decision is made as to what to purchase, this obviously limits the money available for other purchases. In effect, the decision to use resources for some particular purpose or goal reduces the level of contingency by ruling out other potential uses.

Specific "structures" concerned with social integration reflect low symbolic complexity and low contingency by specifying the **specific** normative patterns that will govern actions within **particular** groups or communities. These norms regulate the behaviors that members are expected to follow as they pursue both individual and collective goals and as they interact with one another. Alternative actions are eliminated as members adhere to the prescriptions and proscriptions of their particular normative code. Conformity to the specific norms of a particular group demonstrates and symbolizes membership in that group (or community or society), and the reactions of others may be expected to indicate their inclusion in the community. This basic point can readily be appreciate when we consider how the members of a particular family or friendship circle will need to make adjustments of various kinds in their behavior if they are joined by an outsider. Insiders interact toward one another in ways that differ from the way they would interact with outsiders.

Low symbolic complexity and high contingency are manifested in the "symbolics" of action space representing abstract values. The need for reinforcing shared values is a basic requirement that is represented in Parsons' theory by the functional requirement of latent pattern maintenance. Münch shows that as the theoretical focus shifts from specific and detailed norms to abstract values, the level of complexity decreases. At a sufficiently high level of generality, value commitments tends to revolve around basic but abstract dichotomies involving fundamental choices having to do with issues of right versus wrong, fair versus unfair, good versus evil, appropriate versus inappropriate, and so on, as reflected in society's moral and normative codes. However, even though basic questions of right and wrong may be viewed in abstract terms as a simple dichotomy, the variety of ways in which ideal moral codes can be applied in specific situations involves a high level of contingency. For example, a fundamental moral ideal such as the Golden Rule ("Do unto others as you would have them do unto you") can be manifested in innumerable forms of specific actions, depending on whether it involves relations with family members, neighbors, co-workers, strangers, or abstract categories of people in need, as well as the nature of the situation itself.

To put Münch's model in somewhat simpler and less abstract terms, we might consider all actions as having economic, political, socioemotional, and value orientational dimensions. The "economic" aspect involves individuals' efforts to satisfy their own individual needs and interests. Many different types of resources and many different types of goals may be involved for different people. The "political" component concerns collective goals reflecting the interdependence of people's actions as they adapt to the environment they share. The socioemotional (or structural) dimension involves people's emotional identification with one another and with their community, however this is defined. The value orientation (or symbolic) level reflects abstract moral values that provide ultimate meaning and purpose to people's lives, both individually and collectively. Although all action reflects all of these dimensions to some extent, different types of actions in different institutional environments are likely to vary in terms of which component has priority.

Contrasting Theoretical Perspectives Related to the AGIL Framework

As noted above Münch (1994a, 1994b, 1994c) used his reformulated version of Parsons' AGIL model to classify competing schools of theoretical discourse. The "economic" dimension (reflecting the problem of adaptation), which (as noted above) is oriented toward individuals' own personal needs and interests, is manifested most clearly in market transactions. Individualistic theories such as utilitarianism and exchange and rational choice perspectives deal primarily with this dimension. The "politics" of social action is the primary focus of theories that emphasize the differential distribution of power and resources and the social conflicts that often result. Such theories are consistent with the rational choice emphasis on individual needs and goals, but they highlight the competition and conflict among those with opposing interests plus the tensions between individual versus collective goals.

In defining the "structure" of social action in terms of socioemotional bonds, Münch is consistent with both Parsons and Alexander in emphasizing nonrational normative and moral commitments that transcend individuals' self-interests. This dimension also incorporates the socioemotional bonds that link people together in relationships and communities. It includes the sense of belonging that sometimes leads individuals to move beyond their own interests to include the interests of others as well as the general welfare. The focus on shared values that Münch considers the "symbolics" of social action involves the challenge of dealing with fundamental questions regarding the ultimate meaning and purpose life, both individually and collectively. The theoretical perspectives of both Durkheim and Parsons would fit this dimension because of their emphasis on the importance of shared religious beliefs and values for the social order. Münch also includes Mead, Blumer, and Goffman in the "symbolic" category; in different ways these theorists explored how moral codes guide people's behavior at the micro level. In addition, humanistic psychologists such as Lawrence Kohlberg and Jean Piaget also focus on the development of moral ideals and meaning systems at the individual level.

Both the socioemotional dimension and the value orientational dimension (the "structure" and the "symbolics" of social action in Münch's terms) fit Alexander's notion of the nonrational aspect of social action. These dimensions can be contrasted with the assumptions of rational choice theory—particularly instrumental rationality oriented toward individualistic interests. The "structure" of social action is seen in Münch's terms as reflecting emotional bonds, while the "symbolics" or value orientational dimension deals with ultimate issues of human life, including moral commitments that transcend narrow self-interests, mundane collective goals, and even particular emotional bonds.

Münch (1994a:9–19) argues that many of the differences among various theories result from disagreements in the fundamental dimension of social action that they emphasize as primary. As theorists expand the scope of their analysis, however, and as they respond to criticisms from others with different assumptions, their theories move from the dimension within which they originated into one or more other dimensions. This means in effect that they eventually encroach on the dimensions of "action space" that other theorists with different orientations had emphasized as their primary domain. Thus, despite their different starting points and underlying assumptions, alternative theories tend eventually to converge and overlap with one another, but not without ambiguities and inconsistencies. Moreover, conflicts tend to persist because of the differences in fundamental starting points. Within any single theory, there may be unresolved dilemmas because of the continued emphasis on the original primary dimension. This means that despite the movement toward incorporation of additional dimensions, the limitations of the original focus make it difficult to achieve a sufficient level of generality to deal with these alternative dimensions in a balanced way.

Although all four of the dimensions that Münch identified may be involved in all types of action, there are variations among different people and in different situations. Some people are motivated primarily by their own needs and interests, while others show greater concerns for collective goals or for the inclusion and welfare of others, while still others give priority to transcendent moral ideals. In some situations, individuals' actions may reflect all of these concerns, while in other situations definite priorities must be established. It is always an empirical question as to whether individual interests, group or community goals, socioemotional bonds, or transcendent ideals and values have priority in particular situations.

Münch's focus on the level of social action contrasts with Alexander's emphasis on the social order. At the same time, Alexander seemed to be more explicit than Münch in dealing with voluntary choice as an essential feature of social action. For both theorists, individual action and social structure are inextricably linked; neither level of social reality can be explained without the other and, in the final analysis, "social order" is grounded in the ongoing dynamics of individuals' actions. Both theorists also recognized the need to deal with the inconsistencies that may result from their multidimensional approach.

Alexander and Münch both contrast sharply with Merton's "middle-range" approach in their commitment to developing a theoretical framework that is sufficiently abstract and general that it can embrace and explain the multiple and sometimes inconsistent aspects of social life. Although Parsons had also recognized the need for an all-encompassing theoretical framework in his discussion of the dilemmas represented by his pattern variables, his strong emphasis on shared norms and values seemed eventually to reduce the theoretical space available for competing interests and also for voluntary choice.

The same dilemmas that were implicit (or sometimes explicit) in Parsons—rational choice reflecting self-interests versus nonrational normative commitments, voluntarism versus determinism, social action versus social system or structure—continue to be major concerns in the neofunctional perspectives of both Alexander and Münch. As leading figures in the development of the neofunctional perspective, both Münch and Alexander are committed to a comprehensive theoretical framework that incorporates the valid arguments of Talcott Parsons as well as the arguments of competing theories. Both are deeply concerned with the underlying logic of theoretical discourse. Both theorists also insist on the importance of both the rational and the nonrational dimensions of social action as reflected in the dynamics of social systems as well as individuals' actions.

Summary

This chapter began with a review of Robert Merton's paradigm or framework for functional analysis. Merton disagreed with Parsons' strategy of trying to formulate a comprehensive all-embracing theory in which all institutional structures could be explained in terms of functional requirements that all societies and other social systems must fulfill. Instead, he argued for the strategy of developing "middle-range" theories that would focus on the objective social consequences of individuals' actions as opposed to their subjective motives or intentions. He stressed that the unintended (or latent) outcomes of individuals' actions may differ sharply from the intended outcomes (or manifest functions), and that these outcomes, whether positive or negative, may be different for different groups or different segments of society. Even if a given institutional pattern is beneficial or functional, this does not mean that it is therefore indispensable; the same function could be fulfilled through alternative institutional structures or forms of behavior.

Whether manifest or latent, institutionalized patterns of action may be distinguished according to whether they are beneficial (or functional), harmful (or dysfunctional), or irrelevant to the system, or to different segments of it. In many cases, the outcomes of a particular type of action may benefit some groups but be dysfunctional for others. When latent dysfunctions eventually become manifest in people's consciousness, they may be defined as social problems requiring some form of intervention. However, such efforts themselves may also generate unintended consequences.

A great deal of Merton's work illustrates his development of various middle-range theories. We briefly reviewed his theory of social structure and anomie as related to deviant behavior, his theory of the bureaucratic personality, and his reference group theory. Middle-range theorizing is also widely manifested in the various specialized substantive fields of sociology—even though they may not make explicit reference to Merton's "middle-range" approach.

Following the decline of functionalism in the late 1960s and the theoretical fragmentation of the 1970s, functionalist type theory made a comeback in the 1980s in the form of "neofunctionalism." The multdimensional theoretical perspectives of Jeffrey Alexander and Richard Münch were reviewed to illustrate this development.

In contrast to Merton's preference for middle-range functional theory, Alexander argued that the only way to move beyond the battles of competing theories was to develop an even more abstract theoretical framework that would be sufficiently general and systematic to encompass the opposing perspectives of lower level theories. Focusing primarily on action and order, Alexander insisted that an adequate theoretical understanding of social action must preserve its contingent and voluntaristic character, while an adequate sociological analysis of social order must include subjectively shared normative commitments as well as the conditioning and constraining influence of the material and social environment.

Alexander's analysis of the works of Marx, Durkheim, Weber, and Parsons was reviewed briefly to show why he felt that each of these theories was deficient in terms of providing an adequate account of both social action and social order in ways that would preserve voluntary choice and normative commitments on the one hand and environmental constraints and influences on the other. In some ways, Alexander's work is reminiscent of Parsons' early social action theory in attempting to synthesize the valid insights of previous theories in a more comprehensive theoretical perspective, and also in emphasizing the importance of normative commitments for sustaining the social order. Later on, however, Alexander shifted his attention to focus more explicitly on the cultural level of analysis. This involves analyzing cultural meanings on their own terms rather than as institutionalized in the social system. Elements of culture such as moral codes may themselves be the primary focus of social action.

Münch also argued for a multidimensional model of social action, using Parsons' AGIL framework to identify and analyze these different dimensions. In his theoretical framework, all social action includes "economic," "political," "structural," and "symbolic" aspects. The "economics" of action involves primarily the pursuit of individual interests through market exchanges. The political aspect deals with goals requiring collective effort. The "structural" component consists of socioemotional bonds and shared normative commitments that give rise to a sense of community. The symbolic dimension refers to shared values and beliefs that give meaning to life and that underlie implicitly accepted worldviews.

Münch pointed out that disagreements among different theorists can be traced to their different starting points in this multidimensional framework. Even when theorists expand their perspectives to cover more and more areas of social life, their original starting points continue to influence their analysis. The result is that much theoretical discourse exhibits considerable ambiguities and inconsistencies. The efforts of both Münch and Alexander to promote a highly abstract and general theoretical framework contrast sharply with Merton's advocacy of theories of middle-range but are consistent with Parsons' efforts in the middle decades of the twentieth century.

The next two chapters cover the major macro-level perspectives that contrast with functionalism—namely, conflict and critical theory.

Questions for Study and Discussion

1. Compare and contrast Merton's emphasis on latent functions and dysfunctions with the way symbolic interaction theory and rational choice theory focus on people's conscious interpretations and/or intentions. For some social group in which you are involved, would you consider your network ties or socioemotional bonds to be the result of conscious intention or a latent function of being in the same environment and coping with common problems? Explain.
2. Explain how Merton's distinction between manifest or latent functions and dysfunctions can be used in evaluating alternative policy decisions in some particular area of social life in which you are interested. Explain the positive and negative effects on the different groups or segments of society that might be

affected. What are the challenges of identifying latent functions and dysfunctions, and how might they be addressed through research?

3. Drawing on Alexander's perspective on social action, explain the difference between rational choice and normative commitments in explaining people's social behavior. Would you agree that normative conformity involves motives that are different from (or deeper than) those involved in rational choice? Drawing on the rational choice perspectives discussed in earlier chapters, explain how a person's normative conformity might sometimes be seen as reflecting a rational choice.
4. For some social setting in which you are involved (relationship, group, organization), explain how the different dimensions of action that Münch identified with Parsons' AGIL model can be applied in analyzing recurrent or typical patterns of action with regard to issues involving resources (economic aspect), goals (political aspect), socioemotional bonds (structural aspect), and shared values (symbolic aspect). Do you agree or disagree that these dimensions are useful in identifying some of the key characteristics of social action? Explain.
5. Explain how the neofunctional perspectives of either Alexander or Münch can be used to analyze the contrasting dynamics of markets, formal organizations, and communities as discussed in previous chapters.

Chapter 14
Conflict and Competition: Analytical Conflict Theories at the Macro Level

It is hard to escape the pervasive presence of conflict and competition at all levels of the social world. From the micro world of family squabbles to the macro world of partisan debates in the United States Congress, everyday life seems filled with tensions, disagreements, and conflicts. The mass media regularly report news of disruptive controversies and conflicts among different groups within our society and in international relations. No doubt most of us have had our share of the strains of quarrels and clashes in our own lives, even though we may sometimes try to prevent minor tensions and disagreements from being too disruptive.

Conflict theorists emphasize that the needs and interests of different people and different groups are often incompatible and contradictory, especially with regard to the distribution of scarce material or financial resources. However, none of these theorists proposes that society is characterized by anarchy, as suggested by seventeenth century British social philosopher Thomas Hobbes' speculations regarding the hypothetical pre-societal turmoil that he characterized as the "war of all against all." Nor do contemporary conflict theorists necessarily focus attention on ongoing violence or physical coercion. Instead, conflict often seems to be repressed, due in large part to various strategies that have been developed to prevent, contain, and regulate it. In addition, as suggested in Georg Simmel's perspective in the early classical stage of sociology, processes of conflict and competition are often interwoven in subtle and complex ways with processes of cooperation and social integration.

Conflict is often seen in sociological theory as an important source of social change. However, highly disruptive conflicts typically trigger efforts to control or repress it, thereby restoring stability. This may involve coercive forms of social control, but it may also involve efforts to compromise and settle grievances, and also to develop strategies to deal with future conflicts in ways that are less disruptive. These processes may occur at any level—micro, meso, and macro. For the overall society the result is that conflict may lead to orderly or evolutionary change, as opposed to anarchy or revolutionary change.

In managing conflict, both within and between groups, numerous informal and formal mechanisms of social control are utilized to enforce rules and regulations, to prevent conflict from erupting into widespread rebellion, and to help reduce blatant forms of unfair hostility or coercion of the weak by the strong. These mechanisms for controlling, regulating, or preventing conflict are backed up by hierarchies

D.P. Johnson, *Contemporary Sociological Theory: An Integrated Multi-Level Approach.*

of dominance and by unequal control of the means of persuasion and coercion—and this inequality may itself be a source of conflict. This chapter will cover the following theoretical perspectives on social conflict:

- Lewis Coser's conflict functionalism—Although sometimes considered a conflict theory, Coser's analysis shows how handling conflict realistically can contribute to social integration, particularly in ingroup relations but sometimes extending to outgroups as well.
- Ralf Dahrendorf's analysis of conflict in modern industrial societies—Although Dahrendorf began with a Marxist perspective, he showed how the changes in capitalist society since Marx's time have led to gradual evolutionary change, as opposed to revolutionary class struggle to overthrow capitalism.
- Randall Collins' multidimensional analysis of conflict and social stratification—In Collins' perspective, conflict and competition permeate all areas of social life as a result of people's ongoing struggles to improve their position in terms of material resources, status, and power. Moreover, macro-level institutional conflicts are grounded in micro-level processes of dominance and submission in people's everyday life social relations.
- Immanuel Wallerstein's world systems theory—Our review of Wallerstein's analysis of the capitalist world economy will focus on how dominant societies exploit other societies through their ability to control the terms of international trade.

Functional Analysis of Conflict: Lewis Coser's Contributions[1]

In Parsons' functional theory, the emphasis on social cohesion and integration, based on widespread consensus on values and norms and high levels of functional interdependence, was so strong that conflict and social change seemed to be pushed into the background. Writing at the time when functional theory was still dominant, Lewis Coser analyzed conflict from a functionalist perspective. The title of his 1956 book, *The Functions of Social Conflict*, suggests the term "conflict functionalism" as an appropriate label for his approach.[2]

Coser criticized the functionalist emphasis on value or normative consensus, order, and harmony. He pointed out that conflict, if dealt with at all, was treated as a

[1] This summary of Coser's conflict theory perspective is adapted from D. P. Johnson ([1981] 1986:479–489).

[2] This book was written originally as his doctoral dissertation (see also Coser, 1967). Lewis Coser was born in Berlin, in 1913, but came to the U.S. in 1941. He received his PhD from Columbia University in 1954. He taught at the University of Chicago, the University of California-Berkeley, and Brandeis University (where he founded the Sociology Department). From 1968 until his retirement in 1987, he was Distinguished Professor of Sociology at the State University of New York at Stony Brook. He continued to be active professionally until his death in 2003.

disruptive or dysfunctional problem that potentially could be resolved by the application of appropriate sociological expertise. For example, the growth of the human relations movement in industrial sociology was based on the premise that antagonism and hostility between labor and management were undesirable but could be overcome by open communication and "good human relations" (Coser, 1956:20–29). Coser's perspective was based heavily on the ideas of Georg Simmel. However, while Simmel had viewed conflict as one of the basic forms of social interaction that is linked in complex ways with alternative forms, such as cooperation, Coser's goal was to show that certain kinds of conflict may have positive or beneficial consequences for the larger system in which it occurs. This does not mean that conflict is good in a moral sense; instead, the focus is on its objective sociological consequences. Whether these consequences are good or bad in a moral sense is a separate question.

Conflict Between Groups and In-Group Solidarity

The positive functions of conflict can be seen when conflict **between** groups helps promote solidarity **within** groups. When an in-group is not threatened by conflict with hostile out-groups, the strong emphasis within the group on cohesion, conformity, and commitment may be relaxed. The result is that internal disagreements are more likely to surface and may be negotiated, and deviants are more likely to be tolerated. In the absence of external conflict, individuals often have greater freedom from group pressures for conformity so they can pursue their personal interests, and this can lead to various forms of internal competition and conflict.

However, if conflict erupts between a group and some other group, the internal solidarity and integration of the in-group is likely to increase. The functions of external conflict for strengthening internal cohesion are well known to group leaders. To strengthen their authority, leaders may sometimes exaggerate potential threats by outside groups or remind members of their external enemies in the hope of promoting greater solidarity. Even an imaginary threat may enhance solidarity by providing an enemy to serve as a scapegoat. In a situation of intense conflict, hostility may even be directed toward members of an in-group if they are seen as similar to members of the other group. On the other hand, in the absence of overt conflict, or if the antagonism is less intense, perceived similarities between members of different groups could stimulate increased social bonds, leading eventually to a decline in the level of antagonism.

Groups sometimes rely on opposition or conflict to justify their very existence. Opposition political parties, for example, define themselves as opponents of the current administration and thus may need to make adjustments in their ideology if they gain power. Similarly, the ideology of religious sects usually involves opposition to the dominant religious establishment or the wider society. As a religious sect gradually accommodates to the surrounding society, it tends eventually to be transformed into an establishment-type organization (Troeltsch, 1931). The absence of an officially established church in the United States, coupled with freedom of religion, makes it difficult for sectarian organizations to maintain their anti-establishment characteristics, unless, of course, they are considered excessively deviant.

Does external threat stimulate centralization of power within a society? Coser (1956:87–95) suggests that the answer depends on the nature of the outside threat as well as the society's internal structure. For a modern society with a high division of labor, the outbreak of war is likely to lead to increased centralization, due to the need for highly coordinated, decisive, and rapid action in a complex system. The question of whether a centralized power structure is autocratic and repressive is a separate question, however. Coser suggests that a despotic power structure is more likely to emerge when internal solidarity and cohesion are relatively low. However, maintaining this highly authoritarian strategy may turn out to be counterproductive when the conflict ends because of the resistance it generates. A vicious cycle may develop if such resistance triggers additional repression, which then stimulates more intense resistance, and so on. Whether this occurs or not will depend on the moral investment made by the public in the external conflict, as well as the effectiveness of the political authorities in reducing the sacrifices that had been required once the external conflict has ended.

Conflict and Group Solidarity

Coser also suggests that **internal** conflict may have positive benefits for increasing group solidarity as well. Like Simmel, Coser pointed out that a certain degree of antagonism and tension is likely in all social relationships, due to differences in individuals' needs and goals. The important point is not whether or not tension or conflict exists, but the form that it takes. To a large degree, this will reflect whether conflicting interests are explicitly recognized and negotiated, and also whether the conflict concerns basic principles or secondary issues. If conflict issues are openly acknowledged, particularly secondary issues, and if mechanisms are developed to deal with them, solidarity need not be eroded.

Suppression of conflict is common in some groups, such as families, which ideally are expected to involve emotionally warm relations and high levels of mutual support. Disagreements are sometimes avoided in such relationships because of the fear that solidarity will be undermined. As Coser pointed out, "The closer the relationship, the greater the affective investment, the greater also the tendency to suppress rather than express hostile feelings" (Coser, 1956:62). The result is that hostile feelings accumulate, with each episode of suppression adding to their intensity. Without explicit mechanisms for acknowledging and negotiating opposing interests, the underlying antagonism continues beneath the surface, undermining solidarity and, in some cases, leading eventually to intense bitterness that is too deep and pervasive to be resolved easily (Coser, 1956:67–72).

It is often easier to deal with opposing interests in secondary relationships than intimate ones, and for secondary issues rather than basic principles. Marital relations, for example, will no doubt experience conflict if either party is guilty of marital infidelity, but probably not if one party drinks coffee for breakfast while the other prefers tea. If conflict over secondary or trivial issues were to erupt in an intimate relationship, it should probably be seen as a symptom of deeper problems that are perhaps being repressed. The integrating functions of conflict are most likely to be evident when there is a larger framework of consensus within which the disagreements occur. A married couple or close friends who are committed to their relationship, and who share the same basic values, will manage to tolerate and work through the disagreements which erupt from time to time. However, if there are disparities over fundamental issues, such as the importance of the relationship itself, internal conflict may lead to deterioration of the relationship or fragmentation of the group.

The absence of overt conflict may be misleading as an indicator of a group's solidarity. However, strategies for dealing with conflict vary greatly, depending on the size and structure of the group. In contrast to small groups or families, large bureaucratic organizations often develop formalized procedures to negotiate differences. In either case, acknowledgment of individuals' personal needs, goals, and interests as worthy of attention is likely to generate increased commitment to the group as well as increasing the chances for conflict. In contrast, the absence of conflict may sometimes signal a pattern of emotional withdrawal whereby tensions and antagonistic feelings are avoided. In marital relations, the result is an "empty shell" type of relationship. In groups and organizations, apathy increases. If repressed conflicts should eventually erupt, this is likely to create a crisis that often makes it difficult for the relationship to be sustained. Friendship circles may deteriorate or fragment as a result of members' inability to acknowledge or resolve conflicts.

Realistic Versus Unrealistic Conflict

Theorists who contrast functional and conflict theories often seem to assume that integration is necessarily associated with stability and conflict with change (for example, see Dahrendorf, 1958). Coser (1956:48–55) makes a crucial distinction between "realistic" and "nonrealistic" conflict in terms of the extent or type of change that it may stimulate. Realistic conflict can be a strategy for removing, or at least reducing, the underlying causes of conflict without destroying the relationship. He points out that a social system may have high solidarity and integration at the same time that its members engage in realistic negotiation of conflict issues (Coser, 1967:27–35). In contrast, nonrealistic conflict involves the expression of hostility as an end in itself. Such conflict is often deflected away from the real object of conflict onto a scapegoat. For example, a mother-in-law may be blamed for a couple's marital strains, or a minority group may become the target of collective anger over a society's military defeat. Conflicts are more likely to be realistic if the validity of opposing interests is openly acknowledged instead of denied, and if such opposition leads to negotiation of differences instead of suppression.

The positive functions of conflict in stimulating change may apply even to violent conflict, despite the fact that violence in itself may trigger repressive social control and thus not appear to be a realistic strategy for positive change (Coser, 1967:73–92). At the very least, violence may serve as a symptom of extreme deprivation and hopelessness (Coser, 1967:53–71). In the absence of established procedures for recognizing and negotiating opposing interests fairly, violence may be seen by disadvantaged segments of society as their only option for making their voices heard. Even though violence is usually deplored and criticized on a moral basis, its occurrence can serve as a "danger signal" to alert members of society, particularly those in the power structure, to grievances and hardships of those experiencing extreme deprivation. Moreover, once the threat of violence is understood, participants in an opposition movement may not necessarily have to resort to violent actions to have their claims and demands taken seriously. This is especially likely when an opposition movement itself is split into an extremist faction bent on violence and a moderate faction committed to peaceful compromise. Even though the moderates may disagree sharply with the extremists, the hand of the moderates may be strengthened by the extremists' threats (Coser, 1967:108–109). Many of these principles can be illustrated by the civil rights movement in the 1960s. The late Dr. Martin Luther King was committed to using nonviolent means to pursue the goal of equality for African Americans, but frequent riots in urban ghettoes added a strong note of urgency to his demands for change. Many of the federal civil rights programs developed during President Johnson's administration can be seen as a response to these pressures and the threat of violence associated with them.

Conflict as a Stimulus for Cooperation Between Groups

Changes often occur in the relationship between opposing groups as a result of their conflict. In a prolonged conflict, practical working relationships may gradually be developed between the contending parties themselves as they learn to adjust to one another's strategies and tactics. Sometimes norms may develop that help regulate the conflict. The collective bargaining procedures in labor-management negotiations is a major example. In international relations, even wars have traditionally reflected implicitly shared understandings regarding the goals and the nature of warfare.[3] The termination of warfare is often frequently followed by the establishment of treaties and alliances to establish and maintain peace. For example, following the end of World War II, both Germany and Japan eventually became allies of the United States as well as beneficiaries of American aid in postwar reconstruction.

[3] Contemporary patterns of terrorism represents a new kind of threat because of the way terrorists target civilian populations so as to achieve the maximum possible dramatic effect. Also, the protagonists consist of networks that do not clearly represent a definite territorially based nation-state. In addition, they espouse broad ideological goals that are difficult to settle through traditional patterns of diplomacy.

Similarly, in the decades following the Viet Nam war, both the United States and Viet Nam began the long process of repairing their relationship.

The likelihood that enemies will eventually become allies depends in large part on whether their conflict is realistic or unrealistic. In international relations, when different states refuse to acknowledge the legitimate national security interests of the other side, and when each side defines its own culture as morally superior and is unwilling to make any compromises, it is difficult to find grounds for negotiation. The longevity of the conflicts between Protestants and Catholics in Northern Ireland and between Israelis and Palestinians in the Middle East illustrate persistent conflicts that seem resistant to resolution. Conflicts of this type reveal the limitations of a functional analysis of conflict.

In addition, conflict often stimulates a search for support from other groups (Coser, 1956:139–149). In some cases, too, antagonisms between groups may be overcome as they band together against a common enemy. Whether such a coalition evolves into a highly unified group with high solidarity will vary, depending on the cultural similarity of its members, the number of common interests they share, and the length and intensity of the struggle with opposing groups.

In American society, many forms of realistic conflict are facilitated by "limited purpose" interest groups that are willing to negotiate and compromise. Even though the overall society may seem to be pervaded by continual conflict on multiple issues, these conflicts are usually limited and so do not lead to the formation of deep and pervasive hostility between sharply defined and permanent conflict groups. Instead, the overall society is knit together by crisscrossing lines of limited conflict that is carried out within a larger framework of norms and laws that regulate it. The result is that conflict among such groups does not undermine the solidarity of the overall society but instead helps promote it. On the other hand, however, clashes that occur among violent urban gangs or between them and the police, or the violence that is sometimes perpetrated by vigilante groups in our society, provide an alternative and far less benign picture. In general, however, Coser's emphasis is that conflict can be seen as functional when it is limited and realistic, particularly when it is carried out within a framework of shared rules that regulate it.

Authority Relations and Conflicting Interests: Ralf Dahrendorf's Contributions[4]

The conflict perspective developed by German sociologist Ralf Dahrendorf contrasts with Coser's conflict functionalism in that Dahrendorf began with the opposing Marxist perspective. His intention was to modify Marx's theory to make it relevant

[4] This summary of Dahrendorf's contributions to conflict theory perspective is adapted from D. P. Johnson ([1981] 1986:468–479).

for an analysis of modern "industrial" societies as well as the early capitalism of Marx's time.

Ralf Dahrendorf was born in 1929 and so experienced the rise of Nazism in his youth. After World War II, he became heavily involved in West German political affairs in addition to his academic career, even serving as a member of the West German Parliament. His academic influence extended far beyond Germany, and he was eventually appointed director of the prestigious London School of Economics. Dahrendorf's conflict theory had a strong appeal to American sociologists following the publication of the revised English edition of his major book, *Class and Class Conflict in Industrial Society*, in 1959.

In contrast to Marx's portrayal of the early years of unregulated entrepreneurial capitalism, Dahrendorf pointed out that modern industrial societies are dominated by corporate forms of capitalism that not only operate on a much larger scale but are also more firmly institutionalized in the overall social structure. A key feature of modern industrial societies is that socioeconomic class conflict has been largely contained through various mechanisms that have been developed to reduce and regulate it. As a result, the chances that major disruptive conflicts will erupt and threaten to escalate into an intense revolutionary struggle are far less than Marx had envisioned. Instead, conflict leads to gradual evolutionary change that actually reinforces and strengthens the system.

Dahrendorf focused a great deal of attention on conflict within "imperatively coordinated associations" (formal organizations or "corporate actors" in Coleman's terms) in industrial societies, both capitalistic and socialistic. He regarded conflicts as inevitable because of the divergent class interests of those at different levels in the hierarchies of power and authority in these organizations (Dahrendorf, 1959:36–71). However, he felt that Marx's explanation of class formation and class conflict was relevant only to the early stages of capitalism, not to a "post-capitalist" industrial society. In contrast to Marx's focus on ownership or lack of ownership of the means of production, Dahrendorf argued that **control** is the crucial factor, not **ownership**. As capitalism has gradually been transformed into a "post-capitalist" society, legal ownership and effective control have been separated to a considerable degree. Ownership is widely dispersed among numerous stockholders, while effective control is exercised by professional managers and executives in corporate structures. Although high-level managers and executives often own large amounts of stock, their control is not based on this ownership but on their positions of corporate authority. Professional managers or executives are themselves subject to the oversight of a board of directors, whose members are also likely to be major stockholders even though not actively involved in day-by-day control.

Several other characteristics of modern industrial society distinguish it from early capitalism. These include increased heterogeneity of the labor force, resulting in part from upgrading the skill requirements for industrial jobs, and expansion of the middle class, many of whose members actually participate in exercising delegated authority. Also included are increased social mobility between classes, growth of political equality and citizenship rights, government involvement in various forms of income redistribution to promote social welfare, and establishment of institutional mechanisms for recognizing and negotiating class conflict issues (such as collective bargaining). Each of these developments could be analyzed in great detail, but all of them underscore the point that the dynamics of early capitalism as described by Marx have limited relevance to modern industrial society.

Dahrendorf's strategy of analysis may be applied to any organization, whether controlled by actual owners or professional managers. Drawing on Weber's portrayal of authority relations, Dahrendorf says: "... authority is a characteristic of social organizations as general as society itself." (Dahrendorf, 1959:168)[5] Authority relations exist not only in industrial organizations but in all organizations, including government bureaucracies. With this notion that the distribution of authority is the primary basis for class formation, Dahrendorf (1959:185–173) followed Marx in accepting a two-class model of social structure. In any authority structure there is a dichotomous distinction between those who exercise authority and those who are subject to it. Dahrendorf did not distinguish systematically between the positions of those at the highest level who exercise authority over an entire organization and those in the middle levels who exercise authority over some but are subordinate to others. In most of his discussion, however, all those who participate in the exercise of authority, even limited authority in the middle ranks, are included in the dominant class. This would leave those in the lowest level, who exercise authority over no one, as the subordinate class. Those who are outside these organizational structures but are dependent on them would also be included in the subordinate class.

Authority figures and subordinates inevitably have conflicting interests. However, as Marx suggested, individuals may not be consciously aware of their class-based interests. In Dahrendorf's terms, their interests may be either **latent** (if they are unaware) or **manifest** (if they are aware). Whether latent or manifest, the interests of the dominant class involve preserving their dominance, while the interests of the subordinate class are in challenging or changing the authority structure. For either class, members who lack an awareness of their common interests may be considered as belonging to a class-based "quasi-group" as opposed to a conflict interest group.

Conflict Group Formation

One of Dahrendorf's goals was to identify the conditions under which latent class-based interests become manifest and lead to the formation of conflict interest groups. These conditions are classified as technical, political, and social (Dahrendorf, 1959:

[5] Dahrendorf's assumption that authority relations are a basic feature of all social organization is itself essentially a functionalist notion that might be compared to Parsons' assertions regarding structures and functional requisites. The real difference between Dahrendorf and Parsons is not his revised Marxist foundation but his emphasis on the conflicting interests inherent in any relationship between those who exercise authority and those subject to it. This contrasts with Parsons' view of authority structures in the political realm as reflecting an underlying consensus regarding collective goals, based on widely shared values and norms.

157–205). Technical conditions include the emergence of leaders and a justifying ideology. Political conditions refer to the amount of freedom for groups to organize and engage in collective action. And social conditions refer to the degree of communication between members with common interests who belong to the same "quasi-group."

These conditions vary for different class-based constituencies. Beyond the minimal level necessary for conflict group formation, leaders and ideologies vary greatly in terms of their capacity to mobilize and sustain collective group action. With regard to political freedom, one extreme is represented by totalitarian governments that prohibit opposition political parties, labor unions, or other voluntary associations. At the other extreme, open democratic societies provide a wide range of tolerance for groups to pursue their interests, including opposition groups that advocate social change. Finally, the extent of communication among members of the same class varies for different conflict groups, reflecting in part the level of ecological dispersion of their members or variations in their internal solidarity.

For conflict groups to be formed, latent interests must become manifest; in other words, class consciousness must emerge. Although this process may be stimulated by group leaders and ideologies and by communication with others in the same quasi-group, it is a conceptually distinct process that occurs at the psychological level rather than the structural level. Just as structural conditions are not necessarily the same in all cases, individuals' class consciousness also varies for different people. For example, individuals who anticipate moving into positions of domination in the future are more likely than others to support the legitimacy of the existing authority structure instead of developing class consciousness. Another factor influencing class consciousness and conflict group mobilization is the degree of consistency of individuals' class positions in different settings. Marx had pointed out that those who are subordinate in their occupational role are also subordinate in the political system, in their level of economic well-being, and in their overall status in society. Although occupational status is crucial because of people's dependence on the material resources it provides and the amount of time they spend at work, Dahrendorf pointed out that individuals in modern industrial societies typically belong to a variety of different associations and groups, and their status may vary in these different settings. Some organizational involvements may be a source of high status and other rewards, while others may be low status. Dahrendorf emphasized the notion that individuals differ in terms of whether their material well-being, their level of authority, and other aspects of their status are consistent or inconsistent in the various organizations and social settings in which they may be involved.[6]

Dahrendorf refers to the pattern in which individuals' status is consistent in different social settings as one of high "superimposition." This contrasts with the situation where individuals have low status or are subordinate in one setting but high status and influence in another (Dahrendorf, 1959:213–215). Dahrendorf suggests that the higher the degree of superimposition, the greater the probability that class consciousness will

---

[6]This is consistent with Homans' notion of status consistency, which was discussed in connection with his contributions to social exchange theory.

be developed and class action undertaken. In such situations, conflict is likely to be carried over from one setting or association to other settings and associations. Such generalized conflicts would both reflect and reinforce the emergence of class solidarity and a common class culture (Dahrendorf, 1959:191–193; 201–205).

Intensity and Violence of Conflict

Dahrendorf also attempted to explain variations in the intensity and violence of class conflict as two analytically distinct dimensions. **Intensity** refers to the "energy expenditure and degree of involvement of conflicting parties" (Dahrendorf, 1959:211) and reflects the importance of the outcome to those involved. In contrast, **violence** refers to the means used in engaging in conflict (Dahrendorf, 1959:212). The level of violence can also vary widely, ranging from no violence to threats of violence to actual physical attacks on property or persons (both organized and unorganized). Whether peaceful or violent means are used to attempt to resolve conflicts will depend largely on the availability of alternatives. While intensity and violence of conflict are sometimes related, these variables may vary independently.

Many of the conditions that influence the strength of class consciousness and the extent of conflict group formation also affect the intensity and violence of conflict. Two major variables affecting intensity are the degree of superimposition of conflict in different associations or settings and the degree of mobility between socioeconomic classes. In general, intensity will be high if there is a high degree of superimposition. This increases the likelihood that different issues will coalesce into broadly defined crusades. In an extreme case, the society as a whole may appear to be divided into two large hostile camps. In addition, conflict is more likely to be pervasive and intense if opportunities for upward mobility are limited. On the other hand, as Dahrendorf (1959:222) pointed out: "As mobility increases, group solidarity is increasingly replaced by competition between individuals, and the energies invested by individuals in class conflict decrease."

The intensity and violence of conflict are also influenced by the pattern whereby material rewards and general social status are distributed. A high level of overlap between material resources, other sources of status, and the distribution of authority supports the image of a two-class system. In contrast, individuals' economic rewards, status or prestige, and authority may vary in different organizational settings, resulting in a more complex stratification system in which different dimensions of socioeconomic status crosscut one another instead of overlapping. In addition, if the combined effects of these different dimensions provide a picture of a more or less continuous distribution from the top of the scale to the bottom, this would also undermine the appearance of a clear-cut dichotomous class structure.

In general, the greater the overlap or superimposition between the distribution of authority, material rewards, economic security, social status, and the like, the greater the intensity of class conflict. Whether violence is also greater depends on whether the deprivation of those in the subordinate class is "absolute" or "relative"

(Dahrendorf, 1959:217–219). Absolute deprivation refers to lack of resources above a minimal level of subsistence, giving rise to feelings of having nothing left to lose. Relative deprivation, in contrast, may be felt by persons whose resources provide a reasonably secure lifestyle, but who are nevertheless lower than those above them with whom they compare themselves. Dahrendorf suggests that relative deprivation is less likely to lead to violent conflict than absolute deprivation. Intensity may also be high if there is a high level of superimposition of various forms of deprivation.

One of the most important variables influencing the level of violence in Dahrendorf's model is the extent to which mechanisms are in place to negotiate competing interests and regulate conflict (Dahrendorf, 1959:223–231). This is closely related to the political conditions mentioned earlier that affect class consciousness and interest group formation. When political leaders attempt to suppress conflict by prohibiting the formation of interest groups, conflict is submerged beneath the surface, where it may smolder for long periods of time. From time to time, however, these submerged hostilities may erupt in the form of violence. In contrast to the totalitarian pattern in which conflicts are repressed and conflict regulation procedures are lacking, authority figures may adopt a strategy of acknowledging conflicting interests and providing channels for their expression and negotiation. Paradoxically, therefore, recognizing the validity of conflicting interests leads ultimately to the diminishment of the disruptiveness and violence of conflict. Open democratic societies provide the sharpest contrast to totalitarian ones in terms of their explicit recognition of conflicting interests and in the institutionalization of mechanisms for regulating conflict. But even in democratic societies, political authorities sometimes attempt to stifle debate and dissent or ignore the interests of subordinate groups, and such efforts may be expected to increase the chances for violence.

Consequences of Conflict

Conflict often triggers social change, particularly with respect to the authority structure of an organization or the overall society. Structural change may involve changing the personnel in positions of authority or incorporation of the interests of the subordinate class in the policies of the dominant class (Dahrendorf, 1959:232–233). If members of the subordinate class are actually incorporated into the dominant class, there is a risk they will eventually be coopted and neglect the interests of the subordinate class. One major reason for this is the pattern described by Michels' ([1915] 1949) iron law of oligarchy, whereby persons who move up from the subordinate class into the dominant class often shift their priorities to maintaining their new positions of domination instead of promoting the interests of the subordinate class from which they were recruited.

Dahrendorf also proposed that structural change can be analyzed in terms of how radical and how sudden it is. These variables, like intensity and violence, may vary independently. Radicalness refers to the **extent** of structural change, while suddenness obviously refers to its **speed**. Change may be sudden and radical, as in a revolution, or it may be slow but also radical. In the latter case, the radicalness may not be consciously experienced as such because of the long time period in which it occurs. For example, even though the United States. has never experienced a revolutionary overthrow of the government (despite the Civil War conflict), it can be seen as radically different in many way from what it was a century ago, particularly in terms of the expansion of the welfare functions of government. Similarly, nonradical changes may also be either slow or sudden. A pattern of slow and nonradical change would be manifested when authority figures and their subordinates engage in minor renegotiations from time to time regarding the scope of subordinates' obligations and their level of compensation. In contrast, a rapid but nonradical change may be seen in the process whereby Democrats and Republicans replace one another after national elections in the United States without making fundamental changes in the overall political structure of society. (This sometimes gives rise to the complaint that nothing ever changes despite the election of a new president.)

The radicalness and the suddenness of structural change are themselves related to the intensity and violence of class conflict. Dahrendorf suggested that there is a positive relationship between the intensity of conflict and the radicalness of structural change (even though such radical change need not necessarily be sudden). Similarly, he hypothesized that the violence of conflict is correlated with the suddenness of structural change. Revolutionary political change would illustrate this pattern of sudden change, but smaller-scale changes may also occur suddenly in responds to demands backed up by violence (or the threat of violence).

In Dahrendorf's perspective, Marx's diagnosis of capitalism should be seen as a special case that was relevant only for the earlier years of capitalism. In Marx's analysis, class formation and class conflict took place under the following historically specific conditions: "(a) absence of mobility, (b) superimposition of authority, property, and general social status, (c) superimposition of industrial and political conflict, and (d) absence of effective conflict regulation. Thus, classes are conflict groups involved in extremely intense and violent conflicts directed toward equally extremely sudden and radical changes" (Dahrendorf, 1959:245). However, changes since Marx's time with regard to these conditions have had the effect of decreasing the intensity and violence of class conflict. Institutionalized patterns of conflict regulation, increased mobility, increased material affluence, greater socioeconomic security of persons in subordinate classes, and institutional segregation of industrial, political, and other forms of conflict help prevent serious challenges to the basic structure of the system

Overall, then, although conflict generally creates pressures for social change, whether the change involves revolutionary overthrow of the system and its authority structure or evolutionary development within it is an empirical question. The answer depends on the various factors discussed above that influence conflict group formation and the extent to which conflict regulation mechanisms have been developed. The institutionalization of procedures to regulate conflict may be seen as reinforcing the existing structure but at the same time allowing evolutionary change within it. If such mechanisms are effective, the chances for the kind of revolutionary overthrow that Marx had predicted in the early days of capitalism are drastically diminished.

Conflict Model Versus Functional Model

Although Dahrendorf regarded his perspective as an alternative to the functionalist emphasis on solidarity, integration, and equilibrium, he believed both perspectives are needed for a more comprehensive picture of social structure than either can offer by itself. He described the opposing assumptions of the two perspectives as the "two faces" of society (Dahrendorf, 1959:157–179). Functional theory emphasizes stability, integration, functional integration, and value consensus. Conflict theory, in contrast, emphasizes the ubiquitous nature of conflict, the effects of conflict in stimulating social change, inequalities in resources and power, the way different elements in society contribute to its disintegration, and the use of coercion to maintain social control (Dahrendorf, 1959:161–162). When summarized in this oversimplified form, the contrast between the two models is of course exaggerated. As we have seen, Dahrendorf's own analysis of conflict in modern industrial society is not consistent with the underlying assumptions of conflict theory that he identified. For example, in his conflict model, established patterns of conflict regulation contribute to the maintenance of the existing authority structure, not its disintegration and change.

The challenge is to incorporate both the conflict and the consensus perspectives into a more comprehensive theoretical framework and to identify the conditions in which conflict theory seems more appropriate as opposed to functionalist theory. This is essentially the strategy that Gerhard Lenski (1966) used in applying the functional model to simple, small-scale societies and the conflict model to complex, large-scale societies. But even within a society as it exists at any given stage of its history, both models are relevant to different degrees in different contexts, and the processes they describe are often interrelated in complex ways. In the final analysis, both models are important for understanding social relations and social structures. However, conflict is the major focus of Randall Collins' conflict theory—the next perspective to be considered.

Stratification and Conflict in Interpersonal and Institutional Settings: Randall Collins' Theoretical Synthesis[7]

Randall Collins' 1975 book, *Conflict Sociology*, provides a theoretical framework that is more systematic and comprehensive than either Coser's or Dahrendorf's perspectives. His overall strategy is to build explicitly on individuals' micro-level behavior and interaction patterns as the foundation for social structures of all types and at all levels (see Collins, 1981). Social structures, whether at the micro level of

[7] This summary of Collins' systematic conflict theory perspective is adapted from D. P. Johnson ([1981] 1986:489–499).

friendship groups or the macro level of bureaucratic organizations, consist essentially of repeated interaction patterns. This repetition of similar patterns over time reflects the ability of human beings to remember past interactions and anticipate future ones. Social structures do not even exist in an objective sense except through the recurrent interaction patterns that make them up. However, consistent with the symbolic interactionist and phenomenological perspective, they do exist as a subjective reality in individuals' minds, and these subjective definitions are socially constructed and maintained through interaction. A major source of conflict results from the people's efforts to influence the subjective definitions of others so as to maximize their personal advantages in interpersonal encounters. (The pejorative term "control freak" is widely understood as a description of one extreme form of this strategy.)

The micro and macro levels are linked explicitly in Collins' model of stratification (Collins, 1975:49–89). At the micro level, the effects of stratification can clearly be seen in everyday life relations of dominance and submission. Such relations are symbolized by deference rituals that low-status individuals are expected to enact when interacting with high-status individuals, even in the absence of overt tension and conflict. These may be highly formalized, as in the pattern of military salutes, or they may consist of informal displays of respect (whether sincere or otherwise) and acquiescence (sometimes reluctant) in letting the other party control the flow of conversations. At the macro level stratification is manifested in the differential distribution of resources among different groups or categories of people, including both material assets (such as income or control of the means of production) and nonmaterial resources (such as authority, power, and prestige).

Collins' conflict perspective is not limited to conflict between different authority levels within bureaucratic organization or socioeconomic class conflict. Instead, it can be applied to any area of social life. Collins applies it to conflict between women and men, for example, between different age groups, and between different intellectual communities. In the micro-level context of contemporary families, husbands and wives sometimes experience tension or disagreements over how to spend their money and their time or the quality of their marital bond, and parents' relations with their children are likely to be characterized by increasing conflict as the children move into their adolescent years and seek to establish their independence. At a more institutional level, conflict and competition can readily be illustrated in business firms' competition for market share, in the disagreements among academic departments for resources, and in the way proponents of different schools of thought in philosophy or sociology seek to establish their dominance over alternative schools. Moreover, the model is relevant not only to modern industrial society but to other societies and previous historical stages as well, with differences among different societies explained in terms of the distribution of resources and power, along with the additional variables that are incorporated in the theory.

Essentially, Collins' conflict theory consists of a creative synthesis of several key ideas from Weber, Marx, Durkheim, and Goffman. Of these, Weber's influence is the most pronounced, though Goffman's micro-level perspective on strategies of self-presentation are also crucial. Collins' broad, comparative style of analysis, utilizing information from several different types of society and several historical periods, is somewhat reminiscent of Weber. Incorporating Weber's threefold distinctions among class, status, and power, Collins views individuals as striving always to improve their position in terms of all three of these dimensions. Such efforts would include strategies for increasing one's income (a widely recognized goal) or for seeking to change the social definitions that are involved in the allocation of social approval, respect, and prestige. Collins (1975:58–59) expanded Marx's focus on the differential control of the means of material production by noting that individuals also differ in their control of the means of "mental production," the means of "emotional production," and the means of violence or coercive power. Although Marx had dealt with mental production in his discussion of how ideologies are used to justify the position of dominant groups in society, his primary focus was material production. In comparison to the early-stage capitalist societies of Marx's time, the means of mental and cultural production have expanded greatly in modern societies and would include the educational system, the mass media, and all of the various forms of cultural communication whereby people's subjective consciousness is formed. The means of emotional production refer to resources (both material and nonmaterial) that are used in generating emotional bonds to the group or society, particularly to those in ruling positions. Collins emphasized that shared ritual observances which promote emotional solidarity do not occur spontaneously but are instead orchestrated by leaders explicitly for this purpose. As he put it,

> The creation of emotional solidarity does not supplant conflict, but is one of the main weapons used in conflict. Emotional rituals can be used for domination within a group or organization; they are a vehicle by which alliances are formed in the struggle against other groups; and they can be used to impose a hierarchy of status prestige in which some groups dominate others by providing an ideal to emulate under inferior conditions.
>
> (Collins, 1975:59)

In the clan-type groups that had been analyzed by Durkheim, ritual observances that promoted cohesion and solidarity centered on religious symbols and beliefs. In societies dominated by a secular world view, the same type of process occurs with secular rituals, including patriotic events, such as Memorial Day or July 4 celebrations, that reinforce the legitimacy of the system or honor its past or present leaders and heroes. Even in modern secular societies, however, such ritual celebrations often incorporate various religious symbols as well. Similar processes of ritualistic celebration of various kinds also occur in many other settings, though on a less formal level. Whether formal or informal, ritualized activities are widespread in all areas of social life, including both formal organizations and communities as well as in families and friendship groups.

Collins pointed out that coercion or the threat of violence is always a potential element in any conflict situation, since those who control superior means of coercion are able to impose their will on others through the threat of violence. Individuals generally seek to avoid situations in which they are subject to the threat of violence or the coercive control of others, and this no doubt provides an important part of the motivation for their conformity to laws and norms. Legitimate control over the means of violence or coercive power essentially involves military and police structures as organized by the nation-state. Because of the state's monopoly of the means of legitimate coercion and violence, its coercive power may be invoked in other institutional structures to enforce conformity to legally enacted norms and contracts. For example, an apartment owner may enlist the help of the local police in getting a tenant evicted for not paying the rent. In the final analysis, ideological justification for the existing authority structure, plus emotional attachment to the society and its institutions and leaders, reflect the underlying differential distribution of the means of violence and coercion as organized in the political system of the nation-state. However, the coercive power of the state may remain latent as long as the means of mental and emotional production are effective. This means that people's conformity to laws and norms results from their internalized beliefs and moral values as much as from their fear of legal sanctions. But as demonstrated by the use of the police force or military troops to deal with disruptive forms of deviant behavior, including political demonstrations and riots, this coercive power potential can readily be activated if needed.

Interaction Rituals and Social Stratification

In line with his emphasis on micro-level processes, Collins' perspective provides a link between Durkheim's emphasis on social solidarity through ritual observances with Goffman's analysis of the strategies used in staging interactional performances. Collins treats Goffman's portrayal of the rituals of face-to-face encounters as a micro-level manifestation of Durkheim's insight that social reality at the macro level rests on emotional bonds of solidarity that are created and reinforced through collective rituals. While Durkheim had emphasized how religious rituals reinforce emotional solidarity and shared moral codes for the group as a whole, Goffman concentrated on the deliberate strategies individuals deploy as they seek social support for the identities they seek to project and reaffirmation of their inclusion in the group. Material resources of various kinds are important for successful enactment of shared rituals as well as for stage props that reinforce people's distinctive identity claims and role performances. In large organizational settings, for example, ritualistic events like celebrations or annual meetings are likely to be staged from a raised platform in front of the room with a microphone and perhaps large video displays to establish the dominant presence of the leader and closely related authority figures. If the ritual is successful, those in attendance experience emotional arousal and renewal of their sense of belonging and willingness to participate in the group.

As noted earlier, Collins emphasized that the stratification system of society is expressed and reinforced through micro-level interaction rituals. Those in positions of authority and dominance expect subordinates to exhibit appropriate levels of deference whereby their dominance is symbolically acknowledged and thereby reinforced. As Collins sees it, such ritualistic displays help maintain and reinforce the existing social order by strengthening people's emotional attachments to it.

Although the level of attachment of subordinates is likely not to be as strong as that of authority figures, their conformity to the appropriate rituals and demonstration of respect for authority figures at least signals their willingness to continue their compliance with the established order. Perhaps the most dramatic examples of ritualistic displays are those that express patriotic attachment to the overall society and respect for its institutions, such as the custom of standing during the singing of the national anthem at the beginning of football games, when reciting the pledge of allegiance to the United States flag in a public gathering, or when a judge enters a courtroom.

Despite their overt compliance, those in positions of subordination are probably not likely to share the same level of subjective commitment as those in positions of authority. They may willingly obey orders that they see as legitimate and comply with the expectations of their position so as to avoid the costs and risks of noncompliance or protest, but this does not mean that they have a strong emotional identification with the existing power and authority structure. Instead, their styles of behavior and interaction are likely to express a certain degree of emotional detachment from the power structure, and to demonstrate as much independence and autonomy as possible under the circumstances. On the other hand, people who feel trapped in positions of subordination may sometimes be mobilized to oppose the existing power structure. If authority figures are seen as betraying the values they claim to represent at the expense of subordinates, these values may be used to justify subordinates' resistance to the inequalities and injustice supported by the current authorities. Such a pattern can be seen in the United States civil rights movement as well as in the liberation theology movement in Brazil and other Latin American countries in which religious values supported by the Catholic Church are invoked in the struggles to promote the welfare and improve the opportunities of the poor and the oppressed.

Occupation, Authority Relations, and Socioeconomic Status

Collins emphasized occupation as the major determinant of one's socioeconomic class position. Like Dahrendorf, he treated the authority structure in individuals' occupational settings as the most important dimension of their class position and their general subjective outlook or "class consciousness." In contrast to Dahrendorf, however, Collins did not adhere to a two-class model of authority relations. Instead, he treated power and authority relations as a continuous hierarchical distribution. Those at the top give orders to many persons but take orders from few or none. In the middle level are those who give orders to subordinates at the next level below them but take orders from persons at the next level above them. In large bureaucratic organizations, the middle levels include a wide array of gradations from upper middle to lower middle. Just above the lowest level are the first line supervisors who give orders to subordinates who actually perform the tasks they are assigned instead of giving orders to anyone below.

This emphasis on the hierarchical authority structure of large organizations would not apply to small business entrepreneurs with no employees or to those whose income is based on investments instead of employment. However, as noted in our earlier chapter on socioeconomic class cultures, hierarchical position in one's occupation is strongly related to his or her income, status group membership, and numerous other variables involving lifestyle and cultural tastes. The income people earn is a major influence on the type of housing they can afford and thus the neighborhood where they live. Their lifestyle options, including leisure and consumption patterns, are dependent on what they can afford. In addition, Collins pointed out that the range and level of one's social contacts, both within and outside the occupational context, are highly correlated with occupation, income, and overall status.

Although the potential for physical coercion and violence may be present in any conflict situation, a great deal of Collins' analysis centers on strategies used to avoid the need to resort to the use of physical force. As suggested above, many of these strategies involve the performance of rituals that dramatize individuals' positions in the stratification system or symbolically express their emotional attachments to one another or to their group or society. Those in dominant positions rely heavily on deference rituals from their subordinates, not actual physical control, to reinforce their dominance. Those in subordinate positions tend to comply with these expectations, no doubt partly to avoid the costs of noncompliance, but they also are likely to develop their own rituals to express their alienation or lack of commitment to the existing authority structure, as opposed to engaging in violent rebellion. Within all levels, various rituals are used to enhance emotional solidarity among those whose class positions are similar and also to express their subjective sense of superiority to those at other levels in the stratification system.

Despite his explicit conflict orientation, Collins' perspective thus provides an explanation of how people seek to avoid overt conflict and to maintain social order.[8] In contrast to functional theory, however, Collins treats individual interests as primary and as relatively independent of moral codes. Efforts to promote and reinforce moral and normative commitments are seen as strategies whereby individuals attempt to influence one another's definitions of the situation and their expectations for one another's behavior. Since negative sanctions make it difficult to maintain or enhance one's status, the most rewarding strategy for most people most of the time is to comply with norms as expected (or at least give the impression of doing so) and thereby earn the approval of one's peers as well as authority figures.[9]

[8] This was the same issue that led ultimately to the development of Talcott Parsons' structural-functional theory. In contrast to Collins, however, Parsons' focus on social order based on shared values was so strong that conflict tended to be neglected in his perspective.

[9] It is also relevant to note that persons in subordinate positions often develop alternative ranking systems among themselves in which status is earned by resisting conventional norms and staging behavior that dramatizes this resistance. Such patterns can readily be observed among adolescents who seek to earn the respect of their peers by flaunting their violation of school rules and teachers' expectations. Such patterns are generally more common or more blatant among those who have difficulty in achieving academic success.

The discussion so far has been limited largely to the internal relations of a society. Collins also applies his conflict perspective to competition and conflict which occur among different nation-states as they seek to maintain or improve their international standing. This is done through each society's political leaders, whose strategies may include both diplomacy and warfare as well as regulation or control of international trade. In order to finance the weapons systems needed for a military force, however, a society must have surplus resources over and above the basic survival requirements of the population, plus an effective system of taxation and military recruitment and discipline. Collins emphasized that a high level of political centralization is required to procure and control expensive and technologically advanced modern weapons systems. Depending on a society's relative strength, defensive or expansionist policies may be developed (along with the appropriate justifying ideologies) to try to promote the willingness of the population to invest surplus resources in weapons and military forces. But, a society that attempts to increase its resources and its international position through expansionist policies (as Hitler did in the years leading up to World War II) runs a risk of overexpansion, especially if it must engage in battles on two widely separated fronts. Although modern transportation and communication have reduced the inhibiting effects of physical distance as such, Collins employs the notion of geopolitical constraints to identify the limits to which a society can pursue expansionist policies without becoming vulnerable to internal and external opposition that can sometimes escalate beyond its ability to reestablish control.

Applications of the Model

As noted earlier, Collins intended his conflict perspective to be relevant at all levels of the social world, ranging from face-to-face encounters between authority figures and their subordinates, and husbands and wives in family settings, for example, to macro-level market competition between business firms and military conflict between nation-states. However, it is important to keep in mind that macro-level processes within and between societies do not exist independently of micro-level processes but are instead grounded in them. Collins' analysis is interlaced with numerous formalized propositions that express many of the relationships between the variables in his theory. A few examples will serve to illustrate this style of analysis, as well as demonstrate the strategy for theory construction as it was described in Chap. 4.

On conversational encounters, especially in hierarchical settings: "The more people one gives orders to and the more unconditional the obedience demanded, the more dignified and controlled one's nonverbal demeanor." (Collins, 1975:157); on the tendency of subordinates to express emotional detachment: "The more unequal the power resources and the lower the surveillance, the more perfunctory the compliance with deference rituals, and the greater the tendency for individuals to evade contact..." (Collins, 1975:216); on sexual stratification: "The greater the monopolization of force by political agencies outside the household, the lower the power of men over women." (Collins, 1975:283). This last proposition is intended to contrast modern societies with some premodern societies in which the absence of specialized police or military forces meant that households (often with extended families) were responsible for their own basic security, both internal and external.

At the organizational level, the following examples provide a partial summary of his analysis: "The more one gives orders in the name of an organization, the more one identifies with the organization..." (Collins, 1975:301), and "The more closely a superior watches the behavior of his subordinates, the more closely they comply with the observable forms of behavior demanded." (Collins, 1975:307). Michel's iron law of oligarchy (in which persons in power develop strategies to maintain their power) is explained as follows: "The larger a membership association..." and "the more dispersed the members, the greater the tendency to oligarchy" (Collins, 1975:334). On the means of violence, "The more reliance on *expensive, individually operated weapons,* the more fighting is monopolized by an aristocracy of independent Knights, and the greater the stratification of society." (Collins, 1975:357, italics in original), but "The more reliance on *expensive weapons operated by a group,* the more an army takes the form of a central command hierarchy and a subordinate group of common soldiers" (Collins, 1975:357, italics in original). On religious rituals: "The greater the *equality within the ceremonially united group,* the more likely the religion is to emphasize mass participation rituals, signs of membership, and the ideal of group brotherhood" (Collins, 1975:370, italics in original). A final example, on status-group formation and political power: "The greater the resources for organizing itself as a status group, the greater the political influence of a collection of individuals." (Collins, 1975:386)

This sampling of propositions has been selected from several larger lists included in the various chapters of Collins' *Conflict Sociology.* These examples summarize much of the earlier discussion of Collins' conflict theory perspective and also illustrate the style of relating specific variables through explicit formalization of propositional statements. In contrast to Collins' explicit effort to link micro and macro level, Immanuel Wallerstein's analysis is more macro, focusing explicitly on market transactions among nation-states that vary greatly in terms of resources as well as social organization and political power.

World Systems Theory and International Exploitation: Immanuel Wallerstein's Contributions

Except for the Collins' application of his theory to international conflict, this chapter thus far has concentrated on theories that deal with conflicting interests **within** society. If societies themselves are taken as the unit of analysis, the macro-level theories of both conflict theory and functional theory could be applied to the developing "world system." Functional theory might be expected to focus on the development of patterns of interdependence among different nation-states plus the gradual and often contested emergence of shared values, such as basic human rights, that transcend national boundaries. Conflict theory, in contrast, would concentrate not only on warfare but also on economic competition and exploitation as well as struggles for political and military hegemony.

Despite the expansion of various economic, political, and cultural linkages among different societies, plus the contemporary emphasis among many theorists on the process of "globalization," the world as a whole is less of an organized "system" than its individual nation-states. There is no world government (though there are various types of international alliances), and the widespread insistence of nation-states on national sovereignty and self-determination severely limits any prospects that might be envisioned for a new world order.

For many years Immanuel Wallerstein (1974, 1979, 1980, 1988) has been the leading figure in American sociology to focus on long-term historical dynamics of the world economic system (see Wallerstein [2004] for a brief introduction to his world systems perspective). Despite the lack of an integrated global social order that can be seen as parallel to the social and political organization of nation-states, Wallerstein's analysis makes a highly persuasive case for treating the capitalist world-economy as a single system. In contrast to world empires based on political and military domination, world economic systems are grounded in the economic interdependence that develops from the expansion of international trade. The linkages among different countries that are based on economic interdependence certainly seem today to be more pervasive and more firmly established than their political or cultural interdependence. This economic interdependence has increased substantially over the past several decades, along with the expansion of other dimensions of globalization as well.

Based on his detailed historical analysis Wallerstein showed that the current capitalist world economy actually had its origins in sixteenth century Europe when agricultural surpluses began to be traded beyond the boundaries of local "minisystems." "Minisystems" are self-contained social systems that, in Wallerstein's words, have "a complete division of labor, and a single cultural framework" (Wallerstein, 1979:5). Wallerstein points out that the independence and self-sufficiency of local minisystems have always been vulnerable to erosion through military conquest and political domination as well as trade. However, the results of the types of interdependence that are enforced through political domination differ significantly from interdependence based on trade. The coercive political control that follows military conquest gives rise to empires that are sustained through taxation, with tax revenues invested heavily in the expanded administrative structures and military or police forces that are required to control subject populations. In contrast, economic interdependence gives rise to world economies based on market transactions that presumably reflect the interests of the trading partners. As we know from the exchange theory, however, when trading partners are unequal, the stage is set for the development of power and dependency relations, with levels of inequality tending to expand over time. This applies to international trade as well as transactions between individuals, even though many other factors may be involved in influencing the specific terms of exchange. Whatever the specific terms that are developed, as trade relations expand and economic interdependence increases, local minisystems gradually lose their self-sufficiency and are absorbed into a larger system with an increasingly widespread division of labor. This process has expanded greatly over the years from the level of emerging nation-states to the international level.

The development of a world economy since the sixteenth century has occurred in an environment of heterogeneous political and cultural systems. The beginnings of this process actually preceded the industrial revolution, which is often associated with the rise of capitalism. The essential feature of a capitalist economic system, in Wallerstein's terms, is that it is based on "production for sale in a market in which the object is to realize the maximum profit." (Wallerstein, 1979:15) Thus the products could be agricultural or handicraft products as well as factory goods, and the human labor employed in their production could involve slavery or other systems for harnessing human labor for production for the market (such as agricultural sharecropping, for example) as well as wage labor in factory settings (as Marx emphasized), The widespread shift from production for use in one's household or local region (through "minisystem" transactions) to production for an expanding market system may be compared to Marx's analysis of the long-term capitalist transformation of production from "use value" to "exchange value." Moreover, the ownership and control of productive resources in Wallerstein's perspective may be vested not only in individual capitalists (the dominant pattern in Marx's time), but also in complex corporate structures (as in modern capitalism) or even in the state itself (as in the former Soviet Union).

The underlying dynamics of world economies contrast sharply with world empires based on military and political domination. Both are inherently unstable, but for different reasons. World empires are established through military conquest and are sustained through the redistribution of surplus resources through political means, such as tribute or taxes levied on conquered people or on their own inhabitants. Empires are vulnerable to the increasing administrative costs that result from their own expansion, including the costs of the social control (army and police) that is needed to prevent the outbreak of rebellion among dominated subjects. World economies, in contrast, involve redistributing surplus resources through market transactions. These often tend to be unequal exchanges because of the differences in the resources of the trading partners. The result of trade relations among societies with unequal resources is the emergence or reinforcement of structures of power and domination, and these change over time as the result of each society's ongoing efforts to maintain or improve its position relative to the others.

Economic crises erupt from time to time in the world economy due to the inevitable imbalances that develop between supply and demand for both products and labor. These economic crises are in addition to the internal political crises that may erupt as a result of the way elites exploit their subject populations so as to be able to enrich themselves through international trade. A key point in this process is that capitalists' commitment to maximize profits leads them to try to expand production while keeping the costs of labor and raw materials as low as possible. But to earn a profit they must be able to sell their products, which they cannot do if the income level in a society is too low to generate a demand for the expanded output. Within the most highly developed capitalist societies, wages have risen greatly over the years, partly due to the influence of labor unions. The aggregate purchasing power represented by this increased income has contributed to the strength of the capitalist system by generating a market for the expanded productivity of the system, and also by giving workers a sense of having a stake in the system.[10] All of these market-oriented processes tend over time to expand beyond the boundaries of nation-states. This expansion may occur as capitalists seek to obtain raw materials from other countries at lower costs, or to relocate manufacturing operations to other countries with lower wages. Expansion also occurs as they enlarge their markets, which they are able to do as their own investments in other countries helps raise the income levels in those countries.

The patterns of trade that develop between nations with unequal resources, like exchanges between individuals with unequal resources, always favor the party with more resources. (The rich get richer.) Wallerstein maintains that these dynamics have given rise to three distinct categories of societies: the core and the peripheral societies at the extremes and semiperipheral societies in the middle. The core societies are the most "advanced" in terms of industrial development and mass production, income levels, education, welfare state policies, military strength, and other indicators. The peripheral societies are not industrialized and serve primarily as a source of raw materials for the core societies. Their overall income levels tend to be low, though a large part of their traditional economy involves agricultural production for local use rather than for extended markets, particularly in rural areas where the majority of the population has traditionally lived. Their governments are relatively weak, even though their elites may be able to increase their power by forming alliances with key persons in core societies. Their motivation for such alliances is that these local elites are able to benefit through developing policies that shift their population from subsistence activities to participation in a market economy. Semiperipheral societies are in the middle and may include former core societies that have lost their dominance or former peripheral societies that have managed to move up in the international ranking system. These broad distinctions obviously mask important differences within Wallerstein's primary categories.

The overall structure of the system that Wallerstein defined, with its divisions between core, semiperipheral, and peripheral societies, has persisted since its emergence in sixteenth century Europe. However, because of its inherent instabilities, the system is a dynamic one, and the relative position of each society in the overall structure of the world economy may shift over time. The growth of the economies of the core societies occurred in large part through trade with the "underdeveloped" or "undeveloped" countries in the semiperipheral or peripheral categories that exploited their natural resources. The result was that large segments of the population of the semiperipheral and peripheral countries were impoverished as they shifted from a subsistence economy to low paid wage labor in a market economy. In

[10]This general process within capitalistic societies is consistent with the analysis by Dahrendorf, discussed earlier, of the importance of the growth of the middle class for avoiding revolutionary change.

previous centuries, the pattern of colonialism that European countries imposed on other countries contributed to the development and maintenance of this system. Despite the eventual end of colonialism the pattern of domination continued. In the twentieth century, throughout the decades of the Cold War following the end of World War II, it involved efforts of core societies to try to earn the loyalty of "less advanced" societies by making investments to aid their development.[11] Imbalanced exchanges and exploitation have continued in more recent decades as multinational corporations in the United States have relocated manufacturing operations to less advanced societies with far lower labor costs. There is a substantial risk, however, that this process of deindustrialization in their home country could lead in the long term to the eventual decline of the United States and other core societies. This would occur as developing societies use their gradually increasing income to expand their industrial base and related infrastructure, improve the income and education levels of their populations, centralize their political systems, and perhaps implement reforms to strengthen their internal legitimacy and increase national solidarity.

In the short term, relocating manufacturing operations from core countries with high labor costs to developing countries with significantly lower labor costs enables capitalist enterprises to expand their markets and increase their profits. For one thing, with lower labor costs they can compete more effectively in their home market while still maintaining maximum profit levels. Also, despite the low wages of unskilled laborers in less developed societies, the growing numbers of their population that are involved in administration or commerce may lead gradually to an increase in their income and their ability to purchase various consumer goods. Even for unskilled laborers at the bottom, their meager incomes may nevertheless represent an increase over previous income levels. In addition, the transition away from the pattern of a rural subsistence lifestyle to a market economy may require increased market participation for basic survival, especially with mobility from rural to urban areas. These developments provide the potential for even more capitalist expansion. Although details vary greatly for different industries and different countries, the expansion of global trade has accelerated greatly over the last several decades, and no country, not even the most highly developed, is self-sufficient. This point is dramatically illustrated by the heavy reliance of Americans and other industrialized countries on oil from the Middle East.

Wallerstein (1979:95–118) argues that the countries in the semiperipheral category have played an important political role in insuring the stability and resilience of the overall world economic system. Because of the specific dynamics that develop from the distinctive role of countries in this intermediate category in their

[11] Wallerstein uses this perspective to show why the noncapitalist or "undeveloped" societies of the world would never be able to go through the same process of development and modernization as the current core societies. In effect, they are prevented from doing so because of their exploitation by the core societies. This perspective contrasts sharply with theories of "development" that were popular in the middle part of the twentieth century when functional theory was dominant in American sociology. (For an example of a once-influential "developmentalist" perspective, see Walt W. Rostow [1961].)

relations to those in the other categories, the dominant core societies do not have to face the united opposition of other societies throughout the world suffering from the same level of exploitation. Instead, the semiperipheral societies are themselves involved in exploiting peripheral societies and thus share some interests with the core societies. This means they have a stake in the maintenance of the system—and they are likely to anticipate having an even larger stake in the future. But in the meantime, they are themselves exploited by the core societies.

During times of economic crisis, political conflicts, or other difficulties, semiperipheral societies may find they are able to take advantage of the vulnerabilities of the core societies to improve their position. In their efforts to do so, their governments may adopt policies to improve their international trading position, which may lead to increased levels of exploitation of their own populations, at least in the short run. In the long run, however, their improved position in the world system may lead to increased levels of economic prosperity, at least for some segments of the population. As semiperipheral societies manage gradually to improve their position through this process, they may displace some core societies which thus lose their dominance. For the peripheral societies at the bottom of the hierarchy, however, their relatively weak governments and low level of market-oriented economic development result in a poor bargaining position in the international arena, at least for the time being. But as conditions change, they too may eventually be able to move into the semiperipheral category.

In effect, Wallerstein's model of the capitalist world-economy shifts Marxist analysis from the national to the international arena. Instead of emphasizing class conflict **within** society (which still occurs, of course), Wallerstein focuses instead on competition and conflict **between** societies. Like Marx he sees economic relations as dominant and emphasizes the importance of capitalists' relentless drive to increase profits as the major driving force of the system. He also shows how capitalists seek to influence both internal and external political policies to protect their interests. His analysis of the unequal trade relations between core, semiperipheral, and peripheral societies helps explain how the exploitation of less developed societies has enabled core societies to attain the relatively high levels of material prosperity that make revolution highly unlikely. In effect, their relative stability and prosperity has been at the expense of the less industrialized societies of the world.

Summary

In this chapter the analytical conflict theories of Lewis Coser, Ralf Dahrendorf, Randall Collins, and Immanuel Wallerstein have been reviewed. Coser, Dahrendorf, and Collins gave considerable emphasis to social processes whereby actual overt conflict, particularly the use of coercion and violence, is avoided. Wallerstein, in contrast, focused on the historical development of the capitalist world-economy from the exploitative trading patterns that developed among core, semiperipheral, and peripheral societies as a result of the competition of capitalists in their relentless drive for profits.

In general, conflict theory emphasizes the following features of the internal dynamics of societies: hierarchical distribution of the population in different social strata, reflecting differential access to valued resources; the opposing interests of different groups and social classes; the ability of dominant groups to maintain their dominance by persuading or requiring other groups to conform to its rules and fulfill the obligations of their roles in it; and the struggles of disprivileged and subordinate groups as a major stimulus for social change. However, contrary to the widely accepted image of conflict theory as concentrating on class struggle and drastic social change, the conflict theories we have reviewed devote considerable attention to explaining how disruptive forms of conflict are avoided and institutionalized mechanisms of social change tend to occur within an overarching framework of structural stability.

Lewis Coser's analysis showed how conflict can have positive functions in promoting social integration if conflict issues are openly acknowledged and conflict regulation mechanisms are developed to deal with them. Conflict between groups promotes solidarity within the conflicting groups, and it is often followed by the formation of alliances between them. Moderate conflict within groups prevents tensions and antagonisms from building up to the point that the relationship itself is threatened. Conflict can stimulate positive social change if it is oriented toward realistic goals. In contrast, nonrealistic conflicts may provide emotional release but do not deal with the underlying causes or lead to positive social change.

Ralf Dahrendorf's model of class conflict emphasized the contrasts between modern industrial societies and the early forms of capitalism of Marx's time that render Marx's predictions regarding class conflict and revolutionary change unlikely. With his focus on the authority structure of organizations as the primary basis for class formation (in contrast to Marx's focus on property ownership), Dahrendorf's model specifies the conditions leading to the formation of interest groups that seek to change the authority structure of society and its major organizations. However, there are several features of modern industrial society that make evolutionary change more likely than revolutionary change, including the growth of a large middle class, the limited and crisscrossing nature of conflict issues, and the development of mechanisms to regulate conflict.

Randall Collins' conflict theory represents a theoretical synthesis between the micro and macro levels of analysis, with a strong emphasis on the notion that existing patterns of socioeconomic stratification reflect the enduring outcome of previous conflicts. His view of social structure, including the stratification system, is that it is based on subjective definitions developed and sustained through micro-level interaction processes, particularly interaction between those in positions of dominance and subordination in occupational settings. The resources involved in developing and reinforcing these definitions are differentially distributed and include not only material resources but also the means of mental and emotional production, plus the means of violence and coercive control. People's positions in the authority structure in their employment settings are highly correlated with their income and education as well as with various social status indicators such as residential neighborhood, lifestyle choices, leisure activities, and the types of social groups with whom they identify.

With Immanuel Wallerstein's historical analysis of the rise of the capitalist world-economy, we shifted from the internal dynamics of societies to the world-wide division of labor between societies that developed through the expansion of international trade. His distinctions among core, semiperipheral, and peripheral societies were used to demonstrate how expanded trade relations enabled the more "advanced" core societies to dominate and exploit the "less developed" societies. This pattern of economic domination can be contrasted with the pattern of military and political domination used by world empires. In Wallerstein's perspective, the origins of the modern world economy can be traced back to the trade in surplus agricultural products in sixteenth century Europe. However, the relative positions of different countries shift from time to time as a result of economic crises that develop from the underlying dynamics of economic competition within the capitalist system. These dynamics can be explained as a result of the relentless drive of capitalists to increase profits by seeking constantly to reduce their costs for labor and raw materials and to expand their markets.

The focus in conflict theory on social change contrasts sharply with the functionalist emphasis on social order. However, social change may be either revolutionary or evolutionary, depending in large part on the development of procedures to regulate conflict. The strategy of analyzing evolutionary change from a conflict theory perspective may be contrasted with the implied notion in functional theory that evolutionary change results from a kind of internal dynamic of the system that seems to insure an automatic process of orderly progress. When we look back in retrospect, it may be relatively easy to regard the long-range outcomes of the labor union movement, the civil rights movement, or the women's movement as an inevitable manifestation of steady social progress. However, there is nothing inevitable about this process. Instead, these advances have occurred through struggle, conflict, and sacrifice—and it is in retrospect that the changes that have resulted have been defined as progress.

Do sociologists and concerned citizens have a role to play in coping with conflict and social change? Critical theorists would answer in the affirmative. In particular, they would insist that sociologists should be deeply involved in promoting increased public awareness of how current social structures are based on widespread domination and exploitation. They suggest that purely academic study of how the current system works amounts to de facto support for the status quo. The idealistic goal of critical theorists is to be involved in struggles to reduce the underlying causes of conflict by reducing inequality and promoting changes in the social structure that will improve all aspects of human welfare. This notion of social theory as social criticism will be our focus in the next chapter.

Questions for Study and Discussion

1. Distinguish between realistic and unrealistic conflict and describe an example of each type in a particular social setting with which you are familiar OR within our society. For each type, how do people on each side perceive those on the

other side? Do you agree that realistic conflict can lead to mutually beneficial social change? Explain.

2. Explain how Dahrendorf's explanation of the formation of conflict interest groups can be related to the principles of social exchange and rational choice theory (as discussed in previous chapters), particularly Blau's analysis of how collective action can be developed from imbalanced exchanges and justified through opposition ideologies. What are some examples of conflict interest groups in our society? In addition to trying to change some aspect of the structures of power and authority, what other types of issues in our society lead to conflict between groups?
3. Explain how Dahrendorf's contrast between modern industrial society and early capitalism provides a more comprehensive perspective for comparative analysis than Marx's diagnosis of capitalism. What are the most important features of modern industrial society that decrease the likelihood of revolutionary conflict as predicted by Marx?
4. Drawing on Collins' perspective, explain how rituals can strengthen emotional identification with an organization or the overall society. Do you agree or disagree that the staging of formal rituals in organizational settings is an effective strategy for reinforcing the existing authority structure and preventing overt conflict? Why or why not? How might the meaning and emotional reaction to rituals vary for participants at different levels the hierarchy?
5. What is meant by the concept of the world economy in Wallerstein's perspective, and what are the major differences between the core societies and semiperipheral societies? What factors help account for changes in the positions of different societies over time? What societies appear at the beginning of the twenty-first century to be moving to a higher rank in the world economy and what societies appear vulnerable to future decline? Explain.

Chapter 15
Critical Theory: Social System Requirements Versus Human Needs

In 1776 Thomas Jefferson included the following statement in the well-known document known as the Declaration of Independence whereby the 13 original American colonies in the eastern part of the country declared their independence from England: "We hold these truths to be self-evident, that all men are created equal, that they are endowed by their Creator with certain unalienable Rights, that among these are Life, Liberty and the pursuit of Happiness. –That to secure these rights, Governments are instituted among Men, deriving their just powers from the consent of the governed, …" (U.S. Government Printing Office, 1995:28) Since these lines were written long before the development of the pattern of using gender-inclusive language, we could debate whether the word "men" was used in the generic sense to include women, but we do know that in that period of our history women were not accorded the same rights as men.

Although people may or may not agree with this notion of "natural rights" or their source in the Creator's actions, an appeal to basic human rights can be invoked today as the foundation for a critical analysis of any society and its policies. The notion that the sole purpose of government is to secure human rights has often been used to object to "excessive" government regulation and control of people's lives. This same critical argument could be applied to other institutions and social structures that limit and constrain human beings' freedom and opportunities for the sake of their own survival.

As we saw in earlier chapters, functional theory and conflict theory have contrasting explanations of how social order is maintained. In functional theory individuals' motivations and behaviors are shaped to meet the functional requirements of society, either by deliberate design or as a latent effect. Conflict theory, in contrast, emphasizes how social order is maintained through structures of domination in which relatively high levels of affluence, coupled with widespread acceptance of justifying ideologies, help prevent excessive dissent and overt rebellion.

Is there an alternative to this high priority on the maintenance of existing institutional structures for the sake of social order? For critical theorists, social systems of all types should be evaluated in terms of how they affect individuals' well-being, as opposed to how well they maintain their particular structures or survive. In any case, the survival of particular structures in a society should never be seen as equivalent to the survival or well-being of the individual members of the society's population. The overall goal of critical theory is to raise our consciousness of how existing structures and systems tend to subordinate and repress large segments of the population, molding and shaping people's consciousness and regulating their behavior for the sake of their own maintenance. For critical theorists the overriding priority should be the welfare of people and their development to their full potential as human beings, not the maintenance of particular structures as an end in itself. This often requires major social transformations. The goal of such transformations should be to advance human rights, protect human freedom, and promote the highest possible level of human fulfillment. The critical theorists and perspectives to be reviewed in this chapter are as follows:

- C. Wright Mills' critical description of the American power structure and "mass society"—Mills' perspective, developed in the middle part of the twentieth century, provided a rebuttal to the then-dominant perspective of functionalism in analyzing American society.
- Structural Marxist perspectives as represented by Georg Lukács, Antonio Gramsci, and Louis Althusser—Before Marx became a key figure for American sociologists, these European Marxists focused their analyses on how capitalism is reinforced through the interdependent and mutually reinforcing institutional structures that shape the overall culture through which individuals' consciousness is formed.
- Development of American critical theory, particularly as represented by Frankfurt School theorists Erich Fromm, Theodor Adorno, and Herbert Marcuse[1]—This humanistic neo-Marxist or "new left" perspective emerged in the late 1960s and early 1970s in the context of the protest movements targeting the Vietnam War, racial inequality, and other social problems, and its development helped contribute to the decline of functionalism.
- Jürgen Habermas's critical theory focus on distorted versus open communication—Jürgen Habermas, one of the Frankfurt School's younger members, focused on how people's everyday lifeworlds at the micro level are dominated by the impersonal controls of macro-level systems.
- Michel Foucault's "post-structural" perspective on how professional knowledge and expertise reinforce structures of power and domination—Although Foucault is sometimes regarded as a postmodern theorist, his perspective clearly offers a critical analysis of how systems of knowledge are reflected in forms of discourse that underlie the implicitly accepted differential distribution of power in society.

[1] These Frankfurt School theorists had earlier come to America from Germany to escape the rise of Nazism there.

C. Wright Mills: The Sociological Imagination and Critical Analysis[2]

As described briefly in Chap. 3, C. Wright Mills (1916–1962) was highly critical of functionalism when it was dominant in American sociology.[3] He argued that the "sociological imagination" should uncover the connections between individuals' personal troubles and the overall structure of society (Mills, 1959). The troubles individuals experience, whether material problems such as unemployment and poverty or psychological problems such as alienation, are rooted in the way society is organized. Social structures should therefore be analyzed critically to show how they prevent people from meeting their basic needs or developing to their full potential as human beings.

Mills' image of social reality was influenced by Max Weber, Karl Marx, Karl Mannheim, Thorstein Veblen, George Herbert Mead, and the traditions of pragmatism and symbolic interactionism (Scimecca, 1977:22–36).[4] His writing style can be compared to the sarcastic style of Thorstein Veblen (1934), the American social critic who had earlier debunked the growing middle-class pattern of conspicuous consumption. Like Weber and Mannheim, Mills (1959:165–176) pointed out that individuals have a limited awareness of the complex dynamics of the large-scale bureaucratic organizations in which they are involved. Even so, their freedom is restricted as they adapt to the demands of these organizational structures. Like subsequent critical theorists, Mills shared with both Weber and Marx a central concern with pervasive forms of domination in society, but Weber's influence was probably more important.[5] Mills stressed in particular the institutional basis for power provided by centralized bureaucratic organizations (as opposed to property ownership or prestige).[6] Focusing on American society, his central thesis was that those

---

[2] This summary of Mills' critical perspective on American society, and how his analysis of its "power elite" can be seen as illustrating Michels' "iron law of oligarchy," is adapted from D. P. Johnson, ([1981] 1986:458–468).

[3] Born and reared in Texas, Mills received his PhD from the University of Wisconsin and spent most of his professional life at Columbia University. His earliest interests in pragmatic philosophy and Mead's social psychology were eventually overshadowed by his critical analysis of the American social structure, as well as of Parsons' structural/functional model of society that he felt seemed to justify it. Parsons' structural-functional model could hardly be ignored in the context of the times. Accordingly, Mills devoted one chapter of his book, *The Sociological Imagination* (Mills, 1959:25–49) to a biting and sarcastic criticism of Parsons' "grand theory."

[4] Scimecca suggests that Mills' theory can serve as an "alternative to both structural-functional and conflict models." The influence of symbolic interactionism on Mills' perspective is represented primarily in Hans Gerth and C. Wright Mills' book, *Character and Social Structure: The Psychology of Social Institutions* (Gerth and Mills, 1953).

[5] In collaboration with Hans Gerth, Mills provided American sociologists with an edited volume of Weber's work in English translation (see Weber [1946]).

[6] In this respect his perspective resembles that of Ralf Dahrendorf (1959), discussed in the last chapter, but with a focus on the power elite in the United States.

who occupy the top positions of the economic, military, and political institutions—the "corporate rich," the military "warlords," and the "political directorate"—form a more or less integrated and unified power elite whose decisions determine the basic structure and direction of the society (Mills, 1956).

Mills did not claim that there is a conscious conspiracy among these elites, or that their members always agreed among themselves or shared exactly the same interests. However, the large size and high level of centralization of the dominant economic, military, and political structures mean that the decisions and actions of their elites have wide-ranging ramifications for one another as well as for the overall society, and each can facilitate or hinder the others in achieving their goals. These elites may not be consciously aware of the conflict between their goals and interests and the overall welfare of society; instead, they simply identify their own interests with the general welfare.

Historical Development of the American Power Structure

Both the large size and the high centralization of the dominant institutions that Mills analyzed depend on modern technologies of production, administration, and communication. As Mills stated:

> From even the most superficial examination of the history of western society we learn that the power of decision-makers is first of all limited by the level of technique, by the means of power and violence and organization that prevail in a given society. In this connection we also learn that there is a fairly straight line running upward through the history of the West; that the means of oppression and exploitation, of violence and destruction, as well as the means of production and reconstruction, have been progressively enlarged and increasingly centralized.
>
> (Mills, 1956:23)

In Mills' (1956) historical overview, mid-twentieth century America differs substantially from earlier periods. In the first half of the nineteenth century, the Jacksonian ideal of democratic equality, coupled with the rapidly expanding development of the American frontier, resulted in a much more decentralized system than had existed during the Revolutionary War period. During this period, the economic structure consisted mostly of small businessmen and farmers, none of whom was in a position to have a major impact on the system as a whole. Political power was limited and decentralized, and resistance to government expansion was justified by the ideal of preserving individual liberty.

This decentralized power structure began to change in the economic sector with the growth of large-scale business corporations in the second half of the nineteenth century.[7] The opening years of the twentieth century then witnessed the concentration of political power resulting initially from American involvement in World War I.

---

[7] Mills' analysis of these developments might be compared with the subsequent analysis by Charles Reich (1970) of the historic transformation from the individualism of Consciousness I to the large-scale corporate and technological dominance manifested in Consciousness II. Reich thought he saw a new third stage of consciousness (Consciousness III) beginning to emerge in the middle of the 1960s among those caught up in the spirit of the youth counterculture at the time.

The Great Depression of the 1930s signaled a breakdown in the self-regulating character of the market system and eventually stimulated additional enlargement of the federal government. With various New Deal programs, government became much more active in the economic system, resulting in a tremendous growth in the federal government and expansion of its power. Involvement in World War II then stimulated the permanent expansion and consolidation of the third major co-dominant circle of power: the military system. Although formally under civilian political control, the military system achieved a status that was virtually coequal with the political and economic power structures. Even President Eisenhower (who had formerly been a military general) had issued a warning about the growing influence of the military-industrial complex. The system was justified by the Cold War ideology of the 1950s.[8] Although Mills died before the beginning of the Vietnam war that so divided our country in the late 1960s, his perspective on the American power structure would lead us to evaluate that long, painful, and unproductive struggle as a result of the commanding influence of the military-industrial complex.[9] A similar critique could be applied to the United States invasion of Iraq in the early twenty-first century. Mills summarized his analysis of the growth of the power elite as follows:

> As each of these domains becomes enlarged and centralized, the consequences of its activities become greater, and its traffic with the others increases. The decisions of a handful of corporations bear upon military and political as well as upon economic developments around the world. The decisions of the military establishment rest upon and grievously affect political life as well as the very level of economic activity. The decisions made within the political domain determine economic activities and military programs.
>
> (Mills, 1956:7)

The interpenetrating and interlocking nature of the policies and activities of these dominant institutional orders is based on social psychological as well as social structural factors. Mills pointed out that the elites in these structures had similar social backgrounds and worldviews. In addition to their great wealth, power, and prestige, many of them came from long-established families that traditionally enjoyed high status or had social acquaintances among them. They also tended to have the same kind of educational background, and they intermingled with one another in various clubs and cliques. In addition, some of them moved back and forth between the top of one institutional order and another. In Mills' time perhaps the most dramatic example was the case of General Eisenhower, who became President Eisenhower.[10]

---

[8] It is important to recall that in the historical context of the time, there was a widespread perception throughout the society that this conflict between the United States and the Soviet Union, as the major superpowers of the world, would be decisive for the future of freedom and democracy as well as basic security.

[9] See Mills (1958) for a sequel to the analysis in *The Power Elite* on the growing dominance of the military institution.

[10] Mills mentioned several other types of examples: "...the admiral who is also a banker and a lawyer and who heads up an important federal commission; the corporation executive whose company was one of the two or three leading war material producers who is now the Secretary of Defense; the wartime general who dons civilian clothes to sit on the political directorate and then becomes a member of the board of directors of a leading economic corporation" (Mills, 1956:288).

Despite these overlapping personal and institutional contacts, Mills did not regard the power elite as a closed or static clique with a completely unified set of policies. Different projects or issues could bring together different sets of individuals. On some issues there may be disagreements. Occasionally, too, promising new members were recruited from the middle ranks of power. In short, the power elite was not seen as a single monolithic structure but a series of overlapping and intersecting networks with partially permeable boundaries. But Mills emphasized the institutional and social psychological bonds that set the elites apart from others in the population.

Mass Media and Mass Society

Mills disagreed sharply with the widespread view at the time of the American power structure as amorphous and pluralistic (Mills, 1956:242–268). According to this pluralistic image, there are numerous, largely autonomous centers of power in American society whose members must negotiate and compromise with one another in establishing national policies. Although certain coalitions may achieve temporary dominance on particular issues, these power centers were seen generally as being in a state of balance in which no one center is able to dominate for very long or on all issues. Mills suggested that balance theory was appealing because of its congruence with American democratic ideology, but he also pointed out that it applies more to the middle levels of power than the top levels. Moreover, because the activities and decisions of the top elites are not necessarily always widely publicized, the public at large has little reason to question the pluralistic image. In Mills' time the news media had not yet developed the kind of aggressive investigating and reporting techniques that have become common in recent decades. And certainly it would have been in the interests of the power elite to minimize public visibility of their dominance and to support the pluralistic balance theory.

Mills (1956) viewed the vast majority of people beneath the middle levels of power as a fragmented, passive, and inarticulate mass society whose members are too unorganized to have any significant impact on public policy or even on the middle levels of power (see also Mills, 1951). The passive nature of mass society results largely from the way the mass media are able to manipulate public opinions and attitudes through distorted and simplified presentations of public issues in ways that are not conducive to public dialogue. Thus the elites are able to present their decisions and actions to the public as being in accordance with democratic principles, thereby implicitly justifying the sociopolitical status quo and their elite positions. Beyond this, the media offer escapist forms of entertainment that divert people's attention from sociopolitical issues.

Mills' critique of the mass media and mass society may seem at first to be less relevant today because the mass media themselves are less homogeneous, and their role in criticizing the political power structure has expanded greatly. Moreover, since the late 1960s there has been a higher level of mobilization of various segments of the population to deal with various social problems. Some of the important social movements have developed since Mills' diagnosis of his times include the civil rights movement, the women's movement, the environmental movement, and the gay/lesbian movement. Moreover, through new electronic forms of communication, there are increased opportunities for the public to be heard, even though they may not be organized effectively. In some case, the news media themselves provide opportunities for public feedback. On the other hand, the mass media today also offer multiple options for being diverted to a highly simulated world that they create, thereby avoiding the practical world of public affairs or civic involvement. The key point is that Mills' critique leads us to look at how power elites are able to maintain their position, sometimes by neutralizing or coopting their opponents, in an environment of widespread public apathy. The mass media still play a crucial role in this process.

The American Power Structure and the "Iron Law of Oligarchy"

Mills' analysis of the American power structure is consistent with the organizational processes portrayed by German theorist Robert Michels (1876–1936) as the "iron law of oligarchy." This concept refers to a tendency for power to become concentrated in the hands of an elite group whose decisions and activities are oriented more toward maintaining their positions of power than promoting the interests of the rank and file (Michels [1915] 1949). This process occurred in the political parties and labor unions that Michels analyzed despite their democratic ideology.

The dynamics of this transformation originate in organizational growth and the establishment of paid leadership or administrative positions. With these developments the social distance between rank and file members and official authorities and administrators makes it difficult for the average member to exert influence on organizational policies or administrative decisions. In addition, organizational growth leads eventually to expansion in the number of administrative officials who form their own privileged subgroup and pursue their own distinctive interests. In the meantime, the interest and involvement of rank and file members tends to decline, especially as they discover that their voices will probably not be heard anyway. Widespread apathy may lead members to neglect even minimal opportunities for involvement such as voting. This apathy and indifference make it easier for the authorities to consolidate their power and pursue their interests without undue concern for resistance by the rank and file.

If an opposition movement should develop, those in power may criticize movement leaders as being uninformed and pursuing their own narrow or selfish interests. Moreover, authority figures may use resources they control to "buy off" or coopt potential opponents. In American presidential politics, for example, the incumbent alone has the opportunity to "act presidential" in supporting policies that benefit key constituencies. Not least among the resources of those in power is the opportunity to recruit (or coopt) opponents or potential opponents into the elite circle.

The organizational dynamics implied by the iron law of oligarchy do not mean that overthrowing established power structures is impossible. The history of organizations and societies reveals that power structures are sometimes overthrown and replaced. Nevertheless, enormous odds must be overcome. When such movements are successful, the new power structures are likely to develop the same oligarchical tendencies, despite appeals that may have been made to democratic principles in the struggle to overthrow the old regime.

C. Wright Mills died in 1962, less than a decade before the eruption of the anti-Vietnam war and other countercultural protest movements of the late 1960s and early 1970s. Thus he did not witness the steep decline in the influence of functionalism or the development of a strong critical and neo-Marxist movement within American sociology. Nevertheless, the sociological imagination he advocated represented a critical stance toward society and also toward sociological theorists who fail to develop a critique of existing social structures.

Theoretical Developments Within Marxism

Social theorists can be distinguished according to whether they take a Marxist or non-Marxist approach. Marxism was largely absent from American sociology during the period of sociology's rapid expansion between the end of World War II and the transition period of the late 1960s and early 1970s. Prior to World War II, some aspects of Marxism appealed to various American leftist intellectuals, but sociology's development was influenced more by the ideal of supporting progressive reforms within capitalism than by espousing the kind of critical analysis that would advocate its revolutionary transformation and replacement by some form of socialist system.

The situation was different in Europe, where Marx's influence was stronger. However, European social theorists also tended to concentrate on the strength and resilience of capitalism and the reinforcing effects of its culture and political systems that had developed since Marx's time. Certainly Marx's predictions regarding the increasing misery of the working class that eventually would help foster the formation of revolutionary class consciousness or the eruption of revolutionary struggle had not occurred as he predicted. Even so, the differential distribution of material resources, power, and influence could be seen as a potential target of social criticism.

For Hungarian theorist Georg Lukács in the early 1920s, the modern capitalist system operates according to its own laws that are beyond the ability of individuals to control. Its structures are reified in people's consciousness as inevitable and durable features of the social world to which they must adapt (Lukács [1922] 1968).[11] This process of reification was applied not only to the subjective orientations of industrial workers but also to the mentality of bureaucratic officials as they functioned in accordance with Weber's model of impersonal bureaucratic modes of administration. The "false consciousness" reflected in this widespread reification process prevents the formation of an enlightened form of class consciousness among the working class and thereby inhibits the eruption of revolutionary struggle to challenge or overthrow

[11] The concept of reification refers to the tendency for people to see the outcomes of their own activity as an objective reality that operates according to its own principles beyond their control.

the system. It also leads other segments of the population to accept the dominant patterns of bureaucratic administration and control and thus reinforces the legitimacy and stability of the overall sociopolitical organization of society.

Despite the importance of economic class relations as the foundation of the social structure (which Marx emphasized), other institutions have their own distinctive dynamics and forms of cultural legitimation. These institutions are interrelated with one another and with the economy in ways that are more subtle and complex than Marx had theorized. Writing from prison in the late 1920s and early 1930s, the Italian theorist Antonio Gramsci emphasized the interdependence between the "structure" of actual social relations (including relations of production and other types of institutional relationships) and the "superstructure" of beliefs and ideologies that explain and thereby legitimate the overall system (see Forgacs, ed., 2000). Gramsci's concept of "hegemony" was used to emphasize the overriding dominance of deep-seated cultural beliefs and ideas that support and justify the capitalist system. This emphasis on cultural hegemony contrasts with Marx's focus on material conditions and the differential ownership and control of the means of production as the primary source of domination. The existing system for the differential distribution of economic and political power acquires "hegemony" or cultural dominance through the various socialization processes whereby people's consciousness and fundamental worldviews are developed.

For many Marxist theorists, the political structure plays an even larger and more pervasive role than for Marx himself in maintaining the capitalist system. In addition to serving the interests of the dominant capitalist class (as Marx emphasized), the state has its specific own dynamics of domination, and it provides symbols of political legitimacy that help insure the maintenance of its structure and controlling position. In addition, cultural institutions such as education, religion, and the mass media play a major role in shaping the worldview that helps sustain the legitimacy of the overall system, including its economic and political structures. The high level of convergence between the political structures of the state and the structures of other institutions that support the state was a major theme in the structural Marxism developed by the French theorist Louis Althusser ([1971] 2001) during the Cold War decades of the 1960s and 1970s. By this time period it had become abundantly clear that the communist ideology inspired by Marx and Lenin was being used to justify Soviet domination of Russia and the Eastern European countries in the Soviet Union rather than to promote equality and economic prosperity for the entire population.

Louis Althusser distinguished the "repressive state apparatus" consisting of the legal and law enforcement system and the "ideological state apparatus" that includes the mass media, education, religion, and other structures of cultural production (Althusser [1971] 2001:85–126). However, all of these "structures" of domination—economic, political, and cultural—have their own distinctive dynamics, and the relative importance of each varies for different societies in different historical periods. Despite these variations, however, the underlying foundation consists of material conditions and economic resources. Although there are obvious differences among different social classes in terms of their material well-being and economic resources, the process that Marx predicted whereby the working (or proletarian) class would expand and become more and more impoverished had clearly not occurred with the development of capitalism. Moreover, the overwhelming influence of the various processes of cultural legitimation seemed to make the emergence of class consciousness and revolutionary struggle difficult and unlikely.

Critical theorists influenced by Marx can be contrasted in terms of how much they focus on the external economic and political structures of domination as opposed to the internal domination of people's consciousness through various ideological and cultural superstructures. Both types of analysis are reflected in Marx's own writings. For critical theorists influenced by him, domination through cultural ideologies that shape people's consciousness tends to be more subtle and less obtrusive than economic exploitation or political coercion. In contrast to coercive forms of control, cultural domination leads to tacit acceptance of the system, partly because of an inability to conceive of alternatives. The prevailing mentality supporting the system results in large part from the way the ideologies of society's different institutions reinforce one another, allowing no room for alternative ideological perspectives from which to develop a critical consciousness that could lead to serious consideration of a major social transformation. Without the transformation of consciousness through cultural change, it is difficult even to envision possibilities for revolutionary change in the institutional structures of society.

The dialectical mode of analysis that Marx advocated underscores the numerous internal contradictions and conflicts built into the social structure.[12] Although internal contradictions could theoretically stimulate conflict leading to social change, it turns out that many such contradictions and conflicts have essentially been "contained" through legitimating ideologies and widespread material affluence. These ideologies mask the contradictions by promoting the appearance of consensus and solidarity while the widespread material well-being of large segments of the working class, coupled with the growth of a large middle class, helps reduce class distinctions and the sense of working class deprivation that could otherwise lead to a strong class consciousness.[13] Critical theorists have seen their task as uncovering this containment process to reveal how the workings of the underlying structure of the system help preserve patterns of inequality and domination. The notion of transforming consciousness as the first step in transforming society can be related to the humanistic orientation of Marx's early writings. These early works became highly influential in the "new left" critical theory developments that occurred in the U.S. in the late 1960s and early 1970s (see Horowitz, 1964; Bottomore, 1967, 1974; Birnbaum, 1969, 1971).

---

[12] The strategy of dialectical analysis in Marx's theory was explained briefly in an earlier chapter. For an example of an effort to integrate the opposing implications of dialectical analysis and the functional approach, see Pierre L. van den Berghe (1963).

[13] The ideas of both Erik Olin Wright (1979) and Ralf Dahrendorf (1959) that were reviewed in an earlier chapter provide examples of efforts to revise Marxist theory at the structural level to make it relevant to the organization of capitalist societies in the second half of the twentieth century.

Development of American Critical Theory[14]

The expanded interest of American sociologists since the mid-to-late 1960s in a critical theoretical perspective can be related to the protest movements and social turmoil that erupted in America during these years (e.g., Roszak, 1969, Reich, 1970, Flacks, 1971; Slater, 1970, 1974) and that contributed to the social and cultural fragmentation of that period in our country's history (Berger et al., 1973). These developments had been stimulated initially by the civil rights struggle but later accelerated greatly with widespread opposition to the Vietnam war. Ultimately, the sociopolitical issues were broadened to include many other issues, including abuses of power by those in positions of authority, rigid forms of bureaucratization, perceived unresponsiveness of established institutions to human needs, excessive emphasis on materialism and a consumption-oriented lifestyle, blindness to the environmental pollution resulting from technology, and domination and exploitation in international relations.

Most of those involved in the countercultural movements of the time were not members of the working class but middle class young people, including students, whose youthful idealism was expressed in a yearning for an alternative lifestyle with nontraditional and nonauthoritarian institutions based on a radically different type of worldview. The alternative consciousness they promoted would put a much lower priority on conventional forms of occupational success, technological progress, and material consumption as the foundation for a satisfying and fulfilling life. Those involved with or sympathetic to the countercultural youth movements of the time were unwilling to participate in the perpetuation of what they saw as unresponsive bureaucratic-technocratic systems with their impersonal and manipulative social relationships. Their focus was cultural transformation, as opposed merely to economic restructuring of class relations. Many of them had high hopes that their various forms of protest would somehow lead to increased authenticity in social relations, higher levels of equality, and greater opportunities for human fulfillment.

This widespread critical orientation toward "the Establishment" helped contribute to the growth of critical "new left" sociology in the United States in the late 1960s and early 1970s. This development was also reinforced by the increased availability and popularity of Marx's early humanistic writings (Fromm, 1961). Still another part of the roots of American critical sociology was the influence of the Frankfurt School theorists, including Max Horkheimer, Theodor Adorno, Herbert Marcuse, and Erich Fromm (see Connerton, ed., 1976 and Tar, 1977). The Frankfurt School had its origins at the Institute for Social Research at the University of Frankfurt in Germany in the 1930s. The critical orientation that developed there was no doubt stimulated by the threat represented by the rise of Nazism. By the middle of the 1930s, the Nazi threat effectively disrupted the Institute and many of its members came to America. (Some eventually returned after the war to reestablish the Institute.)

---

[14] This brief description of the development of critical theory in American sociology, including the distinctive neo-Marxist contributions of the Frankfurt School, is adapted from D. P. Johnson ([1981] 1986:450–458).

The impact of critical theory on American sociology was limited prior to the mid-1960s, but there were some notable exceptions. One example was Erich Fromm's (1941) analysis of people's apparent willingness to sacrifice their freedom for the sake of security, as well as his later critique of material consumption as the key to a meaningful life (Fromm, 1976). He drew from Freud and the psychoanalytic tradition as much as from the Marxist perspective. This pattern of linking Marx's concept of oppression and Freud's concept of repression is also reflected in the works of other critical school theorists.

Analyses by Adorno et al. (1950) of the authoritarian personality was also influential in American sociology long before the late 1960s. The authoritarian personality pattern is manifested when subordinates identify with officially established rules and authority figures so strongly that their behavior reflects blind obedience and a failure to show concern for the larger moral implications of their actions. Similarly, authoritarian persons who are in positions of authority are likely to insist on compliance with their orders without questioning their appropriateness. Adorno's influence stimulated a great deal of empirical research designed to measure authoritarian tendencies, its origins in childhood socialization patterns,[15] and the correlations between authoritarianism and other variables. One important line of investigation suggests that authoritarian personality patterns are related to anti-Semitism and negative attitudes toward other minority groups (for example, see Glock and Stark, 1966). This research was consistent with a different stream of research led by Stanley Milgram (1974) that demonstrated how "normal" people could be persuaded in laboratory experiments to be willing to hurt one another by administering painful electric shocks if ordered to do so by an authority figure. (In the experiments, there were no actual shocks, of course, and the "victim" was a stooge of the experimenter.)

By the late 1960s and early 1970s, the works of Herbert Marcuse (1960, 1962, 1666, 1973) had become highly influential, especially among younger members of the discipline. Like Fromm, Marcuse also drew heavily from Freud as well as Marx. In *Eros and Civilization* (Marcuse, 1962), he used the Freudian concept of repression to explain the new and more pervasive forms of domination that had developed within modern society. Marcuse's (1966) concept of the "one-dimensional man" was essentially a critique of how the technological-bureaucratic structures of modern society limit, constrain, and shape the formation of people's consciousness and worldview in ways that restrict their full development as human beings. Whether he intended this concept of the "one-dimensional man" to apply equally to both genders is not clear; although his writings appeared before the contemporary use of gender-inclusive language, he undoubtedly intended it to apply throughout society—even though patterns of repression may well differ for men versus women. Marcuse's influence declined not long after the end of the active countercultural protest movements of the late 1960s and early 1970s.

---

[15] Childhood socialization experiences that were seen as being related to adult authoritarianism include parental insistence on obedience and the use of physical punishment to control children's behavior.

In contrast to Marcuse and the other members of the Frankfurt School as described briefly above, the influence of Jürgen Habermas on sociological theory has continued to the present day. In the next section we turn to his contributions to the development of a systematic critical theory.

Lifeworld Versus System: The Critical Perspective of Jürgen Habermas

Born in 1929, Jürgen Habermas was too young to be involved in the Frankfurt School developments before World War II, and he was not among those who migrated to America in the 1930s. As he developed his theory over the last several decades, he has become the leading contemporary representative of Frankfurt School critical theory. A major theme in his work is the need for open and undistorted communication as a necessary condition for emancipation from repressive sociopolitical domination (Habermas, 1971, 1973, 1984, 1987). This focus on communication is reminiscent of Mead's early perspective that contributed to the development of symbolic interactionism. But in Habermas's more macro critical perspective, the growth of the discourse of instrumental rationality, particularly as embodied in bureaucratic organizations, has the effect of inhibiting communication that does not fit the logic of instrumental rationality. This analysis is comparable to Weber's gloomy prediction of an "iron cage" of bureaucratic rationality.

The Legitimation Crisis in the Political Organization of Capitalism

Like the other Frankfurt School theorists, Habermas focused heavily on the process whereby political and economic systems are legitimated through cultural beliefs, ideologies, and worldviews. However, modern capitalist societies face a legitimation crisis as a result of the long-term transformation from the early forms of entrepreneurial capitalism to modern organized capitalism (Habermas, 1975). This crisis is expressed in contemporary debates regarding the scope of the government's role in society. Its origins lie in part in resistance to the tremendous expansion of the role of government in modern democratic societies. This expansion, accompanying the growth of capitalist enterprises themselves, was triggered in part by the need to deal with the periodic economic crises of capitalism. It also includes the government's increased role in meeting the basic welfare needs that inevitably develop in unregulated market systems. However, the pattern of increasing government regulation is inconsistent with a political ideology that insists on limiting government power for the sake of individual freedom. The goal of limiting traditional restrictions on individual freedom had been important in the early years of capitalism for the development of political democracy. The resulting overthrow of traditional constraints and forms of domination had opened the door for the early development of entrepreneurial capitalism. The result was the separation (or "uncoupling") of economic activity from political control.

The expansion of the role and scope of government that accompanied the expansion of capitalist enterprises was justified in terms of the need to insure economic stability and protect the general welfare. The goal of stability was crucial for capitalist enterprises, while the general welfare goal was important for providing some protection for individual citizens from the growing power of these large-scale corporate enterprises. The overall results of this process were seen by Habermas as a "recoupling" of economic activity and political regulation. Even though justified in terms of the general welfare, a lot of the expansion of government programs and regulations occurred without widespread democratic discussion or clear consensus regarding the proper role of government in insuring the general welfare in a complex society. The long-term outcome was that government policies often seemed to benefit particular groups or "special interests" more than the general welfare. While critical theory is oriented toward increasing individual freedom, the question of when restrictions are needed to prevent exploitation and promote the overall welfare of society are always matters of political debate. The problem in modern societies is that public participation in such discussion tends to be limited and one-sided. This lack of citizen participation makes it possible for large-scale corporate structures to have an inordinate influence on public discourse and political policy decisions.

The restrictions and distortions in the communication process in modern society result in part from heavy reliance on impersonal "steering mechanisms" as a source of control and integration of large-scale complex systems. This leads us to Habermas's (1987) important distinction between **system** and **lifeworld**. Modern societies differ from earlier types of society in terms of their heavy reliance on impersonal procedures of macro-level system integration. Moreover, these mechanisms have become detached (or "uncoupled") from the micro-level processes whereby people's everyday life worlds are integrated through open communication leading to mutual understandings and the possibility of well-informed consensus. This discrepancy between system integration based on impersonal steering mechanisms and social integration based on communication results in large part from the growing size and complexity of society.

Habermas related his distinction between **system** and **lifeworld** to the ideas of several theorists discussed in earlier chapters. His analysis of the **system** is consistent with Durkheim's argument regarding the effects of the expansion of the division of labor in increasing functional interdependence while simultaneously decreasing moral solidarity. This process can also be related to Marx's description of how social ties between members of different socioeconomic classes have been replaced by purely market transactions (or a narrow "cash nexus"). Habermas also incorporated Weber's insights regarding the effects of the strong emphasis on formal rationality of modern society in creating a kind of "iron cage" of administrative efficiency (or instrumental rationality) that undermines concerns with ultimate values or socioemotional expressive needs.

Habermas's discussion of the everyday **lifeworld** drew on the phenomenological perspective of Schutz and Luckmann in highlighting the importance of implicitly shared and taken-for-granted assumptions and stocks of knowledge that are sustained through patterns of micro-level communication. This implicit knowledge provides the underlying foundation for people's ability to make sense of one another's actions and to participate in the social world in a meaningful way. Habermas incorporated Mead's analysis of the importance of communication in enabling people to expand their mutual understanding. He relates this micro level focus to Durkheim's explanation of how moral solidarity is developed and reinforced when people come together to participate in shared rituals. Although Mead focused more on pragmatic adaptation to the environment than ritual action, he recognized the importance of the social solidarity that emerges through communication for promoting normative consensus. The ritual actions and forms of communication that Durkheim emphasized can be seen as helping in a major way to reinforce such consensus.

While micro-level lifeworlds are integrated through communicative action oriented toward the goal of mutual understanding, the integration of macro-level social systems makes use of money and power as "steering mechanisms" that are independent of the subjective (or intersubjective) orientations developed and sustained through communication at the lifeworld level. Money is the key medium for the economy and the market system while power is crucial for the polity and the organization of government at all levels.[16] Both money and power can be deployed in ways that shape human beings' actions without the type of mutual understanding that can be established only through communication. Reliance on these steering mechanisms makes possible the "uncoupling" of macro-level economic and political systems from the lifeworlds individuals share at the micro-level.

In addition to the "uncoupling" of system and lifeworld, Habermas argues also that the dynamics and demands of the **system** have invaded and colonized the **lifeworld**, restricting and distorting the type of open communication that leads to mutual understanding. Thus the fate of individuals, of families, and of local communities is subject to governmental or corporate decisions that are often far removed from local lifeworld scenes. For the society as a whole, basic policy decisions are made by political and administrative elites, with individuals having little meaningful input in comparison to various corporate or organized "special interests."

Habermas' critical perspective is based on a systematic analysis of different forms of communication reflecting contrasting types of rationality. Weber's focus on instrumental rationality based on means/ends relations is limited in Habermas's view; the broader view of rationality that he proposes is grounded in a more comprehensive perspective as manifested in different ways in alternative forms of discourse. In this broader view, statements that are able to withstand criticism when their validity claims are challenged may be said to be rational, as opposed to those that cannot withstand criticism. But there are different criteria by which the implicit validity claims of different types of statements can be criticized or defended. The formal or instruemtnal rationality that Weber

[16] The two media are not exactly comparable, in that money can be more easily detached from its individual possessor and the communication process than can power. Even though we know, since Weber, that power based on authority is associated with the office rather than the person, its exercise cannot be divorced completely from the person exercising it or subject to it.

saw as prevailing in bureaucratic organizations and authority systems represents a limited form of rationality which is concerned only with the effectiveness and efficiency of the means employed to achieve objective ends.

Alternative Forms of Communication and Rationality

Rationality for Habermas is grounded in the communication process whereby people become more reflective regarding their implicit and taken-for-granted common sense assumptions (Habermas, 1973). Such discourse, in the absence of coercion or other restrictions on communication, may lead to questioning and criticizing beliefs and values handed down through tradition and accepted implicitly as "just the way things are." Different forms of communication can be distinguished according to whether they concern the objective world, the intersubjective world, the subjective (or personal) world, or the communication process itself as topics of discourse. Each of these different forms of discourse is associated with its own distinctive type of rationality and its own specific type of action. The four types of action include purposive (or teleological) action, normative action, dramaturgic action, and communicative action (Habermas, 1984:84–87). The kinds of statements associated with these different types of rational action are summarized below.

1. Factual statements and purposive (or teleological) action—Rationality in this area is reflected in the methods of scientific research whereby statements are evaluated against objective empirical facts. The claim that sociology is a science is problematic, however, inasmuch as the social world includes people's subjective experiences, sentiments, beliefs, attitudes, and so on that are not part of the external world—even though the subjective states of other people are clearly external to any particular observer, including sociological observers.

   Purposive or teleological action employs objective factual knowledge in selecting means to achieve goals. This type of action corresponds to Weber's instrumental rationality and is also consistent with the rational choice perspective as described in earlier chapters. Rationality considerations are involved in assessing the effectiveness or efficiency of means in reaching whatever ends are being sought. Habermas uses the concept of **strategic action** to refer to efforts to influence other people's actions as the means for achieving one's own ends. This form of relating to others is not oriented toward reaching mutual understanding. Strategic action is exemplified in market relations, with buyers and sellers interacting or negotiating with one another in terms of the individual interests they seek to satisfy. It is also manifested in authority relations in organizations, where controlling the actions of subordinates is simply the means for achieving the goals of an organization or those of the authority figures within it.
2. Normative statements and normative action—Rationality in this area involves evaluating behaviors in terms of their conformity with widely accepted norms. Such actions may also fulfill various goals for oneself or for others,

but this is not the primary motivation. Instead, the focus is on the norms themselves and the ideals and values they reflect. Communication in this category may include efforts to establish consensus or to evaluate the norms critically. This type of communication is particularly important for the critical theory goal of changing normative patterns and institutionalized structures so as to improve human welfare.

3. Expressive statements and dramaturgical action—Expressive statements reflect one's own personal subjective orientations and intentions. They cannot be evaluated by "checking the facts," since the "facts" are subjective in nature. and their validity also does not depend on social consensus. Rationality with regard to expressive communication would involve discourse that seeks to discover and correct patterns of deliberate deceit or unwitting self-delusion or to improve self-disclosure. This type of action would include dramaturgical action, including the various strategies of presentation of self as analyzed by Goffman that were reviewed in Chap. 5. If a person's self-presentation is intended to manipulate the behavior of others to benefit oneself, it could be seen as a form of strategic action as well. Even if sincere, there are variations in the level of self-disclosure involved in different forms of dramaturgic action.

   A high level of systematic and disciplined expressive self-disclosure is represented by those involved in the creation of cultural products such as art, music, and literature. The goal of these forms of creativity is to communicate a subjective or experiential response to some aspect of the human condition. Expressive communication of this type can be evaluated in terms of intersubjectively shared aesthetic standards. Rational analysis of the meaning of such cultural products would involve evaluating how well they represent common human experiences or convey a meaningful reaction to the human condition that can be shared.

4. Communication and communicative action—Discourse in this category goes beyond establishing facts, norms, or internal sentiments and is oriented explicitly toward communicative competence and mutual understanding. It would include analysis of the grammatical structure of sentences, paragraphs, texts, and speeches, for example, as well as the expressed or implied meanings carried through different forms of communication. Since the goal of communicative action is mutual understanding, this type of action contrasts sharply with purposive or instrumental action as described above. In coordinating people's actions, consensus based on mutual understanding may be contrasted with force, tradition, authority, or manipulation as a basis for control.

Habermas relates these forms of communication and rationality to personality formation, social integration, and the creation and reproduction of cultural meanings and values. His discussion of the socialization process draws heavily on Mead's theory regarding the development of one's self-concept and also on developmental psychologist Jean Piaget's learning theory. For Habermas, however, Mead's micro-level focus does not provide an adequate explanation of the overall framework of beliefs and values shared in the larger social world. To provide this larger picture Habermas draws on Durkheim's theory regarding the way collective rituals reinforce shared meanings and moral codes.[17] This larger perspective is consistent with Peter Berger and Thomas Luckmann's phenomenological analysis of macro-level cultural worldviews as reviewed in Chap. 6.

Habermas argues that **system** integration at the level of the overall society has expanded in modern society at the expense of the **social** integration of the life-world.[18] The process of communication whereby satisfying identities are formed, social solidarity established, and meaningful values sustained at the lifeworld level are overshadowed and swamped by the logic of instrumental action employing the impersonal media of money and power at the macro-system level. The results of such restrictions and distortions may include inadequate levels of socialization, breakdown in normative consensus, and erosion of cultural meanings and values. When such consequences are widespread, the symptoms may include antisocial behavior, disruptive conflict, anomie, and alienation. These problems are more serious than simple misunderstandings that can be corrected through communicative action within individuals' micro-level lifeworlds.

The way social integration at the lifeworld level is subordinated to system integration can be seen in the economic system in the growth of a consumer society. In various ways (particularly through advertising), individuals are encouraged to pursue ever-increasing levels of personal consumption as the key to a fulfilling life. This lifestyle helps compensate them for their subordinate status and lack of autonomy while their enthusiastic conformity to the consumer role promotes the expansion of the economic system. Within the political structure, system integration is promoted as citizens become clients or beneficiaries of the state through their dependence on government for personal benefits or for policies that will serve their interests. Segments of the population as diverse as senior citizens relying on monthly Social Security checks, students who benefit from government-backed loans, and agricultural producers who receive government support illustrate this pattern of dependence. Paradoxically, the roles of both consumer and citizen are also reinforced through ideologies that simultaneously idealize individual freedom and material success, the "free enterprise" economic system, and government responsibility for the general welfare in a democratic system.

From a critical theory perspective, the increased allocation of general welfare responsibilities to the government may be seen as restricting the freedom of individuals and organizations in the private sector in many different ways. Moreover, the limited and subordinate modes of individuals' involvement in the impersonal structures of the system are not a satisfactory substitute for lifeworld integration based on mutual understanding. Specifically, the macro-level "steering mechanisms" of our economic and political structures do not employ the type of communication that creates and reinforces a sense of community or satisfying personal identities at the level of individuals' lifeworlds.

---

[17] This reliance on both Mead and Durkheim for understanding the development of individuals' moral commitments and the role of ritual in reinforcing them may be compared with Collins' (1975) conflict perspective as reviewed in the last chapter.

[18] This contrasts sharply with Parsons' portrayal of modern society as a differentiated but generally well integrated social system.

The distinction Habermas makes between system and lifeworld, and his emphasis on the growth of the former at the expense of the latter, may be seen as a critique of the long-term erosion of close-knit communities where members are bound together in a shared "lifeworld" that sustains their socioemotional and moral solidarity as well as reinforces their personal identities. With this perspective it is easy to discount the possibilities for social movements to emerge from shared lifeworld experiences that may eventually influence and even transform macro-level institutional processes. The civil rights movement, the women's movement, the environmental movement, and the gay/lesbian movement illustrate how shared lifeworld experiences have the potential to encourage communication and mobilize people for attempting to influence the larger system. Sometimes, however, this process leads to the establishment of formal organizations, with responsibilities for specific goals delegated to them. But as these organizations grow and become institutionalized, the logic of instrumental rationality is likely to become dominant as these goals are pursued. When this happens, there is a risk that successful goal accomplishment will again be given priority over mutual understanding. Habermas's emphasis on open communication oriented toward mutual understanding, without restrictions and distortions, is highly idealistic and much more difficult to implement in large-scale systems than in small-scale systems. Even with the new technology of the internet, it is difficult to visualize a "virtual" town hall meeting in which the entire population of a large and complex society could communicate effectively with one another and with government officials or other authority figures representing large-scale institutional structures. In addition to the logistical difficulties, communication would be restricted because the "appropriate" knowledge that is needed to engage in meaningful participation is not likely to be available to all. Habermas's open communication ideal requires all participants to be competent participants—and recognized as competent. Even in small-scale discussion groups with people who appear initially to be roughly equal, differences quickly become apparent in their level of knowledge and expertise, as well as their willingness and ability to contribute. Not all voices are heard, and the collective decisions eventually made are likely to reflect the interests of those who dominate the discussion. In large-scale macro systems, subordinates and others in marginal positions are often left out of the discussion, even though they may be affected in major ways by decisions or actions undertaken by agents for macro-level systems. The close linkage between culturally defined professional knowledge and position in hierarchies of domination is a major focus of Michel Foucault's perspective, which we shall review in the following section.

Knowledge and Power in Michel Foucault's Perspective

Michel Foucault (1928–1984) was a creative French philosopher whose ideas have had a major influence on sociological theory and in wider intellectual circles. He is well known among contemporary sociologists for his analysis of historic changes in the treatment of madness,[19] the development of surveillance and control techniques in prisons, the use of professional knowledge in the medical establishment, and the regulation of sexuality. (For examples of overviews of Foucault's work, see Sheridan [1980], Dreyfus and Rabinow, [1983], and Prado [1995].) In Foucault's perspective, knowledge and knowledge-based forms of discourse serve as the implicit foundation for the development and maintenance of structures of power and domination. His perspective clearly contrasts with the widely acclaimed ideal regarding the importance of knowledge for its own sake. For Foucault, the significance of expert or professional knowledge is that is used to support the claims to power of those who can successfully claim to have a monopoly on such knowledge. This means they are able to dominate discourse in ways that justify and reinforce the differentiation of power between professional experts and lay people.

Foucault's analysis differs in important ways from the critical theory perspectives discussed earlier. Although our goal is not to provide a comprehensive overview of Foucault's work, his insights regarding the way knowledge serves as an implicit foundation for structures of domination can be seen as a form of critical analysis. His perspective can also be related to various ideas from the phenomenological perspective, analyses of language and its use in discourse, and the French structuralist school (as represented by Levi-Strauss [1967], a major leader of this school). French structuralism can be traced back to Durkheim's efforts to explain the social origins of religion in his often-cited distinction between the categories of sacred and profane.[20] It can also be seen in Durkheim's analysis of how identifying and punishing deviants helps sustain the moral boundaries of the group by reinforcing distinctions between "normal" and "deviant" (or "moral" versus "immoral" behavior). Mary Douglas (1966, 1970) also highlighted the importance of socially defined moral boundaries between such categories as "pure" versus "impure" or "clean" versus "dirty" (see also Wuthnow et al., 1984:77–132). This perspective can also be compared with Pierre Bourdieu's focus on how the class structure of society involves the use of dichotomous categories to distinguish people according to various evaluative criteria of superiority and inferiority. At the risk of considerable over-simplification, structuralism can be identified briefly as an effort to discover the invariant underlying structures that exist beneath the surface of people's consciousness and behavior. Such structures may be sought in society itself, in language, or in the mind. A fundamental feature of all forms of structuralism is a system of categories that are widely accepted as everyday common sense and that are used to make distinctions among people or among different objects encountered in the environment.

---

[19] The term "madness" refers most clearly to mental illness, of course. However, definitions of mental illness change over time, and Foucault's type of analysis also applies to criminals and other types of deviants characterized by their "otherness" or their difference from what is considered normal.

[20] Near the end of his book on religion, Durkheim ([1915] 1965) speculated regarding the social origins of the fundamental categories of thought, suggesting that the basic pattern of thinking in terms of categories results from the categorical social divisions that exist within the group itself. This type of analysis became highly influential in French structuralism.

Foucault is sometimes classified as a poststructuralist because of his critique of structural theories.[21] In the perspective of poststructuralism, the categories used to classify and distinguish objects in the environment or people (whether social, linguistic, or mental) are matters of linguistic convention. They do not necessarily reflect fixed distinctions that are grounded in the objective world. In Foucault's analysis, structures dissolve into power relations that are reinforced in the discourse represented by "official" or "expert" knowledge in the interaction of professional experts with untrained laypersons.[22] Foucault's analysis of the exercise of power focused on the process whereby specialized forms of discourse are used to make distinctions among people so as to control, segregate, or punish those who are regarded as outsiders or deviant. The distinctive contributions of Foucault was his focus on the use of professional knowledge to provide a supposedly "objective" analysis of these subjective distinctions.

Surveillance and Social Control

The target of the application of power in much of Foucault's analysis is the human body itself, or whole populations of human bodies. In his historical overview of changing definitions of outsiders, he pointed out that in the Middle Ages it was lepers who were physically confined or expelled as society's dangerous outsiders (Foucault, 1965). In the seventeenth century, the outsider category consisted of the poor. However, instead of being expelled from the community, the poor were to be provided the basic necessities for their survival but kept confined. As urbanization and industrialization advanced, the notion of confinement was gradually replaced by the belief that the poor should be allowed to work (at low wages, of course) and thereby contribute to the advancement of the society. Following the French Revolution in the late eighteenth century, the targets of confinement shifted to the insane and to criminals. However, in the aftermath of the Revolution, social pressures developed for the separation of criminals from the insane.

Prior to the development of prisons, punishment of deviants and law violators took the form of physical torture (floggings or beatings). The public spectacle provided by such punishment was intended to help reinforce royal authority. But with the new mentality that developed after the French Revolution and its attack on the monarchy, prison confinement came to be considered a more humane alternative than torture. Along with confinement as a new method of control, the mechanisms for controlling bodies gradually shifted over time from external to internal forms of control, or self-discipline. This internal control was reinforced by the development of surveillance procedures. The capability for surveillance was evident in the design

[21] In the analysis by Wuthnow et al. (1984:133–178), Foucault's approach is classified as an example of "neo-structuralism."

[22] This preoccupation with power in Foucault's perspective may be seen as reflecting the influence of Nietzsche.

of prisons in which the guard tower is positioned to allow a constant view of inmates and their movements. The type of guard tower Foucault envisioned was one which made it possible actually to see inside each cell (Foucault, 1979). This effect of such a system is that even if a guard tower is temporarily unattended, its physical presence will provide a constant reminder to the inmates that their activities can always be monitored. This threat of surveillance came to be seen as an efficient and effective way to induce "voluntary" compliance with prison rules and routines. In addition, the eventual introduction of various types of treatment strategies such as rehabilitation counseling also represented an increased emphasis on internalized self-discipline.

In our own time techniques of surveillance have been extended far beyond the prison to the society at large. Thus convicted law violators can be monitored not only through periodic visits by a probation officer but also through electronic ankle bracelets that they wear in their own homes and communities instead of being confined in prison. For the population at large, this expansion of surveillance has been accompanied by a decrease in the obtrusiveness of surveillance techniques. Widespread use of video cameras in retail stores, for example, or just inside the entrance to government buildings, demonstrates the use of modern unobtrusive surveillance techniques to insure self-control (e.g., see Staples, 1997). The technology of unobtrusive surveillance and documentation of individuals' activities on a wide scale has expanded greatly with the development of computerized information systems. However, since the tragic events of September 11, 2001, physical inspection of the bodies and baggage of airline passengers can be seen as a shift back to more intrusive forms of surveillance.

Professional Expertise and Social Control

The role that systems of professional knowledge and discourse play in reinforcing power structures can be seen in Foucault's analysis of the development of psychoanalysis and other forms of psychotherapy as well as in modern medical practice. Modern techniques for treating both mental and physical illness reflect the growth of science and the largely unquestioned belief in science as the most important (or sole) source of valid knowledge. Scientific knowledge provides the foundation for the professional expertise of both psychiatrists and physicians and for the power they wield over their patients as well as the prestige they enjoy in society.

However, the validity and superiority of scientific knowledge is not automatically self-evident. Any system of knowledge rests on implicit assumptions in terms of which its validity is accepted. Thus medical knowledge is based on beliefs in modern "science" as valid knowledge (as opposed to magic, for example). Moreover, all knowledge systems, including science, emerge from and are sustained through discourse and the implicit authority of various types of texts. In addition to the formal discursive knowledge that constitutes a formal field of study, such as an academic discipline or professional field of practice, the implicit assumptions and everyday practices of lay people also provide support for the implicit acceptance of such knowledge. Thus, for example, expertise in magic or "alternative" forms of medical treatment is not considered valid or legitimate for treating illness, and those who employ such unorthodox forms of treatment do not enjoy the same level of power or prestige in the overall society as those trained in medical science.

But professional knowledge based on the discursive texts of a discipline is not sufficient by itself for wielding power at the sites where experts and laypersons actually encounter one another. In order to apply their expertise, psychoanalysts or physicians must also rely on personal information from their patients which can then be used in deciding how professional knowledge should be applied to the case at hand. In psychoanalysis or psychotherapy, this involves engaging the patient in a process of extensive discussion whereby the psychoanalyst or psychotherapist elicits information to be used in interpreting the patient's condition as symptomatic of the type of disorder that his or her expertise is relevant to diagnose and treat. Thus, ironically, it is the patient who provides the information which the psychotherapist then uses to establish control over the patient.[23] In this process of self-disclosure, the patient is induced to view himself or herself from the point of view of the psychotherapist. This means not trusting his or her own self-awareness but instead accepting the psychotherapist's analysis. In this way the patient submits to the control of the psychotherapist, even while the psychotherapist uses information provided by the patient to establish this control. The popular image of a patient in psychoanalysis reclining in a subordinate position on the couch while talking to the psychiatrist captures symbolically the power dynamics that are involved.

In the case of physical illnesses, the dynamics of the encounter with a physician are different, due in part to the fact that physical illness manifests itself in objective physical symptoms (such as a fever) that typically can be readily observed or measured (see Foucault, 1975). Even so, the physician relies heavily on the patient's verbal reports of symptoms plus an intensive scrutiny of various parts of the patient's body. Foucault emphasized the importance of the "gaze" whereby the expert obtains information to be used in providing treatment—and also in establishing control over the patient. The authoritative gaze upon the patient's body is crucial at the site where the professional practitioner actually applies abstract scientific knowledge to an analysis of the specific information obtained from a patient that is then used to establish control over the patient.

Despite their high prestige in our society, it is not necessary to assume that physicians are consciously oriented toward maintaining control of their patients. (From a cynical point of view we might assume that their interests in being compensated for their professional services are much greater.) However, the operation of the medical system is sustained by widely shared implicit beliefs regarding medical science and physicians' expertise, which results in widespread acceptance of the power relation between physicians and their patients as inevitable and natural.

[23] The self-disclosure provided by a patient to his or her psychoanalyst may be compared and contrasted with the process of confession to a priest, despite the differences in the way these two kinds of events are interpreted and the underlying type of morality and discourse that each manifests.

Suffering patients are likely actually to welcome their physician's control in the hope of getting medication or other forms of treatment that will help them feel better. However, if physicians did not have the legally recognized monopolistic power to prescribe many types of drugs, we might imagine that many people would discover on their own the medications they need to alleviate their pain and other symptoms of their illnesses.[24]

Foucault's emphasis on the close linkage between knowledge and power goes beyond the treatment of mental and physical illness. In more general terms, the growth of the human sciences is closely related to the formation and operation of new types of power structures based on these disciplines. The ostensible goal of the human sciences is to gain objective knowledge to advance our scientific understanding of people in their various social settings and the different forms of social systems that they develop. In another sense, however, the development of these disciplines can be seen as a greatly expanded and elaborated form of the same type of inquiring mentality that is symbolized by the prison guard tower allowing constant surveillance of prisoners, the therapy sessions conducted by psychiatrists with their patients, or the "gaze" of a physician at particular parts of their patients' bodies. Similarly, the development of the human sciences provides the "knowledge" that serves as the foundation for training experts in various human and social service professions. To the extent that this knowledge is based on research, its ultimate source is the human population that is studied, some of whom may subsequently find themselves subordinated through the application of such knowledge.

The subtle dynamics of power relationships based on authoritative systems of professional knowledge are also revealed in the various ways whereby sexual behavior is regulated (Foucault, 1980). Although the categories of male and female are grounded in biology, Foucault's focus was the way all aspects of sexuality and sexual relations are socially constructed within the particular culture of a society. This social construction process is particularly important because of importance of biological sex is for one's social identity. Cultural definitions include implicit common-sense understandings regarding sex and sexuality as well as the professional knowledge that may be invoked to distinguish "normal" versus "abnormal" forms of sexuality. Both the religious and the medical establishments have long been involved in developing and reinforcing these "official" distinctions, and their definitions are not always consistent.

The effects of power as related to sex may be seen not only in actual sexual relations but in the conflicting social definitions of various types of sexual behaviors as moral versus immoral, legal versus illegal, or desirable versus undesirable. Moreover, such definitions vary greatly in different societies and different historical contexts. The Victorian period in history, for example, was characterized by a heightened level of repressiveness regarding sex and sexuality. Ironically, however, Foucault showed that this very repressiveness gave rise to new forms of discourse

[24] Such a strategy would, of course, have the effect of enhancing the professional expertise of pharmacists. In our society this could mean that people's health is subjected to market forces to an even greater extent than it already is.

about sexuality whereby the power to establish authoritative distinctions between appropriate and inappropriate forms of sexual behavior and to regulate it was strengthened. Foucault's analysis of changing forms of sexuality and sexual regulation can also be applied to the so-called "sexual revolution" of the late 1960s and early 1970s,[25] the widespread concern in recent decades with the dangers of unprotected sex in transmitting the HIV/AIDS virus, and the proliferation of various forms of sex therapy. The popularity of sex therapists in some contemporary social circles also illustrates the belief that personal knowledge based on one's actual experience is inadequate, and that insights and techniques from "experts" are needed to legitimate or to enhance one's own sexual experiences.

Widespread belief in the superiority of expert knowledge in more and more areas of social life leads people to distrust their own judgment and to seek professional help in coping with individual or interpersonal difficulties of various kinds. This tacit reliance on professional knowledge and expertise leads individuals voluntarily to accept the subordination that this requires. This means that the exercise of power based on knowledge does not necessarily involve coercive control. Instead, the professionals who exercise power and the clients who submit collaborate through their shared understanding of the "need" to be governed by professional expertise based on "objective" scientific knowledge. However, coercion may be involved in situations where some form of "treatment" for "misbehavior" is required, or is offered as an alternative to incarceration. Sometimes, too, laypeople may play an intermediate role in such treatment. This would be illustrated when parents, for example, enlist the aid of professionals for helping their adolescent children get over an illegal drug addiction problem or teachers arrange to get legal drugs prescribed for "hyperactive" elementary school children.

Although not exhaustive, this brief overview of some of Foucault's key ideas illustrates the intrinsic linkage he sought to establish between power and knowledge. Specifically, the routine operations of power structures in modern societies rest on systems of knowledge, both implicit and explicit, that are socially constructed through discourse, widely accepted, and reinforced in everyday life practices. Dominant knowledge systems vary greatly in different societies and different historical periods. In addition, the degree of acceptance of particular knowledge systems may vary among different segments of society, and in some cases experts themselves may disagree. There is probably more consensus regarding the application of medical science in treating physical illness than there is with regard to the application of the social sciences in treating youthful violence, for example. However, widespread consensus regarding valid versus invalid forms of knowledge virtually guarantees that "experts" will always carry more weight than "amateurs" or laypersons, even though the latter will usually know more than the former about their own personal situation.

---

[25] The extent to which the changing patterns of sexual relations constituted a revolution in actual behavior is open to debate. Prior to this time, pre-marital sexual relations (as well as extra-marital ones) were kept hidden. The sexual revolution was in part a rejection of the hypocrisy regarding pre-marital sex that had existed earlier.

Foucault's analysis differs sharply from Habermas's faith in the expansion of opportunities for open communication as the key to increasing the level of rationality in society (see Michael Kelly, ed., 1994). For Foucault, the communication process inevitably reflects the differential distribution of knowledge and expertise. Professional knowledge in this perspective can be seen as a form of cultural capital that is always used to justify various forms of domination. Moreover, the differing cognitive orientations of different segments of the population will reflect their particular interests, and the interests of professional experts in insuring their continued dominance will not necessarily coincide with that of laypersons. In more general terms, a course of action that some may regard as increasing rationality could be regarded by others as decreasing rationality (or as mere "rationalization") and as leading to increased regulation and subordination.

This type of critique can be applied to critical analysis itself. The ideal goal for many critical theorists is redistribution of power and resources in order to liberate and empower those who are currently subordinate and disprivileged. But if they were to succeed in promoting this kind of critical orientation in the overall population, the result could conceivably be the empowerment of critical theorists themselves. In Foucault's perspective those who disagree with their critical diagnosis or prescribed solutions would then become the marginalized and subordinated "others."

Summary

Critical theory is oriented toward raising people's consciousness regarding the need for social transformations that will free people from exploitation and domination, move toward higher levels of equality, and expand opportunities for the development of human beings' full potential. These idealistic goals draw heavily from Marx's perspective in showing how prevailing forms of culture and consciousness reflect and reinforce economic and sociopolitical domination in a society's various institutional structures. However, a major challenge that European Marxists faced was that the capitalist economic system was much more resilient than Marx had anticipated and seemed practically impervious to the idea of a proletarian revolution. Also, it eventually became obvious that the Marxist-inspired ideology of communism as practiced in the Soviet Union did not eliminate oppressive structures of exploitation but instead implemented a highly centralized and repressive system of state domination. Marxist theorists varied in their specific diagnoses of modern societies. However, much of their analysis involved efforts to show how institutional structures of economic and political domination were supported by the cultural beliefs and ideologies that shaped people's consciousness, thereby undermining their ability to envision alternatives to the current system.

Even before an interest in neo-Marxist and "new left" perspectives developed in American sociology, C. Wright Mills had applied his "sociological imagination" to an analysis of the United States power structure that differed sharply from the functionalist perspective and the popular image of a pluralistic power structure.

Mills' description of the self-serving power elite in American society is consistent with the process described by Robert Michels as the iron law of oligarchy, which describes a general pattern whereby persons in positions of power and authority give priority to maintaining themselves in these positions.

The development of American critical theory in the late 1960s was triggered in part by opposition to the Vietnam war, along with the civil rights struggle that was already in progress, and various other interrelated countercultural movements of that time. This development was reinforced by the increased availability of Marx's early humanistic writings and also by Frankfurt School critical theorists as reflected in the works of Erich Fromm, Theodor Adorno, and Herbert Marcuse. Even before the turmoil of the late 1960s, Fromm developed a critical orientation that focused on the apparent willingness of people to sacrifice their freedom for the sake of security, while Adorno's analysis of the authoritarian personality stimulated research suggesting that people with this type of personality would voluntarily sacrifice their moral judgments to comply with official authorities. By the late 1960s and early 1970s, Marcuse developed a critical analysis of the "one-dimensional" type of mentality that was reflected in people's conformity to the restrictive roles of a society dominated by bureaucratic control, preoccupation with technical efficiency, and devotion to materialistic values.

The critical perspective of the Frankfurt School was developed most fully by Jürgen Habermas. We reviewed his argument relating the "legitimation crisis" of late capitalism that resulted from the expansion of the government's regulatory and welfare functions. We also examined his distinction between micro-level social integration of the everyday lifeworld through communication and macro-level system integration of economic and political structures through the impersonal steering mechanisms of money and power. Habermas's critical perspective was revealed in his analysis of how the goal-oriented instrumental rationality expressed in modern economic and political structures has invaded the lifeworld, resulting in higher priority being given to regulating human behavior for the sake of maintaining these structures than achieving mutual understanding through open communication. Habermas advocates maximum openness of communication for increasing rationality in all its dimensions, including the expansion of opportunities for increased levels of mutual understanding with minimum distortions in the communication process.

Finally, we looked briefly at Foucault's analysis of the way in which power structures rest on implicit and explicit systems of professional knowledge and expertise. This linkage between knowledge and power is revealed in his analysis of the transition from corporal punishment of deviants to prison confinement, changing definitions of mental illness and strategies for treating those diagnosed as mentally ill, the development of modern medical practice based on scientific knowledge, the growth of the human sciences, and regulation of sexuality. Foucault's critical analysis of knowledge systems can be contrasted with Habermas's notion of the alternative forms of rationality that are grounded in different patterns of communication. Habermas recognized the importance of basic communication competence, but seemed to express an idealistic optimism regarding the possibilities for the advancement of open communication throughout the society. In Foucault's perspective, in contrast, the dynamics of the communication process cannot be separated from the differential distribution of forms of knowledge that serve as the foundation for the operation of power structures in society.

Critical theory tends to be interpretive and philosophical, as the preceding overview reveals. Except for the efforts of Adorno and his followers to measure the authoritarian personality, critical theorists tend to discount the emphasis in American sociology on empirical measurement because such efforts fail to uncover the underlying patterns that are implicit in a society's culture and individuals' subjective consciousness. Indeed, an overriding emphasis on sophisticated methodological techniques may be seen as another manifestation of the logic of instrumental rationality, linked with manipulation and control, that permeates the consciousness of modern industrial society. In contrast to superficial empirical investigation, critical theorists argue that institutional structures, dominant ideologies, and prevailing forms of consciousness should be evaluated from the perspective of human beings' needs for autonomy, self-development, and the like. The ultimate goal is to promote liberation from exploitation and domination, including both external political and economic domination and internal domination of consciousness.

The dual goals of theoretical analysis and social criticism are also revealed in various forms of feminist theory. We turn in the next chapter to the theoretical insights that feminist theorists have provided regarding gender-based conflicts that are grounded in persistent patterns of domination and subordination.

Questions for Study and Discussion

1. In what ways could you see both education and the mass media as providing implicit or explicit support to the basic economic and political structures of our society? Are there some aspects of education or mass media influences that encourage protest or promote change in the system—and are the changes promoted minor evolutionary changes or would they lead to major transformations? Explain.
2. Do you agree or disagree with the argument from critical theory that the structure of our society could be changed to decrease inequality and promote more opportunities for human beings to develop to their full potential? What would be required to achieve these goals? How do different occupations vary in terms of limiting or expanding the opportunities for human beings to develop their potential?
3. Drawing on Habermas's perspective, contrast social integration of the lifeworld with system integration at the level of macro-level economic and political structures? How are individuals' lifeworld experiences at the micro-level influenced by macro-level structures? In what ways do these influences restrict their freedom or opportunities, and in what ways might they expand individuals' choices and experiences?

4. Within the framework of Habermas's perspective on communication and rationality, explain how instrumental rationality oriented toward objective goals contrasts with the rationality involved in communication regarding norms, dramaturgic forms of communication, and communication oriented toward mutual understanding. Cite some examples of each of these types from your own experiences. How would you expect the emphasis on each of these types of rationality to vary in different institutional settings?
5. Explain the relationship between knowledge and power in Foucault's perspective, and cite some examples of how this linkage may be illustrated. In applying his perspective to public policy issues, to what extent do you think professional knowledge is used by political leaders in their decision-making process? Is there a risk that the process of democratic decision making could be undermined by extensive reliance on professional experts? Why or why not?

Part III
Exploring Multi-Level Theoretical Perspectives

Chapter 16
Feminist Theory at Multiple Levels: Analytical and Critical

In the common sense perspective of everyday life it seems obvious that the human species is divided into two distinct sexual categories: male and female. There may be occasional anomalies in which individuals are born with ambiguous physical characteristics, but these are relatively rare. Throughout history people have engaged in endless speculation regarding the differences between men and women and the challenges involved in understanding the puzzling and fascinating conflicts, dilemmas, and ambiguities that often develop in their relations with one another.

The biological differences between women and men are related functionally to the different roles they perform in sexual reproduction. In the perspective of everyday life these differences are assumed to carry over into their "natural" gender roles in society.[1] According to traditional popular beliefs, men are thought to be more independent, competitive, and aggressive by nature and women are seen as more dependent, emotional, and nurturing. This belief in fundamental differences is reflected in descriptions of gender differences such as are found in John Gray's (1992) popular book, *Men Are from Mars; Women Are from Venus*. Reflecting the influence of these implicit social definitions, traditional gender roles for males have included positions of leadership and dominance while those for females have involved positions of support and subordination. This applies to the micro level world of family life and also to the large-scale institutional structures of economics, politics, military systems, religion, and other major institutions. For feminist theorists, this pattern of male dominance, referred to as patriarchy, has been a significant focus of critical analysis and target for major social change.

In opposition to this popular view regarding "natural" gender differences, most sociologists have long agreed with the argument of many feminists that gender and gender roles are socially constructed and reinforced. This emphasis on social definitions is consistent with the symbolic interactionist and phenomenological perspectives as well as Foucault's analysis of the link between forms of discourse and power relations as discussed in the last chapter. Our focus in this chapter is the effects of social construction of gender roles, although biological characteristics will also be noted as appropriate. For both genders there are wide variations within each category.

---

[1] The term **sex** is often used to refer to basic biological differences, while the term **gender** refers to the culturally defined social roles of women and men.

Feminists' contributions to sociological theory and other areas of the discipline have exploded in recent years. Their influence also extends into other social scientific fields and the humanities and has given rise to the emergence of women's studies as a specialized academic discipline. We will not deal with the historical development of the feminist movement but will focus instead on selected contemporary feminist contributions to sociological theory. Feminist theories provide a systematic analysis of the importance of gender definitions in social life, plus a critique of the prevailing patterns of male domination in all areas, including the sociological discipline itself. (For a brief overview of various theoretical approaches within the category of feminist theory, see Janet Saltzman Chafetz [1988]). Our coverage in this chapter is intended to illustrate the contrasts among different perspectives as they apply at the micro, meso, and macro levels of the social world. The following list of topics provides a preview:

- Standpoint theory—developed by Dorothy Smith. This perspective emphasizes the "bifurcated consciousness" that women experience because of the differences between their lived experiences in subordinate positions and the "official" definitions of the social world established by males.
- Gender, race, and class hierarchies. This section will draw on Patricia Hill Collins' analysis of African-American women to highlight differences among them in multiple hierarchies of domination based on race, class, sexual orientation, and nationality as well as gender.
- Micro level gender distinctions. Our focus on this level will allow an exploration of the interdependence among biological, cultural, and social processes. Specific topics include –
  - Nancy Chodorow's analysis of gender differences in early childhood socialization whereby mothering patterns are reproduced;
  - Dorothy Dinnerstein's perspective on how men's and women's emotional reactions to issues of life and death, plus their personal identities, vary because of their different roles in reproducing human life;
  - Jessie Bernard's description of contrasting family experiences of husbands and wives based on inequality in resources and dependency.
- Macro (and meso) gender differences. The theories in this section include the following:
  - Origins of patriarchy—Marxist perspective in Engels' speculations regarding family structure and property;
  - Social organization of violence—Randall Collins' portrayal of the development of specialized institutional control of the means of violence and coercion as applied to gender relations;
  - Miriam Johnson's functionalist perspective on the contributions of the women's movement in the context of the institutional differentiation of modern society;
  - Janet Saltzman Chafetz's analysis of the multiple implications of the differential access of women and men to economic resources and elite positions;

- Dorothy Smith's depiction of how women are affected by the pervasive effects of the "relations of ruling" whereby patterns of domination are mediated through "official" or authoritative texts.

Despite the clear contrasts in their styles of analysis, Chafetz and Smith both emphasize the linkage between macro and micro levels.

Feminist Critique of Sociology: Dorothy Smith's Standpoint Theory

In the perspective of many feminist theorists, mainstream theories in sociology include implicit biases because they were developed mostly by men and thus inevitably reflect male experiences and points of view. These mainstream theories are seen as reflecting the popular beliefs of everyday life in which traditional gender roles result from the obvious biological differences between men and women. With traditional beliefs and norms accepted implicitly, there is no explicit stimulus or theoretical leverage for critical analysis of gender roles, or of the unequal distribution of power, privileges, and resources between women and men that have traditionally been taken for granted. In view of the limitations of mainstream (male-dominated) sociology, Dorothy E. Smith (1987) argues for a "woman-centered" sociological perspective (see also Smith, 1990, 1999). Her perspective, which can be characterized as a feminist "standpoint" theory, emphasizes that the social world is always experienced from the particular standpoints (or social positions) where individuals are located in the social structure. Her analysis leads to a critical orientation toward efforts to develop an "objective" sociology that is not grounded explicitly in the ongoing subjective experiences of people in their everyday lives.

According to Smith, the theories and research findings of (male) academic sociologists purport to provide authoritative accounts of the social world that takes precedence over the experiences and practical knowledge of the people who participate day after day in this world. When the results of such analyses are presented as universally valid knowledge grounded in "objective" facts, the validity of the knowledge based on personal experiences is discounted and dismissed as particularlistic, nonrational, and merely subjective. In this way the voices of women and others without power or influence are silenced in favor of the voices of those (sociologists and others) who claim to base their knowledge on objective scientific facts rather than personal subjective experiences.

Sociological accounts of the social world that fail to correspond to the realities of people's lived experiences contribute to a "bifurcated consciousness," particularly for women (Smith, 1987:6–9). This is a type of consciousness that develops when the actual subjective experiences of everyday life are discounted in favor of professional academic modes of discourse and forms of knowledge that rest on authoritative claims to be objective and thus superior to subjective feelings and impressions. For both genders, this process can be illustrated in the classroom when students are cautioned not to rely on their own limited personal experiences for understanding the social world but to accept instead the authority of "objective" academic discourse for achieving "full" or "valid" or "less biased" understanding. The process is similar is some ways to what happens in marriage relations when a wife's efforts to contribute to discussions with her husband are dismissed as unworthy of consideration because she is being "too emotional," experiencing PMS, or not seeing the "larger picture" objectively.

Despite this tendency for the unique personal experiences of everyday life to be discounted, the micro-level routines in which people engage as they go about their daily lives actually contribute to the reproduction of the larger institutional order, often without participants' conscious awareness. Smith emphasizes in particular the importance of the everyday support that women provide in men's micro-level worlds, whereby men are afforded the opportunity to create and sustain the macro-level institutional structures of society. She points out that large-scale institutional orders actually depend on the supportive work people do at the local sites of their lived experience. This can be illustrated in the traditional type of personal secretary who organizes her boss's schedule and keeps his [typically a male] files up to date as well as by wives who have traditionally taken care of their husbands' clothes, prepared meals for the family, and taken care of routine housework. A lot of this invisible supportive work is behind the scenes. Outside the household, much of it is performed by women in subordinate positions in low-paying jobs. For example, in order for the (typically male) chief executive officers of large corporations to entertain professional associates in their offices or take them out to lunch, they must depend on the labor of those behind the scenes who clean their offices at night or the employees of the restaurant to prepare and serve the food they eat. A large part of this service-type work is performed by women.

The type of sociology Smith advocates begins with actual lived experiences and practical activities in which people engage as they adapt to the realities of their immediate social environment. For women, these realities involve fulfilling the expectations of their subordinate role as they attend to the needs of others (particularly males). These "behind the scenes" support roles are no less essential for the maintenance of institutional structures than the roles of those who are the official "agents" for these structures. Smith insists that by giving more explicit attention to people's lived experiences, sociologists would be better able to understand the everyday social pressures resulting from the impersonal and external "relations of ruling" that confront them daily. Smith describes her alternative strategy for sociological discovery as follows:

> Women's standpoint as a place to begin an inquiry into the social locates the knower in her body and as active in her work in relation to particular others. In a sense it *discovers* the ruling relations. They come into view from where she is in the actualities of her bodily existence, as relations that transcend the limitations of the embodied knower.
>
> (Smith, 1999:4, italics in original)

These ruling relations described by Smith are experienced by women (and other subordinates) at the micro level as they are confronted with the widespread expectations and demands of others who see their own interests and needs as having priority and as giving them the right to assume a position of dominance. Smith's argument is that, all else being equal, gender relations throughout society are governed by the implicitly understood cultural expectation that women will be deferential and compliant in their relations with men and that men will be dominant. All else is frequently not equal, however, especially for women employed in subordinate low-paying service jobs at the bottom of bureaucratic hierarchies. This means they are subordinated not only as women but also as subordinates in the organizational hierarchy at their place of employment.

Smith is highly critical of conventional sociological discourse because of the way it inevitably reflects the particular standpoints and implicit assumptions of those who create and utilize such discourse. This has traditionally been a male perspective. The alternative feminist perspective advocated by Smith emphasizes the way in which the standpoint (or social location) of women, and their experiences of the social world, differ from those of men. This results in large part from the fact that gender provides the foundation for male-dominated "relations of ruling" that pervade all aspects of social life. This concept of the "relations of ruling" refers to how the implicit cultural rules justifying male dominance are expressed in the actual relationships that develop between women and men. Smith argues that these widely accepted cultural understandings are virtually invisible to male sociologists simply because they are so deeply embedded in the taken-for-granted nature of the social world. In short, men don't have a clue as to how to theorize the experience of participating in the social world as a woman because they are on opposite sides of the fence, particularly in terms of thc rclations of ruling.

There are, of course, important differences among different feminist theorists. Some have expanded their focus to show how differences based on class and race, as well as sexual orientation, intersect with gender to give rise to important distinctions in the experiences of different categories of women. Thus different feminist theories can be compared and contrasted in terms of whether they focus primarily on the experiences shared by all women throughout society or the variations among women themselves in different racial/ethnic groups or socieconomic class positions.

Moreover, as shown by Jessie Bernard's (1987) comparative perspective, there are major differences in women's experiences of subordination in different countries around the world. This is clearly evident when we compare highly industrialized Western societies with those that are less developed, or those with different types of political systems and different levels of economic inequality. There are large disparities between the experiences and overall well-being of women in affluent industrial societies with a large middle class and women in less developed societies with high percentages of the population living in poverty (Bernard, 1987:109–122). Specific feminist issues thus differ greatly in different societies. These differences represent a challenge for women as they attempt to develop a strong sense of feminist solidarity in the struggle for gender equality on a global level, despite the universal experience of female subordination. Our primary focus will be on variations in the status of women in the United States. In the next section we look at Patricia Hill Collins' analysis of racial differences among women and how these intersect with both gender and socioeconomic class.

Exploring Differences Among Women in Multiple Hierarchies of Domination in Patricia Hill Collins' Perspective

In her portrayal of black feminist thought, Patricia Hill Collins (2000) emphasized the interrelations of gender, race, and class as intersecting sources of domination, especially for black women. Since a great deal of feminist theory has been developed by white women in academic settings, their analyses may be seen as having limited relevance to the lived experiences of black women. Collins' primary goal is to portray the worlds of black women in their own terms (or from their own standpoints), as opposed to comparing or contrasting their experiences or worldviews with those of white women.[2]

Drawing extensively on the writings and other cultural expressions of African American women, Collins describes their lives and worldviews in the areas of self-identity, "sexual politics," love relationships, motherhood, and community activism. With regard to self-identity, for example, she shows how the heroic struggles of black women within their own social networks enable them to maintain a sense of dignity and self-respect and to resist the negative images that underlie the dominant institutional practices of the wider society. In contrast to the degrading treatment black women receive from others in the wider environment, the loving and mutually supportive relationships they establish with one another in their extended families and communities serve as a source of positive self-esteem and empowerment in a generally hostile and oppressive world.

Collins points out the dilemmas black mothers have in teaching their daughters to resist the system of oppression in which they find themselves and to work for improvements in their life situation. At the same time, however, these mothers understand the need for their daughters to learn how to adapt to their subordinate and marginal position in the larger society in order to survive. In other words, even as black mothers encourage their daughters to try to improve their lives, they must also help them learn to deal with the often humiliating realities they face. Collins shows, too, that motherhood for black women includes an "other mother" role that often involves caring for extended family and other members of the community—a role that often leads to various forms of political activism in the community.

Overall, Collins portrays the world of African American women as involving multiple challenges resulting from their subordination in multiple systems of domination. This means that their struggles to maintain their dignity and to work for justice for themselves and their community must be waged on several different fronts simultaneously. She points out that black women tend to be subordinated to black men in terms of gender identity, but subordinated to white women in terms of racial identity. In other words, the intersecting hierarchies of gender and race

[2] Patricia Hill Collins was elected to serve as president of the American Sociological Association for 2008–2009. She is a member of the faculty at the University of Maryland. She received her PhD from Brandeis University and was formerly affiliated with the University of Cincinnati.

result in a more pervasive form of subordination than that experienced by either black men or white women. In addition, the fact that many employed black women earn minimal incomes means that socioeconomic class position provides yet a third source of subordination affecting their identities and life chances that are independent of their gender and race. This notion of the effects of the intersection of gender, race, and class as multiple hierarchies of domination is one of Collins' distinctive contributions to sociological theory. Her work can be seen as applying Dorothy's Smith's "standpoint" theory to the experiences of black women, especially those near the bottom of the socioeconomic hierarchy.

Moreover, just as the experiences of women in general differ greatly in different social locations, so do the experiences of black women themselves. Although black women are disproportionately represented in the lower socioeconomic class, some of them have managed to move up in the socioeconomic class structure, overcoming obstacles and taking advantage of the increased opportunities that have developed in part as a consequence of affirmative action and equal employment policies. This has led to increasing socioeconomic class differences among black women themselves. The social location (or "standpoint") of black women who have managed to move into middle-class occupational careers differs from the social locations of those who are still working at minimal wage jobs, or who are unable to obtain work and so must rely on inadequate social welfare resources.

In some cases, too, the higher level occupations of upwardly mobile black women involves supervising other black women or providing social services to black clients. The experiences of black women with supervisory or professional careers are qualitatively different from the experiences of black women who continue to be employed in domestic service or other "invisible" types of service jobs. These successful African American women may be seen in some contexts as having been coopted, even when their level of upward socioeconomic mobility is quite limited. In effect, their middle class occupational positions means they are participants in the "ruling relations" (or authority structure) whereby the multiple structures of domination are maintained, even though many of them have not moved very high in the occupational hierarchy. In addition, when upwardly mobile black women are able to move out of African American neighborhoods into integrated neighborhoods, their network ties with other black women are likely to deteriorate. This means that their opportunities to contribute to the multiple forms of self-help exchanged in these communities is diminished at the same time that their resources to do so may have increased.

Other hierarchical differences that Collins analyzed include those of sexual orientation and nationality. The privileged status of heterosexual relationships provides a potential basis for marginalizing black women who are lesbian. Similarly, for black women living in the United States or other wealthy or developed societies, their nationality provides a source of privilege that distinguishes them from black women living in Africa or other poor or less developed regions of the world. Collins' overall emphasis is on the way multiple structures of domination, particularly those based on race, gender, and social class, reinforce one another in perpetuating systematic forms of oppression. But the differences within categories are also important to analyze. Thus race divides black and white women, and gender divides black women and men. Within these broad categories, sexual orientation divides heterosexuals from gays and lesbians, and nationality divides those who are dominated and oppressed in the United States from those in poorer societies who are exploited.

As Collins put it:

> .... All contexts of domination incorporate some combination of intersecting oppressions, and considerable variability exists from one matrix of domination to the next as to how oppression and activism will be organized.
>
> (P. H. Collins, 2000:228)[3]

The pervasiveness of gender stratification and its overlap with other forms of domination and subordination are clearly revealed when we look at how gender relations are expressed at both the micro and macro levels of the social world, as well as in the meso levels in between.

Micro-Level Analyses of Gender Differences

Gender differences begin to be established in the early years of life, as emphasized in the symbolic interactionist perspective on how our identities are formed in the context of face-to-face relationships within the family and other primary groups. Parents and other adults tend to treat infant boys and girls differently. Even if parents succeed in rejecting traditional gender role stereotypes with their children, their daughters and sons cannot escape the sexuality of their own bodies. If a young person of either sex should decide to play basketball in high school, for example, she or he would need to try out for either the girls' or the boys' team. Children also learn a wide range of cultural stereotypes through school experiences, mass media exposure, and other social influences, which also contribute to their implicit understandings of gender differences and the formation of their self-concepts.

The strategies for presentation of self analyzed by Goffman inevitably include various styles of gender display. These displays may indicate acceptance or rejection of traditional roles or some option in between. But even if a nontraditional or egalitarian role is projected, this does not eliminate one's biological characteristics as female or male or prevent other people from reacting accordingly. Moreover, just as one's self-concept, self-presentation, and interaction style reflect one's gender identity, so also one's way of seeing the world is from the point of view of one's female or male identity and one's implicit assumptions about sex and gender differences. As we saw in Chap. 6, the phenomenological perspective and ethnomethodology emphasize the importance of such everyday life assumptions that we usually take for

[3]Collins' analysis of the effects of the way the hierarchies of domination based on gender, race, and socioeconomic class can be compared and contrasted with the arguments by Coser and Dahrendorf, reviewed in Chapter 14, regarding the positive effects of intersecting and crisscrossing lines of conflict in minimizing the disruptiveness of conflict and helping preserve the social order.

granted. The implicit acceptance of cultural definitions of gender roles contributes to the perpetuation of behavior patterns that help sustain these definitions. This section will explore some strategies for explaining gender differences at the micro level.

Biological Sex and Gender Differences

From a biological point of view, one could argue that the most crucial differences between men and women are those related to their reproductive roles. For example, if women can be shown to have distinctive biological predispositions for intense socioemotional attachments, this could be considered to be consistent with their intimate connection with the reproduction of human life. The propensity for forming such attachments may be seen as enhancing the process of socioemotional bonding with their children during the earliest years of their lives. However, even from a biological standpoint, women vary considerably in this regard, and men also share in this same basic human propensity for developing socioemotional bonds with others. This means that whatever gender differences may exist are relative, not absolute. Explicit recognition of differences in biological predispositions, both within and between gender categories, allows ample room for a wide range of cultural and individual variations.

Our primary focus in this chapter is not on the biological differences between females and males but the way social definitions of gender roles are used to provide implicit justification for women's subordination, either implicitly or explicitly.[4] However, Alice Rossi (1984) warned against ignoring biological factors and argued for the importance of integrating both biological differences and cultural influences in explaining gender variations. She pointed out that hormonal differences between men and women may be reflected in their parenting behavior, with mothers giving priority to intimacy and fathers giving priority to independence. Going beyond these differences in parenting styles, she also reviewed studies suggesting that higher levels of male violence in adolescence and young adulthood may have a biological base in their higher levels of testosterone, particularly at that stage in life. Of course, these biological differences do not mean that specific forms of either parenting behavior or violence are biologically determined in a strong sense. Instead, these biological predispositions can be expressed in different ways, depending on cultural influences. Moreover, with regard to aggression, social and cultural influences are commonly employed to try to prevent socially disruptive forms of aggressive behavior through various social control mechanisms, or to allow its expression in harmless or ritualistic ways, such as competitive sports, for example (Lorenz, 1966).[5] The importance

[4] In Chapter 18, the contrasting orientation of sociobiology will be reviewed. As we shall see, this perspective emphasizes the social implications of biological differences in reproductive roles and their importance for long-term species survival.

[5] Konrad Lorenz (1966), who has often been cited for his evolutionary analysis of human aggression and competition, pointed out that overt conflicts are often avoided among subhuman species through subordination displays and rituals.

of Rossi's argument, however, is that it underscores the importance of biological influences in explaining differences between women and men in parenting behavior and how these patterns of parenting influence the development of gender roles. Biological differences may no doubt be expected to affect other types of behavior as well, including patterns of aggressiveness in social relations.

Another possible biological difference between women and men is suggested by some interesting brain research on hemispheric specialization (see Durden-Smith and deSimone, 1983). For both women and men, there appears to be a tendency for the left hemisphere to specialize in language, and perhaps linear forms of thinking, and for the right hemisphere to specialize in more holistic (or contextual) and pattern-type thinking, including perception of spatial relations. (This contrast appears to be greater for right-handed people than left-handed people.) This hemispheric specialization (or lateralization) appears to be somewhat greater for males than for females. In addition, despite the extensive neural connections between the two hemispheres for both women and men, these connections may on average be somewhat more abundant for women than for men. This would suggest that there may be more extensive interchange between the two hemispheres for women. If so, it might imply that their right brain processes could more readily be accessed by their left-brain and verbalized. Of course, the similarities are far greater than the differences, and both women and men vary considerably in both their abilities and their willingness to talk about their subjective feelings.

It is beyond our purpose to analyze this fascinating brain research in detail, especially since their implications for gender differences are not conclusive. Moreover, many brain functions appear to be widely distributed in different regions of the brain. Nevertheless, it is interesting to consider the tantalizing possibility that such differences could have subtle effects on how women and men relate to others. In particular, the somewhat higher hemispheric specialization in men, coupled with their fewer neural connections, may provide some hints as to why men generally seem unable to handle the multifaceted aspects of social relationships or to express their feelings as readily as women. The popular stereotype regarding men's inability to deal with feelings may result not so much from an absence of feelings or a lack of empathy but from less ability than women in representing their feelings in those areas of the brain that would enable them to talk about them. The ability to verbalize one's feelings would presumably involve neural connections between the areas of the brain associated with feelings and those that specialize in speech. But how much of these differences reflect biological predispositions versus the deep and pervasive effects of one's socialization experiences in the earliest years of one's life is a matter of controversy and debate. From the sociological point of view, these differences can be explained largely as a result of cultural learning and social influences. In the next section we will look at Nancy Chodorow's perspective on how differences in gender identity and styles of relating to others may develop in the early years of life in the context of one's family life.

Male-Female Differences in Socioemotional Bonds with Parents

In popular opinion and in some academic research, women and men are seen as differing in terms of independence versus attachment, due either to biological predispositions or to social and cultural influences. In explaining such differences Nancy Chodorow (1978) focused on the contrast in the early life experiences of boys and girls as they are socialized in their families. Her analysis is deeper than simply identifying what type of gender roles parents intend to teach their children. She employs a psychodynamic perspective to show how boys and girls differ in their reactions to their mothers as their usual primary caregiver compared to their fathers. For boys the development of gender identity involves essentially a process of separation or differentiation from their mothers. This need for boys to establish an identity different from their mother gives rise to a strong emphasis on male independence. In contrast, gender identity for girls is developed through identification with their mothers, resulting in a stronger relational capacity or need for attachment rather than independence. In other words, there is a higher level of continuity for girls between their earliest experiences with their mothers and subsequent social relations.

Fathers vary considerably in how they perform their paternal role, but their involvement with their children is typically less than that of mothers, particularly in their children's infancy and early childhood. This greater social distance provides a model for their sons' independence. For daughters, the contrast in their emotional relationship with their father versus their mother helps reinforce their identification with their mother. Through these contrasting processes whereby sons and daughters relate to their mothers and fathers, many of the culturally defined characteristics of women versus men are transmitted as well.

In developing their gender identity, boys are faced with the challenge of dealing with the ambivalence they feel toward their mothers (and women in general). Although they are dependent on their mother and no doubt experience a sense of emotional security through this connection, the need to establish a separate identity leads to ambivalent feelings toward her. As this ambivalence plays itself out in later life in other relationships, usually at a subconscious level, it helps contribute to men's efforts to control women so as to satisfy their own emotional needs for being connected while at the same time maintaining their independence. This clearly has potential implication for how husbands relate to their wives. For women, in contrast, their reaction to the gender subordination they experience involves developing close relationships with one another to help compensate for the frustrations of subordination. During their growing up years, daughters initially experience this compensating alliance through identification with their mothers, whose relation to their fathers serves as a model for how females relate to males. This perspective may be compared with Scheff's (1997) analysis, discussed in an earlier chapter, regarding the differences between women and men in their level and style of attachment versus isolation and the contrasting emotional dynamics that are involved.

Despite this focus on gender differences, it is also important to emphasize that both men and women have the capacity for both independence and attachment, even though the relative importance of these processes may vary by gender (and also within each gender). In her analysis of the influence of gender on people's identities, Ellyn Kaschak (1992) suggests that both women and men have the capacity to move beyond traditional gender identities and thereby achieve higher levels of emotional development and growth. For men this would involve relinquishment of delusions of grandeur and possessiveness toward women. For women it would mean developing their own integrated identity as women who relate to others, including men, in an interdependent fashion instead of in a subordinate and dependent position. For both men and women, the outcome would be relationships of egalitarian interdependence in which the contrasting needs for independence and attachment would be balanced.

The goal of moving beyond the restrictions of traditional gender stereotypes cannot, of course, eliminate all of the differences between women and men in terms of their basic life experiences. We look in the next section at how the differing life experiences of females and males may give rise to variations in their emotional reactions to life and death and the possible effects these differences may have on their social relations.

Matters of Life and Death

Although both men and women have an intellectual awareness of their own mortality, Dorothy Dinnerstein (1976) proposed that their emotional reactions to this reality differ sharply. This contrast results from the crucial differences in the nature of the involvement of women versus men in the reproduction of human life. Dinnerstein's line of speculation suggests that women may tend to suffer less anxiety over their own eventual death than men because they are much more intimately connected than men with the process of producing new life. The result, presumably, is that women are better able than men to develop an implicit and emotionally reassuring awareness of the continuation of their own lives in the lives of their offspring. The biological role of men in the reproductive process does not require the same level of experiential involvement as women. Although they may have considerable emotional involvement with the new human life they help produce, this is not required from a purely biological standpoint; in fact, men can readily contribute to the reproduction of offspring of whom they are not even aware. The result is that men are less likely than women to experience as deep an emotional connection to the process whereby their lives are continued in the lives of their children.

Given their lower level of actual experience in the process of human reproduction, men's anxiety regarding their own eventual death tends to be greater than that of women, according to Dinnerstein. One consequence of the struggle to cope with this anxiety is that men may feel a stronger need than women to create some legacy that will endure beyond their death through efforts to master, control, or somehow change their external environment. This need to create a lasting legacy is manifested in the construction of physical structures of various types (such as impressive monuments at their graves, buildings, works of art, and other material artifacts) as well as in enduring social or cultural products such as successful enterprises, legal and political systems, scientific and philosophical achievements, and so on. In evaluating these speculative ideas, it is important to note that the differences are not absolute. Some women may also experience anxiety regarding their own personal mortality, despite their experience of giving birth to new life. Also, whether or not they experience this anxiety, some women may also develop a strong desire to leave a lasting legacy other than through their children. In addition, both women and men may learn to cope with the knowledge of their own mortality through their religious faith or other ways.

Dinnerstein proposes also that males' anxiety regarding death and the desire to preserve their identity beyond the grave can be expressed in their efforts to dominate women and thereby to control the dramatic and mysterious power women have to produce and nourish new life. These efforts to control women and their reproductive powers provides another option for them as they seek to compensate for their fear of death. Although they cannot insure their personal survival by producing offspring themselves, they can control the women through whom their offspring are produced. Traditional relations of husbands and wives in family life express these patterns of male domination and female subordination. The differences in the power and the resulting benefits that marriage provides to men versus women lead to the distinction that Jessie Bernard identified as **his** marriage versus **her** marriage.

Wives Versus Husbands in Family Life

One of the major challenges that feminists face in their struggles for gender equality is the pervasive pattern of inequality that often prevails in the intimate relations of family life. Jessie Bernard (1982) reviewed several studies showing that men receive more benefits from marriage than women, leading her to distinguish the "husband's marriage" versus the "wife's marriage." Women's disadvantaged position is reflected in the finding that married women have traditionally had higher rates of depression than either married men or single women. In contrast, single men have higher rates of depression than married men. These differences in emotional well-being and mental health may well be the result of traditional gender roles in which wives provide emotional support for their husbands at the psychological and emotional cost to themselves of being dependent and subordinate.

The sharp contrast in husbands' and wives' roles described by Bernard was clearly reflected in the now-outdated functionalist analysis of the contemporary family of the mid-twentieth century provided by Talcott Parsons, Robert Bales, and their collaborators (Parsons and Bales, 1955). In this analysis, as noted earlier, the nuclear family was seen as having become more specialized in modern society in satisfying its members' socioemotional needs, providing for sexual relations between husbands and wives, and meeting the primary socialization needs of the children. Within the family the wife/mother specialized in socioemotional and expressive activities while the husband/father specialized in instrumental or task activities. This micro-level pattern seemed congruent with the long-term process of increasing macro-level institutional differentiation and specialization. With this high level of functional specialization within the family, women were clearly subordinate and were expected to be "on call" and attentive to the emotional needs of their husbands and children. This type of functional analysis should be seen as reflecting the 1950s-style family and thus as more relevant to that historical period than to contemporary dual-career families. At that time the cultural ideal of wives/mothers remaining home and husbands/fathers providing the necessary financial resources through their careers was widely accepted. As is often the case, it appears that Parsons interpreted the social world of his time as confirmation for his general theory, which (as seen earlier) focused heavily on the long-range evolutionary process of increasing differentiation.

But as Bernard's analysis demonstrated, even when it was widely expected that women would prefer to stay home, there were considerable costs they incurred in terms of their one-sided dependence on their husbands, the scarcity of their social contacts outside the family, the burden of having sole responsibility for the never-ending and monotonous household tasks, and the emotional toll of being expected always to be available to meet the emotional and physical needs of other family members. These costs were manifested in the high levels of depression of married women that Bernard noted. Paradoxically, too, the level of opportunities and cultural encouragement for men to satisfy their own socioemotional and expressive needs within the intimacy of the family setting were also limited. Men were expected always to be strong, competitive, and achievement-oriented, to keep their emotions under control, and never to cry. In today's more egalitarian environment, this type of family structure, with its sharply distinguished gender roles, is sometimes referred to as the "traditional family." As a point of fact, however, this type of family system was a reflection of a particular historical period in American history.

From the point of view of feminist theory, Parsons' portrayal of the modern families of his time can be criticized as a pseudo-objective justification of gender role stereotypes that are extremely limiting to both women and men. His theory certainly does not apply to contemporary dual-career families in which both wives and husbands share household and child care responsibilities. Indeed, in terms of fulfilling the human needs of both wives and husbands for developing strong socioemotional bonds with one another, the egalitarian partnership pattern may have the potential to be more functional and emotionally satisfying than the alternative of rigid role differentiation and specialization.

Although Bernard's contrast between **his** versus **her** marriage may be less relevant in contemporary dual-career families than in previous generations, women still tend to take on more domestic and child care responsibilities than their husbands, even in dual-career families with egalitarian gender role ideals. This may be due to differences between wives and husbands in the priorities they give to household tasks and child care needs, but it results in what Arlie Hochschild (1989) refers to as a "second shift" for women who are in paid employment away from home and who are also expected to perform substantially more household and family care tasks than their husbands. This unequal distribution of the work of maintaining a household and raising children reflects the continuing and pervasive influence of traditional gender roles that persist even in "egalitarian" dual-career families.

Many aspects of traditional gender roles continue to be learned and expressed at a very early age—sometimes despite parents' efforts to shape their children's gender identities in a more egalitarian way. To the extent that such traditional patterns seem natural and inevitable at the micro level, the challenge for increasing gender equality at the macro level is all that much greater. We turn in the next section to gender roles and relations at the macro level.

Macro-Level Critique of Male Domination

The critical focus of feminist theory is directed more toward the pervasive patterns of male domination and female subordination than toward gender differences as such. But even if gender roles were completely equal, feminist theorists would insist that other social roles should not be allocated automatically on the basis of gender but should reflect the rights of human beings to make their own choices. Feminist theory can thus be seen as reflecting the humanistic ideal of providing opportunities for each individual person—female or male—to develop her or his own unique potentialities without the constraints imposed by narrow cultural stereotypes or structures of domination.

Feminist theory may thus be compared to Marxist theory in its critical analysis of structures of domination at the macro level. The obvious difference is that feminists focus primarily on gender relations while Marxists emphasize economic class relations. Many feminists are also concerned with socioeconomic class relations, as illustrated, for example, in Patricia Hill Collins' analysis (reviewed earlier) of how class position intersects with gender and race in reinforcing structures of domination. In much feminist theory the overall power structures of society are seen as an extension of patriarchal forms of family relations. Early in the twentieth century, Marx's collaborator Friedrich Engels (1902) linked the origins of patriarchy with the beginning of private property. In this perspective, early hunting and gathering groups were gradually replaced by stable settlements as men began to appropriate land and other forms of private property (some more successfully than others). At the same time, men also began to control women (their wife or wives and daughters) within the context of the family. With higher birth rates than today, multiple wives, and extended families, successful men were able to use the human resources garnered within their households to gain control of more and more land and other productive resources. By controlling their wives men not only benefited from their wives' domestic labor, but they could also be assured that the children their wives bore were indeed their own. This was important for them to be able to pass along the property they had accumulated to their own offspring (particularly males). Males could also offer their daughters as marriage partners to strengthen alliances with other families or groups and thereby reduce the likelihood of external threats.

As we jump forward to the type of capitalist society that Marx and Engels studied, the patterns of domination that working class males experienced in the factories of the early industrial system were reproduced in their homes in their relations with their wives and children. In some cases, women and children themselves also worked in factories. But for the most part women were dependent on their husbands' income, and this helped insure male domination in the family setting. Moreover, the unpaid work that women performed in maintaining their homes and bearing and raising children contributed to the maintenance and the reproduction of the labor force which capitalist employers exploited.

Institutional Differentiation and the Organized Control of Violence

Another perspective that helps explain long-range historical changes in patterns of male dominance is suggested by Randall Collins (who is not necessarily considered a feminist theorist but whose wide-ranging interests included gender roles). In his comparative conflict theory (reviewed in Chap. 14) Collins (1975:225–259; 278–284) argued that the underlying source of male dominance is simply their greater physical size and strength. However, the likelihood that men will use (or threaten to use) coercive power or violence to control women depends in part on the way the means of violence are organized and legitimated in the wider society. Physical coercion and the threat of violence against women are more likely to be used when the right to use violence is institutionalized within households. This would be the case in relatively simple and undifferentiated societies without specialized political or social control institutions. Even in the days of the American frontier, for example, households would rely on their own private forms of "law enforcement" for self-defense or revenge. But in modern societies, the state monopolizes the legitimate use of violence in maintaining "law and order," and the authority of state agencies may be enlisted by women to initiate formal legal action to punish men who are guilty of spouse abuse and rape. Regrettably, even in modern society, the victims of such violence often face immense practical difficulties in getting help from appropriate social control and social service agencies, particularly when abuse occurs within family settings.

Although physical coercion and violence have been largely replaced by other strategies of domination in modern society, Collins suggests that the potential for coercion and violence underlies all forms of conflict, including gender conflict. Understanding the processes whereby the state has monopolized the legitimate use of coercive control and violence while other forms of social control have expanded requires us to look at the long-term historical process of institutional differentiation and growth in the complexity of society. As societies expanded and evolved from simple structures organized primarily around large extended families, separate military, political, and economic institutions were developed. This process of institutional differentiation accelerated greatly with the emergence of modern society, leading to the development of specialized institutions in education, religion, medical care, recreation, social welfare, social control, and so on.[6] Even though the right to use physical violence has been removed from private individuals and households and allocated to formal social control agencies, male domination is no less pervasive. But domination tends to take a "softer" form than physical coercion and violence, and it is reinforced by various ideological justifications that are intended to gain the consent of the governed. Instead of being coerced against their will, people are persuaded to acquiesce in their own subordination in order to achieve their various personal goals.

As this long-range differentiation process has occurred, the patriarchal form of domination, initially established in the family structure, has been extended from one differentiated institution to another. Moreover, as men developed specialized organizations separate from the family to engage in the rational pursuit of various goals, their ability to expand their power and control of resources has been enhanced accordingly. The result is that their power and authority are no longer limited to their own family group but have been extended to subordinates who are employed in the numerous formal organizations they control. As these organizations grew in size, the bureaucratic hierarchy of authority described by Weber became more and more dominant in all major areas of social life, with men much more likely than women to be in the top-level positions.

With specialized bureaucratic organizations dominating more and more areas of the social world, the only option for most people to survive and achieve their personal goals is to seek employment in some formal organizational setting and acquiesce to its authority structure—or to become dependent on someone who is so employed. By having their own careers, women are able to decrease their financial dependence on their husbands and perhaps the level of subordination they experience in their families. But of course, the price that most of them must pay is subordination at work. While many male occupations also involve subordination, the distribution of women and men in occupational hierarchies of power and authority is by no means equal. Instead, the higher one looks in these hierarchies, the lower the proportion of women. In contrast, high proportions of women can be found in positions at or near the bottom of these hierarchies, with their low levels of pay, power, and prestige. While women employed in organizational settings generally have less power and authority and are paid less than men, women whose work is limited to their own households do not get paid at all, and so are economically dependent on their husbands. Moreover, the tasks of household maintenance and child care in the family are not part of the market economy; neither wives nor husbands get paid for fulfilling their domestic responsibilities in the household. However, women tend to perform more of these domestic tasks than men, even in dual-career households, and these

---

[6] As we saw in an earlier chapter, Parsons' general strategy of functional analysis was used to show how all of the various functions requirements that must be performed to insure society's survival are fulfilled by separate institutional structures. This reflects the long-term process of differentiation, which Parsons and Smelser applied to their analysis of the relationship between the family and economy as specialized institutional structures (see Parsons and Smelser [1956]).

domestic arrangements clearly support the more meso and macro level institutional structures of society.

This perspective on how male domination has been solidified in the institutional structures of modern society reflects a critical perspective that emphasizes the importance of gender stratification and the conflicting interests of males and females that result from their unequal access to power, authority, and material resources. However, the dynamic nature of modern society also includes built-in mechanisms of change that have the potential for reducing gender inequality and increasing women's share of power, authority, and material resources. The emergence of the feminist movement is itself a major stimulus for progressive change in this regard. In the next section we draw on Miriam Johnson's feminist perspective to show how the feminist movement can be analyzed in functional theory terms as creating pressures for reducing women's subordination.

Evolutionary Progress from a Feminist Functionalist Perspective

In her feminist interpretation of Talcott Parsons' evolutionary theory, Miriam Johnson (pp. 101–118 in Wallace, ed., 1989) focused on the evolutionary processes Parsons had identified to help analyze the effects of the feminist movement in promoting increased opportunities for women in all areas of social life. She showed how these developments can be interpreted as enhancing the fulfillment of the functional requirements of society by reducing the barriers to women's participation in all areas of society as equals. As discussed in Chap. 12, Parsons used his AGIL model to analyze long-term evolutionary processes in society. His functional requirement of **adaptation** was linked with the long-range evolutionary process of **adaptive upgrading**; **goal attainment** was linked with institutional **differentiation**; **integration** was related to the process of **inclusion**, and **latent pattern maintenance** was connected with the process of **value generalization**.

In Miriam Johnson's analysis, each of these evolutionary processes is seen as being enhanced by greater gender equality and the expansion of opportunities for women brought about in large part by the feminist movement. This improvement in women's status and opportunities is perhaps reflected most clearly with the processes of inclusion and value generalization. Inclusion in this context would apply to the process whereby norms that traditionally excluded women from various social positions in society, particularly in its power structures, have gradually been replaced by policies designed to increase gender equality. In the area of shared values (latent pattern maintenance), the traditional pattern of limited (or particularistic) gender roles and ideals has been changed in favor of applying to women the same universalistic achievement standards that are applied to men. Overall, these evolutionary processes mean that women are expected to have the same opportunities as men and to be judged according to their achievements rather than on the basis of their gender. In the functional areas of adaptation and goal attainment, increased gender equality would be expected to result in more effective adaptation and greater potential for goal achievement. These positive outcomes should be expected as the distinctive talents and abilities of women are developed and incorporated into the macro-level institutional structures of society more fully than in the past.

Feminist theorists have understandably been critical of Parsons' perspective on gender role specialization in family life—a perspective that can be related to the historical context of the times.[7] However, Miriam Johnson's use of his theory to explain the impact of the feminist movement helps to demonstrate the flexibility of functional theory. It is important to emphasize that changes in gender roles and increased opportunities for women did not occur spontaneously as a result of inevitable evolutionary dynamics built into the system. Instead, they involved a great deal of political and moral struggle that was led largely by feminists as they engaged in a compelling critique of the injustice of the patriarchal patterns manifested throughout society, and as they mobilized support for political change. Feminists' own priorities were certainly not oriented toward the system's "functional requirements." Instead, they challenged established structures and traditional gender roles as they fought vigorously to expand women's opportunities and reduce gender inequality. Thus, in contrast to Parsons' emphasis on widespread value consensus, stability, and social equilibrium, growth in gender equality clearly demonstrates the important role of conflict in stimulating change and progress. Feminist theory has played a crucial role in sociological analysis in shifting priorities from fulfilling the requirements of social systems to promoting higher levels of equality with regard to gender roles. But despite the progress that has occurred in gender beliefs and roles, the fact is that gender inequality still persists in modern society. Chafetz's model of gender stratification, to be reviewed in the following section, helps us explain the persistence of gender inequality.

Explaining Gender Inequality: Janet Saltzman Chafetz's Theory of Gender Stratification

In her systematic comparative theory of gender stratification, Janet Saltzman Chafetz (1990) focused on women's independent access to equal economic resources and elite positions in society as the key to reducing gender inequality.

[7] As noted in Chapter 12, Parsons and his colleagues interpreted the specialization of gender roles in the family in the general framework of the overall institutional differentiation of society. Although this analysis may be seen as consistent with cultural ideals that were widespread in the middle of the twentieth century, there were dysfunctional consequences of this pattern even at that time. The contemporary dual-career cultural ideal in which both husbands and wives share in household maintenance and child care tasks may be seen as more functional in reinforcing socioemotional bonds between husbands and wives, provided that both contribute equitably in these tasks.

Although micro and macro level processes tend to reinforce one another in maintaining patterns of gender inequality, Chafetz puts primary emphasis on the macro-level distribution of resources. Inequalities at this level are reflected not only in pay differentials for men and women but also in the fact that men occupy the majority of the elite positions in society's major institutions.

At the micro level, Chafetz focuses on socialization processes in the family and interpersonal relations among women and men in maintaining traditional gender roles. From the beginning of their lives, sons and daughters are rewarded in their families for behaving in accordance with appropriate gender roles. Thus they learn to view such patterns as natural and incorporate them in their self concepts. Among adults, male domination and female submission are manifested in interpersonal encounters as men's definitions and interpretations usually seem to be given more weight, often by women as well as men. The result is that women's behavior often reflects a high level of compliance with traditional gender roles, despite the subordination this involves, partly because of the social approval and other rewards they receive in exchange. This micro level subordination is reinforced at the macro level by the unequal distribution of material resources (especially financial compensation) which leads to an unequal distribution of power. These power differences enable men to impose their definitions on the roles and relations of men and women in all aspects of life, both micro and macro.

In the "traditional" family in which wives are not employed outside the home, the economic dependence of wives on their husbands establishes a clear foundation for husbands' dominance. In contemporary dual-career families, in contrast, wives are somewhat less dependent on their husbands, and thus their power in the family is greater. This greater degree of equality is likely to be manifested in a higher level of joint involvement in decision-making and a somewhat more equitable sharing of household tasks—even though, as noted earlier, even in dual-career families, women tend to do more household tasks and to carry more child care responsibilities (when there are children) than their husbands do.

Moreover, when women are employed outside the home, they typically earn less than men. In addition, in contrast to men, they often give higher priority to their families than to their careers, particularly if there are children in the family. Their lower career priority may then be used by employers to justify the continuing discrepancy in pay. This can sometimes lead to a vicious cycle situation in which the low pay women receive then contributes to their continued low commitment. Experiences are different for women whose primary motivation to work outside the home is economic survival and women who have long-term professional career goals. Single mothers with limited education are particularly vulnerable because of their low wages and economic insecurity. Their situation is particularly bleak if they also have young children who are dependent on them.

Although males are dominant in practically all known societies, there are noteworthy variations among different societies in the degree of male dominance and female subordination. These patterns may change over time within a society, with inequality either increasing or decreasing. Such changes may be either unintentional or intentional. Unintentional changes may result from broad social changes in demography, technology, or economic cycles. For example, women's job opportunities will increase if the economy expands but the population remains stable. In addition, wars help deplete the male labor supply, thus opening up opportunities for women. At the same time, however, wars tend also to lead to a renewed emphasis on traditional values and norms, including those involving family patterns and gender roles. Even though ideals of "normal" family life and gender roles may be suspended during the war, the termination of war is likely to be followed by efforts to restore traditional pre-war gender roles. This process may help explain the strong identification with "family values" in the United States in the decades following the end of World War II. During this time period there was widespread acceptance of the cultural ideal that women should remain home to care for the household and children.

The most obvious example of intentional efforts to change traditional patterns of gender stratification is provided by the women's movement itself. The specific goals and strategies that are used in the struggle to reduce gender inequality are varied and may include advocating for pay equity, increased representation of women in elite positions in society, and redefinition of traditional gender roles in the family and other contexts. Political and legal processes are used to try to promote macro-level change, while micro-level social processes in many different contexts provide opportunities for women to seek to raise the consciousness of both men and women regarding the various subtle ways in which gender norms supporting inequality can be changed.

Chafetz points out that the likelihood that women will get involved in the feminist movement or participate in women's organizations are related to their own socioeconomic class backgrounds. Activists in the feminist movement tend to have middle-class occupations that provide them with the material resources they need to mobilize themselves in the struggle to promote change. The occupational experiences shared by women in middle-class occupations helps raise their consciousness of the numerous ways they are marginalized and subordinated, both blatant and subtle. At the same time, their experience of working for pay outside the home provides a sense of empowerment and confidence that their efforts will be successful.

Some men may also play a role in promoting changes in gender roles and greater equity in pay, prestige, and power in occupational roles. Partly this reflects the ability of women in micro-level contexts to persuade men (including perhaps their husbands and men with whom they work in their occupations) of the need for change. If successful, such efforts raise the consciousness of men so they too understand the issues that are involved in making the system fairer to women. In addition, men in elite positions may themselves become involved in supporting women's issues, particularly when they expect such support to enhance their own power in competition with competing elites. The importance of this process can be seen in the way in which political candidates may seek to earn women's votes by assuring them that they will support policies and legislation to benefit women.

Chafetz also acknowledges the limits the feminist movement and its supporters face in achieving complete gender equality. For one thing, the partial success of the feminist movement may stimulate resistance, giving rise to social movements intended to prevent continued change or even to reverse recent changes. Resistance to the goals of the feminist movement may occur among both men and women who feel their interests are threatened and who have a stake in the maintenance of traditional gender roles. Of course, the justifications for these resistance movements would not be expressed in terms of maintaining unfairness. Instead, their ideology would emphasize the benefits that are thought to result from maintaining traditional gender roles.

Both men and women in conservative or fundamentalist religious groups tend to resist many of the goals of the feminist movement because they see them as undermining traditional family values. The establishment of male groups in recent years such as the Promise Keepers provides an example of an organized effort to reassert male authority and responsibilities in a way that seems contrary to the goals of increasing gender equality (Bartkowski, 2004). Moreover, as the struggle intensifies and the agenda for promoting change expands, opponents are likely to see the movement as becoming more and more radical and so may develop even stronger levels of resistance.

In addition, as the feminist movement is increasingly successful in achieving more and more of its goals, it becomes more difficult to sustain the idealistic enthusiasm of its earlier days. For one thing, the initial success of the movement makes it possible for many women to achieve success in pursuing their own individual goals. For some women, these personal goals then begin to take priority over the collective goals of the movement. For others, fatigue and apathy eventually take their toll, particularly as the movement's ideals seem more and more difficult to achieve in the face of increasing antifeminist opposition. There may be pressures to compromise the movement's ideals so as to continue making progress even with limited goals, and this also may contribute to the erosion of the movement's idealistic enthusiasm.

Chafetz's analysis of the limits of continued progress toward complete gender equality reflects a paradox that is common to other idealistic social movements. As social movements make progress in achieving their goals, their success helps undermine continued enthusiasm as some participants become satisfied with the progress made, even though much may remain to be done before the original goals are achieved. This satisfaction of some with the progress made, coupled with increasing fatigue and apathy on the part of others, makes commitment to the long-term struggle difficult to sustain. In accordance with her overall emphasis on the macro level distribution of resources, Chafetz suggests that future success in achieving higher levels of gender equality will depend heavily on general economic conditions. A strong economy is important for insuring that opportunities for gaining material resources continue to expand for women. In modern society, acquiring resources means having good-paying careers. Thus the key for continued progress has to do with expanding women's opportunities for employment in careers that provide pay comparable to that of men, plus providing greater access to elite positions in society's major institutions, particularly economic and political institutions. It is in these elite positions that policies can be developed and implemented to insure continued progress in achieving the long-term goal of gender equality.

In contrast to Chafetz's emphasis on the objective opportunities for women to gain access to elite positions and the material resources they provide, Dorothy Smith focused on the need for a greater subjective understanding of the subtle and impersonal dynamics employed in the "relations of ruling" that are dominated by men. We turn in the next section to her analysis of these dynamics.

Mechanisms of Macro-Level Domination Through Impersonal Texts

Earlier in this chapter we looked at Dorothy Smith's concept of the "bifurcated consciousness" in which the subjective lived experience of women (and other subordinates) was contrasted with the objective type of knowledge advanced in mainstream (male-dominated) sociology and other "official" forms of knowledge. In addition to emphasizing the importance and the validity of personal knowledge based on lived experience, Dorothy Smith also provided a sophisticated analysis of how the voices of women (and other subordinates) are silenced as those in dominant positions rely on the authoritative texts that they produce to maintain their patterns of domination.

Smith's (1990) analysis of the importance of texts in sustaining the institutional "relations of ruling" in society provides an important and useful bridge between micro and macro levels of analysis. She points out how people located in different positions throughout society (especially subordinates) are grouped together in various institutional settings and actually controlled through the impersonal mechanism of texts. By producing authoritative texts and then using them as an objective source of their authority, those involved in relations of ruling (typically men) are able to expand and consolidate their power and influence beyond the local level to larger institutional contexts. In this way the experiences, behaviors, and actions of individuals in their micro-level social worlds are subjected to the "relations of ruling" of meso and macro level structures. As Smith puts it:

> The ruling apparatuses are those institutions of administration, management, and professional authority, and of intellectual and cultural discourses, which organize, regulate, lead and direct, contemporary capitalist societies. The power relations which come thus into view from the standpoint of an experience situated in the everyday world are abstracted from local and particular settings and relationships. These forms of communication and action are distinctively mediated by texts. The textual mediation of its forms of organization are fundamental to its characteristic abstracted, extra-local forms, and its curious capacity to reproduce its order in the same way in an indefinite variety of actual local contexts.
>
> (Smith, 1990:2)

This perspective on "forms of organization" and reproduction of "order" clearly contrasts with the notion that social order is due to socioemotional cohesion, moral solidarity, or some vague and elusive process of "social integration." It contrasts also with the notion that social systems are based on patterns of functional interdependence that people consciously or voluntarily agree to establish and maintain. Instead, the maintenance of social order results from the fact that individuals throughout society are subjected to the same ruling relations as mediated through authoritative texts. The agents of institutional authority themselves rely on the objective and impersonal authority of these texts to legitimate their exercise of power at the micro level sites of everyday life. These agents of authority may be located in the same micro level social worlds as those they govern but, as agents of institutional or organizational structures, they exercise their authority in an impersonal manner in accordance with the appropriate written rules and procedures.

Numerous examples of the authority and binding power of texts in defining the social world could be cited, but perhaps two of the most obvious examples are the legal codes that control people's behavior in the overall society (and in states and other governmental units as well) and the particular rules and regulations that prescribe their roles and role behavior within the organizations in which they participate, particularly in their occupational setting. This is consistent with Weber's analysis of the importance of written rules and records in bureaucratic settings of all types. This reliance on authoritative texts is manifested in a different context in the reliance on the "objective" knowledge that is available in various academic and professional books and journals that provide the basis for the authority of professionals of all types.[8]

Objective texts are crucial in everyday life for providing authoritative definitions of social reality—so much so, in fact, that verbal agreements carry no legal weight unless written in an official contract in the appropriate language. In addition to rules, regulations, and contracts, other examples of various texts that are crucial in creating the objective social world include academic transcripts and diplomas, professional and marriage licenses, medical and financial records, court transcripts, evaluation and performance reports, minutes of formal meetings, scientific reports and published academic treatises, and many others.

Moreover, particular events of all types become noteworthy as news only when they are presented in objective news reports. Such reports consist not only of written texts but audio and visual representations, especially in our "hi-tech" world of virtually instantaneous communication of both text and pictures around the world via television or the internet. It is the mass media coverage of events both far and near that renders them real and significant in public consciousness and gives them their status as official objective reality, as opposed to mere personal opinion or subjective experience.

Objective texts convey a type of authority that appears to be more certain and valid than mere subjective experiences. Although the creation and interpretation of texts certainly involve subjective processes, once created they become part of the objective world, appearing to transcend the subjective level in the same way that they transcend the local context in which they are produced, interpreted, and enforced.

[8] This is consistent with Foucault's analysis, described earlier, of the connection between professional knowledge and the exercise of power.

The producers of texts need not share the intersubjective social worlds of those who ultimately read and interpret them, or who are subjected to their authority. In fact, producers and interpreters do not even need to be in personal contact with one another. Thus texts appear to take on a life of their own, with an apparent influence and authority that extends throughout society far beyond the local setting where they were produced.

As a text becomes detached from its source, the link that is established between its creators and those who read or listen to it, or who are governed by it, is an impersonal one with minimal levels of intersubjective understanding. This may be revealed, for example, when attorneys, judges, and politicians debate the meaning of certain passages from the United States Constitution to try to legitimate some argument or ruling, even though they cannot know for certain how the authors of the Constitution would apply it to the case at hand. Similarly, members of society who are legally bound to comply with textually mediated rules may have had no say in the creation of the rules or no opportunity to communicate with those who did. The authority of impersonal texts may be unhappily discovered by those who inadvertently violate written rules of which they may not be aware and then find themselves subjected to negative sanctions.

Smith emphasizes the way texts enable persons in positions of power and authority to standardize and expand their "relations of ruling" throughout society and to insure their continuation through time. Her analysis of how texts are used in the relations of ruling helps in a significant way to link micro and macro levels of analysis. Her perspective on this linkage can be contrasted with Habermas's notion of "system" versus "lifeworld" that was discussed in Chap. 15. The ongoing lived experiences that Smith emphasized would correspond roughly to Habermas's notion of the lifeworld. Social processes that are crucial for social integration at this level involve communication aimed at intersubjective understanding. In contrast to the lifeworld, the "system" is integrated through impersonal macro-level mechanisms that sometimes appear to be beyond the level of everyday life understanding and individual control. In Smith's view these impersonal macro-level mechanisms consist in large part of texts.[9]

Of course, Smith's focus on lived experience was quite different from Habermas's analysis of rationalization and communication. However, Smith's contrast between the authority of the impersonal texts of the institutional world and the subjective reality of lived experience may be compared and contrasted with Habermas's distinction between system integration at the level of large-scale institutional structures and social integration at the level of the lifeworld. The texts involved in the impersonal "relations of ruling" identified by Smith may be seen as the medium whereby the instrumental rationality of large-scale economic and

[9] This may be compared to Habermas's explicit focus on money and power as impersonal steering mechanisms. However, both money and power are inscribed in textual form. Money itself is a type of document, while power is reflected in authority structures that are defined through written rules.

political institutions have invaded and colonized the everyday micro-level lifeworld as analyzed by Habermas. As Habermas emphasized, this invasion contributes to the suppression and distortion of communication oriented toward mutual understanding.

Despite this similarity between Smith's distinction between ongoing subjective experience and impersonal objective texts and Habermas's distinction between lifeworld and system, Thomas Meisenhelder (pp. 119–132 in Wallace, ed., 1989) pointed out that Habermas's theoretical perspective contrasts with the arguments of many feminist theorists on the crucial importance of emotions as well as such perspectives as Dorothy Smith's emphasis on lived experience. Briefly, Meissenhelder suggests that Habermas's strong emphasis on rationalization and communication may be seen as failing to provide sufficient theoretical space for analyzing subjective emotional experiences that are not expressed discursively. However, in contrast to Meissenhelder's critique, we saw in the last chapter that Habermas explicitly acknowledged the importance of expressive forms of communication oriented toward the disclosure of feelings and subjective experiences. Even so, the difference in emphasis and style of analysis is readily apparent.

Summary

We do not yet know the full ramifications of incorporating all of the important theoretical insights of feminist theory into all aspects of sociology. However, it should be acknowledged that a separate chapter on women or "feminist theory" in a social theory text can itself, regrettably, be misunderstood as a form of marginalization, despite an author's rejection of such an intention. Presumably, the ultimate goal for feminist theorists would be for their perspectives and insights to be fully incorporated into the heart of sociological analysis rather then being treated separately. (For an assessment of progress made in incorporating the contributions of feminist scholars into mainstream sociology and a selective sampling of these contributions, see Myers et al., eds. [1998].) At the same time, it is important to note that women sociologists do not speak with a single voice. Thus it is not a simple matter to incorporate feminist theory into sociology—due to the fact that there are multiple feminist theories, as we have seen in our brief overview in this chapter.

Although our overview in this chapter is limited, the theorists whose contributions have been reviewed illustrate the variety of approaches represented in feminist theory. One of the main goals of feminist theorists is to provide a critique of the dominant traditions in sociological theory and to show how they implicitly reflect the male viewpoint. We looked in particular at Dorothy Smith's appeal for a distinctive "woman-centered" sociology that would emphasize the subjective lived experiences of women. In her perspective these experiences reflect the oppressive effects of the various "relations of ruling" which she sees as being implicit and therefore unexamined in mainstream sociology. This strategy of developing a separate feminist sociology is obviously inconsistent with the goal stated above of incorporating gender in a comprehensive sociological framework. Smith's argument, however, is based on her belief that the differences between the social experiences of women and men make it impossible for women's experiences to be adequately represented in a male-dominated sociological perspective. If current sociology reflects primarily a male point of view, then perhaps the only alternative for incorporating women's experiences in a more comprehensive framework that includes both men and women is to revise and reconstruct sociology's most fundamental underlying assumptions.

At the same time, however, it is important to remember that not all women share the same position in society or view the social world from the same standpoint. Thus we also examined Patricia Hill Collins' portrayal of black feminist thought to highlight the differences that exist among women themselves who are in different social locations. Collins' overall analysis emphasized the way gender is related to hierarchies of race and class that overlap and reinforce one another in maintaining the existing power structures and their associated patterns of domination and oppression.

Feminist theorists in general emphasize heavily the social construction of gender. The obvious biological differences between males and females provide the foundation for cultural beliefs that exaggerate innate sex differences and lead to gender role distinctions that are used to support patterns of male domination and female subordination. At the micro level, the different socialization experiences of girls and boys in the family and in other institutional settings influence the way gender-related patterns of behavior are learned and reinforced and gender identities thereby developed. At the macro level, feminist theorists focus heavily on the differential distribution of power and material resources in the various institutional structures of society, particularly in political and economic organizations. Patterns of male domination reflect the long-term heritage of patriarchal forms of organization that have persisted through the various social transformations leading to the development of modern and late modern society. Some implications of these long-term social transformations for gender relations are reflected in theories as diverse as Parsons' functional theory and Randall Collins' conflict theory. The specialization of gender roles within the family as analyzed in Parsons' functional theory reflect family life ideals in the middle part of the twentieth century. Despite widespread acceptance of these ideals at that time, the resulting constraints on married women no doubted contributed to their relatively high levels of depression. On the other hand, however, Miriam Johnson incorporated some key ideas from Parsons' functional theory of social evolution to highlight how the feminist movement has led to gender role changes that contributed to long-range evolutionary progress in society. Such changes involved struggle, however, as opposed to emerging automatically from the built-in dynamics of the system.

To illustrate the variety of approaches among different feminist theorists, Dorothy Smith's emphasis on the unique lived experiences of women in subordinate positions can be contrasted with Janet Chafetz's goal of developing an objective comparative theory of gender stratification. The subjective experiences that Smith emphasized are difficult to capture in Chafetz's more objective macro-structural analysis. As we saw, Chafetz emphasized the importance of equal pay and of access to elite positions for providing the material resources needed to reduce gender inequality at both the macro and micro levels, as well as the intermediate meso level. Smith also shifted to the meso and macro levels in her analysis of how objective authoritative texts are used in maintaining the impersonal relations of ruling in the major institutional structures of society.

Despite the differences between Smith's and Chafetz's analyses, both perspectives can be seen as providing an integrated and balanced view of the different levels of the social world. Smith's analysis of the contrast between lived experience and the more impersonal text-mediated relations of ruling provide valuable insights into the tensions between the micro-level and the macro-level social worlds. At the same time, although Chafetz emphasized macro-level gender stratification, she showed in detail how these structural patterns are related to the micro-level world of family relations and interpersonal encounters between women and men. In general, the power of feminist theory is reinforced by its sensitivity to the close linkages between micro, meso, and macro levels of the social world. The next chapter will deal in more detail with the interdependence between these different levels.

Questions for Study and Discussion

1. Explain how Dorothy Smith's "standpoint" theory provides a perspective on authority relations that differs from the exchange and rational choice perspectives developed by Peter Blau and James Coleman (as reviewed in earlier chapters). How would you compare the everyday life experiences of women in subordinate positions and women in positions of authority? Would Smith's perspective be relevant with regard to males in subordinate positions? Why or why not? How might the experiences of male and female subordinates with female authority figures differ from their experiences with male authority figures?
2. Drawing on Patricia Hill Collins' notion of multiple sources of domination, explain how the differences in the structural positions of women in our society might be expected to lead them to focus on different types of issues and challenges in advancing the goal of gender equality. To what extent does the ideal goal of gender equality override these differences and lead to gender solidarity? Explain.
3. What specific strains and dilemmas would you expect in a dual-career family where both wife and husband are successful in their careers? How would these strains and dilemmas differ for a couple with or without children? What guidelines would you propose to insure that both parties will regard their family arrangements as fair?
4. Explain how both micro and macro levels of analysis are incorporated in the feminist perspectives of Janet Saltzman Chafetz and Dorothy Smith. Drawing on your own experience, identify some example that illustrate the

connection between the micro and macro levels with regard to gender roles or relationships.

5. How would you expect the face-to-face encounters between authority figures and subordinates to be influenced by impersonal texts that define their relationship? Describe some examples from your own experiences at school or work? To what extent is it possible for authority figures to take personal experiences or situations into account in applying general rules? Explain.

Chapter 17
Human Agency, the Structuration Process, and Social Systems: Linking Micro, Meso, and Macro Levels of Analysis

The activities in which we engage—going to school or work, attending a movie or religious service, buying groceries or an airline ticket, spending time with family and friends, celebrating a football victory or graduation, registering for classes or applying for a job—are part of our own personal micro-level social world. We have our own individual goals and intentions in mind in performing such activities, but we are likely also to take into consideration the actions and reactions of others. We may also have a general awareness that these activities are part of a larger social world—even though we probably do not consider how our own actions actually help to maintain or reproduce this larger world.

This chapter presents the following three perspectives on how individuals' actions link them together in various social systems—micro, meso, or macro:

- Anthony Giddens' structuration theory—This perspective provides an analysis of the interrelations of agency and structure. **Agency** reflects intentional activities whereby individuals seek to satisfy their needs and goals while **structure** refers to the already-existing rules and resources employed in such actions.
- Walter Buckley's morphogenic open systems theory—In this analysis the cultural patterns and social relations in which people are involved are viewed in terms of feedback cycles that sometimes reinforce novel and innovative behaviors. Through this process social structures are constantly being elaborated and changed.
- Niklas Luhmann's autopoietic model of social systems—Social system are seen in this model as being self-created through communication codes whereby their internal patterns of organized complexity are distinguished from the unorganized complexity of their environment.

These three theories are quite distinct, with none of them developed with specific reference to the others. All three theories make extensive reference to ideas discussed in earlier chapters.

D.P. Johnson, *Contemporary Sociological Theory: An Integrated Multi-Level Approach.*

Structuration Theory: Reproduction and Transformation of the Social World

British sociologist Anthony Giddens has had an enormous influence on contemporary sociology over the last three decades. His writings include critiques of leading European perspectives plus the major American schools of theory discussed earlier in this book (for example, see Giddens, 1982). The structuration theory that he developed was used to provide insightful and critical analyses of key themes discussed in other theoretical perspectives (Giddens, 1979). Giddens (1990) also explored various noteworthy features of contemporary "late modern" social processes and trends, some of which will be reviewed in Chap. 20.

The somewhat unusual term "structuration" suggests a **process** involving human beings' ongoing actions as they occur through the flow of time. Social structures do not exist except as they are manifested in individuals' actions and interactions. Structure is like the rules of a game as opposed to an actual game. Although rules may be recorded in rule books, they become relevant for human behavior only as players take them into account or follow them in their actions during the course of a game. We may think of Giddens' concept of "structure" as a kind of "virtual reality." In contrast "social systems" consist of the actual relationships or patterns of interaction among people. This concept of structure contrasts with perspectives that seem to imply that structures exist as an objective reality that governs individuals' actions independently of their own knowledge and intentions. Thus the "new rules" he proposed contrast explicitly with Durkheim's rules for sociological analysis that focus on external social facts (Giddens [1976] 1993).[1] As Giddens put it:

> *Sociology is not concerned with a 'pre-given' universe of objects, but with one which is constituted or produced by the active doings of subjects.* Human beings transform nature socially, and by 'humanizing' it they transform themselves; but they do not, of course, produce the natural world, which is constituted as an object-world independently of their existence....
> (Giddens [1976] 1993:168, italics in original)

Another way to make the point is that human beings are not passive or unreflective robots, controlled by social structural forces beyond their knowledge and control. Instead, they are active agents whose knowledge and abilities are employed constantly in the ongoing production and reproduction of the social world. As Giddens explained:

> *The production and reproduction of society thus has to be treated as a skilled performance on the part of its members*, not as merely a mechanical series of processes. ... (Giddens [1976] 1993:168, italics in original)

The effects of people's actions are not limited to micro-level face-to-face encounters and relationships. Instead, these effects spread outward beyond their micro-level social worlds and beyond their subjective intentions, particularly when

---

[1] The title of Giddens' book, *New Rules of Sociological Method—A Positive Critique of Interpretative Sociologies*, was obviously intended as a play on words that would suggest a contemporary alternative to the classic argument Durkheim propounded in his book, *Rules of Sociological Method*, regarding the need to focus on objective social facts that are external to particular individuals—a methodological statement that helped establish sociology as a distinct discipline.

aggregated or linked with the micro-level actions of others. Individuals' actions thus provide the foundation for the macro level institutional structures of society. As we shall see, Giddens analyzes the actual "skilled performances" of individuals as reflecting human agency, while the outcome of their performances is the reproduction of society and other social structures. However, this reproduction process does not necessarily result in an exact duplicate. Instead, human beings may engage in innovative actions that sometimes lead (either intentionally or unintentionally) to structural transformation, especially when such innovations are widespread.

Giddens' 1984 book, *The Constitution of Society*, provides his most elaborate and systematic version of structuration theory. He is critical of "micro" level theories such as phenomenological sociology as developed by Schutz, Goffman's dramaturgic perspective, and symbolic interaction theory for failing to deal explicitly with the larger institutional structures within which micro-level social processes occur. He then points out the shortcomings of macro level perspectives, including both functional theory and various Marxist or neo-Marxist perspectives in which the strong emphasis on social and socioeconomic structures fails to incorporate the role of human agency in reproducing such structures. To move beyond these limited perspectives, Giddens proposes to abandon the micro/macro distinction and use instead the agency/structure distinction. **Structures** consist of **rules** and **resources** that human beings employ as they engage in the routine practices whereby such structural rules and resources are continually reproduced. These actions incorporate the **knowledge** and **skills** of human beings as **agents**, and they reflect the ability of human beings themselves to influence the course of events in their social worlds. He regards this perspective as contrasting sharply with the notion that human beings passively respond to structural forces of which they are ignorant and over which they have no control.[2]

The basic argument of Giddens' structuration theory can be expressed in the diagram in Fig. 17.1 (below). The routine practices of everyday life reproduce

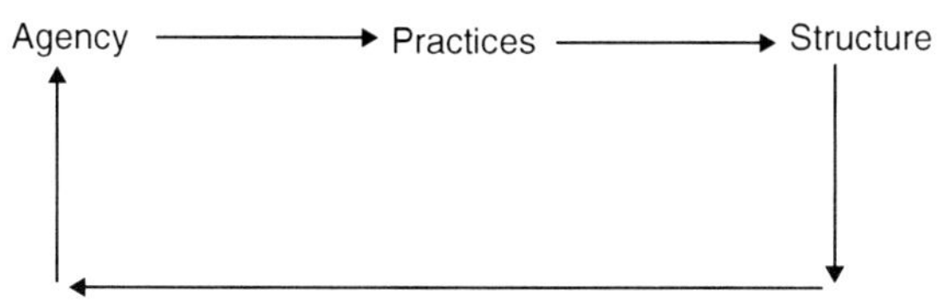

Fig. 17.1 Relation between Agency, Practices, and Structure

[2] Giddens concept of human beings as "agents" differs from Coleman's use of the concept of "agent" as discussed in an earlier chapter. For Coleman, an agent's actions are undertaken on behalf of someone else, the "principal." For Giddens, in contrast, the focus is on the way human beings' behavior reflects their knowledge, skills, and ability to make a difference in the course of events, which he contrasts with the more passive view of human beings that he believes is reflected in "structural" theories such as functionalism and some forms of Marxist or neo-Marxist theory.

(or sometimes transform) the structure, while the structure provides the rules and resources that are used in the practices whereby it is reproduced. The **social system**, then, whether micro or macro or in between, consists of the actual social relations in which people are involved through this structuration process. Thus the structure is both the "medium" and the "outcome" of the routine practices whereby systems of actual social relations are sustained.

Giddens draws on many of the theoretical perspectives that he considered deficient but reformulates them to fit his perspective. The micro-level theories are used to analyze the dynamic nature of human agency, the contingencies involved in social action, and the importance of the interaction process for reaching shared subjective interpretations. But since these processes do not occur in a vacuum, he also acknowledges the contributions that macro-level theories have made in focusing on the larger institutional structures that provide the framework within which micro-level processes occur. In his perspective structure does not merely **constrain** human action but also **enables** it. Even though people cannot always choose the overall conditions in which they find themselves, they do always have the capability as agents to intervene in the course of events and thereby to "make a difference" in what happens. Giddens explained, ".... Structure is not to be equated with constraint but is always both constraining and enabling..." (Giddens, 1984:25). As he put it, "To enquire into the structuration of social practices is to seek to explain how it comes about that structure is constituted through action, and reciprocally how action is constituted structurally" (Giddens [1976] 1993:169).

This notion of structure can be compared to language. Like structure, language involves definite rules. But language does not exist as an objective reality in the external world that is independent of its actual use in speaking and writing. Moreover, although its "virtual" reality is reproduced each time it is employed in speaking and writing, the intention of speakers and writers is not to reproduce the language but to communicate a message. Language is a useful metaphor in this context because, as noted in earlier chapters, the reality of the social world is grounded in the communication process as manifested in speech and written texts. Giddens' structuration theory can be elaborated by reviewing his more detailed analysis of **agency**, **structure**, and **system**.

Agency

The concept of agency includes people's intentions plus their knowledge of how the social world works and how to participate in it as a competent member. As agents, human beings have the ability or power (within limits of course) to make a difference in the world through their actions. This ability to intervene in the course of events to "make things happen" is implicitly understood in everyday life. At the same time, however, many aspects of our social and material environment are beyond our understanding or control. We are also limited in our knowledge and our control of all of the consequences that may follow from our actions. But despite these limitations, people nevertheless are able to engage in an ongoing dynamic process of adjusting their behavior in the light of what they do know regarding the realities of the situation they face and their own goals and intentions. As they participate in the social world, they also take account of the expectations and reactions of other people as well as their own changing needs and wants. This emphasis on shared knowledge, plus the ongoing mutual adjustment of people to one another, involves the communication process as highlighted in symbolic interaction theory, the implicit common sense assumptions of everyday life as emphasized in the phenomenological perspective and ethnomethodology, and the various strategies of presentation of self as analyzed in Goffman's dramaturgic perspective.

In routine situations people typically understand and adjust to one another on the basis of implicitly shared knowledge of one another's expectations without engaging in overt communication to explain their actions. Even so, people would be able to explain their actions if they were asked to do so. This ability to provide reasons for their actions (or to "rationalize") is closely connected with the ongoing process of reflexive monitoring that occurs at a subjective level, and these processes of monitoring and adjusting one's actions are crucial for sustaining its flow and meaning. As Giddens explained, "To be a human being is to be a purposive agent, who both has reasons for his or her activities and is able, if asked, to elaborate discursively upon those reasons (including lying about them)." (Giddens, 1984:3) Although the justifying reasons people offer may not correspond with their "real" reasons (and thus be criticized in everyday life as mere rationalizations), Giddens' broader meaning of rationalization would include any type of explanation or account that would allow others to "make sense" of one's action.

In dealing with people's knowledge and with reflexive monitoring and accountability, Giddens distinguished "**discursive consciousness**" and "**practical consciousness**" (Giddens, 1984:7). Briefly, discursive consciousness includes the knowledge and shared interpretations that can be (and often are) expressed in words. It incorporates the specific forms of knowledge that are needed to participate in the routine practices of everyday life, plus belief systems and ideologies that may be used to explain or justify these practices. Such knowledge may be acquired through both formal and informal modes of socialization. Practical consciousness, in contrast, includes the implicit common-sense knowledge shared among participants in a familiar social world. It may be acquired by observing others and also by one's own experience. It is manifested in the skills with which routine activities are accomplished without verbal explanation. Some activities, such as riding a bicycle or playing a musical instrument, are difficult to learn through verbal instruction alone; one learns by practicing and doing. Verbal instruction may accompany practice for novices but, once the appropriate knowledge and skills are learned, their use in everyday life behavior does not require discourse but is understood implicitly. Discursive consciousness may gradually be transformed into practical consciousness that is incorporated into everyday habits and routines. On the other hand, practical consciousness may become the topic of discourse, such as when newcomers are being socialized. In other words, the boundary between discursive and practical consciousness is permeable.

When people's actions violate widely understood expectations, either intentionally or accidentally, they may feel the need to offer an explanation—or they may be asked for one. If the deviation was intentional, they may seek to justify it as necessary or appropriate in the current situation. If unintentional, they may offer an apology and an explanation of what they intended to do. Giddens emphasized that all behavior, even the most routine practices of everyday life, are potentially transformative. That is, people may vary their routines or engage in innovative behavior—and if such innovations are accepted and repeated by others, the result may be structural transformation. Despite this transformative potential, many of the routine practices of everyday life serve essentially to reproduce the existing structure.

Giddens emphasized that people tend to have a strong interest in maintaining their routine practices because of the way these routines provide a sense of stability and orderliness. It is through the routine practices of everyday life that people are able to satisfy deep-seated and often unconscious security needs.[3] In developing this idea, Giddens moves beyond the distinction between discursive and practical consciousness to incorporate the unconscious level, including unconscious motivations. Drawing on ideas from Freud and psychoanalytic theory, he pointed out that people are likely to repress motivations that generate anxiety or are threatening to their identity and sense of autonomy. But despite this lack of awareness, repressed motives and needs may still have on important influence on their behavior.[4] Giddens' views regarding unconscious security needs that are satisfied through stable routines are based heavily on psychologist Erik Erikson's model of the stages of psychological development (Giddens, 1984:51–60). Although the stages Erikson identified extend throughout one's life, Giddens, like Freud, emphasized primarily the early-life stages, particularly the first stage involving the crisis of trust versus mistrust. The infant develops a sense of security to the extent that his or her basic physical and emotional needs are satisfied in a secure environment, primarily through the relationship with the mother in most cases. Giddens viewed this underlying need for security as a life-long need that provides an unconscious source of motivation for adhering to the stable routines of everyday life.

In addition to trust, however, Erikson's model also included the development of a sense of autonomy. If we expand Giddens' perspective on agency by distinguishing security versus autonomy needs, we could then explore how people may vary in terms of the relative importance of these basic needs. For many people the routine

[3] This explanation of the stability and order that is manifested in social life may be contrasted with Parsons' effort to explain social order in terms of the functional requirements of society as well as with the strategy used by conflict and critical theorists of focusing on structures of domination.

[4] However, Giddens refuses to accept Freud's contention that all forms of unintended or accidental behavior (like "slips of the tongue") should be seen as reflecting repressed motivations. He also contrasts his model of the relation between discursive and practical consciousness and the unconscious with Freud's well-known distinctions among the id, the ego, and the superego. He agrees with Freud and the basic tenets of psychoanalytic theory, however, that repressed motivations may be brought to consciousness through discourse intended to promote self-awareness. This, of course, is an explicit goal of psychoanalysis.

practices of everyday life may well help satisfy basic security needs but frustrate autonomy needs (see D. P. Johnson, 1990). People sometimes complain about getting "stuck in a rut" and needing change in their lives. We might hypothesize that individuals who experience a high level of anxiety and insecurity in their lives (perhaps due to serious abuse or neglect in childhood, radical disruption of present routines, or other reasons) would feel a greater need for stable routines to sustain their fragile sense of security than those who have a stronger psychological or emotional sense of internal security. For others, however, stable routines may not be as crucial because their psychological or emotional security can be satisfied from within, thereby freeing them to express a higher level of autonomy in their behavior. In some cases this may lead to challenging or seeking to change everyday life routines so as to achieve new personal goals or promote some type of positive social change. Giddens (1992) himself focused on how individual autonomy is expressed in the process whereby individuals seek to develop their identities through the exploration of alternative patterns of intimate relations in contemporary life–a pattern that will be described more fully in our discussion of postmodern perspectives in Chapter 20.

Social Structures and Systems

Social structures for Giddens consist of rules and resources but the concept of rules is probably more crucial in his structuration theory (as explained below). Two types or categories of rules may be distinguished: **constitutive** versus **regulative** rules (Giddens, 1984:16–25). Constitutive rules actually establish, define, or create, the nature of the social reality being produced. Although organized games are overly simplistic as a model for social life in general, the definition of what is involved in playing a game may serve to illustrate the way constitutive rules operate. In basketball, for example, if "players" were to try to keep the ball even after scoring or carry it around the court rather than dribbling, we could say that this is simply not basketball. Their activities "count" as basketball only if they follow the rules. However, even constitutive rules may be modified if necessary (though probably not in an "official" contest that "really counts" as a game). If only four or six people are available for a game of basketball, a recognizable form of the game can still be played as long as the players follow the rules as closely as possible. In contrast to the constitutive rules that define the game, regulative rules govern the way it is played and provide sanctions for violations. Although carrying the ball around in one's arms to keep it away from others is clearly not basketball, if a player accidentally takes a quick extra step before starting to dribble (either accidentally or intentionally), this is simply a violation of a rule and results in a turnover if called by the referee.

In contrast to explicit language or game rules, however, the "rules" in many areas of social life are often not so precisely defined, nor is their interpretation or application so explicit. Moreover, in "real life" situations there may be inconsistencies in people's definitions of what is (or should be) going on. The result is inconsistency and ambiguity as to which rules apply. For example, in social encounters between high school students and their teachers outside the classroom or away from the school, should they relate to one another as teachers and students (with the hierarchical distinctions this applies), as acquaintances who recognize each other as fellow-members of the same school system, as having discovered they have something in common by virtue of where they encounter one another (such as at a movie, for example), or as potential friends? When family members have misunderstandings and conflicts (as often happens), should the issue be interpreted as undermining family relationships or as threatening members' independence? Should more family activities be planned, or do members need more time alone? Despite the widespread implicit knowledge that participants share, social life is rife with misunderstandings and disagreements regarding what exactly is going on and the appropriate rules that should be applied.

Two different types of resources are included in Giddens' concept of structure: **allocative** and **authoritative** (Giddens, 1984:33, 258–262). Allocative resources are the material assets used in production or consumption. Authoritative resources consist of the ability or the right to influence the behavior of others. Although material objects (allocative resources) obviously have an objective physical existence, their role in the structuration process is based on rules that provide rights to use them in socially approved ways as well as on actual physical possession. It is also through socially defined rules that relations of power and authority are established and legitimated. Thus both types of resources in Giddens' notion of structure may be subsumed under his general concept of rules. In essence, then, structure may be seen as consisting of constitutive and regulative rules as discussed earlier, plus rules that establish rights to control material objects and/or the behavior of others in their roles as subordinates in some type of power structure.

Although Giddens argued that structures are both constraining and enabling, the balance between constraint and enablement varies greatly for people in different segments of society. Giddens emphasized the differential distribution of resources, highlighting the conflicts and contradictions that are inherent in the socioeconomic class structure of modern capitalist societies. Despite his insistence that people always have the power to "make things happen" by intervening in the course of events, power varies greatly among people in different socioeconomic classes or different levels in a hierarchical structure. It should be emphasized, too, that coercive power is not the same as legitimate authority. The "power" of robbery victims, for example, or of the victims of police brutality or oppressive political regimes, may be limited to either submitting or risking their lives in a futile struggle to resist. In less extreme situations, however, subordinates may exercise power in various ways, ranging from passive resistance to efforts to renegotiate rights and duties to overt rebellion. Throughout history, subordinated and oppressed people have sometimes been able to develop strategies of resistance resulting in various forms of social change that reduced inequalities in power and resources. But resistance is almost always an uphill struggle, and those with limited power and material resources often find it safer or more expedient to play it safe to insure their survival and security. The effect of such safe strategies is to reproduce the relations of power and subordination in which they are involved.

Giddens emphasized the distinction between structures and systems. Although structures do not actually exist in his view as an objective reality, their "virtual" existence is manifested in the ongoing social practices whereby they are either reproduced or transformed. Giddens uses the term "instantiation" to describe the way in which structures come into existence as **instances** of actual social practices. Structure itself has no specific acting subject—even though structural principles are incorporated in the subjective consciousness of human agents and expressed in their actions. But in contrast to structures, social systems can be seen as having an objective existence that can be observed in the ongoing routine practices of everyday life. These interdependent practices reflect the process whereby structural principles or rules are "instantiated." Macro structures, such as the major social institutions of a society, consist essentially of enduring and widespread "instantiations" of various sets of interrelated practices, with each interrelated "set" of practices constituting a particular institution (family, economy, political system, education, or other institutions). Here is how Giddens summarizes the distinction between structure and system:

> ... Structure, as recursively organized sets of rules and resources, is out of time and space, save in its instantiations and co-ordination as memory traces, and is marked by an 'absence of the subject'. The social systems in which structure is recursively implicated, on the contrary, comprise the situated activities of human agents, reproduced across time and space.... Structure is not 'external' to individuals: as memory traces, and as instantiated in social practices, it is in a certain sense more 'internal' than exterior to their activities in a Durkheimian sense.
>
> (Giddens, 1984:25)

But as the effects of structured practices "stretch away" in time and space, they extend beyond the knowledge and control of individual actors. While people's routine practices reproduce the institutional structures of society, they may not be fully aware of how their actions in their own local context are related to these larger institutional structures. But this does not mean that they are totally blind to the effects of their actions on the larger social world. In fact, persons in positions of authority and responsibility in various organizational settings may undertake various actions for the specific purpose of stimulating wide-ranging social consequences. However, people are not omniscient. There are limits to their knowledge, and this applies both to the conditions that may influence their actions as well as the consequences of these actions. Even in local situations, the effects of one's actions for oneself and for others are often unforeseen and unintended.

Despite people's lack of detailed knowledge regarding all of the widespread ramifications of their actions, their shared subjective "knowledge system" may nevertheless include reified conceptions of the larger social world—that is, conceptions in which this larger world **appears** to exist as a separate and objective reality that is independent of the routine practices in which they engage in their micro-level social worlds. Along with such images of the objective reality of their larger social world, people may also develop various ideologies that either support or criticize it. They may also have a general awareness of how their own actions "make sense" as a small part of this larger world, even though their understanding of how these actions actually contribute to reproducing or transforming it may be limited. Moreover, in order for sociologists to make progress in explaining the social world it is essential for them actually to enter into the frame of mind of its participants and to understand their views regarding its essential features. At the same time, sociologists themselves also have the potential for influencing these social definitions. The following section will deal with Giddens' views regarding the reciprocal relations between sociologists and their wider audience in the social world.

Sociological Analysis and Public Discourse

The knowledge and beliefs people share about the social world constitute a kind of implicit (or sometimes explicit) practical sociology regarding how the social world works and how their actions fit together in it. Since people's actions are grounded in their subjective definitions, it is essential for sociologists to take these definitions into consideration in their efforts to explain the social world. This reciprocal relationship between everyday life definitions and sociological analysis represents a sharp contrast with the natural sciences. In addition, it is also important to note that the social world itself may actually change as a result of the dissemination of the results of sociological concepts, insights, and research findings.[5] Giddens refers to this interdependence between everyday life social definitions and sociological definitions as the "double hermeneutic" (Giddens, 1984:xxxv, 284–288). Essentially, this concept refers to the way sociological analysis must necessarily incorporate everyday life definitions at the same time that such analysis has the potential to influence—and thereby change—those very definitions, as well as the social practices which express them.

In seeking to promote a wider public dissemination of sociological knowledge, it is important to steer an intermediate course between two extremes. On the one hand, if the analysis is too far removed from the ordinary concepts and language of everyday life, there is a risk that sociologists will be dismissed as irrelevant "ivory tower" theorists who are not tuned into the "real world." On the other hand, if their analysis is too close to the common sense perspectives of everyday life, they risk being dismissed as simply "explaining the obvious" without adding any new knowledge or insights that people don't already know. (Probably examples of both kinds of analysis could be identified.) Between these extremes, when sociological

[5] An example of how sociological concepts and perspectives have been incorporated into public discourse is provided by Merton's (1968:475–490) concept of the "self-fulfilling prophecy" in which events seem to occur as a consequence of their being predicted. A practical example of how this insight is used in real life is revealed in the way elementary school teachers are challenged to improve students' academic performance by defining them in positive terms as "bright," "capable," or "intelligent." Another example is the way Michels' ([1915] 1949) concept of the "iron law of oligarchy" corresponds to the widespread (and cynical) realization that persons in positions of power are likely to focus heavily on retaining these positions. Both of these processes were discussed briefly in previous chapters.

insights are incorporated into a wider network of public discourse, this may lead to changes in the everyday life social definitions that members of society themselves use to describe and explain their social world. Such changes may subsequently lead to changes in people's behavior or even public policy.

In addition to the rather abstract and technical perspective of structuration theory, Giddens himself provided some provocative insight into several important current issues and trends that can readily be related to widespread public discourse among concerned citizens. These include analyses of the process of globalization, increased reliance on highly technical expert systems, and new types of risks associated with highly routinized expert systems (Giddens, 1990). At a more micro level, he also identified changes in patterns whereby higher levels of autonomy and equality can be achieved in the construction of mutually fulfilling intimate relationships in "late modern" society (Giddens, 1992). (Giddens' analysis of late modern society will be examined in Chap. 20.) In the next section, we note some key features of social systems as background for Buckley's "process model" and Luhmann's perspective on systems as organized complexity.

The Dynamics of Open Systems

Despite Giddens' distinction, the concepts of "system" and "structure" are not always clearly distinguished in sociological analysis. In general, systems can be identified in terms of specific linkages or patterns of interdependence among their component parts, whether intended or unintended, plus input/output transactions with the environment (Bailey, pp. 379–402 in J. H. Turner, ed., 2001). On an everyday common-sense level, the "parts" are often likely to be seen as individual persons. A more accurate sociological view is that the parts actually are social positions and the roles individuals play as their incumbents. Of course, a system cannot exist if its positions are left vacant. However, if a system is defined in terms of positions rather than individual persons, this means it can persist despite changes in personnel over time. Although individuals' involvement is in terms of their particular roles, different individuals will have their own distinctive style in performing their roles. Alternatively, the parts may be various "corporate actors" like formal organizations or other types of social formations in which patterns of interdependence can be identified. The notion of interdependence implies that a change in any one part is likely to have effects on other parts of the system, either direct or indirect. In addition to internal interdependence, all systems can also be characterized in terms of various forms of boundary maintenance as well as input/output transactions whereby they acquire the resources, energy, and information needed for their sustenance. Because of the importance of input and output relations with the environment, this perspective is sometimes referred to as open systems theory.

These ideas regarding internal interdependence and boundary maintenance may be applied to all levels of the social world, ranging from micro-level encounters to macro-level patterns of institutional interdependence. However, it is important to note that social and cultural systems differ in important ways from mechanical and organic systems. They do not have an objective physical existence like electric motors or biological organisms; instead, they are based on social definitions established through communication. This means that the maintenance of their structure and identity requires ongoing interaction to establish and preserve their boundaries, to develop the input/out relations with their environment through which they can be sustained, and to maintain their internal patterns of interdependence. Moreover, the range of variation that is possible in social or cultural systems is far greater than in mechanical systems or organic systems.

To illustrate these processes of input/output transactions with the environment for obtaining resources to maintain their patterns of internal interdependence, manufacturing firms, for example, acquire financial resources, raw materials, personnel, and equipment from outside their boundaries in order to produce goods which are then sold to customers in their environment. The money earned is then used in additional exchange transactions across the system's boundary to gain the additional inputs needed to continue the internal manufacturing process. Similarly, a university receives input from its environment in the form of new students, financial resources, faculty and staff, and provides output in the form of graduates plus scholarly products such as books and professional journal articles, as well as athletic performances and various types of public records. It is through these environmental transactions that the internal patterns of interdependence can be maintained.

This focus on internal interdependence and boundary maintenance is consistent with the general systems theory that biologist Ludwig von Bertalanffy (pp. 115–129 in Demerath and Peterson, eds., 1667; Bertalanffy, 1968) believed could provide a potential unifying framework for all of the sciences. His stress on the emergent organization of interdependent parts to form a larger whole can be contrasted with the traditional scientific strategy in which phenomena are broken down into their constituent components. Bertalanffy insisted that the overall pattern of organized interdependence within a system is not reducible to its individual parts but instead can be analyzed at its own level. Open systems theory captures this larger picture.

Walter Buckley's "Morphogenic Process" Model of Social Systems[6]

Sociologists have long used the concept of "system" to analyze the structure of society and other types of social formations, particularly Parsons (1951) and others influenced by him, as we have seen earlier. During the late 1960s, when Parsons'

[6] This description of general perspective of open systems theory, including in particular Buckley's "morphogenic" model of social systems, is adapted from D. P. Johnson ([1981] 1986:513–519).

structural/functional theory was being largely rejected for reasons discussed earlier, Walter Buckley (1967) advocated a different and more dynamic type of systems theory for sociology. He drew heavily on Bertalanffy's ideas but adapted them to the analysis of social systems so as to avoid the limitations of Parsons' structural/functional theory.

Buckley argued for a "process model" that would concentrate on the inherent tendency of social systems to undergo continuous structural elaboration and change—a process he referred to as "morphogenesis." Although the literal meaning of this term refers to the **origin** of form (or structure), Buckley emphasized the process of more or less **continuous changes in form**, particularly structural elaboration and increasing complexity. He felt that this model was inherent in sociological works as divergent as those of Marx, Simmel, Mead, Cooley, and Blumer.

Buckley contrasted his morphogenic model with the mechanical and organic models that he believed were implicit in some aspects of Parsons' structural/functional theory. The mechanical model, with its concept of equilibrium, suggests stable relationships among the system parts that operate within fairly narrow limits.[7] In such systems disturbances lead to adjustments which restore the system to its steady state, provided the disturbances are not outside the range within which the system is able to adjust. However, unless renewed by outside energy sources that maintain it, mechanical systems tend toward the lowest possible level of inertia; that is, they eventually reach a level of equilibrium where they actually cease operations.

In contrast to machines, organic systems (at the individual, not the species level) have a higher and more complex level of organization that is preserved within narrow limits through the process of homeostasis, despite environment changes and disturbances. This can be illustrated by the built-in processes whereby warm-blooded animals maintain a constant body temperature despite fluctuations in the external environment. If environmental disturbances exceed the organism's coping ability, or if processes of homeostasis should break down, the result is death. Parsons had used the concept of homeostasis to describe the self-maintaining and self-regulating character of social systems. His concept of functional requisites seems to imply an organic model, even though specific functional requirements and limits are much more varied and more difficult to identify for social systems than for biological organisms.

Buckley pointed out that the organic model actually involves two different levels of organization: the individual organism and the species. The concept of harmonious interdependence sustained through built-in processes of homeostasis does not apply to the species level of organization as clearly as to the individual organism. At the species level, the concept of a competitive struggle for survival may be more relevant

---

[7] The mechanical model emerged from the early efforts to explain human behavior and society scientifically, or as part of the objective world of nature. (Comte had used the term "social physics" to refer to the study of society before he coined the term "sociology.")

than harmonious interdependence. As emphasized by the social Darwinists in the early years of the twentieth century, the ecological balance that emerges in nature and in human society results from competition and conflict, not from built-in homeostatic mechanisms that maintain a steady state. Such processes can nevertheless be analyzed in terms of interdependent relationships among different organisms as they adapt to their environment, even though some of the relationships may be competitive or parasitic as well as cooperative.

In contrast to the mechanical and organic models, the process model focuses on interdependent but ever-changing **events** rather than objective "**parts**." As Buckley put it, "In dealing with the sociocultural system, however, we jump to a new system level and need yet a new term to express not only the *structure-maintaining* feature, but also the *structure-elaborating* and *changing* feature of the inherently unstable system..." (Buckley, 1967:14–15, italics in original) This is what he meant by the process of morphogenesis. Buckley described the image of society implied in this model as follows:

> In essence, the process model typically views society as a complex, multifaceted, fluid interplay of widely varying degrees and intensities of association and dissociation. The "structure" is an abstract construct, not something distinct from the ongoing interactive process but rather a temporary, accommodative representation of it at any one time.
> (Buckley, 1967:18)

These ever-changing processes are not random, however. Instead, structural elaboration occurs as participants learn more effective ways of relating to one another and adapting to their environment. These continual improvements in adaptation enable human beings to meet an expanding range of needs and goals in widely varying environmental conditions. The "morphogenetic" model does not include specific assumptions regarding particular functional requirements or the necessity for maintaining a steady state for survival. The model does, however, involve an image of social systems as self-regulating and goal-oriented.

The basic elements of social systems are not individuals as such but their actions and interactions as organized in the various roles they perform, many of which are associated with their particular positions in the system. This means that the units of a social system are not objective entities (such as physical objects or even individual persons) but ongoing events or actions that, as Giddens suggests, are organized as routine practices in which individuals engage as members. This means that structure and process cannot be separated; if the process of action and interaction that make up the system should cease or change, the system itself would disappear or be changed.

Buckley drew heavily on Mead and the symbolic interactionists in analyzing the nature of the actions and interaction patterns that make up social systems (Buckley, 1967:94–100). Individuals' actions should not be seen as automatic responses to environmental stimuli in this perspective; instead, individuals construct their actions in terms of the shared symbolic meanings they attribute to one another and to the objects in their environment. These meanings may change in different situations in ways that reflect individuals' particular goals and plans and that also demonstrate their creativity.

Variations in Social System Dynamics

The open systems model does not include built-in assumptions regarding the precise nature of the relationships among the component parts of the system. In terms of theories discussed earlier, these relations may be cooperative or conflicting; they may be based on shared moral values or individualistic interests; they may be coercive or voluntary; and they may be symbolic or symbiotic in nature. In addition, the strength of the relationships and the level of interdependence may also vary. That is, the component elements may be tightly connected or only loosely coupled. These are all empirical questions that cannot be decided without investigation.

Social systems are also seen as being involved in various kinds of relations with their environments, including input/output transactions as described earlier. Systems vary in terms of boundary permeability, however, and some systems are better able to insulate themselves from environmental intrusions or disturbances than others. For example, members of conservative or sectarian religious groups may develop strategies to avoid becoming excessively involved in secular institutions, such as home schooling their children, for example. In contrast, the major political parties in the United States are extremely open, with membership based solely on individuals' own self-identified party preferences, and they are subject to the sometimes conflicting influences of numerous constituencies and interest groups that they seek to represent. At the societal level, all societies routinely develop procedures for monitoring and controlling the flow of people or goods across their borders and for distinguishing between citizens and tourists or other visitors from other countries.

Identification of a particular system or set of social processes for analysis can vary, depends on one's specific interests. For analysis of a single nation-state, other societies would be part of the environment, and the internal components could be individual citizens or the various institutions, organizations, and other social formations that make up a society. Within a society, various institutions or organizations could be identified as systems in their own right, with other institutions and the rest of the society considered as the environment. Similarly, within a specific formal organization a single department or work group could be analyzed as a system in its own right, with other departments or the overall organization considered the environment of this smaller-scale system. In a global system, nation-states themselves are the relevant "parts" along with multinational corporations or other international organizations. These considerations indicate that the identification of system boundaries, plus the distinction between internal and external relationships, may be seen as somewhat arbitrary, with their specification depending on the scope of the analysis.

One strategy for determining system boundaries would be to use the definitions of participants themselves.[8] Another strategy would be to examine the nature and type of the relationships that might be identified within a particular area of activity

[8] This notion of systems as based on participants' self-definitions will be explored in more detail in the next section when we discuss Niklas Luhmann's perspective on social systems.

and then define a system in terms of the strength of relationships that are above some minimal level. Relationships that fall below this minimal level would be excluded; those that are related above this level would be considered part of the system. For example, for some types of analysis a supervisor with a private office who is not heavily involved in informal sociable relations with subordinates could be excluded from the sociable group made up of these subordinates, despite regular formal interaction. On another level, however, both supervisor and subordinates could be considered a single system in terms of relations with higher levels of management. An additional complication arise from the fact that some system roles may require more interaction outside the system than inside. Salespersons in the field, for example, may interact more frequently with customers in their own locations than with other members of their own organization, despite being part of the organizational system. In general, the task of determining system boundaries may be simplified considerably for many social organizations by using conventional criteria such as geographical boundaries, membership lists or, as suggested above, participants' own definitions.

The linkages among individuals within a social system, and between the system and its environment, are essentially informational linkages based on symbolic codes, not merely physical or energy linkages. As a result of the constant process of individuals' creative adaptation to one another and to their environment, a shared "cognitive map" is developed among participants that consists of their intersubjective representation of the material and social environment and of their relations with one another. This map is not static but changes continuously as participants adapt to one another and the environment. As Buckley emphasized, organized social life involves an ongoing process of sharing or pooling information whereby individuals learn from one another's different experiences as they interact with one another in adapting to their environment.

Feedback Cycles in Goal-Oriented Systems[9]

The process whereby participants in a social system relate to one another and to their environment can be analyzed in terms of feedback cycles involving efforts to match internal conditions and environmental relations to desired goal states. This is an ongoing process in which information about the environment as well as internal relations within the system are continually monitored and corrective actions taken to improve the match with the desired goal state as much as possible. Even a simple mechanical system such as a thermostat can serve to illustrate a type of feedback

[9] An earlier explanation of feedback loops and how they are related to goal-directed behavior was previously published in D. P. Johnson ([1981] 1986:527–531). The basic notion that subjectively desired goals lead to behavioral adjustment in response to environmental feedback lends itself to the formulation of interdependent propositions as described in the theory construction process described in Chap. 4.

cycle in which deviation from the set temperature signals a sensor to turn the furnace or air conditioner on or off. For social systems, the process involves multiple goals and multiple aspects of the environment, plus continuing changes in both internal states and environmental conditions. Actions that fail to achieve desired outcomes may trigger the use of different strategies. As goals are achieved (or given up as not being achievable), new goals may be developed. The multiplicity of goals, plus the fact that some goals may be inconsistent with one another, insures the dynamic quality of social systems. This dynamic quality also results from the need to cope with various types of environmental changes, some of which are themselves the result (intended or otherwise) of human beings' actions.

Numerous everyday life examples could be cited to illustrate the process of ongoing dynamic adjustment to ever-changing environmental conditions. Even a single project like driving an automobile, for example, involves constantly monitoring traffic conditions and making adjustments as needed. Similarly, a person in a conversation who is misunderstood or fails to receive social approval will try to clarify the point or, if unsuccessful, change the subject, seek new conversational partners, or withdraw to pursue other options. Similar processes of monitoring feedback and adjusting behavior can also be identified in larger social systems. Business firms, for example, attempt to evaluate customer satisfaction or public preferences for various types of products or services through market research. If sufficient negative feedback is received, corrective action is likely to be taken. Similarly, national political leaders monitor public opinion polls as well as pressures and complaints from various interest groups and adjust their policies and strategies accordingly.

Buckley describes the feedback process involved in goal-seeking behavior in social systems in terms of the following five stages:

> (1) A control center establishes certain desired goal parameters and the means by which they may be attained; (2) these goal decisions are transformed by administrative bodies into action outputs, which result in certain effects on the state of the system and its environment; (3) information about these effects are [sic.] recorded and fed back to the control center; (4) the latter tests this new state of the system against the desired goal parameters to measure the error or deviation of the initial output response; (5) if the error leaves the system outside the limits set by the goal parameters, corrective output action is taken by the control center.
>
> (Buckley, 1967:174)

Although this description portrays the feedback loop as a formal process (as might be expected in a complex organization), these dynamics are applicable to any level of social system, whether formalized in this way or not. This feedback mechanism allows us to combine functional analysis and motivational analysis without assuming that a future outcome can cause an event in the present. Although future consequences cannot cause present behavior, desired goal states, or subjective images of future consequences, can stimulate or motivate present behavior as well as adjustments in behavior so as to keep "on course" in moving toward the desired goal. In this way social systems can be conceptualized as goal-oriented, self-regulating adaptive systems. This process involves feedback cycles, through which present behavior is adjusted in the light of the consequences of previous behavior as well as desired future goals.

Morphogenesis, Morphostasis, and Entropy[10]

The type of feedback cycle involved in **morphogenesis** may be considered a "deviation-amplifying" feedback cycle. In contrast to mechanical and organic systems, social systems generate an almost-continuous stream of deviation or variety.[11] Given the fact that human beings are not robots, their normal everyday life behavior insures ample variety to serve as the initial stimulus for a "deviation-amplifying" feedback cycle. A deviation-amplifying feedback cycle is one in which some deviations are reinforced and thereby provide the foundation for additional deviations in the same direction. The concept of deviation in this context does not necessarily refer to unacceptable normative or legal violations, but to any form of behavior that differs from established patterns. This would include random variations as well as deliberate innovations that reflect people's efforts to experiment and learn more effective ways of adapting to their environment. Deviations from set routines are exemplified in efforts to promote social progress as well as disruptive forms of legal violations. With this perspective, the long-term development of modern technology may be seen as a lengthy and complex series of numerous interrelated deviation-amplifying feedback loops in which each new technological innovation provides the basis for additional innovations.

The **morphogenic** process can be contrasted with the process of **morphostasis**, which refers to mechanisms that "tend to preserve or maintain a system's given form, organization, or state." (Buckley, 1967:58) The process of morphostasis reflects "deviation counteracting" (or "deviation inhibiting") feedback cycles. Such processes occur whenever deviations stimulate negative sanctions which serve to restore the previous patterns. The responses by law enforcement agents to crimes and other legal violations may serve to illustrate this process of morphostasis.

Both morphogenesis and morphostasis may be contrasted with the process of **entropy** (Bailey, 1990).[12] This concept refers to the process of decay or decline of a social system or simplification of its structure. In extreme cases, the system may fail to survive. For example, a business firm may go out of business, a community may decline as its members move away when employment opportunities disappear, or college buddies may gradually lose contact with one another. The specific type of feedback cycle involved in entropy is just the opposite of that involved in morphogenesis. It involves deterioration in patterns of interdependence. Buckley used the term **negentropy** from general systems theory to argue that social

[10] This portrayal of the contrast between morphogenesis, morphostasis, and entropy, and how these terms relate to the contrast between structural elaboration versus stability versus structural simplification, is adapted from D. P. Johnson ([1981] 1986:531–550).

[11] Of course, natural variation also occurs in biological systems, which is crucial in the evolutionary process, but the time frames involved are typically much longer.

[12] For a popular treatment of this process on a global level, soon after the emergence of a widespread concern with depletion of natural resources, particularly oil reserves, see Rifkin ([with Howard] 1980).

systems (like all other organized systems) must overcome the effects of entropy by importing sufficient energy and resources to prevent decay and maintain (or elaborate) their basic patterns of organization if they are to survive.

Numerous everyday life examples of all three process—morphogenetic, morphostatic, and entropic—may be cited at all levels. At the micro level, the growth of friendships among neighbors or co-workers reflects the process of morphogenesis. If a close-knit circle of friends resists the intrusion of outsiders and insists on doing the same things every time they get together, this illustrates the process of morphostasis. But the process of entropy would result if these friends fail to maintain contact. At the meso level, morphogenesis would be manifested by the growth and development of a residential community or urban area, or by the expansion of a business firm. Morphostasis would be illustrated when a community opposes growth or expansion, perhaps because of fears of increased traffic congestion, crime rates, taxes, or other problems. Finally, the process of entropy may be illustrated by the pattern of deterioration of inner-city areas, which has often occurred at the same time that the outlying suburban areas are growing and experiencing morphogenesis. At the level of the overall society, the opposing patterns of morphogenesis and entropy are reflected in the long-range rise and decline of total societies (see Kennedy, 1987). An example of both processes in the last half of the twentieth century is the growth and expansion of the Soviet Union in the decades of the Cold War following World War II and its collapse in the late 1980s.

Moreover, different aspects (or subsystems) of social systems may exhibit all three processes at the same time. For example, a system may undergo expansion in size and complexity at the same time that its members attempt to preserve certain aspects of its basic identity and traditions. Or, as the population of a community ages, medical services for the elderly may be expanded as the public school system contracts. The question of which of these processes is dominant in a social system, and how their opposing dynamics might be related, is an empirical question requiring investigation. Buckley's major argument, however, is that social systems are characterized by continuous change and structural elaboration more than by rigid structural stability. A focus on the expanding complexity of social systems is also a key theme in Niklas Luhmann's analysis of social systems.

From Unorganized to Organized Complexity: Niklas Luhmann's Perspective on the Self-Creation of Social Systems

Niklas Luhmann's influence on North American sociology has expanded since the middle of the 1980s, due no doubt in part to the 1982 translation of his book, *The Differentiation of Society*, from German into English.[13] A more elaborate and

[13] Niklas Luhmann's career as a sociologist was spent at the University of Bielefeld in Germany, spanning the years from the mid-1960s until his death in 1998.

systematic presentation of his general theory of social systems was provided in the 1995 English translation of his book entitled *Social Systems*. Luhmann contrasted his approach with the structural/functional perspective of Talcott Parsons, with whom he had studied in 1960 (Knodt, "Foreword", pp. xii in Luhmann 1995). Luhmann's analysis is more abstract than Buckley's, and it includes an explicit distinction between social systems and individual-level psychic systems, including consciousness in particular. Luhmann argued that psychic systems and consciousness are actually part of the environment of social systems, despite the fact that psychic and social systems actually interpenetrate one another and influence each other greatly.

Social systems for Luhmann are essentially communication systems, which is consistent with Buckley's perspective and with the emphasis in general systems theory on informational linkages within systems and between systems and their environment. In addition, Luhmann's focus on the importance of communication and texts in the organization of society is largely congruent with the linguistic turn that has occurred in recent years in social theory and also with Dorothy Smith's analysis of the use of texts in the "relations of ruling" as discussed in the last chapter. In Luhmann's perspective, the expansion of communication networks provides the basis for a global society. However, the component parts of the global system are only loosely coupled, lacking a high level of integration and an objective and well-defined center.[14]

Self-Organization and Boundary Formation

In Luhmann's perspective the most crucial distinction between systems and their environments is the self-referential processes of systems themselves (Luhmann, 1995:12–58, 176–209). In other words, social systems are self-defined, self-produced, and self-maintained. Their identity is established by the production of the elements that constitute them, the differentiation of these elements from the wider environment, and the establishment of mutual relations among these elements. Consistent with Buckley's perspective, social systems do not have an objective existence independent of the ongoing elements and processes that compose them. These processes include meaningful patterns of action and interaction whereby the system establishes itself as being distinct from its environment. Luhmann uses the term **autopoiesis** to refer to this process of self-construction. In contrast to the notion that people organize themselves through coordinating already existing roles and identities, autopoiesis does not begin with previously established "parts" that people decide to organize into a system. Rather, autopoiesis refers to a more fundamental underlying process whereby the elements or "parts" themselves are constructed through communication. The system is not made up of individual

[14] These ideas regarding globalization and the absence of a center are both congruent with major themes of postmodern theory, some aspects of which will be described in a Chap. 20.

persons as such, but communication codes that are created and employed to establish the identity of the system, criteria for membership, and the relevance of activities constituting the system.

Like Buckley, Luhmann emphasized information linkages within and between social systems. Moreover, Luhmann's process of self-organization can be seen as foundational for Buckley's concept of morphogenic processes. While Luhmann emphasized the importance of communication codes, it should be noted that this process of self-organization also involves the use of energy to overcome the disintegrating effects of entropy and to insure that the various processes that constitute the system are carried out. Energy is required for communication as well as for engaging in the social actions that actually constitute the system.

Given the importance of communication codes for the creation of social systems, the key distinction in modern communication theory between information and "noise" is important to note. For communication to occur, both the sender and the receiver must share the same code (language or meaning system). Otherwise, the input for the listener is mere noise, as opposed to meaningful communication. Even though limited communication may also occur through gestures, these also must be "decoded" (or interpreted) to be meaningful. Among those who share the same language in a complex society, different subgroups and organizations will develop their own distinctive subcultural codes that are used to distinguish insiders and outsiders. The communication that is possible through the use of shared codes enables members of a system to integrate their activities in ways that reproduce the system of which they are a part. It is this process that distinguishes social systems from psychic systems.

Social Systems Versus Psychic Systems

Luhmann insisted that psychic systems are part of the environment of social systems, just as social systems are also part of the environment of psychic systems. The relation between the two systems is one of interdependence; each system requires the other for its development. In fact, the identity of social systems depends on their being differentiated from members' psychic systems. People implicitly recognize this distinction in everyday life when they try to separate their own personal views, preferences, or needs from their obligations to the team or other groups to which they belong. Here is how Luhmann put it:

> ... We are dealing with social, not psychic systems. We assume that social systems are not composed of psychic systems, let alone of bodily human beings. Therefore, psychic systems belong to the environment of social systems. Of course, they are a part of the environment that is especially relevant for the formation of social systems. We emphasized this ... by examining the concept of interpenetration. Such environmental relevance for the construction of social systems constrains what is possible, but it does not prevent social systems from forming themselves autonomously and on the basis of their own elemental operations. These operations are communications–not psychic processes per se, and also not the processes of consciousness.
>
> (Luhmann, 1995:255)

Psychic systems, in turn, cannot be reduced to the organic level of "bodily human beings." As biological organisms human beings are part of the environment of psychic systems as well as social systems. Unlike biological or organic systems, however, both psychic and social systems are based on meaning. The development of meaning involves processes of selective perception and interpretation of objects or processes, in either the environment or the system, in such a way that some form of organized response, consistent with the system's basic identity, can ensue. Although this terminology is more abstract, the argument is consistent with the symbolic interactionist perspective on how people respond to their environment in terms of shared meanings leading to a socially **organized** response. Luhmann emphasized that the establishment of meaning involves a process of selection from a wide range of environmental stimuli or objects, with each potential selection capable of a virtually inexhaustible array of possible meanings or interpretations.

Consciousness in all its aspects would be included in Luhmann's concept of psychic systems (as would unconscious processes as well). Luhmann's discussion of consciousness drew heavily on Husserl's phenomenological perspective in emphasizing that conscious awareness involves a selective focus of perception and reflection from a virtually unlimited array of possibilities that stretch away into an undefined horizon. There is practically no limit to the thoughts, memories, fantasies, moods, images, or feelings that may drift in and out of consciousness, despite conscious efforts to focus attention on some specific object in the environment or a particular thought. The distinction within consciousness between the focus of attention and the background is not a hard and fast line, however, and one's focus may shift frequently within a fairly short span of time, despite conscious efforts to remain focused. These internal processes of consciousness are not part of the social system, however, although they may become the object of communication. Even so, people often have difficulty responding to a query about what they are thinking about at the moment, particularly when their minds are not consciously focused on anything in particular.

The same selectivity that is involved with consciousness also characterizes communication processes in social systems. For social systems, however, there is a "double contingency" involved.[15] The development of social systems cannot be based on individuals' unique subjective experiences or their own particular choices. Instead, the choices of each individual must be perceived as congruent with the choices of others (at least with regard to what is relevant for the creation of the system), or a social system will not emerge. It is through the process of communication and mutual adjustment that individuals' conscious perceptions may eventually overlap sufficiently for them to develop expectations that their actions will be connected or coordinated in some fashion.

---

[15] Talcott Parsons (1951:10, 36) had also used the concept of double contingency in explaining the development and distinctive characteristics of social systems. However, Luhmann did not feel that Parsons maintained this focus in his analysis of the dynamics of social systems but instead treated psychic systems as virtually encapsulated within social systems through the process of socialization.

Although shared expectations and mutual adjustment are routine, taken-for-granted features of social life, Luhmann emphasizes that there is a large element of chance involved, particularly in the initial formation of social systems. Even when people are physically in one another's presence, in the absence of mutual expectations that define their membership in some social system, they may fail to interact at all. Or, their interaction may fail to progress beyond a one-time encounter. Even when the same individuals engage in subsequent one-time encounters, they may still fail to see themselves as forming an enduring relationship. And even in established social systems, shared meanings are never fixed or permanent. Instead their maintenance depends on a sustained focus of attention, but this focus always has the potential for being diverted to other possibilities.

Luhmann's analysis of the self-construction of social systems makes it clear why social systems cannot be defined in terms of individual persons or psychic processes, including individual consciousness, even though both psychic and social systems are based on meaning. Since social systems are based on communication between people, their reality cannot be reduced to any single individual's consciousness. Luhmann insists that the elements or contents of individuals' consciousness are simply too complex and idiosyncratic to be incorporated fully into social systems. This is consistent with the basic phenomenological idea that the consciousness of no two people is exactly the same, despite the struggles they may undertake to understand one another.

This distinction between individual persons and their psychic systems on the one hand and social systems on the other can be understood in terms of the well-established sociological concept of social roles. Individuals' participation in social systems does not involve all the multiple dimensions and components of their psychic systems or the entire range of their conscious experience. Instead, it involves specific roles they perform as participants in a particular system, with different roles obviously involved in different systems. In this sense social systems can be regarded as **less** than the sum of their parts. Luhmann makes this point in opposition to the argument that is sometimes made in systems theory that the whole is **more** than the sum of its parts because of the emergent relations among these parts. Although the emergent interdependent relations among parts in a system are indeed not reducible to its constituent parts, the "parts" themselves are only partially involved in the system.

The social positions with which roles are associated are the basic elements of the social system, not the individual persons who occupy these positions. These positions are defined in terms of their connections with other positions with which they are linked through communication. This separation of individual persons and their consciousness from their social positions and the roles they play is a well established feature of bureaucratic organizations as well as other social systems. With positions and roles defined in impersonal terms, it is possible to establish continuity in the functioning of such organizations despite periodic turnover in personnel. This same distinction between individual persons and social systems can be made in other aspects of social life as well.

Managing Complexity

In Luhmann's perspective the basic function served by social systems is to manage the complexity of their environments. In one sense the environment consists of the entire world that exists beyond the system's boundaries. However, a large part of a social system's environment consists of other social systems, plus the psychic systems of their members (as discussed above) as well as their biological characteristics. Despite the internal complexity that may develop within social systems, the environment is always more complex than any particular system. The concept of **complexity** in this context refers to the total array of possibilities that the environment offers with regard to the various objects that could be the potential focus of attention, as well as all possible interpretations of these objects. Needless to say, the total array of possible choices is virtually infinite, and people are consciously aware of only a small proportion of these possibilities. Even the possibilities of which they are (or could be) aware are far too numerous for all of them to be selected. Instead, choices must be made, and these choices will reflect the process of selective perception and interpretation as discussed earlier in connection with the development of meaning in psychic and social systems.

Without some strategy to reduce environmental complexity through selective perception and interpretation, the environment would appear chaotic and without order, and we would be unable to respond at all. To illustrate the point, the image of chaos that develops from an unmanageable surplus of options may perhaps be compared in a small way to the situation of a person who has far too many obligations, or too many opportunities, to be able to know what to do and no criteria for establishing priorities. As a result of having too many options and no criteria for making choices among them, an individual may experience a sense of anomie or chaos, unable to decide what to do, and so is virtually paralyzed, unable to act at all.

Through their self-constructing process of autopoiesis, social systems can be seen as restricting the range of choices that are available and providing criteria and guidelines for selecting and interpreting the options that remain. These criteria provide the basis for mutual expectations whereby people's actions can then be connected and coordinated. Without such mutually understood expectations, individuals' behavior would appear to one another to be random occurrences in one another's environment, reflecting nothing more than the organization each person might attempt to provide through his or her individual psychic systems. Although individual differences in perceptions and interpretation are never eliminated, even after the formation of a social system, the ongoing effort to deal with such differences provides a basis for continuing the communication process whereby the system is maintained.

Even as social systems reduce environmental complexity, they also develop their own internal complexity. This varies greatly for different systems, depending on the particular environment to which they must adapt as well as their size and the specific patterns of interdependence that develop internally. A system's internal complexity emerges in large part through the development of strategies to classify and process various types of transactions with different aspects of the environment.

In this way the internal complexity of the system eventually matches the complexity of that part of the environment to which the system must adapt. However, this classification and processing must be in accord with the system's own identity. Elements of the environment that are irrelevant for the system are simply screened out or ignored. For example, the internal complexity of a manufacturing firm will include different subsystems for purchasing raw materials and for selling products. Different subsystems or different procedures may be developed for dealing with small-scale individual consumers versus large business firms, or for new customers versus repeat customers. In addition, there may be subsystems or specialized processes for dealing with regulatory government agencies, personnel recruitment, financial institutions, and various supporting organizations, as well as subsystems or processes for internal integration of the various differentiated components. Similarly, public schools will focus on age categories of the population in their district that define their potential students and will classify them in terms of grade level and perhaps special needs. Adults in the community may be classified as parents or as potential voters and supporters (or opponents); otherwise they are not relevant to the operations of the school system. School systems are likely also to have specific procedures or subsystems for dealing with parents, voters, book suppliers, professional associations, legislative and regulatory bodies, and other school systems.

Although social systems are always less complex than their environment, their internal complexity may reach extremely high levels. However, in contrast with the complexity of the environment, the complexity of social systems may be seen as **organized complexity**. At the same time, particular subsystems within a larger system may develop their own distinct identity whereby they differentiate themselves from the larger system of which they are a part. When this occurs, the larger system may then be seen as part of the environment. For example, different academic departments in a university may regard one another as part of their environment as they compete internally for scarce resources. At the same time, they recognize their shared identity as part of the same university in contrast to other universities and may collaborate in university-wide projects. And the universities within a state's higher education system will distinguish themselves from other state agencies as well as private colleges and universities.

Luhmann's emphasis on the challenges of complexity, plus his clear distinction between individual psychic systems and social systems, contrasts sharply with Jürgen Habermas's communication perspective as discussed earlier. For Luhmann, the ideal suggested by Habermas of promoting maximum mutual understanding through open communication channels would represent an unmanageably high level of complexity. Even though we might imagine a virtual national "town hall meeting" through the internet, it would be impossible for all citizens to participate equally or to achieve mutual understanding beyond a very superficial level, especially with the high diversity that characterizes modern society. In fact, achieving mutual understanding is a major challenge even in fairly small groups in which people are in face-to-face contact with one another. In Luhmann's view, the complexity of modern society requires that communication always be selective. Order can be developed out of chaos only if communication is oriented toward specific issues or themes. Moreover, the more complex the overall society, the less likely it is that any one subsystem can play a dominant role in its members' lives or the overall society. Thus, in contrast to Habermas, for Luhmann it is not **maximum** communication but **selective** communication, coupled with high levels of functional differentiation, that enhances individual freedom and promotes opportunities for personal fulfillment in modern society.[16]

Interaction Versus Organization Versus Society as Systems

Levels of complexity, plus strategies for dealing with complexity through the process of autopoiesis, vary greatly for different kinds of systems. Luhmann (1982:69–89) distinguishes interaction systems, organizations, and societies as alternative types of social systems based on their contrasting principles of organization and levels of abstraction. Interaction systems consist of individuals involved in face-to-face communication. (Voice-to-voice communication by telephone could also be included and perhaps e-mail communication as well.) Interaction systems range from episodic encounters to long-term relationships. Even in long-term relationships, however, actual interaction is likely to be episodic in character, particularly in a complex society in which participants are also involved in numerous other relationships and systems.

At the other extreme, a society consists of the total network of communication possibilities of all types, both direct and indirect. A society, as Luhmann put it, is the "all-encompassing social system that includes everything that is social and therefore does not admit a social environment" (Luhmann, 1995:408). In contrast to interaction systems, societies provide possibilities for maximum levels of complexity to be developed. Within individual societies, this complexity may include high levels of functional differentiation among different institutions. But Luhmann's definition of societies as potential networks of communication possibilities explicitly transcends national boundaries, however. As he put it, "If one accepts the concept of societal system proposed here, society today is clearly a world society" (Luhmann, 1995:430).[17] In this perspective, particular nation-states could be seen as the component parts of the world system, along with multinational corporations, international social movements, and various other social relationships that transcend national boundaries.

[16] This is consistent with Georg Simmel's argument regarding the importance of multiple social involvements for reducing the demands that any one system can make on its members.

[17] The concept of society as an all-encompassing network of communication possibilities excludes an environing social system by definition. Any communication that occurs becomes part of the system by definition. This may seem to imply that societies are by necessity closed systems. However, the material environment, plus the psychic systems and organic systems of their members, are still excluded from the definition of society and thus would be considered as part of the society's environment. This applies to particular nation-states as well as to a globally defined society.

Organizations are intermediate between interaction systems and society and are defined in terms of specific membership criteria. These criteria also include rules that distinguish different positions in terms of expected activities and levels of authority, prescribe particular communication networks, provide members with the resources they need to discharge their responsibilities, and specify how their actions are to be interpreted as being relevant for the system. Luhmann's analysis of organizations as intermediate between micro-level interaction systems on the one hand and societies on the other is consistent with our earlier discussion of organizations as meso-level social formations.

In analyzing the relations between interaction systems and societies, Luhmann insists that neither is reducible to the other (Luhmann, 1995:405–436). Instead, the two types of systems interpenetrate one another, comparable in some ways to the interpenetration of psychic and social systems. Societies reflect a more abstract level of organization than interaction systems, but they could not exist in the absence of interaction systems. Growth in the complexity of modern society has in effect expanded and reinforced the distinction between interaction and society. Particular relationships based solely on interaction processes are expected to have no bearing on system processes. (In some cases, such relationships, like office romantic affairs, for example may be disruptive of organizational processes and thus are often discouraged and sanctioned.) Moreover, societal patterns of organization are not necessarily attuned to the unique aspects of subjective consciousness of their members.[18] A crucial development in the increasing differentiation between societal systems on the one hand and interaction systems and consciousness on the other is the substitution of written forms of communication for face-to-face interaction. Written texts enable meanings to be communicated far beyond the local or temporal situation where they were created. Writers of texts obviously do not need to be in the physical presence of their readers or aware of their conscious experiences for their messages to be transmitted and understood. Moreover, just as society endures beyond the lifespan of any individual, the members of each new generation are the recipients of written meanings from past generations and can transmit their own meanings to the next.

In addition to transmitting meanings, texts make it possible to establish binding decisions and to communicate specific expectations far beyond the spatial and temporal contexts of local interaction systems. Thus, for example, contemporary actions of government officials and law enforcement agents are bound by the United States Constitution, written interpretations handed down through the years by the Supreme Court, and various other laws of the land. Significant forms of societal-level communication are often based on written texts even in situations where individuals are actually in one another's presence. For example, the United States President presents the annual State of the Union address standing in front of the assembled members of Congress and other dignitaries but always reads from a prepared text. Similarly, when

[18] This, of course, contrasts sharply with Dorothy Smith's emphasis, reviewed in the last chapter, of the need to focus on the subjective level of lived experience for advancing sociological knowledge.

police officers inform suspects of their rights, they are likely to recite from a written text they have memorized.

All social systems have the potential for self-reference and self-reflexivity. This is implied by the process of autopoiesis whereby social systems are self-constructed. Despite this self-construction process and the possibilities for self-reflection that it implies, systems differ considerably among themselves in terms of how they define their identity or see themselves **as** systems. Of the three types of systems Luhmann distinguished, intentionally established organizations clearly incorporate the notion of system in their own self-identity. Self-reflection or self-reflexivity may also occur in informal interaction systems as well, even though their participants may be less likely to see their system as intentionally constructed. For long-term interaction systems that are clearly institutionalized, such as marital relations, interaction may sometimes include self-reflection on the nature of the relationship as part of a deliberate effort to improve it or to establish appropriate boundaries between it and the psychic system of its members. For example, members may feel a need to express their desire for more personal space of their own or, conversely, to strengthen their socioemotional bond with their partner. This process of self-reflexivity may involve third parties if couples seek advice from others to resolve difficulties in their relationship.

At the level of societal systems, Luhmann suggests that modern societies have expanded the possibilities for self-reflection and reflexivity, as well as their capacities for implementing changes on the basis of such self-assessment. Some examples of this self-reflection process at the societal level include systematic tracking of economic indicators (inflation rates and unemployment rates, for example), pollsters' surveys of presidential approval ratings, attitude and opinion surveys on various public issues, analyses of crime statistics, and of course the United States Census that is conducted every 10 years. Within sociology, social indicators research may be seen as a strategy for the development of tools for societal reflexivity and self-assessment, the results of which may sometimes be used to support an argument regarding the need for change.

In considering the process of societal reflexivity, it is relevant to note that sociologists (along with economists, political scientists, and other social scientists) sometimes play an important role in the process of societal self-reflection. Since the societal system is the domain of study for sociologists, it should not be surprising that their analyses would be incorporated into the process whereby society (through its members) seeks to understand itself. This is consistent with the point made by Giddens regarding the way in which sociological analysis may gradually become part of the knowledge that society's members use as they engage in the various practices whereby society is continually reproduced and/or transformed. The process of self-reflection and self-understanding is always challenging and never complete. The consequence is that sociologists should always expect to find an audience for their analyses—provided they maintain their openness to the full complexity of the social world and seek opportunities to engage in public discourse. Students and others with some training in the sociological perspective are also able to participate in this process, even without becoming professional or academic sociologists.

Summary

This chapter has explored the relation of human agency to social structures and social systems. The concepts of structure and system are both widely used in analyses of the meso and macro levels of the social world. However, neither structures nor systems can exist independently of the actions and interactions of human beings as competent agents in their micro-level part of the social world. In fact, the concepts of agency, structure, and system are relevant to analyzing the interdependent relations among all levels of the social world—micro, meso, and macro—as well as each of these levels on its own.

We began with Anthony Giddens' structuration theory, in which the concepts of agency and structure were proposed as more useful for sociological analysis than the micro/macro distinction. Structure does not actually exist, however, except as it is reflected in the ongoing practices whereby people produce (and reproduce) the material and social conditions of their lives. Giddens emphasized that structures are the "medium" whereby the routine practices of everyday life are organized, and the reproduction (or transformation) of structures is an important "outcome" of these practices.

The concept of agency refers to the knowledge, skills, and power that people utilize in deliberately and intentionally intervening in the course of events in ways that "make a difference" in what happens in the social world. In this process individuals draw upon both practical and discursive knowledge regarding the conditions as well as the outcomes of their actions, and they are able to explain or account for their actions when appropriate. However, their knowledge of the conditions and the consequences of their actions is never complete. Unacknowledged conditions may even include the motivations underlying their actions, including unconscious security needs that motivate people to maintain their everyday life routines. On the other hand, however, needs for autonomy may lead to deviations from established routines. When this occurs, individuals may be expected to offer an explanation of their action so others can make sense of it and adjust accordingly. When deviations are diffused throughout society, the result can be structural transformation.

The concept of structure in structuration theory consists essentially of the rules and resources that are employed in the routine practices of everyday life. Rules establish rights to various resources, including allocative (or material) resources and authoritative resources (or control of other people's behavior). Although individuals' actions always occur in a micro-level context, when patterns of action are widespread throughout society and endure over time, this leads to the perception that structures exist on their own, independently of the micro-level contexts in which specific actions occur. In contrast to structure, a social system, whether large or small, consists of the actual interdependent practices through which structures are reproduced. Macro-level social institutions may thus be seen as sets of structured practices that are widespread among members of a population and that endure through time, often over many generations.

We then turned our attention to the concept of open systems, focusing on Walter Buckley's morphogenic "process model." Consistent with the open systems theory perspective, social systems are viewed in terms of the internal interdependence among their "parts" as well as their relations with the environment. Input/output transaction with the environment are crucial for obtaining the resources, information, and energy needed for survival (or self-reproduction). Buckley emphasized that social systems are self-regulating and goal-oriented, and that their internal and external relations undergo more or less continuous structural elaboration, change, and development. This often results in more effective strategies for meeting an increasing array of members' needs and goals. The process of structural elaboration and change involves deviation-amplifying feedback cycles whereby minor variations, whatever their source or motivation, are reinforced and thereby provide the basis for additional variations. This process of morphogenesis can be contrasted with morphostasis, which reflects the operation of deviation-inhibiting feedback cycles in which established patterns are stabilized. In addition to these two patterns that Buckley contrasted, still a third pattern of structural change that sometimes occurs in social systems is the process of entropy or decay.

Finally, we reviewed Niklas Luhmann's perspective on social systems as self-organizing responses to the unorganized complexity (or seeming chaos) of the environment. Although social systems may develop their own high level of organized internal complexity, they are always less complex than their environment and represent selections from the options available in the environment. Luhmann's concept of "autopoiesis" refers to the process whereby systems are self-created through their selections of elements and processes whereby their own identity is established.

In Luhmann's perspective, psychic systems and processes of consciousness are excluded as constituent parts of social systems, along with their members' biological or organic characteristics. Only certain aspects of individuals' psychic systems and organic bodily characteristics are relevant for social systems. Each system, however, has its own particular dynamics, and the boundaries separating these different types of systems are never dissolved. The relationships among these systems is one of interpenetration in which each type of system must adapt to the others.

Within the general category of social systems, Luhmann distinguished interaction systems, organizations, and societies. Interaction systems are formed through person-to-person communication. Societies, in contrast, consist of all possible communication networks, including those that transcend national boundaries. Organizations are formed through the development of explicit procedures for incorporating members and structuring and coordinating their various actions and relationships. Each of these three types of systems also exhibits its own distinctive characteristics, and none is reducible to either of the others.

The evolutionary development of modern society involves increasing differentiation between interactional, organizational, and societal systems. The formation and maintenance of societies and meso level social systems beyond the level of interaction systems rely heavily on written texts whereby meanings can be established in objective form, transmitted beyond local situations, and preserved for future generations. Modern societies are characterized by increasing levels of reflexivity or self-reflection and the development of procedures for deliberate implementation of change. Both Giddens and Luhmann highlighted the way in which the efforts of sociologists (and other social scientists) to understand and explain the social world are actually incorporated into that world and thus may become part of the process of societal self-reflection.

Although Luhmann emphasized the distinction between individual persons and social systems, an adequate explanation of human beings' behavior requires us also to understand the biological characteristics of the human species as well as the dynamics of the social and cultural environment they create. The relevance of human beings' biological and genetic characteristics for their social behavior will be explored in the next chapter. These characteristics provide the foundation for cultural influences, which will then be the focus of the following chapter.

Questions for Study and Discussion

1. Drawing on Giddens' structuration theory, explain how structures can be seen as both enabling and constraining. Cite some examples from your own experiences of both of these processes.
2. Compare and contrast the way both discursive and practical consciousness (as distinguished by Giddens) are manifested in everyday life. Under what conditions would you expect implicit practical consciousness to become discursive? How would you expect these two types of consciousness to be demonstrated in routine social practices, as opposed to innovative actions that are intended to stimulate social change?
3. Drawing on Buckley's perspective on open systems, distinguish "morphogenic" and "morphostatic" processes and describe at least one example of each from your own experience or observations. How would these processes contrast with the pattern of entropy? How could you analyze these processes in terms of deviation-amplifying versus deviation-inhibiting feedback cycles?
4. Explain Luhmann's argument that individuals' consciousness, or psychic systems, are part of the environment of social systems. In what ways do social systems manage to reduce the complexity of individuals' consciousness? How do different social systems vary in this regard? Could this process be seen as contributing to the alienation people sometimes experience in the social systems in which they are involved? Explain.
5. Drawing on your own experience or observations, contrast interaction systems with organizations, and explain how each may be seen as analytically independent of the other. How would you relate this distinction to the micro/macro distinction employed in this book?

Chapter 18
The Sociobiological Perspective: Biological Versus Cultural Influences on Human Behavior

The long-lasting debate over nature versus nurture may never be settled completely. Does our development and our behavior as human beings result primarily from the formative influences of our sociocultural environment, or from underlying biological, or genetic factors transmitted through heredity? To what extent does culture itself reflect or express biological needs and impulses? Alternatively, should culture be seen as imposing constraints that inhibit the innate predispositions of human nature for the sake of social order? Moreover, how are human beings enabled by the cultural strategies they have developed to transcend some of their biological limitations, thereby enhancing their welfare and long-range survival? The answers will no doubt depend on the particular behaviors being addressed and the specific features of the material and cultural environment in which they are manifested.

Although sociologists acknowledge the potentialities and constraints of our biological characteristics, their primary emphasis is on the sociocultural environment. The sociobiological perspective, in contrast, explores how human behavior is influenced by underlying biological and genetic characteristics as well as cultural learning. This goal overlaps with the continuing popular interest in questions regarding nature versus nurture. Such questions are especially relevant with respect to people's interest in explaining sex and gender differences, parental motivations, propensities for aggression and violence, and variations in physical and intellectual abilities. The publicity given to the human genome research has no doubt increased public fascination with underlying genetic characteristics. Practical applications of increased knowledge in this area are suggested by the possibilities for developing medical applications of genetic "engineering" techniques to correct potentially harmful biological anomalies.

This chapter will begin with a brief historical description of the evolutionary perspective of social Darwinism, which was described briefly in Chaps. 1 and 3. It is important to emphasize that contemporary sociobiology differs substantially from the perspective of biological and cultural evolution represented by social Darwinism, even though it is also an evolutionary theory. One major difference is that sociobiology is based heavily on recent advances in scientific knowledge regarding genetics that go far beyond what was available in the early twentieth century. Its more sophisticated explanation of genetic variations helps account for a wider range of behavioral strategies that enable human beings to adapt to different types of environments. Moreover, the emphasis on underlying predispositions in contemporary sociobiology is not seen as causing specific behavior patterns in the strong sense. Instead, the way these predispositions are manifested may vary greatly for different people and will always reflect the strong influence of the social and cultural environment. In addition, contemporary sociobiology does not provide support for the unacceptable ideological implications that were developed from social Darwinism. Nevertheless, to show the contrast with contemporary sociobiology, some themes from social Darwinism and their ideological implications will be reviewed briefly.

Following our brief review of social Darwinism, the contemporary sociobiological perspective will be used in exploring the following areas:

- Social emotions and the formation of social bonds
- Reproductive behavior, sex roles, and parenting
- Cooperation and altruism among kin and ingroup members
- Competition and conflict in relations within and between groups
- Religion, morality, and hope
- Cultural evolution

The Historical Background of Social Darwinism[1]

In contrast to the contemporary tendency in sociology to play down biological factors, the popularity of social Darwinism in the last part of the nineteenth and early twentieth centuries in both Europe and America led to a strong emphasis on biological characteristics in explaining human behavior. Essentially, social Darwinism represented an extension of the principles of biological evolution to social evolution.[2] In both realms the competitive struggle for survival in an environment of scarce resources was heavily emphasized. In the biological realm, the competitors could be either individuals or species. In the social realm the competitive struggle may be among individuals or among different groups within a society, different societies, or different racial or ethnic populations. As a result of natural variations in inherited biological characteristics or adaptive strategies, it turns out that some individuals or groups were more successful than others. Those who adapted most successfully were able to reproduce more abundantly than their competitors and

[1] This brief description of the historical background of social Darwinism for contemporary sociobiology is adapted from D. P. Johnson (Johnson [1981] 1986:519–521).

[2] One of the principle representatives of the social Darwinist point of view was William Graham Sumner, whose best-known work, *Folkways* (Sumner [1906] 1979), suggests an evolutionary approach to the development of social customs. For an overview of the influence of social Darwinism in America, see Richard Hofstadter (1944).

become dominant. In contrast, those who are unable to adapt successfully were doomed to extinction or subordination.

The ultimate outcome of this long-term evolutionary process was the survival of the fittest. The differences between those with favorable and unfavorable characteristics were seen as resulting in large part from natural biological variations transmitted through heredity. This means that the evolutionary process involves a gradual selection over many generations of individuals or groups who adapted most successfully to their environment. Although the emphasis was on biological variations, the same pattern applies to social and cultural evolution as well. In other words, sociocultural patterns that proved to be most beneficial in the struggle for survival were gradually selected over those that were less effective. These processes were seen as natural and inevitable, insuring long-term biological and cultural progress.

In America, during the last decades of the nineteenth century and until the outbreak of World War I early in the twentieth century, these ideas provided ideological support for the growth of the gigantic business enterprises that were becoming more and more dominant at the time. Their success was viewed as a natural outcome of the normal evolutionary process and as proof of their superior fitness. The stratification of society into different socioeconomic classes was also seen as natural and inevitable, governed by the same evolutionary processes whereby large business corporations gradually displaced smaller enterprises. A major ideological implication drawn from this evolutionary model was that there should be no artificial interference with this natural process by government or social reformers. Instead, the best strategy for government was a *laissez-faire* policy in which business enterprises (and other groups as well) were free to compete for dominance, despite the exploitation that this sometimes involved. From a long-term perspective, reform efforts were not advisable because of their effects in enabling those who were less fit to survive and reproduce. People's moral sentiments and empathy for others may lead them to engage in acts of charity to alleviate human suffering in individual cases; however, in a long-term perspective, such behavior runs the risk of interfering in the natural evolutionary process.

There were dissenting opinions, however. Some early American social theorists, such as Lester Ward, for example, expanded the evolutionary model to justify intentional efforts to shape the evolutionary process to insure human progress (Hofstadter, 1944:52–67). In his view human intelligence itself was part of the overall process and should be considered part of nature, not in opposition to it. Unlike subhuman species, human beings have the ability to observe, analyze, and influence the course of evolution to promote human welfare instead of relying solely on chance variations or the blind forces of nature. Ward's ideas were consistent with those of George Herbert Mead, who (as shown in Chap. 3) pointed out that the neurological structure of the human brain had itself emerged in the evolutionary process and provides the biological foundation for all mental processes. By using their intelligence, human beings are able to develop shared symbols that enable them to communicate and cooperate with one another in adapting to their environment and pursuing their collective goals.[3]

The prevailing view at the time, however, tended to discourage "artificial" interference in the natural process of competitive struggle and survival of the fittest. However, there was another, more sinister type of interference that some regarded as being consistent with long-range evolutionary principles. The emphasis on hereditary differences provided the basis for various racist proposals such as the development of "eugenics" programs to insure the dominance of "superior" races (Galton, 1869; Pearson, 1909; Stoddard, 1922). Perhaps the most dramatic political implication of this perspective was reflected in the rise of Nazism in Germany. This belief in superior and inferior races may also be seen as providing ideological reinforcement for beliefs in cultural superiority that helped justify European and American efforts to dominate and exploit colonial societies.

Since the horrendous atrocities of the Nazi era in Germany, most social scientists seek to detach themselves as much as possible from any theory based on innate differences among individuals, races, or ethnic groups that could be used to label some groups as biologically inferior or superior, or to justify domination of one group by another. Even so, among some lay persons the belief that certain personality characteristics or behavior tendencies may be due to biology and transmitted through heredity is still accepted. For social scientists, however, differences among individuals or groups are explained in terms of social milieu or cultural conditioning. The lack of success of disprivileged groups is explained in terms of lack of opportunities, not lack of innate ability. In addition to rejecting explanations of behavior based on biological heredity, social scientists today would be reluctant to concede that any one type of cultural system is inherently superior.[4] Also, the *laissez-faire* free market political implications of social Darwinism are not generally accepted among sociologists today. Instead, most sociologists (and other social scientists) recognize the importance of government involvement in regulating a complex economic system, protection of human rights, and reduction of exploitative forms of social inequality.

These changes in social scientists' values and intellectual orientation represent a sharp break in American social theory that was clearly evident by the middle of the twentieth century, especially after World War II. For most contemporary social scientists, social Darwinism was a grievous and embarrassing error, and thus they tend to reject theoretical perspectives that are based on inherited biological characteristics.[5]

---

[3] As noted in Chap. 3, George Herbert Mead's "social behaviorism" was crucial for the development of symbolic interaction theory, in which social definitions are given priority over innate biological characteristics.

[4] This refusal to grant a privileged position to any one pattern of culture or subculture is especially relevant to contemporary postmodern theoretical perspectives, some themes of which will be discussed in Chap. 20.

[5] In fact, the use of social Darwinist ideas to justify the economic and political policies of the time can be seen as illustrating the process Michel Foucault emphasized, as described in Chap. 15, whereby objective knowledge claims were used at the time to provide tacit support for existing power structures.

Exploring the Biological and Genetic Foundations of Social Behavior[6]

Despite the overwhelming contemporary emphasis on cultural influences and the social environment, the influence of natural or species characteristics are not completely ignored. Symbolic interaction theory emphasizes that the ability of human beings to develop and use symbols is grounded in neurological processes within the brain. Noam Chomsky (1965, 1968, 1975) regarded the deep structure of grammatical rules as being innate, reflecting certain aspects of the biological structure of the human brain, despite the great variation in the surface features of different languages. Also, there are numerous features of human nature that form the implicit foundation for all types of sociological analysis. These include, for example, human beings' capacity for intellectual reflection and emotional arousal, their ability to learn from past experience and to make plans for the future, their propensity for forming social attachments and cooperative relationships, and their flexibility in developing and learning cultural rules and technologies that enable them to adapt to different environments.

But in contrast to mainstream sociology, the sociobiological perspective puts a much stronger emphasis on the long-term evolutionary development of underlying biological and genetic characteristics and behavioral predispositions. Despite this emphasis, however, there is ample theoretical space in sociobiology for the formative influence of the social and cultural environment in explaining the wide array of behavioral variations in different environments. Thus, for example, while our basic language ability is innate, specific languages must be learned in the early years of the socialization process. Also, it should also be emphasized that acknowledgment of biological or genetic characteristics does not provide any basis for evaluating different populations as inferior or superior.

Sociobiology is based on the principles of Darwinian evolution in which natural variations in biological or genetic characteristics are related to differences in survival and reproductive success. The basic argument is that genetic code variations give rise to differences in biological characteristics and behavioral predispositions. Variations that improve the ability or organisms to adapt to their environment and reproduce are more likely to be selected for long-term survival than organisms lacking such characteristics. Moreover, it is important to note that variations within and between species that are advantageous in one environment may be disadvantageous in another. Over the long course of evolutionary history, species survival depends on the development of characteristics that increase an organism's "inclusive fitness" in adapting to its particular environment and the replication of these

[6] In a brief overview previously published in D. P. Johnson ([1981] 1986:521–527), the sociobiological perspective was portrayed as being compatible with the general model of open systems theory in being able to incorporate biological and genetic influences on people's social behavior in addition to the usual sociological focus on sociocultural influences.

characteristics in offspring. This concept of "inclusive fitness" refers not only to individual survival, but to the survival of others to whom an individual is genetically related, including offspring in particular. In the long term, however, the concept of survival applies more to the species than to the individual organism. Since the life span of individuals is relatively short, reproduction is obviously crucial for long-term species survival.

The fundamental characteristics of human beings are seen as having evolved over the long course of history in accordance with the fundamental principles of natural selection. Their basic patterns of growth and development reflect the specific instructions provided in the genetic code. Some distinctive biological characteristics of the human species include the following: upright posture, hands capable of sophisticated manipulation of objects in the environment, vocal cords and mouth structure that allow for the production of the complex sounds employed in speech, brains that are capable of developing symbolic codes that are used in abstract thinking and communication, and a capacity for various forms of emotional arousal and socioemotional bonding. Although all human beings share a genetic code that distinguishes them from other species, there are important variations that result in the immense variety we observe in terms of individual characteristics such as appearance and other biological features.

Beyond this, sociobiologists propose that certain distinctive behavioral predispositions may also be genetically encoded.[7] This does not mean that specific behaviors are biologically or genetically determined. It does suggest, however, that there may be underlying biological tendencies or predispositions for certain types of behavior, even though the way these are expressed will reflect the influence of the culture and the social environment as learned through the socialization process. The key question to ask in assessing the potential biological underpinnings of such behaviors is whether they affect individuals' chances for survival and reproductive success. In developing their arguments, sociobiologists frequently compare humans with other species in order to show parallels in behavioral strategies for survival. Our focus will be on human behavior, however, and on how underlying predispositions are manifested through the diverse cultural patterns through which these predispositions are shaped and expressed.

It is important to emphasize that the sociobiological perspective allows considerable flexibility in terms of how biological needs and predispositions may be manifested in particular forms of behavior. Our biological makeup does not provide detailed

[7] Some examples of works that represent the sociobiological approach include: Robert Ardrey, *African Genesis* (Ardrey, 1960) and *The Territorial Imperative* (Ardrey, 1966); David P. Barash, *Sociobiology and Behavior* (Barash, 1977) and *The Whisperings Within – Evolution and the Origin of Human Nature* (Barash, 1979); Konrad Z. Lorenz, *On Aggression* (Lorenz, 1966); Lionel Tiger, *Men in Groups* (Tiger, 1969); Lionel Tiger and Robin Fox, *The Imperial Animal* (Tiger and Fox, 1971), and Edward O Wilson, *Sociobiology, The New Synthesis*, (Wilson, 1975) and *On Human Nature* (Wilson, 1978). For an example of an introductory sociology text based solidly on explicit recognition of the biological foundations of human behavior, see Pierre L. van den Berghe, *Man in Society: A Biological View* (van den Berghe, 1978). See Caplan, ed. (1978) for a wide selection of alternative perspectives on sociobiology, including ethical implications as well as the scientific aspects.

instructions in the form of "hard-wired" genetic programs that determine our behavior in a strong sense. Because of this lack of detailed genetic instructions for successful adaptation, cultural learning is essential. The particular repertoire of knowledge, skills, and abilities that we employ in satisfying our biological needs and expressing our innate predispositions requires the behavioral programming provided through the cultural guidelines that individuals internalize within their particular social setting. This leaves ample room for an immense variety of cultural patterns, thus enabling human beings to adapt to many different types of environmental conditions.

Human beings are probably unique among all species, however, in experiencing tension and conflict from time to time between their natural biological predispositions and impulses and many of the cultural guidelines and regulations to which they are expected to conform. A great deal of the drama of human life involves efforts to balance our "natural" needs, wants, and impulses as biological organisms with our social obligations, shared moral values, and long-range goals, both individual and collective. Even though our innate or "natural" needs and wants are shaped by our culture, this tension is probably never eliminated. The sociobiological perspective can help us understand these tensions between basic biological needs and predispositions and the demands placed on us as members of society or other groups to which we belong.

Human beings' personal needs and predispositions and cultural rules and regulations can both be evaluated in terms of their contributions to individual and group survival. The primary focus in sociobiology, however, is on how individual needs and impulses are related to long-range species survival, not individual survival. In his overview of the sociobiological perspective, Richard Dawkins (1976) proposes that individuals' bodies can be viewed as "survival machines" for the transmission of the genetic code of the species. People's concerns with their own individual survival and well-being are important in this perspective because of how the satisfaction of these personal goals can contribute to the long-range evolutionary "goal" of species survival. In other words, the ultimate goal is not satisfying individuals' personal needs or impulses; instead, the ultimate long-term goal is species survival, not individual survival. In actuality, of course, the species cannot have goals; only individuals do, and their personal needs and goals, including their own survival, are more likely to be paramount in their minds than species survival. But in addition to their personal survival and well-being, individuals may also be concerned with the welfare and survival of their group, particularly their offspring and others who are related to them. This is no doubt a major source of the tension and conflict that are experienced from time to time between individuals' own personal needs, goals, and impulses and their obligations to others in the various social groups to which they belong. In Dawkins' perspective, the ultimate long-range "goal" of species survival is advanced through genetically encoded predispositions that contribute to successful reproduction and support of the next generation. This would imply that there may well be a biological foundation that underlies the pattern whereby human beings discover that behaviors involved in reproducing and caring for the next generation can be intrinsically rewarding. At the same time, however, this may sometimes involve behaviors that involve sacrifice of one's own needs or goals so as to increase the chances for survival of one's offspring and other kin.

In short, patterns of behavior are evaluated in this perspective in terms of their implications for linking individual survival with reproductive success and long-range species survival. We should therefore expect that biologically based behavioral predispositions should be particularly relevant in the areas of reproductive behavior and care for the young. Sexual attraction and gratification are obviously important to motivate reproductive behavior. Providing care for the next generation is crucial because of the relatively long period of helplessness of infants and children. In addition, long-range species survival is also enhanced by the formation of groups whose members cooperate in adapting to the environment. This would include protecting the group and its territory and resources against predators, both human and nonhuman. Since the specific behaviors needed for successful adaptation to the environment are not biologically determined, strategies for adapting must be developed. These are incorporated in the cultural patterns that are transmitted to the next generation through socialization. Promotion of ingroup solidarity is also crucial because of the tensions and conflicts that sometimes develop between the satisfaction of individuals' personal needs and the fulfillment of social obligations to help insure the survival of the groups on which individual survival depends. Moreover, the mental abilities that allow for cultural learning also enable human beings to grasp the precariousness of human life and to anticipate their own eventual death. Thus we might hypothesize that long-term survival would also be enhanced by the development of cultural worldviews that promote confidence and strengthen motivations to persevere despite the risks and struggles of life and the realization that individual lives will ultimately end with death. It is in the areas of group solidarity and positive thinking that religious faith and moral codes may be seen as having a biological foundation. All of these aspects of human behavior are addressed in sociobiology. The next section examines male/female differences in human reproduction in terms of both biological characteristics and cultural influences.

Sex Roles and Reproductive Behavior

In contrast to the emphasis of most sociologists on the social construction of gender roles,[8] sociobiologists begin by highlighting the obvious biological differences between females and males in the human reproduction process. The major challenge is to insure that males and females will be motivated to engage in sexual intercourse and subsequently to work out arrangements to care for the resulting offspring. In sociological theory and in everyday life, developing a sexual relationship is not seen

[8]This emphasis on the social construction and cultural definition of gender roles is perhaps most clearly evident in feminist theoretical perspectives. But it is also widely accepted in other theoretical perspectives as well, including in particular symbolic interaction theory. In the area of the sociology of emotions, differences between women and men are also a major focus of attention, but it isn't always clear whether these differences are due to biological characteristics or pervasive social expectations that are deeply internalized.

as problematic because of the way most human beings are biologically programmed to be attracted to the opposite sex, beginning during puberty.[9] Despite extensive social pressures and cultural values promoting abstinence during adolescence, the biological predispositions that emerge at puberty are difficult to repress, and social control efforts often have limited effectiveness. For all age categories, the motivation to "have sex" is certainly not the same as the motivation to "have children."

Going beyond initial attraction, sociobiologists would note that females and males have different "interests" in their relationship and the offspring they produce (Trivers, pp. 136–179 in B. G. Campbell, ed., 1972). These are not necessarily conscious interests but instead reflect predispositions that are built into the underlying motivations and emotions of women versus men. Although the male's sperm and the female's egg are both essential, a mother's "investment" in her offspring is much greater than the father's from a purely biological point of view. This is because the egg she supplies is much scarcer than the male's sperm, with a maximum for each one egg per month between puberty and menopause, minus nine months for each pregnancy and the time afterwards when she is biologically programmed to nourish her infant by nursing. It should be remembered that it is only in recent times that substitute sources have been available for infants whose mothers who are unwilling (or unable) to breast-feed. In addition to the biological stresses of pregnancy, the infant's long-term dependency limits a new mother's mobility for some time after birth. In addition, the close bodily contact involved in nursing and caring for her new offspring helps promote the formation of a socioemotional bond between mother and infant. Other caregivers may also be involved but, for most of human history, the mother has played the key role.

This extensive investment means that the total number of offspring women are able to produce during their reproductive lives is much more limited than that of men. From a strictly biological point of view, the male's contribution to reproduction of a new life requires no more than one "performance" with a fertile female. Moreover, given the abundance of sperm, males' contribution to the reproductive process is relatively less valuable than the much scarcer biological resource invested by females. Even so, males typically are involved in helping to support their offspring in practically all societies and, from the sociobiological point of view, they may be expected to have a strong interest in insuring that their offspring survive, and also that the offspring they help support are indeed their own. Many of the social customs and rules that surround sexual relations may be seen as strategies whereby females can be assured of support in caring for their infants, and males can be assured of their own paternity of the offspring they help support. Like mothers, fathers also have the capacity to form strong socioemotional bonds with their offspring. Under certain

[9] This general point is not refuted by the fact that some individuals develop homosexual rather than heterosexual orientations. For this and all other predispositions that may reflect biological predispositions, there are natural variations among different individuals. Even if we hypothesize that a homosexual orientation is based in one's biological or genetic make-up, the fact remains that a majority of the population develop definite heterosexual orientations, and this point is obviously relevant for long-term species survival.

circumstances males may also contribute to the support of unrelated offspring and may develop positive socioemotional bonds with them, even though their top priority is usually expected to be their own offspring. Even so, the biological investment that males make is clearly not equivalent to that of females.

The differences in the biological resources that females and males invest in the reproduction and nurturing of human life might be expected to influence the way they relate to one another as well as to their offspring. From a purely biological point of view, males' abundant sperm supply might be expected to give rise to a strategy that maximizes their levels of reproductive activity. The strategy for females, in contrast, should be oriented toward increasing the survival chances of the relatively few offspring they are able to produce. In other words, males might be expected to opt for a high **quantity** of offspring while females would be more likely to give priority to high **quality**. Of course, these strategies are not necessarily selected at a conscious level. Instead, for both males and females it is the intense sensual pleasure of sexual activity itself that is likely to be most relevant in terms of providing the motivational energy for sexual intercourse. Everyday life experience shows that pregnancies and births often occur without being consciously intended. In addition, conscious motivations for having a child may involve such goals as simply starting a family, fulfilling the expectations of others, or, in earlier stages of history, making an investment that will eventually pay off in terms of acquiring help with family survival tasks and insuring one's own long-term welfare, especially in old age.

Due to the helplessness and inability of infants to survive on their own, long-term species survival obviously requires that extensive care be provided. Satisfying this basic survival requirement would be enhanced considerably if males and females could be induced to go beyond their sexual relationship to establish long-term partnerships to care for their offspring. Although mothers' motivation for caring for her offspring should be greater because of her greater investment, the proportion of the offspring's genes that are from the father's sperm is equal to that of the mother's egg. This means the father also should have a strong interest in his offspring's survival, though not as great as the mother's in terms of biological investment. While mothers could theoretically care for their offspring without the father, particularly if other adults are available to help (such as extended family members), the child's welfare would no doubt be enhanced if the mother has reliable help—and the father is a good candidate because of his equal genetic relatedness. Both parents have a stronger genetic relationship than any other adult relations. While the contributions of fathers to their offspring have been important throughout history, the economic vulnerability and insecurity that single mothers face in our society today reveal clearly the problems that ensue from the absence or irresponsibility of fathers.

Despite the differences in their investments, we would expect that the reproductive interests of both mothers and fathers could be satisfied through long-term partnerships that would insure females of the male's support in caring for offspring in exchange for the assurance that these offspring are indeed his own. The likelihood of such partnerships is enhanced by the emotional bonds that develop between men and women—bonds that may be based in part on their mutual sexual attraction but that can be strengthened through additional emotional ties that go beyond the erotic level. Despite the distinction often made between a purely sexual attraction and mature love, the fact that men and women share common human characteristics enables them to provide multiple forms of socioemotional support to one another. Such mutual support is valued for its own sake, but it also strengthens their partnership bonds in the process of caring for their offspring, in addition to their interdependence based on material resources they share.

Thus the sociobiological perspective suggests that the biological differences in women's and men's reproductive strategies underlie and help explain the emotional dynamics of their relations to one another. These patterns are reflected in contemporary cultural definitions that shape the expectations men and women have of each other. With the institutionalization of the pattern of monogamous marriage, the cultural ideal is for men and women to form exclusive partnerships based not only on sexual attraction but also the mutual emotional attachment of a deep friendship and a permanent partnership commitment.[10] These cultural ideals link the interests of society and the long-term survival of its population with the interests of the marriage partners and their potential offspring. In practice, the frequent recourse to the culturally endorsed option of divorce indicates that many marriages fail to conform to this cultural ideal. The widespread practice of divorce and remarriage in modern society implies that serial monogamy has become an acceptable but less-preferred cultural alternative to life-long monogamy. However, the pattern of polygamy or polyandry is culturally unacceptable in American and other modern societies—though both have been endorsed and practiced in other cultures.

In contrast to the contemporary sociocultural institutionalization of divorce and remarriage, actual behavioral strategies sometimes include sexual dalliances outside the marital bond. Extramarital relations typically generate higher levels of social disapproval than premarital sexual relations, due no doubt to the potential damage to the marital relationship that they represent. Despite this disapproval, such relationships nevertheless occur—and men are more likely than women to be the guilty party. From a sociobiological perspective, this higher level of male promiscuity is consistent with the biological propensity for a strategy of maximizing their number of offspring—in other words, giving priority to quantity rather than quality. This does not mean that males are consciously aware of this underlying evolutionary dynamic. On a conscious level, their emotional desires and motivations revolve around their desire for the emotional excitement of a new sexual relationship. Such motivations may become particularly salient if marital partners' mutual sexual attraction or expectations should decline over the years, or if males' sexual preferences eventually fail to match their spouses' desires. Women also engage in extramarital affairs for various reasons. This may reflect an effort to satisfy sexual or emotional needs not being met in their marriage, or perhaps to provide additional sexual variety and pleasure in their own lives. Traditionally, however, women tend to engage in extramarital sexual relations less frequently than men, which may be due in large part to the higher costs involved. Without birth control techniques, these

[10] See Liebowitz (1983) for a description of the differences between the biochemical characteristics accompanying momentary sexual attraction versus the enduring attachment of friendship.

costs would include the possibility of pregnancy, plus higher levels of social disapproval. In any case, in contemporary society the widespread availability of birth control techniques has largely uncoupled the sexual pleasure of intercourse from its natural outcome of pregnancy and childbirth. The result is the potential liberation of women from one of the costs of sexual liaisons.

The ideal of a voluntary monogamous marriage based on love and mutual support is not universal, of course. In some societies of the past, marriages were arranged to help establish or stabilize alliances between extended family groups, with sexual attraction and romantic love a secondary consideration. In some cases, there was considerable toleration for meeting sexual needs outside marital bonds, especially for men. In addition, polygamous marriages were normative in some societies, with males expected to have as many wives as they were able to support (along with their children). On a cultural level, the number of wives and their offspring that a male could support could be seen as a source and indicator of status, but the sociobiological perspective would focus instead on how this pattern enables males to increase their opportunities to replicate their genes in their offspring. Polyandry (women having multiple husbands) is still another pattern that has been acceptable in some societies. Such a pattern helps reinforce mothers' long-term bonds with their daughters and enables matriarchal households to maintain control of their property, but it also increases the likelihood that they and their offspring will have multiple sources of support in protecting their interests. These alternatives demonstrate human beings' flexibility in expressing their underlying biological predispositions for developing sexual relations and thereby replenishing the population. They also underscore the importance of prescribed cultural strategies to insure that the members of each new generation are socialized, nourished, and supported until they can function as adults and reproduce themselves.

Parenting Behavior

To bring new offspring into the world is obviously not the same as caring for them until they can care for themselves. Because of the helplessness of infants and young children for several years after birth, it is essential for adults to invest extensive time, effort, and material resources in nourishing and supporting them until they are able to survive as adult members of society. The specific mechanism for insuring that parents (especially mothers) are motivated to invest the necessary resources, time, and energy in caring for their offspring is the emotional reinforcement and satisfaction that they receive in exchange. In addition, cultural ideals that surround parenting and the various social sanctions (approval or disapproval) that parents receive provide additional reinforcement. Indeed, the pattern of caring for one's offspring is so widespread that people easily assume that there must be an in-born parental (or maternal) instinct that is universal in the human species, and that parents who refuse to provide such care must be suffering from some serious mental or emotional deficiencies. Moreover, as with sexual reproduction itself, caring for offspring is not unique to humans with their extensive cultural conditioning; many nonhuman species also exhibit nurturant parenting behavior. For humans, however, the scope of the care that infants need in order to survive, and the length of time for which it is required, are far greater than for other species.

Given the unformed and helpless nature of infants, sociologists emphasize the importance of being born into an already existing social group (usually the family) and learning gradually to participate in that environment through communication. But until they develop some elementary language skills, infants are unable to express their needs except through crying and unsocialized gestures of distress. For parents and other adults, the sound of a crying baby is not pleasant or intrinsically rewarding. Theoretically, it would be possible for parents to respond by leaving the scene, or simply by strangling their baby to death. We naturally recoil at the thought of such responses. Although, unfortunately, there are too many cases of parental neglect and abuse, the more common pattern is for parents to respond as quickly as possible to their baby's distress by providing the appropriate care. This leads to termination of the crying behavior and stimulates responses indicating satisfaction and well-being, which parents (and other adults) find emotionally satisfying and highly reinforcing. We might consider infants' crying as an innate strategy to alert parents (or other adults) to their needs at a stage in life where they are unable to use language to ask for help or to meet their needs on their own. At this stage in life, their crying behavior is not a result of social conditioning (even though human beings eventually learn to cry when it is socially expected). As babies develop into young children they gradually learn how to communicate their needs and wants verbally instead of crying. They also learn through experience how to act in socially appropriate ways to elicit nurturing and other rewarding responses from their parents (or other caregivers) and even other adults in their environment.

Throughout this process, parents experience a sense of emotional satisfaction as they support and nourish their children, and as their children gradually learn to respond in ways that reinforce and motivate the desire to continue providing support and care. These positive exchanges are often interrupted by negative exchanges, of course, from which both parents and their children may learn to change their strategies. Also, there are many variations in the patterns of interaction between parents and their children in different societies and different historical periods, as well as between children and other adults in the community. Quality of care also varies widely, as well as the age at which young people are expected to care for themselves. In modern societies, this period of dependency has been extended far beyond what it was in earlier stages of human history, even though interaction with other adults in the community occurs primarily in school settings and in various extracurricular activities separate from the routine work activities of adults.

The key point from a sociobiological perspective is that the emotional dynamics of the relations between parents (especially mothers) and their offspring involve a primordial level of emotional experience that cannot be adequately explained by cultural conditioning. Although specific parental behaviors may not be genetically programmed, the biological capacity for positive and negative emotional arousal in the context of interacting with their offspring plays a major role in shaping parental behavior in ways that contribute to the survival and well-being of their offspring. In short, parents feel good about themselves when they are able to alleviate their children's frustrations, satisfy their needs and wants, and contribute to their growth and development. Additional emotional reinforcement is provided as parents experience vicariously their pleasure in seeing their children feel secure and happy, and as they receive appreciative responses from them. Thus parents are emotionally reinforced for doing exactly what is required to contribute to long-term species survival. These underlying, biologically based emotional processes are powerfully reinforced by cultural prescriptions ("It is parents' responsibility to care for their children."). In view of the challenges of maintaining the long-term commitment required to rear children successfully, it is not surprising that cultural mandates would encourage and reinforce parenting and child care, or that failure to care for one's children would lead to high levels of social disapproval and other negative sanctions.

Because of the lower level of biological "investments" on the part of males as compared to females, we might expect that cultural reinforcement would be relatively more crucial for fathers than for mothers to sustain their commitments to help support their offspring. But as parents of both genders could testify, the frustrations and disappointments they sometimes experience might tempt them to question whether the satisfactions outweigh the sacrifices. When such feelings emerge, informal reminders of widespread cultural values can help strengthen appropriate parental behaviors. Also, the anticipation of severe negative sanctions for neglecting parental obligations can make the parental sacrifices seem like a lower cost to pay. In addition to the social reinforcement for parenting, the culture also provides many guidelines regarding specific techniques and strategies for child care, and these may vary greatly in different societies or different historical periods.

The high cultural value placed on parental roles can thus be seen as elaborating an underlying biological or genetic predisposition. This does not mean that all of the many cultural expectations associated with child care necessarily reflect specific genetic influences. Also, cultures vary in terms of how strongly they emphasize the obligation to "be fruitful and multiply" as well as in specific parental expectations. A culture that encourages maximum reproduction would presumably reinforce whatever innate predispositions there may be to have large numbers of offspring. In addition to the emotional satisfaction and social approval this provides, in some societies a large number of children may also provide a kind of "social security" for parents during their old age. This was important for a large part of human history, especially before pensions and our government-sponsored Social Security program, even though the human life span was shorter for most of human history than it is today. On the other hand, if large families are culturally discouraged, as in contemporary China's restrictions of one child per family, this should be expected to have an inhibiting effect on motivations to reproduce as much as possible, even though it does not extinguish it.

Natural or random variations may be expected to occur among individuals (both women and men) in their biological propensities with regard to caring for their offspring. The emotional satisfaction women and men experience in caring for offspring may also vary, as well as their tolerance for the frustrations involved. The level of social support and approval for responsible parenting no doubt also varies in different groups, different societies, and different stages of history within a society. As a consequence of these influences, both biological and cultural, parenting behaviors range from those involved in being devoted and loving caregivers to patterns of gross neglect or abuse. Although care for children may involve considerable costs to parents (and sometimes to others as well), offspring who are well nourished and supported are more likely to survive into adulthood and reproduce themselves. Those who refuse their parental obligations may benefit personally by not being burdened with the responsibilities of parenthood but their offspring (if any) would presumably be less likely to survive and reproduce. However, compensation for this natural evolutionary outcome may be provided through social strategies whereby abused or abandoned children are cared for by relatives or adoptive parents, in orphanages, or through other means.

Whether maximum reproduction is beneficial or not for a particular population will depend on its resource base, infant mortality rates, and overall risks to human life from war, famine, disease, natural disasters, and so on. For a large part of human history, high reproductive rates have been important to compensate for such risks. Nevertheless, the overall reproductive success of the human species is clearly evident in long-term population growth and the distribution of humans over almost all parts of the world. In fact, the current global population picture is quite different from what it has been throughout most of history. Many parts of the world are experiencing problems of severe overpopulation because of the reduced infant mortality and increased human life span that have resulted from dramatic medical advances and increases in the food supply over the last few centuries through improved agricultural techniques. This increased food supply does not necessarily undermine the pessimistic prediction by eighteenth century British social theorist Thomas Malthus that growth in the food supply may turn out to be insufficient to keep pace with the exponential expansion of the human population. This would indicate that the long-range survival and welfare of the human species may require the expanded use of cultural techniques to discourage or inhibit our biological propensity to reproduce, particularly in areas characterized by an increasing imbalance between population size and food supply.

The sacrifices that parents make in investing their scarce resources in supporting their children may serve to illustrate one form of altruistic behavior. Although this occurs within the family household, it involves transfers of resources for the benefit of offspring at the expense of their parents. From a sociobiological point of view, the key characteristic of altruism is that it increases the beneficiary's chances for survival at the cost of decreasing the altruist's chances for **individual** survival. Although parents in modern societies probably do not decrease their own survival chances by taking care of their children, they do invest resources that could otherwise be devoted to their own personal well-being and achievements. Also, unlike previous stages of history, the welfare of individuals in their old age is not as dependent on their offspring as in years past. But according to Dawkins' (1976) "selfish gene" perspective, the benefits parents provide their offspring can be seen as selfishness in disguise, since such behavior helps insure that at least one-half of one's own genetic characteristics will survive in one's offspring. This argument would also apply when resources are provided to other relatives as well, since they share part of the same gene pool, but to a lesser degree. Even so, from a more immediate and personal point of view, altruism is manifested when individuals sacrifice their own personal interests for the welfare of others. Such behavior often goes beyond one's offspring and kin. In the next section we will look at the long-range benefits of altruism beyond the kin network, along with other social processes involving both cooperation and competition.

Altruism and Cooperation Within Groups

Participation in cooperative groups extending beyond family and kin can readily be explained in terms of the exchange and rational choice perspectives (Chap. 7). The benefits individuals receive from such behavior may be evaluated not only for their consequences for the survival and well-being of the cooperating partners and their families, but also in terms of enhancing their "inclusive fitness" and chances for reproductive success (Trivers, 1985, 2002:3–55). In addition, human beings sometimes engage in altruistic behavior, especially toward ingroup members, even when there are no expectations of a reciprocating benefit. Although such behavior may be viewed in exchange theory terms as leading to status, power, or social approval, genuine altruism is not consciously motivated by such benefits. The sociobiological perspective would lead us to look for unintended benefits that accrue to altruists or their kin that enhance their chances for reproductive success, including those deriving from group membership and the positive reputation altruism earns.

As was the case with reproductive and parenting behavior, cooperative and altruistic behaviors can both be seen as reflecting some form of social bond. In explaining the underlying mechanisms that motivate and reinforce such behaviors, it is important to recognize the crucial importance of emotional exchanges as a generalized source of positive and negative reinforcement that can shape a wide variety of behaviors. In Maryanski and Turner's (1992) analysis, human beings' innate capacity for emotional arousal, plus their sensitivity to one another's emotional reactions, are crucial in motivating them to behave in ways that stimulate positive reactions from others and avoid negative reactions. Because of the emotional reinforcement received through their socioemotional bonds, people are motivated to engage in behaviors that will lead to the formation and maintenance of such bonds. The high level of social approval people receive when they show concern for the welfare of others helps reinforce such behavior. This sensitivity to one another's reactions in the context of primary groups also enables people to influence one another's behavior as they cooperate in meeting their needs and insuring their group's survival. In short, despite the strong individualistic propensities that are built into human nature, on an emotional level human beings find it highly rewarding to receive positive reactions from others that indicate inclusion, acceptance, and respect. As a result they are motivated to engage in behaviors that earn these rewards. Even in the absence of specific cooperative tasks to perform, emotional attachments are often expressed through various ritualistic exchanges, as illustrated, for example, by the exchange of greetings among colleagues at the beginning of the work day. In addition to these ritualistic expressions, however, the strength and importance of socioemotional bonds may also be manifested in various forms of cooperative or altruistic behavior. This may sometimes include a willingness to engage in costly or risky behavior for the sake of the group's survival, particularly in conflicts with other groups. Those who engage in such behaviors in military activity earn the prestigious status of hero, and their behavior is publicly celebrated as a model for others to emulate.

According to the sociobiological perspective, the innate emotional characteristics of human beings may be seen as having evolved because of the long-term survival advantages they confer. The attunement of people to one another through their emotional exchanges underlie all forms of social relations, including kin as well as larger groups whose members cooperate in adapting to their environment and defending it against predators and enemies. Emotional sensitivity to others and their needs, particularly among ingroup members, often leads to altruistic behavior as well, and the positive reactions of others to such behavior may be seen as helping to reinforce it and also idealizing it as a model for others. In extending our sociobiological analysis of altruism beyond one's family and kin network, the "kin selection" model must be distinguished from the "group selection" model. As implied by the name, the "kin selection" model involves altruism toward one's offspring and other relatives. The "group selection" model, in contrast, involves altruism toward fellow-members of the groups in which individuals are involved beyond their family and kinship circle. Even though by definition altruism is not necessarily consciously motivated at a conscious level by an expectation of rewards, it certainly leads to high levels of social approval from fellow members of the group, plus gratitude from beneficiaries.

Altruism is not necessarily a one-way street, however. The altruist's situation may change in the future so that he or she is in need of help. Thus a beneficiary of altruistic behavior may eventually have an opportunity to repay his or her benefactor, even though this may not have been anticipated by the original altruist. Other people, too, are more likely to provide aid to those in need who have previously established a positive reputation for their helpfulness. We generally feel good about assisting those who have helped us in the past, as well as others who are known for their generosity. On the other hand, we are probably less likely to aid those who have a reputation of refusing help to those in need. In contrast to the primary emphasis of exchange theory, however, these patterns do not result primarily from rational calculation; instead, they reflect motivations that are grounded in people's emotional identification with one another. The sociobiological perspective would lead us to anticipate that groups in which a high level of altruism develops, whether reciprocal or one-way, are likely to enjoy a survival advantage over groups where such patterns do not emerge. Such behaviors help increase group cohesiveness and strengthen members' willingness to work together cooperatively, thereby improving their ability to adapt successfully to their environment and to respond to threats which may emerge. Long-range survival chances are thereby enhanced. It should be noted, however, that altruism in the sociobiological perspective does not necessarily require subjective feelings of empathy or altruistic sentiments. Instead, all that is required is that such behaviors involve costs or risks to the altruist but benefit others in the group (see Barash, 1977:132–169; E. O. Wilson, 1978:155–175). Even so, the likelihood of altruistic behavior is increased by socioemotional bonds between altruists and beneficiaries, and such behavior is reinforced as well by the social approval received from other members of the group.

In earlier stages of human evolution the groups that benefited from their members' altruism to fellow-members were small primary groups of hunters and gatherers. Over the long course of evolutionary history, however, the socioemotional bonds that led members to identify with their particular group were extended to larger and larger groups, particularly as networks of functional interdependence expanded with the growth in the size and complexity of society. Moreover, through the process of cultural elaboration, the underlying emotional propensity for altruistic behavior beyond one's own group can be encouraged by abstract moral values that are reinforced through cultural ideologies and symbols that individuals internalize. ("It is more blessed to give than to receive.")

Despite the appeal of moral values encouraging altruism beyond the level of particular ingroups, relations between groups are typically dominated by the efforts of each group to promote its own welfare. Even so, cooperative relations may be extended beyond one's own group, based on the benefits anticipated from such relations. In Robert Axelrod's (1984) model of the evolution of cooperative behavior, it is not even necessary for individuals to develop positive sentiments toward one another, or even to be consciously aware of how their independent actions are mutually beneficial. The individualism of Axelrod's model is consistent with the social exchange and rational choice perspectives in which people and groups develop mutually beneficial exchanges in pursuit of their individual and collective goals. Although emotional bonds are not essential for cooperative exchanges to be established, such exchanges are more likely when shared moral commitments provide a foundation for mutual trust. In contrast to these rational choice forms of exchange, patterns of symbiotic interdependence may also develop that require neither rational choice calculations nor socioemotional bonds, and these also may affect a group's chances for long-term survival.

Regardless of their underlying motivational dynamics—whether grounded in socioemotional bonds, rational choice contracts, or unconscious symbiotic relations—the basic argument from the sociobiological perspective is that cooperative and interdependent relations (whether planned or otherwise) may enhance prospects for long-range survival. Populations in which such patterns are widely developed are likely to have higher levels of individual survival and reproductive success than those in which patterns of cooperation fail to develop. This argument is consistent with everyday observations that cohesive groups in which people work together cooperatively tend to be more successful in accomplishing collective goals and surviving than groups characterized by mutual suspicion and hostility.

Competition and Conflict

Conflict, competition, and aggression are also part of the picture, in addition to reciprocal altruism and cooperation. Such patterns may be expected to differ when they occur **within** groups as opposed to **between** groups.[11] Competition and conflict between groups can readily be illustrated by the struggles of rival urban street gangs or of hostile societies to control particular territories or resources, or of different groups to establish dominance over other groups so as to control their behavior. Within groups, competition and conflict can be seen as providing a mechanism for establishing a dominance hierarchy (or "pecking order") within the group, especially when members are in the same age cohort and appear initially to be roughly equal. Competition over territory or dominance is common among other species as well. In addition, conflict can be seen in the aggressive actions of predators against prey of a different species. Among both humans and nonhumans, competition and conflict are more common for males than females. This does not mean that a propensity for aggression or conflict is lacking in females, especially when she or her dependent offspring are threatened by predators. Both between groups and within groups, competition and conflict among human beings often involve issues of honor and reputation. Between groups, the goal is the honor and reputation of the group, while within groups the goal would be the status of its members.

Status Competition and Dominance Hierarchies Within Groups

Dominance hierarchies within groups emerge through competition among their members. The outcome for the group is that dominant members acquire power that can be used to prevent or settle internal conflicts and to mobilize group members to work together in the struggle to achieve collective goals, such as honor and territorial defense.[12] However, it would be a meaningless victory to achieve dominance in a group if its members subsequently disperse or are conquered by a rival group. This means that the winners in the competitive struggle will need to shift priorities from achieving status and dominance within the group to insuring the group's survival. This may involve protecting its members and promoting their well-being. Dominant individuals in human groups vary greatly in this regard, but winners in the competitive struggle for dominance soon learn that earning members' respect and loyalty and gaining their compliance is more likely when their actions help insure their members' security and well-being. Such patterns of leadership are often reinforced by widespread cultural values, but they are seen in the sociobiological perspective as grounded in the biological and genetic features of human nature as reflected in the group formation process.

---

[11] This sociobiological contrast between within-group versus between-group conflict can be compared to Lewis Coser's analysis of the social functions of conflict, discussed earlier.

[12] This notion that dominance hierarchies enable collective action may be compared to Peter Blau's theory of the emergence of power structures that was discussed in an earlier chapter. Blau's emphasis, however, was more on the ability of leaders to earn legitimacy by being able to reward group members rather than by threatening or coercing them through displays of raw power.

Over the long course of evolutionary history, success in the competitive struggle of males for status and dominance within their groups provides not only the reward of high prestige and dominance but also greater access to sexually attractive females. Females themselves are more likely to be attracted to dominant males rather than to the losers in this status game. Their success in forming a sexual partnership with a dominant male will depend in part on whether the group practices monogamy, polygamy, or polyandry, as well as on the sex ratio of the group. The situation in some nonhuman species where dominant males drive their competitors out of the group and thereby gain unrestricted sexual access to all of the females obviously differs from human societies that practice monogamy. However, in human societies, females' attentiveness to the ranking of potential sexual partners can be explained in sociobiological terms as a result of concerns with insuring male support of their offspring. This does not mean that females are consciously motivated by this underlying concern in their assessment of potential partners, just as males are not necessarily consciously motivated by calculating the maximum number of offspring they can produce. Even so, the strategies females employ in attempting to attract the most highly ranked and desirable sexual partner give rise to competition among them, just as males tend to compete among themselves in seeking to attract the most desirable females. The ultimate outcome in monogamous groups is that the pair bonds that are formed involve males and females who are roughly equal in terms of status ranking. The patterns of sexual pairing that result from these competitive processes are related to the overall internal ranking system of family groups within a society and result ultimately in the reproduction of offspring whose life chances vary greatly, mirroring their parents' differential distribution in the society's status hierarchy. Moreover, the pattern of monogamy may itself be seen as limiting male competition and promoting a kind of reproductive democracy.

Tendencies for aggression, conflict, and competition within a group or society may either by encouraged or discouraged by the culture. These tendencies may be expressed in the struggles of rivals to outdo one another in some type of performance that is important for the welfare of group members, or that expresses commitment to the group. Thus, for example, young males whose strength and fighting skills enable them to achieve dominance among their peers may subsequently play an important role in defending the group from external threats or settling internal conflicts. However, competition and conflict may be expected to be somewhat restrained and regulated within a group in which there are also widespread patterns of reciprocal altruism and cooperation and a high level of solidarity. There are large variations among societies in terms of the cultural rules and institutional mechanisms whereby biologically or genetically based behavioral predispositions such as aggression are regulated and controlled. Societies often seek to eliminate blatant and disruptive forms of aggressiveness and violence and to channel the underlying biological predispositions for such behavior in constructive ways such as competitive sports or academic contests.

In explaining how the emergence of dominance hierarchies within groups may enhance its welfare, the sociobiological perspective is largely consistent with social exchange and rational choice theory. However, sociobiology contrasts with the rational choice perspective in that group members' emotions and behavior are explained in terms of underlying genetic and biological predispositions rather than rational calculation of costs and rewards. Moreover, the transformation of dominance hierarchies into legitimate authority structures involves a process of cultural elaboration whereby the development of beliefs and ideologies provides support for the differential distribution of power in exchange for the benefits of group membership.

War and Peace in Intergroup Relations

As suggested above, patterns of aggression, competition, and conflict **between** groups can also be analyzed in terms of their long-range evolutionary effects. According to the evolutionary argument from sociobiology, aggressive policies may enhance survival advantages for certain groups under certain circumstances, particularly if they are able to achieve a position of dominance over other groups. By controlling other groups and exploiting their resources, it is possible to magnify a group's reproductive success and support an even larger population. On the other hand, a group's long-term welfare may sometimes best be served by strategies to adapt to a subordinate position instead of engaging in a struggle that ends in failure. The historical record includes numerous accounts of how different groups and societies have adapted to one another. Depending on their relative strength, they may opt to engage in mutual threats and intense conflict in attempting to establish dominance, focus on defense strategies to resist being threatened or subordinated, struggle to expand their territory and resource base, concentrate on protecting their territorial borders, or seek to avoid arousing the hostility of larger and more aggressive groups. Relations among different groups and different societies are always at least potentially volatile, and the long-range struggle for survival often leads to changes in status and dominance hierarchies. Former enemies sometimes become allies in responding to threats from still other groups. Alliances frequently shift as groups (or societies) adjust to changes in the balance of power and changing levels of resources.

In addition, as an alternative to conflict, intergroup relations may emerge that are based on mutually beneficial exchanges and intergroup social ties, including trade relations, political alliances, and various types of formal or informal cultural exchanges. The increased levels of functional interdependence that result have the potential for improving the welfare of all of the groups involved in this process. But unfortunately, the highly increased interdependence of the modern world has not yet resulted in a decrease in antagonism and hostilities among different peoples. Instead, increased global interdependence seems to have increased the risk that human survival itself can be threatened by the escalation of conflicts on a global level.

At this point in human history, the continued possibility for threats from other groups means that territorial defense should still be seen as an important "functional requirement" of societies. Even when different societies are roughly equal in power, they sometimes engage in strategic probes to identify weaknesses in other societies that they can exploit to strengthen their own position. Societies with more abundant resources, a larger population, higher levels of social cohesion, or other advantages are often able to establish dominance with minimal overt conflict, since weaker societies soon become aware of the futility of resistance. These weaker societies thus settle for the best deal they can get so as to avoid the higher costs of overt conflict and inevitable defeat. But dominant societies are nevertheless vulnerable, partly because their dominance may tempt other societies to devote themselves to developing new strategies to increase their strength or to form coalitions to launch campaigns to seek to bring them down. Societies that insist on pacifist policies become vulnerable to attack by societies pursuing policies of aggression. The risks of unilateral disarmament are widely recognized, at least at our current stage of social and cultural evolution. Nevertheless, even if a certain level of aggressiveness has been beneficial for long-term survival in the past, the sociobiological perspective cannot be used to argue that a policy of conflict and aggression is always beneficial, not even to the victors—particularly in a world in which advances in weapons technology make possible the annihilation of humanity.

Whatever patterns human beings adopt with regard to offensive or defensive conflict and competition between groups, the predisposition for such patterns can be seen as grounded in the biological "raw material" that has emerged over the long course of evolutionary history. These propensities can be either reinforced or inhibited by the prevailing culture, and history provides innumerable examples of how cultural values can be elaborated that encourage "making peace" as well as "making war." These issues of war and peace are of greater urgency for human survival in our time than at any previous period of human history. The availability of nuclear and other weapons of mass destruction means that the risks of continuing to resort to warfare to resolve conflicts when negotiations and peaceful resolution fail could conceivably result in the destruction of the human species and the ultimate loss of its long-term evolutionary struggle for survival. The vision of a world-wide human family that is idealized in the culture of universalistic religions contrasts sharply with the sociobiological emphasis on the struggles of different groups for dominance and long-term survival. However, religion may also be viewed from the perspective of sociobiology.

Religion and Sociobiological Evolution

Even when people's motivations and impulses clearly reflect underlying biological characteristics and genetic predispositions, cultural influences are crucial for shaping the way they are expressed. In addition, various aspects of culture can also be analyzed in terms of their relevance for the long-range survival of the group or society in which they are developed. These considerations can even be applied to religion or other types of belief systems. Since religious beliefs are often closely tied to moral values that regulate and control many aspects of people's behavior and social relations, such beliefs and values should be expected to influence the odds of reproductive success and long-range survival.

In addition to exploring topics such as aggression, sex, and altruism, Edward O. Wilson's (1978:155–217) sociobiological perspective on "human nature" portrays the long-range evolutionary benefits of religion and the propensity for altruism and hope that it encourages. Also relevant is Richard Alexander's (1987) analysis of moral systems as strategies for dealing with conflicts of interest and promoting and preserving systems of indirect reciprocity within groups. Systems of morality may become highly idealized as a result of efforts to encourage behavior that benefits others or the group as a whole, despite the individual costs that may be involved. Processes that promote commitment to the group and conformity to its moral norms may be crucial for long-term success in competing with other groups. Because of the costs that are involved, however, some individuals may be reluctant to apply the same ideal rules to themselves that they do to others. Even so, these ideals may shape and reinforce people's behavior in ways that provide benefits to others and help insure group survival, even though patterns of conformity may be less than some group members might desire. In Brant Wenegrat's (1990) analysis, religious beliefs contribute to the evolution of beneficial strategies that meet human needs for supportive social attachments, regulate their sexual competition, promote mutually beneficial cooperation, and encourage altruistic behavior.

Davis Sloan Wilson (2002) pointed out that adaptation occurs at the group level as well as at the individual level. Applying this notion to religious groups, he showed how their beliefs and normative patterns promote actions that contribute to group survival by encouraging members to see their group as a kind of organism, like a family or community, with high levels of organized interdependence. To the extent that people internalize this perception, their willingness to incur the costs of supporting their group is enhanced. As a result, the survival changes of group members and their inclusive fitness is increased.

In addition to developing and reinforcing normative ideals and behavioral guidelines involving cooperative or altruistic behavior, religious beliefs may also be relevant to long-term survival because of their capacity to provide a sense of psychological security and hope for the future, particularly when linked with conformity to their moral ideals. Specific beliefs and moral codes vary for different religions, and their effects on people's motivations and behavior would need to be examined in particular cases to assess their long-term evolutionary significance. The key point from the sociobiological perspective, however, is that the propensity for religious faith, hope, and morality may well be seen as having been selected through the evolutionary process because of the long-term survival advantages that it confers. The appeal of this argument can be appreciated when we observe, on a more limited and short term basis, the beneficial effects of an optimistic religious faith and a hopeful and positive attitude on individuals' physical, mental, and emotional health and their ability to cope with the frustrations and disappointments they face.

Some beliefs and moral ideals may have a more beneficial effect than others, however, and in some cases beliefs may be developed that actually decrease the odds of individual survival and reproductive success. For example, if a religious group, or a society, were to require celibacy or suicidal forms of terrorism among a large majority of its members, it is difficult to imagine that survival chances would thereby be enhanced. On the other hand, if a limited number of people engage in self-sacrificing behavior, this may serve to provide dramatic examples that inspire others to conform to normative ideals in less extreme ways and with less serious negative individual consequences. Moreover, celibacy norms among some segments of the population may be beneficial in controlling the population size so it does not exceed the carrying capacity of its resource base, even though those following such norms obviously would not reproduce. Overall, therefore, the occasional appearance of genetic predispositions that might motivate self-sacrifice or celibacy instead of reproduction would not be expected to be transmitted to future generations and so would not be expected to be widespread in the population. It must be remembered that biological predispositions within a population vary, as do cultural influences. As a result, people may be expected to make a wide range of choices, even with regard to such basic issues as willingness to take risks or to refrain from sexual activity.

In view of our increased level of global interdependence, it seems plausible to argue that the prospects for the long-term survival of humanity in our time would be increased by universalistic religious beliefs and values that are grounded in a deep appreciation for the shared humanity of all people, regardless of their cultural differences. This goes counter to the long-term pattern whereby antagonistic relations between ingroups and outgroups have often been justified and reinforced through particularlistic forms of religion. However, in addition to the particularism of some of their beliefs, all of the universalistic religions also include abstract ideals regarding our common humanity. In some ways, it is conceivable that these ideals could be manifested more fully now than at any time in the past because of our high level of global communication and interdependence. The prospects for our long-term survival would no doubt be enhanced if the members of different societies throughout the world were to give greater emphasis to these universalistic themes and values. This commitment to universalistic values does not mean that any one group should feel entitled to engage in violence or coercion to try to enforce uniformity on its own terms. Instead, the goal must be to engage in dialogue across different religious and cultural traditions to try to discover the underlying similarities among enduring beliefs and worldviews that on the surface may appear highly divergent. The development of this cultural ideal of global dialogue could prove to be crucial for our survival.

The basic logic of sociobiology would lead us to expect that religious beliefs and moral codes which are less effective in promoting inclusive fitness and reproductive success would gradually be replaced by beliefs and moral values that are more effective.[13] The elimination of particular beliefs and moral codes in the evolutionary process could occur through the elimination of groups carrying these cultural patterns, or it could occur if a group eventually rejects these patterns and replaces them with an alternative system of beliefs and morals. The key point is that it is the

[13] Sociologist of religion Christian Smith rejects the sociobiological explanation of religion and morality but nevertheless regards propensities for morality and belief to be fundamental characteristics of the human species (see C. Smith, 2003:33–43).

beliefs and values themselves that either survive or are eliminated in the evolutionary process. This issue is not the same as whether or not the individuals or groups that carry such beliefs and moral codes survive or not. This distinction is important in helping us understand the dynamics of cultural evolution as a process that is separate from biological evolution.

Sociobiology and Cultural Evolution

Cultural patterns of all types (beliefs, moral values, normative standards, technical skills, and everyday customs) are transmitted to each new generation through the socialization process, not through genetic codes. Even so, cultural strategies must always operate within the parameters of the biological features of human nature. In the long run, behaviors that are prescribed or proscribed by the culture cannot be grossly inconsistent with human beings' biological characteristics, at least for most of the population. Although certain religious groups may encourage fasting or prohibit sexual relations for certain people or on certain occasions, for example, neither long-term fasting nor celibacy could be required for the majority of people if the group or society is to survive. Similarly, some kinds of cultural values may encourage people to long for freedom from the responsibilities of working and rearing offspring; however, no population could survive if its members refused to participate in productive activities or abandoned their offspring to fend for themselves. Whether or not individuals are aware of these underlying biological imperatives, the survival of the human species requires that cultural patterns be developed to pay the biological dues.

In view of the obvious importance of culture in explaining the specific details of human behavior patterns, sociobiologist Richard Dawkins proposed a new concept—"meme"—to refer to a unit of culture that can be analyzed according to the same type of evolutionary principles as biological "genes" (see Dawkins, 1976:203–215). Just as chance variations are important in biological evolutions, random variations in various elements of culture (cultural "memes") can be seen as providing a pool of alternative strategies from which the successful ones are selected over the long course of cultural evolution. The process of selection involves the repetition of successful behaviors and their diffusion and imitation within a population–a process that involves various forms of cultural encoding and communication. Individuals tend to repeat behaviors that are successful or rewarding. Eventually, the behavior in question may become established as a rule or norm (or "meme" in Dawkins' terms) that is routinely transmitted to members of the next generation in the socialization process.

The concept of "coevolution" is sometimes used to highlight the way biological and cultural evolution are interrelated (Durham, pp. 428–448 in Caplan, ed., 1978; see also D. Campbell, 1975). Because of the strong influence of cultural conditioning in shaping actual behavior, it is theoretically possible for cultural evolution to have long-term feedback effects on the genetic code itself. However, the time frame involved in genetic/biological evolution is not nearly as rapid as cultural evolution, and so such feedback effects would be difficult to establish. Moreover, because of the greater short-term adaptability and flexibility represented in cultural evolution, human beings have been able to expand to new environments without "waiting," as it were, for mutations or random changes in their genetic code. In contrast to genetic codes, the component "parts" of cultural codes and the linkages between them are socially constructed and symbolically mediated, and the time frame required to evaluate their outcomes is not nearly as long as in biological and genetic evolution.

It is difficult to use the sociobiological perspective to develop predictive hypotheses to be tested empirically with human populations. The time frame involved in human evolution encompasses thousands of years. Apparent short-term exceptions that do not fit the sociobiological model, such as the widespread practice of birth control or female rejection of maternal roles for occupational careers, are "explained away" as short-term aberrations that are not necessarily significant in the long run. Sociobiologists might predict that in the long run such patterns as these will be selected out or eliminated (as dysfunctional patterns presumably have been in the past), due to the failure of those who follow such patterns to reproduce. On the other hand, the declines in infant mortality rates in industrial societies and the increases in life span that have resulted from modern medical and agricultural technology may mean that cultural strategies to limit reproduction may now be more beneficial than the continuation of the historic pattern of high levels of reproduction. This would suggest that human beings' ultimate survival and welfare may require the development of policies that go counter to long-term biological predispositions. In any case, short-term fluctuations in birth rates or other behaviors are not necessarily considered relevant for evaluating the long-term implications of the sociobiological model.

Despite its controversial features with regard to the nature versus nurture debate, the sociobiological perspective reminds us that human behavior is in part a product of our biological human nature and genetic heritage as well as our cultural heritage. In evaluating its relevance for sociological analysis, it is important to remember that social and cultural systems are not closed systems but receive input from the biological level (as well as from the physical environment itself). Thus the genetic code may be seen as influencing people's underlying behavioral predispositions and motivations as well as being related in complex ways to the cultural systems that govern the specific ways these motivations are expressed.

Summary

The analytical distinctions between biological, social, and cultural systems may be useful for academic study, but to understand people's social behavior it is essential to see these systems as interpenetrating and influencing one another. The overall goal of this chapter involved a shift in the focus of attention from the different levels of the social world itself to the way underlying biological predispositions or propensities may be seen as affecting individuals' social behavior and cultural patterns. This chapter began with a brief overview of the early influence and subsequent repudiation of social Darwinism in American sociology. The strong emphasis of social Darwinism on the notion that progress occurs as a "natural" outcome of the struggle for survival and the survival of the fittest was used at that time as ideological support for the development of a *laissez-faire* economic system, in which the notion of government reforms to deal with the resulting social problems was widely rejected. On the other hand, however, some of those influenced by the evolutionary perspective of social Darwinism saw the emergence of the human mind and the application of human intelligence in social reform efforts as an integral part of this long-range evolutionary process. But largely because of its ideological implications regarding the superiority of some groups over others, plus its support of unregulated and exploitative competition, social Darwinism in America lost influence, and sociologists subsequently tended to reject explanations of social processes in terms of biological factors.

The picture changed for some sociologists with the emergence of sociobiology in the last few decades of the twentieth century. Although this perspective is also an evolutionary theory that emphasizes the biological and genetic foundations of social behavior, it is not a theory involving strong biological determinism, and it provides ample room for biological and cultural diversity. In fact, because of the undeveloped character of genetically programmed behavioral responses that would enable individuals to adapt successfully to their environment, sociobiology emphasizes the importance of the human beings' biological capabilities for creating and learning culturally defined patterns of environmental adaptation through the cooperative relations they establish.

Long-term species survival obviously depends on human beings' reproductive success. Thus a major emphasis in sociobiology is the biological underpinnings that motivate human beings' sexual behavior and patterns of caring for offspring. Gender relations and family forms can be examined within this perspective with respect to their implications for human reproduction and long-term species survival. In understanding reproductive behavior, it is important to keep in mind the differences between females and males and the various ways these biological differences are reflected in their relations with one another and with their offspring.

Numerous other patterns of human behavior were also examined in terms of their long-range survival advantages for the human species. We looked briefly at the following: altruism toward kin and other ingroup members; ingroup processes of cooperation, status competition, and establishment of dominance hierarchies; patterns of conflict and accommodation in intergroup relations, and the development of systems of religious belief promoting hope, social solidarity, and moral behavior. Various aspects of culture may also be evaluated in terms of their consistency or inconsistency with biological or genetic behavioral predispositions and their long-term evolutionary significance for group and species survival.

The conditions of contemporary life present different types of survival challenges from those existing throughout most of the long evolutionary history of the human species. Specifically, global overpopulation pressures and the development of weapons of mass destruction represent serious challenges that make the development of creative new forms of cultural adaptation extremely urgent in our time. In view of the increased levels of global interdependence that have evolved over the past several years, cultural innovations leading to increased dialogue and mutual understanding among different societies are more crucial for our future survival and well-being than ever before. In the next chapter we look in more detail at some aspects of the dynamics of cultural systems.

Questions for Study and Discussion

1. What kinds of differences have you observed in the willingness of mothers versus fathers to sacrifice their own personal needs and interests for the sake of their offspring? How would you explain these differences? Do you think that parents' own career goals sometimes undermine their effectiveness as parents? Explain. How do the variations in parental investments affect their children's well-being and chances for future success?
2. Compare and contrast the kin selection model and the group selection model of altruistic behavior. Also, how would you expect the group selection model to be manifested in small groups involving face-to-face relations as opposed to large groups, particularly in terms of socioemotional bonding, moral sentiments, and functional interdependence?
3. Drawing on your own experience and/or observations of at least two groups, explain the process whereby dominance hierarchies are established and maintained. Also, to what extent have you observed those in positions of dominance demonstrate their concerns for the welfare of their group and its members?
4. From a sociobiological perspective, how can religion be seen as contributing to individuals' survival and well-being as well as the survival of larger groups? Also, despite the fact that religion has often been used to justify conflict between different groups, do you think that religion has the potential to promote peaceful and cooperative relations among different groups? Explain.
5. Would you agree or disagree that the sociobiological perspective should be incorporated in sociological efforts to explain human behavior? Explain. What specific aspects of human behavior seem to you to reflect some form of biological predisposition? Also, what specific cultural rules or regulations seem to you to run counter to our natural biological predispositions? Explain.

Chapter 19
The Dynamics of Cultural Systems

Despite the focus in the last chapter on the biological underpinnings of human behavior, it is virtually impossible to analyze people's behavior or the social world at any level without reference to the formative influence of the cultural environment. Although cultural, social, and biological systems involve different levels of analysis, none of these systems is isolated from the others. All three systems should be seen in terms of mutual dependence and interpenetration, with elements and dynamics of each system being incorporated into, and having profound effects on, the dynamics of the others. The goal in this chapter is to focus primarily on the cultural level.

Sociological analyses of culture have expanded greatly in recent years (Crane, 1994). Our overview in this chapter is highly selective. We will begin with a brief section that is intended to help establish continuity with the sociobiological emphasis of the previous chapter. We will then focus in more detail on three distinct dimensions of culture—cognitive, behavioral, and moral. Following is a list of the topics to be covered, along with the names of the specific theorists whose contributions will be reviewed for each area:

- Cultural learning and human survival—This brief section will provide an overview of anthropologist Paul Bohannan's analysis of how culture builds on human beings' innate ability to learn and enables them to survive, though culture may sometimes inhibit the search for more effective survival strategies.
- Human agency and the morphogenetic process of cultural development—This section will review Margaret Archer's perspective on how cultural ideas and beliefs reflect the efforts of human beings to achieve cognitive consistency in their cognitions and meaning systems.
- Culture as civilized behavioral self-control—Our goal in this section will be to review the historical analysis provided by Norbert Elias to link the origins and diffusion of civilized manners with the collapse of feudalism and the growth of centralized state power.
- Culture as an arena for cognitive and moral struggle—In this section we will highlight Jeffrey Alexander's perspective on how cultural meanings can be analyzed in terms of binary oppositions between good and evil, or right and wrong. These crucial cultural distinctions are deeply connected to the social processes

D.P. Johnson, *Contemporary Sociological Theory: An Integrated Multi-Level Approach.*

involved in defining ingroups and outgroups, and thus are related in a fundamental way to both individual and collective identity.

Cultural Learning and Human Survival

The innate ability of human beings to create and learn culture, particularly in the context of primary groups, is a major emphasis in anthropologist Paul Bohannan's (1995) analysis of the way culture "works." As he put it, "Human beings are hardwired to learn culture; nevertheless all culture is learned. Not a single piece of culture anywhere is itself hardwired into people. Human choices are made, within the limits of hardwired reflexes, on the basis of the biological capacities to choose and act, as well as on the culture-based capacity to reason" (Bohannan, 1995:9). Culture in his perspective includes not only the tools people construct but also the shared meanings that enable them to understand one another and cooperate in adapting to their environment.

Bohannan pointed out that the inborn sociable nature of human beings is crucial for the development and transmission of culture, and also that cultural learning is essential for human development. However, consistent with the theoretical arguments from sociobiology reviewed in the last chapter, some aspects of face-to-face relationships in human groups are comparable to some nonhuman species. These include establishment of dominance hierarchies and patterns of territorial defense, kinship structures and strategies of nurturing the young, specialization of tasks (or a division of labor) that is often based primarily on sex and age, and cooperation in accomplishing basic survival goals (Bohannan, 1995:29–36). In contrast to nonhuman species, however, all of these patterns are culturally organized.

Beyond the level of elementary face-to-face relationships, Bohannan (1995:37–45) emphasizes how larger and more complex groups are based on human beings' capabilities for more elaborate forms of cultural learning. These include the development of contract relations, whereby people are able to expand the level of cooperation beyond their circle of personal relations, plus the creation of social roles that are separate from individual persons. Additional aspects of larger social systems that require extensive cultural learning include social ranking systems, property rules, markets, social networking, and the emergence of mass society and public relations. Cultural systems themselves also evolve, sometimes leading to "cultural traps" and "lock-ins" that may inhibit the search for more adaptive forms of innovation and create the potential for major disaster in changed environmental conditions (Bohannan, 1995:117–131; 173–186). An example of what many people would probably regard as a cultural trap is the way our high reliance on automobiles contributes to such varied negative consequences as traffic congestion, air pollution, and global warning — plus the political vulnerability resulting from heavy reliance on oil imports. Because cultural evolution exhibits its own particular dynamics, it is certainly not feasible to try to analyze all aspects of culture as grounded in biological or genetic characteristics. Instead, as revealed in the following perspectives, an adequate understanding of culture requires it to be analyzed at its own level.

Cultural Morphogenesis: Consistencies and Contradictions in Knowledge and Beliefs in Margaret Archer's Perspective

The role of human agency in the creation and the reproduction or elaboration of culture is a major emphasis of British sociologist Margaret Archer's (1988) cultural analysis. She takes what we might call a "cognitive" or "intellectualist" approach to culture, focusing primarily on the extent to which different beliefs and forms of knowledge are **logically** consistent or inconsistent. In contrast to this cultural level analysis, she treats the level of sociocultural interaction in terms of **causal** relations whereby people influence one another with regard to such beliefs and knowledge and in other areas as well. Archer insists that these levels are analytically distinct and may vary independently, particularly in terms of how well integrated they are. Integration at the cultural level involves logical consistency and coherence, while integration at the level of sociocultural interaction involves social consensus.

Archer contrasts her position of **analytical dualism** with other theoretical perspectives that she sees as "conflating" or blurring the differences between these levels. "Downward conflation" involves the implication that sociological integration is based on a high level of consensus reflecting the overall unity and logical coherence of the cultural system (Archer, 1988:25–45). This emphasis is illustrated in Pitirim Sorokin's argument regarding the way the dominant cultural mentality of a society governs its institutional structures, as well as in Talcott Parsons' subsequent emphasis on widely shared value orientations as the major source of social and institutional integration.[1] In adopting this emphasis, both Sorokin and Parsons were consistent with anthropologists who had earlier emphasized the high level of sociocultural integration of the non-Western societies they studied.

In contrast to downward conflation that emphasizes the governing effects of culture on the social system, "upward conflation" for Archer involves the argument that the coherence and unity of culture is in effect a "manipulated consensus" that serves the interests of the dominant groups in society (Archer, 1988:46–71). Culture in this perspective does not have its own independent influence but instead is developed in ways that support the goals and interests of the ruling class. This type of argument is evident in various neo-Marxist perspectives that emphasize how ideological orientations help reinforce and maintain the existing power structures of society. Archer points out that Gramsci's explanation of cultural hegemony and Habermas's emphasis on technocratic instrumental control both illustrate upward conflation.

Archer also criticizes intermediate forms of "central conflation" in which the culture and patterns of sociocultural interaction are linked together so tightly that it is impossible to show how they may vary independently or exert mutual influence on each other (Archer, 1988:72–96). A major example she provides that we examined in some detail (Chap. 17) is Giddens' structuration theory. Although Giddens' primary focus was at the social structural level, his treatment of language and shared

[1] Pitirim Sorokin's analysis of long-range cycles of "cultural mentalities" was reviewed briefly in Chap. 3 as part of the story of the development of American sociology.

knowledge in the "structuration" process also involved the cultural level. However, Archer believed that Giddens saw these elements of culture as constitutive of the social structure and thus of the interaction process itself. The same critique is applied to Bauman's (1973) analysis of culture as "praxis." For Archer, such a designation suggests that cultural patterns can be identified only in the way that are implemented in the ordering of social life. This tight linkage means that structure and culture cannot be separated to show how they can vary independently or have different kinds of effects on the interaction process.

In analyzing the dynamics of cultural systems Archer's focus is the elaboration of cultural meanings themselves in the process of sociocultural interaction. In her framework, this elaboration involves the process of **morphogenesis**, which can be contrasted with **morphostatis**.[2] Both terms refer to the culture itself in her perspective, not interaction or social structure. Morphogenesis involves positive feedback loops in which cultural deviations are reinforced and so multiply and expand, while morphostasis involves negative feedback loops in which innovations are rejected and existing cultural patterns maintained.[3]

At any one point in time, the existing stock of cultural knowledge provides the basis for the current cultural conditioning of sociocultural interaction. Through this interaction, the culture is either elaborated in various ways or reproduced (Archer, 1988:xxii–xxv). Archer's basic argument regarding elaboration can be diagramed as follows, with the elaborated culture at the end of this cycle then providing the conditions for subsequent sociocultural interaction at the next stage of the cycle:

Cultural Conditioning → Sociocultural Interaction → Cultural Elaboration.
(Archer, 1988:xxii)

Archer's focus in analyzing the component "parts" or elements of culture is primarily on the cognitive components—beliefs, ideas, or knowledge—that she believes can be evaluated in terms of logical consistency or inconsistency. In contrast to "downward conflationists," who argued that high levels of cultural coherence and unity are necessary to explain high levels of consensus and social integration, Archer insists that the ideas constituting particular cultural systems may be logically inconsistent and still support social integration. If there is a high level of consensus in people's acceptance of such beliefs, their logical inconsistency does not necessarily result in a breakdown in social integration. Nor does cultural homogeneity (when it exists) always guarantee high social integration. Even in a society with a unified and coherent cultural system, variations in the material or other interests of different people within the social system provide room for cultural innovations and disagreements, particularly in interpreting the implications

[2] Both of these concepts were introduced in Chap. 17 in reviewing Walter Buckley's analysis of sociocultural systems. In Archer's perspective, Buckley's perspective may also be seen as focusing primarily on the system of sociocultural interaction.

[3] The concept of feedback loops was discussed in Chap. 17 in connection with the dynamics of open systems. The process itself is identical for social and cultural systems.

of cultural beliefs at the level of interaction. In contrast to cultural system integration through logical consistency, consensus and integration within social systems is heavily influenced by the differential distribution of cultural influence, power, and socioeconomic resources in society. Because of the differential distribution of power, people may conform in their behavior to imposed social expectations because they lack the resources to resist, even when they do not agree with the cultural ideas that legitimate their subordinate position. In addition, those with power may seek to repress cultural alternatives that could be used by subordinate groups to resist or undermine the power structure.

A large part of Archer's analysis involves analyzing the various consequences that may result from sociocultural interaction involving "cultural contradictions" versus "cultural complementarities." Cultural inconsistencies and contradictions may be tolerated without leading to social disruption. People may be unaware of such inconsistencies, or they may be aware but see them as irrelevant at the level of social interaction, especially if there is consensus in other areas that are deemed more important. For example, religious adherents and atheists may agree on separation of church and state and collaborate in political activities where they agree. In any case, the dynamics of sociocultural interaction are influenced not only by cultural ideas but also by material conditions and other interests as well.

Inconsistencies may sometimes become salient, however, and have to be faced at the level of sociocultural interaction. This is especially likely when the contradictory ideas overlap with the dynamics of different institutions or groups with different interests and concerns. In this situation cultural beliefs that support the existing distribution of power may be challenged by the development of alternative ideologies that support resistance to the current power structure. Inconsistencies among opposing ideologies become more apparent as opposition groups draw on submerged or repressed beliefs to justify struggles for social change.[4] If the balance of power should eventually shift, these alternative ideas may then become dominant, though of course we would expect them to be modified as they are adapted to the new social realities.

When inconsistencies become salient at the level of sociocultural interaction, the challenge at the cultural level is to reconcile these "**constraining contradictions**" by changing one or more of them so they are mutually consistent and no longer contradictory. One possible result of this effort is cultural **syncretism**. However, whether this process will occur and lead to reconciliation of the social divisions with which the original contradiction was associated is an empirical question (Archer, 1988:158–171). If the contradiction cannot be satisfactorily resolved, the outcome could be the emergence of a "**competitive contradiction.**" This development might be expected to motivate the adherents of both sides to seek to win the struggle by convincing potential adherents of the rightness (or righteousness) of their cause, thereby undermining the other side (Archer, 1988:203–209). When "constraining

---

[4] This emphasis on opposing and inconsistent values may be compared to the role of legitimating values versus opposition values in Peter Blau's explanation of the dynamics of macro-level structures as discussed in Chap. 8.

contradictions" are replaced by "competitive contradictions" the search for common ground is given up and replaced by exaggeration of differences. If neither side is able to win (or if additional factions emerge in the course of the conflict) the result is **cultural pluralism**.

Cultural ideas and beliefs that are mutually consistent may be said to be in a relation of "**concomitant complementarity**" in Archer's terms (Archer, 1988:171–184). Without the challenge of dealing with inconsistencies and contradictions, "cultural agents" in an environment of high cultural coherence are able to elaborate and systematize the culture so it covers more and more areas of the cultural landscape and human experience. One example of this process of cultural growth can be seen in the emergence and growth of Christianity from within Judaism, coupled with the elaboration of specific Christian doctrines, in the first several centuries of the Christian era. Another example is the growth of the scientific mentality in the Western world in the seventeenth and eighteenth centuries. A more limited example of this process that Archer cites is Thomas Kuhn's (1970) analysis of the growth of dominant scientific paradigms.[5]

As a culture of concomitant complementarities expands and covers more and more of the cultural landscape, it becomes more elaborate and dense as more and more elements of culture and human experience are incorporated. As a result, it becomes increasingly difficult for any one person to master the total cultural system. Those who devote time and energy to this task are able to constitute themselves as an elite group distinct from younger and less knowledgeable cultural specialists and from laypersons. These younger cultural agents may respond to their marginal cultural position by seeking to establish their own credentials through the development of new areas of inquiry to which the dominant cultural worldview can be extended. If successful, these additional areas may be seen as "**contingent complementarities**" that are added to the already existing "concomitant complementarities." In some cases, too, additional complementary items may emerge fortuitously and thus become available for incorporation by those with the insight and the interest to do so. The ultimate outcome of the continued expansion of these complementary and mutually reinforcing ideas is the development of high levels of specialization. These different cultural specialties are represented by different groups whose members share a sense of being united under the cultural umbrella provided by the pioneers in the field. Within the field of sociology, for example, despite the high level of fragmentation that exists among different areas of interest and expertise, almost all sociologists today, young and old, acknowledge the pioneering influence of such figures as Durkheim, Weber, and Marx. Similarly, the field of medicine is highly specialized, though united under the umbrella of the "medical science" paradigm.

---

[5] Kuhn's definition of scientific paradigms was reviewed in Chap. 4, along with the argument by George Ritzer that sociology is a "multiple paradigm" area of scientific study (see Kuhn [1970] and Ritzer [1975]). The extension of evolutionary principles from the biological to the social and cultural realms as described in the previous chapter on sociobiology may also be seen as an example of increasing systematization and application of the evolutionary paradigm.

Archer's focus on logical consistencies versus inconsistencies at the cultural level, and the various ways these relate to social integration, contrasts sharply with the sociobiological emphasis of the last chapter on how culture provides tools and adaptive strategies that are beneficial to the long-range evolutionary survival of the human species. Her "intellectualist" approach emphasizes the ideas themselves, and how they are developed, expanded, contested, and modified. However, she clearly rejects the notion that ideas determine human behavior. Her main interest is in distinguishing the dynamics of cultural versus social systems and showing why they should be given equal weight in the influence they have on each other. Like social systems, cultural systems can be either elaborated or reproduced through the actions of human agents. But the specific dynamics of the processes involved in this elaboration or reproduction are not the same for social and cultural systems, despite the influence each has on the other. In a subsequent work, Archer (1995) explores in more detail the interrelations between structure and agency, u sing her perspective of "analytical dualism" to show how the elaboration of social structure also results from the actions of human agency in response to both cultural and structural conditioning.[6]

Contemporary culture is increasingly a global culture with a great deal of cultural and subcultural pluralism and diversity at the local level and a lack of any type of overarching belief system generating high consensus in all areas of social life. In Archer's terms, this pluralism and rejection of ultimate authority may be seen as being at one end of a cultural continuum, the opposite side of which is characterized by high cultural integration as reinforced by the elaborate systematization of "concomitant complementarities." The **cultural fragmentation** end of the continuum also contrasts with the pattern of syncretism, in which serious efforts are made to resolve contradictions, as well as the pattern of "contingent complementarities," in which new areas of knowledge and experience are brought into a larger coherent cultural framework. As will be discussed later in the next chapter, both globalization and cultural diversity are major themes in postmodern theory, along with a repudiation of the notion of any sort of "final word" or ultimate authority, including even scientific knowledge and sociology in particular. These developments support an image of culture as being fragmented rather than integrated.

Archer's intellectualist view of culture seems to suggest that cultural beliefs and ideas can be expressed in propositional statements and their truth or falsity debated on an intellectual level without regard to the group interests they may support. She acknowledges, of course, that cultural ideas may be used to support group interests, but this is not the same as evaluating the validity of the beliefs and ideas themselves. However, there is much more to the dynamics of culture than intellectual debate. There are also behavioral and moral dimensions. The behavioral dimension will be the focus of the next section, in which we review Norbert Elias's explanation of civilized manners as the outcome of the long-term historical process of political centralization.

---

[6] For another example of a perspective that is intended to link culture, social structure, and agency in a theoretical framework that preserves the analytical distinctions among these levels, see David Rubinstein (2001).

Civilized Behavior, Centralization of Power, and Functional Interdependence in Norbert Elias's Theory

German sociologist Norbert Elias is best known among contemporary theorists for his portrayal of the long-term historical developments leading to the type of behavioral and emotional self-control that is reflected in everyday life "civilized" manners.[7] In his perspective this internal self-control resulted in large part from changes in the configurations of external control reflecting a gradual increase in the centralization of political power. The ultimate outcome of these developments was the formation of the modern nation-states of Europe, with their largely successful monopolization of the means of violence and coercion (Elias, 2000).[8] In other words, the development of self-control as manifested in individuals' everyday life behavior and the emergence of modern nation-states were like two sides of the same coin, with self-control developing as a consequence of external political control. The high level of self-control manifested in modern civilized societies involves a process of learning to repress one's impulsiveness and emotional spontaneity so as to improve one's respectability and social status by adherence to refined or "civilized" manners. These changes in manners set the stage for the large-scale expansion in functional interdependence resulting from the long-term growth of the division of labor—a pattern associated with the evolution of modern societies.

Elias's analysis clearly was not limited to the cultural level, since the changes in manners that he described were tied to changing configurations of power and social relations. However, the long-term modifications in people's manners and ways of relating to one another that he emphasized can certainly be seen as the behavioral manifestation of changing cultural customs and expectations. In some ways, Elias's work is outside the mainstream of sociological theory, perhaps in part because its long-range historical scope does not fit the primary emphasis of most sociologists on contemporary issues or styles of research. Elias's overall goal was nothing less than a sociological explanation of the development of civilization in Western European societies, and his theoretical arguments were developed in conjunction with this historical analysis. Although the concept of "civilization" may be seen as including the totality of a society's culture, Elias did not separate cultural analysis from personality formation or the overall configurations of social relations and power

[7] Norbert Elias (1897–1990) did not begin to receive widespread recognition until the 1970s in Europe and still later in the United States. He taught at the University of Frankfurt until he left Germany shortly after Hitler's rise to power. Following a brief sojourn in Paris, he went to England and eventually accepted an academic post at Leicaster. Later he returned to Germany where he became associated with the Center for Interdisciplinary Research at the University of Bielefeld. Between his retirement from Leicaster and his return to Germany, he spent a couple of years as a professor at the University of Ghana and as a visiting lecturer in Amsterdam (Mennell, 1998, Chap. 1).

[8] The 1-volume edition of Elias, *The Civilizing Process*, rev. ed. (Elias, 2000) was originally published in 1939 in German as two volumes. Both volumes were translated into English, the first with the subtitle *The History of Manners* (Elias, 1978), and the second entitled *Power and Civility* (with *State Formation and Civilization* as an alternate title [Elias, 1982]).

structures in which people are involved.[9] Although he focused heavily on macro-level historical developments, he also drew on Sigmund Freud's famous distinctions between the id, ego, and superego in explaining how spontaneous emotional impulses are repressed through the internalization of social controls.[10]

Self-Control and Civilized Manners

Elias's documentation of the historical development of civilized manners highlights the dramatic transformations that had occurred in people's everyday life standards of courtesy, honor, and social respectability that had occurred over the centuries between the late medieval and the early modern period of European history. These changes reflected a steadily increasing level of detailed behavioral self-control, particularly with regard to eating, bodily functions, styles of speech, bedroom behavior, relations between men and women, and patterns of aggressiveness. Although it is impossible to specify a definite beginning point to these processes, Elias focused on the early part of the sixteenth century as a crucial transitional period.

To illustrate these changing standards of courtesy and civility, Elias quotes various sources that provide specific etiquette instructions with regard to the areas mentioned above. Such advice is interpreted as providing indicators of common practices that had become targets of change. Concerning table manners, for example, a thirteenth century source admonishes: "A man of refinement should not slurp from the same spoon with someone else ..." or "gnaw a bone and then put it back into the dish ..." (Elias, 2000:73). Guidelines from the fifteenth century prohibited offering food to someone after taking a bite out of it, or scratching at the table with one's hands or the tablecloth. A 1714 source forbids drinking soup from the bowl (except in one's own family), keeping one's knife in one's hand, "as village people do" (except when it is being used), putting meat back in a common dish after smelling it, selecting the best pieces of meat for oneself, or throwing bones or eggshells on the floor (Elias, 2000:81).

The same level of specificity is applied to other, more private areas of behavior as well. In the sixteenth century, Elias reports, Erasmus advised that young boys should be taught that "It is impolite to greet someone who is urinating or defecating...." (Elias, 2000:110) A 1558 source advocates privacy when it is necessary to

---

[9] In the European context in which he wrote, Elias specifically contrasted the connotations of the German concept of **culture** with the broader meaning he intended by the concept of **civilization**. The concept of culture in German was used to apply to the particular culture of Germany, as opposed to the culture of other societies. The concept of civilization, in contrast, transcends particular societies. For an explanation of how these terms apply in a comparison of Germany and France, see Norbert Elias (2000:5–43).

[10] Sigmund Freud's 1930 book, *Civilization and Its Discontents*, also suggests a link between the overall development of civilization and the increasing social control of basic impulses that are a major source of discontent for people living in a civilized society.

"relieve nature" and also explains that hands should not be washed "on returning to decent society from private places, as the reason for his washing will arouse disagreeable thoughts in people...." (Elias, 2000:111) (Contemporary standards of cleanliness evidently were not salient at that time.)

Nose blowing and spitting were also topics for advice. A 1558 source advised that a handkerchief should not be offered to someone else unless it has been washed, and also notes that it is not ".... seemly, after wiping your nose, to spread out your handkerchief and peer into it as if pearls and rubies might have fallen out of your head" (Elias, 2000:123). A 1774 source offers nothing to match such literary metaphors. Instead, "Every voluntary movement of the nose, whether caused by the hand or otherwise, is impolite and childish. To put your fingers into your nose is a revolting impropriety, ... You should observe, in blowing your nose, all the rules of propriety and cleanliness" (Elias, 2000:125). With regard to spitting, a 1714 source advises against frequent spitting unless necessary, in which case it should be concealed as much as possible and not allowed to soil other persons or their clothes (Elias, 2000:131).

With regard to bedroom behavior, the etiquette instructions Elias quotes suggest that privacy was limited and so guidelines were needed on sharing bedrooms or beds. A fifteenth century source advised that a lower ranking person should allow the higher ranking person a choice as to which side of the bed to use, and then should take the other side only after being invited to do so, followed by promptly bidding his companion good night (Elias, 2000:136). Elias also notes that Erasmus, in 1530, advised that one should be modest when undressing for bed and take care not to expose inappropriate parts of the body. Also, if it is necessary to share a bed, one should take care not to disturb one's bed companion through excessive tossing or by pulling away the blankets.

By1774, lack of privacy aroused different types of concerns, as suggested by the guidelines that should be followed if persons of the opposite sex had to sleep in the same room. Such a situation is described as "a strange abuse" but it can be accommodated if the beds are far apart and care is taken to insure modesty (Elias, 2000:125). Also, if people must share a bed, they should not lie in bed talking when they awaken in the morning; "... nothing more clearly indicates indolence and frivolity; the bed is intended for bodily rest and for nothing else. (Elias, 2000:137).

Even the sexual relations of husbands and wives were less concealed than they had become by the nineteenth century. Elias describes a wedding custom of the Middle Ages in which the wedding party, led by the best men, accompanied the newly married couple into the bedroom where the bridesmaids undressed the bride, and the bride and groom were then " 'laid together' to insure they were " '... rightly wed' [as] the saying went" (Elias, 2000:149–150). "In the later Middle Ages," Elias explained, "... the couple was allowed to lie on the bed in their clothes" (Elias, 2000:150).

Elias's major goal in describing such advice on "good" manners was to show how standards had changed over the centuries. The types of behavior and topics of conversations that cause shame and embarrassment had changed over the years as people gradually became more "civilized" and refined in their manners. Bodily functions that were discussed in an explicit and matter of fact way in late medieval society had become taboo topics by the early modern period.

Changes in the direction of increased self-control were particularly dramatic in the area of aggressive behavior. Elias described in detail the uninhibited enthusiasm of the warfare of the knights of the Middle Ages in expressing their aggressive hostility toward their enemies as they tortured and killed them and destroyed their property. The intense pleasure they experienced in the excitement of battle no doubt helped overcome the fear they might otherwise have felt. Nor was this propensity for violence limited to warring knights in battle. Feuds, private vengeance, and hostility were common in the population at large as well. As Elias explains the widespread violence permeating the social world, "The majority of the secular ruling class of the Middle Ages led the life of leaders of armed bands. This formed the taste and habits of individuals" (Elias, 2000:164). And—"The little people, too–the hatters, the tailors, the shepherds–were all quick to draw their knives" (Elias, 2000:168). As will be explained below, however, the "secular ruling class" was by no means equivalent to the ruling class or political authorities of a modern nation-state. Instead, this class consisted essentially of the victorious warring knights. However, the territory they controlled was limited as well as the type of control they were able to exert, and they were always vulnerable to being plundered by one another.

The picture that emerges is that the level of emotional expressiveness was much more volatile, much less controlled and moderated, in the feudal system of the Middle Ages than it later became. Not only in the excitement of conflict but in everyday life as well, there was less emotional inhibition, and emotional arousal, both positive and negative, was much more extreme. With the changes brought about through the "civilizing process," even the conduct of warfare required higher levels of planning and self-control and less impulsive expressiveness in the spontaneous venting of hostile or aggressive emotional feelings.

As this civilizing process advanced, standards gradually changed in the direction of greater and greater levels of emotional and behavioral self-control. These changes were reflected in the way individuals' personalities were formed by their parents and other adults, shaping and socializing their perceptions of what is natural and unnatural for human beings with regard to appropriate forms of emotional expressiveness. In this way behaviors that seemed natural to people in the Middle Ages eventually came to be seen as barbaric. As civilized forms of behavior were expanded, people gradually came to see the need for children to learn how to behave in a "civilized" way. These new standards of behavior were justified not only as being necessary and normal for living as a civilized member of society but as being in accordance with human nature itself.

Political Centralization and Expansion of Functional Interdependence

For Elias, the formation of individuals' basic personality structures through the socialization process in the context of their families and the configuration of social and political relations at the macro level are part of the same overall process. In the

Middle Ages, people were not compelled to exercise restraint in engaging in spontaneous forms of emotionally expressive behavior, including aggression, due to the lack of a sufficiently strong central political power. As political power gradually became more centralized, the result was an increased demand for self-control of emotional impulsiveness and expressiveness of all types. In other words, internal self-control resulted from external political control. As this internal control gradually expanded and was internalized, behavior that previously had been considered "normal" eventually came to be seen as barbaric and "uncivilized." In making this case, Elias argued that centralization of power gradually eliminated (or greatly reduced) the widespread random violence that permeated social life in the Middle Ages and promoted increased regularity and predictability in people's behavior. This greater predictability made it possible for people to begin to develop long-term cooperative relations and thereby expand the division of labor. This led to gradually increasing levels of functional interdependence among larger and larger segments of the population.

In contrast to the high levels of functional interdependence that gradually developed in modern societies, social life in the Middle Ages had been highly segmented, without a centralized power structure and with frequent outbursts of emotional spontaneity, including violence. In the feudal system of that time warring knights engaged in frequent battles to defend their limited territory or to try to expand it. But as long as the power differentials that emerged through such struggles were small, a stable power structure was impossible to establish. Eventually, however, power differences became sufficiently great to support the beginning of a monarchical system. These early rising monarchies eventually managed to dominate territories that were much larger than the limited and tenuous land holdings of warring knights. As these rising monarchies sought to consolidate their expanding power, they recruited knights and eventually transformed them into the nobility of their courts. Being a member of the nobility in this emerging monarchical court system provided more security than continuing their vulnerable and precarious knighthood.

Life among the court nobility involved constant competition for the favor of the monarch. The elaborate court rituals that gradually developed served to distinguish the monarchy and nobility from the rest of the population and symbolized their higher standing. The challenge for the members of the nobility was to establish or increase their status in their relations with one another and in the eyes of the king. This led to the elaboration of refinements in behavior plus increased levels of self-control. In addition, members of the nobility also learned how to evaluate their own standing in the status hierarchy by detecting subtle changes in the relative standing of fellow members without resorting to violence. In short, palace intrigue had replaced open warfare among the nobility as the dominant form of conflict and competition.

In the meantime, however, the continued growth in the power of kings and the expansion and embellishment of their royal courts gradually became more and more dependent on their power to obtain tax revenues from the emerging bourgeois class. This reduced their dependence on the somewhat less reliable and limited resources extracted from the peasants living on the land they owned or controlled. The security and protection provided by the king to the bourgeois class in return for their tax revenues meant that the rising bourgeois class and the royal court and nobility became more and more dependent on one another. As the bourgeois class in the towns acquired greater economic power, the challenge for the nobility was to elaborate even more the status distinctions that separated them as a group from the bourgeois class, especially as the numbers and influence of the bourgeois class continued to expand. As some members of the bourgeois class acquired greater economic resources themselves, they sought to increase their own status by adopting the manners of members of the royal court, with some aspiring to join their ranks. This general process led to the diffusion of the courtly manners among the bourgeois class. The result was increased levels of "courtesy," heightened sensitivity to others, and various forms of refinement in patterns of behavior and social relations, all of which led to increased self-control among the wider population, especially among the expanding bourgeois class. As the economic power of the bourgeois continued to grow, they gradually developed a greater degree of independence. This meant that their status became less dependent on being able to move into the social circles of the nobility. Even so, the civilized manners they adopted enabled them to distinguish themselves from the lower-level working class, whose numbers were also increasing as the division of labor continued to grow.

The long-term effects of the ongoing competition for power resulted ultimately in the development of absolute monarchies which were able eventually to monopolize the use of violence and thereby pacify the population. In conjunction with this increased power, monarchical rulers eventually managed to acquire monopoly control over taxation, thereby enabling them to consolidate their power without relying so heavily on the court nobility. This process was made possible by the increasing monetarization of the economy, a process that was facilitated by gradual expansion in trade and continuing growth in the size of the bourgeois class. By establishing a steady stream of tax revenues, kings acquired the necessary resources to consolidate and expand their military and administrative power without giving up control of their land. However, this increased their dependence on the growing bourgeois class that was their primary source of tax revenues (Elias, 2000:344–362). This increasing control of the means of taxation also provided the resources needed to insure their control of the means of violence as well.

The widespread diffusion of patterns of increased self-control, sensitivity to others, courtesy, and refinement that followed the centralization of power did not mean people had become less concerned with their own interests. It simply indicated a more refined and less violent pattern of competition for status. In addition, the shift to "civilized" manners and patterns of self-control were diffused among the working class as well, though to a lesser extent. This increase in internalized self-control among the working class helped insure a reliable source of labor for the expansion of bourgeois enterprises. In addition, working class individuals themselves could seek to emulate the self-discipline and other patterns of respectable civilized behavior that had become widespread among the bourgeois class in their own struggles to move up in the emerging ranking system.

In explaining the dynamics of the monarchical configuration of power, Elias points out that kings faced the constant challenge of balancing the conflicting demands and claims of the nobility and the increasing power of the rising bourgeois class in order to maintain their dominance. These competitive dynamics played themselves out in different ways in France, Germany, and England. Court society eventually developed to a high level in France. However, as the economic power and influence of the bourgeois grew, it eventually reached a point where status distinctions of the royal court nobility became superfluous and unnecessary for the continued development of bourgeois society. In fact, the traditional power and privileges of the nobility came to be seen as inhibiting the continued consolidation of the power of the bourgeois class. By the end of the eighteenth century the French Revolution brought a dramatic end to the monarchy and royal court in that country—even though courtly manners and tastes continued to be influential to varying degrees throughout Europe. The differences in the situation in other European societies can be explained in terms of the historical differences in the power and dependency configurations of the different groups that were involved.

Within all European societies, the gradual transition to state formation was based primarily on the process whereby the means of violence and taxation were monopolized by the increasingly centralized political authorities. But there were other changes in the overall social structure that accompanied these processes. Elias emphasizes in particular the importance of higher levels of internal security that resulted from the increased levels of self-control. Because of these developments, people were better able to predict one another's behavior and could therefore develop more and more elaborate patterns of long-term collaboration. In this new environment, it became feasible to expand the differentiation of social functions and thereby increase the level of interdependence among larger and larger segments of the population. This development is essentially the same that Durkheim and other early sociologists described in terms of a steadily increasing division of labor leading to higher and higher levels of functional interdependence in the overall society.

As Elias explained,

> ... As more and more people must attune their conduct to that of others, the web of actions must be organized more and more strictly and accurately, if each individual action is to fulfill its social function. Individuals are compelled to regulate their conduct in an increasingly differentiated, more even and more stable manner.... The web of actions grows so complex and extensive, the effort required to behave 'correctly' within it becomes so great, that beside the individual's conscious self-control an automatic, blindly functioning apparatus of self-control is firmly established.
>
> (Elias, 2000:367–368)

Elias summarized the contrast with the old feudal system of the late Middle Ages as follows:

> In general, the direction in which the behaviour and the affective make-up of people change when the structure of human relationships is transformed in the manner described, is as follows: societies without a stable monopoly of force are always societies in which the division of functions is relatively slight and the chains of action binding individuals together are comparatively short. Conversely, societies with more stable monopolies of force, always first embodied in a large princely or royal court, are societies in which the division of functions is more or less advanced, in which the chains of action binding individuals together are longer and the functional dependencies between people greater.
>
> (Elias, 2000:370)

The total array of changes that Elias described are not consciously planned. Instead, they develop as the outcome of the ever-changing configurations of social relations and power structures in which people are involved. As the civilizing process advances, participants in the various functional groups that emerge in the society may gradually develop a general sense of the larger public and their own role within it, but they obviously do not have the detailed knowledge of the overall web of interdependence within which they are involved. Instead, they sense a vague awareness of larger "social forces" that may affect their lives but that are beyond their understanding and control. It is in this context that sociology itself emerged as a specialized area of inquiry for understanding the larger and more complex social world that was developing.

In addition, as patterns of functional interdependence continue to expand over a larger and larger population, the overall configuration of power relations undergoes additional changes as power gradually becomes more diffused throughout society. With high levels of differentiation and increasing interdependence among a society's major functional groups, any one of these groups could potentially exercise its power to act in ways that undermine the complex configuration of relationships making up the overall system. To maintain the complex patterns of interdependence that have developed, the central government must adjust its strategies to allow these multiple functional power centers to be represented within its structure. This means that it is no longer feasible for the government to exercise power in an arbitrary or authoritarian way, even though it is still central and may be dominant in the overall configuration of power in society. However, its role has been transformed into a kind of public or representative monopoly with regard to the exercise of power. The development of all of the modern nation-states of Europe reflects this overall process of democratization. Instead of maintaining absolute control, the central government wields its power through its overall coordination of the multiple centers of power represented by the different functional groups in society as it seeks to balance their conflicting interests and insure their contributions to the larger system (Elias, 2000:312–344; Mennell, 1998:78–79).

These developments did not occur in a single straight line of development. There were setbacks and uneven patterns in different countries and different areas. Centralizing processes were sometimes reversed as a result of resistance to the efforts of the dominant ruler and the expansion of alternative sources of power. Moreover, the origins of the civilizing processes and the patterns of external and internal control that Elias analyzed can be traced back to the influence of the church and monasteries even prior to the late Middle Ages. Similar in some ways to the strategies developed by the nobility, these earlier structures also developed specific beliefs and styles of behavior that enabled them to distinguish themselves from the surrounding population.

The processes Elias described can be seen continuing in our own society. For example, the detailed protocol that surrounds private citizens' encounters with the United States President or members of Congress on public occasions, or the elaborate rituals of the President's relations with Congress, can be seen in part as a legacy of royal court rituals. In addition, contemporary debates about appropriate versus inappropriate images and language on television and the internet, plus efforts to eliminate disparaging language and tasteless jokes about minority groups in our society, reflect continuing concerns with improving manners and self-control. In still another area, ongoing efforts to prevent armed robbery, homicide, and spouse abuse and to punish offenders indicates that even today the ability of the state to monopolize the means of violence is not yet absolute.

Elias acknowledged the psychic costs that are involved in the introjection of external social controls as they are manifested in the high levels of self-control required in modern civilized societies. As people accept the need for predictability in one another's behavior, their opportunities for spontaneous emotional expression in their social lives inevitably decline. This acceptance is based on an implicit understanding of the need for being disciplined and fulfilling one's various social responsibilities in order to coordinate the actions of different people in a complex division of labor so as to achieve various goals. Various forms of compensation for this combination of external restraint and internal self-discipline may be provided through sports and entertainment, in which socially acceptable opportunities are provided for spontaneous emotional expressiveness, within certain limits, of course (Mennell, 1998:140–158).

Even though Elias's major work was written prior to the midpoint of the twentieth century, his perspective is significant for contemporary sociological theory. It demonstrates the importance of using detailed historical material for increasing our sociological understanding of the dynamics of long-range historical change. His analysis encompasses the multidimensional effects of interrelated changes in cultural patterns, social structure, and personality formation in a way that, arguably, may be compared in its scope to both Pitirim Sorokin's and Max Weber's historical analyses.[11] Elias's major overall concern was to demonstrate how long-term changes in cultural expectations for everyday life behavior were closely related to the changes in the configuration of social relations and power differentials that had led gradually to the formation of the nation-states of the modern world. His focus on the internalization of cultural standards as manifested in behavioral self-control and civilized manners showed how the formation of individuals' basic personality patterns reflect the overall political organization of society. This perspective incorporates both micro and macro levels of analysis and helps transcend the arbitrary distinctions between them.

Although Elias's focus was on European societies, he certainly recognized that social development and the civilizing process take different forms in different regions of the world. In our time, increasing global interdependence, coupled with the increased reach of weapons systems and the availability of nuclear weapons, represents a new stage in the configuration of power and patterns of interdependence among nation-states as well as other groups that are able to gain control of the means of violence. The threat of terrorism, for example, is a clear indication of the willingness of some groups to use violence outside the framework of conventional

[11] Pitirim Sorokin's cyclical theory of long-range cultural change was reviewed briefly in Chap. 3 in connection with the development of American Sociology. Max Weber, of course, has long been recognized as one of the major founders of sociology whose ideas are part of contemporary sociological discourse, and his work included wide-ranging comparative analyses of different societies, particularly with regard to the relation between religious beliefs systems and economic orientations.

state control and beyond the bounds of legitimate or "civilized" behavior. In view of the steadily expanding levels of political, economic, and cultural interdependence that we now experience on a global level, the challenge of developing and implementing shared moral codes to promote increased normative regulation and "civility" in international relations is more urgent than ever. The next section will focus more explicitly on issues of morality.

The Struggle Between Good and Evil: Jeffrey Alexander's Cultural Sociology

Like all other aspects of culture, morality and cultural ideals are socially defined, and these definitions are freighted with symbolic meanings that can be analyzed at their own level, independently of their links to social structure or material conditions. Jeffrey Alexander (2003) argues persuasively for a "strong program" in cultural sociology in which culture is treated as an autonomous area of analysis, having its own structure which must be understood through a process of hermeneutic interpretation of the symbolic meanings that constitute it. This approach can be contrasted with analyses in which culture is explained in terms of institutional needs, socioeconomic interests, or the material environment. To understand cultural meanings at their own level, the analyst must seek to grasp how these meanings themselves are developed and structured, as well as how their symbolic representations shape the way individuals see and understand the social world and their role within it. Alexander cites Clifford Geertz's promotion of "thick" ethnographic description as providing a beginning step in advancing our understanding of how culture penetrates people's lives in local contexts. However, he does not regard Geertz's approach as being sufficient for moving from local description to a more general theoretical analysis that encompasses or links cultural meanings to the structural and institutional features of the macro level (Alexander, 2003:22–23). Alexander's analysis and examples involve an application of this approach to the clarification and symbolic reinforcement of threatened moral values.

To provide a more systematic analysis of the structure of cultural systems and how they apply to moral issues, Alexander relies heavily on the notion of "binary codes" that are used to distinguish between fundamental oppositions, particularly in the area of moral meanings, such as the contrast between good and evil. This idea can be traced back to Durkheim's pioneering distinction between the "sacred" and the "profane" in his analysis of the social origins of religion. In this same vein, as noted in an Chap. 15, Mary Douglas (1966) also underscored the crucial importance of the dichotomous distinctions people make between opposing categories, such as the pure and the impure, clean and dirty, and so on. When applied to people's implicit understandings of their social world, this categorical way of contrasting good and evil easily gives rise to crucial ingroup versus outgroup distinctions. Social theorists themselves also employ various binary distinctions in their analyses, as illustrated for example, by the contrast between the "modern" world from the "premodern" world that preceded it, or primary versus secondary groups.

Language itself can be analyzed as establishing distinctions between that which is named by a particular concept and everything else. With this approach, the development of entire language systems can be viewed as a massive elaboration of a complex series of such distinctions. As a self-contained system, language, like culture itself, can be analyzed on its own terms, independently of its relationship to the social structure. Moreover, the culture of a society can itself be "read" and interpreted like a text—though of course it is not limited to verbal texts but can also include various artifacts such as monuments, works of art, and even material technology. Similarly, the cultural meanings symbolically conveyed through behavior can also be "read" and interpreted, as emphasized in symbolic interaction theory. Some forms of ritualistic behavior, for example, literally make no sense except for the symbolic meanings they are meant to convey.

When applied to cultural ideas of morality or normative conformity, Alexander uses the notion of binary oppositions to argue that the elaboration of moral ideals and their implications for social life (and for individuals' lives) requires that the meanings of immorality and deviance be defined in opposition to morality and normality. In this perspective the type of discourse that is involved in the elaboration of a society's prescribed ideals and values requires an explicit conceptualization of their opposite. To put this point in specific religious terms, the concept of a holy God requires or entails the opposing concept of an evil devil. The challenge is to maintain clear symbolic boundaries to prevent ideals regarding the good or sacred from being undermined or polluted by evil or the profane. God and the devil are clearly on opposite sides of the moral divide, even though the power of both is seen as transcending mere human power.

Alexander devotes considerable attention to the process whereby evil is socially constructed as part of the same process whereby society's sacred ideals and values are socially constructed (Alexander, 2003:109–119). The ongoing struggle to promote the good may involve various types of crucial ritualistic activities that shape and reinforce people's emotional and moral commitments. Among these rituals are those that symbolize or dramatize the ongoing conflict between the forces of good and the forces of evil, and that also seek to purify the social order (and individuals' identities) from the contaminating influence of evil.

Under circumstances of moral uncertainty, anxiety, or conflict, the social order, and the ideals and values that support it, may appear to be contaminated and traumatized by threats represented by the growing influence of the forces of evil. When this occurs, societies may go through an intense and prolonged period of struggle in which concerns are widely expressed regarding the current moral crisis, and challenges are issued by public spokespersons to restore and reinforce the society's moral foundations. This may be accompanied by efforts to assign blame and punish evil doers so as to expunge their contaminating influence from the social order. Different groups vary in their interpretations of such threats and what should be done about them. The characteristics of the ensuing struggle will depend on the ability of various groups to mobilize themselves and influence public discourse in a way that focuses attention on the perceived threats to the moral order and the urgent necessity of expunging these threats and reinforcing the moral commitments that sustain it. Its outcome will be heavily influenced by the differential ability of these various groups to control the means of symbolic production and moral persuasion to define the issues and mobilize support for taking appropriate action. If and when such struggles are eventually resolved, this may be followed in the future by some form of ritualistic celebration and commemoration, and such rituals are designed to reinforce people's emotional and moral commitments to insure that the "evil" will be permanently expunged and the "good" will be triumphant. Thus, for example, our current commemoration of the birthday of slain civil rights leader Dr. Martin Luther King in late January can be seen as a ritualistic pattern for honoring his noteworthy contributions in the long struggle to end the evils of racism and promote equality in American society.

This process of moral struggle can readily be illustrated in our own time by the opposition between "pro-choice" versus "pro-life" advocates, debates over gay and lesbian issues, and the conflict over whether the Ten Commandments should be allowed to be displayed on public property. Such struggles clearly differ from ordinary political conflicts that theoretically can be resolved through negotiation and compromise, as well as economic competition between individuals pursuing their own personal interests. A key feature of moral struggles is that the issues are seen as non-negotiable, giving rise to "cultural wars" between advocates on each side who regard the conflict as a crucial battle between good and evil, with the long-term survival of society or of civilization itself at stake (Hunter, 1991).

Despite this emphasis on the struggle between "good" versus "evil," it should also be pointed out that partisans on both sides in some moral battles seek to justify their opposing positions in terms of ultimate values that both sides would theoretically regard as morally binding, but that clearly have different implications in terms of their application. Instead of seeking common ground, however, the temptation for both sides is to deny the legitimacy of their opponents' moral arguments, to accuse them of insincerity, or to dismiss their arguments as mere "rationalization." In the "pro-choice" versus "pro-life" debate, for example, at one level it seems that it should theoretically be possible for opponents to agree on the abstract ideal of protecting human freedom plus honoring the sacredness of human life. However, the likelihood of finding common ground is decreased by the impassioned arguments that develop regarding the implications of these abstract values with regard to the specific issue of abortion and the conflict between the rights of pregnant women versus the sacredness of the life of the unborn fetus. As another example, most members of our democratic society are likely to endorse the ideal of majority rule at the same time that they also subscribe in principle to the need to protect the rights of minorities. Similarly, while both freedom and security are high priority values, people may have fundamental disagreements on how much freedom should be sacrificed for the sake of security. The disagreement over freedom versus security has become a noteworthy matter of public discourse in the aftermath of September 11. When combatants on both sides of issues such as these are able to invoke widely accepted but conflicting values to justify their position, and when both sides have considerable power and resources to influence public discourse, the result we may expect is a protracted stalemate. As the moral warfare develops, the rhetoric employed may escalate and eventually be transformed from a disagreement over the priorities of different moral values to a struggle between the forces of good versus evil. Moral debates involving the relative priority of different values, or competing notions of how these different values should apply in particular situations, clearly differ from cosmic struggles that all would agree involve a clear battle between generic forces of good versus evil.

Leaning toward the "good versus evil" type of cultural discourse, Alexander applied his strategy for cultural analysis to the gradual development of the meaning of the Holocaust as symbolic of a traumatic outbreak of evil that was seen eventually as so unimaginably horrific that it transcended the mundane world and defied the usual forms of rational explanation. Instead, the Holocaust gradually took on the character of a world-changing sacred or cosmic struggle between good and evil (Alexander, 2003:27–84). The eventual result was the emergence of a sense of urgency in developing universally binding moral codes that would insure that such pervasive outbreaks of evil as were manifested in the widespread slaughter of Jewish victims during the Nazi era in Germany never again be allowed to occur. Although our goal here is not to trace all of the details of Alexander's insightful analysis, he shows how the specific actions that were taken over many years following the end of World War II led to the promotion of a new moral order in which the ever-present threat of the traumatic triumph of this form of evil should never be allowed to be forgotten. Specific actions that were taken in this process ranged from efforts to convict and punish the leading Nazi perpetrators through the Nuremberg War Crimes Tribunal to the establishment of the Holocaust Museum in Washington, D.C. The trials of the perpetrators are designed to expunge the source of the unimaginable evil, while the Holocaust Museum encourages vicarious identification with Jewish victims to insure that they will never be forgotten and to reinforce visitors' conscious awareness of the ongoing cosmic struggle between good and evil in which no one is allowed to be an "innocent" bystander. Underlying these actions is the notion that constant moral vigilance is required to reduce or eliminate the risk of again being contaminated, manipulated, or controlled by the power of the ultimate or transcendent form of evil that the Holocaust represents.

As a symbol of ultimate evil, however, the term "Holocaust" has subsequently been applied in other contexts as well. When this occurs, the implication is that those to whom the term is applied, or their actions, can be regarded as being at risk for being in the same moral camp as Adolph Hitler and those who collaborated in the slaughter of Jews in Nazi Germany (or who remained passive during this process). At the same time, however, there is also resistance to the casual application of the term to "lesser" forms of evil because of the effect this could have in diminishing the seriousness of the evil that the Holocaust represents or the unspeakable suffering of its innocent victims. Alexander points out that the symbolic significance of the use of this term by anti-Vietnam war protesters in the late 1960s and early 1970s in criticizing the American government's military actions against the Viet Cong. The protestors' symbolic representation of the immorality of the war as comparable to the Holocaust provided a dramatic and potent rebuttal to the moral arguments used to support American policy. The wide publicity surrounding these opposing interpretations demonstrated that the government and other "establishment" institutions had in effect lost their monopoly control over the symbolic representation of the morality of American policy—and, by implication, of America's moral character.

Another dramatic example (noted briefly in Chap. 13) of a cultural-level struggle between good and evil that Alexander analyzed was the United States Senate's Watergate hearings during the Nixon presidency in the early 1970s (Alexander, 2003:155–177). Alexander interpreted these hearings as a "democratic ritual" that reflected an effort to purify the United States presidency from the polluting effects of the break-in and burglary of the Democratic Party headquarters during the presidential election campaign. Alexander shows in some detail the way in which this event was elevated from a politically motivated (but potentially ordinary) crime to a high moral drama involving a cultural-level struggle between the ideals and values that define American democracy and their opposite. Closure on this extraordinary event did not end until Nixon resigned from office (thereby expunging the source of the evil) and newly installed President Ford (who had been Nixon's Vice President) could proclaim to the nation that "our long national nightmare is over." It is important to note, as Alexander pointed out, that Ford's loss in the subsequent presidential election may be seen as due in large part to his pardon of former President Nixon, especially when juxtaposed to candidate Jimmy Carter's solemn pledge never to lie to the American people.

Jeffrey Alexander's focus on the discourse employed in symbolic moral struggles between good and evil is a key dimension of cultural analysis as it relates to the challenges of implementing abstract moral ideals within the social order. The process of social construction whereby the transcendent symbolic meanings of the ongoing opposition between good and evil are developed may also be applied to distinctions that are made between ingroups and outgroups, as well as in the construction of personal and collective identities. Extreme forms of nonnegotiable conflict may ensue when the members of opposing groups take the moral "high road" and demonize their opponents as embodiments of evil whose contaminating influence (or presence) must be resisted at all costs. Alexander's focus on moral codes clearly contrasts with Margaret Archer's emphasis on the development of the cognitive dimension of culture as well as Elias's description of behavioral self-control as reflected in civilized manners. Although these three perspectives focus on different dimensions of the cultural level, they also demonstrate the way culture is inevitably and continually manifested in social behavior and social institutions.

Summary

This chapter examined some selected examples of theoretical perspectives that highlight the cultural level of analysis. Culture is based on the innate ability of humans to develop and learn symbolic codes and meaning systems in the context of their primary group relations, but it can be elaborated greatly and analyzed at its own distinct level. Although cultural rules and techniques emerge through interaction as human beings adapt to their environment, rigid adherence to established cultural patterns may sometimes inhibit the development of more effective rules and techniques. This inhibiting effect was noted briefly in our review of Paul Bohannan's perspective on culture. On the other hand, however, the remaining three theoretical perspectives that were emphasized in this chapter deal extensively with dynamic processes whereby cultural systems undergo elaboration and change.

This focus on change is reflected in Margaret Archer's morphogenetic perspective in which the elaboration of culture is explained primarily in terms of responses to logical consistencies or inconsistencies among different cultural beliefs and forms of knowledge. Cultural elaboration and development occur when high levels of cultural coherence trigger efforts to expand dominant beliefs and ideas to more and more areas of people's experience. On the other hand, high levels of inconsistency or cultural contradictions may stimulate efforts to achieve coherence by reconciling these inconsistencies through a process of cultural syncretism. If these efforts are unsuccessful, cultural fragmentation and pluralism ensue. These cultural dynamics influence the patterns of sociocultural interaction in social system, particularly when cultural beliefs and ideas are used to defend or advance people's material and social interests. These processes at the level of sociocultural interaction may lead to ongoing change within the cultural system.

In contrast to Archers' strong cognitive emphasis, Norbert Elias's overall goal was to explain long-term changes in behavioral self-control and the resulting decline in the spontaneous volatility of emotional expressiveness, particularly with regard to violence and aggression. These changes in emotional and behavioral self-control developed in response to the gradual increase in external controls that led ultimately to the development of the sovereign state with its monopoly control of the means of violence and taxation. The resulting increase in the predictability of behavior contributed to the stabilization of the social order and made it possible to expand the level of differentiation and specialization and thus the scope of people's patterns of interdependence. Although the modern state continues to have a monopoly on the legitimate use of the means of violence and taxation, high levels of functional interdependence contribute to a pluralistic power structure in which different functional groups within a society may acquire considerable power to influence the central government.

The inclusion of Elias's comprehensive historical analysis in a chapter devoted primarily to cultural dynamics is somewhat arbitrary, since his analysis also dealt extensively with changing social configurations and power structures as well as individual personality formation. However, the increased levels of self-control reflected in everyday life manners can be seen a manifestation of cultural customs and rules that apply in individuals' relations with one another. The self-control that Elias emphasized was crucial in his analysis in reflecting increased political centralization and also in contributing to the expansion of the division of labor in modern society.

Cultural systems also include moral codes that may be manifested to varying degrees in people's behavior. In Jeffrey Alexander's perspective, moral values, like other aspects of culture, can be viewed in terms of symbolic meanings that can be expressed in binary codes. His analysis focused heavily on the symbolic and ritualistic representations of the moral confrontation between good and evil, insisting that each must be understood in terms of its opposition to the other. This strategy is particularly relevant for understanding people's struggles to implement their moral values in their behavior and social institutions, particularly when manifested in conflicts between groups with competing moral priorities. During times of cultural trauma, transcendent moral ideals and values are believed to be seriously threatened by the forces of evil, which Alexander analyzes as being socially constructed as part of the same process whereby clear moral boundaries between good and evil are established and reinforced. We saw how Alexander applied this perspective to the elaboration of the symbolic meanings associated with the Holocaust, the anti-Vietnam War movement, and the Watergate crisis. The resolution of intense moral struggles between good and evil is likely to be followed by ritualistic reaffirmations of society's fundamental moral values. Such rituals are intended to reinforce the vigilance that is required to assure the ultimate triumph of good over evil.

Alexander's perspective on moral struggle seems to be based on the assumption that clear distinctions can be established between competing moral values or behaviors reflecting a sharp boundary between good and evil. The next chapter will explore the way in which cultural codes of all types—cognitive, normative, and moral—have become highly fragmented in the postmodern world.

Questions for Study and Discussion

1. How could you apply Archer's concept of cultural "morphogenesis" to the elaboration of various areas of specialization within a scientific or academic discipline (such as sociology or biology, for example)? From the review of different theoretical perspectives in this book, do you see the field of sociology as characterized more by cultural consistency or inconsistency? Explain.
2. How does Elias relate everyday life rules of good manners and self-control to the division of labor and the overall political organization of society? From your observations, do you think people from different backgrounds vary significantly in terms of their manners and self-control? Do these variations influence their ability to work cooperatively with others for the achievement of long-range goals? Explain.
3. Based on Alexander's cultural analysis, explain how the binary distinctions used in defining moral boundaries can also be applied in distinguishing ingroups versus outgroups. Would you agree or disagree that viewing moral codes in terms of binary distinctions makes it impossible to compromise? Are there some issues where moral boundaries could (or should, in your view) be redefined in order to compromise? Explain.
4. Explain how the celebration or commemoration of historic events involving conflict and struggle can help reinforce widely shared values that were once contested. To what extent do different groups with different historical experiences and different values engage in their own specific rituals? Cite and discuss at least

two examples of specific groups in our society (or in your own experience) whose rituals reinforce a distinctive identity that is separate from the rest of the society.

5. Both Archer and Alexander highlight the importance of inconsistencies, conflicts, or contradictions at the cultural level. Identify at least two examples of significant cultural contradictions in our society today in terms of basic beliefs, moral values, or other areas of culture, and explain how these contradictions are being expressed. To what extent do these cultural conflicts overlap with conflicts at the level of the social structure itself, such as socioeconomic class conflicts, for example?

Chapter 20
Postmodern Social and Cultural Fragmentation

To be "modern" in the theoretical world of postmodernism is to risk being regarded as obsolete. Modernity in this perspective is not just about being up to date. Instead, it refers to a particular view of the contemporary social world and its ongoing rapid transformations, not just to the recent and current time period.

Sociology itself originated in the challenge of understanding the modern world as it contrasted with the ancient and medieval worlds. The worldview associated with modernity, as we saw in Chap. 2, was grounded in the belief that the steady growth of scientific knowledge would insure continued social and intellectual progress. Postmodern theorists, in contrast, would dispute the notion that any system of knowledge, including science itself, can provide assurance of ultimate truth or guarantee continued progress. Instead, definitions of valid knowledge and progress are relative and vary for people with divergent cultural traditions or different social locations. They see many of the defining features of modernity as having been superseded, rejected, or radically transformed in ways that mark a major transition to a new era.

The postmodern perspective has been widely influential in many academic areas outside sociology. Postmodern theorists in sociology vary in terms of their primary focus of analysis, but they concentrate heavily on contemporary issues and trends. They would generally argue that current trends mark the end of the period of human history associated with the development of modern society, which has long been characterized and largely defined by scientific advance, industrialism, capitalism, urbanism, and bureaucracy. Although these features of the social world continue to be relevant, the focus is on the emergence of a radically different postmodern period. The distinctive characteristics of this new postmodern period are evident in many areas of social life, including personal relationships, lifestyles, and identity formation at the micro level and restructuring of economic hierarchies, increased cultural fragmentation and relativism, and globalization in all its different dimensions at the macro level.

Other theorists, who may be equally interested in understanding the new dynamics of the contemporary world, do not regard current changes and trends as representing a clear or definitive break with the defining features of modernity. Callinicos, for example, rejects the notion of a totally new and different postmodern stage and sees it largely as a "… theoretical construct, of interest primarily as a symptom of the

D.P. Johnson, *Contemporary Sociological Theory: An Integrated Multi-Level Approach.*

current mood of the Western intelligentsia ..." (Callinicos, 1990:9). Both he and Bertens (1995) portray the larger historical context in which the type of orientation represented by postmodernism can perhaps be partially understood as a reaction to the disillusionment that sets in when developments in the social world do not conform to intellectuals' idealistic faith in reason as a foundation for continued progress.

Despite the major shift in worldview represented in postmodern theory, many aspects of the culture of modernity, especially technology and other forms of material culture, clearly continue to be highly relevant in the contemporary world. Continuing progress in such areas as transportation, communication, production, information systems, and computer technology are a significant part of the material environment and exert a major influence on the worldviews and lifestyles emerging in our postmodern era. In addition, scientific work in all disciplines, including sociology, continues to move forward on the basis of the implicit belief that continued progress can be achieved through systematic empirical research and disciplined intellectual inquiry. Likewise, despite the important current transformations that can be identified, many of the most distinctive features of the bureaucratic structures that dominate our economic and political landscape represent a continuation of some of the most important defining characteristics of modernity.

Without being exhaustive, this chapter will highlight the following postmodern themes that various sociologists have highlighted:

- Postmodernity versus late modernity
- Skepticism regarding systems of knowledge and authority
- Increasing global interdependence
- Mass media effects on cultural erosion and fragmentation
- Culture as strategies for escaping mundane reality through expanded and enchanted consumption experiences
- The challenge of identity formation in a late modern or postmodern world
- Cultural expressiveness applied to human beings' bodies

Postmodernity or Late Modernity?

Although certain aspects of the modern world may be undergoing significant change, this does not necessarily mean that we are crossing (or have recently crossed) a threshold to a totally new type of social world in which the modern world is left behind.

In his 1990 book, *The Consequences of Modernity*, Anthony Giddens argues that despite the major transformations and new developments that have occurred in recent times, the continuities with modernity are sufficiently great that the present era (of the late twentieth century when this volume was published) should be characterized as a period of "late modernity" or "radicalized modernity" rather than as a new postmodern period. In spite of the historical discontinuities that can be identified, the fundamental characteristics of modernity are still evident in the continuation of the capitalist organization of economic activity, the use of industrial technology in production, the nation-state as the principle source of societal administration and social control, and reliance on military power in defending and promoting national interests (Giddens, 1990:55–63).

One of the major contemporary changes Giddens emphasizes is the globalization of modernity, which is made possible by the development of more and more effective means of transportation and communication. These technological developments allow for a "disembedding" of social processes from local spatial and temporal limitations. As he put it, "By disembedding I mean the 'lifting out' of social relations from local contexts of interaction and their restructuring across indefinite spans of time-space" (Giddens, 1990:21). At the same time, however, this technology also provides the means for reembedding (constructing or reconstructing) new forms of social relations. People are able to maintain personal relationships and transact business at great distances from one another because of the way technology allows real-time electronic communication between people almost anywhere in the world. These communication linkages are also supported by rapid global travel as well (Giddens, 1990:141–144).

The new freedoms that are available in our late modern period are also reflected in Giddens' portrayal of the experimental and voluntary forms of emotional intimacy that people are able to establish in contemporary society (Giddens, 1992). Instead of fitting into established roles and routines, individuals have a wide array of options that allow them to construct their various relationships in terms that they believe will meet their own distinctive needs. These analyses are largely congruent with postmodern forms of thought that emphasize the process whereby customary boundaries of time, space, and tradition are being dissolved, allowing for more fluidity in social arrangements of all types (see Bauman [2000] for an explicit emphasis on the "liquid" aspects of contemporary modernity).

At the same time, new patterns of trust in the routine operations of larger systems are required that differ dramatically from the kind of personal trust that dominated in premodern or earlier modern forms of society.[1] Modern and late modern societies require implicit confidence in abstract "expert systems" that are based on technical knowledge and that rely on technical and professional experts who are responsible for maintaining and operating such systems. Anyone who travels by airplane can readily appreciate the level of trust that is required to participate in such systems. High levels of trust are routinely demonstrated in the willingness of people to drive their automobiles with the expectation that other drivers will adhere to established rules and customs to avoid accidents. Increased trust in expert systems is also manifested in widespread reliance on the advanced technology of the internet to make purchases or pay bills electronically. In all these cases, trust is extended to a vast network of people that extends far beyond one's

[1] Elias's analysis, reviewed in the previous chapter, suggests that in the Middle Ages the level of random violence was such that mutual trust was extremely limited, perhaps extending no further than one's extended family.

personal network of social relations. This expansion of trust to professional experts who are responsible for the routine operation of highly interdependent systems can be seen as an extension of Elias's analysis of the importance of the increased ability of people in a civilized society to predict one another's behavior.

There are, of course, new kinds of risks that emerge from relying on expert systems and those responsible for them (including automobile drivers and airline pilots) to perform as expected. Modern or late modern society exposes people to potential new dangers that were unknown in previous periods of history. At a more general level, an even larger concern than localized accidents emerges from the way the overall dynamics and direction of late modern society appear to be beyond anyone's control. This lack of control leads to high levels of vulnerability to the increased levels of new kinds of risk that could result in major catastrophic accidents. In addition, the dangers posed by the proliferation of weapons of mass destruction, including nuclear weapons, are far greater than the risks posed by previous forms of warfare. As Giddens put it, ".... There are 'environments' of risk that collectively affect large masses of individuals—in some instances potentially everyone on the face of the earth, as in the case of the risk of ecological disaster or nuclear war" (Giddens, 1990:35). Giddens uses the image of the "juggernaut" to portray how the routine patterns of everyday life in our current period of radicalized modernity are vulnerable to spinning out of control in ways that threaten our well-being and even our survival (Giddens, 1990:151, 173).

Giddens' emphasis on the risks of our contemporary period of "radicalized modernity" is consistent with the analysis of German sociologist Ulrich Beck (1999) regarding the unanticipated risks resulting from the technological advances of our advanced industrial society. However, both Giddens and Beck emphasize the increase reflexiveness of advanced modernity as well. This concept refers to the ability of society's members to monitor and reflect on their condition, assessing the potential dangers and learning how to predict the future consequences of their actions more effectively. Definitions of risk are themselves socially constructed, and Beck points out that efforts to minimize or contain risks, including those resulting from technology, always involve important political issues, the resolution of which could lead to changes in our concepts of progress and freedom (Beck, 1999:133–152). The erosion of our unquestioned faith in progress resulting from our increased awareness of our vulnerability to humanly constructed dangers could well be a major stimulus for new forms of theoretical analysis. As Beck put it, "... I feel strongly that we have to be imaginative yet disciplined if we are to break out of the iron cage of conventional and orthodox social science and politics. We need a new sociological imagination which is sensitive to the concrete paradoxes and challenges of reflexive modernity ..." (Beck, 1999:134). These challenges include the management of risks resulting from human action.

Both Giddens and Beck emphasize the crucial importance of understanding the interrelated changes that characterize the transition from modernity to "late" or "radicalized" modernity. But despite these major transformations, they also see significant continuities. The ambiguities and uncertainties inherent in the concept of postmodernity are also reflected in Ritzer and Goodman's (pp. 151–158 in Jonathan H. Turner, ed. 2001) argument which they introduce with the statement that "Modernity is already postmodern." (p. 151) In Ritzer and Goodman's view postmodernism reflects a heightened awareness of the "contingency" that has always been associated with modernity. The social world of modernity is seen in this perspective as always having been characterized by a great deal of uncertainty and numerous "historical accidents." This orientation toward postmodern theory highlights these contingent and unpredictable features of the modern world instead of relegating them to the background. Ritzer and Goodman's perspective clearly contrasts with the main thrust of the major theories of modern society, in which the goal was to discover underlying deterministic principles or "essential forces" through systematic scientific investigation. They suggest that sociological analysis should focus on the alternative possibilities inherent in modern social life instead of continuing a futile search for an ultimate comprehensive explanation that aims at prediction or control. Nevertheless, for some postmodern theorists the interrelated changes of our time indicate a qualitative transformation of all levels of the social world that cannot adequately be described as a continuation of the defining features of the "modern" world. Or, at least the magnitude of current social changes requires a radical revision of our theoretical understanding. This suggests that models of linear change and progress that had earlier been developed to explain the dynamics of the modern world must be replaced by new paradigms that are not burdened or distorted by the underlying ballast of the implicit assumptions associated with modernity.

Although postmodern perspectives are certainly not limited to the cultural level, their development coincides with the emergence of a strong sociological interest in cultural analysis. Beyond this, however, major areas of emphasis in various postmodern analyses include the rapidly changing dynamics and high volatility of the economic system, changes in the configuration of power relations within and among nation-states, and an increase in the confrontation of an emerging globalized culture with local traditions. Coupled with increasing insecurity and risk in various aspects of life, the interrelations among these dynamics can be seen in some ways as a development of new forms of critical analysis that are designed to fit the new realities of the political economy and culture of advanced capitalism. The postmodern emphasis on the increasing globalization of capitalism expands the perspective on the world economy pioneered by Wallerstein (as reviewed in Chap. 14) in ways that reflect the more fluid and dynamic nature of economic transactions today as compared to previous stages of capitalism. These transformations are accompanied by an increasing globalization of culture as well, particularly as manifested in the diffusion of American forms of entertainment and consumption and their confrontation with local cultural traditions.

A great deal of postmodern theorizing examines various aspects of the dynamic relations among cultural meanings and value systems, social institutions, and individual identity. This involves showing how alternative cultural symbols and meanings are being created and combined in various ways for different purposes in the process of constructing or transforming individual and group identities. This process is particularly salient in an environment where traditional sources of institutional authority and cultural meaning are being questioned or seem irrelevant. (For a sampling of several different examples of postmodern forms of analysis, see A. A. Berger, ed. [1998].) Several interrelated themes of postmodern analysis will be reviewed in the following sections. Perhaps one of the most crucial is the widespread breakdown in all type of authority structures, including those involved in defining valid forms of knowledge.

Skepticism Regarding Knowledge and Authority

A key feature of postmodern forms of thought is that no system of knowledge can be regarded as providing absolute or ultimate truth. Instead, all types of knowledge are conditioned by the social locations and interests of those who develop them and reflect the implicit biases and limitations of the knower's particular perspective. This skeptical orientation applies to scientific knowledge as well as to all other belief systems. Like other forms of knowledge, scientific knowledge also reflects the specific social and material circumstances of its development. This skepticism represents a break with the "modern" era's faith in scientific knowledge, as well as implicit reliance on rational analysis to discern "ultimate" or at least objective truth. Since the 18th century Enlightenment, truth claims based on reason or scientific evidence were seen as beyond dispute, and these claims were often used by some to criticize or debunk traditional customs and religious beliefs. For postmodernists, however, rational analysis and scientific evidence can be regarded as valid only within the particular cognitive framework where are developed, and these implicit frameworks vary for people in different social locations and reflect their divergent interests. These social locations can be defined in terms of socioeconomic class location, gender, race and ethnicity, nationality, sexual orientation, various group memberships, and so on. The material and social interests associated with these positions influence the pursuit or promotion of systems of knowledge in various ways. The effect of these influences is to provide implicit support for particular group interests.

This type of critique is consistent with Michel Foucault's perspective regarding the linkage between knowledge and power (reviewed earlier in Chap. 15), and also with Dorothy Smith's analysis of how mainstream sociology inevitably reflects the biases resulting from the social standpoint of its male founders and dominant representatives (as described in Chap. 16). (This skeptical orientation is actually consistent with Auguste Comte's 19th century criticism of the 18th century Enlightenment faith in reason [as reviewed in Chap. 2], which he categorized as reflecting the "metaphysical" stage of human evolution, and which would eventually be replaced by the "positive" stage and its more open-ended commitment to the growth of scientific knowledge through detailed empirical research.) For sociologists today, the implication is that no theoretical orientation can be seen as providing an objective and authoritative account of the social world or a scientific explanation of it that must be regarded as universally true.

The modern world is characterized by widespread acceptance of the notion that scientific knowledge mirrors and explains the objective world, although this applies more to the natural than the social sciences. In the postmodern world, however, scientific knowledge in all areas of inquiry can be evaluated and criticized in the same way as any other form of knowledge. This is because scientific claims to objective truth inevitably reflect the particular linguistic and cultural frameworks within which they are developed. More than this, all systems of knowledge can be analyzed as self-referential patterns of discourse, as opposed to providing objective representations of the external world. Words, concepts, ideas, and paradigms in all areas of study are defined and elaborated linguistically, and their significance and validity are established in terms of other linguistic constructions. In this way, systems of knowledge are socially constructed and constitute a symbolic world of their own as much as (or more than) mirroring the real world or providing objective representations of it.

If carried to the extreme, the implication of this argument is that it is impossible to have irrefutable objective knowledge of the external world as it really is; instead, we can know it only through the forms of discourse and categories of thought that we use to describe and explain it. A less extreme version would hold that knowledge based on experiential sensations of the external world do not necessarily require linguistic formulation. For example, a person may experience the pain of being struck with a sharp or hard object or touching a hot surface, and may thereby learn to avoid such situations, even without knowing the words "hurt" or "hot" or being able to communicate these unpleasant sensations. Despite the differences in their styles of analysis, both Richard Rorty (1989) and John R. Searle (1995) deal with these issues in moderate terms that are largely consistent with the basic assumptions of pragmatism and symbolic interaction theory.[2] Although bodily sensations and perceptions do not necessarily require language to be experienced, language is obviously required to communicate such experiences. And once linguistic categories are internalized, individuals inevitably make use of them even in their own subjective reflections on their perceptions and experiences.

This skeptical orientation regarding knowledge claims extends to theoretical models that purport to identify any primary master trend or grand narrative that may be seen as dominating the overall direction of social change or insuring long-term evolutionary progress (Lyotard, 1984). As described earlier in this volume, the initial development of sociology was stimulated in part by the growth of science and technology and the long-term transition from a rural-agricultural society grounded in fairly stable traditions to a more dynamic urban-industrial society governed by a strong orientation toward the promotion of progress through the application of instrumental rationality. Despite the strains resulting from these social transformations, there was a strong belief in the prospects for long-term progress in terms of material technology as well as social organization.[3] This faith in long-term linear progress was reflected in functionalist

---

[2] John Searle's (1995) analysis of the way social reality is constructed symbolically was reviewed in Chapter 5 in connection with symbolic interaction theory. Searle distinguished between the objective world, as it exists independently of human beings' social definitions, and the symbolic forms whereby the external world is represented in people's consciousness and in their communication.

[3] These beliefs in long-range progress were certainly not uniform. As we saw in Chap. 2, Durkheim was optimistic that sociological insights could provide the foundation for the development of a modern moral code that would promote a type of social solidarity that would be consistent with the increased division of labor, while Marx felt that long-term progress would be based on increasing class conflict leading to a social revolution. Weber, in contrast, was concerned with the way modern instrumental rationality was leading to an the construction of an "iron cage" that stifles emotional expressiveness and reduces the salience of concerns with idealistic moral commitments.

models of social evolution as well as in the aspirations of neo-Marxists and critical theorists to point the way to a less exploitative and oppressive social order.[4]

Postmodern theorists reject the notion of an overarching narrative of linear change and progress that is governed by any single master trend. Instead of a single dominant story of human progress, there are multiple narratives that can be told, no one of which should be seen as more authoritative than the others. For example, the history of the development of modern capitalism can be described in terms of the struggles of working class men and women to cope with the new economic hardships and uncertainties they faced as well as in the success of capitalist entrepreneurs in developing large-scale enterprises leading to widespread improvement in people's living standards. Still another story could be told by their competitors who were eliminated in the process. Similarly, American history can be narrated from the point of view of native Americans as well as European settlers, or from the point of view of Spanish settlers in the Southwest as well as English settlers in the Northeast. The same point can also be made with regard to the contrast between European and American versions of history as opposed to Middle East Islamic versions, for example, Southeast Asia Islamic versions, or Chinese versions.

This strong emphasis on the relativity of all forms of knowledge leads postmodern theorists to refuse to grant a more privileged position or greater authority to some forms of knowledge or grand narratives than others in any area, or to exclude or discount any claim to knowledge or any historical narratives as necessarily invalid for those holding them. The same critique can also be applied to all cultural worldviews. There is no rational or scientific basis for claiming that any particular worldview is inherently superior or inferior. Instead, all cultural worldviews should be assessed in the light of their historical development and current conditions—though any of them could be criticized if they provide implicit support for structures of domination that lead to marginalization of disprivileged segments of the population or promotion of any form of cultural imperialism. This relativism sometimes leads to a kind of fascination with cultural and subcultural pluralism and diversity, in addition to a skeptical orientation regarding claims of cultural superiority. The expansion of this more pluralistic perspective may readily be related to the increased level of cross-cultural and international contacts associated with globalization.

Globalization and its Impact on Nation-States and Local Settings

An important part of the background for postmodern types of theory is the way the globalization process is eroding the autonomy of nation-states, expanding the level of interdependence among the different societies and regions of the world, and

---

[4] A major contrast between functionalists and critical theorists in this regard is that functionalists focused heavily on the evolutionary progress already achieved, while critical theorists emphasized the need for additional social transformations. But both seemed to reflect a belief in the possibility of progress.

setting the stage for what Huntington (1996) refers to as a potential "clash of civilizations." The notion that increased levels of global interaction will increase the risk of a major civilizational conflict obviously reflects an orientation toward cultural diversity that contrasts with the nonauthoritarian or nonjudgmental postmodern response to pluralism as described in the preceding section. Tolerant acceptance of cultural pluralism is clearly a pattern that not everyone would accept. For some, the confrontation with beliefs and lifestyles that are different leads to a sense of being threatened and therefore determined to maintain their own particular culture as superior to others and to defend it against the contaminating influence of competing cultures. This is the basic orientation that today is reflected in various forms of cultural fundamentalism. A major contrast in worldviews can be identified in American society, and globally, between those who are open to cultural diversity and those who insist on the superiority of their own culture. For some of the latter, the desire to defend their own culture is sometimes transformed into a desire to expand its influence and displace other cultures in the process. It is this process that can lead to the clash of civilizations that Huntington analyzed.

The increased levels of both interdependence and conflict on a global level include several interrelated dimensions: economic, political, military, cultural, and social.[5] Robertson (1992) points out that the entire world is increasingly perceived as a single place, while Urry (2003) uses the concepts of networks and flows to analyze the complexity of the emergent global system. Dennis Smith (2006) highlights how struggles to achieve economic and political domination may stimulate conflicts that are motivated by the determination to redress the collective humiliation experienced by those who are dominated by the major powers. He points out, too, that the ability of particular nation-states to forestall such conflicts through such strategies as promotion of human rights is threatened by the declining power of nation-states in an increasingly globalized system. Featherstone (1995) emphasizes the high level of cultural fragmentation resulting from the juxtaposition of divergent cultural traditions through increased levels of global communication and their confrontation with the worldwide diffusion of many aspects of America's consumer culture. Wallerstein (1999) suggests that we are currently witnessing major interrelated crises that threaten the future of the capitalist world system and that make the long-term future difficult to predict, and Giddens' (1990:151, 173) metaphor of the juggernaut implies that the dynamics of the global system in which we are involved are inherently risky and out of control (see also Giddens, 2000).

The origins of the contemporary process of globalization can be traced back at least as far as the early stages of modernity. As explained in Chap. 14, in Immanuel Wallerstein's world systems theory, the modern world economy had its origins in sixteenth century trade in agricultural products among European societies. Increased levels of economic interdependence are manifested today not only in traditional patterns of trade in raw materials and manufactured goods but in the way financial capital can be moved rapidly across the political boundaries of different

[5] For analyses of several different dimensions of globalization as they are related in various ways to global capitalism, see Will Hutton and Anthony Giddens, eds. (2000).

societies through electronic transfers. In addition, multinational corporations operating in a global environment in the emerging postmodern era have demonstrated their willingness to relocate manufacturing operations from high-wage societies to low-wage societies to save labor costs and increase profits. The lack of loyalty to particular societies or communities that this pattern of job relocation reflects obviously increases economic insecurity in high-wage industrial societies and also decreases employees' loyalty and their expectations of relatively stable life-long career paths. The overall picture that emerges is one of high volatility and long-term insecurity. This increased density and volatility of global economic processes have major implications for national and local autonomy, as well as undermining the economic security of large segments of the population, including the middle class.

In addition to economic interdependence, the emergence of postmodern global systems also includes increased levels of political and cultural interdependence and conflict as well. In a global political environment with multiple transnational and regional centers of power, it is difficult even for dominant societies to act unilaterally in their relations with one another, or with the multinational corporations located within their borders. Although various types of alliances among different nation-states are established to defend national interests (economic, political, and military), such relationships create a web of constraints and obligations that limit the rights and the ability even of dominant societies to act in disregard of the interests and power of other societies. Although international treaties and alliances are certainly not new, their role in the postmodern world is in many ways more crucial and more complex than ever. This is partly because of the need to manage the multiple effects of high levels of economic interdependence, partly because of the increased risks resulting from the expanded reach and destructiveness of military power, and partly because the way in which communication and transportation technologies greatly reduce the effects of geographical distance and increase the possibilities and the challenges of coordination of human activities on a global level.

In the area of culture, the consumer and entertainment industry of American and other Western societies has been diffused throughout much of the world. This is due in part to the expansion of business enterprises into international markets (such as McDonald's fast food in Moscow, Russia, for example) and partly to the influence of the mass media (such as Hollywood movies) and international celebrities in the world of entertainment and other areas. Increased international travel and communication have also helped foster the emergence of a more homogeneous cultural landscape around the world among large segments of the population. The emerging globalized worldview includes an increased level of awareness of multiple cultures in different societies. Nevertheless, iconic representations of America and Western cultural patterns often exert a dominant influence, stimulating reactions that range from fascination to resentment.

The perceived American domination of an increasingly homogenized global culture has not gone unchallenged. Other societies have resisted this influence by mounting deliberate efforts to preserve their own distinctive values, symbols, and ways of life. Even within the United States, countervailing pressures are sometimes launched to preserve local cultural enclaves in the face of the expanding influence of an increasingly homogenized culture. In some cases these preservation efforts are intended to promote tourism and economic development. When this occurs, the influx of tourists and of businesses to cater to their needs inevitably undermines the ability of local communities to maintain their culture in its authentic or pristine form. Instead, the commodification and packaging of nostalgic representations of local cultures are combined with various tourist-oriented business enterprises. Many of the latter are franchise operations that contribute to the standardization and homogenization which undermine the presumed authenticity of the local cultural experiences that are offered for sale for tourists' consumption. These developments obviously have important effects on local communities' employment patterns and occupational and wage structures.

Beyond the borders of individual societies, the influence of a globalizing culture always has to be adapted to the specific characteristics of local communities and their traditions. Multinational corporations have major headquarters in particular cities, and their high concentration in certain large and well-known cities around the world leads to their designation as "global cities" in the postmodern world (Abrahamson, 2004). In addition, local communities in many countries serve as sites for various types of operational activities of multinational corporations. The dynamic interplay between globalism and localism is thus an important issue for economic, political, and cultural analysis. The emergence of global cities that serve as the hub of multiple international business operations provides a clear indication of the confrontation between global forces and local traditions. Those who are actively involved in global networks often seem oblivious to the issues and concerns of local residents in their immediate area.

The mass media are also a major influence in the emergence of global culture. In addition to the global diffusion of Hollywood-style entertainment, the almost instantaneous global transmission of "breaking news" that occurs anywhere throughout the world gives those who tune in a sense of "real time" connection to such events. In addition to the one-way flow of information provided by satellite television networks, the global expansion of the internet enables people throughout the world to exchange ideas and information and to collaborate at a distance in cooperative projects. These projects may include participating in a wide range of social movements as well as taking care of business for formal organizations. Contemporary strategies for gaining intelligence regarding terrorist networks, for example, include eavesdropping on their electronic communication. Terrorists themselves contribute to this process as they post news of their activities and threats on the internet. The next section will focus on the increased contributions of the mass media to the production of a virtual form of social reality that overlaps and penetrates the objective reality of the actual social environment within which people live.

Mass Media and the Representation Versus the Simulation of Reality

Increasing levels of global communication and transportation contribute to the erosion of traditional geographical and cultural boundaries. This blurring of boundaries is itself a major theme in postmodern analysis. This theme can be related to the increased diversity that occurs when the cultural or subcultural patterns of a particular area or group are diffused to other areas or groups and combined in various ways with their local traditions. The result of this process is that the boundaries between different local cultures, and between them and an emerging global culture, intersect and overlap in diverse ways in different societies and local communities. As a result of the invasion of global influences, local groups learn to see their own local culture in a new light. As a result they are faced with the challenge of how to adapt as they seek to determine what aspects of the global culture to embrace or to resist, and how to preserve the distinctive local traditions they value.

The mass media are a major vehicle for the diffusion of global culture in local communities around the world. They may also contribute to the diffusion of some aspects of local cultures by providing background for their featured story of the day. In many ways the social world seems to be saturated by their influence. Actual events in far-off places become "real" in people's minds—or at least "significant"—by being reported by the mass media. However, the mass media themselves are not as homogeneous as they once were. Despite the enormous impact of their influence in expanding people's social worlds beyond their own local context, the mass media themselves are fragmented. The images and perspectives they present are also inevitably limited and often distorted in ways that may be difficult for viewers to detect. In addition to the total volume and great diversity of entertainment and news coverage they provide, the mass media have also contributed in a major way to the erosion of traditional boundaries. National and international events become part of the face-to-face conversations of people in innumerable local contexts, and sensational local events quickly become elevated to the status of breaking national or international news. In addition, the mass media's distinctions between news, political commentary, entertainment, and marketing easily become blurred. News stories are selected and packaged to highlight their sensational aspects and public appeal, while advertisers pay the bills to induce the members of their audiences to expand their level of consumption. Political leaders as well as social movement spokespersons stage their messages to get maximum positive news coverage. Critical reactions to official government policy statements are sometimes provided by the opposition as well, thereby enabling the news media to foster a reputation of fairness and also to appeal to the largest possible audience. "Infomercials" designed to sell new products may be framed as much like news items as possible. Movies and television may provide implicit political messages or commentary, and celebrities in the world of entertainment may use their celebrity status for political purposes.[6]

---

[6] An example of this linkage between entertainment and politics is provided by the late Ronald Reagan, whose political career as president of the United States and earlier as governor of California followed a career as a Hollywood actor. Arnold Schwarzenegger is another example of how celebrity status earned as an actor provided the public visibility necessary for generating political influence sufficient to be elected governor of California.

The impact of the mass media on the culture and the public mentality has long been recognized as an important characteristic of modernity. In a once-influential book entitled *The Medium is the Massage* (McLuhan and Fiore, 1967), Marshall McLuhan and Quentin Fiore highlighted the notion that the influence of the television medium itself was as noteworthy as the messages conveyed, even though the media were fewer and the messages more standardized at that time. In the current postmodern era, however, in addition to the proliferation of cable and satellite television channels, the world wide web of the internet provides another vehicle for the electronic dissemination of traditional types of news, plus many other types of information. Unlike traditional television, the internet also allows for various forms of public discourse regarding all types of current events, both serious and trivial. In fact, news stories transmitted via the internet are sometimes accompanied by an invitation for public response. Like the "letters to the editor" that are featured in local newspapers, these electronic venues for public discourse may provide the illusion of meaningful participation in public life, despite the often unstructured and unorganized nature of such participation. These various forms of mass media in the postmodern world are seen not only as reflecting social reality but as actually creating a simulated version of it that seems to displace the "real" world in people's consciousness. This type of influence is a major theme in French social theorist Jean Baudrillard's (1983) perspective (see also Douglas Kellner [1989] and Paul Hegarty, [2004]). In Baudrillard's analysis, one of the major contemporary effects of the mass media is to create a simulated and self-contained cultural reality that seems to replace or to supersede the real world. An extreme form of this emphasis is expressed in the title of his book, *The Gulf War did not take place* (Baudrillard, 1995). The assertion in the title can be seen as reflecting Baudrillard's intention to convey the idea that the reality of the war was experienced by the public largely in terms of how it was packaged for mass media representation.

Despite the often arbitrary and tenuous relation between media-represented reality and the objective reality of the real world, media versions contribute in a major way to people's perceptions of the larger social world and how it may relate to the local circumstances of their lives. The overwhelming saturation of popular culture by the mass media contributes to the erosion of the dividing line between the reality of social life as it is actually experienced and media representations or simulations of it. In addition, the opportunities available for electronic networking through the internet allows for the creation of still another virtual reality, the boundaries of which may overlap or intersect with other communication media and local interaction in complex ways. For example, celebrities who are publicized heavily by the mass media become influential role models with whom young people identify in their efforts to develop a satisfying identity as they face the uncertainties of their lives. Their identification with these public celebrities may be reinforced through electronic network contacts with other fans across the country. The influence of the alternative realities provided through television and the internet is magnified as a result of the erosion of a stable social environment which might otherwise provide meaningful guidelines and real life role models for one's social identity in local settings.

Popular Culture and Experiments in Identity Construction

The impact of mass media constructions at the macro level in permeating and dominating the micro level social world is clearly manifested in the world of popular entertainment and the consumer culture. As noted above, the stories generated by entertainment celebrities are featured regularly in television and internet-based news stories as well as popular magazine articles. In fact, personal details of the private lives of major celebrities are often treated as being equal in significance to news of actual public affairs with significant social impact. In any case, public celebrities offer a wide array of iconic images and symbols from which people may draw as they construct their own personal social worlds and their identities in ways that are at least partially independent of local contexts and personal ties. This is reflected in the way many young people imitate the fashions of their favorite rock stars, professional athletes, or movie celebrities, or wear iconic representations of them on their tee-shirts. This identification process may be extended to include fellow fans, providing a sense of bonding even in the absence of personal ties. Such bonds are reinforced through the emotional arousal that occurs at celebrities' public performances, such as rock concerts, and being there can be commemorated by tee-shirts or other material memorabilia. Moreover, one's status and identity in local peer groups may be enhanced by regular attendance at such events as well as by keeping up with the details of celebrities' lives. Zygmunt Bauman (1992) pointed out how the shared identification of fans with their favorite public celebrities leads to the emergence of abstract "tribal communities" that extend beyond the networks of the actual social relations in which people are involved in local peer groups. Symbols of "membership" in such tribal communities can be displayed through visible symbols or iconic representations in clothing, styles of expression and behavior, tattoos, and popular culture tastes.

Overall, a large part of contemporary popular culture is seen by some postmodern analysts as consisting of an immensely wide array of images, symbols, meanings, and iconic representations from various sources and contexts that are often highly fragmented and discordant. Individuals are able (and sometimes are expected) to "pick and choose" from these various cultural resources in constructing symbolic representations of whatever identity or meaning system they would like to claim. These claims are matters of personal taste and preference, and they sometimes seem to override the mundane and routine reality of everyday life. This contrasts with earlier periods (including the modern era) in which individuals' identities and meaning system were grounded in the everyday life routines of their local social environment. Although individuals could make choices, within certain limits, these choices were more clearly structured and less likely to be arbitrary selections from a free-floating array of cultural options from the wider social world. The background for these contemporary individualized forms of cultural expression is a social world that is characterized by rapid institutional change and widespread cultural fragmentation. The resulting instability and uncertainty contribute to an erosion of people's sense of security about the "real" social world and their social location and identity within it.

There are many different types of responses to the insecurities resulting from this deterioration of well-established and widely accepted cultural expectations. The emergence of "tribal" pseudo-communities as described by Bauman is one response to this breakdown. Highly personal experimentation with symbolic or iconic representations of various cultural or subcultural meanings that can readily be adopted and incorporated into one's identity is another. Still another response would involve a search for security through private forms of spirituality, or through identifying with various social networks whose members are also involved in a quest for a deeper or transcendent meaning system. In the area of religion, identification with a fundamentalist religious group may be an option that will provide a sense of security and ultimate meaning by insulating its members from the contaminating influences of the surrounding culture and enabling them to resist its fragmentation and uncertainty. In addition, as Denzin (1991) points out, some elements of the disparate cultural resources that are widely available may be selected to reinforce particularistic identities such as those associated with race, socioeconomic class or status group, gender, or sexual orientation.

The erosion of established expectations and traditions provides an expanded array of options for new experiences and new forms of human relationships and identities. Richard Gergen (1991) expresses considerable optimism regarding these possibilities in postmodern society. He acknowledges that individuals' meaning systems and identities are threatened with erosion by the overwhelming effects of an increasing array of divergent cultural symbols and meanings, but suggests that this opens up new possibilities for individual choice. In developing their distinctive lifestyles and identities, individuals today have a degree of freedom that is far greater than would be possible with the fewer options and the more stable and restricting social expectations of the earlier "modern" period. The options available today have increased in large part through the expanded range of travel and communication that modern technology makes possible in contemporary societies, as well as through their dissemination in global markets and the mass media.

Anthony Giddens (1992) also emphasized how the erosion of traditional expectations and constraints makes possible and encourages the "transformation" of intimate relations in ways that increase the freedom of the parties involved to develop the terms of their relationship through the consensus they themselves negotiate. This freedom is seen by him as allowing for a fuller manifestation of democratic values, with increased opportunities for individual autonomy and equality. For relations between women and men, the availability of contraception techniques as well as increasing levels of gender equality allow for the development of what Giddens describes as "pure" relationships involving emotional intimacy and/or sexual pleasure that are not undermined or distorted by concerns relating to reproduction or economic or emotional dependency. The has obvious relevance for enhancing the quality of marital relations and increasing the level of personal fulfillment that both women and men are able to experience through their intimacy. In addition, the choices people make regarding how their sexuality is incorporated into their basic identity can be detached from the constraining effects of social expectations related to other aspects of their social positions. As choices expand and autonomy increases, individuals are increasingly able to discover new options for constructing their identities and relationships in ways that break out of traditional boundaries and allow for the expression of their personal choices.

At the same time, however, the dissolving of stable expectations and social arrangements result in a highly fluid situation in which the security of stable structures and established boundaries has eroded (Bauman, 2000, 2003). Just as the stability of occupational careers has been undermined by transnational relocation of business enterprises, so also the freedom to establish new forms of social relations implies that the parties involved are free to terminate them as well. The breakdown of traditional barriers, constraints, and expectations has led to increased freedom and more opportunities in terms of people's relationships, but it also increases their vulnerability. The security and personal fulfillment that individuals achieve through their voluntary choices are undermined when the other parties involved in these relationships choose otherwise. Without the social anchorage provided by a stable environment, such relationships endure only on the basis of the mutual commitments of the parties involved.

Enchanted Consumption as a Source of Identity and Status

Individuals' lifestyles and leisure patterns have long been seen as expressive of their identities. Even before the Great Depression and World War II era, Thorstein Veblen's 1934 book, *The Theory of the Leisure Class*, highlighted the way lifestyles and conspicuous consumption patterns symbolized status distinctions that went beyond basic economic survival issues and objective differences in income. However, in the postmodern period, consumption and leisure activities are sometimes seen as assuming even greater importance for establishing and confirming people's identities than in previous periods of history. This is because of the way rapid social change and cultural fragmentation have undermined long-established social and cultural supports that anchored people's social positions and reinforced their relationships. With the potential for frequent changes in occupation, social network contacts, family status, residential location, and primary group memberships, individuals are faced with the ongoing challenge of how to manage their identities and their relationships in a fluid social and cultural environment with multiple options. For those with sufficient resources, lifestyle choices are reflected in distinct patterns of consumption and leisure activities which postmodern theorists would regard as a major contemporary source of individual status and identity.

George Ritzer (1999) described the expanding opportunities for new forms or styles of consumption as a strategy of providing the experience of "enchantment" in an otherwise "disenchanted" world.[7] The concept of "disenchantment" had been used by Weber to describe the emerging modern world of his time in terms of the growth of bureaucratic organizations and increasing instrumental rationality in more and more areas of life. We might see disenchantment as characteristic of the modern world while enchantment becomes possible with the increased options of a postmodern world. The logic of capitalist development involves a relentless effort to increase profits through the commodification and sale of more and more goods and services. The last half of the twentieth century has seen a proliferation of business enterprises that exhibit this process. With more and more goods, services, and experiences "commodified" and offered for sale, opportunities for affluent consumers to seek to enrich or enchant their lives through new or expanded forms of consumption are constantly being heavily promoted by advertisers as the key to a satisfying and meaningful life. Ritzer described in fascinating detail several different types of "cathedrals of consumption," including shopping malls, discount stores, superstores, specialty restaurants (ranging from fast food to theme restaurants), casinos, "old-town" markets, and even cruise ships (Ritzer, 1999:8–22).

Ritzer also points out that the success of these establishments in attracting large numbers of customers requires them to resort to the potentially disenchanting strategies of rationalization so as to manage the flow of customers and maintain the consistency of the products and experiences they offer. This means, of course, that the employees of such establishments do not necessarily experience the enchantment themselves, even though they are expected to maintain the "enchanting" experiences that will lure customers and entice them to spend their money. But the "inside" view of such establishments, as opposed to the view intended for consumers, can be seen as manifesting the well-known modern form of bureaucratic rationality that Weber described—and from which their costumers presumably are offered a temporary escape. The predictability expected of employees as they fulfill the obligations of their bureaucratic positions can thus be seen as a continuation of the disenchanting pattern of modernity, even though the intended outcome from the consumer's point of view is postmodern enchantment.

The enchantment associated with these "cathedrals of consumption" is related as much to customers' status and identity as to the "use value" of the commodities or services they purchase. Part of the enchantment is due to the feeling of temporary escape from the "real world" into a simulated world, though this simulated world may nevertheless incorporate some aspects of the real world in idealized form. Thus, for example, a modern enclosed shopping mall provides the juxtaposition of numerous types of stores that might be found in a traditional downtown "Main Street," but with the stores closer together and their doors always open, and without the risks

---

[7] George Ritzer's numerous contributions to contemporary sociological theory cover both "modern" and "postmodern" types of theory. For example, in the area of contemporary consumption patterns, his widely cited portrayal of the McDonalidization process makes extensive use of Weber's classic analysis of bureaucracy and the high level of standardization and predictability it fosters in the fast food industry and other franchise enterprises (see Ritzer, 1993). The concept of bureaucratization has long been central in "modern" sociological theory.

of automobile traffic (once a parking spot has been found), unpleasant weather, potential robbers, or panhandlers. Restaurants, movies, games, and other forms of entertainment or leisure activities may also be handily available in these settings. More extreme forms of this pattern of simulation are found in places like Disney World and Las Vegas in which the goal is total immersion in an enchanting environment that clearly is intended to provide an appealing alternative to the mundane real world, even while duplicating some of the distinctive appeal of various potentially enchanting real world vacation destinations. Thus, for example, the Las Vegas experience not only encourages unrealistic fantasies of untold wealth through gambling but also the simulated experience of being in New York, Egypt, Paris, Venice, and so on—all within an afternoon's walk or a short drive.

Ritzer also identifies various strategies for providing everyday life forms of enchantment that do not require escape to the simulated reality of a Disney World or Las Vegas. Residence in upscale gated communities, for example, provides the promise of an ongoing form of everyday life enchantment which can be integrated with routine consumption patterns that are expressive of one's distinctive cultural tastes and identity. The option of occasional trips to the local shopping mall or attendance at popular entertainment venues (concerts or athletic events of various types) provides additional everyday life forms of enchantment. Moreover, gated communities promise a higher level of security than can be guaranteed by a highly bureaucratized government with regard to being kept safe from the "dangerous classes" of people who lack the resources needed to participate in the "good life" of the enchanted postmodern society. Overall, in contrast to modernity, the promise of a satisfying and fulfilling life and identity is provided in the postmodern period through a consumption-oriented lifestyle, much of which involves participating in a simulated and enchanted world that contrasts sharply with productive activity and mundane routines.

Sociology of the Body: Body Shaping and Decorating as Expressive Reactions to Individual Anonymity

The postmodern challenges of identity construction and meaningful self-expression overlap with another emerging new emphasis in sociology: the sociology of the body. As we saw in Chap. 15, Michel Foucault emphasized how social control is exerted through monitoring, restricting, and regulating the movements of individuals' bodies. This applies both to individual bodies (as with the control of prisoners or probationers, for example) as well as to populations of bodies in public settings (crowd control). In addition, Bryan Turner (1996) has been highly influential in emphasizing the way human beings' bodies are employed to express cultural meanings. Turner regards the somewhat disembodied character of much social theory as due to the strong emphasis on instrumental rationality and its implications regarding the need to control the body and its unsocialized impulses. This tension between deliberate efforts to control the body and the ongoing experience of bodily desires and impulses is consistent with the historic dualism in Christianity between the "flesh" and the "spirit" and the never-ending warfare between these two aspects of "human nature." This conflict is often played out in efforts to regulate or control human beings' sexuality and, as suggested earlier, such control efforts have historically been stricter for women than men.

The human body is the actual site where the objective material and biological characteristics of human beings intersect with cultural patterns and social expectations. The body is obviously the source of various desires and potentialities for pleasure and pain that individuals are expected to learn to manage and control in the course of their everyday life behavior. The body also provides the energy for this everyday life behavior, even though biological capabilities and human anatomy set limits to people's performances. Moreover, as emphasized in the work of both Norbert Elias and Sigmund Freud, considerable effort and self-discipline are often required to control one's natural impulses and to fulfill the expectations of others as well as one's own internalized self-expectations. As suggested earlier, the motivation to engage in these self-control efforts is often reinforced by the anticipation of positive emotional arousal through social approval, or avoidance of a negative arousal through disapproval, and both kinds of emotions are grounded in innate biological processes that individuals readily recognize and learn to manage, at least to some extent.

The process of social construction as emphasized in symbolic interaction theory can also be applied to individuals' bodies. In other words, people not only construct their sociocultural world and their actions within it; they also engage in various forms of "body construction" (or reconstruction) as well. This is manifested in many different ways, including, for example, dieting and exercise programs whereby individuals seek literally to control their physical shape and appearance. Motivations for these regimens vary and may include concerns with insuring good health, postponing the effects of the aging process, or conforming to a culturally defined ideal body type with which they identify. In addition, through tattoos, body piercing, and jewelry that may be attached to their bodies, individuals use their bodies for iconic artistic expressions that serve to represent their identities, group affiliations, and cultural meanings with which they identify (see DeMello, 2000).

The effort to shape and decorate one's body to reflect symbolic meanings appears to go beyond the strategies portrayed by Erving Goffman regarding the use of clothes, cosmetics, and detachable jewelry to manage one's appearance in particular settings. As seen in Chap. 5, Goffman's dramaturgic perspective regarding the presentation of self emphasized how people attempt to control the impressions they make on others so as to reflect the identity or persona they seek to project. In his perspective, the flexibility they exhibit in different situations calls into question the notion of an inner core self that remains stable in different social environments. After all, people can readily change their clothing styles, jewelry, and even their hair styles, as well as their demeanor and behavior patterns as they move from one situation or social encounter to another. The situation is different with their bodies, however. The effects of people's efforts to construct and decorate their bodies seem to be intended to have a greater degree of permanence. Tattoos and body piercing cannot be washed off at the end of the day as readily as cosmetics or changed like tee-shirts and baseball caps. Although such characteristics as weight and overall appearance change gradually over time, the intention of developing and preserving an idealized body can be seen in the ongoing commitment and self-control that is manifested among those who adhere strictly to their diet and exercise programs.

In a pluralistic and fragmented culture, individuals have a wide range of symbolic options from which to choose in this body construction process. Styles of bodily self-expression differ for men versus women and young versus old, and there are significant variations within these broad categories as well. But despite these differences, people's determination to control the shape and appearance of their bodies, or to inscribe it with cultural meanings and symbols, may perhaps be seen as expressing a deeper sense of their unique personal identities than clothing preferences which can be changed on a daily basis. Such "body construction" and decoration serve to portray one's distinctive identity in a durable way that is not limited to particular social positions or situations, or to the clothes one wears and changes daily.

The discipline and self-control that are reflected in people's efforts to shape and control their bodily appearance through diet and exercise may be seen as a contemporary manifestation of the long-idealized discipline of the work ethic, the modern origins of which Weber identified in Protestantism. In addition, however, such strategies fit the contrasting emphasis in contemporary postmodern culture on hedonism and pleasure. This is because of the way people tend to see physical fitness as enabling them to "feel good" about themselves. The pattern is consistent with the overall shift in late capitalist or postmodern society from production to consumption. It also reflects the notion that one's identity and its expression are matters of personal preference and individual assertion, as opposed to being ascribed on the basis of family background, social location, tradition, or even one's age and "natural" appearance. Moreover, the uniqueness of the particular styles of artistic expression demonstrated in tattoos and body piercing with attached jewelry are another manifestation of the long-term individualism of contemporary society.

This individualism that is demonstrated through people's efforts to shape and decorate their bodies may be seen as particularly important in the context of the fluid and fragmented world of postmodern culture. Because of the widespread feelings of vulnerability and insecurity that result from the disintegration of consistent and meaningful social supports, individuals must rely primarily upon themselves for their sense of stability and security, and for constructing an identity that they feel will be personally fulfilling and meaningful to them. Indeed, the erosion of stable and well-defined social anchors means that individuals have no choice but to accept the challenge of taking an active role in constructing their own identity. Since people have a constant awareness of their own bodies throughout their waking hours, the power that is manifested in being able to control their bodies, and to employ their bodies in asserting a distinctive identity, may provide a reassuring sense of constancy and certainty that contrasts with the fluid and impermanent character of the larger sociocultural environment. Through the strategies they adopt in shaping and decorating their bodies, individuals manage to demonstrate control over at least one aspect of their lives that they experience as being relatively stable and uniquely their own. In this way they may partially compensate for their lack of control of the larger social world in which they participate.

This "sociology of the body" perspective and the sociobiological perspective reviewed in Chap. 18 can be compared and contrasted in terms of how they deal with the interface between human beings' biological characteristics and the socio-cultural world they construct. Despite their differences, in both perspectives human beings' bodies are the source of basic desires and impulses as well as the capacity for pleasure and pain. In both perspectives, too, there is a major concern with the need to control and regulate the body, either through external enforcement or self-discipline. The emphasis in sociobiology is on the behavioral and cultural strategies whereby innate biological predispositions and propensities are channeled in ways that serve the ultimate purpose of reproduction and long-term species survival. In contrast, in the sociology of the body perspective, the body serves as the site for inscribing and expressing symbolic cultural meanings, often in unique creative ways. People attempt through such strategies to establish their distinct identities in the face of social pressures designed to control and regulate their bodies in order to fit into an uncertain and often impersonal social world.

Ironically, however, despite the goal of individualized self-expression that body decorations such as tattoos and attached jewelry reflect, the pattern whereby increasing numbers of people opt to decorate their bodies in this fashion demonstrates that they are in fact following a growing social trend. The same point could also be applied to individualized clothing fashions as well but, as noted earlier, clothing is less permanent than tattoos. It is noteworthy that even these individualized forms of self-expression can be viewed through the distinctive lens of sociology and explained in terms of the conditioning effects of the social environment. It turns out that the social construction process applies not only to the social world but to individuals' bodies as well.

Summary

Our goal in this chapter has been to examine some selected themes in postmodern forms of sociological theory. Postmodern perspectives apply to all aspects and all levels of the contemporary social world, but the emphasis on the cultural level is particularly strong. One of the key characteristics shared by all postmodern forms of theory is a rejection of the notion that any theory, or any mode of scientific analysis, can represent ultimate objective truth. Instead, all forms of knowledge reflect the social conditions in which they originate and the cultural and linguistic frameworks through which they are developed and communicated. This leads to a highly pluralistic and relativistic view of truth and knowledge in which no form of knowledge is privileged as superior or more valid than any other form. This would, of course, have to apply to postmodern theoretical analyses as well.

Contemporary theorists vary in terms of whether or not they base their analyses on the notion that we have reached the end of modernity and entered a qualitatively different postmodern period. As indicated by Anthony Giddens, many of the crucial trends of our time may be seen as a continuation of the defining characteristics of modernity, but with significant changes that distinguish our contemporary "late modern" period from earlier periods of modernity. Some of these new trends include the emerging new patterns of global economic and cultural interdependence, the decline in the ability of nation-states to act unilaterally in the international arena, and the increased vulnerability of the population to risks that have emerged as an unintended byproduct of technological progress.

Postmodern forms of theorizing are highly diverse. But there is underlying agreement regarding the crucial discontinuities with modernity. Some of the key themes that were reviewed include rejection of any source of knowledge or authority as ultimate or universal, increasing cultural fragmentation and widespread breakdowns in traditional boundaries, the fluid and rapidly changing character of the contemporary world, the dynamic interrelations between the processes of globalism and localism, the influence of the diverse forms of mass media in defining social reality, and the expansion of various forms of reality simulation, coupled with the blurring of the line between real and simulated worlds. New forms of economic insecurity emerge from the expansion of global markets as multinational corporations seek to increase their profits by relocating to low-wage societies. Among the affluent segments of the population, individuals face the challenges of establishing a satisfying identity and managing their social relations in an environment of rapid social change, fragmented meaning systems, dissolving boundaries, widespread anxiety and uncertainty, and vulnerability to global social and cultural forces that seem beyond anyone's control. The erosion of traditional expectations and the proliferation of new options have expanded individual freedom, making possible new patterns of social relations and new types of identity construction. However, the particular arrangements that individuals manage to work out for themselves with regard to their social relations are also vulnerable because they are dependent on the congruence of other people' voluntary choices. In this context of change and uncertainty, the proliferation of various types of "cathedrals of consumption" provide a means for temporary escape from everyday life routines in order to pursue the quest for a more enchanting and satisfying lifestyle. As opposed to finding meaning and identity through mundane productive activities, the primary goals of life in the postmodern world revolve around steadily expanding consumption of material goods as well as (real or simulated) cultural experiences. In addition, the recent development of the "sociology of the body" perspective demonstrates how individuals draw on various cultural symbols as they seek to shape and decorate their bodies in ways that anchor their identities and express their individuality in an impersonal and uncertain world. In this way, they can at least depend on their own bodies to provide a sense of social stability and security.

As reflected in this volume, the development of sociology throughout a large part of the twentieth century, especially the second half, is grounded in modern schools of theory more than postmodern perspectives. If we review the history of the discipline, however, it is clear that major issues, and also dominant texts, change over time. It is obviously impossible to make predictions regarding the future; however, it will be interesting to see how the postmodern analyses that are sometimes seen as the new frontiers of the discipline will fare in the future.

Will the postmodern perspectives of today be included among the classical texts of the future, to be read in the middle or later decades of the twenty-first century and regarded as crucial for defining or redefining the major issues of the field? If so, this would certainly be ironic in view of postmodern refusal to regard any texts as a final authority regardless of how brilliant or insightful they seem to be.

If past patterns provide any basis for making predictions regarding the future of sociological theory, we can expect future developments to build selectively on current and past perspectives, even though these orientations may be subjected to critical analysis and transformed in the process. As the social world continues to change, the theories that are dominant today will no doubt seem less relevant, and the need for new insights and new paradigms will become more and more urgent. But the struggle to get an intellectual grip on the emerging new social world never begins from scratch. Despite the limitations of existing theories, the growth of knowledge in all areas occurs through a cumulative process in which current developments always build on past efforts. Theoretical perspectives are eventually evaluated as "classics" to the extent that they prove to have enduring relevance as a foundation for trying to understand and explain the emerging new issues and problems that make their appearance as the social world continues to change. It is perhaps too early now for us to try to predict which of the various postmodern themes reviewed in this chapter will prove to be most relevant for the remainder of the twenty-first century.

Questions for Study and Discussion

1. What does the postmodern critique of the authority of scientific knowledge imply regarding sociology as a scientific discipline devoted to discovering general principles of human behavior? How would you contrast your own views regarding the social world with those of your parents' generation? Are there some basic concepts and principles of the "sociological imagination" that you feel would always be relevant and appropriate for understanding people's social behavior, regardless of their own personal characteristics or social location? Explain.
2. Based on your experiences and observations, to what extent are various aspects of life in your own hometown influenced by the globalization process (economic, political, cultural, social)? Do you regard these effects as positive or negative? Explain. To what extent do you feel that exposure to a different culture, through travel or through your own social network contacts, is important for your identity and social awareness?
3. Discuss how the mass media today can serve both to unite and to divide people without regard to their geographical location. From your own experience, do your social contacts and network ties reflect some form of shared experience with the simulated reality that is created through television or the internet? Explain.
4. Based on your own personal experience or your observations of others, to what extent do "enchanted" consumption patterns and/or purely voluntary social

relationships provide an escape from everyday life routines and social obligations? What are the costs and benefits of these types of "escape?" What are their implications for your identity (or the identities of others in your social network)?

5. Explain how the social construction process can be applied to individuals' bodies? From your own experience or your observations of others, what types of cultural meanings are expressed in various tattoos, jewelry, clothing, and diet and exercise programs?

Chapter 21
Conclusion

All of the theories covered in previous chapters can help us expand our understanding of how the social world works, but none of them provides a complete picture. By comparing and contrasting multiple theories in a critical and reflective way, we are able to synthesize their valid insights into a more insightful and comprehensive analysis. The theoretical perspectives that have dominated sociological theory since the middle of the twentieth century can be distinguished in terms of their micro or macro emphasis. This contrast between microscopic versus macroscopic views provided our organizing frame, with a focus on selected meso-level social formations in between. These levels are linked in multiple ways in real life, however, and all of the theories we have discussed have been extended and elaborated to show their implications beyond the level of their primary starting point. This summary chapter will provide a brief review in terms of the major divisions of the book as follows:

- Preliminary stage setting
- From micro to meso to macro levels
- Toward theoretical integration: strategies and challenges

Preliminary Stage Setting

Chapter 1 contrasted the implicit theories of everyday life with explicit theories that are developed as part of a scientific discipline. The value of explicit theories is that they expand and clarify our vision of the social world and raise our consciousness regarding underlying beliefs and assumptions that we may have taken for granted. The quest for greater understanding often begins when we encounter people whose social and cultural backgrounds are different, or when we reflect on how our lives will be affected by the social changes of our time. As our understanding grows, we learn to appreciate that our own particular views about the social world reflect our own background and local (micro-level) environment. The origins of sociology as a distinct discipline are explained as resulting from efforts to understand the major social transformations involved in the emergence of the distinctive characteristics of the modern world.

Chapters 2 and 3 provided a brief historical overview of the development of sociology. Chapter 2 focuses on the early European sources. Brief descriptions were provided of the key ideas of the major figures who are today considered crucial in establishing sociology as a distinct discipline. These include Karl Marx, Émile Durkheim, Max Weber, and Georg Simmel. In addition, we also examined the contributions of several others whose works have long been neglected, despite being relevant and influential earlier. These include Harriet Martineau and Marianne Weber (whose ideas were important for demonstrating the early contributions of women), Auguste Comte (who coined the term "sociology"), Alexis de Tocqueville, Vilfredo Pareto, and Ferdinand Tönnies. Marx was neglected in American sociology prior to the mid to late 1960s but has had a major impact on contemporary conflict and critical perspectives since that time. Durkheim's analysis of social solidarity contributed to the development of functionalism. Weber has had a major impact on numerous areas, particularly his analysis of the formal legal rationality expressed in bureaucratic organizations and the religious and moral foundations of the work ethic. Simmel's perspective was important for focusing attention on the basic forms of interaction, particularly at the micro level, as the foundation for society. Of the remaining theorists whose ideas were reviewed briefly, Martineau's account of her visit to America provided an early critical analysis of the inconsistencies between people's claimed beliefs and values and their actual behavior. Comte emphasized growth in scientific knowledge for promoting evolutionary progress while preserving social order. De Tocqueville described the vitality of American civic life that he observed on his visit to America. Pareto focused on underlying sentiments as the key to understanding human behavior and applied this perspective to his cyclical analysis of changes in power structures. Tönnies is remembered today primarily for contrasting community (*Gemeinschaft*) and society (*Gesellschaft*)—a distinction that is still relevant in analyzing different types of social formations.

Chapter 3 then described the origins of American sociology, particularly as represented in the Chicago School of the early years of the twentieth century. Key figures in this development included George Herbert Mead (whose influence contributed to the symbolic interactionist perspective), Jane Addams, William I. Thomas, and Robert Ezra Park. Other early contributors discussed in this chapter include Charles Horton Cooley, W. E. B. Du Bois, and Charlotte Perkins Gilman. By the middle of the twentieth century, functionalism emerged as the dominant theoretical orientation, following a shift from the micro-level emphasis of the Chicago School to a more macro-level approach developed in large part at Harvard University. This transition was initiated by Pitirim Sorokin's portrayal of the long-range historic patterns he identified in the cyclically recurring worldviews of different cultural systems, but it became even more pronounced with Talcott Parsons' functional analysis of how social order is maintained. Alternative versions of functional theory were developed in Robert Merton's "middle-range" perspective and in Lewis Coser's functional analysis of conflict. Contrasting perspectives were promoted by Herbert Blumer (symbolic interaction), C. Wright Mills (critical theory), and George C. Homans (exchange theory based on psychological behaviorism), but functional theory was the dominant paradigm in American sociology from the early 1950s until the rise in the mid-to-late 1960s of various critical or "new left" perspectives. All of these developments were influenced by the European theorists highlighted in Chap. 2. However, the influence of Parsons' functional theory, with its emphasis on widespread value consensus and high levels of functional integration, can be seen in large part as reflecting the American spirit of the times.

Chapter 4, dealing with formal theory construction, provided the final part of the stage-setting for the contemporary theories presented in the subsequent chapters of Part II. Formal theory construction involves a strategy for developing explanations of important variations in social life in terms of relationships between independent and dependent (or interdependent) variables. The goal is to formulate these expected relationships in propositional statements to be used in generating researchable hypotheses that can be tested in a variety of settings. The ideal is for theory to guide research (both quantitative or qualitative), with the results of research then used to evaluate the validity of the theory. In this way the continued development of sociology as a scientific discipline can be grounded in empirical data, as opposed to philosophical speculation or subjective impressions. Although most of the theories in Part II do not explicity reflect this model of formal theory construction, it should be possible in principle to formulate the key social processes they highlight as sets of interrelated propositional statements that can be used to interpret or predict the basic underlying patterns that are manifested in people's social behavior in various social settings. In this way, these theoretical principles would be supported by empirical research findings. Alternative theoretical orientations should be expected to lead to different kinds of research questions and hypotheses and different types of research strategies. These alternatives may sometimes be equally valid, even though they involve a different focus or angle of vision. As indicated near the end of Chap. 4, sociology is indeed a multiple-paradigm discipline, as manifested in the great variety of perspectives presented in Part II.

From Micro to Meso to Macro Levels

The first four chapters in Part II focused primarily on the micro level. Symbolic interaction theory (Chap. 5) and phenomenological sociology (Chap. 6) both deal extensively with the dynamics of face-to-face relationships and how they reflect the ongoing interdependence between communication and subjective interpretation. The symbolic interaction perspective emphasizes the importance of human beings' ability to create and use symbols (as indicated in the name of the theory) and the symbolic nature of the social world they construct through interaction. In addition to creating the external social world, the formation of individuals' identities and all aspects of their subjective consciousness also occurs through this same process of symbolic communication. People's perceptions and interpretations of themselves and their material and social environment are thus shaped and molded through participation in their particular micro-level social worlds. An equally important emphasis is that people also make their own distinct contributions to their social worlds through their participation and interaction and through the particular identities that they project in this process. The phenomenological perspective deals even more explicitly with subjective consciousness and thus differs somewhat from the symbolic interactionist focus on the interdependence between overt communication and covert interpretation. Although each individual's consciousness is unique in many ways, phenomenological sociology emphasizes that organized social life is grounded in the widespread sharing of intersubjective forms of consciousness that are simply taken for granted and so do not require extensive overt communication. These implicit understandings are sometimes disrupted for various reasons (both intentional and unintentional), and ethnomethodology highlights the efforts people make to resolve the confusion and restore order. Even in the process of overt communication, however, people's ability to understand one another depends on unspoken background knowledge and their implicit interpretations of the general social context in which they are involved.

The processes emphasized by the symbolic interactionist and phenomenological perspectives serve as the underlying foundation for all forms of social life, including those at the meso and macro levels as well as the micro. Major variations exist among different people and in different segments of the population, of course, in terms of the specific symbolic codes they develop, the extent to which they are shared, and the level of consensus, disagreement, or misunderstanding there may be in their interpretations. But despite these variations, all social formations are based on the fundamental processes of symbolic communication and subjective interpretation as these are involved in the formation and expression of individuals' distinct identities and in organized social action of all types.

Chapters 7 and 8 also dealt primarily with the micro level but the emphasis was on how individuals seeks to satisfy their personal needs and interests (both material and nonmaterial) through various social encounters involving direct or indirect exchanges of costs and rewards. Chapter 7 highlighted the development of exchange theory in the works of George Homans and Peter Blau and showed how it was incorporated in the rational choice perspectives of Michael Hechter, James Coleman, and others. Homans' efforts to explain social behavior were grounded in the principles of behavioral psychology, which he contrasted with the functional theory emphasis on the needs of society. He showed how both the development and the deterioration of social relations reflect the exchange of positive and negative sanctions in face-to-face relations that result from people's efforts to shape one another's behavior to achieve favorable reward/cost outcomes for themselves. Since expressions of social approval can serve as highly general reinforcers, individuals tend to be strongly motivated to engage in sociable and conforming behavior that earns such rewards or that avoids disapproval. Peter Blau distinguished exchanges that are intrinsically linked to particular relationships from more impersonal market-type transactions. This distinction is based largely on the level of socioemotional bonding that is involved and thus can be related to the sociology of emotions perspective discussed in Chap. 8. Blau's exchange theory also incorporated Richard Emerson's analysis of how power and dependency relations develop from imbalanced exchanges. The power structures that emerge from imbalanced exchanges provide the foundation for collective action and the formation of macro structures (a process that was described in more detail in Chap. 9).

Although macro structures exhibit their own distinctive dynamics, they have their foundation in the ongoing exchange of compliance for rewards. We reviewed Michael Hechter's application of rational choice theory in explaining how group solidarity results from favorable reward/cost outcomes for participants, plus the ability of members to monitor one another's level of conformity and administer positive or negative sanctions accordingly. And James Coleman's rational choice theory goes beyond individuals' personal decisions and independently negotiated exchange transactions to show how social consensus develops regarding the need to regulate and control people's behavior for achieving various collective benefits. With widely accepted rules that prescribe or proscribe certain forms of behavior, individuals' conformity can be explained in terms of their desire to avoid negative sanctions as well as to share in the benefits of group membership, both of which may be independent of particular exchange transactions that people negotiate on their own.

Despite the straightforward way that people's motives and interests are explained in the social exchange and rational choice perspectives, real-life applications and predictions are often difficult because of the risks and uncertainties people face in evaluating alternatives and predicting their outcomes. Achieving the best outcomes in reward/cost terms is often contingent on the actions of other people, and we frequently are unable to predict these actions, or to anticipate how others will respond to our own actions. As explained in Raymond Boudon's analysis of perverse effects, when large numbers of people undertake actions that appear to be the most rational from their own individual points of view, the collective outcomes may turn out to be less beneficial for all of them than if at least some of them had selected some other alternative.

Another challenge in using the rational choice perspective by itself to explain people's social behavior is the difficulty of accounting for their distinct preferences, interests, and goals. Some basic human needs and interests are always potentially salient, of course, including needs for food, shelter, and security, plus innate desires related to sexual gratification and sociability. But the specific ways such needs and interests are satisfied vary greatly in different sociocultural settings, as well as their priority for different people. Within the framework of rational choice theory, the specific goals and interests that people pursue are taken as given and left unexplained. The sociology of emotions perspective reviewed in Chap. 8 may be seen as providing a large part of the explanation for many of the underlying preferences reflected in the rational choice process. Despite the differences in emphasis between rational choice theory and the sociology of emotions, all social exchanges, even the most fleeting, are likely to involve various forms of positive or negative emotional arousal that can be evaluated in the reward/cost terms of rational choice theory. In addition to whatever other goods or services may be exchanged, these emotional exchanges are crucial in understanding the dynamics of all social encounters, influencing individuals' overall evaluation of them as rewarding and worth preserving, or otherwise.

Moreover, the type of exchanges in which people engage, and the resulting balance of positive or negative emotions they experience, are likely to be influenced by how similar they are to one another, particularly in terms of power, status, and group membership, as well as how closely involved they are with one another. Thus we also looked in Chap. 8 at Peter Blau's analysis of how structural patterns of heterogeneity and inequality affect individuals' opportunities for encountering and developing relationships with different types of people. People vary greatly in terms of the structure of their social networks, with the social contacts they develop ranging from casual acquaintances who are rarely contacted to intimate relationships that involve intense interaction on a daily basis. In addition, network structures themselves also vary, ranging from closed networks with high levels of socioemotional bonding to more open bridging networks with less intense internal ties. But despite these important variations, the emotional dimension is always potentially relevant in the maintenance of network ties, in addition to whatever other rewards and costs may be involved.

The sociology of emotions perspective emphasizes the importance of the micro-level social processes that structure the arousal and expression of emotions in all types of encounters, ranging from the most casual network contacts to the most intimate relationships. However, the underlying human capacity for emotional arousal and expression is innate and may be considered an important part of the biological foundation for social solidarity and conformity to group norms. Our sensitivity to the reactions of others for our own self-esteem is crucial for inducing us to restrain our impulses and curb the selfishness that we might otherwise be expected to exhibit in our ongoing efforts to satisfy our interests and achieve our goals. In highly intimate relationships, and in groups with high levels of socioemotional solidarity, this process of mutual identification may result in changes in our own personal needs and goals to incorporate the needs and welfare of others. Although this process does not eliminate our concerns with our own personal welfare, it may lead us to see our well-being as tied closely to the welfare of others and thus help insure positive emotional exchanges.

Drawing on the works of Thomas Scheff and Diane Rothbard Margolis, we looked at the tensions that are sometimes experienced in individuals' efforts to balance their own personal needs, interests, and goals with their obligations and the expectations of others. Such differences are often related to gender roles, but there are differences within gender categories as well. Beyond the level of personal relationships, Arlie Hochschild illustrated the importance of organizational rules for managing emotions and emotional displays in interpersonal encounters. There are noteworthy variations in different institutional settings with regard to the normative expectations governing emotional arousal and expression. Moreover, while emotional exchanges are inherent in all face-to-face contacts, the emergence of electronic networks in recent years provides another option that can be used in developing or maintaining social relations as well as in impersonal market transactions.

Going beyond personal relations and social networks, Chap. 9 draws on the work of Peter Blau and James Coleman to show how meso and macro structures emerge from micro-level exchanges. Blau emphasized how power differentials emerging from imbalanced exchanges provide the foundation for hierarchical structures of power and authority. Power structures are based on the ability to provide rewards (or withhold punishments) in exchange for compliance and the dependence of recipients on such rewards. Power is transformed into legitimate authority when the beneficiaries of these rewards develop a consensus that the level of compliance expected in exchange is fair. This consensus may be reevaluated from time to time, however, particularly when there are changes in cost/reward outcomes. Moreover, participants tend to compare their current cost/reward outcomes with past outcomes or with the outcomes of others in similar situations. In addition, norms and values may emerge to help stabilize exchange patterns that are regarded as fair or to promote changes when they are perceived as unfair. James Coleman used the rational choice perspective to account for the establishment of formal organizations as corporate actors to accomplish goals, both individual and collective, beyond those that individuals could achieve on their own. When this occurs, the stage is set for such corporate actors to develop their own exchange transactions, through their agents, either with individuals or with other corporate actors. The power of such corporate actors as expanded greatly in modern society, giving rise to a decrease in the perceived power of individuals as "natural persons" to have a significant impact on the social world.

Despite the implicitly acknowledged importance of intermediate-level structures and processes, most theories tend to emphasize either the micro or macro level, or the relations between them, without explicit attention to social formations in between. Chapter 10 covered communities and organizations as meso-level social formations, while Chap. 11 dealt with markets and socioeconomic classes. Communities are seen as based on perceived socioemotional bonds, and thus their dynamics may be related to the general perspective of the sociology of emotions. These bonds sometimes extend beyond particular relationships to encompass others with similar characteristics, interests, or life experiences. Major attention was given to residential location as sites for community formation and the multiple neighborhood-based communities that emerge within larger urban areas, but residential location is by no means the only basis for the development of a sense of community. Whatever the specific basis for the socioemotional bonds that develop among people, identification with particular communities often reflects distinctions between insiders and outsiders. But, different communities vary in terms of how particularistic or inclusive they are, as well in the density of network ties among their members. Highly particularistic orientations present major challenges for creating a sense of community and shared responsibility for the common welfare in large, complex, and highly heterogeneous societies, as well as in our emerging global society. (The macro-level perspective of functional theory [Chaps. 12 and 13] emphasizes the importance of social processes promoting a sense of community solidarity at the level of the overall society.) Communities also vary greatly in terms of whether they are organized to pursue collective goals. In contrast to communities, organizations are seen as reflecting the rational choice perspective. But by bringing people together on a regular basis, organizations may also be sites for the emergence of a sense of community as socioemotional bonds develop among colleagues or co-workers.

The establishment of organizations involves the identification of goals to be pursued, a division of labor in which individual members are authorized to perform specific actions as agents of the organization, a hierarchy of authority, and a system of incentives to motivate members to contribute to organizational goals. Organizations are also involved in various types of environmental transactions with other organizations and with individuals, and the total population of organizations within a society constitutes a major part of the societal landscape.

In Chap. 11, markets were portrayed as consisting essentially of direct and indirect exchange networks whereby individuals seek to satisfy their individual interests, both material and nonmaterial. It is in markets that the individualistic image of the social exchange and rational choice perspectives is manifested most clearly. However, this applies more to markets for material and financial resources than socioemotional exchanges. Differences in resources is manifested in the emergence of power/dependency relations that result from transactions in which those with more resources are able to dominate the terms of the transaction to their advantage. The inequalities resulting from pure market systems can be moderated through governmental or voluntary organizations that redistribute material wealth, or through normative or legal regulations or community sentiments that discourage or prevent the development of excessively exploitative transactions. In addition, the dynamics of markets for nonmaterial social rewards are heavily influenced by socioemotional bonds that sometimes lead individuals to show concern for the welfare of others as opposed to their own personal interests.

Nevertheless, inequality persists in all societies, as reflected in distinct socioeconomic classes. In many ways the differential distribution of material or financial resources is the most crucial aspect of the socioeconomic class structure, but this tends to be strongly related to differences in power, privilege, education, prestige, and general lifestyle. We looked at Erik Olin Wright's analysis of the class structure of American society in terms of control of the personnel and financial resources involved in production. We also reviewed Randall Collins' multidimensional perspective on the socioeconomic class structure. He emphasized in particular the interpersonal dynamics of authority relations in occupational settings, plus differentials in earnings and their effects on status and lifestyle variations. Pierre Bourdieu's perspective was used to highlight the correspondence between objective class position and subjective dispositions regarding appropriate styles of behavior. Macro-level inequalities in socio-economic class structures are emphasized heavily in conflict and critical theoretical perspectives (Chaps. 14 and 15).

The next four chapters (Chaps. 12–15) shifted to macro-level orientations. Macro-level structures do not exist on their own, however, separate from the micro-level interaction patterns and social processes that constitute them. Chapters 12 and 13 focused on functional and neofunctional theory, respectively, while Chap. 14 dealt with conflict theory and Chap. 15 with critical theory. The major topic of Chap. 12 is Talcott Parsons' structural/functional model, which was highly influential in the mid-twentieth century. Even though Parsons was clearly oriented toward the macro-level institutional structures of the overall society, his functionalist analysis was grounded in a theory of social action that stressed the importance of subjective normative orientations and widely shared values for maintaining social order. He emphasized how cultural values and norms are internalized in individuals' consciousness and expressed in the differentiated institutional structures of modern society. These structures were analyzed by him in terms of their contributions to fulfilling the basic functional requirements of adaptation to the environment, achievement of collective goals, promotion of social integration, and maintenance of underlying value commitments (symbolized by the AGIL acronym). He considered modern society to reflect a high level of evolutionary progress with regard to all of these basic requirements.

Parsons' emphasis on value consensus and functional integration was subjected to numerous criticisms, and these became particularly severe by the late 1960s. By the 1980s, however, alternative versions of functional theory (neofunctionalism) were developed that were intended to avoid the limitations of Parsons' model. Even prior to the decline of Parsons' perspective, Robert Merton advocated a less abstract and less comprehensive ("middle-range") form of functional analysis that involved identifying latent dysfunctions as well as positive functions, and that emphasized the importance of specifying the particular groups or segments of the population for which particular patterns were either functional or dysfunctional.

Chapter 13 described Merton's "middle range" strategy for functional analysis in more detail, including some examples of how he applied this approach, plus the later neofunctional perspectives developed by Jeffrey Alexander and Richard Münch. Like Parsons, Alexander also emphasized normative commitments in explaining social order. However, he insisted that this focus must be balanced by explicit recognition of conflicting interests among different segments of society, particularly those based on the differential distributions of resources, privileges, and prestige. Moreover, to understand the achievement of social order at the societal level, it is necessary to deal with the micro-level dynamics of social action. These dynamics involve individuals' efforts to cope with the uncertainties and contingencies they face as they adapt to their particular situation and attempt to balance their personal needs and interests, the expectations of others, and their normative commitments.

In Münch's neofunctional perspective, the functional requirements identified in Parsons' AGIL model were seen as fundamental dimensions of all types of social behavior. This means that social actions always have an economic component (adapting to the environment), a political dimension (dealing with collective goals), a structural aspect (involving integration and socioemotional bonds), and a symbolic level (reflecting moral values and ultimate meaning). Moreover, alternative theoretical perspectives can be distinguished in terms of which of these dimensions is seen as primary. In Münch's perspective, functional theorists deals primarily with the structural and symbolic components, while conflict theorists focus heavily on the political aspect, and rational choice theorists emphasize the economic dimension.

Conflict and critical theories have long been considered the major macro-level alternatives to functionalism. The conflict perspectives reviewed in Chap. 14 take an analytical approach in which conflict and competition are seen as pervasive and inevitable in all aspects of social life, both micro and macro. This is due to the opposing interests of individuals and groups throughout society and the unequal distribution of resources, power, and privileges as manifested in the socioeconomic class structure.

We looked at Lewis Coser's analysis of conflict in functional terms, showing in particular how conflict can sometimes promote group solidarity. While this is perhaps most clearly evident in conflict between groups, even conflict within groups can be functional, if it is realistic, in insuring that their members' personal needs and interests are taken seriously, thereby increasing their commitment to the group.

We then examined Ralf Dahrendorf's more macro perspective. His primary concern was to show how various features of modern industrial societies, plus the development of strategies to manage and regulate conflicting interests, help reduce the intensity and violence of conflict. Emphasizing the contrast with the early forms of capitalism that Marx had criticized, Dahrendorf pointed out that the socioeconomic class structure of modern industrial societies reflects hierarchies of authority in bureaucratic organizations more than ownership of the means of production as Marx had argued. Moreover, because of the structural changes that have occurred since the early days of capitalism, conflict is more likely to lead to evolutionary change within the system, as opposed to the revolutionary overthrow of capitalism that Marx had predicted. These changes include: expansion of the middle class, widespread dispersion of ownership of the means of production through stock holdings, a relatively low level of overlapping and mutually reinforcing lines of conflict for most of the population, and the development of procedures for dealing with opposing interests and resolving conflict issues.

Randall Collins' multidimensional analysis of conflict also focused heavily on authority structures. He saw the process of giving or taking orders in occupational settings as crucial for people's micro-level subjective experiences of their socioeconomic class position, as well as their subjective identities and styles of relating to other people. In addition to giving orders and controlling the distribution of positive and negative sanctions, persons in authority positions often seek to promote positive emotional identification of subordinates with the organization and its values and authority structure, often through various rituals. Moreover, people's positions in such hierarchies are strongly related to their income, education, and social status, as well as the scope of their social network contacts and overall lifestyle. Going beyond the opposing interests reflected in occupational and income hierarchies, Collins' perspective was sufficiently broad to deal with conflict in many other contexts as well, ranging from gender and youth/adult relations, for example, to military confrontations between nation/states. In all such contexts, conflict can be seen as related to the differential distribution of resources of all types, as well as to individuals' desires to maintain or improve their overall socioeconomic position.

The final theoretical perspective reviewed in Chap. 14 was Immanuel Wallerstein's analysis of the development of the modern world economy. His perspective was important for shifting the level of analysis from class conflicts within society to the conflicting interests of different societies as manifested in international trade. Due to inequalities in their resources and level of development, the societies making up the world economic system can be seen as divided into core, semi-peripheral, and peripheral categories. The core countries use their superior resources and power to dominate the terms of trade and thereby exploit the semi-peripheral and peripheral countries, while the semi-peripheral countries dominate and exploit the peripheral countries below them. The positions of different countries in these categories do not remain stable, however, but change over time as a result of shifts in resources, level of development, and internal political conditions.

The critical theorists discussed in Chap. 15 also recognize explicitly the pervasiveness of conflict and competition and the inequalities that are built into the economic and political structures of a society and are reinforced by cultural ideologies. In contrast to analytical conflict theory, however, critical theorists advocate ideals oriented toward the promotion of social transformations that promise to reduce conflict and inequality and expand opportunities for human fulfillment. At the same time, however, their analyses emphasized the obstacles that must be faced in the ongoing struggle to implement major social changes. These obstacles result from the resilience of the interrelated institutional structures of the system in supporting existing systems of domination. A large part of the resilience and stability of the system is due to the influence of dominant cultural beliefs and ideologies in shaping people's consciousness and subjective worldviews to accept the basic structure of the system as simply "the way it is."

Chapter 15 began with an overview of C. Wright Mill's critical analysis of the American power structure and the widespread apathy that he believed was characteristic of mass society. We then looked briefly at selected European neo-Marxist perspectives that emphasized how the underlying economic foundation of modern societies is reinforced by other major institutional structures, particularly political, as well as by the dominant cultural ideologies through which individuals' consciousness and worldviews are formed. The development of "new left" critical sociological perspectives in American sociology in the late 1960s was influenced by the neo-Marxist orientation and by Marx's own early humanistic writings. We reviewed briefly the critical orientations of Erich Fromm, Theodore Adorno, and Herbert Marcuse.

Jürgen Habermas's contributions were described in more detail, in view of their continuing relevance for contemporary theory. Like other critical theorists, Habermas was critical of the limitations of the logic and the discourse of instrumental rationality, as manifested in large-scale bureaucratic economic and political systems. He contrasted the impersonal nature of this particular form of rationality with the patterns of everyday life communication at the micro level that are oriented toward mutual understanding. The ideal he advocated was to reduce barriers to communication as well as the domination of the (micro-level) lifeworld by the intrusion of impersonal (macro-level) system controls.

Finally, we reviewed Michel Foucault's perspective on how systems of knowledge and forms of discourse are inevitably linked to power structures and serve to reinforce them. This perspective is manifested in his analysis of changing penal codes and forms of punishment as well as in the development of the medical, mental health, and social service professions. Although Foucault's orientation is sometimes considered "post-structuralist" or "postmodern," his critical orientation is evident in his analysis of systems of domination, which he saw as reflecting the differential distribution of specialized types of knowledge that are manifested in forms of discourse that distinguish professional experts from laypersons and that lead the latter to accept their subordination to the former.

Toward Theoretical Integration: Strategies and Challenges

The four chapters in Part III cover a variety of contemporary orientations that may be seen as moving beyond the distinctions among different levels of the social world as represented by the different perspectives in Part II. The feminist theories reviewed in Chap. 16 are concerned with both micro and macro levels and their interrelations. Chapter 17 bypasses the micro-macro contrast and deals instead with the interrelatedness of human agency and the underlying structural patterns manifested in social systems at all levels. Chapter 18 then emphasizes the underlying biological foundations of social behavior, while Chap. 19 focuses explicitly on culture as analytically distinct from social systems. Finally, the postmodern theoretical themes reviewed in Chap. 20 do not distinguish contrasting levels but implicitly reflect the linkages among current cultural and social transformations in many areas of social life and their effects on individuals' lifestyles, social relations, and identities.

A wide range of feminist perspectives was presented in Chap. 16. Consistent with the orientation of symbolic interaction theory, feminist theories of all types share a strong emphasis on the way gender roles are socially constructed and reinforced in ways that go far beyond the obvious biological differences between men and women. These definitions are sustained and reinforced by widespread cultural beliefs and social practices that reflect and perpetuate male domination in all areas of social life. Feminist theorists' critical analyses of gender inequality in the distribution of power and resources are consistent with the basic orientation of conflict and critical theory perspectives. Wide-spread patterns of male domination and gender inequality range from relations between wives and husbands in household settings to macro-level gender differences in wages and salaries and occupancy of elite positions in society.

Of the various feminist theorists whose works were reviewed, the contributions of Dorothy Smith and Janet Saltzman Chafetz are noteworthy for the linkages they established between micro and macro levels. Smith argued explicitly for a feminist sociology as an alternative to what she considered the male-dominated mentality of mainstream perspectives. In developing this position, she emphasized the importance of knowledge based on personal subjective experiences, particularly those of subordinated groups, such as women, whose voices are often discounted. She also emphasized how written texts and documents are employed in the widespread exercise of power and authority at the macro level in ways that fail to acknowledge the real-life conditions of local contexts. In contrast to Smith's emphasis on subjective experience, Chafetz's theory of gender stratification focused on objective differences in the economic resources of women and men and their access to elite positions in the major economic and political institutional structures of society. These structural inequalities are reflected and reproduced in interpersonal encounters as men and women conform to socially defined gender roles. These gender roles are also perpetuated in the context of family life in the socialization of children and the relations of husbands and wives. In addition, the contributions of Patricia

Hill Collins are significant because of her portrayal of the overlapping and intersecting relationships between gender stratification and structures of domination based on race and socioeconomic class. Her analysis emphasizes that the social locations and experiences of women vary greatly, depending on their race and socioeconomic status, despite the widespread subordination they share as women.

The concepts of agency, structure, and system that were analyzed in Chap. 17 can be applied to all levels of the social world—micro, meso, or macro. Our discussion of these concepts began with Anthony Giddens' structuration theory. He insisted that structures do not have an objective existence except as manifested in actual social practices. People's behavior is not determined by social structures, however. Instead, it reflects their power to act, plus their socially acquired knowledge of how to do so in ways that reflect their specific intentions and that enable them to be accountable for their actions. Structures consist essentially of rules and resources that human agents employ in the routine practices whereby such structures are reproduced. Obviously, rules and resources vary for different segments of the population or different socioeconomic classes. But Gidden's concept of agency underscores the intentionality underlying people's behavior, plus the knowledge, skills, and power that their intentional behavior reflects. Giddens regarded the routine practices of everyday life as helping to satisfy people's underlying security needs. However, it is always possible for innovative behavior to lead to transformations of social structures, especially when such changes are widespread within the population. The motivation for intentional innovative behavior may be seen as reflecting individuals' autonomy needs as well their explicit commitments to changing structural rules or the distribution of resources.

In contrast to this concept of structure as rules and resources, social systems are seen as comprised of patterns of interdependent social actions grounded in symbolic communication processes. Like all other open systems, social systems can be analyzed in terms of the nature and strength of these patterns of interdependence as well as the processes whereby they maintain their boundaries while engaging in input/output exchanges with their environment. We reviewed Walter Buckley's morphogenic model, which emphasized the creativity of human beings in developing increasingly elaborate systems as a result of their ongoing cooperative efforts to adapt more effectively to the environment. This process of morphogenesis can be contrasted with morphostasis, which involves actions that serve to maintain system stability, and entropy, which refers to system decay. All of these processes can be seen as reflecting different types of interrelated feedback cycles which serve to amplify or counteract deviations that develop within the system. Such deviations may be random or they may reflect intentional efforts to implement change.

The final perspective reviewed in Chap. 17 was Niklas Luhmann's systems theory. He emphasized that social systems are self-created through communication codes that are developed to manage and reduce complexity. Social systems are always less complex than their environment, but their internal organization manifests its own internal complexity that emerges in the course of dealing with various aspects of the environment. For any particular social system, its environment includes not only the objective material world and other social systems, but also the psychic systems and subjective consciousness of its participants, plus other social roles that members may have that are not relevant to their membership in the system. (These distinctions are reflected, for example, in the expectation that people should not allow their personal worries or daydreams or their family lives to interfere with their occupational roles.) Luhmann also distinguished interaction systems, formal organizations, and societies as distinct categories of social systems, with each of these being regarded as part of the environment for the others. Interaction systems involve relations between individual persons, while formal organizations consist of relations between social positions whose occupants may change over time. A society is made up of all possible communication networks, both direct and indirect, including those that extend beyond nation/states to the global level.

The sociobiological perspective presented in Chap. 18 contrasts with the main emphasis of the other theoretical orientations we reviewed in emphasizing the genetic and biological foundations of social behavior. Advocates for sociobiology do not propose that human behavior is determined in a strong sense by biological characteristics. Instead, their argument is that certain predispositions may be built into the genetic code, but there are numerous ways these propensities can be expressed in behavior, reflecting the specific influences of the sociocultural environment. Moreover, these genetic characteristics themselves may vary, giving rise to differences in behavioral predispositions, just as specific biological or bodily characteristics vary for different individuals. In fact, the evolutionary model emphasizes how random variations in genetic and biological characteristics may affect individuals' survival chances as they adapt to their particular environment. The key to assessing the potential influence of genetic or biological influences on behavior patterns is whether or not the behavior in question contributes to reproductive success and long-term species survival. Even the survival of individuals is significant in this perspective because of their contribution to species survival—and obviously individual life spans are limited. Some of the specific types of behavior that have been addressed in sociobiology include sexual relations and parenting behavior, status competition and the formation of dominance hierarchies within groups, altruism toward kin and in-group members, and aggression, territorial defense, and other forms of adaptation to other groups. All of these categories of behavior are relevant for survival and reproduction and can be observed in all types of societies and among many nonhuman species as well.

In addition, human beings are biologically equipped for creating elaborate systems of symbols, including those involved in language. The ability to communicate through symbols enables human beings to develop elaborate systems of cooperation in adapting to their environment as well as to collaborate in intellectual reflection and problem-solving. The belief systems, worldviews, and meaning systems developed through symbolic language may also contribute indirectly to long-term survival by encouraging hope and confidence for the future despite human beings' ability to anticipate their eventual death as individuals. Patterns of culture, ranging from mundane techniques and tools to religious and scientific beliefs systems, may also be evaluated in terms of their relevance to the promotion of successful individual adaptation and long-range species survival. Over the long run, cultural patterns that decrease the chances for individual survival and reproductive success should be selected out in the evolutionary process, as people either abandon them or else fail to survive and reproduce. Such counterproductive patterns may be followed in the short run, however, or for limited segments of a population. However, it is easy to understand why cultural rules that would require practices such as celibacy or infanticide, for example, could never become long-term dominant patterns for the entire society if it is to survive beyond the current generation.

Chapter 19 shifted explicitly to the cultural level. Although cultural systems vary greatly in different societies, the innate human ability to create, transmit, and learn the appropriate cultural patterns of their society through participating in their particular social world is essential for their individual survival as well as the long-range survival of their society. We reviewed Margaret Archer's morphogenetic model of cultural beliefs and worldviews that develop through the actions of human agents and that are reflected in their interaction. These beliefs and cognitions can themselves become the focus of intellectual reflection as people strive to expand their perspectives and to achieve cognitive consistency. Cultural systems can be distinguished in terms of how comprehensive and consistent they are in providing explanations of people's experiences. High levels of consistency may serve as the foundation for cultural elaboration as a dominant worldview is expanded through people's efforts to explain more and more of the world they experience. On the other hand, the cultural pluralism that results from inconsistencies and contradictions in beliefs and cognitions may trigger cultural-level competition or efforts to syncretize or reconcile opposing beliefs. Examples of both of these patterns may be seen in the efforts of different groups in America to deal with the relations between science and religion, for example, as alternative belief systems.

In contrast to Archer's strong intellectualist view of culture, we looked next at Norbert Elias's portrayal of the long-term historical development of civilized manners. In his analysis, the basic norms of courtesy and self-control that constitute "civilized" behavior can be traced back to the emergence of the early European monarchies and the aristocratic court societies they developed. The consolidation of power that they achieved provided the foundation for the eventual rise of nation/states and their establishment of monopoly control over the legitimate means of violence and taxation. In addition, various aspects of the manners and self-control of the aristocratic class were gradually diffused among the expanding bourgeois class, due in large part to their efforts to increase their status and distinguish themselves from the emerging urban working class as well as rural peasants. With the increased self-control that developed from these interrelated processes, it became easier for people to predict one another's behavior, including the behavior of both acquaintances and strangers. This increased predictability made possible the expansion of the division of labor, the lengthening of chains of interdependence throughout the society, and the emergence of a more pluralistic power structure. Elias did not explicitly treat culture as analytically distinct from the overall configuration of social relationships in the population. Instead, in explaining the gradual development of civilized manners, he emphasized the long-term changes that led to the centralization of power and how this resulted in the internalized self-control that was manifested in the formation of individuals' personality structures. However, the normative patterns defining civilized behavior can certainly be seen as an important dimension of culture as these patterns are implemented in social systems and in individuals' conscience.

Our final theoretical orientation in Chap. 19 was Jeffrey Alexander's cultural sociology. Like Archer, Alexander advocated analyzing culture on its own level. However, his primary focus seemed to be the moral ideals expressed in the dichotomous distinctions people make between good and evil. Culture is seen primarily as systems of meaning represented through symbolic codes. When people move beyond secondary issues and concerns and seek to interpret the ultimate meaning and significance of their lives, both individual and collective, the resulting cultural codes involve symbolic representations of fundamental binary oppositions. The contrast between good and evil in this context can be compared with that between the sacred and the profane, for example. These basic cultural distinctions sometimes seem to merge in people's consciousness with the contrast between in-groups and out-groups as reflected in behaviors indicating inclusion or exclusion. Alexander illustrated this form of cultural analysis by tracing the processes whereby the Holocaust was socially constructed as demonstrating a horrific form of evil that must never again be allowed to contaminate the culture or be manifested in any form in people's behavior. When related to relations between in-groups and out-groups, this type of analysis is particularly relevant as our increasingly globalized social world leads to higher levels of contact between people from highly diverse social and cultural backgrounds.

Chapter 20 portrayed several interrelated themes that illustrate postmodern forms of analysis. Although the themes reviewed in Chap. 20 are generally consistent with the underlying orientation of postmodern theory, not all of the theorists whose works were mentioned would necessarily be considered "postmodern." We began with a review of Anthony Gidden's diagnosis in which he argued that we are living in a period of "late modernity" as opposed to a qualitatively new "postmodern" stage. Nevertheless, there are important new trends that he highlights, including the globalization of capitalism and industrial production, increased risks resulting from modern technology, and increased levels of freedom in intimate relationships.

Despite their differences, proponents of postmodern perspectives regard current social and cultural developments as indicating a significant transition that contrasts with many of the defining features of modernity. Many aspects of modernity continue to be vitally important, of course, such as high levels of technological development, for example, and a complex division of labor. Even so, for postmodern theorists, the social and cultural transformations we are now experiencing represent a new era that is fundamentally and qualitatively different from the modern period that originated with the development of urban-industrial society.

A major feature of postmodern perspectives is widespread erosion of well established systems of knowledge and belief, the fragmentation of moral values, and the decline in institutional authority systems. These developments can be related to expanding levels of cultural diversity as well as to the strong individualistic emphasis of contemporary American culture. In this context, any claims that might be made regarding ultimate or absolute standards of truth or morality are regarded as relevant only to the individuals or groups that make such claims or choose to accept them. It is up to each individual or group to decide what is to be accepted as valid forms of knowledge, standards of morality, or lifestyles. This high level of cultural relativism can be related in part to the increased contacts between societies with different cultural traditions that have resulted from the globalization process. The advance of globalization has also increased the scope of tensions and conflict between societies with different cultural traditions, as well as between local and national interests on the one hand and global interests on the other. Along with the fragmentation and uncertainties of this postmodern period, the mass media play a major role in defining social reality and sometimes offering simulated versions of it in their efforts to expand their influence in a competitive cultural environment. The social and cultural fragmentation and uncertainty of the postmodern world are seen as undermining and eroding the stability of long-term relationships and the sociocultural anchors of the modern period, leaving individuals on their own in their quest to construct a satisfying and meaningful identity and lifestyle from among the expanding range of social and cultural alternatives they find available in the wider environment. Their responses vary greatly, and may include increasing levels of material consumption, expanding the scope of their (sometimes simulated) cultural experiences, experimenting with alternative social relations, or identifying with particular groups whose fundamentalist-type subcultures provide a sense of security through rejection of the pluralism and relativism of postmodern culture. Another possibility in our increasingly globalized world is to seek to expand the level of communication and mutual understanding among persons with alternative cultural orientations and lifestyles in a quest for peace and friendships without borders.

The challenges of understanding our fascinating and puzzling social world will no doubt continue to engage our attention at all levels, ranging from micro-level face-to-face encounters and personal relations to the various meso-level social formations that have been highlighted in this volume (networks, groups, markets, communities, and organizations), the macro-level dynamics of nation-states, and the still-emerging global system. Continuing study and additional research will probably never provide final answers. However, the results can continue to be richly rewarding for providing new knowledge and insights that we may dare to hope will enable us to work for the kind of changes in our increasingly interdependent social world that will improve the well-being of all people.

The range of theories reviewed in this volume may serve to demonstrate that no single theory so far has been regarded as able to capture all the essential details of social life. For postmodern theorists this should not be surprising; no perspective in any discipline can claim to provide universal or ultimate knowledge. The challenges for sociology are especially great in view of the pluralism, the complexity, and the ever-changing nature of the social world. It is perhaps impossible to envision or explain the entire social world in all the varied forms of its multidimensional complexity and, as postmodern theorists would emphasize, each point of view reflects the limitations and biases inherent in the vantage point of the observer. Unlike the physical world, the social world is constructed largely of subjective definitions, and these differ greatly and change in multiple ways over time among different segments of the populations. This means that the theorizing process in sociology should never go out of date. And this applies to professional sociologists as well as to all others who are intellectually curious and who wish to increase their understanding of our social world and its current metamorphosis.

Questions for Study and Discussion

1. Explain how the micro-level perspectives of symbolic interaction theory, phenomenological sociology, and social exchange theory can be extended to an analysis of the culture or social structure at the macro level.
2. Compare and contrast the way rational choice theory and the sociology of emotions can be incorporated into an analysis of the differences between markets, organizations, and communities.
3. Explain how the macro-level perspectives of functional or neofunctional theory and analytical conflict theory can be used to analyze micro-level interaction processes.
4. In what ways can feminist theories be used to analyze the interdependence between micro, meso, and macro levels of analysis?
5. Compare and contrast way individuals' actions and social systems are related in structuration theory and open systems theory.
6. Drawing on the appropriate theoretical perspectives reviewed in this volume, discuss the interrelations between social systems, subjective consciousness, human beings' biological characteristics, and cultural systems.

Glossary

Agency Refers in Anthony Giddens' structuration theory to knowledge, ability, and intentionality as manifested in individuals' actions (in opposition to the view that behavior is determined by social structures).

Agent A person in James Coleman's rational choice theory whose actions are performed on behalf of another party (either another person or an organization) and who is expected to give priority to the interests of this other party instead of his or her own personal interests.

Alienation Feeling of estrangement from one's self or others due to lack of control over one's own actions or the products of one's own labor as emphasized in Marxist theory.

Analytical dualism Theoretical orientation advocated in Margaret Archer's perspective in which equal weight is given to social structure and interaction processes on the one hand and to elements of culture (knowledge and beliefs) on the other.

Anomie Feelings of normlessness or meaninglessness that result from inadequate social integration in Émile Durkheim's theory, from fragmentation or inconsistency in ultimate meaning systems in Peter Berger and Thomas Luckmann's perspective, and from lack of opportunities to pursue culturally prescribed goals in Merton's orientation.

Asceticism Pattern of self-discipline, self-denial, or deferred gratification, often associated with one's religious commitment; applied by Max Weber to development of the Protestant work ethic (which contrasts with monastic forms of asceticism that involve withdrawal from secular life).

Autopoiesis Concept used in Niklas Luhmann's systems theory to refer to the process where social systems are self-created through symbolic codes whereby they differentiate themselves from their environment.

Axiom Term often used in theory construction to denote a highly abstract propositional statement that cannot be tested directly but that serves as the foundation for the development of less abstract propositions to be tested.

Bifurcated consciousness Concept used by feminist theorist Dorothy Smith to highlight the inconsistency between personal knowledge based on lived experience versus that provided through various authoritative texts, including those developed in academic sociology.

Breaching experiments Procedure used in ethnomethodology in which a disruption is introduced in a particular social setting in order to observe the process whereby people seek to "make sense" of it and to restore a sense of order.

Bureaucratic personality A personality pattern described by Robert Merton in which compliance with bureaucratic rules is given priority over the goals to be achieved through the rules; seen as leading to rigidity and an inability to deal innovatively and flexibly with new situations in organizational settings.

Bureaucracy A type of formal organization that is based on a rational-legal authority structure (as analyzed by Max Weber); characterized by a clear division of labor, a hierarchy of authority, reliance on established rules, and definitions of rights and duties associated with official positions as opposed to the individual persons who occupy such positions.

Charismatic authority A type of authority that is based on extraordinary personal qualities of a leader; it is one of three types of authority identified by Max Weber, the other two being rational-legal authority and traditional authority.

Collective consciousness (or conscience) A concept emphasized heavily by Émile Durkheim that refers to subjective orientations widely shared among the members of a group or society, including in particular their moral ideas and underlying cognitions and patterns of thinking.

Compensatory groups A concept used by rational choice theorist Michael Hechter to refer to groups whose activities or goals are not necessarily intrinsically rewarding to participants, as a result of which members must be compensated to make contributions.

Compliance structure A term used by Amatai Etzioni to distinguish organizations according to whether they rely primarily on coercion, compensation (usually financial), or moral values to motivate their members, as well as whether their members' orientation to such power are positive or negative.

Conflict functionalism Refers to the perspective developed by Lewis Coser regarding the way conflict can be "functional" by contributing to social integration.

Consolidation A term in Peter Blau's structural theory that denotes a high level of overlap between the various characteristics that are used to distinguish and classify people.

Constitutive rules In Anthony Giddens' structuration theory, rules that define the nature of the activity in which people are involved.

Contradictory class position A position in Erik Olin Wright's analysis of the American socioeconomic class structure in which a person may be in a position of authority over others but not control productive resources, or may control productive resources but have no authority to control the labor of others.

Corporate actor Formally established organization in James Coleman's rational choice theory, to which individual persons transfer certain rights and resources to act on their behalf.

Critical theory A basic theoretical orientation, inspired in part by Marxist-type theory, that emphasizes the need to evaluate existing social structures in terms of their effects in repressing and dominating certain segments of the population and the challenge of transforming such structures to reduce inequality and increase opportunities for human fulfillment.

Cultural capital Knowledge, expertise, or cognitive orientations that can be employed in the exchange process to advance one's interests.

"Definition of the situation" Concept often associated with William I. Thomas, member of the early Chicago School, that highlights the importance of subjective definitions and the significance of social outcomes that result from actions based on such definitions.

Derivations A term that Vilfredo Pareto, early Italian sociologist, used to highlight the underlying sentiments that are involved in motivating people's behavior, with such sentiments regarded as more important than the rationalizations people themselves offer to explain their behavior.

"Double consciousness" The experience that W. E. B. Du Bois described whereby African Americans attempt to deal with the contradictions between the negative reactions they experience in the dominant culture of whites and their own sense of their worth and dignity as human beings

Dialectical analysis Strategy of analysis that emphasizes the process whereby social change occurs through the conflict between opposing forces within society; a concept applied by Marx to class conflict and also to the conflict between present social structures and emerging new structures–which he saw as reversing Hegel's emphasis on the opposition of ideas in promoting progress through increasing rationalization; the concept is sometimes also used to describe the paradoxical process where individuals create society at the same time that society shapes the development of its members, as emphasized in Berger and Luckmann's "social construction of reality" perspective.

Dramaturgic perspective Theoretical perspective developed by Erving Goffman that highlighted the various strategies individuals employ to make a good impression on others and thereby gain support for the identities they seek to project in particular situations.

Elementary social behavior Behavior manifested in face-to-face interaction in which individuals are involved in direct exchanges with one another—a primary focus of George Homans' exchange theory.

Emotional labor Concept that Arlie Hochschild used to describe the process whereby employees (flight attendants in particular in her research project) were expected to display certain types of positive emotions in their public encounters (with airline passengers) and the challenges they faced in actually feeling these emotions so their displays would be seen as sincere.

Enlightenment Orientation that developed among many 18th century intellectuals which involved an optimistic faith in reason as a basis for criticizing traditional beliefs and practices (particularly religious beliefs) and for reorganizing society so it would conform to the principles of natural law as discovered through reason or rational analysis.

Entropy A concept used to describe the deterioration and decay of open systems when the energy and other resources needed to sustain them can no longer be obtained from the environment.

Ethnomethodology Refers to the "methods of people" that they use, often on the basis of tacit understandings, in interpreting and making sense of one another's behavior and maintaining a sense of social order

Exchange behaviorism A term that can be applied to George Homans' exchange theory because of his explicit focus on using the principles of behavioral psychology to explain how individuals seek to shape one another's behavior so as to gain experience favorable reward/cost outcomes.

Externalization The process described in Berger and Luckmann's "social construction of reality" perspective in which individuals are actively involved in creating or reproducing their social and cultural worlds.

Extrinsic rewards A term used in Peter Blau's exchange theory to refer to rewards people seek that do not necessarily reflect any type of social bond to a particular exchange partner.

False consciousness According to Marx and Marxist perspectives, a lack of awareness of one's true class interests or of knowledge as to how the structure of society could be changed to advance these interests; often seen as manifested among working class individuals who support the capitalist system because they see no alternative, and sometimes because they believe they can advance within it.

Feedback cycles (positive and negative) A concept used in systems theory to describe whether the reactions to a particular type of action reinforce or inhibit the continuation of that action or its elaboration; can readily be applied to whether innovative or deviant behavior patterns are followed by positive or negative reactions.

Free rider Pattern identified in rational choice theory whereby individuals seek to benefit from their membership in some group without incurring the expected costs of membership.

Functionalism Basic theoretical orientation that emphasizes the way individuals' actions and patterns of organization contribute to various intended and unintended social outcomes, including in particular outcomes that benefit the social system in which they are involved by contributing to its survival requirements and overall welfare.

Gemeinschaft Literally translated "community," a term that highlights the importance of socioemotional bonds as a major source of solidarity and cooperative behavior, as opposed to formal establishment for the pursuit of individualistic interests.

Generalized exchange A term used in exchange theory that refers to various patterns of indirect exchange in a system in which individuals may incur costs in some relationships without receiving direct benefits, while the opposite is true in other transactions.

Generalized other A term used by George Herbert Mead to describe the general expectations and normative guidelines of the larger community that individuals use in evaluating their own behavior, as opposed to the expectations of specific individuals.

Gesellschaft Literally translated "society" or "association," refers to a social system that may be formally established, but that is characterized by impersonal relationships in which individuals are oriented primarily toward satisfying their own individual needs.

Graduated parameters In Peter Blau's structural theory, characteristics that can be used to distinguish individuals and that allow for ordinal ranking (less or more), such as income or age, for example.

Group selection A process emphasized in sociobiology whereby individuals' survival and reproduction chances are enhanced through behaviors that may be risky or costly to them personally, but that are beneficial for the survival of the group to which they belong, even though they may not be genetically related to other group members.

Habitus Objective conditions of one's material and social situation as analyzed by Pierre Bourdieu, particularly as determined by socioeconomic position; contrasts with subjective predispositions, despite the high level of congruence that usually exists between habitus and subjective disposition.

Hierarchy of conditioning Refers to the idea in Parsons' theory regarding the hierarchical relationship of cultural systems, social systems, personality systems, and behavioral organisms in which the lower level systems set limits and constraints for the control exerted by higher-level systems (e.g., limits set by biological characteristics of human organism on the behaviors that can be expected in individuals' social roles).

Hierarchy of cultural control In Parsons' perspective, the pattern whereby cultural orientations, particularly values and norms, govern the organization of social systems and the actions of individuals in performing their roles within them.

Historicism Orientation reflected in classical stage German social theory that emphasizes the importance of understanding a society's distinctive cultural traditions and how these are manifested in individuals' subjective consciousness—an emphasis that contrasts with the positivist emphasis on universal laws governing overt behavior.

Imbalanced exchange Transaction in which individuals receive more rewards or incur greater costs than are considered appropriate for a balanced relationship and which, in Peter Blau's exchange theory, gives rise to differentiation in status or power in order to achieve balance.

Implicit theory The everyday life assumptions people share regarding their social world that may not necessarily be incorporated in their conscious awareness or reflection; contrasts with explicit theory as developed in academic sociology.

Inclusive fitness A term used in sociobiology to refer to the outcomes of biological characteristics or behavior patterns that improve the "fitness" of others to whom one is genetically related as well as oneself in being able to adapt successfully to the environment and thereby improve long term prospects for survival and reproductive success.

Internalization Process whereby individuals acquire the cultural patterns of society in their own subjective consciousness through socialization and through participation in society; emphasized in Berger and Luckmann's perspective (along with externalization and objectification) to explain the reciprocal relationship between individuals and society (i.e., individuals create society, but society also shapes and forms its individual members).

Intersection In Blau's structural theory, the pattern whereby the characteristics used to classify different types of people crosscut one another in various ways so that individuals may be seen as similar in terms of some characteristics but different in others; contrasts with the pattern of consolidation in which these differences overlap with one another.

Intersubjective consciousness In phenomenological sociology, the consciousness that is shared among people; contrasts with the unique components of individuals' consciousness that cannot be experienced by others in the same way.

Intrinsic rewards Concept used in Peter Blau's exchange theory to refer to rewards that are linked to particular individuals, often because of their socioemotional bonds.

Instrumental rationality Type of rationality in which calculation and choice are involved with regard to the ends to be pursued as well as the means for achieving them; emphasized by Max Weber in his explanation of capitalism and bureaucracy and by Jürgen Habermas as one of the distinct forms of rationality that he identified.

Iron law of oligarchy Process described by Robert Michels in which persons in positions of power engage in strategies to maintain their power—a process that occurs in democratic organizations as well as other types.

Kin selection Concept from sociobiology in which reproductive success and long-range species survival are enhanced by behaviors that may be risky or costly to an individual but that enhance the survival chances of those to whom the individual is genetically related, particularly his or her offspring.

Laissez-faire Can be translated as "leave it to do" (meaning leave it alone), a term describing an orientation which advocates minimal interference in the market or the "natural" evolutionary process, particularly by government, reflecting a belief that social welfare and long-range evolutionary progress are best achieved when individuals have maximum freedom to pursue their individual interests.

Latent dysfunction and function Consequences of individuals' actions that are not consciously intended or recognized, including both negative (dysfunctions) or positive (functions) consequences, particularly as emphasized in Robert K. Merton's strategy for middle-range functional analysis of widespread institutional patterns of action.

Latent pattern maintenance A basic functional requirement in Talcott Parsons' structural/functional theory for maintaining society's basic values and norms through processes of socialization, social control, and various other mechanisms that serve to reinforce these underlying cultural patterns.

Lifeworld In Jürgen Habermas's theory, the everyday micro-level world as experienced by individuals in their daily lives which, in his view, is characterized by a high level of communication that is oriented toward mutual understanding (as opposed to impersonal social control).

"Looking-glass self" Term used by Charles Horton Cooley in the early years of American sociology to describe how an individual's self-concept reflects and incorporates the reactions of others, particularly in primary group settings, and the positive or negative feelings (such as pride and shame) that result from these reactions.

Mechanical solidarity In Émile Durkheim's theory, a form of solidarity that is based on similarities among people in experiences and shared consciousness.

Meme A concept introduced by sociobiologist Richard Dawkins to refer to basic units of cultural evolution that may be seen as corresponding in some ways to genes in biological evolution, and that may be evaluated in terms of their contributions to long-range human survival and reproductive success.

Middle-range functional theory An approach to theory development advocated by Robert K. Merton that was intended to be less abstract than the type of theory represented by Parsons' comprehensive structural/functional theory, but more general than the empirical generalizations that that emerge from specific research projects.

Morphogenesis In open systems theory, a process of structural or cultural elaboration that is based on positive feedback cycles—a concept used by Walter Buckley to describe elaboration of the structure of social systems and by Margaret Archer to describe the elaboration of cultural knowledge and beliefs.

Morphostasis In open systems theory, a process of maintaining existing social structural patterns through deviation-inhibiting feedback cycles.

Negative externalities In rational choice theory, a term used by James Coleman to refer to the consequences of individuals' actions or exchange patterns that affect other people or the general public in a negative way.

Negentropy A term used by Walter Buckley to describe how social systems overcome the disintegrating or decaying effects of entropy by importing sufficient energy and other resources to maintain themselves.

Neofunctionalism Theoretical orientation that emerged in the 1980s in which the basic strategy of functional analysis was revived and revised in an attempt to address the criticisms that had been directed against earlier forms of functionalism (particularly Talcott Parsons' version) by explicitly incorporating analyses from the conflict, symbolic interactionist, and phenomenological perspectives.

Necessary cause A condition which must be present for a particular outcome to occur (though the condition does not in itself insure that the outcome will occur and thus is not equivalent to a sufficient cause).

Nominal parameters A term used in Peter Blau's structural theory to describe individual characteristics that are used to categorize different types of people but that do not involve ordinal ranking (in contrast to graduated parameters which do involve ordinal ranking).

Objectification The process identified in Peter Berger and Thomas Luckmann's "social construction of reality" approach in which the products of human beings' actions appear to them as an objective external reality to which they must adapt.

Obligatory groups A term used in Michael Hechter's rational choice perspective to identify groups in which members are expected to incur the costs of their contributions in exchange for the benefits or intrinsic gratifications they receive through their participation; contrasts with groups in which individuals must be compensated because the goals or activities are not necessarily otherwise beneficial or intrinsically gratifying.

Organic solidarity In Durkheim's theory, a form of social solidarity that is based on high levels of functional interdependence reflecting a high division of labor.

Paradigm The underlying assumptions and presuppositions that serve as the implicit foundation for explicit theory development, with different underlying paradigms seen as a major reason for the development of multiple theories that focus on different aspects of the social world.

Parental investment In sociobiology, the resources that parents spend in reproduction and in caring for their offspring.

"Part/whole analysis" Term used in the sociology of emotions perspective developed by Thomas Scheff to indicate the way emotional experiences and expressions at the micro-level can be related to the collective emotions that are shared and sometimes expressed throughout society.

Particularistic values Values that promote solidarity among individuals who share particular characteristics (such race/ethnicity, gender, age, occupation, for example) that distinguish them from others in the population; contrasts with universalistic values in Peter Blau's exchange theory and also in Talcott Parsons' functional theory.

Pattern variables A set of five dichotomous choice in Talcott Parsons' functional theory that can be used to classify social relations in terms of the normative orientations that govern people's perceptions and the expectations they have of one another.

"Perverse effects" In rational choice theory, a term used by Raymond Boudon to refer to the unexpected irrational (or less beneficial than expected) consequences that sometimes result from individuals' rational actions in pursuit of their interests, especially when they anticipate that others will also act rationally in terms of their interests.

Phenomenological sociology A basic theoretical orientation that emphasizes the widely shared and often implicit subjective orientations and cognitive schema in terms of which individuals view all aspects of their external world.

"Plausibility structures" A term used in Peter Berger and Thomas Luckmann's "social construction of reality" perspective to highlight the way major institutional structures society reflect and reinforce the dominant cultural worldview shared within a society.

Political economy The overall institutional context of the economic market system, particularly as influenced by government policy.

Positive externalities In James Coleman's rational choice theory, the positive social consequences of individuals' behavior or their exchange transactions, sometimes unintended, that benefit other people or the public welfare.

Positivism A view of knowledge, particularly scientific knowledge, that emphasizes the importance of objective empirical investigation for discovering universal laws, an approach that was advocated for sociology by Auguste Comte and Émile Durkheim (especially in his earlier works) and that is widely regarded as being reflected in contemporary research involving quantitative data analysis.

Postmodern theory An orientation reflecting the view that various characteristics of the contemporary world represent a definite break with many of the defining features of modernity, particularly in terms of skepticism toward all forms of knowledge and authority, widespread erosion and fragmentation of the institutional structures, and increased individualism and cultural diversity.

Postulate In the theory construction approach, a basic statement that helps define the underlying assumptions and presuppositions of the subject to be investigated, or that serves as the basis for an explicit propositional statement to be researched.

Pragmatism A basic intellectual or philosophical orientation that was widely accepted in American social thought and was associated specifically with the early Chicago School, and that emphasizes the way human knowledge is developed through the process of adapting to the environment and solving problems.

Primary group A group based on socioemotional bonds and mutual identification of its members with one another, usually with regular face-to-face contact; analyzed by Charles Horton Cooley and others as important for one's self-concept and typically contrasted with more impersonal secondary groups.

Principal A term used in James Coleman's rational choice theory that indicates the person (or organization) on whose behalf an agent is authorized (and expected) to act.

Proposition In theory construction, a statement of a relationship that is expected to exist between at least two variables, often designated as independent or dependent variables, that serves as the basis for specific research hypotheses.

Rational-legal authority A type of authority analyzed by Max Weber and subsequent theorists that is based on formal enactment of rules that define the scope and terms of its exercise and that subordinates accept as legitimate; contrasts with authority based on personal charismatic qualities and on traditional customs, with all such authority structures contrasted with power as a basis for controlling people's behavior.

Reference group In Robert K. Merton's perspective, a group with which an individual identities, even though not currently a member, that may lead to normative deviations from groups of which they currently are members, with such identification serving an "anticipatory socialization" function for future membership.

Regulative rules In Anthony Giddens' structuration theory, rules that regulate how routine structured activities are to be performed, as contrasted with constitutive rules that define the basic nature of such activities.

Repressive laws In Émile Durkheim's theory, laws that are intended to insure uniformity of people's behavior or beliefs (in contrast with restitutive laws), with punishment of deviants serving to reinforce mechanical solidarity.

Residues In Vilfredo Pareto's theory, the underlying sentiments that motivate human behavior, in contrast to the explanations (or rationalizations) that individuals might offer.

Restitutive laws In Émile Durkheim's theory, laws that are intended to preserve patterns of functional interdependence that develop with a high division of labor (which contrast with repressive laws), with punishment of deviants serving to restore such patterns of interdependence and thereby preserve organic solidarity.

Restricted exchange A direct exchange of material or nonmaterial rewards in social exchange theory that does not involve third parties.

Role identity In George McCall and J. L. Simmons' symbolic interactionist perspective, a component of one's self-concept, often associated with a particular type of social position or relationship, that may vary in terms of its long-term importance to an individual as well as its salience in particular situations.

"Sacred canopy" A metaphor used in Peter Berger and Thomas Luckmann's "social construction of reality" perspective to describe an overarching worldview, or set of beliefs and values, that gives meaning and purpose to individuals' lives and that legitimates and reinforces the major institutional structures of society.

Self-fulfilling prophecy A pattern described by Robert Merton in which people's definitions of future outcomes leads to behavior that insures such outcomes will indeed occur (though such outcomes may not otherwise have occurred).

Significant gesture In the perspective of Chicago School theorist George Herbert Mead, a gesture (or initial phase of an act) which has the same meaning for others who observe it as it does for the individual performing it, and which can therefore serve as a form of intentional symbolic communication.

"Social behaviorism" A term used by Chicago School theorist George Herbert Mead to distinguish his perspective from psychological behaviorism—an approach that emphasized explicitly the processes of subjective interpretation and communication for determining how individuals respond to environmental stimuli.

Social capital In James Coleman's rational choice theory, a term that refers to social relationship people develop that potentially can be employed in achieving various collective (or individual) goals.

"Social construction of reality" A term used to describe the phenomenological perspective developed by Peter Berger and Thomas Luckmann which emphasizes that all aspects of the sociocultural world are constructed through human beings' actions and interaction as well as the way this socially constructed world influences individuals' subjective worldview and behaviors.

Social Darwinism An perspective that was influential in the classical stage of sociological theory and that was based heavily on the evolutionary theory of Herbert Spencer (and was highly consistent with Charles Darwin's theory of biological evolution); emphasized the long-term process whereby social progress was thought to result from ongoing competition among different individuals, groups, and organizations, and the "survival of the fittest" through this competitive struggle.

Social evolution Long-term development of a society—a process that in the classical stage of sociological theory was explained in terms of the social Darwinist principles of the "struggle for survival and survival of the fittest" but that since the middle of the twentieth century indicates a pattern of gradual change **within** the system, as opposed to revolutionary change.

Social integration A general term that is used to indicate how individuals' actions and the institutional structures of society are coordinated or fit together to insure at least a minimal level of social order in dealing with individual and collective needs and goals, plus feelings of solidarity that provide individuals a sense of belonging—a major emphasis in the general perspective of functional theory and one of four basic functional requirements in Talcott Parsons' structural/functional theory.

Social networks A pattern of direct and indirect relationships in which individuals are involved and that can be analyzed in terms of the relations of various social positions to one another without explicit attention given to the specific individuals in these positions or their motivations or subjective orientations.

Standpoint theory A perspective developed by feminist theorist Dorothy Smith that emphasizes how people's subjective experience and knowledge of the social world reflects their particular social location (or standpoint), with a particular emphasis on the notion that the knowledge based on women's experiences cannot be captured or portrayed adequately in a male-dominated sociological framework, in large part because of the widespread gender subordination that women experience.

Strategic action A concept used in Jürgen Habermas's critical theory perspective in which individuals relate to one another in terms of how they can influence one another's actions to achieve their own personal goals (as opposed to relating to them in ways that are intended to achieve mutual understanding).

Structural/functional theory An theoretical orientation developed largely by Talcott Parsons and his colleagues and students that was highly influential in the middle decades of the twentieth century and that emphasized the need to analyze the institutional structures of society, and individuals' role performances within these structures, in terms of their contributions to the fulfillment of the functional requirements of society.

Structuration A fundamental process emphasized by Anthony Giddens in which individuals' actions serve to reproduce (or transform) the social structures at the same time that structural rules and resources are intentionally and skillfully employed in such actions but without actually determining individuals' behavior.

Sufficient cause A condition that is always produces a particular outcome (though such an outcome could also result from other conditions as well, thus distinguishing a sufficient from a necessary cause).

Suicide—egoistic, anomic, altruistic, and fatalistic Categories of suicide highlighted in Émile Durkheim's theory of how suicide rates are related to level of social integration in society, with egoistic suicide resulting from inadequate social attachments, anomic suicide resulting from inadequate regulation of individuals' aspirations, altruistic suicide resulting from excessive normative integration in which suicide may be expected under certain conditions (particularly when individuals fail to conform adequately with group norms, for example), and fatalistic suicide resulting from excessive social control.

Symbolic interaction A basic theoretical orientation that emphasizes the interrelated processes of subjective interpretation and communication through the use of linguistic symbols; heavily influenced by George Herbert Mead's "social behaviorism" but developed extensively in the middle years of the twentieth century, with the term itself coined by Herbert Blumer.

Taxonomy A set of categories used to make distinctions (among individuals, groups, organizations, societies, or other phenomena) on the basis of a clearly defined set of criteria.

Twenty Statements Test (TST) A strategy for measuring individuals' self-concepts developed by Manford Kuhn in which respondents are asked to complete twenty statements beginning with "I am_____."

Universalistic achievement The specific cultural value orientation that Talcott Parsons attributed to American society, based on his pattern variable analysis, in which individuals are evaluated according to universalistic norms on the basis of their achievements.

Universalistic values Values that are intended to apply to all people throughout society (or around the world) and that are seen as a potential source of unity among people despite their individual differences; emphasized in Peter Blau's social exchange theory and in Talcott Parsons' functional theory in terms of how such values contrast with particularistic values.

Utilitarianism An theoretical orientation that emphasizes that human behavior can be explained and evaluated in terms of its "utility" or benefits, either for the individual engaging in such behavior or for the public good—a concept that was reflected in classical economic theory (as represented by Adam Smith, for example), in Herbert Spencer's classical-stage theory of social evolution, and in contemporary social exchange and rational choice theoretical perspectives.

Value-oriented rationality A form of rationality in Max Weber's theory in which rational calculation or evaluation does not apply to the ends or goals of action (which often reflect ultimate religious or moral commitments) but only to the means employed for achieving such ends; contrasts with instrumental rationality in which rational calculation and choice are applied to both the ends and the means.

Voluntaristic theory of action A theory of action developed in a major early work by Talcott Parsons in which he emphasized that individuals make choices with regard to their behavior and the goals they seek (as opposed to having their behavior determined by external or internal forces beyond their control), but that their choices are normatively regulated by widely shared values and norms.

References

Abrahamson, Mark. 2004. *Global Cities*. New York: Oxford University Press.

Addams, Jane. 1905. "Problems of Municipal Administration." *American Journal of Sociology*, 10:425–444.

Addams, Jane. 1907. "Survivals of Militarism in City Government." Chapter 2 in *Newer Ideals of Peace*. New York: Macmillan.

Addams, Jane. 1910. *Twenty Years at Hull-House*. New York: Macmillan.

Addams, Jane. (1902) 1920. *Democracy and Social Ethics*. New York: Macmillian.

Addams, Jane. 1930. *The Second Twenty Years at Hull-House*. New York: Macmillan.

Adorno, Theoder W., with E. Frenkel-Brunswick, D. T. Levinson, and R. Newitt Sanford 1950. *The Authoritarian Personality*. New York: Harper & Row.

Aldrich, Howard. 1979. *Organizations and Environments*. Englewood Cliffs, NJ: Prentice-Hall, Inc.

Alexander, Jeffrey C. 1982a. *Theoretical Logic in Sociology. Vol. 1—Positivism, Presuppositions and Current Controversies*. Berkeley and Los Angeles, CA: University of California Press.

Alexander, Jeffrey C. 1982b. *Theoretical Logic in Sociology, Vol. 2—The Antinomies of Classical Thought: Marx and Durkheim*. Berkeley and Los Angeles, CA: University of California Press.

Alexander, Jeffrey C. 1983a. *Theoretical Logic in Sociology, Vol. 3—The Classical Attempt at Theoretical Synthesis: Max Weber*. Berkeley and Los Angeles, CA: University of California Press.

Alexander, Jeffrey C. 1983b. *Theoretical Logic in Sociology, Vol. 4—The Modern Reconstruction of Classical Thought: Talcott Parsons*. Berkeley and Los Angeles, CA: University of California Press.

Alexander, Jeffrey C. 1998. *Neofunctionalism and After*. Malden, MA: Blackwell Publishers.

Alexander, Jeffrey C. 2003. *The Meanings of Social Life—A Cultural Sociology*. New York: Oxford University Press.

Alexander, Jeffrey C. 2006. *The Civil Sphere*. New York: Oxford University Press.

Alexander, Richard D. 1987. *The Biology of Moral Systems*. New York: Aldine de Gruyter.

Althusser, Louis. (1971) 2001. "Ideology and Ideological State Apparatus (Notes Towards an Investigation)." Pp. 85–126 in *Lenin and Philosophy and Other Essays*. New York: Monthly Review Press.

Anderson, Benedict. 1991. *Imagined Communities*. London: Verso.

Archer, Margaret S. 1988. *Culture and Agency: The Place of Culture in Social Theory*. Cambridge: Cambridge University Press.

Archer, Margaret S. 1995. *Realist Social Theory: The Morphogenetic Approach*. Cambridge: Cambridge University Press.

Ardrey, Robert. 1960. *African Genesis*. New York: Atheneum.

Ardrey, Robert. 1966. *The Territorial Imperative*. New York: Atheneum.

Aristotle. 1971. "Organon: Posterior Analytics." Book 2, Chapter 11 in *Basic Works of Aristotle*, edited by Richard McKeon. New York: Random House.

Axelrod, Robert. 1984. *The Evolution of Cooperation*. New York: Basic Books.

Bailey, Kenneth D. 1990. *Social Entropy Theory*. Albany, NY: State University of New York Press.

Bailey, Kenneth D. 2001. "Systems Theory." Pp. 379–401 in *Handbook of Sociological Theory*, edited by Jonathan H. Turner. New York: Springer.

Barash, David P. 1977. *Sociobiology and Behavior*. New York: Elsevier.

Barash, David P. 1979. *The Whisperings Within—Evolution and the Origin of Human Nature*. New York: Penguin Books.

Bartkowski, John. 2004. *The Promise Keepers: Servants, Soldiers, and Godly Men*. Rutgers, NJ: Rutgers University Press.

Baudrillard, Jean. 1983. *Simulations*, translated by Paul Foss, Paul Patton, and Philip Beitchman. New York: Semiotext(e), Inc.

Baudrillard, Jean. 1995. *The Gulf War Did Not Take Place*, translated and with an Introduction by Paul Patton. Bloomington and Indianapolis, IN: Indiana University Press.

Bauman, Zygmunt. 1973. *Culture as Praxis*. London: Routledge & Kegan Paul.

Bauman, Zygmunt. 1992. *Intimation of Postmodernity*. London and New York: Routledge.

Bauman, Zygmunt. 2000. *Liquid Modernity*. Cambridge, UK: Polity Press.

Bauman, Zygmunt. 2003. *Liquid Love*. Cambridge, UK: Polity Press.

Beck, Ulrich. 1999. *World Risk Society*. Cambridge, UK: Polity Press.

Bell, Daniel. 1973. *The Coming of Post-Industrial Society—A Venture in Social Forecasting*. New York: Basic Books.

Bellah, Robert, M. Richard, S. William, S. Ann, and T. Steven. 1985. *Habits of the Heart: Individualism and Commitment in American Life*. Berkeley, CA: University of California Press.

Bem, Sandra L. 1974. "The Measurement of Psychological Androgyny." *Journal of Consulting and Clinical Psychology* 42:155–162.

Bem, Sandra L. 1993. *The Lenses of Gender*. New Haven, CT: Yale University Press.

Bendix, Reinhard. 1962. *Max Weber: An Intellectual Portrait*. Garden City, NY: Anchor.

Berger, Arthur A., ed. 1998. *The Postmodern Presence—Readings on Postmodernism in American Culture and Society*. Walnut Creek, CA: AltaMira Press.

Berger, J., M. Zelditch, and B. Anderson, eds. 1972. *Sociological Theories in Progress*, Vol. 2. Boston: Houghton Mifflin.

Berger, Peter. 1963. *Invitation to Sociology: A Humanistic Perspective*. Garden City, NY: Doubleday Anchor.

Berger, Peter. 1964. *The Sacred Canopy*. Garden City, NY: Doubleday.

Berger, Peter, Brigitte Berger, and Hansfried Kellner. 1973. *The Homeless Mind*. New York: Random House.

Berger, Peter, L. and Thomas Luckmann. 1966. *The Social Construction of Reality*. Garden City, NY: Doubleday.

Bernard, Jessie. 1982. *The Future of Marriage*. New Haven, CT: Yale University Press.

Bernard, Jessie. 1987. *The Female World from a Global Perspective*. Bloomington and Indianapolis: Indiana University Press.

Bertalanffy, Luduig von. 1967. "General System Theory." Pp. 115–129 in *System, Change and Conflict*, edited by N. J. Demerath III and Richard A. Peterson. New York: Free Press.

Bertalanffy, Ludwig von. 1968. *General System Theory: Foundations, Development, Applications*. New York: George Braziller.

Bertens, Hans. 1995. *The Idea of the Postmodern: A History*. London: Routledge.

Birnbaum, Norman. 1969. *The Crisis of Industrial Society*. New York: Oxford University Press.

Birnbaum, Norman. 1971. *Toward a Critical Sociology*. New York: Oxford University Press.

Black, Max, ed. 1961. *The Social Theories of Talcott Parsons*. Englewood Cliffs, NJ: Prentice-Hall.

Blalock, Hubert M. 1969. *Theory Construction: From Verbal to Mathematical Formulations*. Englewood Cliffs, NJ: Prentice-Hall.

Blau, Peter. M. 1955. *The Dynamics of Bureaucracy*. Chicago: University of Chicago Press.

Blau, Peter M. 1964. *Exchange and Power in Social Life*. New York: John Wiley & Sons.

Blau, Peter M. 1977. *Inequality and Heterogeneity: A Primitive Theory of Social Structure*. New York: Free Press.

Blau, Peter M. 2001. "Macrostructural Theory." Pp. 343–352 in *Handbook of Sociological Theory*, edited by Jonathan H. Turner. New York: Springer.

Blau, Peter M. and W. Richard Scott. 1962. *Formal Organizations—A Comparative Approach*. San Francisco, CA: Chandler Publishing Co.

Blumer, Herbert. 1962. "Society as Symbolic Interaction." Pp. 179–192 in *Human Behavior and Social Processes–An Interactionist Perspective*, edited by Arnold M. Rose. Boston: Houghton and Mifflin.

Blumer, Herbert. 1969. *Symbolic Interactionism: Perspective and Method*. Englewood Cliffs, NJ: Prentice-Hall.

Bohannan, Paul 1995. *How Culture Works*. New York: The Free Press.

Bottomore, Thomas B. 1967. *Critics of Society: Radical Thought in North America*. London: G. Allen & Unwin.

Bottomore, Thomas B. 1974. *Sociology as Social Criticism*. London: George Allen & Unwin.

Boudon, Raymond. 1982. *The Unintended Consequences of Social Action*. New York: St. Martin's Press.

Boudon, Raymond. 1979. *The Logic of Social Action*. London: Routledge and Kegan Paul.

Bourdieu, Pierre. (1980) 1990. *The Logic of Practice*. Stanford, CA: Stanford University Press.

Bourdieu, Pierre. 1984. *Distinctions: A Social Critique of the Judgment of Taste*. London: Routledge.

Bourdieu, Pierre and James S. Coleman, eds. 1991. *Social Theory for a Changing Society*. Boulder, CO: Westview.

Bourdieu, Pierre and Jean-Claude Passeron. 1979. *The Inheritors—French Students and Their Relation to Culture*, translated by Richard Nice. Chicago: The University of Chicago Press (originally published in French, 1964, by Les Editions de Minuit).

Buckley, Walter. 1967. *Sociology and Modern Systems Theory*. Englewood Cliffs, NJ: Prentice-Hall.

Burgess, Ernest W. (1925) 1967. "The Growth of the City: An Introduction to a Research Project." Pp. 47–62 in *The City*, edited by Robert E. Park, Ernest W. Burgess, and Roderick D. McKenzie. Chicago: University of Chicago Press.

Burgess, Ernest W., H. J. Locke, and M. M. Thomes. 1963. *The Family from Institution to Companionship*. New York: American Book.

Burns, Tom. 1992. *Erving Goffman*. London: Routledge.

Burt, Ronald S. 1982. *Toward a Structural Theory of Action: Network Models of Social Structure, Perception, and Action*. New York: Academic Press.

Button, Graham and John R. E. Lee, eds. 1987. *Talk and Social Organization*. Clevedon, England: Multilingual Matters Ltd.

Calhoun, Craig. 1991. "Indirect Relationships and Imagined Communities: Large-Scale Social Integration and the Transformation of Everyday Life." Pp. 95–121 in *Social Theory for a Changing Society*, edited by Pierre Bourdieu and James S. Coleman. New York: Russell Sage Foundation.

Callinicos, Alex. 1990. *Against Postmodernism: A Marxist Critique*. New York: St. Martin's Press.

Campbell, Bernard G., ed. 1972. *Sexual Selection and the Descent of Man, 1871–1971*. Chicago: Aldine.

Campbell, Donald. 1975. "On the Conflict Between Biological and Social Evolution and Between Psychology and Moral Tradition." *The American Psychologist* 30:1103–1126.

Caplan, Arthur L., ed. 1978. *The Sociobiology Debate—Readings on the Ethical and Scientific Issues Concerning Sociobiology*. New York: Harper & Row.

Castells, Manuel. 1996. *The Rise of the Network Society*. Malden, MA: Blackwell.

Chafetz, Janet S. 1978. *A Primer on the Construction and Testing of Theories in Sociology*. Itasca, IL: F. E. Peacock.

Chafetz, Janet S. 1988. *Feminist Sociology—An Overview of Contemporary Theories*. Itasca, IL: F. E. Peacock Publishers, Inc.

Chafetz, Janet S. 1990. *Gender Equity—An Integrated Theory of Stability and Change*. Newbury Park, CA: Sage Publications.

Chambliss, Rollin. 1954. *Social Thought*. New York: Dryden Press.

Chodorow, Nancy. 1978. *The Reproduction of Mothering*. Berkeley and Los Angeles: University of California Press.

Chomsky, Noam. 1965. *Aspects of the Theory of Syntax*. Cambridge, MA: M.I.T. Press.

Chomsky, Noam. 1968. *Language and Mind*. New York: Harcourt.

Chomsky, Noam. 1975. *Reflections on Language*. New York: Pantheon.

Cicourel, Aaron. 1973. *Cognitive Sociology: Language and Meaning in Social Interaction*. Harmondsworth, England: Penguin Education.

Coleman, James S. 1961. *The Adolescent Society*. New York: Free Press.

Coleman, James S. 1982. *The Asymmetric Society*. Syracuse, NY: Syracuse University Press.

Coleman, James S. 1990. *Foundations of Social Theory*. Cambridge, MA: The Belknap Press of Harvard University Press.

Coleman, J. S., E. Q. Campbell, C. J. Hobson, J. McPartland, A. M. Moody, F. D. Weinfeld, and R. L. York, 1966. *Equality of Educational Opportunity*. Washington, DC: U.S. Government Printing Office.

Collins, Patricia H. 2000. *Black Feminist Thought–Knowledge, Consciousness, and the Politics of Empowerment*, 2nd edition. New York: Routledge.

Collins, Randall. 1975. *Conflict Sociology*. New York: Academic Press.

Collins, Randall. 1979. *The Credential Society: An Historical Sociology of Education and Stratification*. New York: Academic Press.

Collins, Randall. 1981. "On the Microfoundations of Macrosociology." *American Journal of Sociology* 86:984–1014.

Collins, Randall. 1986. *Weberian Sociological Theory*. New York: Cambridge University Press.

Collins, Randall. 2004. *Interaction Ritual Chains*. Princeton, NJ: Princeton University Press.

Comte, Auguste. 1858. *The Positive Philosophy of Auguste Comte*, freely translated and condensed by Harriet Martineau. New York: Calvin Blanchard.

Comte, Auguste. 1877. *System of Positive Polity*, 4 vols., translated by Richard Congreve. New York: Burt Franklin.

Connerton, Paul, ed. 1976. *Critical Sociology*. New York: Penguin Books.

Cook, Karen S., R. M. Emerson, M. R. Gilmore, and T. Yamagishi, 1983. "The Distribution of Power in Exchange Networks: Theory and Experimental Results." *American Journal of Sociology* 89:275–305.

Cooley, Charles H. (1902) 1964. *Human Nature and the Social Order*. New York: Schocken Books.

Coser, Lewis A. 1956. *The Functions of Social Conflict*. Glencoe, IL: Free Press.

Coser, Lewis A. 1965. *Georg Simmel*. Englewood Cliffs, NJ: Prentice-Hall.

Coser, Lewis A. 1967. *Continuities in the Study of Social Conflict*. New York: Free Press.

Coser, Lewis A., ed. 1975. *The Idea of Social Structure: Papers in Honor of Robert K. Merton*. New York: Harcourt Brace Jovanovich.

Coser, Lewis A. 1977. *Masters of Sociological Thought*. New York: Harcourt, Brace, Jovanovich, Inc.

Crane, Diana, ed. 1994. *The Sociology of Culture*. Cambridge, MA: Blackwell Publishers.

Dahrendorf, Ralf. 1958. "Out of Utopia: Toward a Reorientation of Sociological Analysis." *American Journal of Sociology* 64:115–127.

Dahrendorf, Ralf. 1959. *Class and Class Conflict in Industrial Society*. Stanford, CA: Stanford University Press.

Dawkins, Richard. 1976. *The Selfish Gene*. Oxford: Oxford University Press.

Deegan, Mary J. 1997. "Introduction: Gilman's Sociological Journey from *Herland* to *Ourland*." In *Charlotte Perkins Gilman, With Her in Ourland—Sequel to Herland*, edited by Mary Jo Deegan and Michael R. Hill. Westport, CT: Greenwood Press.

DeMello, Margo. 2000. *Bodies of Inscription—A Cultural History of the Modern Tattoo Community*. Durham, NC: Duke University Press.

Demerath, N. J., III and Richard A. Peterson, eds. 1967. *System, Change, and Conflict*. New York: Free Press.

Denzin, Norman K. 1991. *Images of Postmodern Society: Social Theory and Contemporary Cinema*. London: Sage International.

Devereux, Edward C., Jr. 1961. "Parsons' Sociological Theory." Pp. 1–63 in *The Social Theories of Talcott Parsons*, edited by Max Black, Englewood Cliffs, NJ: Prentice-Hall.

Dinnerstein, Dorothy. 1976. *The Mermaid and The Minotaur—Sexual Arrangements and Human Malaise*. New York: Harper & Row.
Douglas, Mary. 1966. *Purity and Danger: An Analysis of the Concepts of Pollution and Taboo*. New York: Pantheon Books.
Douglas, Mary. 1970. *Natural Symbols: Explorations in Cosmology*. New York: Pantheon Books.
Dreyfus, Hubert L. and P. Rabinow. 1983. *Michel Foucault—Beyond Structuralism and Hermeneutics*, 2nd edition. Chicago: University of Chicago Press.
Du Bois, W. E. B. 1970. *W. E. B. Du Bois—A Reader*, edited and with an Introduction by Martin Weinberg. New York: Harper & Row.
Du Bois, W. E. B. (1903) 1999. *The Souls of Black Folk*, edited by Henry Louis Gates, Jr. and Terri Hume Oliver. New York: W. W. Norton.
Du Bois, W. E. B. 2001. *The Education of Black People—Ten Critiques*, edited by Herbert Aptheker. New York: Monthly Review Press.
Dubin, Robert. 1969. *Theory Building*. New York: Free Press.
Durden-Smith, Jo and D. deSimone. 1983. *Sex and the Brain*. New York: Warner Books.
Durham, William H. 1978. "Toward a Coevolutionary Theory of Biology and Culture." Pp. 428–448 in *The Sociobiology Debate—Readings on the Ethical and Scientific Issues Concerning Sociobiology*, edited by Arthur L. Caplan. New York: Harper & Row.
Durkheim, Émile. (1893) 1964. *The Division of Labor in Society*, translated by George Simpson. New York: Free Press.
Durkheim, Émile. (1895) 1964. *The Rules of Sociological Method*, translated by Sarah A. Solovay and John H. Mueller and edited by George E. G. Catlin. New York: Free Press.
Durkheim, Émile. (1915) 1965. *The Elementary Forms of the Religious Life*, translated by Joseph Ward Swain. New York: Free Press.
Durkheim, Émile. (1897) 1966. *Suicide*, translated by John A. Spaulding and George Simpson and edited with an Introduction by George Simpson. New York: Free Press.
Ekeh, Peter. 1975. *Social Exchange Theory and the Two Sociological Traditions*. Cambridge, MA: Harvard University Press.
Elias, Nobert. 1978. *The Civilizing Process: The History of Manners*, published in German in 1939 and translated by Edmund Jephcott. Oxford: Basil Blackwell, Ltd.
Elias, Nobert. 1982. *Power and Civility* (alternative title *State Formation and Civilization*), published in German in 1939 and translated by Edmund Jephcott. New York: Pantheon Books.
Elias, Nobert. 2000. *The Civilizing Process*, rev. edition. Oxford: Blackwell Publishers.
Elshtain, Jean B. 2002. *Jane Addams and the Dream of American Democracy*. New York: Basic Books.
Elshtain, Jean B., ed. 2002. *The Jane Addams Reader*. New York: Basic Books.
Elster, Jean. 1986. *An Introduction to Karl Marx*. New York: Cambridge University Press.
Emerson, Richard M. 1962. "Power-Dependence Relations." *American Sociological Review* 27:31–41.
Emerson, Richard M. 1972. "Exchange Theory, Part II: Exchange Relations and Networks." Pp. 58–87 in *Sociological Theories in Progress*, Vol. 2, edited by J. Berger, M. Zelditch, and B. Anderson, Boston: Houghton Mifflin.
Engels, Friedrich. 1902. *The Origin of the Family, Private Property, and the State*, translated by Ernest Untermann. Chicago: C. H. Kerr & Co.
Etzioni, Amatai. 1961. *A Comparative Analysis of Complex Organizations*. New York: Free Press.
Etzioni, Amatai. 1993. *The Spirit of Community—The Reinvention of American Society*. New York: Touchstone.
Featherstone, Mike. 1995. *Undoing Culture—Globalization, Postmodernism and Identity*. London: Sage.
Fielding, Nigel G., ed. 1988. *Actions and Structures: Research Methods and Social Theory*. London: Sage.
Flacks, Richard. 1971. *Youth and Social Change*. Chicago: Markham.
Forgacs, David, ed. 2000. *The Antonio Gramsci Reader—Selected Writings 1916–1935*. New York: New York University Press.
Foucault, Michel. 1965. *Madness and Civilization: A History of Insanity in the Age of Reason*, translated by Richard Howard. New York: Pantheon Books.

Foucault, Michel. 1975. *The Birth of the Clinic: An Archaeology of Medical Perception*. New York: Vintage.
Foucault, Michel. 1979. *Discipline and Punish: The Birth of the Prison*, translated by Alan Sheridan. New York: Vintage/Random House.
Foucault, Michel. 1980. *The History of Sexuality, Vol. 1: An Introduction*, translated by Robert Hurley. New York: Vintage/Random House.
Fox, Renée C., Victor Lidz, and Harold J. Bershady, eds. 2005. *After Parsons: A Theory of Social Action for the Twenty-First Century*. New York: Russell Sage Foundation.
Frank, Robert H. 1999. *Luxury Fever—Why Money Fails to Satisfy in an Era of Excess*. New York: The Free Press.
Frank, Robert H. and P. J. Cook, 1995. *The Winner-Take-All Society*. New York: The Free Press.
Freud, Sigmund. 1930. *Civilization and Its Discontents*. New York: J. Cape and H. Smith.
Friedrichs, Robert W. 1970. *A Sociology of Sociology*. New York: Free Press.
Fromm, Erich. 1941. *Escape from Freedom*. New York: Holt, Rinehart & Winston.
Fromm, Erich. 1961. *Marx's Concept of Man*. New York: Frederick Ungar.
Fromm, Erich. 1976. *To Have or to Be*. New York: Harper & Row.
Gadamer, Hans-Georg. 1989. *Truth and Method*, 2nd rev. edition, translated by Joel Weinsheimer and Donald G. Marshall. New York: Crossroad Publishing Co.
Galton, Francis. 1869. *Hereditary Genius: An Inquiry into Its Laws and Consequences*. London: Macmillan.
Garfinkel, Harold. 1967. *Studies in Ethnomethodology*. Englewood Cliffs, NJ: Prentice-Hall.
Garreau, Joel. 1991. *Edge City—Life on the New Frontier*. New York: Doubleday Anchor Books.
Gergen, Kenneth J. 1991. *The Saturated Self—Dilemmas of Identity in Contemporary Life*. New York: Basic Books.
Gerth, Hans and C. Wright Mills, 1953. *Character and Social Structure: The Psychology of Social Institutions*. London: Routledge and Kegan Paul.
Gibbs, Jack P. 1972. *Sociological Theory Construction*. Hinsdale, IL: Dyrden.
Giddens, Anthony 1979. *Central Problems in Social Theory*. Berkeley and Los Angeles, CA: University of California Press.
Giddens, Anthony 1982. *Profiles and Critiques in Social Theory*. Berkeley and Los Angeles, CA: University of California Press.
Giddens, Anthony. 1984. *The Constitution of Society*. Berkeley and Los Angeles: University of California Press.
Giddens, Anthony. 1990. *The Consequences of Modernity*. Stanford, CA: Stanford University Press.
Giddens, Anthony. 1992. *The Transformation of Intimacy—Sexuality, Love, and Eroticism in Modern Societies*. Stanford, CA: Stanford University Press.
Giddens, Anthony. (1976) 1993. *New Rules of Sociological Method—A Positive Critique of Interpretative Sociologies*, 2nd edition. Stanford, CA: Stanford University Press.
Giddens, Anthony. 2000. *Runaway World—How Globalization is Reshaping Our Lives*. New York: Routledge.
Gilligan, Carol. 1982. *In a Different Voice: Psychological Theory and Women's Development*. Cambridge, MA: Harvard University Press.
Gilman, Charlotte P. (1892) 1973. *The Yellow Wallpaper*. New York: Feminist Press.
Gilman, Charlotte P. 1900. *Concerning Children*. Boston: Small and Maynard.
Gilman, Charlotte P. 1904. *Human Work*. New York: McClure and Phillips.
Gilman, Charlotte P. 1911. *The Man-Made World, or Our Androcentric Culture*. New York: Charlton Co.
Gilman, Charlotte P. 1898. *Women and Economics*, edited and with an Introduction by Carl N. Degler. New York: Harper and Row.
Gilman, Charlotte P. 1979. *Herland*, with an Introduction by Ann J. Lane. New York: Pantheon Books.
Gilman, Charlotte P. 1997. *With Her in Ourland—Sequel to Herland*, edited by Mary Jo Deegan and Michael R. Hill. Westport, CT: Greenwood Press.
Gladwell, Malcolm. 2000. *The Tipping Point: How Little Things Can Make a Big Difference*. New York: Little, Brown and Co.

Glaser, Barney G. and Anselm L. Strauss, 1967. *The Discovery of Grounded Theory: Strategies for Qualitative Research*. Chicago: Aldine Publishing Co.
Glock, Charles Y. and Rodney Stark. 1966. *Christian Beliefs and Anti-Semitism*. New York: Harper & Row.
Goffman, Erving. 1959. *The Presentation of Self in Everyday Life*. Garden City, NY: Doubleday.
Goffman, Erving. 1961. *Asylums*. Garden City, NY: Anchor.
Goffman, Erving. 1963. *Stigma*. Englewood Cliffs, NJ: Prentice-Hall.
Goffman, Erving. 1974. *Frame Analysis: An Essay on the Organization of Experience*. Cambridge, MA: Harvard University Press.
Goffman, Erving. 1983. "The Interaction Order." *American Sociological Review* 48:1–17.
Goleman, Daniel. 1995. *Emotional Intelligence—Why It Can Matter More Than IQ*. New York: Bantam Books.
Gouldner, Alvin W. 1959. "Reciprocity and Autonomy in Functional Theory." Pp. 241-270 in *Symposium in Sociological Theory*, edited by Llewellyn Gross. New York: Harper & Row.
Gouldner, Alvin W. 1960. "The Norm of Reciprocity." *American Sociological Review* 25:161–178.
Gouldner, Alvin W. 1970. *The Coming Crisis of Western Sociology*. New York: Basic Books.
Granovetter, Mark. 1973. "The Strength of Weak Ties." *American Journal of Sociology* 78: 1360–1380.
Gray, John. 1992. *Men are from Mars; Women are from Venus*. New York: HarperCollins.
Gross, Llewellyn, ed., 1959. *Symposium in Sociological Theory*. New York: Harper & Row.
Habermas, Jürgen. 1971. *Knowledge and Human Interests*; translated by Jeremy J. Shapiro. Boston: Beacon Press.
Habermas, Jürgen. 1973. *Theory and Practice*, translated by John Viertel. Boston: Beacon Press.
Habermas, Jürgen. 1975. *Problems of Legitimation in Late Capitalism*. Boston: Beacon Press.
Habermas, Jürgen. 1984. *The Theory of Communicative Action*. Vol. 1: *Reason and the Rationalization of Society*, translated by Thomas McCarthy. Boston: Beacon Press.
Habermas, Jürgen. 1987. *The Theory of Communicative Action*. Vol. 2: *Lifeworld and System: A Critique of Functionalist Reason*, translated by Thomas McCarthy Boston: Beacon Press.
Hage, Jerald. 1972. *Techniques and Problems of Theory Construction in Sociology*. New York: Wiley.
Hage, Jerald. 1994. *Formal Theory in Sociology: Opportunity or Pitfall?* Albany: State University of New York Press.
Hechter, Michael. 1987. *Principles of Group Solidarity*. Berkeley: University of California Press.
Hegarty, Paul. 2004. *Jean Baudrillard: Live Theory*. New York: Continuum.
Heise, David R. 1979. *Understanding Events–Affect and the Construction of Social Action*. London: Cambridge University Press.
Heise, David R. 2007. *Expressive Order–Confirming Sentiments in Social Actions*. New York: Springer.
Herman, Nancy J. and Larry T. Reynolds, eds. 1994. *Symbolic Interaction—An Introduction to Social Psychology*. DIX Hills, NY: General Hall, Inc.
Hochschild, Arlie Russell. 1983. *The Managed Heart—Commercialization of Human Feeling*. Berkeley and Los Angeles: University of California Press.
Hochschild, Arlie Russell. 1989. *The Second Shift: Working Parents and the Revolution at Home*. New York: Viking.
Hofstadter, Richard. 1944. *Social Darwinism in American Thought*. Philadelphia: University of Pennsylvania Press.
Homans, George C. 1950. *The Human Group*. New York: Harcourt, Brace, and Co.
Homans, George C. 1962. *Sentiments and Activities*. New York: Free Press of Glencoe.
Homans, George C. 1964. "Bringing Men Back In." *American Sociological Review* 29:809–818.
Homans, George C. (1961) 1974. *Social Behavior: Its Elementary Forms*, rev. edition. New York: Harcourt, Brace, Jovanovich.
Homans, George C. and David M. Schneider. 1955. *Marriage, Authority, and Final Causes: A Study of Cross-Cousin Marriage*. New York: Free Press.

Horowitz, Irving L., ed. 1964. *The New Sociology: Essays in Social Science and Social Theory in Honor of C. Wright Mills*. New York: Oxford University Press.
Howard, Roy J. 1982. *Three Faces of Hermeneutics—An Introduction to Current Theories of Understanding*. Berkeley, CA: University of California Press.
Hunter, James Davison. 1991. *Culture Wars: The Struggle to Define America*. New York: Basic Books.
Huntington, Samuel P. 1996. *The Clash of Civilizations and the Remaking of World Order*. New York: Touchston.
Hutton, Will and Anthony Giddens, eds. 2000. *Global Capitalism*. New York: The New Press.
Johnson, Doyle Paul. 1979. "Dilemmas of Charismatic Leadership: The Case of the People's Temple." *Sociological Analysis* 40:315–323.
Johnson, Doyle Paul. (1981) 1986. *Sociological Theory: Classical Founders and Contemporary Perspectives*. New York: Macmillan.
Johnson, Doyle Paul. 1990. "Security Versus Autonomy Motivation in Anthony Giddens' Concept of Agency." *Journal for the Theory of Social Behaviour* 20:111–130.
Johnson, Doyle Paul. 2003. "From Religious Markets to Religious Communities: Contrasting Implications for Applied Research." *Review of Religious Research* 44:325–340.
Johnson, Doyle Paul and Larry C. Mullins. 1987. "Growing Old and Lonely in Different Societies: Toward a Comparative Perspective." *Journal of Cross-Cultural Gerontology* 2:257–275.
Johnson, Miriam M. 1989. "Feminism and the Theories of Talcott Parsons." Pp. 101–118 in *Feminism and Sociological Theory*, edited by Ruth A. Wallace, Newbury Park, CA: Sage Publications, Inc.
Johnston, Barry V. 1995. *Pitirim Sorokin—An Intellectual Biography*. Lawrence, KS: University Press of Kansas.
Kanter, Rosabeth Moss. 1977. *Men and Women of the Corporation*. New York: Basic Books.
Kaschak, Ellyn. 1992. *Engendered Lives—A New Psychology of Women's Experience*. New York: Basic Books.
Kelly, Michael, ed. 1994. *Critique and Power—Recasting the Foucault/Habermas Debate*. Cambridge, MA: MIT Press.
Kellner, Douglas. 1989. *Jean Baudrillard—From Marxism to Postmodernism and Beyond*. Stanford, CA: Stanford University Press.
Kemper, Theodore D. 1978. *A Social Interactional Theory of Emotions*. New York: John Wiley & Sons.
Kennedy, Paul. 1987. *The Rise and Fall of the Great Powers*. New York: Vintage Books.
Knodt, Eva M. 1995. "Forward." In Niklas Luhmann. *Social Systems*, translated by John Bednarz, Jr. with Dirk Baecker. Stanford, CA: Stanford University Press.
Knottnerus, J. David and Christopher Prendergast. 1994. *Recent Developments in the Theory of Social Structure*, Supplement 1 of *Current Perspectives in Social Theory*. Series Editor: Ben Agger. Greenwich, CT: Jai Press.
Kuhn, Manford H. 1964. "Major Trends in Symbolic Interaction Theory in the Past Twenty-Five Years." *The Sociological Quarterly* 5:61–84.
Kuhn, Manford H. and Thomas S. McPartland. 1954. "An Empirical Investigation of Self-Attitudes." *American Sociological Review* 19:68–76.
Kuhn, Thomas S. 1970. *The Structure of Scientific Revolutions*, 2nd edition. Chicago: University of Chicago Press.
Lakatos, Imre and Alan Musgrave, eds. 1970. *Criticism and the Growth of Knowledge*. Cambridge: Cambridge University Press.
Lawler, Edward J. and J. Yoon. 1996. "Commitment in Exchange Relations: A Test of a Theory of Relational Cohesion." *American Sociological Review* 61:89–108.
Lawler, Edward J. and J. Yoon. 1998. "Network Structure and Emotion in Exchange Relations." *American Sociological Review* 63:871–894.
Lawler, Edward J. and J. Yoon. 2000. "Emotion and Group Cohesion in Productive Exchange." *American Journal of Sociology* 106:616–657.
Lefebvre, Henri. 1969. *The Sociology of Marx*. New York: Random House.

Lengermann, Patricia Madoo and Jill Niebrugge-Brantley. 1998. *The Women Founders—Sociology and Social Theory 1830–1930: A Text/Reader*. Boston, MA: McGraw-Hill.

Lenski, Gerhard. 1966. *Power and Privilege: A Theory of Social Stratification*. New York: McGraw-Hill.

Levi-Strauss, Claude. 1967. *Structural Anthropology*. Garden City, NY: Anchor.

Liebowitz, Michael R. 1983. *The Chemistry of Love*. Boston, MA: Little, Brown.

Lipset, Seymour Martin, Martin Trow, and James Coleman. 1956. *Union Democracy—What Makes Democracy Work in Labor Unions and Other Organizations?* Garden City, NY: Anchor Books.

Lorenz, Konrad Z. 1966. *On Aggression*. New York: Harcourt, Brace and World.

Luhmann, Niklas. 1982. *The Differentiation of Society*, translated by Stephen Holmes and Charles Larmore. New York: Columbia University Press.

Luhmann, Niklas. 1995. *Social Systems*, translated by John Bednarz, Jr., with Dirk Baecker. Stanford, CA: Stanford University Press [originally published in German by Suhrkamp Verlag Frankfurt am Main].

Lukács, Georg. (1922) 1968. *History and Class Consciousness*. Cambridge, MA: MIT Press.

Lukes, Steven. 1973. *Émile Durkheim—His Life and Work: A Historical and Critical Study*. Middlesex, England: Penguin.

Lundberg, George A. 1939. *Foundations of Sociology*. New York: Macmillan.

Lyotard, Jean-François. 1984. *The Postmodern Condition*. Minneapolis: University of Minnesota Press.

MacIver, Robert M. 1937. *Society: A Textbook of Sociology*. New York: Rinehart.

Marcuse, Herbert. 1960. *Reason and Revolution*. Boston: Beacon Press.

Marcuse, Herbert. 1962. *Eros and Civilization*. New York: Vintage.

Marcuse, Herbert. 1966. *One-Dimensional Man: Studies in the Ideology of Advanced Industrial Society*. Boston: Beacon Press.

Marcuse, Herbert. 1973. *Counter-Revolution and Revolt*. Boston: Beacon Press.

Margolis, Diane Rothbard. 1998. *The Fabric of Self—A Theory of Ethics and Emotions*. New Haven and London: Yale University Press.

Martineau, Harriet. 1836/1837. *Society in America*, 2 vols. New York: Saunders and Otley.

Martineau, Harriet. 1838a. *How to Observe Morals and Manners*. London: Charles Knight and Co.

Martineau, Harriet. 1838b. *Retrospect of Western Travel*, 3 vols. London: Saunders and Otley.

Marx, Karl. 1964. *Early Writings*, translated and edited by T. B. Bottomore. New York: MacGraw-Hill.

Marx, Karl. 1967. *Capital*, 3 vols., translated by Samuel Moore and Edward Aveling. New York: International Publishers.

Marx, Karl and Friedrich, Engels. (1848) 1972. "Manifesto of the Communist Party." Pp. 335–362 in *The Marx-Engels Reader*, edited by Robert C. Tucker. New York: Norton.

Maryanski, Alexandra and Jonathan H. Turner. 1992. *The Social Cage—Human Nature and the Evolution of Society*. Stanford, CA: Stanford University Press.

Masterman, Margaret. 1970. "The Nature of a Paradigm." Pp. 49–89 in *Criticism and the Growth of Knowledge*, edited by Imre Lakatos and Alan Musgrave. Cambridge: Cambridge University Press.

McCall, George and J. L. Simmons. (1966) 1978. *Identities and Interactions*, rev. edition. New York: Free Press.

McKeon, Richard, ed. 1941. *Basic Works of Aristotle*. New York: Random House.

McLuhan, Marshall and Quentin Fiore. 1967. *The Medium is the Massage*. New York: Random House.

McLellan, David. 1971. *The Thought of Karl Marx: An Introduction*. New York: Harper Torchbooks.

Mead, George Herbert. 1932. *The Philosophy of the Present*, edited and with an Introduction by Arthur E. Murphy. LaSalle, IL: Open Court.

Mead, George Herbert. 1934. *Mind, Self, and Society*, edited and with an Introduction by Charles W. Morris. Chicago: University of Chicago Press.

Meisenhelder, Thomas. 1989. "Habermas and Feminism—The Future of Critical Theory." Pp. 119–132 in *Feminism and Sociological Theory*, edited by Ruth A. Wallace. Newbury Park, CA: Sage Publications, Inc.

Mennell, Stephen. 1998. *Norbert Elias—An Introduction*. Dublin, Ireland: University College Dublin Press.
Merton, Robert K. 1968. *Social Theory and Social Structure*, enlarged edition. New York: Free Press.
Michels, Robert. (1915) 1949. *Political Parties*. Glencoe, IL: Free Press.
Milgram, Stanley. 1974. *Obedience to Authority*. New York: Harper and Row.
Mills, C. Wright. 1951. *White Collar*. New York: Oxford University Press.
Mills, C. Wright. 1956. *The Power Elite*. New York: Oxford University Press.
Mills, C. Wright. 1958. *The Causes of World War III*. New York: Simon and Schuster.
Mills, C. Wright. 1959. *The Sociological Imagination*. New York: Oxford University Press.
Mintzberg, Henry. 1983. *Power In and Around Organizations*. Englewood Cliffs, NJ: Prentice-Hall.
Mitchell, Jack N. 1978. *Social Exchange, Dramaturgy and Ethnomethodology: Toward A Paradigmatic Synthesis*. New York: Elsevier.
Mitzman, Arthur. 1970. *The Iron Cage: An Historical Interpretation of Max Weber*. New York: Alfred A. Knopf.
Molm, Linda D., N. Takahashi, and G. Peterson. 2000. "Risk and Trust in Social Exchange: An Experimental Test of a Classical Proposition." *American Journal of Sociology* 105:1396–1427.
Moreno, J. L. 1934. *Who Shall Survive?* Washington, DC: Nervous and Mental Disease Publishing Co.
Mouzelis, Nicos. 1995. *Sociological Theory: What Went Wrong—Diagnosis and Remedies*. London: Routledge.
Münch, Richard. 1994a. *Sociological Theory. Vol. 1—From the 1850s to the 1920s*. Chicago: Nelson-Hall Publishers.
Münch, Richard. 1994b. *Sociological Theory—Vol. 2, From the 1920s to the 1960s*. Chicago: Nelson-Hall Publisher.
Münch, Richard. 1994c. *Sociological Theory—Vol. 3, Developments Since the 1960s*. Chicago: Nelson-Hall Publisher.
Myers, Kristen A., Cynthia D. Anderson, and Barbara J. Risman, eds. 1998. *Feminist Foundations—Toward Transforming Sociology*. Thousand Oaks, CA: Sage Publications.
Nisbet, Robert A. 1953. *The Quest for Community*. New York: Oxford University Press.
Padilla, Efren N., ed. 2006. *Perspectives on Urban Society: From Preindustrial to Postindustrial*. Boston: Pearson Education.
Pareto, Vilfredo. (1916) 1935. *The Mind and Society*, 4 vols., edited by Arthur Livingston; translated by Andrew Bongiorno and Arthur Livingston, with the advice and active cooperation of James Harvey Rogers. New York: Harcourt, Brace and Co.
Park, Robert Ezra. 1952. *Human Communities: The City and Human Ecology*. Glencoe, IL: The Free Press.
Park, Robert E. and Ernest W. Burgess. (1921) 1969. *Introduction to the Science of Sociology*. Chicago: University of Chicago Press.
Park, Robert E., Ernest W. Burgess, and Roderick D. McKenzie, eds. (1925) 1967. *The City*. Chicago: University of Chicago Press.
Parsons, Talcott. 1937. *The Structure of Social Action*. New York: McGraw-Hill.
Parsons, Talcott. 1949. *Essays in Sociological Theory*. New York: Free Press.
Parsons, Talcott. 1951. *The Social System*. New York: Free Press.
Parsons, Talcott. 1961a. "An Outline of the Social System." Pp. 30–79 in *Theories of Society* (1-vol. edition), edited by Talcott Parsons, Edward Shils, Casper D. Nagel, and Jesse R. Pints. New York: Free Press of Glencoe.
Parsons, Talcott. 1961b. *Structure and Process in Modern Society*. New York: Free Press of Glencoe.
Parsons, Talcott. 1964. "Evolutionary Universals in Society." *American Sociological Review* 29:339–357.
Parsons, Talcott. 1966. *Societies-Evolutionary and Comparative Perspectives*. Englewood Cliffs, NJ: Prentice-Hall.
Parsons, Talcott. 1969. *Politics and Social Structure*. New York: Free Press.

Parsons, Talcott. 1970. "On Building Social System Theory: A Personal History." *Daedulus* 99:826–881.
Parsons, Talcott. 1971. *The System of Modern Societies*. Englewood Cliffs, NJ: Prentice-Hall.
Parsons, Talcott. 1978. *Action Theory and the Human Condition*. New York: Free Press.
Parsons, Talcott and Robert F. Bales, in collaboration with J. Olds, M. Zelditch, Jr., and P. E. Slater. 1955. *Family, Socialization and Interaction Process*. New York: Free Press.
Parsons, Talcott and Gerald M. Platt. 1973. *The American University*. Cambridge, MA: Harvard University Press.
Parsons, Talcott and Edward A. Shils, eds. 1951. *Toward A General Theory of Action*. New York: Harper & Row.
Parsons, Talcott and Neil J. Smelser. 1956. *Economy and Society*. Glencoe, Ill: Free Press.
Parsons, Talcott, Robert F. Bales, and Edward A. Shils. 1953. *Working Papers in the Theory of Action*. New York: Free Press.
Parsons, Talcott, Edward Shils, Casper D. Nagel, and Jesse R. Pints, eds. 1961. *Theories of Society*, 1-vol. edition. New York: Free Press of Glencoe.
Pearson, Karl. 1909. *The Scope and Importance to the State of the Science of National Eugenics*. London: Dulau.
Phillips, Bernard. 2001. *Beyond Sociology's Tower of Babel: Reconstructing the Scientific Method*. New York: Aldine de Gruyter.
Prado, C. G. 1995. *Starting with Foucault—An Introduction to Genealogy*. Boulder, CO: Westview Press.
Prus, Robert. 1996. *Symbolic Interaction and Ethnographic Research—Intersubjectivity and the Study of Human Lived Experience*. Albany: State University of New York Press.
Psathas, George. 1995. *Conversation Analysis: The Study of Talk-in-Interaction*. Thousand Oaks, CA: Sage.
Putnam, Robert D. 2000. *Bowling Alone—The Collapse and Revival of American Community*. New York: Simon and Schuster.
Rabaka, Reiland. 2007. *W. E. B. Du Bois and the Problems of the Twenty-First Century*. Lanham, MD: Lexington Books.
Reich, Charles. 1970. *The Greening of America*. New York: Random House.
Residents of Hull-House–A Social Settlement 1895. *Hull House Maps and Papers—A Presentation of Nationalities and Wages in a Congested District of Chicago*. New York: Thomas Y. Crowell.
Reynolds, Paul Davidson. 2007. *A Primer in Theory Construction*. Boston, MA: Allyn and Bacon.
Rifkin, Jeremy, with Ted Howard. 1980. *Entropy—A New World View*. Toronto: Bantam Books.
Ritzer, George. 1975. *Sociology: A Multiple Paradigm Science*. Boston: Allyn and Bacon.
Ritzer, George. 1981. *Toward an Integrated Sociological Paradigm: The Search for an Exemplar and an Image of the Subject Matter*. Boston: Allyn and Bacon.
Ritzer, George. 1993. *The McDonaldization of Society—An Investigation into the Changing Character of Contemporary Social Life*. Thousand Oaks, CA: Pine Forge Press.
Ritzer, George. 1999. *Enchanting a Disenchanted World—Revolutionizing the Means of Consumption*. Thousand Oaks, CA: Pine Forge Press.
Ritzer, George. 2000. *Modern Sociological Theory*, 5th edition. Boston: McGraw-Hill.
Ritzer, George and Douglas Goodman. 2001. "Postmodern Social Theory." Pp. 151–169 in *Handbook of Sociological Theory*, edited by Jonathan H. Turner. New York: Springer.
Robertson, Roland. 1992. *Globalization: Social Theory and Global Culture*. London: Sage.
Rorty, Richard, ed. 1967. *The Linguistic Turn: Recent Essays in Philosophical Method*. Chicago and London: The University of Chicago Press.
Rorty, Richard. 1989. *Contingency, Irony, and Solidarity*. New York: Cambridge University Press.
Rose, Arnold M., ed. 1962. *Human Behavior and Social Processes–An Interactionisti Perspective*. Boston: Houghton and Mifflin.
Rossi, Alice. 1984. "Gender and Parenthood." *American Sociological Review* 49:1–19.
Roszak, Theodore. 1969. *The Making of a Counter Culture*. Garden City, NY: Doubleday.
Rostow, Walt W. 1961. *The Stages of Economic Growth: A Non-Communist Manifesto*. New York: Cambridge.

Rubinstein, David. 2001. *Culture, Structure & Agency—Toward a Truly Multidimensional Society*. London: Sage.

Scheff, Thomas J. 1997. *Emotions, the Social Bond, and Human Reality—Part/Whole Analysis*. Cambridge, UK: Cambridge University Press.

Schegloff, Emanuel A. 2001. "Accounts of Conduct in Interaction—Interruption, Overlap, and Turn-Taking." Pp. 287–321 in *Handbook of Sociological Theory*, edited by Jonathan H. Turner. New York: Springer.

Schneider, Louis. 1975. *The Sociological Way of Looking at the World*. New York: McGraw-Hill.

Schutz, Alfred. 1967. *The Phenomenology of the Social World*, translated by George Walsh and Frederick Lehnert. Evanston, IL: Northwestern University Press.

Schutz, Alfred and Thomas Luckmann. 1973. *The Structures of the Life-World*. Evanston, IL: Northwestern University Press.

Scimecca, Joseph A. 1977. *The Sociological Theory of C. Wright Mills*. Port Washington, NY: Kennikat Press.

Scott, John Finley. 1963. "The Changing Foundation of the Parsonian Action Scheme." *American Sociological Review* 28:716–735.

Scott, W. Richard. 2003. *Organizations—Rational, Natural, and Open Systems*, 5th edition. Upper Saddle River, NJ: Prentice-Hall.

Searle, John R. 1995. *The Construction of Social Reality*. New York: The Free Press.

Sheridan, Alan. 1980. *Michel Foucault—The Will to Truth*. London: Tavistock Publications.

Simmel, Georg. 1950. *The Sociology of Georg Simmel*, translated, edited and with an Introduction by Kurt H. Wolff. New York: Free Press.

Simmel, Georg. 1955. *Conflict and the Web of Group-Affiliations*, translated by Kurt H. Wolff and Reinhard Bendix. New York: Free Press.

Sjoberg, Gideon. 1967. "Contradictory Functional Requirements and Social Systems." Pp. 339–345 in *System, Change, and Conflict*, edited by N. J. Demerath III and Richard A. Peterson. New York: Free Press.

Slater, Philip. 1970. *The Pursuit of Loneliness*. Boston: Beacon Press.

Slater, Philip. 1974. *Earthwalk*. Garden City, NY: Doubleday.

Smith, Christian. 2003. *Moral, Believing Animals—Human Personhood and Culture*. New York: Oxford University Press.

Smith, Dennis. 2006. *Globalization: The Hidden Agenda*. Cambridge, UK: Polity Press.

Smith, Dorothy E. 1987. *The Everyday World As Problematic—A Feminist Sociology*. Boston: Northeastern University Press.

Smith, Dorothy E. 1990. *Texts, Facts, and Femininity—Exploring the Relations of Ruling*. London: Routledge.

Smith, Dorothy E. 1999. *Writing the Social—Critique, Theory, and Investigations*. Toronto: University of Toronto Press.

Smith-Lovin, Lynn and David R. Heise, eds. 1988. *Analyzing Social Interaction: Advances in Affect Control Theory*. New York: Gordon and Breach.

Sorokin, Pitirim A. 1927. *Social Mobility*. New York: Harper.

Sorokin, Pitirim A. 1941. *The Crisis of Our Age*. New York: E. P. Dutton.

Sorokin, Pitirim A. 1957. *Social and Cultural Dynamics*, 1-vol. edition. Boston: Porter Sargent.

Sorokin, Pitirim A. 1959. *Social and Cultural Mobility*. New York: The Free Press of Glencoe.

Spencer, Herbert. 1967. *The Evolution of Society: Selections from Herbert Spencer's Principles of Sociology*, edited and with an Introduction by Robert L. Carneiro. Chicago: University of Chicago Press.

Spykmann, Nicholas J. 1964. *The Social Theory of Georg Simmel*. New York: Russell and Russell.

Staples, William G. 1997. *The Culture of Surveillance—Discipline and Social Control in the United States*. New York: St. Martin's Press.

Stewart, Thomas A. 1997. *Intellectual Capital*. New York: Doubleday/Currency.

Stinchcomb, Arthur L. 1968. *Constructing Social Theories*. New York: Harcourt, Brace and World.

Stoddard, Lothrop. 1922. *The Revolt Against Civilization*. New York: Scribner's.
Strauss, Anselm. 1990. *Basic of Qualitative Research: Grounded Theory Procedures and Techniques*. Newbury Park, CA: Sage Publications.
Stryker, Sheldon. 1980. *Symbolic Interactionism: A Social Structural Version*. Menlo Park, CA: Benjamin/Cummings Publishing Co.
Sumner, William Graham. (1906) 1979. *Folkways*. Boston: Ginn.
Sumner, William Graham. 1934. *Essays of William Graham Sumner*, 2 vols., edited by Albert G. Keller and Maurice R. Davie. New Haven, CT: Yale University Press.
Swartz, David. 1997. *Culture and Power—The Sociology of Pierre Bourdieu*. Chicago: The University of Chicago Press.
Tar, Zoltan. 1977. *The Frankfurt School—The Critical Theories of Max Horkheimer, and Theodor W. Adorno*. New York: John Wiley.
Thibaut, John W. and Harold H. Kelley. 1959. *The Social Psychology of Groups*. New York: John Wiley.
Thomas, William I. 1923. *The Unadjusted Girl*. Boston: Little, Brown.
Thomas, William I. and Florian Znaniecki. 1958. *The Polish Peasant in Europe and America*, 2 vols. New York: Dover.
Tiger, Lionel. 1969. *Men in Groups*. New York: Random House.
Tiger, Lionel and Robin Fox. 1971. *The Imperial Animal*. New York: Holt, Rinehart & Winston.
Tocqueville, Alexis de. 1945. *Democracy in America*. New York: Knopf.
Tönnies, Ferdinand (1887) 1963. *Community and Society*, translated and edited by Charles P. Loomis. New York: Harper and Row.
Trivers, Robert. 1972. "Parental Investment and Sexual Selection." Pp. 136–179 in *Sexual Selection and the Descent of Man, 1871–1971*, edited by Bernard Grant Campbell. Chicago: Aldine.
Trivers, Robert. 1985. *Social Evolution*. Menlo Park, CA: Benjamin/Cummings.
Trivers, Robert. 2002. *Natural Selection and Social Theory: Selected Papers of Robert Trivers*. New York: Oxford University Press.
Troeltsch, Ernst. 1931. *The Social Teachings of the Christian Churches*, 2 vols., translated by Oliver Wyon. New York: Macmillan.
Tucker, Robert C., ed. 1972. *The Marx-Engels Reader*. New York: Norton.
Turner, Bryan S. 1996. *The Body and Society*, 2nd edition London: Sage.
Turner, Jonathan H. 1985. *Herbert Spencer: A Renewed Appreciation*. Beverly Hills, CA: Sage Publications.
Turner, Jonathan H., ed. 1993. *Classical Sociological Theory: A Positivist's Perspective*. Chicago: Nelson-Hall Publishers
Turner, Jonathan H., ed. 2001. *Handbook of Sociological Theory*. New York: Springer.
Turner, Jonathan H. 2003. *The Structure of Sociological Theory*, 7th edition. Belmont, CA: Wadsworth Thomson Learning.
Turner, Jonathan H., Leonard Beeghley, and Charles H. Powers. 2002. *The Emergence of Sociological Theory*, 5th edition. Belmont, CA: Wadsworth Thomson Learning.
Turner, Ralph H. 2001. "Role Theory." Pp. 233–254 in *Handbook of Sociological Theory*, edited by Jonathan H. Turner. New York: Springer.
Turner, Stephen Park and Jonathan H. Turner. 1990. *The Impossible Science—An Institutional Analysis of American Sociology*, Sage Library of Social Research 181. Newbury Park, CA: Sage Publications.
Urry, John. 2003. *Global Complexity*. Cambridge, UK: Polity Press.
U.S. Government Printing Office. 1995. *The Declaration of Independence and the Constitution of the United States of America*, with an Introduction by Richard G. Stevens. Washington, DC: National Defense University Press.
van den Berghe, Pierre L. 1963. "Dialectic and Functionalism—Toward a Synthesis." *American Sociological Review* 28:695–705.
van den Berghe, Pierre L. 1978. *Man in Society: A Biological View*, 2nd edition. New York: Elsevier.
Veblen, Thorstein. 1934. *The Theory of the Leisure Class*. New York: Modern Library.

Vidich Arthur J. and Joseph Bensman. 1960. *Small Town in Mass Society*. Garden City, NY: Doubleday.

Wagner, Helmut R. 1970. *Alfred Schutz on Phenomenology and Social Relations*. Chicago, IL: University of Chicago Press.

Wallace, Ruth A., ed. 1989. *Feminism and Sociological Theory*. Newbury Park, CA: Sage Publications, Inc.

Wallerstein, Immanuel. 1974. *The Modern World System I: Capitalist Agriculture and the Origins of the European World-Economy in the Sixteenth Century*. New York: Academic Press.

Wallerstein, Immanuel. 1979. *The Capitalist World-Economy—Essays by Immanuel Wallerstein*. London: Cambridge University Press.

Wallerstein, Immanuel. 1980. *The Modern World System II: Mercantilism and the Consolidation of the European World Economy 1600–1750*. New York: Academic Press.

Wallerstein, Immanuel. 1988. *The Modern World System III: The Second Era of Great Expansion of the Capitalist Economy, 1730–1840*. New York: Academic Press.

Wallerstein, Immanuel. 1999. *The End of the World as We Know It: Social Science for the Twenty-First Century*. Minneapolis, MN: University of Minnesota Press.

Wallerstein, Immanuel. 2004. *World Systems Analysis—An Introduction*. Durham, NC: Duke University Press.

Ward, Lester F. 1883. *Dynamic Sociology*, 2 vols. New York: Appleton.

Weber, Marianna. (1926) 1975. *Max Weber: A Biography*, translated and edited by Harry Zohn. New York: Wiley.

Weber, Max. 1946. *From Max Weber: Essays in Sociology*, translated and edited by Hans Gerth and C. Wright Mills. New York: Oxford University Press.

Weber, Max. 1947. *The Theory of Social and Economic Organization*, edited by Talcott Parsons and translated by A. M. Henderson and Talcott Parsons. New York: Free Press.

Weber, Max. (1916) 1951. *The Religion of China: Confucianism and Taoism*, translated by H. H. Gerth. New York: Free Press.

Weber, Max. (1917–1919) 1952. *Ancient Judaism*, translated by H. H. Gerth and Don Martindale. New York: Free Press.

Weber, Max. (1916–1917) 1958. *The Religion of India: The Sociology of Hinduism and Buddhism*, translated by H. H. Gerth and Don Martindale. New York: Free Press.

Weber, Max. 1996. *The Protestant Ethic and the Spirit of Capitalism*, translated by Talcott Parsons (original translation 1930), Introduction by Randall Collins. Los Angeles, CA: Roxbury.

Weinberg, Meyer, ed. 1970. *W. E. B. Du Bois–A Reader*. New York: Harper and Row.

Wenegrat, Brant. 1990. *The Divine Archetype—The Sociobiology and Psychology of Religion*. Lexington, MA: Lexington Books.

Wiley, Norbert. 1994. *The Semiotic Self*. Chicago: The University of Chicago Press.

Wilson, Davis Sloan. 2002. *Darwin's Cathedral—Evolution, Religion, and the Nature of Society*. Chicago: The University of Chicago Press.

Wilson, Edward O. 1975. *Sociobiology, The New Synthesis*. Cambridge, Mass.: Harvard University Press.

Wilson, Edward O. 1978. *On Human Nature*. Cambridge, Mass.: Harvard University Press.

Wirth, Louis. 1938. "Urbanism as a Way of Life." *American Journal of Sociology* 44:1–24.

Wright, Erik Olin. 1979. *Class Structure and Income Determination*. New York: Academic Press.

Wright, Erik Olin. 1997. *Class Counts—Comparative Studies in Class Analysis*. New York: Cambridge University Press.

Wuthnow, Robert, James Davison Hunter, Albert Bergesen, and Edith Kurzweil. 1984. *Cultural Analysis—The Work of Peter L. Berger, Mary Douglas, Michel Foucault and Jürgen Habermas*. London: Routledge and Kegan Paul.

Zanden, Vander James W. 1984. *Social Psychology*, 3rd edition. New York: Random House.

Zetterberg, Hans L. 1965. *On Theory and Verification in Sociology*, 3rd edition. Totowa, NJ: Bedminster.

Zito, George V. 1984. *Systems of Discourse—Structures and Semiotics in the Social Sciences*. Westport, CT: Greenwood Press.

Index

Lightning Source UK Ltd.
Milton Keynes UK
UKOW03n1814160714

235224UK00001B/17/P

9 780387 765211